THE
BANNER OF TRUTH
MAGAZINE

ISSUES 1–16

THE
BANNER OF TRUTH
MAGAZINE

ISSUES 1–16

THE BANNER OF TRUTH TRUST

THE BANNER OF TRUTH TRUST
3 Murrayfield Road, Edinburgh EH12 6EL, UK
P.O. Box 621, Carlisle, PA 17013, USA

*

First published in one volume 1961
Reprinted 1967
Reprinted 2005

© Banner of Truth Trust 2005

ISBN-10: 0 85151 919 9
ISBN-13: 978 0 85151 919 7

*

Printed in the U.S.A. by
Versa Press, Inc.,
East Peoria, IL

CONTENTS

NOTE: All unsigned articles were written by the Editor, Iain H. Murray

Contents

* The U.S. edition reprinted here was issued in July 1958 (see p. 334).

Contents

INTRODUCTION

*T*he volume now reprinted is made up of issues of *The Banner of Truth* magazine, from the first issue, September 1955, to the sixteenth, August 1959. It had its origin in the small church of St John's, Summertown, Oxford, where the minister was Sidney Norton, and where I came to assist him in May 1955. The vision for the magazine came to us that summer, but our resources were so limited that after the first issue there was no income for a second until February of the following year (1956). The truth is, there were no resources to pay salaries let alone publish a magazine. Yet we were constrained to make an attempt to do something. Sidney Norton (1907–94) was not a popular preacher but he was a man of prayer and faith. A text that he had written and pinned prominently to his desk-top at this time read, 'He hangeth the earth upon nothing' (*Job* 26:7). Our burden was not for a magazine as such; it was for a recovery of the truths that present salvation as the work of divine grace. Our hope was for the republication of an older Christian literature as the best means to that end, for little of that kind was available in Britain in 1955.[1]

Oxford as the publisher's address served to catch attention. It was about the last place in the country identified with the message the magazine contained. It was three hundred years since Puritan beliefs had fed many in that city, and subsequent ministries of that persuasion – with the exception of a few brave Church of England evangelicals – had been few and far between. Although neither Mr

[1] The main exceptions were Calvin's *Institutes* (1949) and Ryle's *Holiness* (1952), both reprinted by James Clarke at the instigation of Dr Lloyd-Jones. In the United States, the Sovereign Grace Book Club, initiated by Jay Green, was just beginning.

Norton nor I had any connection with the University, the history of the city certainly had a strong influence upon us. There is scarcely any part of Oxford's ancient centre not connected with memorable men and events: the spot outside Balliol College, where Latimer and Ridley were burned to death on 16 October 1555; St Mary's Church, where Cranmer finally repudiated the Pope, and where Wesley would later offend the clergy of his day; Christ Church, where students were imprisoned for circulating Tyndale's New Testament and where John Owen later presided – these, and a score of other memories, were an inspiration to us and ought to be to every Christian. It was in Oxford that Latimer said, 'We shall this day light such a candle, by God's grace, in England, as I trust shall never be put out.' What moved us in 1955 was that the message of these men was so largely forgotten and that because the history, and the literature it produced, was so very little known.[2] The purpose of *The Banner* magazine was not to speak in our own name - there was nothing of a personal nature in all those early issues - it was to let others speak. Thus the principal voices in the first issue were those of William Gurnall, Martin Luther, Thomas Goodwin, and John Calvin.

I owe much to Sidney Norton; I was the main writer and the editor from the start; he was only to provide one article for the first issue. But it was his faithfulness and praying that provided the foundation. I recall that after I had written the first editorial, and given the new magazine a title, my senior friend went over it and changed the title from *Gospel Banner* to *The Banner of Truth*. I respected his opinion, for the words of Psalm 60:3–4 were a compelling part of his motivation, and they duly appeared on the front cover of the first number: 'Thou hast showed thy people hard things: thou hast made us to drink the wine of astonishment. Thou hast given a banner to them that fear thee, that it may be displayed because of the

---

[2] To find out more about the glorious testimony of these men, see Sir Marcus Loane's *Masters of the English Reformation*, recently republished by the Trust (ISBN 0 85151 910 5).

truth.' The change of title was certainly settled by 19 July 1955, for I have a diary note for that date, 'Went up to pray with Mr Norton early this morning concerning *The Banner of Truth.*'

By the time of the third issue of the magazine, October 1956, I had removed to London, and that led, the following year, to the publishing house we named 'The Banner of Truth Trust'. By that means a major re-issue of Christian classics began. I can only explain it in terms of the hand of God.

From St John's, Oxford, I had moved to Westminster Chapel and Dr Lloyd-Jones in London. The latter had been an encourager of the magazine from the start, although he had some misgivings about it, and these I can understand better now than I did then. A difference between the two pastors whom I first served deserves comment. Before 1955 I had never met a man so articulate in his Calvinistic convictions as Sidney Norton. He was possessed by the persuasion that a superficial evangelicalism, which left the will of man as the determining factor in salvation, had done immense harm. It had skewed the prevailing thought among evangelicals in a man-centred direction, so that little attention was given to how salvation is for the glory of God. In this his belief was close to that of Dr Lloyd-Jones, but he differed from the latter in the way he wanted 'free grace' spelled out in terms that none could miss. Luther, he used to say, blamed Erasmus for being 'like a man trying to walk on eggs without breaking them', and he did not mean to repeat that mistake. Accordingly he used such terms as 'Calvinist' and 'Arminian' very freely. Dr Lloyd-Jones preferred to teach the meaning of the words rather than to use the labels. He wanted Christians to be won to a change of view as they came to understand the Scriptures; a slower route, perhaps, but at the end of the day, the one he believed was more likely to produce permanent change and to avoid needless divisions. In this regard Norton resembled A. W. Pink, while Lloyd-Jones followed the method that John Newton had used with Thomas Scott, and which the latter has recorded in his testimony, *The Force of Truth.*

This difference between Sidney Norton and Martyn Lloyd-Jones needs to be understood in relation to their circumstances. The latter inherited a large city congregation that needed to be moved into doctrinal Christianity; Sidney Norton never had a congregation of more than two dozen people at most, and I think he had never really adjusted to our Lord's pattern of speaking 'as they were able to bear it'. In his eyes the Lloyd-Jones policy of 'little by little' seemed almost akin to compromise. Be that as it may, his zeal for the truth and his confidence in God to honour the truth were very salutary to me. I should also add that, in his strong emphasis on grace, he did not fail to appreciate the necessity of evangelism. He loved Spurgeon, and it was at St John's, where he kept most of his books, that I first set eyes on a whole set of the sixty-three black volumes that made up Spurgeon's *New Park Street Pulpit* and *Metropolitan Tabernacle Pulpit*.

The reader of this volume will see that Dr Lloyd-Jones' policy was not always well followed in these pages. I will not try to enumerate faults that I can see now, fifty years later. I still believe what I believed then but I also believe more. When the magazine began I was only twenty-four years old, and it is doubtful if that is the age when one should attempt to be a reformer. Youth is ever possessed with more confidence than wisdom. We had much to learn. James Denney once wrote: 'Even Christian ministers, who ought to know the mind of Christ, almost universally, at least in the beginning of their work, when they preach about evil, lapse into a scolding tone. It is of no use whatever in the pulpit.'[3] The same is true of writing.

The contents of these pages have been left just as they were written.[4] They were designed for the situation that then existed in England. Initially we had no thought, still less experience, of the

[3] James Denney, *The Second Epistle to the Corinthians*, 5th ed. (London: Hodder & Stoughton, n.d.), p. 70.
[4] It should therefore be remembered that addresses given are long out of date. But it is a matter for gratitude that many book titles mentioned continue to be available.

wider world beyond. This should be kept in mind. The truth is needed in all places and at all times, but not with the same emphasis in all times and places. Our hope in the 1950s was that the magazine would prompt serious thought and lead Christians to search more deeply into their heritage of Christian literature. With thankfulness it can be said that there has been a great change in that regard. An abundance of good literature now exists, and yet this in itself is not enough. Revival and reformation are even more sorely needed today than they were fifty years ago, and our desire is that these reprinted pages may serve further to that end.

IAIN H. MURRAY
August 2005

INTRODUCTION TO 1961 EDITION[1]

*T*his volume is made up of the sixteen numbers of the *Banner of Truth* which were published during the five years 1955–59. The earlier numbers have been out of print for some time, and such is the ephemeral character of magazines that it is not likely that many copies of other issues will survive the passing years unless given this more permanent form. There is, no doubt, a sense in which it would not matter if all these back numbers passed into oblivion; they were intended for what we conceived to be the needs of the hour and as those needs are never precisely the same from one decade to another, there must inevitably come a time when the message of old magazines is no longer as relevant as it once was.

We believe, however, that there is still a need for the emphasis these pages contain and at least some of the material will have enduring value, for there is a good deal of quotation from writers whose works − often inaccessible to most Christians − will give light to the church till the end of time. There is also a further reason why we have brought these articles together in one volume. In its own way the book may serve as a testimony to the fact that God always honours his Word and owns his truth. There will be some who will remember that this magazine, after its birth in Oxford in September 1955, soon had a very mixed repute. In so far as the *way* in which we said things may have provoked needless controversy we have cause for regret, but in the main it was *what* was said that caused the stir. Our witness was simple, but we were convinced it was true and urgent, so we spoke plainly: the ills of our land and

---

[1] Although '1960' appeared on the title page of the first printing, the actual publication date was May 1961.

the spiritual poverty of the church arise from the fact that we have offended God and that he has a controversy with us. Our problem lies not in empty churches nor in indifferent multitudes but in our own disobedience to the Word of God. We have diluted the gospel by turning it into a man-centred message and we have ceased to make the Scriptures the rule of all our practice. In short, before everything else, we need to clear out of our lives and out of our pulpits and out of our churches all the things that have caused God to depart from us.

At any rate this message did not meet with an indifferent response, and if we found censure and opposition on the one hand we were not left without much encouragement on the other. By the summer of 1957, the providence and grace of God had brought a few of us into close fellowship and, in a way in which it is probably not yet time to record, we experienced the fulfilment of a long-felt desire in the formation of a Publishing Trust designed to make available books which set forth the free grace of God. The principle upon which we have selected books for republication is exactly the same as that upon which we sought to base this magazine from the start. We try to consider not what people may like or want but what they *need*. In other words we determined to print books regardless of how they might sell. Some prophesied that this publishing venture would soon collapse, but it did not; and it did not for the same reason that the magazine was not swamped by opposition at the outset: that is because God is ever pleased to bless a sincere, even if feeble, attempt to make his truth known.

Regarding the magazine, there are perhaps one or two things that might be said by way of introduction. We have not issued it as a regular periodical at fixed dates, and that for two reasons. Firstly, had we tied ourselves to publication dates we should have been obliged to print whether we had anything worth saying or not. Having few to contribute to our pages this was an evil into which we were more likely to fall than others and we sought to avoid it. Secondly, we never planned to make the magazine a permanent addition to the number of Christian magazines in circulation. That it has tended to become so is not by design and once there are indications that its function has been fulfilled we shall not seek to preserve its existence. When we first put pen to paper in 1955 it was because, as far as our limited knowledge went, there was no other magazine in England expressing the burden which we felt. Happily the situation today is considerably changed. We are now in the midst of a movement back to the theology of the Reformers and the New Testament. Not for many a long year has there been such an awakening to the value of Reformed and Puritan writings. These are early days and no one can predict what this rising interest in old truths may lead to, yet there can be no question that through various influences which God has raised up, a movement is quietly progressing; the waters, as it were, are now about our ankles; soon they may reach our knees and who knows but we may yet see again in our land that blessed vision of Ezekiel, 'the waters were risen, waters to swim in, a river that could not be passed over'.

It would seem that in those periods when God is pleased to restore his church to her former glory, there are always two sides or stages that are apparent in his work. The first is negative, 'to root out, and to pull down, and to destroy' (*Jer.* 1:10). The extent to which this work is necessary, and the duration of its continuance, depends upon how far the church has departed from the truth. The levelling of long-established practices, traditions and teachings that are not in accord with the Word of God is often not 'a work of one day or two' (*Ezra* 10:13). It is also noticeable that this early stage of demolition work is generally characterized not so much by original thinking, as by a re-discovery of the past and a consequent critical re-assessment of the present: Josiah first goes back to Moses (*2 Kings* 22), Augustine to Paul, Luther to Augustine, Whitefield to the Puritans, and so on. But there is a second phase, the positive, 'to build and to plant', when it is no longer a question of finding out what is wrong but of establishing what is right. The old truths have to be re-applied in new ways and the visible church has to be reformed so that once again she becomes 'the perfection of beauty'. Of this second stage the reader may find little in this present volume. To create an awareness of need, to help Christians to discern error, to bring the light of Scripture and church history to bear upon the religious superficiality of our times, these were our immediate aims. That there are more important ultimate objectives we have no doubt, but it is apparent that little can be done in the positive reconstruction of the visible church until there is first created a body of Christians who are alive to the needs. It is only a consciously sick man who will look for positive remedies.

There is also another factor which is closely connected at this point. The present theological awakening to the doctrines of free grace is as yet largely confined to students and ministers. Such has often been the starting point of revival and reformation, but whether the present interest will lead to such events will in a sense depend on whether the masses, and Christians in general, become involved. The difference between the Reformation in England and in Spain has something to teach us here. In England, where William Tyndale and others set themselves to win the heart and mind of the common ploughboy, the people themselves became deeply involved. In Spain, on the other hand, the Reformation was, for the most part, confined to the intellects of the higher classes. It is not surprising therefore that the former movement went from strength to strength, while the latter was stamped out in the fires of the *autos-da-fé*. A Reformation by its very nature requires to be a popular spiritual movement. As men like Luther and Calvin well knew, ministers may expose abuses but they cannot themselves reform churches. The order of events, surely must be this: first the clearing away of error and the recovery of a pure gospel; then, positively, the proclamation of that gospel in the power of the Holy Ghost to the people; leading on to a reformation of the church according to the Word of God. None of these steps is in our power and in each one of them we are absolutely dependent on the sovereign Spirit of God. Sometimes he does not choose to grant all these blessings. The Holy Spirit is now doing a work of spreading the light of truth in the minds of a number of Christ's servants; it may be that he is but strengthening a remnant who will have to stand fast, like Noah and Jeremiah, through a flood of apostasy, sin and judgment; or it may be that this is but a step to a further blessing and that he is now preparing ambassadors who, amidst a general outpouring of the Holy Spirit, will again blazon the gospel throughout our land. It may even be that this land will see once more the church of Christ appearing in all her beauty and 'terrible as an army with banners'.

Although these things are dark to us now, they are clear to God, and in his providence the future is already infallibly decreed. It is ours to cry, as did Martin Bucer on his deathbed in Cambridge in 1551, 'He reigns! He reigns! He governs all', and we may rest in the assurance that he is ordering all things for the glory of his Son and towards the preparation for that day when the kingdoms of this world shall 'become the kingdoms of our Lord and of his Christ'.

IAIN MURRAY
October 1960

BOOKS REFERRED TO

THE BANNER OF TRUTH

BOOK INDEX

The

Banner of Truth

SEPTEMBER . 1955

" Thou hast shewed thy people hard things;
Thou hast made us to drink the wine of
astonishment. Thou hast given a banner to
them that fear thee, that it may be displayed
because of the truth."   Psalm 60, 3-4

THE BANNER OF TRUTH

Dear Reader,—We are living in the midst of a dying nation. Throughout this century successive partial judgements—wars and bloodshed—testimonies of the displeasure of God, have fallen upon us. These providential warnings have gone unheeded. The land abounds in sin, God is against us, and at any time may pronounce that final, fatal sentence, "I will not again pass by them any more." Partial judgements unregarded ever terminate in total ruin (Amos vii). The Lord has said "Shall not a land tremble for this, and everyone mourn that dwelleth therein?" Yet such is our desolate state that there is no trembling at God's Word, no mourning, no repentance, but rather, like a dying man—with eyes dim, and senses decayed— our poor country is unable to see or hear what God is plainly declaring against us. Blindness, apathy, and false security, are always the marks of a nation not far from Judgement, as it was with Israel of old, "Grey hairs are here and there upon him, yet he knoweth not", so it is with us. It is true that some appear to feel the seriousness of our days, that the issue at stake is nothing less than our national survival, but how can they provide a remedy who are not even aware of the cause of our present condition ? Various designs and schemes are continually brought forward, vain desires and hopes are expressed, but they are all doomed because the mind of God who smites us is not enquired after. The true cause of all our troubles and dangers, with the only remedy for them, is utterly neglected. The providences of God, the manner in which He is ordering the events of our days, will only be understood by them that know and fear Him : it is to such readers that we now send this out, praying that the Lord will cause it to fall in your path. God's people to-day are a scattered remnant, "Thou hast shewed Thy people hard things", we need rallying to a Banner, the Banner Of Truth. We are in an evil day, only those who have their loins girt about with truth shall be able to withstand.

God values nothing in a nation apart from His Church, for only regenerate people can rightly glorify God—and those that glorify Him not are useless dross, they render God no revenue of praise. God no longer values a professing church where His truth is not acknowledged, for God cannot be glorified apart from a knowledge of the truth. Therefore when the church in a nation departs from the truth, God has no longer any cause to keep that nation in being. It was the fall of truth in the church in Israel that brought the overthrow of the whole land, God tells us so in Hosea iv. Again when Jerusalem rejected the truth in the time of Christ there was nothing left for them but to be given over to the sword—as they were in 70 A.D. To possess the Truth of God is a nation's greatest privilege and honour, the strength and security of a land lies not in its arms but in its acknowledgement of the Truth of God ; to such a land God says "I will contend with him that contendeth with thee."

But when God's Truth, the Gospel, departs, all other blessings depart with it. His truth is a land's greatest mercy, and therefore the removal of it must be the greatest misery. As an old writer says, " When the Gospel of Peace removes, eternal peace goes with it, temporal peace flies after it ; and whatsoever is safe, profitable, prosperous, takes wings and departs also. God hath no other intention in the removing of the truth, and unchurching a nation, but the utter ruin and destruction of that nation. Other judgements may be medicinal ; this is killing. The torments of Hell are not inflicted for the conversion of the damned, nor is the setting of the Gospel sun for the conversion of a nation." In our land to-day, although true believers remain scattered in different denominations, the visible church as a whole has departed from the truth—" they that handle the Law knew me not ". God is not tied to any particular visible church, and will reject those who reject His Truth, " because thou hast rejected knowledge I will also reject thee." The fall of the church is being followed, of necessity, by the fall of the nation, and there is but one hope, but one remedy, that is that before the day of God's patience becomes the day of His wrath, He will, in mercy, revive His truth. If a land will not glorify God by the revealed truth—the Bible—God has another manner of making His Truth known and acknowledged, " The Lord is known by the judgements which He executeth ". That is, He will pour out His wrath, and make a land feel that He wrote not in vain " the nation and kingdom that will not serve Thee shall perish." " And the slain shall fall in the midst of you, and ye shall know that I am The Lord " (Isaiah lx. 12 ; Ezek. vi. 7).

There are many to-day who regard truth and error as matters of small consequence ; if a man lives rightly, they say, it matters not much what his beliefs and opinions are. Such statements do not surprise us. Night and day are all one to a blind man, truth and error are all one to an ignorant man. None can value the truth except those who have been brought to know it ; such have a very different estimation of it. The Word of God says that man's immortal soul, his eternal state, depends upon his right knowledge of the truth. There are certain definite doctrines, and those that hold them not are already marked out in the Scriptures as lost men. Error is a work of such evil consequences that God commanded the Israelites that all who should propagate it should be put to death (Deut. 13). Nor is God changed in His judgement in the New Testament ; He threatens the church at Thyatira which was infected with errors, " I will kill her children with death " (Rev. ii. 22). The Apostles, taught by the Spirit of truth, held the same view of error. Paul calls down the curse of God upon all that pervert the truth. " I would," he says, " they were even cut off " (Gal. i. 8-9 and Ch. v. 12). Men will be questioned at the Last Day concerning whether they were in the faith, and what truths they held. Though truth may seem a small matter now, the Apostle Paul tells us that at that Day, heretics will meet the same condemnation as drunkards (Gal. v. 21). Likewise the Apostle Peter calls heresies " damnable heresies ", because he declares they bring " swift damnation " upon those that hold them (II Pet. ii. 1). As an old servant of God rightly said, " I pray you observe what an accent he lays on the damnation that comes by these corrupt doctrines, he calls it ' swift damnation '. Would any make it a shorter voyage to Hell than ordinary, let him throw himself into this stream of corrupt doctrine, and he is not likely to be long in going."

Never was there a day when plain, certain, decided statements of Scriptural truth were more needed to guide the Lord's children. We are aware that there is much apparently Evangelical literature in circulation, yet the majority of it is so mixed with error as to denote the absence of the work of the Spirit of truth ; the root of God's controversy is not laid bare ; true causes and true remedies are for the most part passed over, and statements are made in such a mild and moderate fashion that we are led to doubt how much such writers are aware of the mind of God towards this present age. More serious still is the false confidence that is spreading abroad amongst professing Evangelicals. This has arisen out of certain recent events and evangelistic campaigns. If numerical success was the test to apply we should be happy, but when we consider that the Lord of Hosts is not concerned with numbers, when we read in the Scriptures that God loves the glory of His Truth more than the souls of men, then we are ill at ease. The chief end of preaching is to declare the glory of God's grace, this truth is a " sweet savour ", acceptable to God, whether men receive it or reject it, whether its proclamation results in the salvation or damnation of hearers (II Cor. ii. 14). To gather as many souls as possible is obviously, on the face of Scripture, not the design of God. If it were so, why then did He hide the Gospel from the world for thousands of years, revealing it only to the Israelites while hundreds of generations of Gentiles were allowed to perish in their sins ? When anything else besides the declaration of the truth of God to His glory is made the foundation of evangelism it is a false foundation. The evangelism of the past few years has been on this false foundation. Emphasis has not been upon the Truth, plain statements concerning the verbal inspiration of Scripture have been avoided, heresies have been mildly overlooked — so that Modernists, Romanists, and Ritualists, whose soul-destroying errors have aided in the eternal undoing of thousands, have been allowed to " assist " and join hands in these campaigns. Such compromise leads to the very overthrow of Truth. The Scriptures plainly declare that none are in the way of salvation except those who hold what is now called " evangelical " truth ; it is the ONLY saving truth. Without it none can be regenerate, and all unregenerate are wicked in God's sight ; those who pretend union or agreement with such men, need to pay heed to God's solemn warning—" He that saith unto the wicked, Thou art righteous ; him shall the people curse, nations shall abhor him ", that is, those shall curse and abhor who have been led by such compromising statements into eternal fire.

But there is a more serious fact which shows that any confidence in such evangelism as is now prevalent is misfounded. (Though we do not deny that God has in His sovereign pleasure in some cases used such preaching to the salvation of souls.) Ministers are commanded " to rightly divide the Word of Truth ", that is to preach according to the Scriptures, a preacher is to say neither less nor more than the Word of God. Now to speak plainly, there is a manner of preaching from the Bible that is not Biblical. It is possible to preach that Christ died for sinners and yet not preach it according to the Scriptures. An example is necessary. In the seventeenth century an error arose strongly under the teaching of a man named Arminius, which became known as " Arminianism ". His teaching briefly was that God has provided mercy for all men in Christ, and that once a man has heard the Gospel, it depends upon the free-will of man whether he is saved or not. The twin principles of Arminianism are that the grace of God is universal—extending to all, and that the efficacy of that grace depends finally upon the free-will of man. The success of the Gospel, in their mind, depends upon the willingness of man to receive it. Some will ask were not such opinions held before Arminius spread them ? They were, but not by the true church of God. Heretics in the early centuries held similar views, but they were overthrown by the leaders God gave to the church such as Augustine. An apostate medieval Roman church held these errors while the true servants of God in those dark centuries, such as Wycliffe and Huss, rejected them. At the Reformation when the pure light of God's Word once more shone upon Europe, though the church of Rome in her Council of Trent desperately sought to defend " Arminian " principles, the Reformers to a man declared against them. That any man can be saved by the exercise of his free will they utterly repudiated. To attribute the denial of free-will solely to Calvin of Geneva is a plain ignorance of facts. The Spirit of truth led Luther to reject it before ever Calvin began his historic Genevan ministry ; in England already by 1538 such Reformers as Lambert—who died at the stake with those glorious words on his lips : " None but Christ. None but Christ "—were ready to lay down their lives rather than assent to such unscriptural doctrines as man's free-will in his salvation. In his trial for life Lambert fearlessly opposed his Romanist persecutors with such words as these : " Concerning free-will I mean altogether as doth St. Augustine :

That, of ourselves, we have NO liberty nor ability to do the will of God ; but are shut up and sold under sin." But such is the desolate state of the church to-day that Arminianism passes for the truth ; it cannot be true for truth does not change with the centuries. What the Holy Spirit has testified to be false in times past is false now. Though Arminianism may be regarded as a small matter in men's eyes, it has never been so to those whom God has instructed in His Word. Those Christians who were God's instruments in bringing the Bible to us in our own language were not contending about nothing when they were ready to oppose " Arminianism " with their lives. What were the grounds upon which they rejected it, and upon which we must reject it to-day ? It is to be rejected because the Word of God rejects it.

Arminianism strikes at the very foundation of the Gospel. The Scriptures show God to be eternally sufficient in Himself, that which is infinite—that is God—cannot be added to ; the glory and happiness of God cannot be added to, therefore they could not be the moving motive in His creation of man because He needs not any glory or happiness that arises from man. God was under no necessity to create, but at perfect liberty ; it was His will alone that brought this world into being. But having willed it, the end of His design was the manifestation of His glorious nature. None of God's actions, the Scriptures declare, are primarily for man's sake, but "for Thy pleasure they are and were created " (Rev. iv. 11 ; Rom. xi. 36). " For of Him, and through Him, and to Him, are all things, to whom be glory for ever. Amen." To be ignorant of this is to be ignorant of both the beginning and the end of all the purposes of God. It was the Sovereign pleasure of God alone that gave man a being and did not leave us eternally in the womb of nothingness.

Now God retains this sovereignty in all His actions. When the angels fell they were all immediately condemned, and none could reply unto God " What doest Thou ". So when man fell and became all alike corrupt and undone, the objects of the righteous wrath of God, God was under no necessity to deliver any from the consequences of sin. He would have remained eternally righteous if He had rejected all. But out of that corrupt mass God had an election, those whom He chose, though nothing in them led Him to do it, but solely " according to the good pleasure of His will " (Eph. i. 5). " For He saith unto Moses, I will have mercy on whom I will have mercy." The grace of God is that free love which He bestows upon some, while others are passed by in their sins. Grace is more than love, it is that sovereign favour of God cast upon some totally without any meriting cause in themselves. The elect were the objects of God's grace in eternity (when they had no existence except in the mind of God) (II Tim. i. 9). These were given to Christ before the foundation of the world (Eph. i. 4), and as the Fall necessitated the removal of sin from the elect, Christ became responsible for removing all the consequences of the Fall from those which the Father had given Him. For them alone He took a human nature, and died to satisfy justice (John vi. 37-39 and Ch. xvii. 2, 9). They alone have the truth revealed to them (Matt. xiii. 11), and are granted the gift of faith (Eph. ii. 8 ; Acts xiii. 48). The salvation of any soul depends solely upon the eternal grace of God, none are saved except those whom grace predestinated, and the end of it all—the end of all true preaching—is " to the praise of the glory of His grace."

Reader, reject not these things because they are not fashionable in these degenerate days. What the Reformers thought worthy of sealing with their blood ought, at least, to be worthy of your earnest attention. We do not ask you to assent to the opinions of men, but to examine the Word of God. You will then find that Arminianism overturns the very design of God, it denies God the right to be sovereign, it declares God is obliged to show mercy to all, it rejects the free grace of God and asserts that any fallen creature can " decide " to have grace by the exercise of his free-will. That man is impotent, " shut up in unbelief ", and fettered in sin, it overlooks. Salvation is no longer the outworking of the eternal Counsel of God, but the action of man. The chief design of God, " the praise of the glory of His grace ", is no longer the chief design in Arminian preaching. Such teaching is a corruption of the truth, it is not what the Spirit of truth has written in the Word, and the God of truth has a controversy with any church based on such a system.

Arminian principles are common to the minds of natural men (therefore believers often retain Arminian opinions for some time after their conversions). Whenever a church falls from revealed truth, it falls into Arminianism. Therefore the Apostle Paul, knowing by inspiration that the church at Ephesus would be assaulted by error, and knowing that error begins by denying the sovereignty of God, he sets out in the Epistle to the Ephesians those doctrines of eternal predestination and sovereign grace which are the corner stones of the whole revelation of God.

To-day one thing is certain for Britain : God will have His truth glorified, either actively by our acknowledgement of it, or passively by declaring His truth through our destruction. One hope stands between our land and ruin, the hope that He will in mercy revive His truth. Believer, this is the day for you to make the truth of God the object of your prayers and earnest attention. All things else will pass away, " the grass withereth, the flower fadeth : but the Word of our God shall stand for ever." That the Lord will bless this magazine to your soul, and that you may stand on the side of truth, is the prayer of your servants in the Gospel,

SIDNEY NORTON. 162 Banbury Road, Oxford.
IAN MURRAY. 85 Kingston Road, Oxford.

" . . . STAND THEREFORE, HAVING YOUR LOINS GIRT ABOUT WITH TRUTH."

Extracts from WILLIAM GURNALL on Ephesians vi. 14.

What is here meant by loins that are to be girt with this girdle? Peter will help to interpret Paul : " gird up the loins of your minds " (I Pet. i. 13). It is our minds that must wear this girdle of Truth, and very fitly may our mind be compared to the loins. The loins are the chief seat of bodily strength. If the loins fail the whole body sinks ; hence to " smite through the loins " is a phrase to express destruction and ruin (Deut. xxxiii. 11). Weak loins, then a weak man. Thus it is with our minds ; if the understanding be clear in its apprehensions of truth then he is a strong Christian, but an uncertain mind is ever accompanied by feeble spirits. So just as our loins need a girdle for support, our minds need this girdle of truth, or else we shall do nothing vigorously. Let us mark some reasons why it should be the first care of every Christian to get an established judgment in the truth.

A true love to God will make the soul inquisitive to find out what is near and dear to God. Now upon a little search we shall find that the great God sets a very high price upon the head of truth (Ps. lxxxviii. 2). " Thou hast magnified Thy Word above all Thy Name ". That is called God's Name by which He is known, every creature hath God's Name upon it ; by His created works God is known, even the least pile of grass displays His Name. But to His Word God hath given pre-eminence above all other things that bear His Name. The Word is the glass in which we see God, it is the " word of truth " because it sets out The God of Truth in all His glory. Not only is His Word the extract of His thoughts and counsels which from everlasting He took up, but it is, chiefly, the most full and perfect representation that God Himself could give of His own being—that is His Name or attributes. Although God's glorious nature is seen in His other works it is nowhere else seen so fully as in His Word, and therefore He values it more than all His other works ; He cares not much what becomes of this world and all in it, so long as He keeps His Word and saves His Truth. Ere long we shall see the world in flames ; " the heavens and earth shall pass away, but the Word of the Lord endures for ever ". When God will, He can make more such worlds as this ; but He cannot make another truth, and therefore He will not lose one jot thereof. Let us mind this, and know that as we deal with " the Word of Truth ", so we deal with God Himself ; he that despiseth that, despiseth Him. He that abandons the truth of God, renounceth the God of Truth. Though men cannot come to pull God out of His throne, and deprive Him of His Godhead, yet they come as near this as it is possible, when they let out their hatred against the truth : in this they do, as it were, execute God in effigy. But such is God's care for His own Glory that He will preserve that Word of Truth which conveys a knowledge of His Glory to men. However much Satan works to deface and disfigure the Word by unsound doctrine, God will maintain His especial care of His Truth ; whatever else is lost, God looks to His Truth. In shipwrecks at sea, and fires by land, when men can save but little they use not to choose lumber. and things of no value, but what they esteem most precious. Likewise in all the great revolutions, changes, and overturning of kingdoms, and churches also, God hath still preserved His Truth. Thousands of saints' lives have been lost, but that which the Devil hates more than all the saints ; yea, which alone he hates them for (that is the truth) this lives, and shall to triumph over his malice ; and sure if truth were not very dear to God, He would not be at this cost to keep it with the blood of His saints ; yea, which is more, with the blood of His Son ; whose errand into the world was by life and death " to bear witness to the truth " (John xviii. 37). In a word, in that great and dismal conflagration of heaven and earth, when the elements shall melt for heat, and the world shall come to its fatal period, then truth shall not suffer the least loss, but the Word of the Lord endureth for ever. There is reason we see, why God should so highly prize His Truth, and that we that love Him should have our minds girt with it.

A further powerful reason why believers ought to be established in the Truth comes from the days in which we live. Never was there a more giddy age than ours ! What unsettledness of judgment possesses this unconstant age ! Truths to the minds of most professing believers, are not as stars fixed in the heavens, but like meteors, that dance in the air ; they are not as characters engraven in marble, but writ in dust, which every wind and idle breath of error defaces. If the heathen (who did not glorify God with the light of nature they had) were given over to a reprobate mind, then how much more has a land like ours, which has dishonoured God with the revealed light of Scripture truth, deserved to have been given up to believe lies and errors. A heavy curse indeed to wonder and wilder in a maze of error and yet think they are walking in the way of truth. Well, shall believers, in such days as these, remain spectators in the struggle of God's Truth ? Does not a Prince expect his subjects to be in the field, to declare their loyalty, by owning his quarrel against an invading enemy ? O it were shame with a witness, that any effeminate delicacy should be found amongst Christ's servants, that they cannot break a little with their worldly rest to attend upon Him and His Truth ! Let us get the girdle of truth close about us, that we may be able to hold fast the profession of it, even in the face of danger and death, and not be offended when persecution arises. Blessed be God, it is not yet come to that, we have truth at a cheaper rate ; but how soon the market may rise, we know not. Truth is not always had at the same price. And let me tell you, there has, is, and will be a spirit of persecution in the hearts of the wicked unto the end of the world. Satan comes first with a spirit of error, and then of persecution ; he first corrupts men's minds, and then enrages hearts against those who hold the truth. It is impossible, that error being a brat of Hell, should be peaceable, it would not be like its father. That which is from beneath cannot be peaceable. How far God has suffered this sulphureous spirit of error to prevail, is so well known (or ought to be) that no apology can cover the nakedness of these unhappy times. It is therefore high time to have our girdle of truth on, yea, close girt about us. Let us mind the damning nature of error and what God has for all who fall from the truth. When we know what God has prepared for the " fearful " (Rev. xxi. 8) and all that run away from Truth's colours (Hebrews x. 39) then we will lose the fear of man. " Pardon me, O Emperor," said a godly man, " if I do not obey your command ; you threaten a prison, but God a Hell." Man's wrath, when hottest, is but a temperate climate, to the wrath of the living God.

Finally let us mark that Truth shall be victorious. It is great and shall prevail at last. It is the great counsel of God, and though many plots may be in the hearts of men, yet the counsel of the Lord shall stand. Sometimes I confess, the enemies to truth get the control of this lower world into their hands, and then the truth seems to go to the ground, and yet it is more than error can do to keep truth in the grave. Who loves not to be on the winning side ? Choose Truth for your side and you have it. News may come that truth is sick, but never that truth is dead. No, it is error that is short lived ; " a lying tongue is but for a moment ", but truth's age runs parallel with God's eternity. It shall live to see the heads of all who oppose it laid in the dust. Live, did I say ? Yea, reign in peace with those who now are willing to suffer with, and for it. Wouldest thou not (Christian) be one of those among the train of victors who shall attend on Christ's triumphant chariot into the heavenly city, there to take the crown, and sit down in thy throne with those that have kept the field when Christ and His Truth were militant here on earth ? Thus wouldest thou but wipe away—in your thoughts—the tears and blood which now cover the face of suffering truth, and present truth to thy eye, as it shall look in glory, thou couldest not but cleave to it with a love stronger than death.

ELECTION

" Election having once pitched upon a man, it will find him out and call him home, wherever he be. It called Zaccheus out of accursed Jericho ; Abraham out of idolatrous Ur of the Chaldees ; Nicodemus and Paul, from the College of the Pharisees, Christ's sworn enemies; Dionysius and Damaris, out of superstitious Athens. In whatsoever dunghills God's elect are hid, election will find them out and bring them home."—ARROWSMITH.

" Predestination when rightly understood, never leads to sloth ; it has been frequently, in human history, of tremendous force for the production of the most daring and determined action and it shall be so again. ' Since God wills it we will it '."

Spurgeon - A Call to Prayer & Testimony

MARTIN LUTHER : CERTAINTY IN THE TRUTH

It was a day of grace for Europe when Martin Luther was born at Eisleben, in Germany, in 1483. Entering first the University of Erfurt in 1501, then an Augustinian monastery, Luther was ordained in the Church of Rome in 1507. But the death of a friend in a thunderstorm, a visit to Rome—revealing its corruption—and an increasing sense of his sinfulness, arrested Luther's promising career. Made aware of the emptiness of all human wisdom, its inability to give peace to the soul, he was drawn to study the Word of God. So great was his anguish of soul that sometimes he would lay " three days and three nights upon his bed without meat, drink, or any sleep, like a dead man." In this condition he learnt to read each verse in the Bible like a drowning man would clutch at any piece of wood to save his life, and thus sometime between the years 1513–1517 he found that man can be justified by faith in Christ alone, and that in salvation God takes no account of man's works, merit, or will. " This doctrine," Luther writes, " is not learned or gotten by any study, diligence, or wisdom of man, but it is revealed by God Himself." Henceforth he stood upon the Word of God alone, it was his store-house from whence he drew those truths which, in his writings, flashed like thunderbolts through Europe. In 1519 Erasmus writes to Luther that " his books had raised such an uproar at Louvain, as it was not possible for him to describe." God had begun a conflict for His Truth, and it was bitterly opposed. " I had " Luther says, " hanging on my neck the pope, the universities, all the deep learned, and the devil ; these hunted me into the Bible, wherein I sedulously read . . ." An " illiterate monk " thus became, in the hands of God, too much—as Margaret the Emperor's sister confessed—for all the academics in Paris to answer. By 1520 there was an irreconcilable break with the Church of Rome ; the pope was determined that Luther and his gospel should perish together.

A man-made religion will ever contest with those who preach that salvation is solely of the grace of God. There is a clean differ-ence between the two. This was exemplified in Luther's disputation with Eckius, the Romanist champion, in 1519, when the first point of dispute was over free-will. " We condemn," Luther proclaimed, " man's free-will, his strength, his wisdom, and all religion of man's own devising ; in short, we say that there is nothing in us able to deserve grace." The compromising Erasmus rightly saw free-will to be a chief issue between Luther and Rome, and fearing the displeasure of man, he wrote in defence of man's free-will in salvation. This brought forth in reply Luther's mighty work on " The Bondage of The Will ". Erasmus rather than attempting the hopeless task of showing that the Bible teaches free-will and not God's eternal election, had sought to avoid the issue by complaining that there could be no usefulness in teaching doctrines of election and predestination. Luther, sweeping aside his evasions, demands to know whether the

doctrines are of God or not ? " Where, alas ! Erasmus, are your fear
and reverence of God, when you roundly declare that this branch
of truth, which He has revealed from heaven, is at best, useless ?
What ! Shall the Glorious Creator be taught by you, His creature,
what is fit to be preached ? Is the adorable God so very defective
in knowledge, as not to know, till you instruct Him, what would be
useful and what pernicious ? Could He not know the consequence
of His revealing this doctrine, till those consequences were pointed
out by you ? Who art thou, O Erasmus, that thou shouldst reply
against God ! Paul, discoursing of God, says, " Whom He will
He hardeneth." And again, " God willing to show His wrath . . ."
and the Apostle did not write this to have it stifled among a few
persons, and buried in a corner, but wrote it to the Christians at
Rome ; which was, in effect, bringing this doctrine upon the stage
of the whole world, stamping a universal imprimature upon it, and
publishing it to believers at large throughout the world. What can
sound harsher to carnal men than those words of Christ, ' I know
whom I have chosen ' ? Now these and similar assertions of Christ
and His Apostles, are the very positions which you, O Erasmus, brand
as useless and hurtful ! " Luther then goes on to show why the
doctrines of election and grace are to be preached, " Whilst a man
is persuaded that he has it in his power to contribute anything, be it
ever so little, to his salvation, he remains in carnal self-confidence ;
he is not a self-despairer, and therefore is not duly humbled before
God, he believes he may lend a helping hand in his salvation, but
on the contrary, whoever is truly convinced that the whole work
depends singly on the will of God, such a person renounces his own
will and strength ; he waits and prays for the operation of God, nor
waits and prays in vain . . ."
        Luther's characteristic is certainty in the Truth. " A man must
be able to affirm, I know for certain, that what I teach is the only
Word of the high majesty of God in Heaven, His Final conclusion
and Everlasting Unchangeable Truth, and whatsoever concurs and
agrees not with this doctrine is altogether false, and spun by the
devil . . . To God's Word will I remain, though the whole world
be against me." Commenting on Paul's certainty in the truth on
Galatians i. 9, he writes, " he dare curse all teachers throughout the
world and in heaven, which pervert the Gospel that Paul preached,
or teach any other ; for all men must either believe that Gospel that
he preached, or else be accursed and condemned." Such was
Luther's certainty of the truth that he cared not for any man : ex-
communicated by the pope, he replied by throwing the papal bull
into a fire with the prayer " Because thou hast troubled the Holy One
of God let eternal fire trouble thee." When King Henry VIII of
England was incensed to write against the truth, Luther answered
him very plainly, and defends his sharpness of language thus : " nor

ought it to be considered as a great matter if I affront and treat sharply an earthly prince, who has dared to blaspheme the King of Heaven in his writings, insulting His Name with lies." Again we see his boldness in stating God's truth that all relying upon their works for salvation, not justified by faith in Christ alone, are under the curse of God (Gal. iii. 10). "This the pope and his proud prelates do not believe. Yet must we not hold our peace but must confess the truth and say, that the papacy is accursed ; yea the Emperor is accursed ; for according to Paul, whatsoever is without the promise and faith of Abraham, is accursed."

Luther was a man void of ambition. He took no money for his written works. His consuming desire was the declaration of the Truth of God. The Bible was the beginning and end of his thoughts, without it, he said, all the learning in the world is not worth a straw. His dying prayer was that God would preserve His church in the truth, and his last words : " Thee, O Christ have I known, thee have I loved, thee have I taught, thee have I trusted, into thy hands I commend my spirit." It would be a happy day indeed, should God cause His children to return and study the works of His servant, Martin Luther, then we could say : " Earth still enjoys him, tho' his soul is fled, his name is deathless, tho' his dust is dead."

SALVATION BY GRACE

Comments on Ephesians Ch. 2, taken from the writings of Thomas Goodwin, President of Magdalen College, Oxford, 1650.

In Ephesians chapter two, the Apostle having described our lost condition by nature goes on to enumerate the benefits we have in and by Christ. But not sooner does Paul state the first blessing a soul experiences " quickening " (that is conversion) in ver. v., than he must break in with the cause of this salvation, " by grace ye are saved," this abrupt manner with which he brings the cause in—before he finishes his sentence—argues that he had this thing in his thoughts, his thoughts were full of it, and it must break out. " By grace ye are saved," he states it briefly at first, but then repeats it again and again ; he opens it more largely in ver. viii, showing it to be the cause of our salvation excluding all things else ; he cuts off all pleas whatsoever that might share the honour with free grace. There is nothing that hath been more corrupted in all ages than the truth that free grace alone is the cause of our salvation, therefore Paul states it both briefly and largely, to the end that we might have in our eye this as the chief result and scope of his discourse.

Furthermore it is no wonder he should so repeat the truth of grace, for grace is the first great end and design of God. So ver. vii, you have it, " That in the ages to come, He might shew the exceeding

B

riches of His grace." Therefore let us observe that the dependency our salvation hath upon free grace, is the greatest thing in the Gospel. It is that which the Apostle would have these Ephesians above all things, else to take notice of. He sets therefore this mark upon it by this parenthesis in ver. v, as if he had said, " Remember this, as the great result of my discourse, to hold forth this to you, to beget thoughts of this in you, that ' by grace ye are saved '."

Let us then enquire what is meant by " grace " here. In ver. iv. the mercy and love of God were stated to be the cause of salvation. But here in ver. v. he brings grace in as a cause distinct in some way from mercy and love. " The Lord, gracious and merciful " (Exod. xxxiv. 6), grace you see is a distinct thing from mercy . Grace is the same thing for substance with love and mercy, yet it holds forth something more eminently than both ; this expression " grace " is more than mercy and love, it superadds to them. It denotes, not simply love, but the love of a sovereign, transcendently superior, one that may do what he will, that may wholly choose whether he will love or no. There may be love between equals, and an inferior may love a superior ; but love in a superior, and so superior as he may do what he will, in such a one love is called grace : and therefore grace is attributed to princes ; they are said to be gracious to their subjects, whereas subjects cannot be gracious to princes. Now God, Who is an infinite sovereign, Who might have chosen whether ever He would love us or no, for Him to love us, this is grace. In Exodus xxxiv. 6, when God proclaims His Name, what is the first word ? " The Lord, The Lord," and " Gracious " is the next. I am the sovereign Lord of all creatures ; if I shew mercy, this is grace. Grace notes the greatest freeness, God is not necessitated to love any, and when He loves He loves freely—that is, His love is not caused or motivated by anything in the creature (Man fallen in sin has forfeited any hope that God is " obliged " to love him). Therefore, where the Apostle uses the word " grace " or " graciously ", our translators often render the word, to " give us freely ". Thus in I Cor. ii. 12, and Romans viii. 32, " freely " is the same word, " graciously ". Now for God to give us freely implies this truth, that He set His heart on us merely out of His own good will. Mark how His will and grace are joined together in Eph. i. 5-6. In the 5th verse he said God " predestinated us . . . according to the good pleasure of His Will "; and in the 6th verse he says, " to the praise of the glory of His Grace." When God doth thus choose and predestinate merely out of the motion of His own will, this is freeness, and this makes it grace. Grace signifies the sovereignty of God's will, that He may love whom He will, and do what He will, merely as a sovereign. " Behold the heaven and the heaven of heavens is the Lord's thy God, the earth also, with all that is therein. Only the Lord had a delight in thy fathers, to love them, and to choose

We can love God : we can't be gracious to God.

their seed after them, even you above all people " (Deut. x. 14). If I would choose, saith God, I have choice enough, I have the heaven of heavens, I could have filled all those with creatures ; and there were the angels that fell, I might have chosen those, and fixed them as stars, never to have fallen ; but I let multitudes of them tumble down to Hell. And I have the earth also, and all the nations thereof before me ; but to shew my love in a special manner I have chosen you. " You only have I known of all the families of the earth " (Amos iii. 2). God casts His grace upon what persons He will. Amongst men there is no difference, " but all have sinned ", as the Apostle says (Rom. iii. 22), then comes in, " being justified freely by His grace ". God has a freedom, in respect of persons, to this person or that person, and not to others. Therefore in Romans xi. 5, whereas all were in a like condition, this free taking of a remnant, this choosing of these and not others, is out of grace ; it is therefore called " the election of grace ". Moreover, as God respects no persons, so He respects no conditions upon which He gives salvation to us. I say in giving pardon of sin, justification, and heaven at last, He doth it freely without conditions. Faith is not a condition of salvation, but the Apostle terms it plainly an effect of grace—" the grace of God was exceeding abundant in faith and love," that is, in working faith and love. So also in ver. viii. of this chapter two of Ephesians, faith is not a condition, but " the gift of God ".

Mind this then, that in the work of salvation God has so ordered, and designed, and plotted all things, to the advancement of His free grace. In Rom. iv. 21 it is said " grace reigned " . . . It reigneth, mark it ; of all things else, God hath set up His free grace as a monarch, and hath so set it up as that it shall reign ; and there is no work of man, or anything in man, that shall in the least impair the sovereignty of it. We are therefore said to be " under grace " in Rom. 6. and that therefore " sin shall no more have dominion over us," because we are under the dominion of grace, implying that grace is a mighty king and sovereign. God has so ordered salvation that free grace alone shall be magnified.

Free grace is the sole cause of all the parts and benefits of salvation. The election of those whom God would hereafter call is attributed solely to " His own purpose and grace, which was given us in Christ Jesus before the world began " (II Tim. i. 9). Then in time they are " called by grace " (Gal. i. 15). What is it that caused God to call, and convert a man ? .It is that original grace of God given to His chosen in eternity, conversion is a fresh act of that same grace ; by that same grace we are justified (Titus iii. 7), and our whole state afterwards is one of being " under grace ", " the grace wherein we stand." Paul attributes his ministry solely to grace, he attributes the generosity of the Macedonians solely to God's grace, he attributes the sanctification of believers to grace working in us "both to will and to do His good pleasure". Lastly, for heaven, though God must give holiness before it, when God comes to bestow it He doth it out of the same grace by which He chose a man at the first, and as freely ; therefore eternal life is called " a gift of grace ". How are Christians described, their persons, and the work of grace upon them ? Read the New Testament : how are their persons expressed ? " They that receive abundance of grace " (Rom. v. 17). He might have said believers. No, but " those that receive abundance of grace ", and he contrasts them with unbelievers and men condemned : they are free-grace receivers, you may well call them so. And so in Acts xv. 11, they are called such as believe through the grace of God. And how is the work of God upon them described ? How is the work of conversion described ? Col. i. 6 : " Since ye knew the grace of God in truth ". So then we say that salvation, both the whole and every part of it, is attributed solely to the grace of God.

Let us finally observe that our salvation by grace is of the greatest moment for believers to know and to be acquainted with. The Apostle here you see in Eph. ii. 5, cannot hold speaking out his whole sentence before he brings in this ; as soon as ever he had said " we are quickened by Christ ", he comes in with, " by grace ye are saved." He would have it with a treble impression on their hearts, so he enlarges in verses vii and viii. This is the great axiom, the great principle he would beget in their hearts. It is the sum and substance of the gospel, and to advance the glory of His grace is the sum of the great design of God. Therefore the advancement of His glory by grace being the design of God, you will find that when a man doth step out of the way and road of free-grace unto anything else, he is said to turn aside from God. See Gal. i. 6 : " I marvel that you are so soon removed from Him that called you "—it was because they did not hold the doctrine of free grace—" into the grace of Christ, unto another gospel " ; implying that it is a turning aside from God. It being God's great design to advance grace, and therefore he calls their stepping aside from the doctrine thereof, a frustrating of the grace of God (Gal. ii. 21), which men do by mixing anything else with it. It is a frustrating of the grace of God because it frustrateth the great design of God, for to frustrate is to make void a design. By mingling anything else with it you frustrate the design of God, and turn from Him unto another Gospel. The ministry which Paul received, what was it ? To testify the grace of God. And to divert from it the Apostle interprets to be a turning to another gospel, and he pronounceth a curse to any that shall do it, even unto angels themselves. My brethren, grace is the main thing of the gospel, and to trust perfectly in grace, not by halves, but fully, is the greatest thing in the world. " I have written to testify unto you that this is the true grace in which ye stand " (I Peter v. 12).

IGNORING THE ANALOGIES

The work of regeneration or conversion is an operation performed by the Lord the Spirit in the hearts of all the elect, and in none else. The prophet Ezekiel attributes it to the sovereign will of God (see Ezek. xxxvi. 26), and what this prophet says comports with the general teaching on regeneration found in the Bible. It has pleased the Lord to show His people the nature of this work by giving it various names, or descriptions, each of which is designed to teach that it is performed by His almighty power and that the creature's will can have no share in it. These names are God-given types or analogies of regeneration, and to the minister of the glorious gospel of the grace of God it is essential to observe them, for they carry the most important instruction. Among those that are found in the Scriptures three stand out prominently. They are the analogies of Creation, Birth, and Resurrection. We find the first in 2 Cor. v. 17. Paul under inspiration calls conversion a creation. What is the main teaching of this figure ? Surely it is this, that God created the heavens and earth, the old creation, without the co-operation of any creature, and that He performs the new creation, a far more stupendous work, likewise without creature assistance. Take the second which is the analogy of birth (John i. 13). What is the basic instruction here ? Is it not plainly seen when we answer another question : Is there a living creature in the whole universe who asked to be born ? Can one be found who exercised his own will in the matter of his birth or who had any say in it initially ? The answer is in the negative. The third analogy, that of resurrection, conveys most important instruction, too (Eph. ii. 5-6). Can the power of man call the dead to life ? No ! In the frightful presence of death man is powerless to do anything.

The church of God is troubled with so-called evangelists whose method of preaching betrays an ignorance of basic truths. Attention given to the God-given analogies of conversion would do much to disperse a kind of evangelism that lacks Scriptural warrant, and is a source of grief to many of God's servants who know that such evangelism will have the baneful tendency of confusing natural excitement and human decisions with the supernatural work of God in conversion. The slogan of contemporary evangelists shows that they believe that human nature can exert its will and generate the great work of regeneration. Preposterous as it is, the idea has gained ascendancy that the will of our Holy God is dependent on the carnal and corrupt will of the sinner, that the Lord must surrender His sovereignty to the " sovereignty " of a creature. The term " will you let God ", used so frequently, conveys the erroneous idea that God's will needs the assistance of man's will to perform the work of regeneration. Such an idea is opposite to the God-given figure of creation which shows that none can assist the Lord in this. The phrase " decide for Christ " which is extravagantly used at campaigns today, reverses the Scriptural teaching that man, in his natural state, is dead in trespasses and sins. How can the dead decide? The analogy of birth is completely ignored by the constant appeals made to the creature to take the initiative. Surely there is great need for a return to the evangelism that is supported by Scriptural authority. This means a reversal of the order that is now accepted which denies the sovereign will of God. We need not be apprehensive of the question whether sinners will be saved. The Lord will see to that. Evangelism that is not based upon the truth is the most fertile soil for the production of counterfeit Christians, but that which has God's authority is productive both to His glory and the salvation of sinners.

S. NORTON.

OBSERVATIONS ON ROMANS, CHAPTER NINE
From "The Eternal Predestination Of God,"
a treatise by John Calvin, 1552.

The salvation of believers depends upon the eternal election of God for which no cause or reason can be rendered but His own gratuitous good pleasure. God calls (converts), justifies, and glorifies, no one but him whom He had ordained unto eternal life. Conversion is the seal or ratification of His eternal election. Let those roar at us who will, let them pretend this truth to be against the goodness or justice of God. But if we do God an injury who set His election above all other causes, Paul taught this doctrine long before us. Let these enemies of God dispute the matter with the Apostle. "Therefore", Paul says in Romans ix. 18, "He hath mercy on whom He will have mercy, and on whom He will He hardeneth", that is, he resolves salvation solely into the will of God.

The rejection of Christ by the Jews, who called themselves the church, was a great obstacle and a formidable barrier to the weak, therefore the Apostle undertakes to explain their unbelief in the following manner :— He by no means makes the fleshly seed, the legitimate children of Abraham ; but accounts the children of promise alone for the seed, and those were the children of promise whom God chose before they were born. Therefore the rejection of Christ by the Jewish nations was not a failure in God's purposes ; that those who professed to be the church should oppose the truth ought not to make believers stumble. No, but just as Jacob and Esau were separated in the womb to a different destiny, so the Apostle assigns the cause of the present difference—the unbelief of the Jew and the salvation of Gentiles—to the Counsel of God.

But our opponents assert that grace was offered to both Jacob and Esau ; and one was willing to accept, what by his free will he could accept ; and the other refused it. So that, election they say, depends on the future works or will of man which God forsees ; God

foresaw how men would react to the truth. But the Apostle takes for
a fact what is wholly overlooked by these excellent theologians—that
all men are alike unworthy, and equally corrupt—they dream of some
good in man, but the Apostle, knowing the true nature of man, knew
that none would be obedient unless they were first elected.

Paul knew that election without works would raise the objections
of men, which he anticipates by stating what carnal would reply
against this doctrine in verses xiv and xix : " Thou wilt say then unto
me, Why doth He yet find fault ? For who hath resisted His will ? "
If indeed the solution is so plain and satisfactory—that God offers
grace to all, and only makes a difference from respect to their future
works—there would be no need to anticipate objections, for none
would object against the justice of that. When our opponents place
the cause of election or reprobation in the works of men's coming
lives, they seem to escape and solve this very objection which Paul
supposes them to put. Whence it is fully evident, that the Apostle
was not instructed in this new wisdom. For be it so—that works
foreseen are the cause of election—then the Apostle introduces these
men quarrelling with the justice of God quite out of place ; and were
it so, why does he not say so, instead of entangling himself deeper
and asserting that the cause of the difference between Jacob and Esau
rested in the will of God alone ? Why then did he turn to Moses,
and bring forward God's own claim and free right to exercise His
mercy as, and towards whom, He pleased ? For God declared he
would be the Master, Lord, and Arbiter, of His own mercy. He
did not say that His choice of them depended on themselves, but
rather that He would spare whom He would spare, as being bound
by no necessity to choose either one or another. And the Apostle
next infers, that which of necessity follows from the above declaration
of God to Moses, that " it is not of him that willeth, nor of him that
runneth, but of God that showeth mercy." For if the salvation of
men depends on the mercy of God alone, there can be absolutely
nothing left for men to do, will, or determine, in the matter of salvation. " Most absurd," therefore says Augustine, " is the cunning
device of certain ones who spin, out of these important questions, a
conclusion that there is a kind of concurrence, or half-way meeting,
between the mercy of God and the endeavours of man—as if Paul
meant, that men can do very little . . . whereas the Apostle reduces
man to nothing, that he may give all to the mercy of God. Paul does
not answer the objection that he knew would be raised by the interpretation of election invented by our adversaries—" Because God
foresaw their future works." The Apostle does nothing of the kind.
On the contrary, he introduces the all-conclusive word of God to
Moses, " For He saith to Moses, I will have mercy on whom I will
have mercy." Where are merits now ! Where are works either
past or future, either fulfilled or to be fulfilled, as by the power or

strength of free-will ! Does not the Apostle openly declare his mind in commendation of free grace only ? ''

The Holy Spirit condemns in this chapter the impious pride of all who measure the justice of God by their own comprehension, and who presume to subject the tribunal of God to their own judgment— " O man who art thou that repliest against God ! " Let them beware therefore, who assert that they vindicate the justice of God and fear lest it be endangered by the doctrine of election. Such men speak according to their own natural understanding. God would have us know that His honour is not to be protected by our lies. God Himself not only rejects such a protection as this, but declares in the Book of Job, that it is hateful to Him. Let such defenders take care, lest by affecting greater caution than the Lord prescribes in His Word, they become guilty of madness and folly. For believers to praise the goodness of God worthily it is necessary to know how much we are indebted to Him ; those who remain ignorant of the cause of the difference between themselves and others have never yet learned to render unto God the glory due unto Him for making that difference. The justified may learn from the condemnation of the rest what would have been their own punishment had not free grace stepped in.''

Dear Reader,

The object of the ministry of this paper is to send out sound words of truth, with the conviction that there can be no greater matter of concern to the church of God than the truth of God. "When a nation is to perish in its sins, 'tis in the church the leprosy begins," says a godly poet. A great part of knowledge lies in the knowledge of causes : the true cause of a disease found out goes far to the reaching of the cure. What is the cause of the dread leprosy upon the church which has sapped its strength and rendered it incapable of giving a cogent answer to the power of Satan today ? We believe it is this, that the church has dethroned the sovereign will of God and has enthroned the sinful will of man in its place. This is the root cause of our trouble today. We believe there are those of God's children who share this conviction. If you, dear reader, having read this paper, are moved with concern, let me ask you to fill in the form enclosed and send the same to the Rev. Sidney Norton, 162 Banbury Road, Oxford. If you know of others who would be interested, please give us their names and addresses, so that copies can be sent to them also. According to the measure in which we are enabled, our desire is to continue to propagate the truth as fully, widely, and often as possible. There are great stores of written treasure, amassed by God's servants in past generations, now lying buried under the dust of time. We wish to unearth this treasure and disperse it far and wide on the printed page. We earnestly solicit your prayerful attention.

" When heaven is shut up, and there is no rain, because they have sinned against Thee ; if they pray toward this place, and confess Thy Name, and turn from their sin, when Thou afflictest them : then hear Thou in heaven, and forgive the sin of Thy servants, and of Thy people Israel, that Thou teach them the good way wherein they should walk, and give rain on Thy land, which Thou hast given to Thy people for an inheritance."—I Kings viii. 35.

Printed by Geo. T. Bailey. 335 Harold Road. Hastings. and Published by S. Norton. 162 Banbury Road. Oxford.

The
Banner of Truth

FEBRUARY :: 1956

" Thou hast shewed thy people hard things ;
Thou hast made us to drink the wine of
astonishment.   Thou hast given a banner to
them that fear Thee, that it may be displayed
because of the truth."   Psalm 60 : 3-4

EDITORIAL COMMENTS

Dear Reader,—What awe and reverence ought to possess us when we begin to consider the revelation of God's Truth! The great intention of God in teaching His children is that our souls might be continually transformed and restored into His image : the knowledge of this intention ought to produce in us an earnest desire to apprehend the truth, in order that God might be glorified in us by a thankful and holy life. When we are taught by the Spirit of God every truth will have a practical effect upon us, we shall be increasingly filled with faith, love, humility, and wonder at the condescension of God. The primary purpose of Scripture then is to promote godliness.

Now it is a sad fact that although the Word of God was given for the above purpose, it also has another effect upon men, it arouses controversy and strife. Opposition to the truth is inevitable in a world where men's minds are alienated from God by sin, ' the carnal mind is enmity against God,' Rom. 8 : 7. Moreover when truth appears Satan ceases to slumber and sleep ; it is when truth disturbs the profound darkness which Satan and sin has brought upon man that tumult arises. So it was that the witness of Elijah, and of Paul, and of ' the Lord Himself ' while upon earth, was met with violent opposition and contention. All believers are for the same reason involved in controversy with the world—" I have given them Thy Word and the world hath hated them," Jn. 17 : 14. This controversy is a grief to their heaven born souls, but avoid it they cannot, for they dare not sit in Gallio's seat (Acts 18 : 17), nor act as the inhabitants of Meroz (Judges 5 : 23) when the struggle for God and His truth is taking place. Nevertheless although we are thus forced into controversy, our motives are to be very different from those which cause unconverted men to contend with each other. It is no party spirit nor personal interest which moves us, no, but we are moved by that which moved the Psalmist when he wrote, ' Rivers of tears run down mine eyes, because they keep not thy law.' God and His Word were dishonoured, this is what broke the Psalmist's heart. It was chiefly this same feeling which made Paul say, ' I could wish that myself were accursed from Christ for my brethren, my kinsmen according to the flesh,' Rom. 9 : 3. The Apostle felt it as a great obscuring of the glory of Christ that the Jews rejected their own Messiah, it also prejudiced many against the Gospel that it had not been received by those to whom it was first preached, therefore he supposes that if the common salvation of the Jews was more to the glory of God than His own particular salvation, then he valued the glory that would redound to God more than his own happiness. Unless we have this same motive— the glory of God—in opposing error, then we have nothing more than a carnal spirit.

A true love for God and His glory will also manifest itself by a fervent love towards men, both unconverted and brethren in the Lord. When we see men deluded by Satan ; in that condition which was ours by nature—' foolish, disobedient, deceived,' it would be a very false love which did not speak plainly to them. As for our brethren, we desire to state those positive truths which will preserve us from the prevailing errors of our days by which we are all liable to be affected, Ephesians 4 : 14-15. We say these things lest the purpose of a magazine such as this should be misunderstood. May both writer and reader desire only that God might be glorified in all things!

We send out this second issue of *The Banner of Truth* with thankfulness to God Who alone can make His truth prosper in these days. The response for the first issue of last September was very encouraging ; warm letters were received from Cornwall to the North of Scotland ; these have indicated that there is a true concern among the Lord's people. We are sorry that sometimes we have not been able to answer these letters personally, we were thankful to read each letter which has been received. Various obstacles at present prevent us from publishing this magazine at stated times, these may be removed according to the will of God, in which case we could publish more frequently and at a regular time. Printing costs are heavy, and having no financial resourses we have been, and are dependent on God for the supplies He sends us through His people. For the information of our readers this present issue costs approximately sixpence per copy. If only one copy of the magazine reaches you, and you can use more, please let us know ; we will gladly send copies to addresses which are sent to us.

We would like to record our gratitude to Mr. Geoffrey Williams, the Librarian of the Evangelical Library, 78a Chiltern Street, London, W. 1, for his constant help in supplying us with necessary books. Members of the library (sub. 10/- per annum) can have good books sent to them in all parts of Britain. We warmly commend this fine work.

This present issue is more historical than we generally intend the contents to be, though we hope to be able in the near future to refer to the mighty works of God in Scotland in times past. May the knowledge that we possess those· truths committed by God to our forefathers stir us to prayer and diligence, ' Be strong all ye people of the land, saith the Lord, and work : for I am with you saith the Lord of hosts ' Hag. 2 : 4. ' We will rejoice in thy salvation, and in the name of our God we will set up our banners " Ps. 20 : 5. We take this opportunity of conveying our Christian love and greetings to all readers, earnestly soliciting your prayerful concern in the truth as it is circulated.

FORMER GENERATIONS CALLED TO WITNESS

Why hath the Lord done thus unto this land, and unto this house ? And it shall be answered, Because they forsook the Lord God of their fathers. 2 Chron. 7 : 21-22.

Those that forsake their father's God, shall be rejected by the Lord God of their fathers. This was the sin that ruined Judah in the time of Jeremiah ; possessed with a false confidence that the God of their fathers was still their God, they refused to consider their ways, and ask for the old paths. ' The Lord hath rejected thy confidences,' was the message sent unto them, ' This is a nation that obeyeth not the voice of the Lord their God : truth is perished, and is cut off from their mouth ' (7 : 28). Whenever God visits a nation in mercy the whole of that nation's posterity is involved in greater responsibility ; thereafter the relation of the people to their fathers' God becomes a matter of solemn importance, to forsake Him will prove their ruin.

England is a land which has been visited by God, and we ought therefore to enquire what is our land's present relation to the God of our fathers ? Have we forsaken Him or not ? To determine this we need to know whether we worship the same God Who revealed Himself to our fathers, do we hold the same truths as were held by them ? We must recall therefore, as Israel was commanded to do, how God has manifested Himself in our national history, and we will look particularly at the history of Oxford from where we write.

At the beginning of the sixteenth century in England there was no visible church, where God's Word was purely preached. Believers existed only in scattered handfuls, being known as Lollards, and such were there times that one of them was tortured and burnt to death at the instigation of the Archbishop of Canterbury in 1517 for denying purgatory. Ignorance, superstition, and immorality reigned supreme in the Church of Rome which occupied the land. The Bible was an almost unknown book. Oxford could be best described in the words of Latimer, ' *Where the devil is resident—there away with books and up with candles ; away with Bibles and up with beads ; up with the decking of images and down with God's most Holy Word . . .* ' Into this ancient city, slumbering in its medieval learning, there came a book in 1516, it was the New Testament in Greek printed on the Continent for the first time. Through this book a mighty awakening was to take place within the next few years. The Reformation—as this awakening was named—was nothing else than a direct return to the Word of God ; the doctrines of the Reformers were the doctrines of Scripture.

At Oxford this New Testament came into the hands of a student from Gloucestershire, William Tyndale (1484-1536), he was converted but the wrath of the monks soon forced him to leave. Nevertheless the truth could not be silenced and soon arose in another quarter of the city. In 1523 Cardinal Wolsey—a patron of learning—founded a new College (now called Christ Church) and brought several scholars from Cambridge to direct its learning, little knowing that some of these men had been recently awakened to the truth of God. Under the leadership of Clark these diciples of the Gospel in the University steadily increased. Meanwhile Tyndale, consumed with the desire that his countrymen might have the Bible in their native tongue, had crossed over into Europe and was working night and day translating the New Testament into English ; his great task was done by 1525 ; towards the end of that year the first printed copies of the New Testament were smuggled into London and lodged in the house of a converted priest named Garret. Brave Garret then undertook to convey some of the precious books to Oxford—the city of his student days. How he was there seized by the agents of Rome in the middle of the night, how he escaped but was recaptured, how twenty other brethren were arrested and flung into a deep underground cellar beneath Christ Church, we cannot now relate. The damp foul air, the salt fish (their only food), soon removed their health but not their spirit. After six months four of them lay dying, including Clark. They were released, but it was too late ; the severities of Popery had killed these noble men who had the honour to be the first witnesses to die for the Reformed Faith in England. The remainder of the twenty were also released, some of them like Ferrar and Fryth were later to be burnt at the stake for the sake of the Gospel.

Now the above mentioned, along with their brethren at Cambridge—particularly Bilney, Latimer, and Barnes—were those appointed by God to lay the foundations of the Reformation in England. What then were the foundation truths which God gave them from His Word ? Their common testimony was to the great doctrine that man is justified by faith in Christ alone, and to establish this truth they saw that it was necessary to assert that neither man's works nor his will led to his justification. Salvation, they apprehended, was determined solely by the distinguishing grace of God, faith was His gift granted unto those whom He had predestinated unto life. Rome held that salvation depended on the twin principles of free-will and justification by good works, the Reformers denied both, and held two opposite principles, the eternal election of God and justification by faith. The God they knew and loved was the sovereign ruler of all persons and events. 'The will of God,' writes Tyndale to Fryth, 'Be fulfilled ! And what He hath ordained to be, ere the world was made . . . There falleth not an hair till God's hour be come ; and when His hour is come necessity carrieth us hence.' In his preface to Paul's Epistle to the Romans, Tyndale tells us that in chapters 9 to 11, ' *the apostle teaches us of God's predestination, from whence all things spring ; whether we shall believe, or not believe ; be loosed from sin, or not be loosed ; by which predestination, our justifying and salvation are clear taken out of our own hands, and put into the hands of God only: which thing is most necessary of all. For we are so weak, and so uncertain, that if it stood in us, there would of truth be no man saved: the devil no doubt would deceive him. But now God is sure of His predestination ; neither can any man withstand or hinder Him.'*

Tyndale's herculean labours ended with his martyrdom in Belgium in 1536 ; though he died separated by distance from his brother martyrs—Bilney, Lambert, and Barnes—who suffered in England about the same time, they were all undivided in the truth. Let the testimony of Barnes to the sovereign grace of God suffice, ' *Sayest thou that God giveth to the one mercy ; and to the other none ? I answer, what is that to thee ? Is not His mercy His own ? Is it not lawful for Him to give to whom He will ? For, if He will shew His wrath and make His power known, over the vessels of wrath ordained to damnation ; and to declare the riches of His glory ; unto the vessels of mercy, whom He hath prepared and elected unto glory ; what hast thou therewith to do ? But here will subtle blindness say, God forsaw before, that Jacob should do good ; He saw also that Esau should do evil ; therefore did He condemn him.' Alas, for blindness! What ? Will you judge of that which God forsaw ? These children being yet unborn, they had done neither good nor bad : and yet one of them is chosen, and the other of them is refused. St. Paul knoweth no other cause, but the will of God ; and will you need discuss another ? He saith not, I will have mercy on him whom I see shall do good ; but I will shew mercy to whom I will.'*

These early English martyrs all died confident that the truth would not die with them. Barnes declared, ' If they burn me, what will they gain by it ? The sun, and the moon, fire and the elements—yea, and also stones shall defend the cause against them, rather than the truth should perish.' And Bilney prophesied, ' A new time is beginning. Someone is coming unto us, I see Him, I hear Him—it is Jesus Christ.' His words were true. In 1547 the pious young King Edward VIth ascended the throne, and the errors of Rome no longer received the protection of the monarchy. Under the leadership of men like Cranmer (Archbishop of Canterbury) and Ridley (Bishop of London), godly men, a true church began to be established founded on the Bible. The Articles and Catechism drawn up at this time, reveal to us the truths these men held. In the Catechism we read, ' *The first, principal, and most proper cause of our justification and salvation, is the goodness and love of God, whereby He chose us for His, before He made the world. After that God granted us to be called by the preaching of the Gospel of Jesus Christ.*[4]

The bright reign of Edward VIth terminated suddenly by his death on July 6th, 1553 ; the dying prayer of this boy of sixteen was, 'Bring me into Thy Kingdom, free this kingdom from Antichrist, and keep thine elect in it.' It was a dark day for the elect ; once more they found themselves under a Roman Catholic sovereign ; Mary, a woman filled with all the superstition and persecuting fervour of her religion, succeeded to the throne. She was wise enough to know the foundations upon which Romanism rested ; she knew how the doctrines of Wickliffe and Huss, who had preached that the eternal election of God was the cause of salvation, had been condemned by Martin Vth in his Papal bull of 1418 ; she knew also how these doctrines had revived again in that present century under men like Luther and were the very basis of Protestantism. The Tenets essential to the interests of Popery, such as free-will and the merit of works before justification, could not be re-introduced without the suppression of the contrary. No wonder then that the English Bible was removed from all churches and publicly burnt ; no wonder that the possession of books by Luther, Calvin, Cranmer, Latimer, and other predestinarians was forbidden ; no wonder that all who held these truths were forthwith removed from Oxford and Cambridge, and an oath appointed for all students that they should not 'keep, hold, maintain, and defend, at any time during your life, any opinion erroneous, or error of Luther, Wickliffe, Huss, or any other condemned of heresy : And that you shall namely and specially, hold as the Catholic church holdeth in all these articles, wherein lately hath been controversy, dissention, and error ; as concerning faith and works, grace and free will . . . '

There were many who had no intention of taking such an oath and the truth was still going to be heard though it cost men their lives. In the spring of 1554 the three leaders of the Reformed Faith, Cranmer, Latimer, and Ridley, having passed a bitter winter imprisoned in the Tower of London, were brought to Oxford. These three men were to meet the most eminent of the popish divines in public debate before the University. All things were combined in an attempt to remove their confidence and to make their public statements despicable. They were flung into a common prison, deprived of all books and papers that might aid their defence, and finally not allowed to appear together in debate, but singly on separate days. Nevertheless it was a victory. Latimer confounded his enemies by his silence and his refusal to hear any argument not drawn from Scripture. Ridley (who in youth had memorized all Paul's Epistles) rapidly showed his ability to meet his adversaries on every point, at length he was shouted down and refused a hearing. Both were condemned as heretics and both died together, burnt at the stake outside the north wall of Oxford, 16 Oct.,1555. 'We shall this day brother, light such a candle in England as shall never be put out,' were Latimer's parting words ; and Ridley prayed, 'I beseech Thee, Lord God, have mercy on this realm of England.' Cranmer followed them to heaven by the same fiery chariot the following March.

We will give an instance of the doctrines these martyrs held fast till death. While they were imprisoned in Oxford a letter arrived addressed to 'My dear fathers, Dr. Cranmer, Dr. Ridley, Dr. Latimer, prisoners in Oxford for the testimony of the Lord Jesus, and His Holy Gospel.' It was from that mighty evangelist John Bradford, who wrote on behalf of the believers imprisoned in London. Bradford's great concern was to oppose an error that had appeared among a small sect of professing Protestants who asserted that man's free-will was necessary to his salvation. ' *Great evil*,' he writes, ' *is like to come hereafter to posterity, by these men . . . Christ's glory and grace is like to lose much light if your sheep be not something holpen by them that love God, and are able to prove that all good is to be attributed only and wholly to God's grace and mercy in Christ . . . The effects of salvation they (the free-willers) so mingle with the cause, that, if it be not seen to, more hurt will come by them, than ever came by the papists, inasmuch as their life commendeth them more to the world than the papist.. In freewill they are plain papists ; yea, Pelagians. God is my witness that I write not this, but because I desire God's glory and the good of His people . . . I complain of it to you as the chief captains of Christ's church here. And truly I must complain of you even unto God at the last day if you will not, as far as you can, help that the truth of doctrine may remain among those that come after . . . My brethren here with me have thought it their duty to signify that this need is not less than I make it.*'

With this letter Bradford sent a short treatise entitled ' A Defence of the doctrine of Election and Predestination,' concerning which Bradford wrote, ' All the prisoners hereabouts in manner have seen it and read it ; and therein they agree with me, nay rather with the truth.' The treatise opens with these words,' *Faith in God's election, I mean to believe in very deed we are the children of God through Christ, is of all things that God requires of us not only the principal, but also the whole sum.*' Bradford goes on to show that the mercy of God is nowhere more magnified than in election, nor can humility be rightly seen save in the elect ' for they alone reckon nothing at all due to themselves but damnation, that their whole glory may be in God only and forever.' This treatise was approved by Cranmer, Latimer, and Ridley, and in reply to Bradford's exhortation, Ridley himself wrote on Predestination at this time. **The fact is that the Reformers were all un-**

divided in these great truths, they viewed them as a most essential part of the faith once delivered to the saints.

After the martydom of the leading Reformers, the above mentioned sect of free-willers attempted to stir confusion among believers by their pretension of likeness of doctrine with the martyrs, and the Reformed faith. But this attempt was overthrown by the surviving Protestant ministers who, says Strype the historian, ' deemed it a scandal ' to be numbered with those fanatics, who ' denying predestination ' held ' free-will and justification by works.' In order to disclaim any connection with these free-willers, and to publicly own the doctrines which Cranmer, Ridley, and the foregoing martyrs had sealed with their blood,' these orthodox ministers drew up ' A Protestation of the Christian Faith.' Towards the beginning this document asserts the subtlety of Satan in corrupting the truth. *' Some denying the doctrine of God's firm election and free election in Jesus Christ ; which is the very certainty of our salvation. And as he (the devil) hath caused them to deny all these things, even so hath he made them affirm many mad and foolish fantasies, which the Word of God doth utterly condemn: as man's free-will, man's righteousness, and justifying works ; to the great dishonour of God, to the obscuring of His glory ; yea to the utter destruction of many a simple soul that cannot shift from these subtle sleights of Satan, except the Lord show His great mercy upon them.'* This Protestation continues, *' I do undoubtedly believe in God the Holy Ghost, Who is the Lord and giver of Life, and the sanctifier of all God's elect . . . I do confess that Adam by his fall, lost from himself and all his posterity, all freedom, choice and power of man's will to do good . . . I do acknowledge that God, in Jesus Christ, ordained, predestinated, appointed, before the foundation of the world was laid, an innumerable multitude of Adam's posterity, to be saved from their sins through the merits of Christ's death . . . in whom His mercy shall be magnified forever.'*

We must pass from this glorious generation of believers who preferred to die with truth rather than to live with error ; nearly 300 were martyred before this terrible period ended with the death of ' Bloody ' Mary in 1558. Many years were to pass before Englishmen began to forget the horrors of Romanism.

In the following reign of Elizabeth those doctrines for which the martyrs suffered became the recognized truths of the Word of God. When a new edition of the Bible (known as the Bishops' Bible) was published in 1568, the leaders of the restored Church of England supplied the prefaces and marginal notes. In the preface to the New Testament we read, ' By Him (Christ) hath He (God the Father) decreed to give, to His elect the life everlasting.' On Romans 11 : 11. the note is, ' The will and purpose of God is the cause of election and reprobation : for His mercy and calling through Christ are the means of salvation ; and the withdrawing of His mercy is the cause of damnation.'   In 1576 a further improved edition of Scripture was published, the Quarto Bible. On Matt. 11 : 26, the note is ' Faith cometh not of man's will, nor power ; but by the secret illumination of God, which is the declaration of His eternal counsel.'   On John 10 : 26, where the text says, ' Ye believe not because ye are not my sheep,' i.e., because ye are not of the number of the elect ; the marginal note is, ' The cause whereof the reprobate cannot believe.'

In the latter Bibles of Elizabeth's reign a form of questions and answers were added to aid the understanding of Scripture. They begin thus—

' *Question.*   Why do men much vary in the matters of religion ?

Answer.   Because all have not the like measure of knowledge, neither do all believe the gospel of Christ.

Question.   What is the reason thereof ?

Answer.   Because they only believe the gospel and doctrine of Christ, which are ordained unto eternal life.

Question.   Are not all ordained unto eternal life ?

Answer.   Some are vessels of wrath ordained unto destruction ; as others are vessels of mercy prepared to glory.

Question.   How standeth it with God's justice, that some are appointed unto damnation ?

Answer.   Very well : because all men have in themselves sin, which deserveth no less.   And therefore the mercy of God is wonderful, in that He vouchsafeth to save some of that sinful race, and to bring them to the knowledge of the truth.

Question.   If God's purpose and determination must of necessity take effect; then why need any man to care ?   For he that liveth well must needs be damned, if he be thereunto ordained ; and he that liveth ill must needs be saved, if he be thereunto appointed ?

Answer.   Not so : For it is not possible that the elect should always be without care to do well ; or that the reprobate should have any will thereunto.   For, to have either good will, or good work, is a testimony of the Spirit of God, which is given to the elect only; whereby faith is so wrought into them, that, being graft in Christ, they grow in holiness to that glory whereunto they are appointed.   Neither are they so vain, as to think they may do as they please, because they are predestinate unto salvation ; but rather they endeavour to walk in such good works as God in Christ Jesus had ordained them unto, and prepared for them to be occupied in, to their own comfort, stay and assurance, and to His glory.

Question.   But how shall I know myself to be one of those whom God hath ordained to life eternal ?

Answer. By the motions of spiritual life—lothing of sin ; love of righteousness ; the hand of faith reaching unto Christ ; the conscience comforted in distress, and raised up to confidence in God, by the work of His Spirit.

Another proof—from among many that could be given—of those truths loved by our forefathers of this period, is a great book by Dr. Willet entitled ' *A General View of Popery,*' this was dedicated to the Queen and published by authority. Concerning free-will, Willet writes, ' They that affirm that God offereth grace and faith equally to all, do consequently hold, that, to believe, is either wholly or in part, in man's power. The absurdity of which opinion we decare thus : All cannot have faith ; but such as are ordained and elected thereunto, John 10 : 26 ; John 12 : 39 ; Acts 13 : 48. Faith and every good gift, the beginning, perfecting, and end, is only of God, Rom. 9 : 16 ; John 6 : 44. They that are drawn of God must needs come to Christ.'

In the beginning of the seventeenth century free-will teaching began to invade England from the Continent where it was being promulgated by a Dutchman named Arminius. To show how contrary this teaching was to the recognized truth, we will quote some of the statements laid down by the University of Oxford at that time necessary for students to hold before they could pass a degree in divinity—

' *Man's will is not free.*'—' *The grace of regeneration is irresistible.*'—' *The will of man is entirely passive, in the first reception of grace.*'—' *Christ's death did not procure reconciliation with God for every man.*'—' *Man's will cannot resist the efficacious grace of God.*'—' *Faith itself and the righteousness of faith, are peculiar to the elect.*'...' *Predestination unto life is not for faith and good works forseen.*'—' *God's grace is not determined by man's will.*'

When a young preacher named Laud ventured to preach views in Oxford in 1606 which had little resemblance to the Word of God, he was called to account by Dr. Airay, the Vice Chancellor. In 1614 when Laud had risen to be President of St. John's College, his opinions were publicly denounced in St. Mary's Church by Dr. Abbot as ' Popery.' The fact is that Laud was one of those few in the Church of England who having no love of the faith of the Reformers was willing to receive Arminianism.

On the ascendency of Charles Ist to the throne in 1625 Arminians began to enjoy more of the royal favour and ecclesiastical power was placed in their hands. Laud became Bishop of London and then Archbishop of Canterbury. The preaching of predestination was forbidden, and many ministers who obeyed God rather than man found themselves removed from their churches, imprisoned, or exiled. Parliament stood true to the Word of God in this struggle, and in 1629 passed a resolution that ' *Whosoever shall bring in innovation of religion, or by favour or countenance*

*seem to extend Popery or Arminianism, or other opinion disagreeing
from the true and orthodox church, shall be reputed a capital
enemy to this kingdom and commonwealth.'* Francis Rous pleaded
with the House in the manner of a prophet, and denounced that
*' error of Arminianism which makes the grace of God lackey it
after the will of man,'* and called upon his fellow members of
Parliament to postpone other questions for this question, which
concened ' eternal life, men's souls, yea, God Himself.' The truth
is that Englishmen of that generation had been brought up to
believe the doctrine of predestination. Had not their fathers seen
the Reformation martyrs die rather than surrender this truth ?
Had not Arminius openly sought to remove the doctrine in order
to re-unite the Reformed church to Rome—that corrupt church
under which their forefathers had suffered for centuries ? Was
it not concerning the very errors of free-will teaching that Bradford
and other martyrs had implored those left behind to take heed
lest they were deceived ? If this error was allowed would not the
whole truth of God be corrupted ? No wonder then that
Parliament acted against it, and believers fasted and prayed
against it ! The King silenced Parliament by dissolving it,
and attempted to rule the nation with the same despotism
with which Laud was ruling the church. The dreadful and
inevitable result was the Civil War which broke out in 1642, it
ended in the restoration of liberty and freedom to teach the truth.
These years form the great Puritan period. Great, because of the
mighty working of the Spirit of God upon the land ; godly men
were in the government of the nation ; godly ministers were raised
up in numbers who preached with tremendous authority, power,
and fervour ; never in English history was the Gospel more known
and loved ; prayer, praise, and Bible reading were the usual employment for many of the common people in their leisure hours.
What kind of preaching produced these effects ? The answer can
plainly be seen from reading the great Westminster Confession of
Faith. What kind of men were the Puritans ? The historian
Macaulay will tell us—

*' The Puritans were men whose minds had derived a peculiar
character from the daily contemplation of superior beings and
eternal interests.*

*Not content with acknowledging, in general terms, an over-
ruling providence, they habitually ascribed every event to the will
of the Great Being for whose power nothing was too vast, for
whose inspection nothing was too minute. To know Him, to
serve Him, to enjoy Him, was with them the great end of existence.
If they were unacquainted with the works of philosophers and poets,
they were deeply read in the oracles of God. If their names were
not found in the registers of heralds, they were recorded in the
Lamb's Book of Life. If their steps were not accompanied by a*

*splendid train of menials, legions of ministering angels had charge
of them. The very meanest of them was a being to whose fate
a mysterious and terrible importance belonged, on whose slightest
actions the spirits of light and darkness looked with anxious interest,
who had been destined, before Heaven and Earth were created to
enjoy a felicity which should continue when Heaven and Earth
should have passed away.'*

The Puritan period was over by 1662. In that year, Charles
II having come to the throne, two thousand ministers were ejected
from the Established Church because they could not bow to the
commands of men. Some were imprisoned, all were silenced, and
the truth was silenced with them. The Reformed faith was now
to be scarcely heard from the pulpits of the Established Church,
as a result the moral condition of the people deteriorated until 1730
such was the profanity and godlessness of the masses that one would
scarcely have known there had ever been a Reformation or a
Puritan period. The truths of election and salvation by grace
almost entirely disappeared. Nothing but a mighty awakening
to the truth brought by the Spirit of God could alter England's
downward path. Such an awakening did take place, it brought
a return to the Scripture and therefore a return to the doctrines
of Scripture. The movement began with students at Oxford
between 1730-1740. Men like George Whitefield, Walker, Romaine,
Grimshaw, and Venn were raised up to preach salvation by grace
through the righteousness of Christ. These men were pre-eminently
evangelists, they were burdened with love for men's souls ; Whit-
field, it is said, scarcely every preached without weeping, but their
evangelism knew nothing of any belief in man's will. Let us hear
Whitefield, who preached sometimes 40 sometimes 60 hours a week,
thousands would assemble in the open air in the early hours of the
morning to hear him preach, and multitudes were converted—

' *Oh amazing, Oh infinitely condescending love! . . . I have
offered you Christ's whose wisdom, Christ's whole righteousness,
Christ's whole sanctification, and eternal redemption, if you will
but believe it. If you say you cannot believe, you say right ; for
faith, as well as every other blessing is the gift of God. But then
wait upon God, and who knows but that He may have mercy upon
thee.'*

In Oxford Thomas Haweis raised an uproar by preaching the
Word of God in the power of the Holy Ghost from the pulpit of
St. Mary Magdalene where he was the curate.

These eighteenth century leaders met the same opposition
as the Reformers because they preached the same truths ; Whitefield
was threatened with arrest if he preached in Oxford again ; Haweis
was ejected from Mary Magdalene in 1762, for the bishop declared
he was determined to suppress ' heretical doctrine in the University.' Although the truth was no longer received by the

Universities or the majority of the Established Church it profoundly effected the nation at this time.

This then is an account of some of the works of the God of our forefathers. The truths which He honoured in His servants preaching were the truths of His Holy Word. Examine any period when the Spirit worked mightily in England and you will find that the sovereign grace of God was extolled, election was maintained, and man's free-will in salvation was denied. It will always be so, the Spirit of Truth will never work contrary to the written Word of Truth. Dear reader, there is no need to bring forward meloncholy proofs that the God of our fathers is a stranger in the land to-day. We have forsaken Him and His Word. What was preached in Oxford recently, that ' the new birth is entirely voluntary, you can at this moment surrender your life to Him,' is being preached everywhere. Where is the Lord God of the Reformers and Martyrs ? Where is the Lord God of the Puritans and eighteenth century leaders ? ' O children of Israel, fight ye not against the Lord God of your fathers ; for ye shall not prosper.' ' I beseech Thee Lord God have mercy on this realm of England ' was Ridley's dying prayer, and it ought to be ours. Generally before God gives a land over to judgment, He gives it up to error. But His arm is not shortened, His mercy is still infinite. Let us plead with God lest His wrath fall upon us to our utter ruin, and men shall say ' Why hath the Lord done thus unto this land ? And it shall be answered, Because they forsook the Lord God of their fathers.'

THE VALUE OF TRUTH.

" Solomon bids us buy the truth (Prov. 23 : 23), but does not tell us how much to pay for it, because we must get truth though it be never so dear. Every parcel of truth is precious as filings of gold ; we must either live with it or die for it. As Ruth said to Naomi, ' Whither thou goest I will go ; and where thou lodgest, I will lodge . . . and nothing but death shall part thee and me ' ; so must believers say, ' Where truth goes I will go, and where truth lodges, I will lodge, and nothing but death shall seperate me and truth.' A man may lawfully sell his house, land, and jewels, but truth is something that exceeds all price and must not be sold ; it is our heritage—' Thy testimonies have I taken as my heritage for ever '—Ps. 119 : 111. It is a legacy that our forefathers bought with their blood, which should make us willing to lay down anything, and lay out anything, that we may purchase this precious pearl, which is worth more than heaven and earth, and which will make a man live happily, and die comfortably, and reign eternally."

THOMAS BROOKS.

34

THE GREAT AWAKENING IN WALES

" We have heard with our ears, O God, our fathers have told us, what work Thou didst in their days, in the times of old."
Psalm 44.

If ever a land sat in darkness and under the shadow of death it was Wales in the early eighteenth century. The churches of the Establishment were dead and formal, from many pulpits a sermon would not be heard for months on end, while the chapels of the Dissenters were for the most part desolate and forsaken. The majority of the people had no more concern for religion than had their cattle. According to an eye-witness, " There being at that time (1735) a general slumber over the land, the generality of the people spent the Lord's Day contrary to the laws of God and man ; it being by none rightly observed ; neither had any whom I knew, the true knowledge of that God whom we pretended to worship. An universal deluge of swearing, lying, revelling, drunkenness, and fighting had overspread the land like a mighty torrent." A thick, heathen darkness covered gentry, clergy and common people all alike. In short, the whole country was in a corrupt state, careless, thoughtless, and godless.

In such a scene as this, events began to take place which are in no way explainable apart from a recognition of a visitation from God. At Trefecca, in the county of Brecon, Howell Harris was born in 1714. In the summer of 1735 he was powerfully awakened and soundly converted ; in the autumn of that year he went as a student to Oxford, but amazed at the immorality and vanity of the place he remained only one term (largely spent in secret prayer and public worship) before returning to " dear Wales." Burdened by the realization of the state of the neighbourhood around his home, he began to press the truth upon souls " Seeing both rich and poor going hand in hand to ruin, my soul was stirred up within me. The ministers were the first that lay on my heart. I saw that they were not in earnest, and did not appear to have any sense of their own danger, or experience of the love of Christ ! Their deadness and indifference therefore made me speak . . . Death and Judgment were my principal subjects of conversation. Now the fire of God did so burn in my soul that I could not rest day or night, without doing something for my God and Saviour." Harris at first only addressed people in their houses, but shortly, such vast numbers assembled to hear him that he commenced preaching in the open-air. " The Word was attended with such power, that men cried out on the spot for the pardon of their sins."

In 1737 Harris preached in Radnorshire, and finding the power of God continually present upon his preaching, he began to itinerate throughout the whole of South Wales. The effects of his visit to St. Davids, in Pembrokeshire, are typical of what happened elsewhere. He found the place, like the inhabitants of Laish, "Quiet and secure." Some attended the formal service of the Established Church on Sabbath mornings, while the multitude flocked together into houses where music, dancing, and all manner of amusements imaginable were going on. Suddenly (the account goes) came Mr. Harris into the midst of this careless people, and information that a stranger would preach at an appointed time caused a great crowd to assemble. Without delay Harris proceeded to deliver the Word of God as an herald from another world, "exposing the sins in which the town and country lay and were guilty of; every particle of his speech flashed and gleamed so vividly, as lightning on the consciences of the hearers, that they were terrified and feared that the day of judgment had overtaken them : yea, so powerful were the effects accompanying his words, that bold, hardy men, being seized with fainting fits through fear and terror, fell as corpses in the street." Harris declared the truth in this terrific and alarming manner in every place, preaching either in houses, or standing upon a wall or table in the open air; his sermons, at this time contained little more than destruction towards sinners.

Satan was not long in rousing his subjects to defend his kingdom, and Harris's persecutions daily increased. "My life," he says, "was now endangered in several places by the violence of the mob." A pistol was discharged at him while he preached; at Bala he was nearly beaten to death; Seward, who accompanied Harris, died after being stoned in 1742. "We have ventured our lives," writes Harris, "under all manner of discouragements, in the face of an angry world, frequently in danger of being stoned to death, sometimes having our blood mingled with the dust, because we invited sinners to the only Saviour! We have travelled incessantly, day and night, through rain and wind, frost and snow . . . What are we that we should be counted worthy to suffer for His sake? Oh, how humbly then, we should lie at His feet, admiring His free electing love, if He in the least distinguishes such poor, vile worms as we are!"

The overwhelming effects of Harris's preaching may be judged from the following incident. Harris was preaching along with Whitefield in Wales in 1740. At one place Whitefield preached, but a stageplayer was procured by some of the mob to mock the preacher and he was successful enough to force Whitefield to terminate his sermon. Harris then came forward; his text was "The great day of His wrath is come; and who shall be able to stand?" The player said, "I am able." "What!" said Harris, with piercing eyes and strong voice, "What, such a poor, contemptible worm as thou art?" Upon which the wretched man fell down, a peculiar awe having seized him, from which, it is said, he never recovered!

Simultaneously with this awakening in South Wales, God was raising up a mighty instrument in the South West, in Cardiganshire. In this county, in the parish of Llancwnlle, which borders on the parish of Llangeitho, Daniel Rowlands was born in 1713. Ordained as a curate to these parishes in 1733, Rowlands was as destitute of the truth as the previous incumbents had been before him. After prayer and preaching on a Sunday morning, Rowlands was foremost among the foolish, the vain, and the dissolute, who met for sports to fill the rest of the day. Sometime about the year 1737 a great change was wrought in Rowlands' soul, he was no longer the same man. From the pulpit now, Owen, his biographer tells us, "he proclaimed eternal perdition to a sinful world. Awful and extremely terrific was his message. His own spirit seemd to have been filled with great terror. He appeared as if he wished to kindle the fire of Hell around the transgressors of God's law. He unfolded the indignation of Heaven against sin with amazing earnestness, clearness and vigour. But there was no harshness in his voice, rather he spoke as one overflowing with compassion, and under the deepest conviction of his own unworthiness."

" There is a great revival in Cardiganshire, through one Mr. D. Rowlands, a church minister," wrote Harris to Whitefield in 1739; and again later to Whitefield, " I was last Sunday with brother Rowlands at the Ordinance, where I saw, heard, and felt such things as I cannot communicate any idea of on paper. It is very common, when he preaches, for scores to fall down by the power of the Word—pierced and wounded by the love of God, and a sight of the beauty and excellency of Jesus—and lie down on the ground—nature being overcome by the sight and enjoyment of God, given to their heaven born souls, so that it cannot bear any more . . . His congregations consist of, I believe, far above two thousand." Rowlands himself writes to Whitefield, " The Lord comes down among us in such a manner that words can give no idea of. Though I have, to prevent nature mixing with the work, openly discountenanced all crying out, yet such is the light, view, and power God gives very many in the Ordinance —of preaching—that they cannot possibly help crying out, praising and adoring Jesus, being quite swallowed up in God."

One of Rowlands' hearers gives us this description of him— " His doctrine was Calvinistic . . . I seem to see him now, dressed in his black gown, opening the little door that led from the outside to the pulpit, and making his appearance to the multitude." When he preached, " The people drew nigh, as it were, in the cloud, to Christ and to Moses and Elias, and eternity and its realities rushed into their minds." Another hearer gives this account of his preaching on John 3 : 16, " He dwelt with such overwhelming thoughts on the love of God, and the vastness of His gift to man, that I was swallowed up in amazement. I did not know where I was, whether on earth or in heaven." Christ crucified was Rowlands' great subject; such was his realization of the Saviour's sufferings, that on one occasion while in prayer before the sermon he cried out, " Oh, empty veins ! Oh, pale countenance ! " and then he fainted away in the pulpit. On recovering he preached with astonishing power and energy.

Rowlands was first led to go beyond his own neighbourhood by a woman who—like many others—came over twenty miles, along hilly, mountainous roads each Lord's Day to hear the Word preached; at length she found courage to address Rowlands in this manner, " Sir, if what you say to us is true, there are many in my neighbourhood in a most dangerous condition, going fast to eternal misery. For the sake of their souls come over, Sir, to preach to them." In this way Rowlands' ministry was extended beyond Cardiganshire. In 1743, Harris writes, " The Kingdom of God is coming on everywhere with great power—I am now in Pembrokeshire where Rowlands has been preaching. The power at the conclusion of his sermons was such that multitudes continued weeping and crying out for the Saviour and could not possibly forbear." By this year the alarm of the Gospel had spread throughout the whole South and South-West of Wales, other ministers were raised up, who, along with Harris and Rowlands, preached to thousands in the open air. " He pours down His Spirit upon us more abundantly than ever, and that in various places ! Great is the power that goes with the Word everywhere. God seems to make all fall before the Gospel of His dear Son."

The tremendous itinerating labours of Harris for some seventeen years were over by 1752. His zeal was unabated but his physical strength was broken; after this time, apart from a few years more itinerant preaching, Harris's preaching was confined to Trefecca till his death in 1773. The ministers who were to take his funeral service were all too overcome with grief, so he was buried without one, amidst great weeping. The ministry of Daniel Rowlands at Llangeitho continued, with its same power, for over fifty years. He died in 1790. During this time there were, it is said, seven revivals, that is times when the Spirit was poured out in an uncommon and extraordinary manner. The third of these movements of the Spirit. " The Great Revival," so called because it spread throughout the southern counties, began about 1763 while Rowlands was preaching in Llangeitho. His son says on this occasion. the whole chapel seemed as if it were filled with some supernatural element, the whole assembly was filled with extraordinary emotions. A verse of Scripture, " I thank Thee, Father,

Lord of heaven and earth, because Thou hast hid these things from the wise and prudent and hast revealed them unto babes; even so Father, for so it seemed good in Thy sight " (Matt. 11 : 25), had such an overwhelming effect upon the people that it exceeded all description.

We can say no more on this occasion, about the great awakening in Wales in the eighteenth century. It would be of incalculable blessing if the lives of Harris and Rowlands, both excellently written by Morgan, could be republished.

But let us note some characteristics of the awakening. The first is this, God Himself came down upon Wales. Nothing else is sufficient to explain the facts. It was this presence of God that made people say of Llangeitho, " There was something solemn and awful in the place; " it was the sense of the presence of God, that made believers meet at five in th morning " to adore and worship the Lord together." " Their singing and praying is indeed full of God;" so Harris wrote. Not to live as those who were created and redeemed to glorify and enjoy this great God was to them the greatest evil. " Did we see more of the evil that is in every forgetfulness of God, and in every thought, word, and look that is not full of God, and springs not from Him in our souls, there would be more inward mourning and brokenness of spirit."

Secondly, we note that this awakening had lasting results, indeed it is true to say that it transformed the whole principality of Wales. Moreover such historic events as the formation of the Bible Society came from the Welsh awakening, and a great impetus was given to missionary societies. These permanent effects can be largely traced to the foundations of sound doctrine which characterized the ministry of men like Rowlands and Harris. What their doctrine was, may be rapidly judged by the fact that from their preaching grew up a great Association of believers known as the Calvinistic Methodists. The title was unfortunate, for, as Harris said, " We, being dead to all names, will contend for nothing but who shall love the other the most, and desire no other distinguishing name but that of Christian." Nevertheless their being associated with the name of the great Reformer was inevitable in an age which had ceased to regard the doctrines of the Reformation as the doctrines of Scripture. " I think we all agree with the good old orthodox Reformers and Puritans; I hold their works in great esteem," so Harris wrote. These evangelists saw that no evangelism was sound which was not based on doctrinal truths. To preach a gospel that was conditional, depending on any will or assent in man, was entirely foreign to them. They strongly opposed any teaching that Christ died for everyone on condition they will believe. Referring to one who had not entered into these truths, Whitefield writes to Harris, " Oh, that the Lord may batter down his free-will scheme, and compel him to own God's sovereignty and everlasting love." " The Sovereign Lord wrought faith in me," writes Harris, " Oh ! that free, sovereign, and everlasting love, that calls those in time who were elected in eternity ! " Rowlands, Williams who assisted him tells us, opposed both Arminianism and Baxterianism, he proclaimed an entirely free salvation—free in its origin, free in its progress, free in its consummation, granted without any condition to be fulfilled on the part of man. " Man says, " What can I do nothing? Have I no power of myself? Am I a stick or a stone? We are indeed as hard, dead, and senseless to God's calling and love as a stone ! But we are worse than this ; the stone abides where you leave it, but we run away from God." (Harris). It was because they knew these truths that the revivals were attributed solely to the sovereign purpose of God ; in the intervals between these visitations no unusual meetings were called to attempt to promote the outpouring of the Spirit ; at Llangeitho, Rowlands' biographer tells us, only the ordinary means were attended to—public worship and preaching ; " there was no praying for individual conversions, nor many praying together." There was no approach made to those who were apparently impressed by the proclamation of the truth. These ministers knew that while the preaching of the Word belonged to them, the conversion of souls belonged wholly to God ; and when He works there will naturally be a desire on the part of the soul concerned to unite with believers. They saw that any methods apart from this would result in scores of unsound professions

That faith in these doctrines of the absolute sovereignty of God does not make a man less earnest, compassionate, and burdened for souls can in no way be better seen than in the lives of Rowlands and Harris. Once when Rowlands was riding up the vale of Aeron with Thomas Gray, when they came to the highest point of the ascent, Rowlands looked down on the extensive valley and, speaking of the irreligious state of the inhabitants, shed many tears. On another occasion when Rowlands was lodging with Harris, he found the latter in bed one morning with tears rolling down his face. Having asked what was the matter with him, Harris replied, that in a dream he had been preaching to ruined sinners on the brink of Hell, and that he felt so much for them that he had been entreating them with all his might to return to God. These were men overpowered with compassion, and while they believed none but the elect would be saved, they applied the Gospel in the most vehement manner to suit the case of all sinners. Let Rowlands being dead yet speak :—

" Rise, sinner, He calls thee. Come to the Lord and say, Behold here I am. If I have no grace, I come at Thy word of grace. If I cannot call Thee Father, I can say that I am fatherless, for I forsake all others ; and if fatherless it is with thee that I can find mercy. If I am not a son, Thou canst make me a son. Oh! is there not a blessing left for me. Bless me, yea, even me, O Lord. I will not go from Thee : I cannot go; for where can I go? With Thee are the words of eternal life. I dare not say, ' be just to me a saint ; ' and yet I do say, and will say, yea, I must say, ' be merciful to me a sinner.' "

Much more could be said; we could contrast our days with theirs; contrast what is preached now, with what was preached then; but we need say no more, only add the exhortation of Williams, Rowlands' assistant.

> " O'er the gloomy hills of darkness
> Look, my soul, be still and gaze,
> While the promises are pointing
> To a glorious day of grace :
> Blessed Jubilee,
> Let thy glorious morning dawn."

The following excellent books may be obtained from the Evangelical Book Shop, 15 College Square East, Belfast. *The Shorter Catechism,* 4d. *The Westminster Confession of Faith,* by post 2/10. *The Institutes of the Christian Religion,* John Calvin, 2 vols., 30/-. *Commentary on Romans,* by Martin Luther, by post 18/6. *Commentary on Galations,* Luther, by post 17/6. *The Reformed Doctrine of Predestination,* Boettner, 15/-. *Summary of Christian Doctrine,* Berkhof, by post 11/7. These are as advertised in *The Irish Evangelical Magazine.*

' Whosoever therefore shall confess me before men, him will I confess also before my Father which is in heaven. But whosoever shall deny me before men, him will I also deny before my Father which is in heaven. Think not that I am come to send peace on earth : I came not to send peace but a sword.' Matthew 10 : 32-34.

" As Satan ever from the beginning hath declared himself an enemy to the free grace and undeserved love of God, so hath he now, in these last and corrupt days, most furiously raged against that doctrine which attributes all the praise and glory of our redemption to the eternal love and undeserved grace of God alone."

—JOHN KNOX.

SCRIPTURAL DIFFICULTIES RELATING
TO THE DOCTRINE OF ELECTION

The aim of the first issue of the *Banner of Truth*, last September, was to declare that error in matters of religion is a dangerous thing. Error is a departure from that truth revealed by God in His Word, and it is punished by plagues from Him whose authority has been disregarded (Rev. 22 : 18). The worst plague of all that can fall upon men in this world is to be given up to a ' rebrobate mind ' (Rom. 1 : 28), a mind no long able to discern truth, but given over by God to ' strong delusion that they should believe a lie.' Not only does God deal with individuals in this manner, as Ahab (2 Chron. 18 : 21-22), but also with nations whose ingratitude and sin renders them fit for judgment ; thus God sent ' a perverse spirit '—that is a spirit of error—upon Egypt (Isaiah 19 : 14), and deceived prophets in Israel—' If the prophet be deceived when he hath spoken a thing, I the Lord have deceived that prophet,' Ezek. 14 : 9. This being so, when we find ourselves living to-day in a land where the truth of God was once feared and loved, but where now deceptions and delusions everywhere abound, we have abundant reason to conclude that the solemn displeasure of God is upon the nation. ' Woe unto the inhabitants of the sea coast, the Word of the Lord is against you.'

Our second purpose in the last *Banner of Truth* was to show those particular truths which have been cast off not only by the professing church but also by many professing evangelicals, namely those truths concerning the Sovereignty of God, that ' He worketh all things after the counsel of His own will,' granting salvation to some who are called (converted), not according to their works present or forseen—for all men are equally corrupted by the fall of Adam—' but according to His own purpose and grace ' 2 Tim. 1 : 9. This purpose of God to save those ordained to eternal life shall ' stand ' (Rom. 9 : 11), that is, be irresistibly carried out, because it depends not in any respect upon man for its execution and completion. The soul that is given to Christ by being ' chosen in Him before the foundation of the world ' (Eph. 1 : 4), ' shall come unto Him ' (Jn. 6 : 37) ; the enmity to God that is in him by nature being overcome by the mighty operation of the Holy Spirit Who works faith in all God's elect (Eph. 2 : 8 ; Titus 1 : 1 ; Acts 13 : 48). The whole work of conversion or repentance is attributed in Scripture to God alone, He gives and grants repentance (Acts 5 : 31), and all who are predestinated in eternity are also called in time as the Holy Spirit states in Rom. 8 : 30. The purpose of God is thus infallibly carried out.

These truths will always be an offence to the natural man, but it is not with such readers that we are now directly concerned.

We write primarily to brethren in the Lord, to those who have experienced the love of God in their souls and thereby love Him and His Word ; all such have a sincere desire to understand the truth and dare not reject what is confirmed by Scripture. Among these our brethren, whom we trust we love, there are several who when they hear the doctrine of election, dare not deny it, yet feel it is impossible to reconcile it with other passages of Scripture. These other passages of Scripture they have been always accustomed to interpret in a manner plainly contrary to election, and therefore they conclude that God has allowed truths to exist in His Word which are apparently contradictory ; but before they drew this conclusion (which throws all Scripture into confusion, so that there is no hamony left between the various parts of the whole revelation of God) they ought rather to have doubted their interpretation of the particular passages.

Before looking at some of these passages let us consider what is necessary for a right study of Scripture. First the love of God in our souls out of which will arise the desire for His teaching ; next, before fixing the meaning of a particular verse or word, the context is to be diligently studied, the aim of the Holy Spirit is to be considered, and lastly individual words are to be understood not by how they sound to us by what they generally signify in Scripture. The same word may be used in Scripture with different meanings, for instance ' that which is born of the Spirit is spirit,' spirit in the first place is the Spirit of God in the second that spiritual life derived from Him. Other examples could be given to prove that the meaning of particular words must be determined by the context and the rest of Scripture. The word ' world ' cannot be rightly interpreted apart from this rule ; take John 1 : 10, ' He was in the world, and the world was made by Him, and the world knew Him not.' It would be obviously foolish to take these three references to ' the world ' in the same sense. The first refers to the inhabited world of men where Christ manifested Himself, the second to the material world—the whole fabric of heaven and earth, and the third speaks of the majority of men living in the world, namely unbelievers. Sometimes the word world in Scripture means every individual living in the world, as in Rom. 3 : 9, but far more often it means only a multitude or many, as in John 12 : 19, ' Behold, the world is gone after Him! ' which world signified only many of one small nation ; or Luke 2 : 1, ' That all the world should be taxed,' where only the chief inhabitants of the Roman Empire are meant. Again ' The whole world lieth in wickedness ' (1 Jn. 5 : 29), plainly refers not to every individual but only to un- believers. Several times the many who are left in their sins are spoken of as the ' world,' this is the ' world ' that will be condemned (1 Cor. 11 : 32), concerning whom Christ says " I pray not for the world ' (Jn. 17 : 9), and suffered ' that He might deliver us from this present evil world ' (Gal. 1 : 4). On the other hand the world

sometimes refers to that multitude of believers who are called out
of every tongue and nation, this is the world spoken of in Psalm
22 : 27, and Rom. 4 : 13, to mention only two undisputable
passages..

Now to come directly to the particular passages that raise
difficulties in the minds of some believers. John 3 : 16. 'God so
loved the world,' is quoted and interpreted in the sense that Christ
died for every individual that ever lived. But why should ' the
world ' be interpreted in such a sense ? It does not, as we have
seen, usually mean that in Scripture. Moreover many Scriptures
express that Christ died for ' His people ' Matt. 1 : 21 ; His ' sheep '
Jn. 10 : 11-14 ; His ' church, which He redeemed by His own
blood,' Acts 20 : 28 ; His ' elect,' Rom. 8 : 32-34 ; His ' children,'
Heb. 2 : 12-14. On what grounds therefore can anyone assert that
' the world ' in Jn. 3 : 16, must necessarily mean every single
individual ?

Furthermore the intention, aim, and purpose of God in so loving
this world spoken of in verse 16 is its salvation, ' that the world
through Him might be saved.' God intends the salvation of those
thus loved, therefore plainly if the world here means every individual person either all men must be finally saved or else God
has failed to carry out His great intention in sending His Son ! Yet
it may be objected that the love of God is general to all men but
it depends upon whether men will believe, ' Whosoever believeth.'
But the verse does not say anything about God's love being conditional depending upon faith, literally it says, ' He gave His only
begotten Son that every believer in Him should not perish,' the
purpose of the words being to show how God communicates life
to those for whom He gave His Son ; we participate in this love by
means of faith, the sentence states only who God intends to save—
that is believers. What sense then can there be in interpreting the
world as every individual when God purposes that none but believers should benefit from His love ? Did not God know who
would believe in Christ ? Rather did not God know upon whom
He would bestow faith ? Do not the Scriptures say that to those
for whom God gave His Son to them He will also give all things ?
Is not faith one of these ' all things ' which God gives ? (Eph. 2 : 8).
Therefore as all men have not faith, Christ was not given for all
men. The truth is that only those ordained to eternal life believe
Acts 13 : 48. What possible sense then can there be in asserting
Christ died for all men, when God intended that none but the
elect should believe and benefit from that death ?

Thus we take Christ's words to Nicodemus in a manner which
is fully consistent with the rest of Scripture when we understand
it to mean—' God so loved the world,' miserable, sinful men of all
sorts, not Jews only as Nicodemus thought, but the elect scattered
over all the world, subject to all the iniquities of the world, ' that,'

intending their salvation, ' He gave His only begotten Son, that whosoever believeth in Him,' all believers whatsoever, signifying the persons whose good God intended, who are loved for no good in themselves—not because of any external or national difference from others—but distinguished solely by faith.

Further light on the use of the term world in the Bible is gained by understanding the erroneous persuasion which prevailed among the Jews that the salvation to be brought by the Messiah would be confined to them alone (see 1 Thess. 2 : 16). The Apostles themselves were misled by this persuasion until Acts 11 : 18, and thereafter they sought to use general expressions contrary to their former error ; such expressions as the world, all men, all nations, knowing that the Gospel was not to be restricted to one nation and family as the Jews supposed. There is an example of this in John's first Epistle chapter 2, verse 2, where John (there is evidence to conclude) writing to fellow Jews, writes ' He is the propitiation for our sins,' that is our sins who are believers of the Jews, but lest he should appear to confirm their former error he adds, ' And not for ours only, but for the sins of the whole world,' or ' for the children of God scattered abroad,' as John 11 : 51-51, living throughout the whole world, as opposed to the inhabitants of one place or country. The aim of John is clearly to console believers against their sins and failings, and he does so by reminding them of the effectual remedy provided for them in the death of Christ. If by the whole world he meant every individual what consolation would it have been to tell them that Christ died for innumerable that shall be damned ? Would it encourage them to know that they had no remedy except that which is common to multitudes that shall perish eternally ? We can therefore conclude that neither John 3 : 16 nor 1 John 2 : 2 contain anything contrary to the doctrine of election. The difficulty only arises from the ambiguous word ' world,' and it disappears when the word is interpreted in the light of the rest of Scripture.

A further ambiguous word, which has different meanings according to the passage in which it is used, is the word ' all.' Sometimes ' all ' refers to every individual of a certain class of people none excluded, so ' all ' in 1 Cor. 15 : 22 ; Eph. 4 : 6 ; Rom. 5 : 18 is limited to the class of believers (plainly the gift of justification which the last verse speaks of is only to all believers). That the term ' all ' does not in Scripture refer to every individual that is, was, or will be, can be made manifest from nearly five hundred instances. A general use of ' all ' is to signify some of all sorts, as in Matt. 9 : 35 ' every sickness ' which can scarcely mean that Christ cured every disease of every man, but only that He cured all sorts of diseases. That ' all ' often signifies ' all manner of ' is demonstrated by the translation on Luke 11 : 42, where clearly the Pharisees did not tithe every individual herb, though

C

the original says 'every herb,' therefore the translators rightly render it 'all manner of herbs,' or herbs of all sorts. The same is the case in Acts 10 : 12 when Peter sees a sheet containing 'all beasts,' and the translators naturally render it 'all manner of beasts.' The use of the term all in Acts 2 : 17, John 12 : 32, Matt. 3 : 5, Rom. 14 : 2, etc. further confirms this. Therefore when we find 'all' used in connection with redemption nothing but inattention to how the term is generally used in Scripture can make us conclude that it must necessarily mean every single individual. When Paul writes of praying 'for all men' (1 Tim. 2 : 1-4), he appears to interpret himself as referring to all classes of men, 'for kings and for all that are in authority,' men of all sorts, ranks, and conditions. The same as in Jerem. 29 : 1-2 where Nebuchadnezzar is said to have carried away 'all the people,' and the 'all' there means—as the following verses show—some of all classes of the people. So the aim of Paul in 1 Tim. 2, is to exhort believers to pray even for rulers who might be persecuting them, because God has now opened the door of salvation to all classes of men, He 'will have all men to be saved,' the time being come that Old Testament distinctions have been removed, and the Lord purposes to save some of all sorts and nations. Rev. 5 : 9.

When 'all' is understood in this Scriptural manner there is no contradiction between God's promise to wipe away the tears from 'off all faces,' and His declaration that some shall be left weeping and wailing for their sins.

There are a further class of Scriptures that are brought forward and interpreted as contrary to the doctrine of election. Such texts as these, 'Preach the Gospel to every creature' ; 'Warning every man and teaching every man' ; 'God now commandeth all men everywhere to repent.' From verses like these the following kind of statement is drawn—'If the Gospel contains universal exhortations to repent and believe, and men have not the ability to do this, then such exhortations are meaningless and useless.' To this we reply that it is necessary for the Gospel to be preached in an indiscriminate manner to all, as the elect and non-elect are mixed in this world and ministers cannot distinguish between them. Therefore the invitations and exhortations of the Gospel fall upon the ears of all men alike ; nevertheless though the non-elect are also called by the outward hearing of the Word, confronted with their duty of believing God, and left inexcusable for remaining in their sins, yet it was never the intention of God to overcome their disobedience by inwardly illuminating their minds and moving their wills—as He does in the elect. Thus 'many are called' by the outward hearing of the Word, 'but few are chosen,' that is chosen to be given faith. Though sin is the immediate cause of unbelief in those who hear the Gospel, yet the final cause why some are left in unbelief is the will of God ; so Isaiah assigns the cause of the Jew's unbelief by asserting that the arm of the Lord is not revealed to all, Is. 53 : 1, and John states that they could not believe the doctrine of Christ because this curse from God lay upon them, John 12 : 37-38. Again the Holy Spirit proclaims the same truth in Romans 11 : 7-8 ' The election hath obtained it, and the rest were blinded (According as it is written God hath given them the spirit of slumber, eyes that they should not see . . .).. Therefore although men resist the truth because of sin, God has sentenced some to remain in their state of sin, with whom He intends His Word to have no effect, thus the sons of Eli would not listen to warnings ' because the Lord would slay them ' (1 Sam. 2 : 25), nor would Pharoh listen because he was appointed to be a monument of God's just wrath against sinners (Exodus 9 : 16). It can thus be seen that though the Gospel is offered indiscriminately to all, and God declares Himself ready to show mercy upon all who desire and implore it, such Scriptures serve to console the elect who find themselves inwardly drawn by God to believe these free offers, while the same offers render the non-elect inexcusable. In short, both Scripture and experience testify that though the Gospel finds all men equally involved in disobedience and guilt, God magnifies His sovereign mercy in granting faith to some, while others are left in their natural state of enmity to Him. In this God can be charged with no injustice for He gives freely to some what He owes to none, no man being in any sense deserving of the grace of God. Nor do these truths in any way lessen a man's responsibility for his sins—for which his own conscience condemns him as the author. Because God is not pleased to deliver a man from his sins it by no means excuses his guilt.

There are several other passages which could be examined as they are often interpreted as contrary to election, but if believers would weigh well the context, the intention of the words, the teaching of the rest of Scripture, they would cease to hold doctrines contrary to each other, nor be satisfied with such meaningless assertions like ' truth lies in both extremes,' (an assertion that reduces all truth into confusion). Rather they would see in Scripture a Divine harmony, though the view of this harmony indeed causes us to cry out, ' Thy judgments, O Lord are a great deep.' "After all has been said, that can be said upon this stupendous subject ; let the short but awe-filled exclamation of the Apostle terminate all our disputations. Let us with him stand in awe of the unsearchable mind of God, and breath ' O the depth! ' " (Augustine).

The Banner of Truth is written (unless otherwise stated) and published by Sidney Norton and Iain Murray, Ministers of St. John's Church. Summertown, Oxford. COMMUNICATIONS SHOULD BE SENT TO 162, BANBURY ROAD, OXFORD. (Tel. Oxford 55163). (We are willing to travel out of Oxford in order to meet those who are truly concerned).

Printed by the Wickliffe Press, 104 Hendon Lane, N. 3

THE
BANNER of TRUTH

OCTOBER, 1956

(3rd Issue)

EDITOR:

MR. IAIN MURRAY, B.A.,
11 Lawrence Street, London, N.W. 7.

*　　*　　*

" Thou hast shewed thy people hard things ;
Thou hast made us to drink the wine of
astonishment.　Thou hast given a banner to
them that fear Thee, that it may be displayed
because of the truth."　　　　Psalm 60 : 3-4

*　　*　　*

CONTENTS

EDITORIAL COMMENTS

Nothing worse can happen to us in this world than to be deprived of the means of possessing a true knowledge of God. The loss of those ways by which the Word of God is spread and expounded is a loss greater than any other which a people can suffer. It is this loss which has overtaken our nation, and it is to this loss that our troubles may be traced. Faithful ministers, the preaching of sound doctrine, the powerful influences of the Holy Ghost, these are God's means of establishing the truth, and the widespread absence of these means is the loss to which we refer. But there is another means which may still be used. By the printed page truth may be read where it cannot be heard. Deprived as we are of a strong body of true teachers, by the printed page a great host of Christ's ministers in former generations may be summoned to our aid. It is by this means that the testimony of Reformers and Martyrs, Puritans and Covenanters, may again sound forth in the lands which once so prospered under their preaching. These are some of our convictions as we send out this publication.

In the providence of God, Mr. Norton and I, are no longer working together in the ministry at Oxford, as I have been called to move to London. Will readers therefore please note the change in address for all correspondence. It was from Oxford that the *Banner of Truth* was first published under a joint editorship. Although this joint editorship will now be discontinued the believers there will continue to be closely associated with this work, and the benefit of Mr. Norton's aid and counsel will not be lost.

For the benefit of friends this magazine costs (due to a recent rise in printing prices) approximately 9d. to produce, with another 2d. for postage. If the Lord directs us, we will shortly seek to issue the *Banner* bi-monthly or at some other regular interval, at which time it would seem best to run the magazine on a subscription basis. We will gladly forward any stated quantity to ministers or individuals for distribution, on the understanding that they return any copies which they are unable to sell. All gifts received will be gratefully used to send out free sample copies to addresses which are sent to us, thereby extending the circulation.

The uncertainty and solemnity of our days, our insufficiency and lack of means, all lead us to pray that God may arise and have mercy on Zion. " The afflicted's prayer He will not scorn ; All times this shall be on record ; And generations yet unborn shall praise and magnify the Lord." (Psa. 102). With Christian love and greetings to all readers.

50

COMING EVENTS AND PRESENT DUTIES

J. C. RYLE, Bishop of Liverpool (1880-1900).

*" Then shall the Kingdom of heaven be likened unto ten virgins, which
took their lamps, and went forth to meet the bridegroom. And five of them
were wise, and five were foolish . . . at midnight there was a cry made,
Behold, the bridegroom cometh . . . Watch therefore, for ye know neither
the day nor the hour wherein the Son of man cometh."*
(Read through Matt. 25: 1-13).

These thirteen verses make up one of the most solemn parables
that our Lord Christ ever spoke. This parable stands as a beacon
to the Church of Christ in all ages. It is a witness against carelessness and slothfulness—against apathy and indifference about
religion.

The figures and emblems used in the parable call for some
explanation. I will give my own view of their meaning. I believe
the parable to be a prophecy all the way through. I believe the
time spoken of in the parable, is the time when Christ shall return
in person to this world, and a time yet to come. The very first
word, the word " then," compared with the end of the twenty-fourth
chapter, appears to me to settle that question. I believe the ten
virgins carrying lamps represent the whole body of professing
Christians—the visible Church of Christ. I believe the Bridegroom
represents our Lord Jesus Christ Himself. I take the wise virgins
to be the true believers, the real disciples of Christ, the converted
part of the visible Church. I take the foolish to be the mere
nominal Christians, the unconverted, the whole company of those
who have no vital godliness. I take the lamps which all alike
carried, to be that mere outward profession of Christianity. I take
the oil, which some virgins had with their lamps, and others had
not, to be the grace of the Holy Ghost—that " unction of the Holy
One " which is the mark of all true Christians.

Let us then learn, first of all, that the visible Church of Christ
will always be a mixed body, till Christ comes again. I can gather
no other meaning from the beginning of the parable we are now
considering. I there see wise and foolish virgins mingled together
in one company, and I see this state of things going on till the very
moment the Bridegroom appears. I frankly say that I can find
no standing ground for the common opinion that the visible Church
will gradually advance to a state of perfection—that it will become
better and better. I fully admit that the Gospel appears sometimes
to make rapid progress in some countries ; but that it ever does
more than call out an elect people, I utterly deny. It never did
more in the days of the Apostles. It never has done more in any
country, from the time of the Apostle down to the present day.
There never yet was a parish or congregation in any part of the

world—however favoured in the ministry it enjoyed—there never was one, I believe, in which all the people were converted.   I believe that now is the time of election, not of universal conversion.

I fully admit that missions are doing a great work among the heathen.   I do not under value these things, I would to God that all professing Christians would value them more.   But as for any signs that all the ends of the earth shall turn to the Lord, under the present order of things, there are none.   God's work is going forward, as it always has done.   The Gospel is being preached for a witness to every quarter of the globe.   The elect are being brought to Christ one by one, and there is everything to encourage us to persevere.   But more than this no missionary can report in any station in the world.   I would not hesitate to preach the Gospel, and offer Christ's salvation to every man and woman alive ; but that there always will be a vast amount of unbelief and wickedness until the second coming, I am fully persuaded.   A large proportion of tares will be found growing together with the wheat, at the time of harvest.

Reader, the visible Church of Christ is made up of these two classes.   There always have been such.   There always will be such until the end.   Gracious and graceless, wise and foolish, make up the visible Church of Christ.   You yourself are described and written down in this parable.   You are either one of the wise virgins, or one of the foolish.   You have either the oil of grace, or you have got none.   You are either travelling towards heaven, or towards hell.   Never for a moment forget this.   The wise are they who have that wisdom which the Holy Ghost alone can give.   They know their own sinfulness.   They know Christ as their own precious Saviour.   They look on life as a season of preparation for eternity—not as an end, but as a way—not as a harbour, but as a voyage—not as a home, but as a journey.   The foolish are they who are without spiritual knowledge.   They neither know God, nor Christ, nor sin, nor their own hearts, nor the world, nor heaven, nor hell, nor the value of their souls as they ought.   There is no folly like this.   To expect wages after doing no work—or prosperity after taking no pains—or learning after neglecting books—this is rank folly.   But to expect heaven without faith in Christ—or the Kingdom of God without being born again—or the crown of glory without the cross and a holy walk—all this is greater folly still, and yet more common.   Alas, for the folly of the world !

Learn secondly, from this parable, that the visible Church is always in danger of neglecting the doctrine of Christ's second advent.   I draw this truth from that solemn verse, " While the bridegroom tarried, they all slumbered and slept."   I believe our Lord's meaning was simply this, that during the interval between His first and second advent, the whole Church, both believers and unbelievers, would get into a dull and dim-sighted state of soul about the blessed doctrine of His own personal return to earth. And, reader I say deliberately, that so far as my own judgment goes, there never was a saying of our Lord's more thoroughly verified by the event. I say that of all doctrines of the Gospel, the one about which Christians have become most unlike the first Christians, in their sense of its true value, is the doctrine of Christ's second advent. I have long felt it is one of the greatest shortcomings of the Church of Christ that we ministers do not preach enough about this advent of Christ, and that private believers do not think enough about it. A few of us here and there receive the doctrine, but we none of us live on it, feed on it, act on it, work from it, take comfort in it, as much as God intended us to do. In short, the Bridegroom tarries, and we all slumber and sleep.

It proves nothing against the doctrine of Christ's second coming, that it has sometimes been fearfully abused. I should like to know what doctrine of the Gospel has not been abused. Salvation by grace has been made a pretext for licentiousness—election, an excuse for all manner of unclean living. But if men will draw wrong conclusions we are not therefore obliged to throw aside good principles. Separate the doctrine from the mistakes and blunders of many who hold it. Do not reject the foundation because of the wood, hay, and stubble which some have built upon it. Do not condemn it and cast it aside because of injudicious friends.

Learn, in the third place, that whenever Christ does come again, it will be a very sudden event. It will come on men suddenly. It will not have been talked over, prepared for, and looked forward to by everybody. It will awaken men's minds like the cry of fire at midnight. It will startle men's hearts like a trumpet blown at their bedside in their sleep. Like Pharaoh and his host in the Red Sea, they will know nothing till the very waters are upon them. Like Dathan and Abiram, and their company, when the earth opened under them, the moment of their hearing the report of the visitation will be the same moment when they will see it with their eyes. Before they can recover their breath and know where they are, they shall find that the Lord is come. Everything which is written in Scripture on this point confirms the truth. " As a snare shall it come," says one place—" As a thief in the night," says another—" As the lightning," says a third—" In such an hour as ye think not," says a fourth—" When they shall say, Peace and safety," says a fifth. (Luke 21 : 35 ; 1 Thess. 5 : 2 ; Luke 17 : 24 ; Matt. 24 : 44 ; 1Thess. 5 : 3). When the Lord came on the earth in Noah's time, there was no appearance beforehand of anything so awful being near. The days and nights were following each other in regular succession. The grass, and trees, and crops were growing as usual. The business of the world was going on . . .

The flood took the world by surprise—so also will the coming of the
Son of Man. (Luke 17 : 26).

Ah, reader ! When shall this thing be ? Truly we may say,
" Lord God, Thou knowest." A thousand years in His sight are
as one day, and one day as a thousand years. But we do know
that yet a little while He that shall come, will come, and
will not tarry. Yet a little while, and the last sermon shall be
preached—the last congregation shall break up. Yet a little while,
and carelessness, and infidelity shall cease, perish and pass away. The
believers among us will be with Christ, and the unbelievers in hell.
The night is far spent, and the day is at hand . . . Now God delays
the final glory, and allows things to go on as they do in this world.
It is not that He is not able to prevent evil—it is not that He is slack
in the fulfilling of His promises—but the Lord is taking out for
Himself a people by the preaching of the Gospel. (Acts 15 : 14 ;
2 Peter 3 : 9). He is longsuffering to unconverted Christians.
" The Lord is not willing that any should perish, but that all should
come to repentance." Once let the number of the elect be gathered
out of the world—once let the last elect sinner be brought to repentance— and then the kingdom of Christ shall be set up, and
the throne of grace shall be exchanged for the throne of glory.

Reader, the suddenness of the Lord's second advent is a truth
that should lead every professing Christian to great searching of
heart. Learn what an immense change this event will make to the
members of the visible Church, both good and bad. I draw this
truth from the concluding portion of the parable—from the discovery of the foolish virgins that their lamps were gone out, from
their anxious address to the wise, " Give us of your oil,"—from their
vain knocking at the door when too late—from the happy admission
of the wise who were found ready, in company with the bridegroom.
It will be an immense change to the ungodly—to all who are found
mere nominal Christians. All such persons, when Christ comes
again, will see the value of real spiritual religion. They will do in
effect what the parable describes under a figure—they will cry to
the godly, " Give us of your oil."

Who does not know, as things are now, spiritual religion never
brings a man the world's praise ? It entails on a man the world's
disapprobation—the world's persecution—the world's mockery . . .
Who has not heard of nicknames in plenty, bestowed on those who
follow Christ—Puritans, Methodists, Calvinists, and many more ?
Who does not know the petty family persecutions which often go on
in private society to-day ? Let a young person go to every ball,
and opera, and race-course, and worldly party, and utterly neglect
his soul, and no one interferes ; no one says, " Spare thyself "—no
one says " Take care : remember God, judgment, and eternity."
But let him only begin to read his Bible, and be diligent in prayer—

let him decline worldly amusements, and become particular in his employment of time, let him live like an immortal being ; let him do this, I say, and all his friends and relatives will probably be up in arms. "You are going too far. You are taking up extreme views." There will be an end of all this when Christ returns to the world. The light of that day will at length show everything in its true colours. The scales will fall from the poor worldling's eyes. The value of the soul will flash on his astonished mind. The utter uselessness of a mere nominal Christianity will burst upon him like a thunder-storm. Just as Saul wanted Samuel when it was too late, and Belshazzar sent for Daniel when the kingdom was about to be taken from him, so will the ungodly turn to the very men they once mocked and despised, and cry to them, " Give us of your oil, for our lamps are gone out."

Let me draw from the whole subject a solemn question for all into whose hands this address may fall. That question is simply this : Are you ready for the great change ? Are you ready for the coming of Christ ?

"Ah ! " I can imagine some saying, " this is asking far too much. —To be ready for Christ's appearing ! this is far too high a standard. This is extravagance. There would be no living in the world at this rate. This is a hard saying. Who can hear it ? "— I cannot help it. I believe this is the standard of the Bible. I believe this is the standard Paul sets before us when he says the Thessalonians were " waiting for the Son of God from heaven," and the Corinthians " waiting for the coming of our Lord Jesus Christ." (1 Thess. 1 : 10 ; 1 Cor. 1 : 7). And surely this is the standard Peter sets before us, when he speaks of " looking for and hasting unto the coming of the day of God." (2 Pet. 3 : 12).

It is useless to tell me that, in asking this, I put before you too high a standard. It is vain to tell me that a man may be a very good man, and yet not be ready for the kingdom of Christ. I deny it altogether. I say that every justified and converted man is ready, and that if you are not ready you are not a justified man. I say that the standard I put before you is nothing more than the New Testament standard, and that the Apostles would have doubted the truth of your religion, if you were not looking and longing for the coming of the Lord. I say above all that the grand end of the Gospel is to prepare men to meet God. What has your Christianity done for you if it has not made you meet for the kingdom of Christ ? Nothing ! nothing at all ! Oh, that you may think on this matter, and never rest till you are ready to meet Christ !

In the next place let me offer an invitation to all readers who do not feel ready for Christ's return. That invitation shall be short and simple. I beseech you to know your danger,and come to Christ without delay. I entreat you this day to " flee from the

wrath to come," to the hope set before you in the Gospel. I pray
you in God's stead, to lay down your enmity and unbelief, and at
once to be reconciled to God. (2 Cor. 5 : 20). Cast away everything that draws you back. Cry mightily to the Lord Jesus to
reveal Himself to your soul.

Last of all, let me draw from the subject an exhortation to all
who know Christ indeed, and love His appearing. That exhortation
is simply this, that you will strive more and more to be a " doing "
Christian. (James 1 : 22). Labour more and more to show forth
the praises of Him Who hath called you. Improve every talent.
Let your conformity to the mind of Christ be unquestionable and
unmistakable. Never was there a greater mistake than to fancy
that the doctrine of the personal return of Christ is calculated to
paralyze Christian diligence. Surely there can be no greater spur
to the servant's activity than the expectation of his master's speedy
return. This is the way to attain a healthy state of soul. Alas,
there are not a few of God's saints who complain that they want
spiritual comfort in their religion, while the fault is altogether in
themselves. " Occupy, occupy," I would say to such persons.
Lay yourselves out more heartily for the glory of God . . . Oh,
brethren believers, it would be well indeed if we did but see clearly
how much it is for our interest and happiness to occupy every
farthing of our Lord's money—to live very near to God.

I ask every reader of this address to bring the light of the day
of Christ to bear upon his inner man. Set your years, and months,
and weeks, and days, and hours in the full blaze of that day. Try
all your employment of time by the test of Christ's second coming.
Live as if you thought Christ might come at any time. Lie down
in bed at night ready, if need be, to be awakened by the midnight
cry—" Behold the Bridegroom cometh." Do everything as if you
did it for the last time. Say everything as if you said it for the
last time. Read every chapter in the Bible as if you did not know
whether you would be allowed to read it again. Pray every prayer
as if you felt it might be your last opportunity. This is the way to
be found ready. This is the way to turn Christ's second appearing
to good account.

Whether the last days of old England have really come—
whether her political greatness is about to pass away—whether her
Protestant Church is about to have her candlestick removed—
whether in the coming crash of nations England is to perish like
Amalek, or at length be saved, and escape " so as by fire "—all these
are points which I dare not attempt to settle ; a very few years will
decide them. But I am sure there never was a time when it was
more imperatively needful to summon believers to " cease from
man," to stand on their watch towers, and to build all their hopes
on the second coming of the Lord.

AUGUSTINE, BISHOP OF HIPPO

Augustine, the son of a Roman official, was born at Tagaste in North Africa in A.D. 354. Endowed with brilliant talents, strongly motivated by vain glory and the desire of praise, he was by the age of nineteen studying and teaching rhetoric in the ancient city of Carthage. Here, with his mind bent on the pursuit of worldly wisdom, and his heart captivated by the pleasures of sin, Augustine remained consuming the prime of his life. " Woe, woe !" he later wrote, " By what steps was I brought down to the depths of Hell ! Toiling and turmoiling through want of truth ! " The various philosophical systems of thought which in turn occupied his attention, only plunged him deeper into a maze of error. By the age of thirty-one, mental despair and heart misery led him to take up the doubts of the Academics, who believed that nothing was certain. " I was overcharged with most gnawing cares, lest I should die ere I found the truth." Now, in his downward path, consciousness of sin began to torment him. Lashed by fear and shame, made painfully aware that sin had diseased his mind and bound his will, he began to abhor himself.

Little did Augustine realize that a vessel of mercy was being formed, that a servant of Christ was being made, that he should be by grace, one of the mightiest champions of the truth that God has ever given to His Church. So it was, that in a garden in Milan in the year A.D. 386, a voice fell upon his ears as from heaven, commanding him to take up and read the Bible. " Thou calledst, and shoutedst, and burstedst my deafness." Opening a copy of God's Word at Romans 13 : 13-14, he said, " A light of serenity infused into my heart, and the gross darkness which had floated before my eyes dissolved in an instant. Thy powerful voice said, Let there be light and there was light." Henceforth Augustine, humbled in the dust, had only one consuming desire, to love and serve his Saviour. " I taste no other pleasure but that which results from speaking, hearing, writing, conferring and perpetually dwelling upon the meditation of Thee and Thy glory."

It was the appointed time of God for the raising of this servant. The age was one full of cause for alarm and solemn fears. The Church of Christ was threatened with errors from within, while from without the fall of the Roman Empire was bringing confusion. invasions of barbarians, and centuries of disorder and darkness over Europe. In the years following his conversion we see Augustine being moulded into the instrument of God's purpose. Day by day, year by year, he was solely engrossed in the Word of God : often he would be studying it till half way through the night, learning it upon his knees, unweariedly digesting its contents. Foundation truths were being laid deep in his soul, truths from the

Word of God which were to shine like beacons for future ages of the Church.

In the spring of 392, the prayers of the aged Valerius, Bishop of Hippo, for another pastor for his flock were answered by the sending of Augustine to that place. There he was ordained a presbyter at the age of 39, and subsequently became the bishop. Unhappily for the Church, the apostolic equality of presbyters and bishops was disappearing. Although at Rome the office of bishop had already begun to be associated with lordly arrogance and priestly pretension, it was not so at Hippo in North Africa. Augustine as Bishop of Hippo held all things in common with fellow believers, he himself never being preferred. At his death he left no money, and in his life he not only parted with all his own means, but even melted down the silver vessels of the Church for the sake of the poor. From the pulpit he would plead with souls in a startling fashion. His one authority was the Word of God which he treated with the most profound reverence. "Wondrous depths of Thy Word!" he exclaimed one day in preaching, "whose surface behold is before us little ones ; yet are they a wondrous depth, O my God, a wondrous depth!" Towards the end of his life this apostolic minister declared "that though he should with better capacity and greater diligence study all his lifetime, from the beginning of his childhood to decrepit age, nothing else but the Holy Scriptures ; yet they are so compacted and thickly set with truths, that he might daily learn something which before he knew not." Augustine preached from his heart, and his deep love for souls made him long to preach his hearers into Christ. He had learned in his own daily life to gaze so intently on Christ, that in his preaching all other themes dwindled into nothing.

"Oh unspeakable love," he would cry, "that God for man should die in the flesh ; had not man been ransomed at so vast expense, he must have unavoidably suffered eternal damnation." He eschewed wisdom of words, and preached in a vehement, plain, downright manner, often reducing his hearers to tears.

What were the doctrines of this godly man ? What errors did God raise him up to oppose ? Let none say that the remoteness of Augustine's times has caused his writings to outlive their usefulness. The world, as Augustine said, with its glory and grandeur will soon perish, but the truth of God abides, eternal and unchanging. Likewise, although error appears in countless differing forms, the foundation upon which error stands is one and the same in all ages. In fact, it is true to say that the doctrines which Augustine expounded from the Scriptures are of such momentous importance that to be ignorant of them renders one unable to judge the issues that are at stake to-day. The error which he opposed then, is the error which is alive with devastating effects in the Church now.

Heresy never appears as heresy. In Augustine's day it arose from a man named Pelagius, apparently a blameless, mortified, modest monk, who zealously exhorted others to follow the example of Christ. The teaching of this man was so subtle and ambiguous that it passed undetected before a counsel of 14 bishops in Palestine. It was left to Augustine to expose the foundations of Pelagianism. Through many years of trial and humbling God had prepared his servant for this task. The root of Pelagian teaching lay in its view of human nature. Man, Pelagius said, was not in a condition of original sin, but possessed free-will as Adam did before the Fall. Sin was inherited by example rather than by nature. Therefore, in salvation, the grace of God was not an inward power renewing the ruined nature and restoring the fallen will of man to its freedom, but rather grace was something external, which the will may grasp if it so chooses. Pelagius asserted that the grace of God was extended equally to all, and therefore it was the choice of man that determined whether grace was received or not. In short, Pelagianism is the belief that salvation is the result of the co-operation of God and the sinner.

What led Augustine to contend so strongly against such statements as these ? He was not the man to engage in controversy for the sake of non-essentials, a controversial spirit was quite foreign to his tender love towards all men. His only concern on earth was the glory of God through His Church, but because he knew that the safety of the Church lay in the preservation of the truth, he was ready to denounce Pelagianism as a pernicious error. " The great sin of Pelagianism," he declared, " is that it makes a man forget why he is a Christian." Upholding the Scriptures, he asserted that the conversion of the sinner proceeds solely from the free election of God, and that the reason why He calls some and leaves others reprobate, lies solely in His own unsearchable will. In his work, " *Concerning the Predestination of the Saints*," Augustine writes as follows : " Lest anyone should say, My faith or my righteousness distinguishes me from others, the great teacher of the Gentiles asks ' What hast thou that thou hast not received ? ' Faith, therefore, from its beginning to its perfection, is the gift of God. But why faith is not given to all, ought not to concern the believer, who knows that all men by the sin of one, came into the most just condemnation. Why God delivers one from this condemnation and not another, belongs to His inscrutable judgments. And if it be investigated how it is that the receiver of faith is deemed worthy of God to receive such a gift, there are not wanting those who will say, It is by their human will. But we say that it is by grace ; or Divine Predestination." Following the Bible, he shows election to be the first great cause of all, and demonstrates the absurdity of making the foreseeing of faith by God the cause of election. " Paul does not declare that the children of God were chosen, because He foreknew they would believe, but in order that they might believe. God did not choose us because we believed, but so that we might believe ; lest we should appear to have first chosen Him.   Paul loudly declares that our very beginning to be holy is the fruit of election.   They act most preposterously, therefore, who put election after faith.   When Paul lays down, as the cause of election, that good pleasure of God which He had in Himself, he excludes all other causes whatsoever."

It was claimed by Augustine's adversaries that the authority of the Church was against his doctrines, whereupon he replied that before the heresy of Pelagius the fathers of the primitive church did not deliver their opinions deeply upon predestination, which reply was the truth.   And he adds, " What need is there for us to search the works of those writers, who, before the heresy of Pelagius arose, found no necessity of devoting themselves to this question. Had such necessity arisen, and had they been compelled to reply to the enemies of predestination, they would doubtless have done so. What was it that compelled me to defend those passages of Scripture in which predestination is set before us ?   What, but the starting up of the Pelagians who say that the grace of God is given to us according as we render ourselves worthy of it ! "

How the Pelagian controversy was fought out, how the Council of Ephesus condemned the positions of Pelagius in A.D. 431, how the godly bishop of Hippo, filled with love for Christ, laboured till his dying breath, how he died three months before the Roman garrison at Hippo was overwhelmed by the barbarian invasion ; these are things we cannot speak of now.   Nor is there space to draw out the lessons from this man's life, except to mention one. The life of Augustine disproves once and for all the objection that faith in God's Eternal Predestination is inconsistent with earnest preaching and evangelism.   " They say," writes Augustine, " that the doctrine of predestination is enemy unto preaching, that it should do no good.   As though it had been an enemy unto the the Apostle's preaching.   Hath not that excellent teacher of the Gentiles so oftentimes commended predestination, and yet ceased not to preach the Word of God ? . . . For as godliness is to be preached, that God may be truly worshipped, so also is predestination : that he which hath ears to hear, may glory of the grace of God, in God, not in himself."

The old world of Augustine's day has passed away, but the errors he fought have not.   They revived powerfully in Arminianism in the seventeenth century, and to-day these same errors—this great sin as Augustine called it—have overspread the visible Church. God has pronounced a solemn curse on those who seek to undo His work by building up what He has cast down (Joshua 6 : 26). Let us then weigh well in closing the following words of Richard

Sibbes, once a Doctor of Divinity at Cambridge :—

" The heresy of Pelagius was damned to Hell by the ancient Councils. The African Councils, divers of them, divers synods, wherein Augustine himself was a party, they condemned Pelagius's heresy. Are there not men now abroad who will revive these heresies ? We can expect nothing but a curse to prevail when men go about reviving heresies that God has condemned. They are opinions cursed by the church of God, that have been led by the Spirit heretofore ; such opinions, I mean, as speak meanly of the grace of God, and advance the strength of free-will, and make an idol of that ; and so, under the commendation, and setting up of nature, are the enemies of grace."

(I.M.)

THE DOCTRINE OF THE LEADERS OF THE ENGLISH REFORMATION

" The Reformation from Popery in the sixteenth century was the greatest event, or series of events, that has occurred since the close of the canon of Scripture ; and the men who are really entitled to be called the ' Leaders of the Reformation ' have a claim to more respect and gratitude than any other body of uninspired men that have ever influenced or adorned the church . . . In point of intrinsic merit as authors, as successful labourers in expounding and establishing Christian truth the Reformers are immeasurably superior to the theologians of preceding generations—the Fathers and the schoolmen are mere children compared with the Reformers . . . The Reformers were God's instruments in bringing out to a large extent the permanent truth revealed in His Word, and in restoring the church to a large measure of apostolic purity."—(Dr. William Cunningham).

" England requires now more than ever to study the Fathers of the Reformation in their writings, and to be animated by their spirit."—(Dr. Merle D'Aubigné).

God's Predestination and Absolute Will.

Bradwardin (Archbishop of Canterbury, 1349, one of the earliest Reformers) defines predestination as " God's eternal fore-ordination, or pre-determination of His will, respecting what shall come to pass." " Whatever things come to pass, they are brought to pass by the providence of God."

Wycliffe (1324-1384, ' the greatest English Reformer '—D'Aubigné). " All things that happen do come absolutely of necessity."

Latimer (Bishop of Rochester, martyred 1555). "He fills the earth :

that is to say He rules and governs the same : ordering all things according to His will and pleasure." "No man's power is able to stand against God, or disappoint Him of His purposes."

Thomas Becon (Cranmer's private chaplain and one of his six preachers at Canterbury). "Predestination is the secret unchangeable appointment of God ; before all beginnings, by His counsel and wisdom, to life everlasting concerning His elect and chosen people."

Martin Bucer (appointed by Cranmer as the King's Professor of Divinity at Cambridge, 1549, and called by Bishop Hooper Cranmer's "inseparable companion.") "Predestination is an appointment of everything to its proper use ; by which appointment, God does, before He made them, even from eternity, destine all things whatever to some certain and particular use."

John Bradford (martyred 1555—"I thank God heartily that ever I was acquainted with him."—wrote Bishop Ridley). "We should certainly know that it is God which is the ruler and arbiter of all things, and that having determined all things that He will do, now of His power doth in His time put the same into execution, according as He hath decreed with Himself."

Salvation Depends on God's Will alone.

Cranmer (first Protestant Archbishop of Canterbury, martyred 1556). "Certain it is, that our election cometh only and wholly of the benefit and grace of God."

William Tyndale (martyred 1536—"the Apostle of England," Foxe). "Why doth God open one man's eyes and not another's ? Paul (Romans 9) forbiddeth to ask why ; for it is too deep for man's capacity. God we see is honoured thereby . . . But the Popish can suffer God to have no secret, hid to himself . . . they go and set up free will with the heathen philosophers, and say that a man's free-will is the cause why God chooseth one and not another, contrary unto all the Scriptures. Faith cometh not of our free-will ; but is the gift of God."

Foxe. "Concerning election, if the question be asked, 'Why was Abraham chosen and not Nahor ? Why was Jacob chosen and not Esau ? Why was Moses elected, and Pharaoh hardened ? ' It cannot be answered otherwise than thus : because it was so the good will of God."

Lancelot Ridley (appointed by Cranmer one of the six preachers at Canterbury, 1541). " 'According to the pleasure of his will' (Eph. 1 : 4). No other cause is to be asked why God has elected and chosen us to be his children by adoption."

The Catechism of 1553. "The first, principal, and most proper cause of our justification and salvation is the goodness and love of God, whereby He chose us for His, before He made the world."

George Carleton (Bishop of Chichester, 1626). " If the question be proposed, why God receiveth one to mercy, and not another ? why this man, and not that ? to this question the Orthodox that have taught in the Church after St. Augustine's answer, that of this taking one to mercy, and leaving another, no reason can be given but only the will of God. The Pelagians and Arminians say, that God's will herein is directed by somewhat fore-seen in men predestined. Now that predestination dependeth only upon God's will without respect to anything foreseen in men, is, as I said the received doctrine of Augustine, and of the Church following. And this has hitherto been the received doctrine of the Church of England."

All Those Elected Shall be Converted, and Can Never be Finally Lost.

Cranmer. " The elect shall not wilfully and obstinately withstand God's calling." " The elect, in whom finally no fault shall be, but they shall perpetually continue and endure." " The elect shall follow Christ's precepts, or when they fall, they shall repent and rise again, and obtain remission . . . "

Foxe. " Whom God hath chosen, the same He hath justified." " Election is the cause of vocation. Vocation (which is the working of God's Spirit by the word) is the cause of faith."

Coverdale (Bishop of Exeter). " In the faith of the Gospel were saved all they that from the beginning were preserved and ordained to salvation."

Bale (Bishop of Ossory, Ireland). " They only possess the kingdom of God, which are written in the Lamb's book of life, that were predestinate thereunto in Christ before the world's constitution."

Sandys (Archbishop of York). " Neither filthy Sodom, nor superstitious Egypt, nor idolatrous Babylon, nor corrupt Cessarea, was able to infect Lot, or Joseph, or Daniel, or Cornelius ; whom the Lord had chosen according to His good pleasure. ' The foundation of God remaineth sure, and has this seal ; The Lord knoweth who are his'. ' I will have mercy on whom I will have mercy.' "

Nicholas Ridley (Bishop of London, martyred 1555). " In all ages God has had His own manner, after His secret and unsearchable wisdom, to use His elect, sometimes to suffer them to drink of Christ's cup . . . yet the Lord is all one towards them in both, and loveth them no less . . . No man can take us out of the Father's hands—Who shall lay anything to the charge of God's elect ! "

Martin Bucer. " God's election cannot be made void by any creature whatever. Seeing, then, that the purpose of God, according to election, may stand, not of works, but of him that calleth (Rom. 9 : 11) ; He not only elected His own people before they were born, and had done good or evil (Rom. 9 : 11), but even before the very foundations of the world (Eph. 1 : 4). Hence our Lord said concerning his apostles, I pray not for the world, but for them whom thou hast given me ; for they are thine : that is, they were chosen by thee unto life." (Jn. 17). " My Sheep hear my voice," (Jn. 10 : 27). " In these words our Lord expressly teaches, that all good things are dependent on God's election ; and that they, to whom it is once given to be sheep, can never perish afterwards."

Bradford (probably the most greatly used preacher in England during the reign of Edward VI). "Faith and belief in Christ is the work and gift of God ; given to none other than to those which be the children of God : that is, to those whom God the Father, before the beginning of the world, hath predestinate in Christ unto eternal life."

Fallen Man Deserves Nothing from God, and has been so Ruined by Sin that He can Excercise Neither Will, Choice, nor Desire Towards Salvation.

Latimer. " If we shall be judged after our own deservings, we shall be damned everlastingly." " I am of myself, and by myself, coming from my natural father and mother, the child of wrath . . . a lump of sin, and working nothing of myself, but all towards Hell, except I have better help of another than I have of myself." " The Devil's will and our own fight against God's will."

Becon. " Man has no power to seek for salvation, but rather continues still in his old wickedness, and seeks to be far from the face of God, coveting rather to be damned than he would once approach unto the sight of God ; sin has so slain his courage, Satan in him has so great dominion . . . he hates God, and wishes that there were no God, that he might escape unpunished."

Cranmer. " Our faith and trust that we be in God's favour and His own children hangs not of our applying of our will to His motions."

Barnes (martyred in 1540—"The great restorer of good learning to Cambridge."—Strype). " A man hath no free-will." This same assertion was charged against Luther in a Papal Bull published in England in May, 1521, and against the Evangelicals by the Lower House of Convocation in 1536. For maintaining this truth several Reformers—such as Lambert, Legat, and Harrison, were martyred during the reign of Henry VIII.

Christ Died to Fulfil The Father's Eternal Purpose.

Cranmer. " Our Saviour Christ, according to the will of His eternal Father, when the time thereof was fully accomplished, taking our nature upon Him, came into the world, from the high throne of His Father ; to give light to them that were in darkness and the shadow of death, and to preach, and give pardon and full remission of sins to all His elected."

N. Ridley. " The death and passion of Christ was and is the one only sufficient and available sacrifice satisfactory for all the elect of God."

Bale. " He died for all them which were create to be saved."

Norden. His blood was shed " for many, for the remission of sins : not for all."

Bradford. " The world, John the Baptist speaks of, whose sins Christ takes away, and the world which Paul says has been reconciled, is to be discerned from that world for which Christ prayed not (Jn. 17 : 9), for look, for whom He prayed not, for them He died not."

Tyndale. " ' God which will have all men to be saved,' that is, some of all nations and all degrees, and not the Jews only. (Tim. 2 : 4)." Likewise he expounds 1 John 2 : 2.—" Christ died not only for our sins, who are Jews, but for the whole world, that is, all who should believe unto the world's end, of whatsoever nation or degree (kind) they be."

All Men Are Not Elect, But God Has Rejected (Reprobated) Some.

Wycliffe. " The prayer of the reprobate prevaileth for no man."

John Frith (martyred1533). " Whomsoever He chooseth, them He saveth of His mercy : and whom He repelleth, them of His secret and unsearchable judgment, He condemneth."

L. Ridley. " Whosoever be not glad to hear the word of God, but despise it, and care not to keep God's commandments but are all set to seek the pleasures and the glory of this world : whosoever is so affected, it is a token that they be not the children of salvation, but of perdition and eternal damnation : of these works that follow (the hearing of God's Word), we may have a conjecture, who be ordained of God to be saved, and who to be damned."

Bucer. " Scripture does not hesitate to affirm, that there are persons, whom God delivers to a reprobate sense, and whom He forms for destruction : why, therefore, should it be deemed derogatory from God, to assert, that He not only does this, but resolved beforehand to do it ? " " The doctrine of reprobation is useful to the elect ; inasmuch as it influences them to a greater fear and abhorrence of sin, and to a firmer reliance on the goodness of God."

Peter Martyr (" He was thought," writes Melchior Adam, " the properest divine, on earth, to preside in the divinity chair at Oxford. He was accordingly, with the King's concurrence, invited to England by Cranmer." 1547. Between the Archbishop and Martyr, says Strype, there existed " a great and cordial intimacy and friendship : for of him he made particular use in the steps he took in our reformation "). " Reprobation may be defined, that most wise determination of God, whereby He did, before eternity, immutably decree not to have mercy on those whom He loved not, but passed by : and this without any injustice on His part."

Dr. Whitaker (Queen's Professor of Divinity at Cambridge during the reign of Elizabeth). " Peter Martyr and Martin Bucer, of honor. able memory, did profess this doctrine of absolute and irrespective Reprobation, in both our famous Universities ; and our Church did always hold it as the undoubted truth, ever since the restitution of the Gospel to her."

(For Scripture relevant to this solemn doctrine see Exodus 9 ; Deut. 2 : 30 ; 1 Sam. 2 : 25 ; Prov. 16 : 4 ; Luke 4 : 26-27 ; John 12 : 39-40 ; 1 Pet. 2 : 8 ; 2 Pet. 2 : 12 ; Jude 4 ; Rev. 13 : 8, etc.)

The Above Truths are of Great Importance, and Practical Use, and are therefore to be Openly Maintained.

John Knox (Chaplain to Edward VI, his preaching was a mighty instrument in the English Reformation). " Some do think that because the reason of man cannot attain to the understanding how God shall be just, making in His counsel this diversity of mankind, that therefore it were better to keep silence in all such mysteries . . . But yet, I say, that the doctrine of God's eternal predestination is so necessary to the Church of God, that without the same, faith can neither be truly taught , nor surely established."

Bucer. " Those persons are not to be heard, who would have the doctrine of election laid (as it were) asleep, and seldom or never make its appearance in the congregations of the faithful."

Cranmer, Martyr, Haddom, and Taylor. " An earnest and correct contemplation of our predestination and election (respecting which it was appointed by the will of God before the foundations of the world were laid) . . . soothes the minds of pious men inspired with the Spirit of Christ."

Bradford. " But what go I about to recount the commodities (blessings) coming out of the doctrine of God's election, in that they be innumerable ? This is a sum, that, where a Christian man's life has respect to God, to man, and to himself, to ' live godly, justly, and soberly,' all is grounded in predestination in Christ. For who lives ' godly,' but he that believes ? and who believes but such as are ' ordained to eternal life ' ? (Acts 13 : 48). Who lives ' justly,' but such as love their neighbours ? and whence springs this love, but of God's election ' before the beginning of the world, that we might be blameless by love ? ' (Eph. 1). Who lives ' soberly,' but such as be holy ? and who are they but only those that be endued with the Spirit of sanctification ? which is the seal of our election, which by election do believe."

Antonie Gylbie. " This doctrine is so necessary that upon all occasions it ought with reverence to be uttered to the glory of God, which so wonderfully appeareth in His rich mercy towards us, whom He choseth from the filth of sin."

66

THE SOVEREIGN GRACE BOOK CLUB

Under this name Mr. Jay Green, a United States citizen, has not long begun the great work of republishing some of the finest Christian books—books which have for many years been unobtainable both in Britain and the U.S.A. The re-appearance of these books in Britain should be a matter of real thanksgiving for all believers. Upon the presence or absence of the truth hangs the future of our nation. Such was the concern of the Reformers to circulate the truth that at Basle in 1525 they sold their possessions to buy printing presses ; at Geneva 30 printing presses were in continuous use ; in England imprisoned martyrs for want of pen and ink tore strips of lead out of the windows and recorded the truth with their blood ! Can anything be of greater concern to us to-day than this ?

The work Mr. Green has begun is desparately needed. It has already in the U.S.A. been greatly blessed by God. The work which began without any financial capital, depended on the co-operation and support of believers. The manner in which the difficulties which faced such a project have been overcome, demonstrates how a few united men acting together can be instruments of the power of God. So far the following books have been printed.

Exposition of Romans, by Robt. Haldane, 5 vols,, 8/6 per vol., 42/- per set.

Exposition of First Peter, by John Brown of Edinburgh, 3 vols., 47/6 per set.

Songs of Sovereignty, Sermons by John Owen, 8/-.

The Saints Everlasting Rest, by Richard Baxter, vol. I 10/6 (2nd vol. to follow).

A *Mute Christian, and Apples of Gold,* by Thomas Brooks, 15/-.

Keeping the Heart, by John Flavel, 3/6.

Prayer, by John Bunyan, and *Return of Prayer,* by T. Goodwin, 3/6.

Within the next year, Mr. Green hopes to publish other rare works, including such authors as Thomas Goodwin, Thomas Manton, Jonathan Edwards, Augustus Toplady, and others.

It is possible that some of our readers may not be familiar with the above works. Several of them are 300 years old, and due to their rarity their great worth has been little known. The fact is, as Jay Green writes, " The cream of the Puritan writers of the golden age of theology, the 17th century, are represented in this series ; in addition such men as Edwards, Haldane, and Carson who followed in the spirit of the great Puritans in their writings."

A few comments on the above books are needed.   Haldane's
Commentary on Romans (first published in Scotland between 1835
and 1839) is believed by many to be the finest commentary on this
great Epistle ever written.   Haldane, a Scotsman, first expounded
it informally to a group of students at Geneva in 1816-17.   The
outcome was a great revival of truth in that ancient city.   His
commentary was the result of some 30 years' study, and though it
went through 9 editions in less than 100 years, it is to-day one
of the scarcest books on the second-hand market.   Certainly these
volumes form an exposition superior to anything that has been
published in England in this century.   The reappearance of this
one book could have a profound influence upon the whole land.
John Brown was another great expositor of the last century.
Spurgeon said of him, " Brown is a modern Puritan.   All his expositions are of the utmost value ; " and of his commentary on
1 Peter , " It is one of the best, a standard work, at once evangelical,
doctrinal, and practical."   The set of 3 vols. contain 1408 pages.
Flavel's small work on *Keeping the Heart* when first published in
London 300 years ago, was purchased by a gentleman who had
entered a book shop with the intention of buying a play or a novel.
Shortly he returned and asked the shopkeeper for a further 100
copies, declaring " It hath saved my soul : blessed be God that
ever I came into your shop ! "   The scope of this work is to direct
a believer into a close daily walk with God.   Owen, Brooks, Baxter,
all these writers wrote works of peculiar and lasting value.

These books are all finely printed and bound (except the 3/6
copies which are paper backed).   To all who are familiar with
the prices of American books they are cheap.   These publications
are entirely non-profit making.   We urgently exhort all readers,
especially ministers, to purchase and circulate as many as possible.
Jay Green adds some reasons why you ought to do this.

" *You will grow in grace and knowledge*!   *In Grace* because
you will be brought face to face with Him Who is the Author and
Finisher of your faith . . . These old writers did not write to please
men but to please a pure and holy God !   They bring Scripture to
bear on your sin, and then they take you before your God—modern
writings generally miss this mark.

In Knowledge because these old authors are so exhaustive in
their searchings into Scripture.   They will, by their deep probings
into God's Word, convince you of your ignorance of Scripture—
and the beginning of knowledge is to realize that you are ignorant.
We promise you that you will read many times more hours in the
Bible after you have read these books.   That has been my own case.

By the overpowering and abounding grace of God, there is
in my heart a sincere, single-hearted desire to surround you with
the *GOLD* of human writings ; and to ruin your appetite for the

brassy, adulterated writings of this day. It is a short life, and one who redeem the time must heed to *WHAT* he read."

Jay Green is also the editor of a fine bi-monthly magazine— *The Way, The Truth, and The Life,* those who would like a sample copy should writ direct to him at

1124 S.E. FIRST ST., EVANSVILLE, INDIANA, U.S.A,

The subscription is approximately 15/- per year ; money can be sent to U.S.A. by obtaining a necessary permit from any Post Office. The organization of the Sovereign Grace Book Club in Britain, Mr. Green has entrusted to us.

Mr. Thomas Watson, B.A., 48 Thorncliffe Road, Oxford, England, is taking charge of this work.

Readers in the sterling area should write to Mr. Watson direct to order any of the above books. *Readers in the U.S.A. and Canada* should write direct to Jay Green.

Lastly, we ought to state that the Sovereign Grace Book Club has no connection with the organization of a similar name which exists in England.

" *Worship God in your family.*—If you do not worship God in your family, you are living in positive sin ; you may be quite sure you do not care for the souls of your family. If you neglectd to spread a meal for your children to eat, would it not be said that you did not care for their bodies ? And if you do not lead your children and servants to the green pastures of God's Word, and to seek the living water, how plain is it that you do not care for their souls! *Do it regularly,* morning and evening. It is more needful than your daily food, more needful than your work. How vain and silly all your excuses will appear, when you look back from Hell ! *Do it fully.* Some clip off the psalm, and some the reading of the Word ; and so the worship of God is reduced to a mockery. *Do it in a spiritual, lively manner,* go to it as to a well of salvation. There is, perhaps no mean of grace more blessed. Let all your family be present without fail, let none be awanting."

—(*R. M. McCheyne*).

A most fragrant and spiritually valuable biography was published privately recently, *Durable Riches*, being the memoirs of the late Miss May Shaylor, 4/6. Few books could be more calculated to promote godliness, we hope this book will have a wide circulation. Write for copies to Miss L. Shaylor, 84 Kingston Road, Oxford.

The autumn number of the Evangelical Library Bulletin contains a fine article by an Anglican minister on " The Doctrine of Election from the Reformers to the Puritans." The subject is truthfully and forcefully presented. We advise all readers to obtain a copy from The Evangelical Library. 78a Chiltern Street, London, W. 1.

WHEN I AM WEAK, THEN AM I STRONG

2 Corinthians 12 : 10

Notes from a Sermon of the Rev. Thomas Jones (1752-1845).

The subject before us can be understood only by Christian warriors, and it is understood by all who have any knowledge of themselves. Though it appears a contradiction, yet it agrees exactly with the experience of every believer; the more he feels of his own weakness, the more he applies to his Lord; and the more he applies, the more strength is communicated. If ever we are strong, it must not be in ourselves, but strong in the Lord, and in the power of His might; strong in the grace that is in Christ Jesus: we are commanded to have no confidence in the flesh. This weanedness from self and oneness with the Lord is the main study of a Christian's life; it is one of the greatest difficulties, to learn that we are perfect weakness. We may learn the truth in a study; I could teach you all in a fortnight: but life is short enough to learn, that of ourselves we have no power to help ourselves. What strength have we to stand before the holy law of God? to break through all the chains that tie down our captive souls from glorious liberty—from running the race set before us? What strength have we to open prison doors—to subdue spiritual enemies—Satan, the world, and the cheating of our own hearts? What power to do all the work, which the Lord has given us to perform?

We are prone to think more highly of ourselves, than we ought to think; it is called "the pride of life," because it is with us all our life long: but lofty looks must be humbled—self must be denied. A hard lesson. How often have we failed, where we had the greatest confidence; and fallen, where we thought ourselves most secure; enemies we disdained overcame us, temptations we thought light of have thrown us down. To be sensible of our own weakness, is the way to be strong: none will trust God but those who cannot trust themselves; none lean on Christ, till they feel themselves sinking.

We will consider the advantages of being convinced of weakness. First, it will teach us to be on our watch-towers: so long as we think we have strength, we run into this and that temptation, read this and that book, go into this and that company, etc. The man who has discovered danger everywhere, has his eyes about him—dares not trust himself. Lot thought he could live in Sodom; had he stayed one day longer he would have been burned with it; Abraham thought he might go into Egypt, and be safe; temptation took hold of him, he fell, he told a falsehood: Peter had strong confidence in himself, he would go into the judgment-hall—thought he was a rock, but found he was a reed; the breath of a woman threw him down.

Where there is self-sufficiency there is little self-knowledge, little safety; we always find the self-confident one the first to fall. He who cries, " Hold Thou me up," having Christ to lean upon, may walk upon the waters.

Secondly, who are the praying souls amongst us? who are the men that live in prayer, on their legs, on their knees, in bed and out; those who have sweet intercourse with heaven? It is those who have no confidence in the flesh. The rich do not go begging; those alone will go to the door of God who are driven out by pinching poverty; and of all trades this is the best—begging at the door of One who gives according to the riches of His glory in Christ Jesus.

This accounts for there not being more prayer : people think they have strength, wisdom, righteousness, of their own. When we know how guilty, how foolish, how helpless we are, we cannot help but pray, " Give me this day, daily bread." This is the life God has ordained for us. The more we feel our poverty, the more we pray; and after praying most earnestly, we turn again with renewed desires as the child to the breast. Though the Lord fed us yesterday, we cannot do without Him to-day.

Thirdly, who are they who will lean on Christ, but those who feel sinking. God, by various means, convinces His own children that they have no strength; they find their old corruptions too strong for them; they get entangled in the wilderness. The Lord restores His wandering child, sets his feet upon the rock, establishes his goings. What does the restored one now say? He goes on a little way, but soon omits prayer; gets into a dry spirit : the enemy comes, and overcomes him by the very same temptations which caused him to fall before : this teaches him the desperate wickedness of his own heart, and drives him with fresh earnestness to Christ : this is the end of all falls and troubles, to convince us of our weakness, and send us to Christ.

We ought not to be too much dejected under infirmities; they are painful to feel ; but it is God's appointed way ; he has ordained that they shall cleave to us all our way home. It is no accident, but in order to instruct our blind souls where our strength lies. Thank God that you feel your great infirmities. When we really know that we are without strength, our language is not what it used to be, but—" I will go in the strength of the Lord."

Look at David, when Goliath threatened to give his flesh to the fowls of the air; did David trust in his arm of flesh to sling the stone? or in his skill to make it penetrate the giant's skull? No, no : " I come to thee in the name of the Lord of hosts, the God of the armies of Israel." Every Christian who thus leans on the name of the Lord must conquer.

" SEARCH THE SCRIPTURES "

John 5 : 39.

The attitude of a man to the Scriptures is indicative of the state of his soul before God.   The language of a Christian is, " O how I love Thy Law."   He desires to treasure the Word of God more " than thousands of gold and silver " (Ps. 119), whereas the ungodly are marked out as those who have no delight in the Law of the Lord, and such " shall not stand in the judgment." (Ps. 1).   Believers, like Joshua, are commanded to search and meditate in this Book day and night ((Josh. 1 : 8), but those who fail to tremble at the authority of this Word (Is. 66 : 2), and carelessly despise its divine origin, " shall be destroyed." (Prov. 13 : 13).   Judge the state of your soul by whether you have learned this fear of God, and His Word, " which is the beginning of wisdom."

But not only may the temporal and eternal condition of individuals be judged from their regard of Scripture, there is also no surer test of the state of the visible church than the prevailing attitude towards the Bible.   The prosperity of the church is invariably in proportion to her valuation of God's Word.   The Reformation in the sixteenth century is a clear proof that the church flourishes when the Word is exalted.   Consider the Reformers' view of Scripture.   Luther affirmed " That he would not take all the world for one leaf of the Bible."   And Luther proved his regard for God's Word by his knowledge of it.   During his early ministry, he tells us, there was not verse in Scripture which if quoted to him he could not instantly place !   Ridley knew by heart the whole of Paul's Epistles.   Beza, when over 80 years of age, could relate exactly all the Psalms and the Epistles in their original.   Such a hunger to know Scripture was not confined to ministers.   During the reign of Henry VIII (while the possession of any portion of the Bible was punished by burning at the stake) an English farmer gave a whole cartload of hay for only one page of James' Epistle !   Many of the English martyrs, though only laymen, were able at their trials mightily to use the Scripture they had memorized in answering their adversaries.   How greatly did the cause of God prosper when this attitude to The Word of God prevailed !

On the other hand, when the church is in a declining, and powerless condition, the cause will always be found to be connected with an absence of a true and deep knowledge of God's Word. Never for four hundred years in England, perhaps, has the Bible been so little known in the church—even in evangelical churches— as to-day.   The direct result is that the visible church is in a desperately low condition.   But as few will be prepared to accept that ignorance of Scripture is the characteristic mark of the religion of

our times, let us confirm the statement by some proofs.   When a
low view of Scripture prevails it will always betray itself by certain
definite marks.   Three of these marks we will consider.

1. *Error is regarded as comparatively harmless, and the importance of purity of doctrine is minimised.*

This is a sure mark of ignorance.   Error, heresy, and ignorance
of Scripture are soul-destroying things.   " My people are destroyed
for lack of kowledge." (Hosea 4 : 6).   " That the soul be without
knowledge, it is not good." (Prov. 19 : 2).   It is a fearful threatening, " They shall die without knowledge." (Job 36 : 12).
Ignorance makes a man the object of Divine wrath.   Christ shall
come " in flaming fire taking vengeance on them that know not
God." (1 Thess 1 : 8).   Eusebius records that the aged Apostle
John so feared heresy, that he refused to enter a building when he
learnt that the heretic Cerinthus was inside, saying " Let us depart,
lest the house wherein the Lord's enemy is should fall on our heads."

Where shall we go to-day to find men who have such a view
of the importance of sound doctrine ?   Is the doctrine of men who
are allowed to join in on evangelistic campaigns examined ?   Are
converts told not to go to certain churches?   Do not young men preparing for the ministry attend Colleges where the Word is not purely
taught ?   What is all this but a disregarding of God's displeasure
over error, and a failure to recognise that where error prevails there
God's judicial blindness reigns.   Errors are God's bullets with which
He destroys gainsayers—" O stand not where God's bullets fly,"
says old Gurnall.   " Take heed what ye hear ! " (Mark 4 : 24 :
Prov. 19 : 27).

2. *Lack of desire or concern to grow in knowledge becomes
evident.*

Man was made a rational creature, and endowed with the
noble faculty of understanding in order to know God.   The result
of the Fall was to remove from his mind any saving knowledge of
God—" There is none that understandeth." (Rom. 3 : 11).   The
great purpose of redemption is nothing less than to restore men to a
knowledge of God, " This is life eternal, that they might know
thee " (John 17 : 3)), and only by this means is a man able to glorify
and enjoy God forever.

While all regenerate persons, all believers, have a desire to
know God, they have it in varying degrees of strength.   We can
unmistakably test the measure of our desire by our diligence in
studying Scripture—for by this Book alone can we increase in a
true knowledge of God.   Who can doubt that the seventeenth
century Puritans were the greatest searchers, expositors, and
preachers of God's Word our land has ever seen ?   The great
power and force of their ministry lay in the tremendous emphasis

they put on a profound understanding. of the Scripture. The biographer of the mighty Puritan Oliver Heywood (whose ministry affected much of the north of England) says, " He spent much of his time in his study. It was his custom to rise at an early hour . . . he was assiduous in the pursuit of knowledge." Heywood himself recorded in his diary, " I prize learning above all sublunary excellencies, and I might have been more useful had I improved my time better therein—Prov. 10 : 14, ' Wise men lay up knowledge.' " John Cotton, the great leader of the New England Puritans, lived under a conviction of that sacred precept, " Give attendance to reading, to exhortation, to doctrine." " He rose early, and commonly studied twelve hours a day, accounting that a scholar's day." (Brook's Lives of the Puritans). Likewise of Thomas Manton it was written, " His great delight was in his study." The prolocutor of the Westminster Assembly, William Twisse, when dying cried with his departing breath, " Now at length I shall have leisure to follow studies to all eternity ! " The consuming passion of the Puritans was to know God. " To know Him," records the historian Macaulay, " was with them the great end of existence." They therefore unceasingly searched the Scriptures, and advanced far beyond any other generation of Englishmen in their ability to unfold their contents.

The duty of giving all diligence to add knowledge to faith, is laid by God upon all believers. (2 Pet. 1 : 5). Listen to Jonathan Edwards exhorting his hearers—" We should make growing in knowledge a great part of the business of our lives . . . There is no doctrine of divinity whatever, which doth not some way or other concern the eternal interest of every Christian. The Scriptures were written that they might be understood : otherwise they are not instructions . . . we can receive benefit by no more of the Scriptures than we understand . . . You all have by you a large treasure of divine knowledge, in that you have the Bible in your hands ; therefore be not content in possessing but little of this treasure. God hath spoken much to you in Scripture : labour to understand as much of what he saith as you can."

A concern such as this to grow in knowledge is markedly absent amongst the generality of professing believers to-day. Superficiality abounds in every direction. Shallowness is excused as simplicity. Sermons that require no diligent preparation suit the taste of congregations that are not accustomed to girding up the loins of their minds. It is presumed that the contents of Scripture are easy to understand. Granted that the saving facts of the Gospel are simple, the whole revelation of Scripture concerning God, His Being, Attributes, and Purposes, is a subject that the minds of prophets and angels can only " search " and " look into," (1 Pet. 1 : 11-13) ; a subject that staggered the understanding of the Apostle

Paul so that he could only cry out, " O the depth " (Rom. 11 : 33),
and call the Gospel a " great mystery " (1 Tim. 3 : 16). This
attitude towards Scripture always prevails amongst those who are
no longer babes in the truth. " Religion itself is a deep mystery,"
says Richard Sibbes, " it requires a great deal of learning." Listen
again to one of the greatest Puritans, John Owen—" Do not suppose
that you have learned anything of God in Christ, of the mystery
of His grace, *unless you see therein such evidence of infinite wisdom,*
goodness, holiness, love, in all things so suited unto the eternal glory
of God and advantage of your own souls, as that you may admire,
adore, delight in them, and cleave unto them with a holy, prevalent,
unconquerable love. When you do so, then will you be established
in the truth."

3. *The Lack of praise and spiritual joy becomes apparent.*

When believers are little acquainted with Scripture this mark
is always manifested. The Word of God is the ground and foundation of true joy and praise—" These things *write* we unto you
that your joy may be full." (1 Jn. 1 : 4). The Word was written
for this purpose. There is no such thing as joy in the Holy Ghost
apart from the knowledge and belief of God's Word—" *Believing,*
ye rejoice with joy unspeakable and full of glory." (1 Pet. 1 : 8).
The only way for a believer to be established in a joyful assurance
is *to know* his privileges and the exalted position to which God has
raised him in Jesus Christ. Satan's constant work is to keep us
ignorant, or make us forget the dignity and strength that we have.
Truly, Sibbes says, " A Christian is a more excellent creature than
he thinks." " Unacquaintedness with our mercies, and our privileges, is our sin as well as our trouble," writes John Owen. " We
hearken not to the voice of the Spirit which is given unto us ' that
we may *know* the things that are freely given to us of God.' (1 Cor.
2 : 12. This makes us go heavily, when we might rejoice."

Let us then ask how much spiritual joy is to be seen to-day
and we shall immediately be able to judge how much or little the
Scriptures are known. Oh, who is not aware that in most evangelical circles, carnal mirth, frivolity, " foolish talking and jesting "
(Eph. 5 : 4), are accepted as signs of a healthy Christian life, and
have replaced joy in the Holy Ghost ! We read recently in a well
known Christian newspaper the report of a campaign meeting of
a man who is now being acclaimed as a leading evangelist—" He
pummelled the audience into warmth and enthusiasm. He cracked
jokes about the Cup ties. More singing . . . more jokes about the
Cup ties. Everybody singing and laughing . . ." How could
such ' evangelism ' as this flourish except amongst people who are
grossly ignorant of Scripture ! True spiritual joy is accompanied
by deep seriousness. The soul is overpowered by eternal realities

and walks in the fear of God. That this work of the Spirit is rarely to be seen is a sure mark of the neglect of Scripture.

We have thus far been largely considering some evidences of the ignorance of Scripture that abounds in our times. We could summarise the conclusion to be drawn in such words as these— " Not one in a hundred read their Bible to be called reading." The subject could be much enlarged, but we have said sufficient to establish in our minds that the first requisite to a diligent study of the Bible is this :—*We must be convinced of the necessity of searching the Scriptures.* And this conviction will not be impressed upon us until we see the perils of ignorance, and the desirability of knowledge—" Blessed is the man that findeth wisdom, and the man that getteth understanding." (Prov. 3 : 13-14). We must be aroused to walk contrary to the spirit of our times and fear to be infected by the prevailing attitude to the Scriptures. It is hard to live in the midst of a plague and be kept unaffected.

A brief application remains. We can draw from the solemnity of our days arguments to increase our diligence in the Scriptures. Just as Egypt was made to know the worth of light by the want of it (Exod. 10 : 21-24), and just as a sick man learns the value of health by the absence of it, so God makes men value His Word by sending a famine for it. Contempt of the Word is punished by judicial blindness, so that though men may still possess the Scriptures and read them (as the Pharisees and Sadducees did at the time of Christ), they are given over to blindness and a true understanding is removed from them. (John 12 39-40). The famine is a famine " of *hearing* the words of the Lord," (Amos 8 : 11), that is God removes those who truly expound it. Unless God in mercy reverses His present sentence against us, there are surely awful judgments ahead. " How guilty (in neglect of Scripture) our English nation is, is too manifest to write, and what we have cause to expect for it, I tremble to write." Three centuries of God's longsuffering have passed over the land since Elnathan Parr wrote those words. It may be that now our guilt has reach its limit. " I have written to him the great things of my law, but they were counted as a strange thing . . . Now will He remember their iniquity, and visit their sins." (Hos. 8 : 12-13).

But the children of God need not fear the future, " For wisdom is a defence." (Eccles. 7 : 12). They who have let the Word of Christ dwell in them richly in all wisdom (Col 3 : 16) will be like Joseph who while there was time and opportunity laid up stores for the time of need. Believers shall overcome the world and the devil, " By the blood of the Lamb, *and by the word of their testimony.*"   (I.M.)

(To be continued D.V.)

Printed at the Wickliffe Press, Wickliffe Avenue, 104 Hendon Lane, Finchley, N. 3

THE
BANNER of TRUTH

(4th Issue)

Price 9d.

Subscription 5/6
for six issues.

EDITOR:

MR. IAIN MURRAY, B.A.,
11 Lawrence Street, London, N.W. 7.

*   *   *

"Thou hast shewed thy people hard things ;
Thou hast made us to drink the wine of
astonishment.   Thou hast given a banner to
them that fear Thee, that it may be displayed
because of the truth."   Psalm 60 : 3-4

*   *   *

CONTENTS

D

EDITORIAL NOTES—February, 1957

We have increasing cause to be confident not only in the need of a magazine such as this, but in the fact that many of God's people are recognising that need and giving their support to the furtherance of our common desire. It is from the belief that the efficiency of the magazine and the frequency of its appearance can be considerably improved by the adoption of a subscription basis of support, that we have given information on this subject on the front cover.This obviously does not apply to those who do not receive their copy by post. The major hindrance to a more frequent publication hitherto has been that from want of capital we have had to await the incoming of support, following each issue, before we could proceed to print another. We are indeed thankful that this support has always been forthcoming, but if sufficient numbers of our readers are willing to contribute a subscription, this will enable us to proceed to print further issues at regular intervals, and without the delay that the previous method has involved. Any not familiar with printing would be amazed at the cost of publishing a magazine even of this size. Those who are able to contribute above the subscription cost will greatly aid the circulation of the magazine to the new readers—who are sent copies free of charge.

Of previous issues of the *Banner of Truth,* only the third is still available. It is important to remind readers that our object is not so much to set out every truth in its Scriptural proportion, as to declare those truths particularly relevant to our own times. That which is being most attacked, needs to be the most defended. As an old Scottish divine says—" What would you think of the man who, when the city was besieged, should buckle on his armour, and run to the east gate, where there was no danger, while the enemy was at the west." Articles have been written with that in mind.

Publications of The Sovereign Grace Book Club.
Publisher Mr. Jay Green, 1124 S.E. First St., Evanville, Indiana, U.S.A. British agent, Mr. T. Watson, 48 Thorncliffe Road, Oxford.

Exposition of First Peter, by John Brown of Edinburgh, 3 vols., 47/6 per set.

Songs of Sovereignty, Sermons by John Owen, 8/6.

The Saints Everlasting Rest, by Richard Baxter, vol. I, 13/6 (2nd vol. to follow).

A Mute Christian, and Apples of Gold, by Thomas Brooks, 15/-.

Keeping the Heart, by John Flavel, 3/6.

Prayer, by John Bunyan and *Return of Prayer,* by T. Goodwin, 3/6.

Exposition of James, by Thomas Manton, 17/6.
Available March, 1957.

Absolute Predestination, by Jerome Zanchius, 6/- (paper), 10/6 (cloth). Available April, 1957.

Exposition of Romans, Robt. Haldane. The reprint of this great work has already been sold out, but a further reprint is planned early in 1957.

" It rejoices my heart to know that as the result of the efforts of Mr. Jay Green in the U.S.A. it is possible for us to obtain many of the Puritan classics and other standard evangelical works, which have long since been out of print, and which only rarely appear in the 2nd hand catalogues. It is my fervent prayer that as God used these works to stimulate and to feed many of the leaders of the evangelical awakening in the eighteenth century He may do so again in this period of spiritual darkness and desperate need. I would therefore urge all who are concerned to see the name of God made glorious in the land to avail themselves of this wonderful opportunity of obtaining these precious volumes." *Dr. D. M. Lloyd-Jones.*

" The Puritans of the last century—burning and shining lights —wrote and preached after they were cast out of the Church (of England), as men having authority. A peculiar unction attends their writings to this day ; and for these thirty years I have remarked, that the more true and vital religion hath revived, either at home or abroad, the more the good old Puritan writings have been called for." *George Whitefield.*

" It is vain to deny that we have fallen on trying times for Christianity. Heresies of the most appalling kind are broached in quarters where they might have been least expected. Principles in theology which were once regarded as thoroughly established are now spoken of as doubtful matters. In a time like this, I believe that the study of some of the great Puritan divines is eminently calculated, under God, to do good and stay the plague. I commend the study especially to all young ministers . . . I fear it is not a reading age. Large books, especially, have but little chance of a perusal. Hurry, superficiality, and bustle are the characteristics of our times. Meagreness, leanness, and shallowness are too often the main features of modern sermons. Nevertheless, something must be attempted in order to check existing evils. The churches must be reminded that there can be no really powerful preaching without deep thinking, and little deep thinking without hard reading. The republication of our best Puritan divines I regard as a positive boon to the Church and the world, and I heartily wish it God speed." *J. C. Ryle.*

The above books may be obtained, postage extra, from The Evangelical Book Shop, 15 College Square East, Belfast, Northern Ireland. The Bookroom, Westminster Chapel, Buckingham Gate, London, S.W.1.

PURITAN EVANGELISM

Rev. J. I. Packer, M.A., Lecturer at Tyndale Hall, Bristol

In the report of the Archbishop's Committee on Evangelism, published in 1945 under the title : *Towards the Conversion of England,* the work of evangelism is conveniently defined as follows : ' so to present Christ Jesus in the power of the Holy Spirit, that men shall come to put their trust in God through Him, to accept Him as their Saviour, and serve Him as their King in fellowship of His Church.'

Did the Puritans tackle the task of evangelism at all ? At first sight, it might seem not. They agreed with Calvin in regarding the ' evanglists ' mentioned in the New Testament as an order of assistants to the apostles, now extinct ; and as for ' missions,' ' crusades ' and ' campaigns,' they knew neither the name nor the thing. But we must not be misled into supposing that evangelism was not one their chief concerns. It was. Many of them were outstandingly successful as preachers to the unconverted. Richard Baxter, the apostle of Kidderminster, is perhaps the only one of these that is widely remembered to-day ; but in contemporary records it is common to read statements like this, of Hugh Clark : ' he begat many Sons and Daughters unto God '; or this, of John Cotton, " the presence of the Lord . . . crowning his Labours with the Conversion of many Souls' (S. Clarke, *Lives of* 52 . . . *Divines,* pp.131, 222, etc.) Moreover, it was the Puritans who invented evangelistic literature. One has only to think of Baxter's classic *Call to the Unconverted,* and Alleine's *Alarm to the Unconverted,* which were pioneer works in this class of writing. And the elaborate practical ' handling ' of the subject of conversion in Puritan books was regarded by the rest of the seventeenth-century Protestant world as something of unique value. ' It hath been one of the glories of the Protestant religion that it revived the doctrine of *Saving Conversion,* and of the *New Creature* brought forth thereby . . . But in a more eminent manner, God hath cast the honor hereof upon the Ministers and Preachers of this Nation, who are renowned abroad for their more accurate search into and discoveries hereof ' (T. Goodwin and P. Nye, Preface to T. Hooker, *The Application of Redemption,* 1656).

The truth is that two distinct conceptions and types of evangelism have been developed in Protestant Christendom during the course of its history. We may call them the ' Puritan ' type and the ' modern ' type. To-day we are so accustomed to evangelism of the modern type that we scarcely recognise the other as evangelism at all. In order that we may fully grasp the character of the Puritan type of evangelism, I shall here set it in contrast with the modern type, which has so largely superseded it at the present time.

Let us begin, therefore, by characterising evangelism of the modern type. It seems to presuppose a conception of the life of the local church as an alternating cycle of converting and edifying. Evangelism almost takes on the character of a periodical recruiting campaign. It is an extraordinary and occasional activity, additional and auxiliary to the regular functioning of the local congregation. Special gatherings of a special sort are arranged, and special preachers are commonly secured to conduct them. Often they are called 'meetings' rather than 'services'; in any case ,they are thought of as sómething distinct in some way from the regular public worship of God. In the meetings, everything is directly aimed at securing from the unconverted an immediate, conscious, decisive act of faith in Christ. At the close of the meeting, those who have responded or wish to do so are asked to come to the front, or raise a hand, or something similar, as an act of public testimony to their new resolutions. This, it is claimed, is good for those who do it, since it helps to make their 'decision' definite, and it has the further advantage of making them declare themselves, so that they may be contacted individually by 'personal workers.' Such persons may then be advised and drafted forthwith into local churches as converts.

This type of evangelism was invented by Charles G. Finney in the 1820's. He introduced the 'protracted meeting,' or, as we should call it, the intensive evangelistic campaign, and the 'anxious seat,' a front pew left vacant where at the end of the meeting 'the anxious may come and be addressed particularly . . . and sometimes be conversed with individually.' At the end of his sermon, he would say: 'There is the anxious seat ; come out, and avow determination to be on the Lord's side.' (See *Revivals of Religion,* esp. ch. xiv). These were Finney's much opposed 'new measures.'

Now, Finney was a clear-headed and self-confessed Pelagian in his doctrine of man ; and this is the reason why his 'new measures' were evolved. Finney denied that fallen man is totally unable to repent, believe or do anything spiritually good without grace, and affirmed instead that all men have plenary ability to turn to God at any time. Man is a rebel, but is perfectly free at any time to lay down his arms in surrender. Accordingly, the whole work of the Spirit of God in conversion is to present vividly to man's mind reasons for making this surrender—that is to say, the Spirit's work is confined to moral persuasion. Man is always free to reject this persuasion : 'Sinners can go to Hell in spite of God.' But the stronger the persuasion is, the more likely it is to succeed in the breaking down of man's resistance. Every means, therefore, of increasing the force and vividness with which truth impinged on the mind—the most frenzied excitement, the most harrowing emotionalism, the most nerve-racking commotion in evangelistic meetings—was a right and proper means of evangelism.

Finney gave expression to this principle in the first of his lectures on *Revivals of Religion*. 'To expect to promote religion without excitements is unphilosophical and absurd . . . until there is sufficient religious principle in the world to put down irreligious excitements, it is in vain to try to promote religion, except by counteracting excitements . . . There must be excitement sufficient to wake up the dormant moral powers . . .' And, since every man, if he will only rouse up his 'dormant moral powers,' can at any time yield to God and become a Christian, it is the evangelist's work and duty always to preach for immediate decision, to tell men that it is their duty to come to Christ that instant, and to use all means—such as the rousing appeal and the 'anxious seat'—for persuading them to do so. 'I tried to shut them up,' he says of a typical mission sermon, 'to present faith and repentance, as the thing which God required of them : present and instant acceptance of His will, present and instant acceptance of Christ' (*Autobiography*, p. 64). It is hardly too much to say that Finney regarded evangelistic preaching as a battle of wills between himself and his hearers, in which it was his responsibility to bring them to breaking-point.

Now, if Finney's doctine of the natural state of sinful man is right, then his evangelistic methods must be judged right also, for, as he often insisted, the 'new measures' were means well adapted to what he held to be the end in view. 'It is in such practices that a Pelagian system naturally expresses itself if it seeks to become aggressively evangelistic' (B. B. Warfield). But if his view of man is wrong, then his methods, as we shall see, must be judged disastrous. And this is an issue of the first importance at the present time ; for it is Finney's methods, modified and adapted, which characterise most evangelism to-day. We do not suggest that all who use them are Pelagians. But we do raise the question, whether the use of such methods is consistent with any other doctrine than Finney's, and we shall try to show that, if Finney's doctrine is rejected, then such methods must be judged inappropriate and, indeed, detrimental to the real work of evangelism. It may be said that results justify their use ; but the truth is that the majority of Finney's 'converts' backslid and fell away, and so, it seems, have the majority of those since Finney's day whose 'decision' has been secured by the use of such methods. Most modern evangelists seem to have given up expecting more than a small percentage of their 'converts' to survive. It is not at all obvious that results justify such methods. We shall suggest later that they have a natural tendency to produce such a crop of false converts as has in fact resulted from their use.

The Puritan type of evangelism, on the other hand, was the consistent expression in practice of the Puritans' conviction that *the conversion of a sinner is a gracious sovereign work of Divine power*. We shall spend a little time elaborating this.

The Puritans did not use 'conversion' and 'regeneration' as

technical terms, and so there are slight variations in usage. Perhaps the majority treated the words as synonyms, each denoting the whole process whereby God brings the sinner to his first act of faith. Their technical term for the process was *effectual calling ; calling* being the Scriptural word used to describe the process in Rom. 8 : 30, 2 Th. 2 : 14, 2 Tim. 1 : 9, etc., and the adjective *effectual* being added to distinguish it from the ineffectual, external calling mentioned in Mt. 20 : 16, 22 : 14. *West Conf.*, X. i., puts ' calling,' into its theological perspective by an interpretative paraphrase of Rom. 8 : 30 : ' All those whom God hath predestinated unto life, and those only, he is pleased, in his appointed and accepted time, effectually to call, by his Word and Spirit, out of that state of sin and death in which they are by nature, to grace and salvation by Jesus Christ.' The *Westminster Shorter Catechism* analyses the concept of ' calling ' in its answer to Q. 31 : ' Effectual calling is the work of God's Spirit whereby, convincing us of our sin and misery, enlightening our minds in the knowledge of Christ, and renewing our wills, he doth persuade and enable us to embrace Jesus Christ, freely offered to us in the gospel.'

Concerning this *effectual calling,* three things must be said if we are to grasp the Puritan view :

(i) It is *a work of Divine grace ;* it is not something a man can do for himself or for another. It is the first stage in the application of redemption to those for whom it was won ; it is the time when, on the grounds of his eternal, federal, representative union with Christ, the elect sinner is brought by the Holy Ghost into a real, vital, personal union with his Covenant Head and Redeemer. It is thus a gift of free Divine grace.

(ii) It is *a work of Divine power.* It is effected by the Holy Ghost, who acts both *mediately, by* the Word, in the mind, giving understanding and conviction, and at the same time *immediately, with* the Word, in the hidden depths of the heart, implanting new life and power, effectively dethroning sin, and making the sinner both able and willing to respond to the gospel invitation. The Spirit's work is thus both *moral,* by *persuasion* (which all Arminians and Pelagians would allow), and also *physical,* by *power* (which they would not).

Owen said : ' There is not only a *moral,* but a *physical* immediate operation of the Spirit . . . upon the minds or souls of men in their regeneration . . . The work of grace in conversion is constantly expressed by words denoting a real internal efficacy; such as creating, quickening, forming, giving a new heart . . . Wherever this work is spoken of with respect unto an active efficacy, it is ascribed to God. He creates us anew, he quickens us, he begets us of His own will ; but when it is spoken of with respect to us, there it is passively expressed ; we are created in Christ Jesus, we are new creatures, we are born again, and the like ; *which one observation is sufficient to avert the whole hypothesis of Arminian grace.'* (*Works,* ed. Russell 11, II. 369). 'Ministers knock at the door of men's hearts (= persuasion), the Spirit comes with a key and opens the door' (T. Watson, *Body of Div.,* 1869, p. 154). The Spirit's regenerating action, Owen goes on, is 'infallible, victorious, irresistable, or always efficacious' (*loc cit.*); it 'removeth all obstacles, overcomes all oppositions, and infallibly produceth the effect intended.' Grace is *irresistible,* not because it drags man to Christ against his will, but because it changes men's hearts so that they 'come most freely, being made willing by His grace.' (*West. Conf.* X. i). The Puritans loved to dwell on the Scriptural thought of the Divine power put forth in effectual calling, which Goodwin regularly described as the one 'standing miracle' in the Church. They agreed that in the normal course of events conversion was not commonly a spectacular affair; but Goodwin notes that sometimes it is, and affirms that thereby God shows us how great an exercise of power every man's effectual calling involves. 'In the calling of some there shoots up very suddenly an *election-conversion* (I use to call it so). You shall, as it were, see election take hold of a man, pull him out with a mighty power, stamp upon him the divine nature, stub up corrupt nature by the roots, root up self-love, put in a principle of love to God, and launch him forth a new creature the first day . . . He did so with Paul, and it is not without example in others after him.' (*Works,* ed. Miller IX. 279). Such dramatic conversions, says Goodwin, are 'visible tokens of election by such a work of calling, as all the powers in heaven and earth could not have wrought upon a man's soul so, nor changed a man so on a sudden, but only that divine power that created the world (and) raised Christ from the dead.'

The reason why the Puritans thus magnified the quickening power of God is plain from the passages quoted: it was because they took so seriously the Bible teaching that man is *dead* in sin, radically depraved, sin's helpless bondslave. There is, they held, such a strength in sin that only Omnipotence can break its bond; and only the Author of Life can raise the dead. Where Finney assumed plenary ability, the Puritans taught total inability in fallen man.

(iii) Effectual calling is and must be *a work of Divine sovereignty.* Only God can effect it, and He does so at His own pleasure. 'It is not of him that willeth, nor of him that runneth, but of God that showeth mercy' (Rom. 9: 16). Owen expounds this in a sermon on Acts 16: 9, 'A vision of unchangeable, free mercy in sending the means of grace to undeserving sinners' (XV 1 f.). He first states the following principle: 'All events and effects, especially concerning the propagation of the gospel, and the Church of Christ, are in their greatest variety regulated by the eternal purpose and counsel of God.' He then illustrates it. Some are sent the gospel, some not. 'In this chapter . . . the gospel is forbidden to be preached in Asia or Bithynia ; which restraint, the Lord by His providence as yet continueth to many parts of the world'; while 'to some nations the gospel is sent . . . as in my text, Macedonia ; and England . . .' Now, asks Owen, why this discrimination ? Why do some hear and others not ? And when the gospel is heard, why do we see 'various effects, some continuing in impenitency, others in sincerity closing with Jesus Christ ? . . . In effectual working of grace . . . whence do you think it takes its rule and determination . . . that it should be directed to John, not Judas ; Simon Peter, not Simon Magus ? Why only from this discriminating counsel of God from eternity . . . Acts 13 : 48 . . . The purpose of God's election, is the rule of dispensing saving grace.'

Jonathan Edwards, a great Puritan evangelist, often makes the same point. In a typical passage from a sermon on Rom. 9 : 18, he lists the following ways in which God's sovereignty (defined as 'His absolute right of disposing of all creatures according to His own pleasure') appears in the dispensations of grace : '(1) In calling one nation or people, and giving them the means of grace, and leaving others without them. (2) . . . In the advantages He bestows upon particular persons ' (e.g. a Christian home, a powerful ministry, direct spiritual influences, etc.) ; (4) In bestowing salvation on some who have had few advantages ' (e.g. children of ungodly parents, while the children of the godly are not always saved) ; '(5) . . . In calling some to salvation, who have been heinously wicked, and leaving others, who have been very moral and religious persons . . . ' (6) In saving some of those who seek salvation and not others ' (i.e., bringing some convicted sinners to saving faith while others never attain to sincerity) (*Works*, 1838, II, 849 f.). This display of sovereignty by God, Edwards maintained, is glorious : ' it is part of the glory of God's mercy that it is sovereign mercy.'

It is probably true that no preacher in the Puritan tradition ever laid such sustained stress on the sovereignty of God as Edwards. It may come as a surprise to modern readers to discover that such preaching as his was evangelistically very fruitful ; but such was the case. Revival swept through his church under his ministry, and in the revival (to quote his own testimony) 'I think I have found that no discourses have been more *remarkably blessed*, than those in which the doctrine of God's *absolute* sovereignty, with regard to the salvation of sinners, and his *just liberty*, with regard to answering prayer, and succeeding the pains, of natural men, continuing such, have been insisted on ' (I. 353). There is much food for thought here.

God's sovereignty appears also in the *time* of conversion. Scripture and experience show that ' the great God for holy and glorious ends, but more especially . . . to make appear His love and kindness, His mercy and grace, hath ordained it so ' that many of His elect people ' should for some time remain in a condition of sin and wrath, and then He renews them to Himself' (Goodwin, VI, 85). It is never man, but always God, who determines when an elect sinner shall believe. In the *manner* of conversion too, God is sovereign. The Puritans taught that, as a general rule, conviction of sin, induced by the preaching of the Law, must precede faith, since no man will or can come to Christ to be saved from sin till he knows what sins he needs saving from. It is a distinctive feature of the Puritan doctrine of conversion that this point, the need for 'preparation' for faith, is so stressed. Man's first step toward conversion must be some *knowledge*, of God, of himself, of his duty and of his sin. The second step is *conviction*, both of sinfulness and of particular sins ; and the wise minister, dealing with enquirers at this stage, will try to deepen conviction and make it specific, since true and sound conviction of sin is always to a greater or less degree particularised. This leads to *contrition* (sorrow for and hatred of sin), which begins to burn the love of sinning out of the heart and leads to real, though as yet ineffective, attempts to break off the practice of sin in the life. Meanwhile, the wise minister, seeing that the fallow ground is now ploughed up, urges the sinner to turn to Christ. This is the right advice to give to a man who has shown that with all his heart he desires to be saved from sin ; for when a man wants to be saved from sin, then it is possible for him genuinely and sincerely to receive the One who presents Himself to man as the Saviour from sin. But it is not possible otherwise ; and therefore the Puritans over and over again beg ministers not to short-circuit the essential preparatory process. They must not give false encouragement to those in whom the Law has not yet done its work. It is the worst advice possible to tell a man to stop worrying about his sins and trust Christ *at once* if he does not yet know his sins and does not yet desire to leave them. That is the way to encourage false peace and false hopes, and to produce 'gospel- hypocrites.' Throughout the whole process of preparation, from the first awakening of concern to the ultimate dawning of faith, however, the sovereignty of God must be recognised. God converts no adult without preparing him ; but 'God breaketh not all men's hearts alike' (Baxter). Some conversions, as Goodwin said, are sudden ; the preparation is done in a moment. Some are long-drawn-out affairs ; years may pass before the seeker finds Christ and peace, as in Bunyan's case. Sometimes great sinners experience 'great meltings' (Giles Firmin) at the outset of the work of grace, while upright persons spend long periods in agonies of guilt and terror. No rule can be given as to how long, or how intensely, God will flay each sinner with the lash of conviction. Thus the work of effectual calling proceeds as fast, or as slow, as God wills ; and the minister's part is that of the midwife, whose task it is to see what is happening and give appropriate help at each stage, but who cannot foretell, let alone fix, how rapid the process of birth will be.

From these principles the Puritans deduced their characteristic conception of the practice of evangelism. Since God enlightens, convicts, humbles and converts through the Word, the task of His messengers is to communicate that word, teaching and applying law and gospel. Preachers are to declare God's mind as set forth in the texts they expound, to show the way of salvation, to exhort the unconverted to learn the law, to meditate on the Word, to humble themselves, to pray that God will show them their sins, and enable them to come to Christ. They are to hold Christ forth as a perfect Saviour from sin to all who heartily desire to be saved from sin, and to invite such (the weary and burdened souls whom Christ Himself invites, Mt. 11 : 28) to come to the Saviour who waits to receive them. But they are not to do as Finney did, and demand *immediate* repentance and faith of all and sundry. They are sent to tell all men that they must repent and believe to be saved, but it is no part of the word and message of God if they go further and tell all the unconverted that they ought to ' decide for for Christ ' (to use a common modern phrase) *on the spot.* God never sent any preacher to tell a congregation that they were under obligation to receive Christ at the close of the meeting. For in fact only those prepared by the Spirit can believe ; and it is only such whom God summons to believe. There is a common confusion here. The gospel of God requires an immediate response from all ; but it does not require the *same* response from all. The immediate duty of the unprepared sinner is not to try and believe on Christ, which he is not able to do, but to read, enquire, pray, use the means of grace and learn what he needs to be saved from. It is not in his power to accept Christ at any moment, as Finney supposed ; and it is God's prerogative, not the evangelist's, to fix the time when men shall first savingly believe. For the latter to try and do so, by appealing to sinners to begin believing here and now, is for man to take to himself the sovereign right of the Holy Ghost. It is an act of presumption, however creditable the evangelist's motive's may be. Hereby he goes beyond his commission as God's messenger ; and hereby he risks doing incalculable damage to the souls of men. If he tells men they are under obligation to receive Christ on the spot, and demands in God's name that they decide at once, some who are spiritually unprepared will try to do so ; they will will come forward and accept directions and ' go through the motions' and go away thinking they have received Christ, when all the time they have not done so because they were not yet able to do so. So a crop of false conversions will result from making such appeals, *in the nature of the case.* Bullying for ' decisions ' thus in fact impedes and thwarts the work of the Holy Spirit in the heart. Man takes it on himself to try to bring that work to a a precipitate conclusion, to pick the fruit before it is ripe ; and the result is ' false conversions,' hypocrisy and hardening. For the appeal for immediate decision presupposes that men are free to ' decide for Christ ' at any time ; and this presupposition is the disastrous issue of a false, un-Scriptural view of sin.

What, then, were the principles that should govern evangelistic preaching ? In the first place, the Puritans would insist, it must be clearly understood that evangelistic preaching is not a special kind of preaching, with its own distinctive technique. It is a part of the ordinary public ministry of God's Word. This means, first, that the rules which govern it are the same rules which must govern all public preaching of God's Word ; and, second, that the person whose task it primarily is is the local pastor. It is his duty in the course of his public and private ministry of the Word, ' diligently to labour for the conversion of souls to God ' (Owen). What God requires of him is that he should be faithful to the content of the gospel, and diligent in imparting it. He is to seek by all means to make his sermon clear, memorable and relevant to the lives of his hearers ; he is to pray earnestly for God's blessing on his preaching, that it may be ' in the demonstration of the Spirit and of power '; but it is no part of his business to to study to ' dress up ' the gospel and make it ' appeal ' to the natural man. The preacher's calling is very different from that of the commercial traveller, and the ' quick sale ' technique has no place in the Christian pulpit. The preacher is not sent of God to make a quick sale, but to deliver a message. When he has done that, his work in the pulpit is over. It is not his business to try and extort ' decisions.' It is God's own sovereign prerogative to make His Word effective, and the preacher's behaviour must be governed by his recognition of, and subjection to, Divine sovereignty in this matter.

Does not the abjuring of appeals, and the other devices of high-pressure salemanship which have intruded into the modern type of evangelism, make the preaching of the gospel a somewhat forlorn undertaking ? Not at all, said the Puritan ; those who argue so have reckoned without the sovereignty of God. The Puritan pastor had the same quiet confidence in the success of his evangelistic preaching as he had in the success of all his preaching. He was in no feverish panic about it. He knew that God's Word does not return void ; that God has His elect everywhere, and that through the preaching of His Word they will in due course be called out—not because of the preacher's gifts and ingenuity, but by reason of God's sovereign operation. He knew that God always has a remnant faithful to Himself, however bad the times—which means that in every age some men will come to faith through the preaching of the Word. This was the faith that sustained such Puritan pioneers as Richard Greenham, who after twenty years of faithful ministry, ploughing up the fallow ground in a Cambridgeshire country parish, could not point to any converts bar a single family. This was the faith that God honoured in Richard Baxter's Kidderminster ministry, during which, over a period of seventeen years, by the use of no other means but sermons twice a week and catechetical instruction from house to house, well over six hundred converts were gathered in ; of whom Baxter wrote, six years after his ejection, that, despite constant exposure to ridicule and obloquy for their ' Puritanism,' ' not one that I know of has fallen off from his sincerity.' *Soli Deo gloria*!

The issue with which we are confronted by our study of Puritan evangelism is clear. Which way are we to take in our endeavours to spread the gospel to-day ? Forward along the road of modern evangelism, the intensive big-scale, short-term 'campaign,' with its sustained wheedling for decisions and its streamlined machinery for handling shoals of ' converts ' ? Or back to the old paths of Puritan evangelism, the quieter, broader-based, long-term strategy based on the local church, according to which man seeks simply to be faithful in delivering God's message and leaves it to the sovereign Spirit to draw men to faith through that message in His own way and at His own speed? Which is loyal to God's Word? Which is consistent with the Bible doctrine of sin, and of conversion? Which glorifies God? These are questions which demand the most urgent consideration at the present time.

REMEMBRANCER OF DAILY DUTIES

JOHN LOVE, D.D.

1. Return solemn thanks for the night's mercies. Beg assistance for the day.
2. In all acts of devotion, let me first collect my thoughts. Let me have them at their bent before I begin. Speak directly to God. Give way to no external, nor internal diversion.
3. Let me read the Scriptures—(a) with a serious, practical view ; and (b) with comment.
4. Never trifle with a book with which I have no present concern. And, in reading any book (a) let me reflect what I may learn by it, and (b) beg Divine assistance.
5. Never lose one minute of time.
6. Watch against undue expenditure, that I may have the more to spend for God.
7. When abroad, let me be desirous of doing and receiving good. Let me have some subject of contemplation, in readiness to occupy my thoughts as I walk along. Let me render myself agreeable and useful to all, by tender, compassionate, friendly behaviour. Let me avoid trifling, impertinent stories. Imprudence is sin.
8. Use great moderation in meals. Watch against hypocrisy in thanksgiving.
9. Let me never delay a duty, unless I can prove that another time is more fit—or that some more important duty stands in the way of it.

ROBERT MURRAY McCHEYNE

Minister of St. Peter's, Dundee, 1836 - 1843.

Two men were working beside a fire in a quarry, one day in winter, when a stranger approached them on horseback. Alighting from his horse he began to enter into conversation on the state of their souls and drew some alarming truths froms from the blazing fire. The men were surprised, and exclaimed ' Ye're nae common man.' ' Oh yes,' he replied, ' just a common man.' One cannot meet Robert McCheyne either in his biography (so powerfully written by Andrew Bonar) or in his sermons, without receiving the impression which these men received in their personal encounter with him so long ago. His brief ministry of seven-and-a-half years ' stamped an indelible impress on Scotland,' and though he died in his twenty-ninth year, more was wrought by him that will last for eternity than most accomplish in a lifetime. If we could summon but one life from the past, the lessons of which would apply most directly to this slothful and careless generation, perhaps it would be the life of Robert McCheyne. After his death, a fellow minister wrote, " Indolence and levity and unfaithfulness are sins that beset me ; and his living presence was a rebuke to all these, for I never knew one so instant in season and out of season, so impressed with the invisible realities, and so faithful in reproving sin and witnessing for Christ."

Robert McCheyne was born in Edinburgh in May, 1813, the youngest child in a family of five. His father was a prosperous lawyer and a man of social importance. Their spacious home, with its gardens, commanded a glorious view across to the shores of Fife. Here in Edinburgh McCheyne spent his childhood and youth. After passing successfully through the High School, he entered the Arts Faculty of the University in autumn 1827. " He was of a lively turn "—his father later recorded—" and, during the first two or three years of his attendance at the University, he turned his attention to elocution and poetry and the pleasures of society . . . " McCheyne became at this time an eager participant in the city's fashionable entertainments, and scenes of gaiety—card playing, dancing, music—occupied his leisure hours. But he was the subject of his elder brother's fervent prayers, and the early death of this brother in 1831 was a stroke which was used to awaken Robert from the sleep of nature. It was " the first overwhelming blow to my worldliness." He began to be serious, and to sit under an evangelical ministry. Soon we read entries like this in his diary :—" March 10, 1832. I hope never to play cards again." " March 25. Never visit on a Sunday evening again." " April 10. Absented myself from the dance . . ." Having himself once followed such fading pleasures, McCheyne was often in later years to declare in his preaching—" O Christless man, you have pleasure, but it is only for a season. Laugh on if you will—your candle will soon be out. Your games, your dance, your social parties, will soon be over. There are no games in hell."

In the winter of 1831, following his desire to enter the ministry, he entered the Divinity Hall of the University. Under the leadership of men like Chalmers and Welsh there was a new stir of spiritual life in the College at this time, indeed it proved to be a new stir in the life of the Church in Scotland. We can trace from his diary in the following years a growing grasp of Scriptural truth, a growing desire to live in communion with God and under the power of the world to come. Entries like the following speak for themselves :—" June 22. Bought Edwards' works. Truly there was nothing in me that should have induced Him to choose me. I was but as the other brands upon whom the fire is already kindled, which shall burn for evermore ! " " August 15. Awfully important question, Am I redeeming the time ? " " February 23. Sabbath. Rose early to seek God, and found Him whom my soul loveth. Who would not rise early to meet such company ? " Reading the biographies of past ministers had a profound influence on McCheyne at this time, especially such lives as Jonathan Edwards, Brainerd, Martyn, Payson, and Halyburton. In fact he became so familiar with the works of the first named, that Edwards' ' Resolutions ' became exemplified in McCheyne—" Resolved never to lose one moment of time, but to improve it in the most profitable way I possibly can. Resolved, That I will live so, as I shall wish I had done when I had come to die. Resolved, To live with all my might, while I do live . . ." From a letter McCheyne later wrote to a student, we can see what rules he applied to himself—" Do get on with your studies. Remember you are now forming the character of your future ministry, if God spare you. If you acquire slovenly or sleepy habits habits of study now, you will never get the better of it. Do everything in earnest. Above all, keep much in the presence of God. Never see the face of man till you have seen His face who is our life, our all." The last entry of his student days is " March 29, 1835. College finished on Friday last. My last appearance there. Life itself is vanishing fast, make haste for eternity." So ended his preparatory discipline, both of heart and mind. " His soul," writes Bonar, " was prepared for the awful work of the ministry by much prayer, and much study of the word of God ; by inwards trials ; by experience of the depth of corruption in his own heart, and by discoveries of the Saviour's fulness of grace."

McCheyne was licensed by the Presbytery of Annan on July 1st, 1835 and became " a preacher of the Gospel an honour to which I cannot name an equal." After a further period, largely of preparation for the future, as assistant to Mr. John Bonar the minister of Larbert and Dunipace, he was ordained minister of St. Peter's, Dundee, in November, 1836. It was a new church built in a sadly neglected district containing some 4,000 souls. " A city given to idolatry and hardness of heart," was his first impression. " A very dead region," is Bonar's description, " the surrounding mass of impenetrable heathenism cast its influence even on those few who were living Christians." " He has set me down among the noisy mechanics and political weavers of this godless town," McCheyne wrote. There was nothing in his message to please such a people ; " If the Gospel pleased carnal men it would not be the Gospel," he declared. He was deeply persuaded that the Spirit's first work in salvation is to convict of sin, and to bring men to despair of their condition by nature, it was therefore on this note that his ministry commenced and continued—" Men must be brought down by law work to see their guilt and misery, or all our preaching is beating the air. A broken heart alone can receive a crucified Christ. The most, I fear, in all congregations, are sailing easily down the stream into an undone eternity, unconverted and unawakened." Urgency and alarm characterized his message. " God help me to speak to you plainly ! The longest lifetime is short enough. It is all that is given you to be converted in. In a very little, it will be all over ; and all that is here is changing —the very hills are crumbling down—the loveliest face is withering away—the finest garments rot and decay. Every day that passes is bringing you nearer to the judgment-seat. Not one of you is standing still. You may sleep ; but the tide is going on bringing you nearer death, judgment, and eternity."

McCheyne was enabled to walk in a continual awareness of these truths—" I think I can say, I have never risen a morning without thinking how I could bring more souls to Christ." In his diary we find records like this :—" As I was walking in the fields, the thought came over me with almost overwhelming power, that every one of my flock must soon be in heaven or hell."

But there is another feature of McCheyne's life which is perhaps even more prominent than his constant longings for the salvation of souls. " Above all things, cultivate your own spirit," he wrote to a fellow minister. " Your own soul is your first and greatest care. Seek advance of personal holiness. It is not great talents God blesses so much as great likeness to Jesus. A holy minister is an awful weapon in the hand of God. A word spoken by you when your conscience is clear, and your heart full of God's Spirit, is worth ten thousand words spoken in unbelief and sin." " Get your texts from God—your thoughts, your words, from God." From his diary we gather his own private observations :—" I ought to spend the best hours of the day in communion with God. It is my noblest and most fruitful employment . . . The morning hours, from six to eight, are the most uninterrupted . . . After tea is my best hour, and that should be solemnly dedicated to God, if possible." Bonar writes, " the real secret of his soul's prosperity lay in the daily enlargement of his heart in fellowship with his God,

Meditation and prayer were the very sinews of his work." Even when pressed by duties, " he kept by his rule, ' that he must first see the face of God before he could undertake any duty.' " It was McCheyne's constant aim to avoid any hurry which prevents " the calm working of the Spirit on the heart. The dew comes down when all nature is at rest—when every leaf is still. A calm hour with God is worth a whole lifetime with man . . . "

McCheyne was ever concerned to deepen his ministry by continual study. " Few," says Bonar ; have maintained such an " undecaying esteem for the advantages of study." Though always conscious that souls were perishing every day, he never fell into the error of thinking that a minister's main work consists of outward activity. " The great fault I find with this generation is, that they cry that ministers should be more in public ; they think that it is an easy thing to interpret the word of God, and to preach. But a minister's duty is not so much public as private." Two thick notebooks in quarto remain from his early years at Dundee, which show that he was constantly storing his mind by reading the Puritans, and Reformers. This emphasis on personal growth he never lost. " Oh," he declared to a friend, " we preachers need to *know* God in another way than heretofore, in order to speak aright of sin and of salvation. The work of God would flourish by us, if it flourished more richly in us."

" The want of ministerial success," says Robinson, " is a tremendous circumstance, never to be contemplated without horror." Never to rest without success was McCheyne's unvarying aim ; though from his earliest days at St. Peter's his preaching was attended with saving power, and produced deep convictions and distress in the hearts of many, he and his people ever prayed for further manifestations of God's glory. But towards the end of 1838 the course of his ministry was interrupted by symptoms which alarmed his friends. He was attacked by violent palpitation of heart—the effect of unremitting labour. It soon increased, so that his medical advisers insisted on a total cessation of work. Accordingly McCheyne with deep regret returned to his parents home in Edinburgh, to rest until he could resume his ministry. This separation from his people occasioned some of his richest letters. " Ah ! " he writes, " there is nothing like a calm look into the eternal world to teach us the emptiness of human praise, the sinfulness of self-seeking, the preciousness of Christ." From the ten lengthy Pastoral Letters which he sent to his flock, we can quote but a paragraph of one :—

" Consider what fruit there is of *believing* in you. Have you really and fully uptaken Christ as the Gospel lays Him down ?— John 5 : 12. Do you cleave to Him as a sinner ?—1 Timothy 1 : 15. Do you feel the glory of His person ?—Revelation 1 : 17 ; His finished work ?—Hebrews 9 : 26 ; His offices ?—1 Corinthians 1 : 30. Does He shine like the sun into your soul?—Malachi 4 : 2.

Is your heart ravished with His beauty ?—Song of Solomon 5 : 16. Again, what fruit is there in you of *crying after holiness* ? Is this the one thing you do ?—Philippians 3 : 13. Do you spend your life in cries for deliverance from this body of sin and death ?— Romans 7 : 24. Ah ! I fear there is little of this. I fear you do not know " the exceeding greatness of His power " to usward who believe. I fear many of you are strangers to the visits of the Comforter."

Prolonged illness prevented McCheyne's speedy restoration to his people, and in the spring of 1839 it was proposed in Edinburgh that he should accompany a party of ministers who were to visit Palestine to make personal enquiries into the state of Israel. The voyage and climate it was thought would prove beneficial to him. His acceptance, and their subsequent travels to Jerusalem and Galilee we cannot pause to describe. Even when far from them, the spiritual prosperity of his people in Dundee was uppermost in his heart. After surveying the barren spot beside Galilee where Capernaum once stood, he wrote to them, " If you tread the glorious Gospel of the grace of God under your feet, your souls will perish ; and I fear Dundee will one day be a howling wilderness like Capernaum." " Ah ! would my flock from thee might learn, How days of grace will flee ; How all an offered Christ who spurn, shall mourn at last, like thee."

Not long after the party had begun to return homewards through Asia Minor, McCheyne was taken dangerously ill. Towards the end of July, 1839 as he lay apparently dying near Smyrna, he believed it was not to his native Scotland but to his eternal home that he was going. " My most earnest prayer was for my dear flock." " The cry of his servant in Asia was not forgotten," writes Bonar ; " the eye of the Lord turned towards his people. Their pastor was lying at the gate of death, in utter helplessness. But the Lord had done this on very purpose ; for He meant to show that He needed not the help of any." W. C. Burns—a young man of twenty-four—was supplying McCheyne's place at Dundee in his absence. It was under his preaching on 23rd of July that the great Revival at Kilsyth took place. " All Scotland heard the glad news that the sky was no longer brass. The Spirit in mighty power began to work from that day forward in many places of the land." As soon as Burns resumed his ministry in Dundee early in August, the same effects occurred. The truth pierced hearts in an overwhelming manner—" tears were streaming from the eyes of many, and some fell on the ground groaning, and weeping, and crying for mercy." Services were held every night for many weeks— often lasting till late hours. The whole town was moved. The fear of God fell upon the ungodly. Anxious multitudes filled the churches.

When McCheyne, restored to health, returned to St. Peter's in November of that year, he viewed an unforgettable scene. A deep concern and impression of eternal realities possessed the vast congregation. In worship " the people felt that they were praising a present God." Such a sight as this was not uncommon throughout the remainder of his ministry. The grief at sin which filled the hearts of many could only be expressed by tears ; the distress expressed by one awakened sinner to McCheyne represented the feelings of scores—" I think," he said, " hell would be some relief from an angry God." Such was the anxiety which now prevailed to hear the Gospel that even when McCheyne was preaching in the open air in the meadows at Dundee, and heavy rain began to fall, the dense crowd stood till the last. The Word was listened to on these occasions with " an awful and breathless stillness."

It was McCheyne's custom never to accept mere professions of faith as signs of conversion. " It is holy-making Gospel," he declared. " Without holy fruit all evidences are vain. Dear friends, you have awakenings, enlightenings, experiences, a full heart in prayer, and many due signs ; but if you want holiness, you will never see the Lord. A real desire after complete holiness is the truest mark of being born again. Jesus is a holy Saviour. He first covers the soul with His white raiment, then makes the soul glorious within—restores the lost image of God, and fills the soul with pure, heavenly holiness. Unregenerate men among you cannot bear this."

As his ministry drew towards its solemn close, he became increasingly conscious of the brevity of time. " I do not expect to live long . . . Changes are coming ; every eye before me shall soon be dim in death. Another pastor shall feed this flock ; another singer lead the psalm ; another flock shall fill this fold . . . There is no believing, no repenting, no conversion in the grave— no minister will speak to you there. This is the time of conversion. Oh ! my friends, you will have no ordinances in hell—there will be no preaching in hell . . . Oh that you would use this little time ! Every moment of it is worth a world."

In his last year at St. Peter's we find him preaching with terrible clearness on the eternal punishment of the unconverted— four sermons were devoted to this subject. He ever dreaded the reproach a dying woman addressed to John Newton—" You often spoke to me of Christ ; but oh you did not tell me enough about my danger." " Brethren," McCheyne warned fellow ministers, our people " will not thank us in eternity for speaking smooth things, and crying Peace, peace, when there is no peace. No, they may praise us now, but they will curse our flattery in eternity." At his last communion service in January 1843 he preached on " Paul a Pattern " (1 Timothy 1 : 16). In February he was away in the north west of Scotland, and preached twenty-seven times, in twenty-four different places often travelling through heavy snow. On his return to Dundee he confessed he felt " very tired." March

12th proved to be his last Sabbath in the pulpit of St. Peter's, his final sermon was from Romans 9 : 22 and 23. " What if God, willing to shew his wrath . . ." " It was observed," writes Bonar, " both then and on other occasions, he spoke with peculiar strength upon the sovereignty of God." The following Tuesday he felt ill but took a wedding service, and afterwards spoke to a group of children, who informally gathered round him, on " The Good Shepherd." It was his last public appearance ; that evening he succumbed to the fever which was prevalent in the parish at the time. After lying helplessly for a week with burning fever, a delirium overtook him on Tuesday 21st. His utterances now showed the thoughts which were uppermost in his mind. As if addressing his people he cried " You must be awakened in time, or you will be awakened in everlasting torment, to your eternal confusion." Then he prayed, " This parish, Lord, this people, this whole place ! " Robert Murray McCheyne died on Saturday, March 25th, 1843. " Live for eternity. A few days more and our journey is done." The truth, he had so often preached was accomplished. His desire was fulfilled—" Oh to be like Jesus, and with Him to all eternity ! "

We have finished our outlines of the life of one who declared he was " just a common man." But our impression must surely be that such a ministry is very uncommon in our times. It is then no small question for ministers to ask—" Where lies the difference between his ministry and ours ? " No other questions are so vital as this, the answer is far from the minds of many. *First, McCheyne was different in doctrine.* His preaching was clearly and definitely in line with the faith of the Reformers and Puritans. That glorious Puritan document, in which every doctrine is given its true Scriptural proportion—The Westminster Confession of Faith—was his constant text book. " Oh for the grace of the Westminster divines," he writes, " to be poured out upon this generation of lesser men." Ruin by the fall, Righteousness by Christ, and Regeneration by the Spirit was the substance of his preaching. Sin has so ruined man's mind and heart that he has no will to be saved. " You will only have yourselves to blame if ye awake in hell. If you die, it is because you *will* die ; and if you *will* die, then you must die." Like all who apprehend this to be the true condition of men by nature, McCheyne clearly saw that without God's electing love and without the Divine power He exercises in conversion no soul would be saved. Unless He makes them willing in the day of His power they never will come. After declaring the text ' As many as were ordained to eternal life believed,' he says " Every thinking man must know and feel that none will ever come to Christ but those who were given Him by the Father from all eternity." " The only power that can bring a child of Satan and make him a child of God, is God Himself. Ah ! dear friends, the power is not in creatures. It is not in the power of man—it is not in the power given to ministers ; God alone can do it . . . Ah! my friends, this is a humbling doctrine.   There is no difference between us and the children of wrath ; some of us were more wicked than they, yet God set His love on us.   If there are any here that think they have been chosen because they were better than others, you are grossly mistaken."   In conversion therefore the Divine work of re-generation must precede faith.   The Spirit convicts the sinner that Christ *alone* is able to save him.

The constant aim of McCheyne's preaching to the awakened and converted was to bring them to see the vastness, completeness, and freeness of the salvation brought by Christ.   " Remember Jesus *for us is* all our righteousness before a holy God, and Jesus *in us* is all our strength in an ungodly world . . . He justifies sinners who have no righteousness, sanctifies souls that have no holiness. Let Jesus bear your whole weight.   Remember, He loves to be the only support of the soul.   There is nothing that you can possibly need but you will find it in Him."   The most prominent cause of the absence of such ministries as McCheyne's to-day lies in the absence of his doctrine, for it is only the truth of God which the Spirit will honour and bless.

Secondly, McCheyne was different in his life.   I do not mean he was exempt from the conflict with indwelling sin known by the Apostle Paul (Romans 7) and by every Christian.   On the contrary it was (as we see in his diary) the constant awareness of the " abyss of corruption " in his heart, that brought him into such continual dependence on Christ.   " Our wicked heart taints all we say and do ; hence the need of continual atonement in the blood of Jesus. We must have daily, hourly pardons."   But he was different in that he ever lived as one on the brink of eternity, as one who longed for a " full conformity to God," and prized communion with Him as his chief joy.   He was ever reminding himself—" If I could follow the Lord more fully myself, my ministry would be used to make a deeper impression than it has yet done."   Are we not re-buked by this minister who was given hundreds of souls as his reward ?   Have we not failed to estimate aright the value of near access unto God ?   Is such a ministry not needed in our times ? The same Jesus reigns ; the same Spirit is able ; and the same source of grace is open to us.   " Oh! brethren, be wise.   ' Why stand ye all the day idle ? '   In a little moment it will be all over.   A little while and the day of grace will be over—preaching, praying will be done.   A little while, and we shall stand before the great white throne—a little while, and the wicked shall not be ; we shall see them going away into everlasting punishment.   A little while, and the work of eternity shall be begun.   We shall be like Him—we shall see Him day and night in His temple—we shall sing the new song, without sin and without weariness, for ever and ever."

*Notes of a sermon preached by R.M. McCheyne on Electing Love.
(A Basket of Fragments. Sermon XII).*

John 15 : 16 " Ye have not chosen me, but I have chosen you."

I. *Men naturally do not choose Christ.*   This was true of the Apostles ; this is true of all that will ever believe to the end of the world . . . It is quite true, that when God opens a sinner's heart, he chooses Christ and none but Christ. But, brethren, the truth here taught us is this, that every awakened sinner is willing to embrace Christ, but not till made willing. You do not choose Christ because you see no beauty in Him : " He is a root out of dry ground, in which there is no form nor comeliness." You see no beauty in His person, no glory in His cross. You do not choose Christ because you no not want to be made holy by Him. " He shall save His people from their sins." But you love your sin—you love your pleasure. So you can never come to terms with Christ.

II. *Christ chooses His own disciples* : " I have chosen you." I observe that the time when He chose them was before they believed. " Ye have not chosen me," as much as to say, I began with you, you did not begin with me. " We are bound to give thanks always to God for you, brethren, beloved of the Lord, because God hath from the beginning chosen you to salvation through sanctification of the Spirit, and belief of the truth." 2 Thess. 2 : 13. " According as He had chosen us in Him before the foundation of the world." Eph. 1 : 4. It was before the foundation of the world that Christ choose His own ; when there was neither sun nor moon ; when there was neither sea nor land—it was from the beginning. Ah! He might well say, you have not chosen me.

Now, it is a very natural question, why did He choose me ? I answer, that the reason why He chose you was, the good pleasure of His will.   You see this illustrated in Mark 3 : 13, " And he goeth up into a mountain, and calleth unto him whom he would." There was a great crowd round about Him : He called some, He did not call all. The reason here given why He did it is, " He called whom He would."   There is no reason in the creature ; the reason is in Him who chooses—You will see this in Malachi 1 : 2. " Was not Esau Jacob's brother ? saith the Lord ; yet I loved Jacob, and I hated Esau. Were they not of the same mother? yet I loved Jacob, and I hated Esau." The only reason given, you see, is " I will have mercy on whom I will have mercy."   You will see this also in Rom. 9 : 15-16. This is the only reason given in the Bible why Christ loved us—and if you study till you die you will not find another. O, my brethren, be humbled under the sovereignty of God.

III. *" I have ordained you that ye should go and bring forth fruit, and that your fruit should remain."*   Christ not only chooses who are to be saved, but He chooses the way—" through sanctification of the Spirit and belief of the truth." 2 Thess. 2 : 13 ; Rom. 8 : 30 ; Eph. 1 : 4. " He hath chosen us in Him . . . that we should be holy." Ah ! how this takes away the feet from all objections raised against this holy doctrine of election. Some here, perhaps say, If I am elected, I will be saved, live as I like. Some may say, If I am not elected, I will not be saved, do as I like. Whether you are elected or not, I know not, but this I know—if you believe on Christ you will be saved. Have you believed on Christ ? Do you bear His whole image ? then you are elected and will be saved. But are there any here who have not believed on Christ, and who do not live a holy life, then, whatever you think now you will find it true that you were among those who were passed by.

THE PRESENTATION OF THE GOSPEL AND THE DOCTRINES OF GRACE

" Preach Christ and leave doctrines alone," has been the popular outcry. As though it were possible to declare who Jesus is, and the necessity and nature of conversion, without teaching doctrine! Beneath such a statement there lies the common delusion that it matters not what a man believes so long as he rests on Christ in some vague way. We are here concerned to assert that not only doctrine in general, but the doctrines of grace in particular are necessary for a correct presentation of the Gospel. We mean such doctrines as fallen man's total inability, the sovereign mercy of God in election and the almighty work of the Holy Ghost in conversion. Now the objection which confronts us is one which is widely accepted by evangelicals, namely that whatever be the truth of these doctrines, they have no essential place in the preaching of the Gospel, they are not necessary for Scriptural evangelism. There can be no question that this commonly accepted view has governed the presentation of the Gospel for many years, yet when we stand aside for a moment from the opinions of our times and look back across the centuries, we are met with the plain fact that this view is in reality a radical departure from the evangelical witness of former generations. We are not therefore raising this matter in a controversial spirit but out of the conviction that the spiritual barrenness of our days, the withdrawal of the powerful operations of the Holy Ghost, the widespread absence of the fear of God among the people, may well be related to this variance in our presentation of the Gospel.

Now of course the only way to ascertain whether such variance does in fact exist is to examine some church history. Let us then direct our attention to periods when the Spirit of God was mightily poured out upon people under the ministry of the Word. How was the Gospel presented in such times ? Under what kind of doctrines were multitudes savingly converted ? We will look at three periods during the last 300 years when the operations of the Spirit in great power have been in evidence.

Between the years 1625-1630, there was a widespread revival of serious religion in Scotland, wrought through preaching attended by the authority of the Holy Ghost. Five hundred persons traced their conversion to one sermon preached by John Livingstone in 1630 at Kirk of Shotts. At Irvine, multitudes under deep concern for their souls attended the preaching of David Dickson. "Few," says Howie "were more instrumental in this work than he." On Monday evenings (being market day) Dickson preached to large congregations, many coming in from the countyside. This was accompanied by such distressing, then saving effects, that a revival known as the "Stewarton sickness" broke out in the area. Listen then to something of Dickson's preaching ; from his text 2 Tim. 2, v. 19, he concludes : " that the doctrine of election and reprobation is a doctrine which may be safely taught and propounded unto people, albeit men say it should not be meddled with, because (say they) it makes some men despair, and others become careless what they do. I answer, let God make an answer for His own doctrine, who has commanded us to teach it . . . The apostle says boldly, the election obtained it and the rest were blinded. Would Christ have propounded this doctrine if it had been dangerous ? Therefore we oppose to such carnal men, secure sleepers in sin, this doctrine of Christ and His apostles, clearly set down in scripture. Let none take offence at this doctrine, for Christ's sheep will hear His voice and if any will startle away, let them go . . . This doctrine is a strong attractive to draw back those who are fallen in error or vice, that they lie not in it ; for this doctrine forces such men to turn to God, or else, to take on the name of reprobates . . . It is a doctrine meet for this age, wherein God is mocked and blasphemed by the lewd lives of those who are called Christians, to tell them that they must either turn to God, or take home with them those black tidings, that they are vessels of dishonour, fitted for destruction. *This doctrine is very needful to put men to their decisions ;* and yet it condemns not a man to hell presently, who is lying in sin ; but it tells him that there are some elect who will come home ; and some reprobate, who will not come home. Therefore, if a man be elect, albeit for the time he be a deboshed villain, this doctrine will serve him for the third and last summons : for when he hears that he must either quit his sinful courses, or have no portion with God, presently he must resolve, I will renounce my old lovers, my uncleanness, worldliness, and turn in to God, and seek a covering to hide my vileness, and a garment to make me beautiful in the eyes of God. *This effect will this doctrine work in the elect.*" Such was the preaching which accompanied the great Scottish awakening of the seventeenth century.

The next period when the soul-saving effects of the Gospel were so gloriously displayed was at the time of the New England revival. Jonathan Edwards, the foremost instrument in this movement has left us a full account of it, and of the sermons which he preached at that time, in his works. . New England had flourished in the seventeenth century under the Gospel ministries of several eminent Puritans, but early in the eighteenth a marked decay in piety and seriousness became evident. " Mirth and jollity " and vain amusements began to engage the young. Concerning the year 1734, Edwards wrote, " Arminianism seemed to appear with a very threatening aspect upon the interest of religion here.. The friends of vital piety trembled for fear of the issue. Many who looked on themselves as in a Christless condition seemed to be awaked by it, with fear that God was about to withdraw from the land, and that we should be given up to heterodoxy and corrupt principles ; and that their opportunity for obtaining salvation would be past." Yet, as Edwards says, this event led to wonderful consequences. Despite the censure of some he began to oppose these errors in his preaching, and it was attended with a very remarkable blessing of heaven to the souls of the people. " In the latter part of December " (1734, Edwards' narrative continues) " the Spirit of God began extraordinarily to set in, and wonderfully to work amongst us . .. a great and earnest concern about the great things of religion, and the eternal world, became *universal* in all parts of the town, and amongst all persons of all degrees, and all ages . . . religion was with all sorts the great concern, and the world was a thing only by the bye. The only thing in their view was to get the kingdom of heaven. It was then a dreadful thing amongst us to lie out of Christ . . . the number of true saints multiplied ; the town seemed to be full of the presence of God : it never was so full of love, nor of joy, and yet so full of distress, as it was then . . . This remarkable pouring out of the Spirit of God extended from one end to the other of this country." This is but a brief extract of the amazing account Edwards gives, we are chifly concerned with the doctrine preached at this time. " The drift of the Spirit of God in His legal strivings," writes Edwards, " seemed most evidently to be to bring persons to a conviction of their *absolute dependence* on His sovereign power and grace . . . I think I have found that no discourses have been more *remarkably blessed*, than those in which the doctrine of God's *absolute sovereignty*, with regard to the salvation of sinners, and His just liberty, with regard to answering the prayers of natural men have been insisted on . . . As to those in whom awakenings seem to have a saving issue, commonly the first thing that appears is a conviction of the *justice of God* in their condemnation. In giving an account of this, they expressed themselves very variously ; some that they saw God was sovereign and might receive others and reject them ; some, that they were convinced, God might justly bestow mercy on every person in the town, in the world, and damn themselves to all eternity ; some that if they should seek, and take the utmost pains all their lives, God might justly cast them into hell at last, because all their labours, prayers and tears cannot make atonement for the least sin . . . some have declared themselves to be in the hands of God, that He may dispose of them just as He pleases.

Whatever Minister has a like occasion to deal with souls under such circumstances, I cannot but think he will soon find himself under a necessity, greatly to insist upon it with them, that God is under no manner of *obligation* to show mercy to any natural man . . . It appears to me, that if I had taught those who came to me under trouble, any other doctrine I should have taken a most direct course to undo them. I should have directly crossed what was plainly the drift of the Spirit of God in His influences upon them, and blocked up their way to that humiliation before the *Sovereign* Disposer of life, and death, whereby God is wont to prepare them for His consolations."

In 1745 similar effects followed David Brainerd's evangelistic ministry among the Indians, resulting in a widespread revival. Scores of instances similar to the following could be quoted from Brainerd's narrative—" Those whom I have reason to think in a Christless state, were almost universally seized with concern for their souls. It was an amazing season of power among them, and seemed as if God had ' bowed the heavens and come down.' So astonishingly prevalent was the operation upon old as well as young, that it seemed as if none would be left in a secure and natural state . . . numbers of men and women, old and young, might be seen in tears, some in anguish of spirit . . . so that there seemed here a lively emblem of the solemn days of accounts ; a mixture of heaven and hell, of joy and anguish inexpressible." Concerning his presentation of the Gospel Brainerd writes, " Those doctrines, which had the most direct tendency to humble the fallen creature, to show him the misery of his natural state, to bring him down to the foot of *Sovereign Mercy*, and to exalt the great Redeemer— discover His transcendent excellency—were the subject matter of what was delivered." Brainerd records the effect of these doctrines upon numerous individuals ; he is assured of the conversion of one man for " his heart echoes to the soul humbling doctrines of grace, and he never appears better pleased than when he hears of the absolute sovereignty of God." A woman who had long quarrelled against God " because He would, if He pleased, send her to hell," " was brought to a comfortable calm, and seemed to be bowed and reconciled to divine sovereignty ; and told me ' she now saw and felt it was right God should do with her as He pleased.' Others," continues Brainerd " were refreshed to find that love to God in themselves, which was an evidence of His electing love to them."

Finally let us look briefly at the revival which began at Kilsyth in Scotland in 1839, and which spread to other parts of the land. The occasion of the outbreak of this awakening was the preaching of William Burns on the text Psalm 110 : 3, " Thy people shall be willing in the day of Thy power." Burns tells us that the heads of his sermon were these " I. The person spoken of—they are God's elect—those given to Christ of the Father. II. The promise of the Father to Emmanuel regarding those persons—' they shall be willing.' III. The time of the promise—the day of Emmanuel's power." In opening his discourse Burns insisted on man's inability to will what was pleasing to God, " it is the crowning part of man's depravity that his will is opposed to the will of God . . . this is the state of the fallen soul by nature ; and therefore, my friends, when God brings back in His infinite love the souls of His elect people, He makes them willing." At the end of this sermon while he was pleading with the unconverted to close with God's offers of mercy, the Spirit of God descended upon the people. " During the whole of the time that I was speaking, the people listened with the most rivetted and solemn attention ; but at the last their feelings became too strong for all ordinary restraints and broke forth simultaneously in weeping and wailing, intermingled with shouts of joy and praise from some of the people of God. The appearance of a great part of the people from the pulpit gave me an awfully vivid picture of the state of the ungodly in the day of Christ's coming to judgment. Some were screaming out in agony ; others, and among these strong men, fell to the ground as if they had been dead . . . "

Now what do all these quotations prove ? *They demonstrate that these doctrines have been predominant in times when God mightily honoured the preaching of the Gospel.*

It remains for us to briefly summarize some reasons why these doctrines are essential to a Scriptural presentation of the Gospel. The natural man is content to live "without God in the world " (Eph. 2 : 12) until he sees the dreadfulness of his condition and the desirableness of conversion. This discovery comes to him by the apprehension that he is a creature of God, bound to obey His Law in every point, yet because of his sin unable to do so. His duty to meet God's righteous claims is the same as when God created him perfect and holy ; his inability is a proof of the fall and of his sin. He is still a creature and has not lost his responsibility, but as a sinner he is now " not subject to the law of God, *neither indeed can be* " (Rom. 8 : 7). He has lost his ability to obey God. Guilt and helplessness are the causes of the sinner's misery, and only when he comes to self-despair does he start to " fear God which is the beginning of wisdom " (Psa. 111 : 10). Pride is the grand obstacle to conversion, and nothing more humbles man than to realise that he depends upon the sovereign mercy of God, and that Christ alone is able to save him.

Man's sinful inability applies equally to the commands of the

Gospel. Faith and repentance are his duty, God has commanded them just as He has commanded the Law ; but he can no more believe and love Christ than he can believe and love God—which is the first commandment.. The natural man is no more able to decide for Christ than he is able to decide to keep the Law. Therefore while the preacher is to exhort men to believe on Christ, he is at the same time to plainly declare that conversion is a work of Divine power. Saving faith is a gift of God (Eph. 2 : 8) and not to teach this leads to the fatal error of accepting a mere profession of assent to the Gospel as a sign of salvation. There is a ' temporary faith ' (Matt. 4 : 16-17), and there is the faith of devils who believe and tremble (James 2 : 19). " The faith of God's elect " (Titus 1 : 1) is of an entirely different nature and origin ; it involves a renewal of the whole person ; God makes a new creature, implants new principles in the soul—hatred of sin, love of holiness, desires for heaven. To teach that a soul has a saving faith before these marks of his " calling and election " (2 Peter 1 : 10) by God are evident, leads to Antinomianism, carelessness, and the eternal delusion of multitudes. Unless these truths of God's Sovereignty in conversion are taught, Luther rightly says, " every man will bolster himself up with a delusive hope of a share in that salvation which is supposed to lie open to all ; and thus genuine humility and fear of God would be kicked out of doors." In conclusion we would assert that unless the doctrines of Grace underlie the presentation of the Gospel, a true view of the glorious nature of conversion is impossible. Edwards tells us that prior to the revival in New England there had been " a great deal of talk about conversion and spiritual experiences," but when persons became the subjects of conversion they declared their former idea of it was " brought to nothing . . . they have seen themselves brought down, and become nothing ; that free grace and divine power may be exalted in them."

Publications of The Inheritance Publishers.
P.O. Box 334, Grand Rapids I., Michigan, U.S.A.

The object of these publishers is to print, in the form of approx. 30 page booklets, extracts from some of the finest writings and sermons of the Puritans and their successors. Out of the several series that have already been published the following titles represent the value and standard of the rest :—*The Christian Man's Calling,* by George Swinnock. *Praying in the Spirit,* by Wm. Gurnall. *Life a Journey,* by A. M. Toplady. *Of the Assurance of Faith,* by John Newton. *Of Original Sin and Man's Misery,* by Thomas Watson. *The Method of Grace,* by George Whitefield. *The Importance and Advantages of a Thorough Knowledge of Divine Truth,* by Jonathan Edwards. These booklets and others may be obtained free and postpaid upon application to the Publishers.

Wickliffe Press, Wickliffe Avenue, 104 Hendon Lane, Finchley, N.3.

THE
BANNER of TRUTH

(5th Issue)

Price 9d.

Subscription 5/6
for six issues.

EDITOR:

MR. IAIN MURRAY, B.A.,
65A BLENHEIM TERRACE, ST. JOHN'S WOOD,
LONDON, N.W. 8.

*   *   *

" Thou hast shewed thy people hard things ;
Thou hast made us to drink the wine of
astonishment.   Thou hast given a banner to
them that fear Thee, that it may be displayed
because of the truth."   Psalm 60 : 3-4

*   *   *

CONTENTS

EDITORIAL—April, 1957

It is the duty of every believer to understand the times in which he lives. The tribe of Issachar are commended as "men that had understanding of the times to know what Israel ought to do." (1 Chron. 12 : 32). Whereas the Jews were condemned for failing to know "the time of their visitation." "O ye hypocrites ye can discern the face of the sky ; but can ye not discern the signs of the times ? " (Matt. 16 : 3). Just as the approaching changes of weather are known from the face of the sky, so the mind and purposes of God are revealed by the workings of providence. The heathen Egyptians suffering under the plagues had rightly apprehended their origin when they cried, " This is the finger of God! " (Exodus. 8 : 19). " The Lord is known by the judgment which He executeth." What then are the events of our days telling this generation ? What is the mind of God towards us ? What do the times especially demand of us ?

We are aware that modern man will not countenance the fact of God's providence. God may be allowed to have made the world but not to govern it. He may have framed the universe but He does not manage it. God may no longer be viewed as the orderer of all events, the judge of men, and the disposer of nations. Reader, if these are your thoughts you will never know the signs of the times. You must either profess yourself an unbeliever, or face the truth everywhere declared in Scripture that God is the governor and manager of all things here below. Who sent the flood on the world in the days of Noah ? It was God (Gen. 6 : 17). Who sent disease upon the Philistines ? It was God (1 Sam. 5 : 7 ; 6 : 3-7). Who sent the pestilence in the days of David ? It was God (2 Sam. 24 : 15). Who sent war upon Israel and Judah in the time of the prophets ? It was God (2 Chron. 15 : 6, etc.). Prosperity and adversity, war and peace, are not accidents, they come to us from the hand of God. Nations rise and fall at His will, " He increaseth the nations and destroyeth them " (Job 12 : 23). The most preeminent people God by His acts of providence brings to nothing, " Amalek was the first among the nations, but his latter end shall be, that he perish for ever." For nations there can be no future judgment day. The sins of nations, the Scriptures teach, God judges in time.

Let us then consider what there is in the workings of providence in our days which summons our attention. The truth is that God is using a multitude of events to address us by—two world wars and the expectancy of a third ; the collapse of our Empire ; the ill-feeling of nations ; the removal of strong national leaders ; the disunity of Parliament ; and the economic unrest. All these things are as messages from heaven. *They declare that God is against us as a nation.* Would that all Englishmen were as wise as those Egyptians who could recognise the finger of God! Until we recognise these signs and their meaning all our expectations will be blasted. For Jonathan Edwards truly asserts that "It is the manner of God before He removes any awful judgments which He has brought upon a people for their sins, first to cause them to forsake those sins which procured those judgments." Sins must be recognised before they can be forsaken. We must therefore do what David did long ago when his land was visited with famine, " David inquired of the Lord," concerning the cause. (2 Sam. 21 : 1). "Show me wherefore thou contendest with me," said Job (10 : 2). "Wherefore doth a living man complain, a man for the punishment of his sins ? Let us search and try our ways, and turn again to the Lord " (Lam. 3 : 39-40). This is a principle taught throughout Scripture. God's judicial acts of providence are rods (Micah 6 : 9) and their purpose is to bring us to search and try our ways. God loves to be clear when He judges (Ps. 51 : 4), that is to have the reason of His dispensation seen ; He never revokes afflictions before the offence which caused them is acknowledged— " I will go and return to my place, till they acknowledge their offence." (Hosea 5 : 15).

Now we are not here concerned with an application of this principle to the nation as a whole, or even to the professing church at large, for this truth is meaningless to those who do not recognise the authority and infallibility of Scripture. But what do the times demand of us who are professors of orthodoxy and of the evangelical faith? One thing is plain to all, namely that we are failing to command the attention and hearing of the masses of the people. Our first duty then, it is said, must surely be to reach the people, ' to get the Gospel across to them,' and to use all modern methods to attain that end — campaigns, advertisements, modern translations of Scripture, films, etc. Such proposals, we believe, have arisen out of a wrong veiw of the nature of our failure, and an underestimation of its seriousness. Our need is a much more fundamental one than the need of new methods. The cause of our spiritual impotency can only be adequately explained as nothing less than an absence of the powerful operations of the Holy Spirit; it is to be feared that many are too active to stop and recognize this. Some are ready to see that our need is a spiritual one, and immediately they commence to think of a remedy in terms of more prayer. But surely it is insufficient to stop at this. Are there not times when God has cause to be angry with the prayers of his people and to refuse to hear them ? (Psa. 80.4 ; Isa. 59.2). Are we not at this point still overlooking the true cause of our low spiritual condition? It is only when we pause to consider the implications of the following statement of Luther's that the vital matter comes into view, ' While doctrine flourishes, everything in the church flourishes also.' If everything else is not flourishing ought we not to look first to our doctrine ? Is anything more offensive to God than dishonour to his written word? Is it not an astonishing instance of Satan's ability to work within the church as an angel of light — obscuring the real issues at stake — that though the Scriptures give us so many warnings to '*take heed unto the doctrine*' (1 Tim. 4.16.), we take it for granted that our failure could not be related to the doctrinal views which generally prevail among evangelicals? Yet surely this is a possibility which demands a solemn consideration, for nothing more certainly promotes the absence of the Spirit of Truth, and a rejection of prayers, than erroneous views of the Word of God. 'He that turneth away his ear from hearing the law, even his prayer shall be abomination.' (Prov. 28.9.)

To seek to produce such a consideration is the purpose of this magazine. The enquiry will not be a popular one, for although doctrine held first place in importance in the apostolic church (Acts 2.42), many reasons conspire to promote its neglect today. Among these reasons two perhaps are predominant. First, the fact that doctrine generally leads to controversy causes many to avoid it. But as Ryle says,' There are times in which controversy is a positive duty. Peace is an excellent thing, but it can be bought too dear. Unity is a mighty blessing, but not at the expense of truth.' Secondly, there is a complacent opinion abroad that the doctrine current amongst evangelicals does not call for a re-examination in the light of Scripture, therefore such an enquiry as this is irrelevant to the needs of the times. It is because we believe that such a complacency could never exist were the facts of church history thoroughly known, that we usually devote considerable space to historical articles. In this issue we draw attention to John Knox and John Elias, both leaders of the church in former generations, and two of the foremost ministers the land has ever seen — their preaching being mightily accompanied by the power of God. These men, though two centuries apart, were of one faith, and represented the mind of the church of their time, yet the fact is that their doctrine is fundamentally at variance with what is commonly accepted as ' evangelical belief ' today. Church history of itself can prove no doctrine finally, but when we find that the preaching which prevailed in those glorious periods when God so powerfully visited the land is so different to our own, we must surely question whether it is not we that have misunderstood the Scriptures, and whether this is not the primary cause of our spiritual condition?

There can be no more urgent consideration than this . For the preservation of the nation, depends upon the prosperity of the church, and prosperity of the church depends upon the possession of sound doctrine. It is upon us who profess the truth that the responsibility lies. Now is the time of our opportunity, it is still the day of our visitation, but who knows how long it will be before that word goes forth against us, '*A fire is kindled in mine anger, and shall burn unto the lowest hell . . . For they are a nation void of counsel, neither is there any understanding in them. O that they were wise, that they understood this, that they would consider their latter end*'! (Deut. 32. 22-29.)

JOHN ELIAS 1774 - 1841

There have been men who made the most profound impression upon their own generation, yet whose very names are well-nigh forgotten by posterity. Man 'fleeth as a shadow and continueth not,' and another generation takes his place upon the stage of life. Such is the shortness of life that few find time to obey that Scriptural command—'Inquire, I pray thee, of the former age . . . Shall not they teach thee, and tell thee?' (Job. 8 : 8-10). As a result those glorious works which God wrought among their forefathers are unknown, and the lessons they ought to have learned from them wholly lost. One cannot consider the life of John Elias without being sadly persuaded that such observations are true. Though he died only some hundred and sixteen years ago, though his preaching was attended by such evidences of Divine power as have not often been seen in these British Isles—promoting a great awakening in North Wales—though his influence as a minister of Christ in his own day was second to none, yet the fact is that his life is now neither known nor remembered by the vast majority.

John Elias was born near Pwllheli, Carnarvonshire, on March 6, 1774. His parents were not religious, but under the hand of his godly grandfather he was brought to fear God at a tender age. By the age of seven he had read through the Bible from Genesis to the middle of Jeremiah. Soon after when his aged grandfather was unable to walk with his grandson on Sabbath days to hear the preaching of the Methodists, the young boy would continue to walk without a guide or friend upwards of ten miles to hear the Word of God. His distress at his parents' failure to observe God's commands caused him to weep much, and at length prevailed upon them to hold family worship. Though between the age of fourteen and sixteen (Elias tells us) he experienced great inward conflict —'there was a strong inclination to become light and trifling like my contemporaries'—yet these serious impressions did not leave him, and the concerns of his soul remained the one thing needful in his mind. From his earliest days he had heard stories of the great work of God in South Wales and of the revivals which had occurred under the preaching of Howell Harris and Daniel Rowlands. The former Elias could never hear for he had died in 1773, but Rowlands in his old age was still preaching with great power at Llangeitho. As soon as he felt strong enough for the walk of 80 miles Elias was determined to journey south to Llangeitho.

E

But one Sabbath morning, in his seventeenth year, upon going to church in Pwllheli he was overwhelmed with the mournful tidings of Mr. Rowlands' death. Little did Elias realise at this time that he himself was to be in the north what Rowlands had been in the south!

North Wales at this time was a scene of spiritual darkness. The Established Church was dead, and the people were given over to all manner of ungodliness. When Harris had preached in the north in 1741 he had very nearly lost his life. But there were some in the north who had been converted under Rowlands or Harris and who began to form Methodist societies as in the south. Their leader was Thomas Charles who settled at Bala in 1783. God's time to favour them was about to come. In 1791 a great awakening occurred at Bala. Charles writing in that year says—' We have had a very great, powerful, and glorious out pouring of the Spirit on the people in general. Scores of the wildest and most inconsiderate of young people of both sexes, have been awakened. Their convictions have been very clear and powerful . . . divine truths have their own infinite weight and importance on the minds of the people . . . at one time there were but very few who had not felt awful impressions on their minds, producing foreboding fears respecting their future existence in another world.' The following year Elias, now eighteen, joined a large company of young people who were to attend the Association meeting at Bala. (These Associations were regular meetings among the Welsh Methodists, when believers gathered to be addressed by several ministers). As they walked to Bala, a distance of 40 miles, Elias says their time was filled with praise or discourse concerning the Bible or sermons —" They were indeed most anxious for the unspeakable favour of meeting with God. When we came there we observed crowds from different places, meeting together, and the whole multitude appearing as persons of one mind, and engaged in the same important business . . . God owned the preaching in an extraordinary manner, making his servants like a flame of fire. The saving operations of the Spirit were most clear and powerful on the people ; and the divine glory rested on them . . . I had such delight and pleasure in the fellowship of these godly people that I could not live separate from them. I determined to join them."

It was about this time that Elias was brought to a state of peace in his own soul, and he began to be burdened towards the work of the ministry. In 1793 Thomas Charles wrote, "A very general awakening now prevails through the greatest part of the county of Caernarvon." At Christmas 1794, the monthly presbytery meeting in Carnarvonshire received John Elias as a preacher. ' Brethren,' said an old minister, ' when I am in the dust this young lad will be a great man.' Never was the ministry undertaken with more gravity and solemnity. Apart from one or two Puritan works he had read few books, but, says Morgan, his biographer, 'he was so well acquainted with the chief subjects in every chapter in the Bible from the beginning to the end, that he could easily make use of them on any occasion.' On Elias's first appearance as a minister at an Association meeting he opened in prayer, the effect of which was, says one who was present, that 'all around me were in tears as well as myself ; indeed we trembled as if we were going to appear before the judgment seat of Christ.' It made a deeper impression than all the sermons they were to hear at that Association. After he had preached a few times the rumour travelled the country that a great servant of God had been raised. At one church, where he was sent to preach in the place of another, because of his youthful appearance the members felt doubtful at first whether they would allow him to preach ; 'but before the sermon was over he appeared unto them as a seraph come from heaven.'

Elias's ministry was of an itinerant nature, and even after 1799 when he married and settled at Llanfechell in Anglesey, he continued to visit all parts of the land awakening a dead and sleeping people. The effects which accompanied his preaching are truly indescribable. Though many might come to hear him only out of idle curiosity, 'in the twinkling of an eye their souls and spirits were absorbed with greater things. Trifles vanished ; great realities appeared ; God became great, and Jesus Christ and His precious blood ; and they left the meeting in an agonising struggle for their own salvation.' At Denbigh in 1800 when many assembled in the open air to hear him, such a real dread of punishment and hell fire fell upon the people that many screamed in despair. In 1802 Elias visited Rhuddlan, one of the strongholds of Satan, where thousands attended Sunday fairs—scenes of riot, revelry, and all manner of evil. On one such Sunday afternoon Elias and a party of believers took up their stand outside the New Inn. The sound of fiddling and dancing from the taverns was loud in their ears, and there were some hundreds of pleasure bent people before him. Elias gave out Psa. 24 to be sung, then prayed in such a manner that awe and dread took possession of the dense throng. The din of the fair was gone when he read his text, Exod. 34 : 21, 'Six days thou shalt work, but on the seventh day thou shalt rest ; in earing time and in harvest thou shalt rest.' After expounding the verse, he showed from Scripture how God visited Sabbath breakers with punishment. He answered any excuse which might arise in their minds. Then he cried to the people with all his might, with his arm lifted up and tears flowing down his face : 'Oh robbers, Oh robbers, Oh thieves ! Alas ! stealing the day of the Lord ! What ! robbing my Lord of His day ! Oh robbers, the most vile and abominable.' These words shook the people like the shock of an earthquake ; they were filled with fear ; many said after the sermon was over that they would not for the world go there again. It put a complete end to these fairs. Rarely has the power of the

world to come been so present in a man's preaching as it was in
that of Elias.   People listened to him ' as men that were going to
the Judgment Day.'   He would at times suddenly say, ' Stop !
Silence !   What are they saying in heaven on the subject ? '   Or
he would exclaim, ' Stop !   Silence !   What do they say in hell on
this awful subject ?   Consider the shortness of time, and the
approach of eternity.   Everything will be over with us here below
very soon, and we shall be in an eternal world before long.'

No ministers of the Gospel in Wales at this time doubted that
' the fear of the Lord is the beginning of wisdom,' and they lived
under the impression, that, ' it is a fearful thing to fall into the
hands of the living God.'   The famous incident of Michael Roberts
at Llanidloes in 1819, demonstrates the effects which followed this
manner of preaching by others besides Elias.   Roberts, on arriving
at this place the evening before he was due to preach, was deeply
stirred in his spirit by beholding the evident marks of ungodliness
in the speech and actions of the inhabitants.   ' After going into
his house for the night,' reports Owen Jones, ' he could eat nothing :
and during the whole of the night he slept none at all, but wrestled
with God in prayer ; nor could he take anything to eat the following
morning.   The service was to be at ten o'clock before the Red Lion
Hotel.   As it was an Association, there were a great many people
present from all parts of Montgomeryshire.   His text was Psa. 1 :
5, " Therefore the ungodly shall not stand in the judgment."   He
described the judgment with such vividness that a great solemnity
came over the whole multitude.   He described the ungodly losing
the trial, and unable to ' stand.'   He described them as overwhelmed with extreme despair, the pallor of death on their faces,
and their knees trembling.   The preacher turned to the Judge,
and said : ' O, mighty Jesus ! withhold Thine hand ; say not a word
more unto them ; they are already in the agony of death ; they are
already overwhelmed.'   The reply was : ' No ; I have one word
yet more to say to them ; and that word I *must* say to them ; after
that—not another for ever !   And this is it : DEPART FROM ME,
YE CURSED, INTO EVERLASTING FIRE ! ' . . .   Some
hundreds of ungodly men were immediately cast into the condition
of the jailer of Philippi after the earthquake . . .   Some had forgotten altogether where they stood, some swooned and fell down,
some wept, many were sstricken with the paralysis of guilt, and
others seized with the pangs of despair.   After Michael Roberts
had finished, Ebenezer Morris, one of the greatest preachers of his
day, was unable to fix the attention of the people ; he finished, after
a few minutes, and the service was closed."

But although they considered that the greatness, purity, and
justice of God in punishing sin was to come first in preaching the
Gospel, they were equally instrumental in declaring the all
sufficiency and excellence of Christ in an overwhelming manner to

needy sinners. More was accomplished then by single sermons than is accomplished in years of preaching to-day! Once Elias was called to preach at Pwllheli where the state of religion was known to be very low and discouraging. 'A great spiritual darkness and lethargy had prevailed there for upwards of 10 years,' writes Morgan. 'Elias was greatly moved, when he rose up to preach, and took those words for his text, "Let God arise, let his enemies be scattered." Psa. 78 : 1. The truths delivered by him then, had, under God's blessing, the most happy and astonishing effect ; many of the people fell down to the ground in great terror, crying for mercy. It is said that no less than 2,500 persons were added to the church in Carnarvonshire that year, in consequence of the powerful impetus which was given by that extraordinary sermon.'

It was in Anglesey itself that the effects of Elias's preaching were most visible. 'Awful indeed was the state of things there, and evil beyond expression,' writes Morgan. Drunkenness, fighting, smuggling, and adultery were prevalent. The societies of believers were few and small. Within a short time the whole island was transformed, these sins became uncommon ; smuggling was done away with ; those who had plundered wrecked vessels took their booty back to the sea shore ; horse racing and play acting were given up ; owners of windmills stopped them on the Sabbath day ; and within 40 years 44 chapels were built, and filled with congregations.

Very high views of church membership were held in these times, and Elias tell us that such questions as the following were to be put to professed converts. '(1) Have I been brought to see and consider the greatness and infinite purity of God, before whom I am, at all times ? (2) Have I seen that I am a responsible creature, bound to give an account of my thoughts, words, and actions ? (3) Have I believed that I fell awfully in Adam ? Have I seen myself an enemy of God, and that I deserve the wrath of God to all eternity on its account ? (4) Have I discovered the value of Christ as a Saviour to lost sinners ? Is He precious to my soul, and is He in my estimation altogether lovely ? (5) Does my soul desire to know Him more, and to love Him better, to enjoy more of His fellowship, and to be more conformable to His image ? '

Four children were born into the humble Elias home, but only two survived infancy. Elias's wife kept a shop in the village to provide for them all till her death in 1829. When it was necessary for the children to be away from home at school, the kind of loving counsel they received from their parents illustrates the spirit which reigned in the homes of believers in those days. Elias writes thus to his son—'Avoid more carefully the things that injure thy soul : abhor those things as the most bloody murderers, yea the murderers of thy soul : thou knowest what they are ; levity and jesting, hastiness and passion . . . Think of the great God, who is everywhere present with thee, and seeth thee at all times—think of thy soul, which is immortal, and to endure everlastingly—think of the shortness of thy time, it is but little ; when a day has passed, there is no possibility of recalling it in order to be spent again. Think frequently of death ; of the judgment day ; of eternity, we shall soon be there ! Think of Jesus dying, and be amazed and happy.' ' My dear daughter,' he writes in another letter, ' spend not the time of thy youth in vanity and sin ; thou must ere long give an account to God of every day and every hour of thy life, and for every word and action ! Do not allow thyself to live in any known sin, nor in the neglect of any known duty. O ! do not neglect secret prayer, but go to the throne of grace as you are, and humbly commend thyself to God through the Mediator Jesus Christ—implore His mercy to pardon you, His Spirit to direct you, His providence to protect you.' Both children grew up to adorn the Gospel.

It is not possible in an article of this size to give a chronological account of Elias's life, but surely enough has been said to cause us seriously to attend to the following questions. Wherein lay the power of this man's ministry ? Why has such power departed from us to-day ? What was there in his life and doctrine which led to the great usefulness of his preaching ? Where is the contrast between him and us most evident ? In an understanding of such questions lies the only hope for the visible church to-day. We can answer them by looking at Elias first in terms of his private life, in reference to his doctrine.

Elias obtained his strength and authority from very close communion with God. ' Satan is not afraid of the soldiers,' he writes to a fellow minister, ' though they are armed—of the knowledge or gifts of any preacher ; but he is afraid of the presence of God, the leader of the true army. As the Philistines cried out, ' Woe to us, God is come to the camp.' So a cry would be made in hell, and a great alarm in the regiment of Satan, if God should be pleased to appear among you.' Elias was well acquainted with ' appearances ' in his own home. His daughter said of him, ' To live in his family was to a great degree heaven upon earth. I can never forget the light that followed our family worship. And never can I forget the tears I saw on the chair in his study by which he bent on his knees ; though nothing was heard, we were well aware that he was pouring out a profusion of tears in his secret prayers. Many times did I observe him coming out from his chamber, like Moses coming down from the mountain, with so much of the image of God upon his countenance that no one could look him in the face.'

Sentences like the following recur throughout his letters, and illustrate what was uppermost in his heart—' The ministers of the Gospel are under great necessity of being experimentally acquainted with the work of the Holy Ghost . . . Oh, that we might have more of the communion and fellowship of the Holy Ghost! '—' O, may each carefully observe that nothing separates or darkens between his soul and God. Cherish a tender conscience, and a broken heart ; avoid an indifferent spirit, a hard heart, and a sleepy conscience. Press on for more intimate fellowship with God in private . . . O, brethren, be not easy without his presence. I often fear that many are now in the churches that know no difference between the hiding and the shining of his countenance. O, be not satisfied with anything instead of him. Let us cry earnestly that we may be made more heavenly continually ; we shall be here but a short time.'—' The greatest loss I feel, is that of the Spirit, and earnestness of secret prayer.'—' If private prayers were more frequent and earnest, the public ministry would be more effectual.' There is room to give only one instance of the remarkable answers which attended Elias's prayers. Once at Carnarvon, he found some mountebanks were corrupting the place with their sinful amusements. On their refusing to desist, Elias in a Chapel meeting prayed to the Lord to put a stop to their proceedings. 'Many,' says Morgan, 'were struck with the fervency, and power of his prayer, as being extraordinary. The next day, awful to relate, three of the players came to an untimely death ; the waggon in which they travelled was overturned, and they were killed! Two others, in the act of dancing on the rope, fell and broke their necks ! '

' Elias's character,' writes Morgan, ' was composed of determination, perseverance, and mental energy, to a high degree . . . The character of pious gravity was stamped on all he did. He reflected Christ's image upon the world. He was never known to have cast off the livery of his noble calling upon any occasion. The seriousness of his appearance would repel any disposition in others to levity and frivolity.' Owen Jones truly comments, ' The strength of his character as a preacher *lay in the hold which the great truths of the Gospel had taken upon his own spirit.*' This was in no small measure due to the high value Elias placed upon study. He never allowed his constant preaching and long itinerant journeys to lessen his deep conviction of the relationship between hard study and powerful preaching. Although he never had any regular schooling, he not only mastered the English language (having been brought up to speak only Welsh), but studied sufficient Greek and Hebrew to be able to consult the original Scriptures. Such writers as John Owen, and Jonathan Edwards were his constant text books ; in his letters we find him recommending such Puritans as Brooks and Flavel. Dr. Jenkyn said of Elias ' that he had collected more of the Puritan theology into his mind than any man of his age.' Reflecting on his early ministry Elias wrote—' I was enabled to persevere day and night at my studies without fatigue and delay. I am now even in my 67th year, learning ; and see greater need of knowledge daily.' Again he writes ' It is not in an easy, careless manner, that we get learning, understanding, and knowledge ; no, it must be by labour, industry, and toil. Prov. 2 : 3-4.' 'Those who knew him best,' says Morgan, ' testified that his sermons cost him many a tear, many an earnest prayer, yea many a sleepless night! ' His chief delight was in his study, and he would even bring his Bible down with him to his meals.'

In the latter years of Elias's life there was a noticeable withdrawal of the powerful operations of the Spirit from the land in general. Writing in 1837, he says, ' The light, power, and authority, formerly experienced under the preaching of the word, are not known in these days ! The ministry neither alarms terrifies, nor disturbs the thousands of ungodly persons who sit under it . . . No experimental, thoughtful Christian, can deny but that God has withdrawn Himself from us, as to the particular operations of His Spirit, and its especial manifestations of His Sovereign grace.' The explanation Elias gives of this declension illustrates his doctrinal position, and his consciousness that the preservation of the favour of God depended upon their maintenance of the Word in its purity. He believed that nothing so ruined churches or dishonoured God as erroneous teaching—' It is an awful thing to misrepresent God and His mind in His holy word ! ' ' The Lord,' he wrote, ' hath favoured us, poor Methodists, with the glorious truths of the gospel in their perfection. Alas ! errors surround us, and satan, changing himself into an angel of light, sets these pernicious evils before us, as great truths ! ' These evils, as the following quotation from his diary shows, were the appearance of Arminian errors in Wales in the nineteenth century. ' The connexion ' (that is, the church, which arose in Wales in the eighteenth century awakening) ' was not called Calvinistic Methodists at first, as there was not a body of the Arminian Methodists in the country. *But when the Wesleyans came amongst us, it was necessary to add the word Calvinistic, to show the difference.* There were, before this, union and concord, in the great things of the gospel, amongst the different denominations of Christians in Wales. The Independents agreed fully with the Methodists in the doctrines of grace. They used to acknowledge the Westminster Catechism, as containing the substance of their doctrine . . . All from the least to the greatest, preached very clearly and plainly. The chief subjects of their discourses were these : the fall and total corruption of man ; his miserable state under the curse, and the just indignation of God : his total inability to deliver and save himself ; free salvation, by the sovereign grace and love of God . . . ' It was a departure from these truths that caused his deep concern. ' The great depth of the fall, and the total depravity of man, and his awful misery, are not exhibited in many sermons in scriptural language, it is not plainly declared that all the human race are by nature, " the children of wrath,"—that none can save himself—that no one deserves to be rescued, and that none will come to Christ to have life. There are but few ministers that fully show that salvation springs entirely out of the sovereign grace of God.'

The Arminian teaching was that Christ has purchased redemption for all, but that the effectual *application* of that redemption is limited and determined by the will of man. To Elias such teaching involved a denial of the completeness of Christ's work and offices, it led to an underestimation of the effects of the fall upon man, and therefore to correspondingly low views of the necessity of the Spirit's Almighty work in conversion. ' I do not know,' he writes, ' how those that deny the total corruption of the human nature, and that salvation as to its plan, its performance, its application, is of grace only, can be considered as faithful ministers . . . *Unsound and slight thoughts of the work of the Holy Spirit are entertained by many in these days, and he is grieved thereby.* Is there not a want of perceiving the corruption, obstinacy, and spiritual deadness of man, and the consequent necessity of the Almighty Spirit to enlighten and overcome him ? He opens the eyes of the blind ; subduing the disobedient, making them willing in the day of His power ; yea, He even raises up the spiritually dead ! It is entirely the work of the Holy Ghost to apply to us the free and gracious salvation, planned by the Father in eternity, and executed by the Son in time. Nothing of ours is wanted to complete it . . . *Man, under the fall, is as incapable to apply salvation to himseslf, as to plan and to accomplish it.*'

No one saw the dangers which threatened the visible church from these errors more clearly than Elias. Towards the end of his life he writes—' It is a dark night on the church, the depth of winter, when she is sleepy and ready to die. It is still more awful, if while they are asleep they should think themselves awake, and imagine that they see the sun at midnight ! . . . The watchmen are not very alert and observant. The multitude of enemies that surround the castle walls, bear deceitful colours ; not many of the watchmen know them ! They are for opening the gates to many a hostile regiment ! Oh let it never be said of the Welsh Calvinistic Methodists, " Their watchmen are blind." ' He knew of no remedy for such a situation save a restoration of the truth in its purity.— ' If people are anxious for the favour of God's presence, as the early fathers in the connexion were blessed with, *let them take care that they be of the same principles*, under the guidance of the same Spirit . . . When the Spirit is more fully poured on people, those precious pillars of truth will be raised up out of their dusty holes ; then the things of God shall be spoken in " words taught by the Holy Ghost," and the corrupt reasonings of men will be silenced by the strong light of divine truth. May the Lord restore a pure lip to the ministers, and may the old paths be sought, where the road is good, and may we walk in it ; there is no danger there.'

John Elias died on June 8, 1841. Some 10,000 people attended his funeral at Llanfaes in Anglesey, a multitude of solemn feelings possessing their hearts. 'Ah,' writes Morgan, ' the thought of seeing him no more till the last day ! the day he frequently and seriously dwelt upon in his discourses, with power almost inspired. Oh Mona ! Oh Wales ! Oh ye multitudes of men, how wilt it be with you, when you will next see that most eminent minister ? ' ' Remember them,' commands the Apostle, ' who have spoken unto you the word of God : whose faith follow, considering the end of their conversation. Jesus Christ the same yesterday and to-day, and for ever.' Heb. 13 : 7-8.

PUBLICATIONS

Works by three of the authors recommended by John Elias on another page of this issue have recently been republished by the *Sovereign Grace Book Club.* " *Keeping the Heart,*" by John Flavel, 3/6. " *Songs of Sovereignty,*" Sermons by John Owen, 8/6. " *A Mute Christian, and Apples of Gold,*" by Thomas Brooks, 15/-. Order from the British agent, Mr. T. Watson, 48 Thorncliffe Road, Oxford.

We believe many readers would be glad to have their attention drawn to the following booklets. " *Sound an Alarm,*" the report of a sermon delivered by Dr. D. M. Lloyd-Jones on Isa. 22 : 8-14. Price 6d., from The Bookroom, Westminster Chapel, Buckingham Gate, London, S.W.1. " *How I learnt to love the doctrines of Sovereign Grace,*" by Walter C. Brehaut. Price 3d. This booklet by a minister in the Channel Islands is worthy of a wide circulation. Order from E. J. Harmer, 47 Albion Road, Tunbridge Wells. " *The Puritans and the Doctrine of Election,*" duplicated copies of this lecture given by the Editor, ought to have been received freely by all subscribers. Further copies are available, price 3d.

Man's responsibility for disobedience. ' Is it our *duty* to do what is commanded, without divine assistance ? The granting or withholding such assistance has nothing to do with the consideration of our duty ; whatever God commands, it is our duty to do whether we can or not. God requires nothing of us, that was unreasonable or impossible for us to do in the state we were in before the fall of Adam. And though our condition is changed by the fall, yet God was under no obligation to change or abrogate his law on that account. Our inability to do anything that God requireth of us. is altogether a sinful inability. Divine assistance is not necessary to make obedience to God's commandments, to be our duty. To give that assistance to a sinful creature is an act of sovereign grace.'
—*John Elias.*

A PLEA FOR ZEAL

' *Be zealous* ' (Rev. 3 : 19). This watch-word of Christ, it be
not now a word in season, I know not when ever it was, or will be.
If God should now send through the earth such surveying angels
as Zechariah mentions, chap. 1, could they return any other observation of their travels than this, ' The whole world lies in lukewarmness ' ?   Zeal hath been little practiced, less studied.   Zeal
is everywhere spoken against ; it hath many enemies and few
friends.   The world can no more abide it, than beasts can the
elementary fire.   Oh ! that I had so much zeal as to set it forth in
its colours, that I might regain the decayed credit of it with the
sons of men . . .   He is earnest, or a zealot, whose affections are
passionately disposed ; his love is ever fervent, his desires eager,
his delights ravishing, his hatred deadly, and his grief deep.   This
being the nature of zeal in general, Christian zeal differs from
carnal and worldly chiefly in its causes and objects.   It is a spiritual
heat wrought in the heart of man by the Holy Ghost, improving
the good affections of love, joy, etc., for the furtherance of God's
glory, His word, His house, His saints, and salvation of souls ;
directing the contrary of hatred, anger, grief, etc., towards God's
enemies, the devil, his angels, sin, the world, with the lusts thereof.
A zealot, like David (Psa. 119), has zeal in every affection.   *Love—*
' How do I love thy law, O Lord.'   *Hatred—*' Thine enemies I
hate with a perfect hatred.'   *Joy—*' Thy testimonies are my delight'.
Grief—' Mine eyes gush out rivers of tears . . . because they destroy
thy law ! '   The fervency of the true zealot is in the spirit, not in
show ; for God, not himself ; guided by the word, not by his
humours ; such a man's worth cannot be set forth with the tongues
of men and of angels.

It is good to be zealous in good things, and is it not best in
the best ?   Is there any better than God, or the kingdom of
heaven ?   Is it fitting whatever we do, to do it with all our might ?
(Eccles. 9 : 10).   Only not fitting when we serve God ?   Is mediocrity in all excellent arts excluded, and only to be admitted in
religion ?   And were it not better to be of no religion, than to
be cold or lukewarm in any ?   Is it good to be earnest for a friend,
and cold for the Lord of hosts ?   What aileth the world ?   Is it
afraid, think we, that God can have too much love ?   Ought not
all the springs and brooks of our affection to run into this sea ?
Who, or what can be sufficient for Him, our Maker and Saviour ?
In other objects fear excess ; here no ectasy is high enough.

What makes one Christian differ from another in grace, as
stars do in glory, but zeal ?   All believers have a like precious
faith ; all true Christians have all graces in their seeds ; but the
degrees of them are no way better discerned than by zeal.   All
Christians are the excellent of the earth ; but the zealot surmounteth
them all.   One of these is worth a thousand others, one doth the

work of many ; these are the agents for doing God good service.
There is no standing for any of God's enemies before them ; they
make havoc of their own and others' corruptions.   All difficulties
are but whetstones of their fortitude.   The sluggard saith, ' There
is a lion in the way.'   Tell Samson and David so ; they will the
rather go out to meet them.   Tell Nehemiah of Sanballat ; he
answereth, ' Shall such a man as I fear ? '   Tell Caleb there are
Anakins, and he will say, ' Let us go up at once,' etc.   Let Paul
be told that in every city bonds await him ; he is not only ready
for bonds, but for death.   Tell Luther of enemies in Worms ; he
will go, if all the tiles of the houses were devils.   They that mean
to take the kingdom of God by violence, provide themselves to
go through fire and water and carry their lives in their hands ;
they say to father and mother, ' I know you not,' to carnal counsellors, ' Get you behind me, Satan.'   Zeal is as strong as death,
hot as the coals of Juniper, floods of many waters cannot quench it.

If zeal were not some admirable good, the devil and world
would not so hate it.   Let Festus be the speaker for the rest, for he
speaks what all the rest think ; you know his mad objection, and
Paul's sober answer in that place, Acts 26 : 24. and the like, 2Cor.
5 : 13 ; whether we be mad or sober, it is for God and you.   A
Christian indeed is never right, till he seems to the world to be
beside himself ; Christ's own kindred were afraid of Him.   The
apostles are said to be full of new wine, Acts 2 ; besides, with these
the world is mad, they run at Stephen like mad men, Acts7 :
Nicodemus, and such as he, never offends them.

You know what Ahab laid to the charge of Elijah, with the
apology he made for himself.   This is a stale imputation in ages.
The apostles are said to be troublers of the whole earth.   In the
primitive church all contentions were laid to the martyrs.   True
it is, where zeal is there is opposition, and so consequently troubles.
Christ sets this fire on earth, not as an author, but by accident.
The thief is the author of the fray, though the true man strikes
never so many blows ; the Ahabs of the world trouble Israel, then
complain of Elijah.

Oh, say they, but some discretion would do well.   It is true,
but take withal Calvin's warning to Melancthon, that he affect not
so the name of a moderate man, and listen to such syrens' songs
till he lose his zeal.   I have observed that which the world miscalls
discretion to eat up zeal, as that which they call policy doth wisdom.
The fear of overdoing makes most come too short.   Of the two
extremities we should most fear lukewarmness.   Rather let your
milk boil over than be raw . . .   As this objection will not do, they
fall to right down railing.   ' These puritans, these singular fellows,
unfit for all honest company ! '   With that which most call puritanism I desire to worship God.   For singularity, Christ calls for it,
and presseth and urgeth it.   What singular thing do you ? or what
odd thing do you ?   Shall God's peculiar people do nothing

peculiar ? I believe none shall ever please Christ till they appear odd, strange, and precise men to the common sort. Let him that hath a right ear hear what Christ saith to the churches ; *Be zealous.*

Yea, but by what means shall a Christian attain this fire, and maintain it when he hath gotten it ? Thou mayest fetch it from heaven by thine own prayer, as did Elias and the apostles, men of infirmities as well as thyself. Pray constantly and instantly. Sermons are bellows ordained for this purpose. Let the word dwell richly in thine heart. Excite thy dullness by spiritual hymns. Read or sing the 116th psalm ; and if thou be not zealous, every verse will stick in thy throat. Meditation is another help—Behold the Lord God, especially thy Lord Christ, in His glorious titles and majesty. Consider and reason thus with thyself (O man), canst thou tolerate a sluggard in thy work, if thou be of any spirit thyself ? And shall he that is all spirit (for whom the angels are slow and cold enough) take pleasure in thy drowsy and heavy service ? Even to Judas He saith, ' That thou doest, do quickly ' ; so odious is dullness unto Him. Behold Him as one that seeth thee and knoweth thy works. Behold Him as the beginning of creatures, especially of the new creature. Oh, what love hath He shewed thee in thy redemption ! Out of what misery into what happiness, by what a price, to what end, but that thou shouldest be zealous of good works. Behold Him as a speedy and royal rewarder of His followers. Take thyself into paradise, represent to thyself thy crown, thy throne, thy white robes. Look upon these, and faint if thou canst. Behold, also, He is a consuming fire, a jealous God, hating lukewarmness, not only destroying Sodom with fire and brimstone, and providing Tophet for his enemies, but awakening also his drowsy servants by judgments (as Absalom Joab, by firing his corn), his Israelites by fiery serpents. Whom He loved He chasteneth, and keepeth them in the furnace of fiery trials, till they come to their right temper. He standeth and knocketh. If nothing will arouse us, a time will come when heaven and earth shall burn with fire, and Christ shall come in flaming fire, to render vengeance with fire unquenchable. We, therefore, that know the terror of that day, what manner of persons ought we to be ?

From God turn thine eyes unto man ; set before thee the pillar and cloud of fiery examples, that have led us the way into Canaan. The stories of the Scriptures, the lives of the fathers, the acts and monuments of the church, have special virtue for this effect. If thou canst meet with any living examples, follow them, as they follow Christ, and frequent their company. If thou findest none, let the coldness of the times heat thee, as frosts do fire. Let every indignation make thee zealous, as the ignorance of the monks made Erasmus studious. One way to be rich in times of dearth, is to engross a rare commodity, such as zeal is. Now, if ever ' they have destroyed thy law,' it is now high time to be zealous . . . Consider and emulate the children of this generation, to see how eager every

121

Demas is for worldly promotion. It angered Demosthenes to see a smith earlier at his anvil than he was at his desk.

But here methinks I hear the lukewarm worldling of our times fume and chafe, and ask what needs all this ado for zeal, as if all God's people were not zealous enough. Such as think they are, or can be zealous enough, need no other conviction to be poor, blind, naked, wretched, and pitiful Laodiceans. Fire is ever climbing and aspiring higher ; zeal is ever aiming at that which is before ; carried toward perfection ; thinking meanly of that which is past, and already attained, condemning his unprofitable service, as Calvin in his last will ; this rule tries full conceited Christians.

' What would you have us to do ? We profess, attend church, hear sermons, as Christians ought to do.'—To such God may well say, Let us have some of this zeal at home and in private. God respects the devotions of those whose families, closets, fields, beds, walks do testify of their worship, as well as churches. ' We would have you know, that we are such as have prayers said or read in our families and household ; or else we say some to ourselves at our lying down and uprising ; and what more than that is needed ? ' —First, know that zeal knows no such unmannerly courses as to slubber over a few prayers, while you are dressing and undressing yourselves ; as most do, half asleep half awake. Know further, that such as hold only a certain course of daily duties, as mill-horses their round, out of custom or form, are far from that mettle which is ever going forward, growing from strength to strength, and instant in duties, in season, out of season ; and this says hard to lazy Christians.

' May not we go too far on the right hand ? '—It is true ; but liberality fears covetousness and niggardness more a great deal than prodigality ; so does zeal, lukewarmness, and coldness more than too much heat and forwardness ; the defect is more opposite and dangerous to some virtues than the excess.

' There are but few such, no, not of the better sort you speak of.'—Grant there be any, and zealous emulation seeks the highest examples. He that hath true zeal, will strive to purge himself, as Christ is pure. ' Will you have us run before our neighbours, or live without company ? '—Cowards stand and look who goes first ; soldiers of courage will cast lots for the onset and fore-rank, for desperate services and single combats.

' Some indeed care not whom they offend, they are so harsh and fiery.'—Will true Christianity allow us to bear with any sin ? Can hot iron choose but hiss if cold water be cast on it ? Can a righteous soul choose but vex itself at evil ? Such persons as can listen to profane and filthy speeches, shew what mettle they have for the Lord of hosts.

' All are not by nature of so hot disposition, or so fiery-spirited as others.'—If there be such a dull, phlegmatic creature as hath no life or spirit in anything he goes about, or whom nothing will move ;

he may plead temperament ; and yet grace is above nature. But the best way is, see every man compare his devotion in matters of God with his spirits and mettle in other affairs, wherein his element or delight lies. If the one equal not the other, the fault is not in nature : the oldest man hath memory enough for his money, and the coldest constitution heat enough where it likes.

'Well, our hearts may be good as the best, though we cannot shew it.'—Fire cannot be long smothered, it will either find a vent or go out ; zeal will either find word or deed to express itself withal.

'All have not so much leisure to spend so much time and study about matters of religion ; they have somewhat else to do.'— There are indeed many vanities which distract and divide the mind of worldlings ; but zeal counts one thing needful, to which it makes all other stand by. Is there any so good a husband of his time, that will not steal some hour for his pleasure ? that cannot spare his God and his soul half an hour, morning and evening ? If thou beest not a vain and willing deceiver of thyself and others, deal honestly and plainly with thy soul, try thyself by these few rules ; and if thou judgest thyself to come short of them, amend and 'be zealous.'

The Spirit, knowing that which is spoken to all to be in effect as spoken to none, directs that this message be addressed particularly to the angels, that is ministers, of the churches. . . . As in the time of the Old Testament, the custody of the fire and light was the charge of the priest, so here I observe Christ to lay it upon His ministers, interpreting His rule by His practice : 'Tell the church, tell the angel of the church.' Implying that they should exceed as far the people as angels do men, and that He will reckon with them for the religion of the people, because cold ministers make bold sinners. We therefore, brethren, upon whom it lies to keep life and heat in the devotion of the world, to consume the dross of heresies, that have fallen into the sink of our times ; we that are to make ready our people for the second coming of Christ, is the spirit of Eli, think we, sufficient for us ? What manner of person ought we to be, burning in spirit, fervent in prayer, thundering in preaching, shining in life and conversation ? Why is it then, my brethren, that some of us pray so rarely and so coldly in private (the evils of our times will not out but by frequent fasting and fervent prayer), in public so briefly, so perfunctorily, and feebly, that we scarce have any witnesses of what we say ? Do we love Christ more than ordinary ? Would we give proof of our treble love to Him ? Let us, then, feed His flock with a treble zeal, expressed in prayer, preaching, and living. Let us make it appear to the consciences of all, that the top of our ambition is God's glory ; and that we prefer the winning of souls to the winning of the world.

Chiefly mine affections burn within me for the good of mine own nation. For I must bear it record, it hath knowledge, I would

I could say according to zeal. Where is it in divers places of the land to be seen ? I had almost said, in my haste and heat, there is none that hath zeal, no, not one, there is no courage for the truth ; but that I remember that Elijah was checked for overshooting himself in his too short and quick computation. I hope the Lord hath His fifties amongst us, though but thin sown in comparison of the swarms of church-papists, of profane atheists, key-cold worldlings, and lukewarm professors. Do we think He will ever tolerate us, in the temper we are in ? What is it but a state of neutrality, indifferency, or such mediocrity as will just serve the time, or stand with reputation of neighbours ? But behold, He stands at the door and knocks, by plagues, by the hammer of dearths, discontents, fires, inundations, especially by the word ; His locks are wet with waiting. He hath indeed brooked and borne us a long time. O, before He shakes off the dust of His feet against us, and turn to some other nation more worthy, let us open the door, that He may come in and sup with us.

The Lord give us not only understanding, but zeal in all things ; He baptize us with fire ; He breathe on us, and inspire into us the Spirit of life and power. So shall we run the ways of His commandments.

Samuel Ward, Town preacher at Ipswich, 1603-1639.

'Ye should earnestly contend for the faith which was once delivered unto the saints.' (Jude 3). The contention to which Jude exhorts these Christians is an eminent and extraordinary one ; the word contend means, to strive, to fight, to labour fervently ; it is a contention which requires all their strength and utmost force, they are to be as those who fought for their lives, nay, that which was dearer than life itself, even the life of their souls. This imports a serious and weighty cause and ground for contention. Men account not trifles worth any, much less vehement strife. It is for the faith that we must contend vigorously, fervently, with all our might 2 Tim. 4 : 5-7. A lazy, slender, slight contention will not serve the turn. Lukewarmness neither pleases our Captain, nor prevails over our adversary. Holy fervour is never so seemly as in contending for a holy faith. Indifference better becomes our worldly contentions between man and man, than spiritual contentions between men and devils. We must contend for the faith against error universally, impartially, for every doctrine of faith, and against every opposite error. We must contend for discountenanced, disowned, persecuted, faith and take it in doors when the most would have it laid in the streets, and give it entertainment when it is death to harbour it. We must contend for the faith constantly. We must never give over our conflict as long as one enemy is left. We must be faithful to the death if we expect a crown of life. Moderation is not always commendable. Moderation that hinders a real and earnest contending for the faith, is no better than loathsome lukewarmness. I fear there is much neutrality, sinful halting and indifference gilded over with the name moderation. He who is not for Christ is against Him. There may be a sinful, damnable moderation. Following Christ afar off in this world is no sign that we shall be near Him in the next. No man will be afraid of being too professed a Christian at the day of judgment, or will think he has lost too much for Christ when he is to presently lose all things by death. If the time wherein we live be a night of profaneness, it is our duty the more brightly to shine as lights. A Christian should be best when the times are worst. Cursed be that patience that can see error and say nothing. The Apostle saith that the mouths of decievers are to be stopped, and gainsayers must be convinced. I know not how it comes to pass, but among many the opposing of seducers is either accounted bitter or needless ; and it is still the policy of Satan not to suffer a sword in Israel. But if there be ' damnable heresies,' 2 Pet. 2 : 1, I see not but there may be a damnable silence in those who should oppose them. Everyone must give account for his idle words, and for his idle silence.

The goodness of any cause exempts it not from opposition. What more precious than faith, and what more opposed ? Hatred is ever the companion of truth. The reason of Satan's peculiar rage against the saints, is because they have the faith delivered to them which is the bane and battery of his kingdom ; that truth which is an antidote against his poison ; that doctrine which discovers his deeds of darkness. Satan's policy is ever to disarm a place of the Word. But this faith is ' once delivered,' that is firmly irrevocably delivered. It shall ever be, it shall never be quite taken away from the church, it endures for ever. The doctrine of faith shall never cease in the world. It is the candle that all the winds of Hell shall never blow out, a flame that all the waters of trouble can never extinguish. Thus it is called the eternal gospel, Rev. 14, never to be destroyed. It is as easy for enemies to pluck the sun out of the firmament, as this faith out of the church. The whole power and policy of Hell have been employed for that purpose sixteen hundred years. Could they have done it, it had been done long before now. Then let us earnestly contend for this faith once delivered to the saints.

William Jenkyn on Jude.

Jenkyn, a mighty puritan divine, died in prison in London on Jan. 19, 1685. We are told that when the news reached the court, a nobleman in waiting had the courage to tell James II, " May it please your majesty, Jenkyn has got his liberty." Upon which he asked with surprise " Aye, who gave it him ? " The nobleman replied, " A greater than your majesty, the King of Kings."

MORAL INABILITY OF MAN
John Elias.

There is much confusion respecting man's ability, or inability, though the Scriptures are clear on the subject. In order to shew the truth on this point, I will make some observations on what the Scripture states respecting man's weakness, in consequence of sin, to spiritual and holy things, and then on the nature of his inability.

The Holy Scriptures plainly declare, that man, in his fallen state, is WEAK, or without strength for spiritual things, "For when we were yet without strength, in due time Christ died for the ungodly." Rom. v. 6. So the Father viewed sinners, when he gave his son and sent him to redeem them ; so Christ considered men, by coming to live and die for them : and so the Holy Ghost finds them, when he calls sinners to Christ, and applies salvation to them. For what things are they then incapable ? They can do many things as men ; yet there are some things, and those of the greatest importance, yea all the things that belong to their peace, which they cannot do.

They cannot be *subject* to the law of God ; they cannot give that obedience which he requires, to *love* him with all their heart, and obey him at all times and in all things. So it is evident they cannot please God ; for none can please him, without being subject to his law. Rom. viii. 7, 8. And as they cannot please God, they cannot be saved ; for those that displease him, are under his wrath and indignation. Rom. viii. 3 ; Ps. xxii. 29 ; vii. 11. Though God did, in his infinite mercy, send his Son to die for sinners, so that whosoever believeth in him, shall not perish, yet none can *go* to Christ, and believe in him, and receive life. John iii. 16 ; 1 Tim. i. 15 ; John vi. 44. They cannot *understand* the Gospel, or the things of the Spirit ; neither can they think correctly of the things of God, however correctly explained ; the "natural man cannot know them." 1 Cor. ii. 14 ; 2 Cor. iii. 5. They cannot either turn or change themselves, neither believe nor repent. In a word, man, without Christ, can do nothing holy ; he is as incapable of acting in a holy manner, as a body without soul is in a natural manner. Jer. xiii. 23 ; Acts v. 31 ; xxvi. 18 ; John v. 25 ; 2 Tim. ii. 25 ; Eph. i. 19, 20 ; Phil. i. 29 ; John xv. 5. Man, under the fall, is as incapable to *apply* salvation to himself, as to plan and to accomplish it. There is as much need of the Spirit to apply salvation, as of the Mediator to work it out ; though he became the Author of eternal salvation unto all them that obey him. Heb. v. 9. Yet no one *will* nor can obey him, except the Spirit, in his infinite and overcoming power, works in him. The grace of God appears as clear in turning man, giving faith and repentance to him, as in redeeming him on the cross. Man is not only incapable of, but *opposed* to, the application of salvation. He has no inclination to come to Christ, nor to live under his government ; incapable and unwilling to be made willing and obedient. John v. 40 ; Ps.

lxxxi. 11 ; Math. xxiii. 37 ; Luke xix. 14, 27. We cannot shew man's miserable state, without setting forth his inability to all spiritual things ; for there is a great degree of man's misery in this. And we cannot, without this, exhibit the glorious plan of salvation, by grace, especially the work of the Spirit in applying it. Though salvation is so free and complete, and so clearly set forth in the Gospel ; and though it is preached in the most gifted, clear, and winning manner, and though the danger of neglecting it, and the misery of those that reject it, be set forth in a most lively and awakening way ; yet man will not, neither can he, of himself, receive or use it!

Now we will make a few observations on the NATURE of man's inability to holy and spiritual things.

Though man fell awfully in Eden, by disobeying and breaking God's covenant, yet he did not cease to be man ; he still has the essential properties of man though he fell, the body and all its members and senses ; the soul and all it faculties : he is, as a reasonable creature, yet accountable to God for all his conduct. The Lord did not give up his right to require obedience from man, and his obligations to obey God, did not cease.

But, when man broke the covenant, he lost the peace of God, and he lost his holy image also, and in this he *lost* the principle and holy disposition, the root of good works, so that there is in no man under the fall, the nature, principle, or disposition to do any spiritual good ; there is no principle, a holy operation, within him ; so he is dead in sin. Eph. ii. 1 ; Col. ii. 13. Not only is man destitute of a nature, principle, and a disposition to act in a holy manner—but " his heart is fully set in him to *do* evil ; the carnal mind is enmity against God." The soul is under the dominion of a nature and disposition that is sinful and hostile to God and every good. Eccles. viii. 11 ; Jer. xvii. 9 ; Gen. vi. 5 ; Rom. viii. 7 ; i. 30.

The moral inability is not less because there is no want of natural ability, members, senses, or faculties in man ; the need of a nature, principle, and disposition to act in a holy manner, is as great an inability to it as if there was a want of members or faculties to operate in a natural manner. As the body cannot act without the soul, so the soul cannot do any thing that is holy without the divine nature. 2 Pet. i. 4. As the eye cannot behold any thing without the humour, so the soul cannot act in a holy manner, though possessed of all the faculties, without a holy principle and disposition to do so. A spiritual life is as necessary to act in a holy manner, as natural life is for its actions. There is no spiritual life but in Christ, "He is our life, without him we can do nothing." Col. iii. 4 ; John xv. 5.

All the faculties of the soul are unable to act in a holy manner, the one as well as the other, and entirely opposed to every thing that is godly. The understanding is dark, it cannot perceive the things of God ; the will is obstinate, so man will not come to

Christ ; the affections are earthly and carnal—the conscience is corrupt. 1 Cor. ii. 14 ; John v. 40 ; 2 Tim. iii. 4 ; Tit. i. 15. So a man must be regenerated, risen, yea created anew, in order to act and live in a holy manner. John iii. 3 ; 2 Cor. v. 17 ; Eph. ii. 1. For he has entirely lost all power to spiritual and divine things. It is not the ceasing of action to holy things, as it is with men in sleep ; and it is not the absence of strength in some part, as with men in complaints ; but the man is altogether without strength and inclination to perform holy things in a spiritual and godly manner ; he is dead ! He is unable to be willing, and unwilling to be able to do what is good. The godly man has experienced his inability to holy things ; there is no need to say much to prove this to him. But the natural man does not feel his weakness, neither does he receive the things the Spirit declares respecting him.

There is great danger to hear, read, and converse, in an unfeeling and unsuitable manner, on human inability. There is a danger of mistaking, or drawing INFERENCES from this doctrine, respecting man's weakness to holy things.

We ought to be on our guard, lest we think that man's inability should make him *excusable* in his sin, or in neglecting his duties, or the great salvation. He, by his inability, does not become unaccountable to God. The Lord's authority to demand obedience from man, and man's obligations to obey his Maker, are the same. Our disobedience is not less sinful, because we are naturally sinners ; and our sins are not less aggravating, on account of our strong inclinations to sin ; and our vileness is not less evil, because of our strong opposition to be holy. Let us beware lest we imagine that it is not sinful for us to be sinners. We should also beware that as man is unable to change his nature, he is therefore excusable in living in his sin ; it is no excuse whatever to him, neither does it lessen his fault at all—for he delights in his sin, and hates to be kept from it. He does not like to live a godly life, nor to be made willing and able. He contends with his Master, opposes his Spirit, and rejects his invitation. Gen. vi. 3 ; Acts vii. 51 ; Prov. i. 24, 25.

We ought to take care, on the other hand, lest, by proving that it is not the need of members, senses, or faculties, which is man's inability to act in a spiritual manner, we should set forth that weakness as something *small,* and that man may remove it by some endeavour of his own ; or that ministers may overcome it by strong reasons, awful, alarming threatenings, and winning, captivating invitations ; and by that disregard and lose sight of the truth respecting the Spirit's work in man's salvation. There is danger lest ministers and people should fail in observing the need of the Holy Ghost working by his grace and infinite strength in man's salvation. There is as much need of his applying it, as of the Son's accomplishing it, as already observed. There is room to fear that preachers and hearers grieve the Holy Spirit, by losing sight of this ; and are, consesquently, left destitute of his powerful influences and operations, because they do not seriously consider, nor humbly acknowledge, the necessity of the Spirit working powerfully by the ministry of the Word for man's salvation.

The application of salvation is as entirely of God as its plan ; it is all of God, and the glory altogether belongs to him for ever, and he shall have it from the redeemed most freely throughout eternity.

Bibliography. Memoir of John Elias, by Edward Morgan. Letters and Essays of John Elias, edited by Morgan. Obtainable from The Evangelical Library, 78a Chiltern Street, London, W.1. Members of the Library may receive books by post.

JOHN KNOX AND THE DOCTRINE OF PREDESTINATION

" We should not only call to mind the histories of ancient times, but also we should diligently mark what notable works God hath wrought, even in this our age."—Knox, 1565.

Neglect of church history always leads to serious consequences ; it leads to many assumptions being taken for granted which would be utterly discredited if viewed in the light of historical facts. A most important instance of such a false assumption is the prevailing opinion that the so called evangelical faith to-day is the same as the faith so powerfully established by God in Britain in the sixteenth century. No more suitable witness could be summoned to expose this opinion than Knox, for in him were combined in the most eminent degree the qualities which shone in the lives of other British Reformers. Not as friendly partisan but as a Professor of history, Froude of Oxford wrote : " No grander figure can be found, in the entire history of the Reformation in this island, than that of Knox . . . but for whom the Reformation would have been overthrown among ourselves ; for the spirit which Knox created saved Scotland ; and if Scotland had been Catholic again, neither the wisdom of Elizabeth's ministers, nor the teaching of her bishops, nor her own chicaneries, would have preserved England from revolution."

When Knox was born in Scotland in 1504 the land was under the strong and uncontested tyranny of Romanism ; by his death in 1572 there was in existence a militant visible church, deeply instructed in the truth, and already accomplishing its task of transforming the nation into a people characterised by piety and godliness. Carlyle says, " This that Knox did for his nation we may really call a resurrection as from death." Knox entered the University of Glasgow in 1521, and was ordained in the Church of Rome before 1530. It appears his conversion to the Gospel took place between 1535 and 1542—the year when he professed himself a Protestant. The light of Reformed doctrine had been lit in Scotland in 1528 by the martyrdom of Patrick Hamilton ; from then till the death of James V in 1542 the growing body of believers were exposed to almost constant persecution. In the early years of the regency of the Earl of Arran (the heir to the throne being the infant Mary Stuart) the Reformation made considerable progress, aided at first by his patronage, and especially by the return of Wishart from England in 1544. But Wishart was martyred in 1546, and the following year Knox and others who had taken refuge in St. Andrew's Castle were forced to capitulate to the besieging French forces. The triumph of Romanism appeared secured. For the following two years Knox was a slave chained to the oars of a French galley. The fine treatise which he was later to write on prayer was largely the outcome of his experience during that confinement. From his liberation in February 1549 till January 1554, Knox was in England, inspiring the English Reformers by his zeal, and arousing many parts of the countryside by his fiery preaching. He refused the Bishopric of Rochester, but as chaplain to Edward VI he exerted a wide influence.

The next four years, apart from a temporary visit to Scotland (autumn 1555 - June, 1556), Knox spent largely with Calvin at Geneva, finding that city to be what he termed " the most perfect school of Christ that ever was on the earth since the days of the Apostles." When Knox finally returned to Scotland in 1559, being then fifty-four years old, the most vital part of his life's work still lay before him. Matters were in a critical state. The French Queen-mother (who had replaced Arran in the regency in 1554) had openly avowed her determination to suppress the Reformation, and behind her was the support of the French throne and army. The believers, although now greatly increased in number and including in their ranks many of the nobility, had no recognised standards of discipline and doctrine ; moreover ; they had for several years been leaderless. The Lord had prepared Knox for this very hour. The land soon shook under the power of his preaching— " Wouldst thou, O Scotland ! have a king to reign over thee in justice, equity, and mercy ? Subject thou thyself to the Lord thy God, obey his commandments, and magnify thou the word that calleth unto thee, ' This is the way, walk in it ' (Isa. 30), and if thou wilt not, flatter not thyself ; the same justice remains this day in God to punish thee, Scotland, and thee Edinburgh especially, which before punished the land of Judah, and the city of Jerusalem. Every realm or nation, saith the prophet Jeremiah, that likewise offendeth, shall be likewise punished " (Jer. 9). " The voice of this one man," wrote a contemporary, " is able in an hour to put more life in us than six hundred trumpets continually blustering in our ears." None were spared his solemn exhortations—" I come, in the name of Jesus Christ," he declared to the Queen Regent, " affirming that the religion which ye maintain is damnable idolatrie." On another occasion he was ready to tell the fashionable and gaily dressed ladies-in-waiting at Mary Stuart's court, that death would make a fine havoc with all their finery ! Such authority was the fruit of much wrestling with God in prayer ; which even the Queen Regent recognised when upon a particular occasion she said she was more afraid of his prayers than of an army of ten thousand men.

The history and incessant conflict of the years 1559-1572 is too detailed to relate here. Suffice it to let Knox's part be summarised by Froude : " His was the voice wh.ch taught the peasant of the Lothians that he was a free man, the equal in the sight of God with the proudest peer or prelate that had trampled on his forefathers. He was the one antagonist whom Mary Stuart could not soften nor Maitland deceive ; he it was that raised the poor Commons of his country into a stern and rugged people whom neither king, noble, nor priest could force again to submit to tyranny." Knox's zeal was unabated till the last. Towards the close he was so worn with incessant toil that he had to be " lifted up to the pulpit, where he was obliged to lean at his first entrance ; but before he had done his sermon he was so active and vigorous, that he was like to beat the pulpit to pieces, and fly out of it." " He died in the sixty-seventh year of his age," writes M'Crie, " not so much oppressed with years as worn out and exhausted by his extraordinary labours of body and mind. Few men ever were exposed to more dangers, or underwent such hardships. From the time that the standard of truth was first raised by him in his native country, till it dropped from his hands at death, Knox never shrunk from danger—never consulted his own ease or advantage—never entered into any compromise with the enemy—never was bribed or frightened into cowardly silence ; but keeping his eye singly and steadily fixed on the advancement of religion and liberty, supported throughout the character of the Reformer of Scotland."

Some of the most notable of his parting words and dying prayers were these—" The time is approaching for which I have long thirsted, wherein I shall be with my Saviour for ever ; and now, God is my witness, that I have taught nothing but the true and solid doctrines of the Gospel. I am not ignorant that men have blamed me, and yet do blame my too great rigour and severity : but God knoweth, that in my heart I never hated the persons of those against whom I thundered God's judgments : I did only hate their sins, and laboured to gain them to Christ . . . Come Lord Jesus, sweet Jesus ! Grant true pastors to thy church, that purity of doctrine may be retained. Grant us Lord, the perfect hatred of sin, both by the evidences of thy wrath and mercy." " In this manner," writes a contemporary, " departed this man of God : the light of Scotland, the comfort of the Church within the same, the mirror of godliness, and pattern and example of all true ministers, in purity of life, soundness of doctrine, and boldness in reproving of wickedness ; one that cared not for favour of men, how great so ever they were."

The principal and most important theological work of John Knox, from which we are about to quote, was his treatise on Predestination—a work that extends to some 450 pages. This book was the fulfilment of a promise made to the brethren in Scotland by Knox during his exile. After warning them by letter of the appearance of some sectaries who were questioning the absolute sovereignty of God in salvation, and of the serious consequences involved, Knox wrote—" The fountain of this their damnable error (which is, that in God they can acknowledge no justice except that which their foolish brain is able to comprehend), at more opportunity, God willing, we shall entreat." His great treatise on the subject appeared in 1560 ; we can do no more than give some extracts from the preface.

Knox commences by speaking of the effects of God having offered the great and infinite benefit of his truth to the world at that time. " After darkness light has appeared," yet the result has been, he says, " that vice, cruelty and blasphemies, have so abounded that the imprudent beholder of such confusion is given occasion to prefer the darkness of superstition which before time did reign, to the light of salvation, which God of his great mercy has now of late years offered again to the unthankful world." Why, asks Knox, should the preaching of righteousness by faith be the occasion of sin ?   Why should the preaching of grace inflame men with rage and cruelty ?   Why, when God's glory is declared should man blaspheme against it ?   The natural man cannot perceive why such confusion should follow God's Word, a great number denying it, while only a few embrace it with reverence.   These same effects followed the preaching of Christ and the apostles as well as ours, Knox continues, therefore they ought to be the occasion for us more steadfastly to cleave to the truth.   Then coming to his point, he boldly declares the reason why such enmity and disorder was stirred by the preaching of the Reformers.   " As Satan ever from the beginning has declared himself an enemy to the free grace and undeserved love of God, so has he now in these last and corrupted days, most furiously raged against that doctrine, which attributes all the praise and glory of our redemption to the eternal love and undeserved grace of God alone.   Eph. 2 : 8.

" By what means Satan first drew mankind from the obedience of God the Scripture doth witness.   Namely, by pouring into their hearts that poison—that God did not love them . . .   This same practice Satan ever from the beginning has used, to infect the the Church with all kinds of heresy ; as the writings of Moses, of the prophets, of the apostles and of the godly in the primitive Church do plainly witness.

"But alas! to such blasphemy the devil never did draw mankind as now of late days, in which no small number are become so bold, so impudent and so irreverent that they fear not openly to affirm God to be unjust, if he in his eternal counsel has elected more of one sort of men than another, to life everlasting in Christ Jesus our Lord." The opposition to this doctrine of predestination which has of late become manifested, he proceeds, is the cause of his undertaking this written work. "But lest that some should think that my labours might have been bestowed in some other exercise, I thought it expedient to admonish all my brethren, and charitably to require of them *not to esteem the matter to be of small weight and importance.* For seeing that God's free grace is openly impugned and disdainfully refused, I judge it the duty of every man that looks for life everlasting, to give his confession to Christ Jesus, whose glory is by these blasphemers, to the utmost of their power, suppressed.

"Some do think that because the reason of man cannot attain the understanding how God shall be just, making in his Counsel this diversity of mankind, that therefore it were better to keep silence in all such mysteries . . . I willingly confess that all curiosity ought to be avoided . . . But yet, I say, that the doctrine of God's eternal predestination is so necessary to the church of God, that without the same, faith can neither be truly taught, nor surely established ; man can never be brought to true humility and knowledge of himself, neither yet can he be ravished in admiration of God's eternal goodness, and so moved to praise him aright.

"And therefore, we fear not to affirm that, even as it is necessary that we brought to unfeigned humility, and that we be brought to praise him for his free grace received, that true faith be established in our hearts ; so also is the doctrine of God's eternal predestination necessary. For first, there is no way more proper to build and establish faith, than when we hear and undoubtedly do believe that our election, which the Spirit of God doth seal in our hearts, consists not in ourselves, but in the eternal and immutable good pleasure of God. And that in such firmness that it cannot be overthrown, neither by the raging storms of the world, nor by the assaults of Satan, neither yet by the wavering and weakness of our own flesh. Then only is our salvation in assurance, when we find the cause of the same in the bosom and counsel of God.

" . . . Unless the very cause of our faith be known our joy and comfort cannot be full. For if we shall think that we believe and have embraced Christ Jesus preached, because our understandings are better than the understanding of others, and because we have a better inclination, and are by nature more tractable than the common sort of men, Satan, I say, can easily overthrow all comfort builded upon so weak a ground." For Knox goes on to show that true believers are so changeable in heart and feelings that, though once zealous for godliness, they can be soon overcome by disobedience, temptation, and barrenness. " Therefore, I say, that except our comfort be grounded upon that foundation, which never can be moved, it is not perfect. And that ground is this ; that when we understand, we now believe in Christ Jesus, because we were ordained before the beginning of all times to believe in him ; as in him we were elected to the enjoyment of eternal life (Rom. 8 : 29 ; Eph. 1 : 4) ; then is our faith assuredly grounded, and that because the gifts and vocations of God are without repentance, and he is faithful that hath called us. (2 Thess 2 : 13 ; 2 Pet. 1 : 2-20 ; Rom. 11 : 29).

" Howsoever we are changeable, yet is God in his counsel stable and immutable ; yea, how weak, how feeble, how dull soever we are, yet is there nothing in us (even when we are in our own judgment most destitute of the Spirit of God) which he did not see to be in us before we were formed in the womb, yea, and before the beginning of all times. Which imperfections, infirmities and dullness, as they did not stop his mercy to elect us in Christ Jesus, so can they not compel him now to refuse us. And from that fountain doth flow this our joy, that with the apostle we are bold to cry, " Who is able to separate us from the love of God, which is in Christ Jesus ? " Rom. 8. For seeing that the Father who has given us for a peculiar inheritance to his only Son, is so mighty that out of his hand none is able to take us away ; what danger can be so great, what sin so grievous, or what desperation so deep, that is able to devour us ! . . . The comfort of this do none feel except the chosen children of God, and that in the day when man's justice fails and the battle of their conscience is most grievous and fearful. Therefore, as faith springs from election, so it is established by the true knowledge of that doctrine only, which this day is most furiously oppugned by those who do not understand the same.

" And from that same doctrine flows the very matter of true humility. For while we behold the condition of those whom nature has made equal, to be so far diverse the one from the other, it is impossible but that the children of God in their own hearts unfeignedly be humbled. For whithersoever they shall direct their eyes, they shall behold fearful examples of blindness, and of such iniquity as all men justly ought to abhor ; but when they consider themselves to be sanctified in the midst of so wicked a generation, from what fountain can they say that this proceeds ? Who has illuminated their eyes while others abide in darkness ? Who doth bridle their affections, while others do follow the same to perdition ? If they say nature hath done it, their own conscience shall convict them ; for nature hath made us all equal—by nature are we the children of wrath, even as others (Eph. 2). If they say education, reason, or their own study, common experience shall declare their vanity. For, how many have been nourished in virtue, and yet become most filthy in life! And by the contrary, how many have long remained without all virtuous education, and yet in the end have attained to God's favour! And therefore we say that such as attribute anything to themselves in the grace of their election, have not learnt to give to God the honour which to him appertains, because they do not freely confess what makes them to differ from others.

" Such as cannot abide the mention of God's eternal election," Knox concludes, " can never be rightly humbled nor thankful, for they cannot acknowledge that God according to the good pleasure of his eternal counsel, has made separation betwixt those who fell into equal perdition, as touching the offence and sin committed. Such as desire this article to be buried in silence, and would that men should teach and believe that the grace of God's election is common unto all—but that one receives it and another receives it not, proceeds either from the obedience or disobedience of man —such deceive themselves and are unthankful and injurious unto God. For as long as they see not that true faith and salvation spring from election, and are the gift of God, and are not of ourselves—so long are they deceived and remain in error (Eph. 2 : 8). And what can be more injurious unto God's free grace than to affirm that he gives no more to one than to another ; seeing that the whole Scriptures do plainly teach that we have nothing which we have not received of free grace and mercy, and not of our works, nor of anything in us, lest any man should boast.

" And therefore let wicked men rage as they list, we will not be ashamed to confess always, that grace only makes difference betwixt us and the rest of the world. And further, we fear not to affirm, that such as feel not that comfort inwardly in their conscience, can never be thankful to God, neither yet willing to be subject to his eternal counsel ; which is the only cause that these wicked men most irreverently do storm and rage against that doctrine which they do not understand. Let us, dear brethren, be assured, that none other doctrine doth establish faith or make men humble and thankful unto God. And, finally, that none other doctrine makes man careful to obey God according to his commandment, but that doctrine only which so spoils man of all power and virtue, that no portion of his salvation consists within himself ; to the end that the whole praise of our redemption may be referred to Christ Jesus alone ; whom the Father, of very love, has given to death for the deliverance of his body, which is the Church, to which he was appointed Head before the beginning of all times. (1 Cor. 1 : 30 ; 1 John 4 : 10 ; Eph. 1 : 22). To Him, therefore, with the Father and Holy Ghost, be all praise and glory for ever and ever."

FOR WHOM CHRIST DIED

C. H. Spurgeon.

Now, you are aware that there are different theories of Redemption. All Christians hold that Christ died to redeem, but all Christians do not teach the same redemption. We differ as to the nature of atonement, and as to the design of redemption. For instance, the Arminian holds that Christ, when He died, did not die with an intent to save any particular person; and they teach that Christ's death does not in itself secure, beyond doubt, the salvation of any one man living. They believe that Christ died to make the salvation of all men possible, and that by the doing of something else, any man who pleases may attain unto eternal life; consequently, they are obliged to hold that if man's will would not give way and voluntarily surrender to grace, then Christ's atonement would be unavailing. They hold that there was no particularity and speciality in the death of Christ. Christ died, according to them, as much for Judas in hell as for Peter who mounted to heaven. They believe that for those who are consigned to eternal fire, there was as true and real a redemption made as for those who now stand before the throne of the most High. Now WE believe no such thing. We hold that Christ, when He died, had an object in view, and that object will most assuredly, and beyond a doubt, be accomplished. We measure the design of Christ's death by the effect of it. If any one asks us, "What did Christ design to do by His death?" we answer that question by asking him another—"What has Christ done, or what will Christ do by His death?" For we declare that the measure of the effect of Christ's love, is the measure of the design of it. We cannot so belie our reason as to think that the intention of Almighty God could be frustrated, or that the design of so great a thing as the atonement, can by any way whatever, be missed. We hold—we are not afraid to say what we believe—that Christ came into this world with the intention of saving "a multitude which no man can number"; *and we believe that as the result of this, every person for whom He died must, beyond the shadow of a doubt, be cleansed from sin, and stand, washed in blood, before the Father's throne.*

The greatness of Christ's redemption may be measured by the EXTENT OF THE DESIGN OF IT. He gave His life a "ransom for many." We are often told that we limit the atonement of Christ, because we say that Christ has not made a satisfaction for all men, or all men would be saved. Now, our reply to this is, that, on the other hand, our opponents limit it: we do not. The Arminians say, Christ died for all men. Ask them what they mean by it. Did Christ die so as to secure the salvation of all men? They say, "No, certainly not." We ask them the next question—Did Christ die so as to secure the salvation of any man in particular? They answer "No." They are obliged to admit this, if they are consistent. They say "No; Christ has died that any man may be saved if"—and then follow certain conditions of salvation. Now, who is it that limits the death of

Christ ? Why, you. You say that Christ did not die so as to infallibly secure the salvation of anybody. We beg your pardon, when you say we limit Christ's death ; we say, " No, my dear sir, it is you that do it." We say Christ so died that He infallibly secured the salvation of a multitude that no man can number, who through Christ's death not only may be saved, but are saved, must be saved, and cannot by any possibility run the hazard of being anything but saved. You are welcome to your atonement ; you may keep it. We will never renounce ours for the sake of it.

EXPOSITION BY C. H. SPURGEON

Isaiah LXIV.

Verse 1. *Oh that thou wouldest rend the heavens,*

God's ancient people were in great trouble, and the prophet saw no way out of their perplexity ; but God can make a way of escape where there is not one, he can rend even heaven itself, if need be, in order to deliver his saints. Therefore, the prophet, or the people pray, " Oh that thou wouldest rend the heavens,"—

1. *That thou wouldest come down,*

" Come down thyself, great God, in all the majesty of thy glory ; burst through the firmament, and appear in divine splendour! "

1. *That the mountains might flow down at thy presence,*

The eternal hills are made to melt at the touch of God's foot. Mountains are the things that are last to move ; but God moves them when he once comes near. How often we forget omnipotence! That is a factor we are too apt to leave out of our calculations ; and yet, my brethren, omnipotence is at the back of all our feebleness, when that feebleness is with the truth and the right, and is engaged in the service of God. If the Lord's presence is manifested, even the mountains will flow down, as we read in Michah's prophecy, " For, behold, the Lord cometh forth out of his place, and will come down, and tread upon the high places of the earth. And the mountains shall be molten under him, and the valleys shall be cleft, as wax before the fire, and as the waters that are poured down a steep place."

2, 3. *As when the melting fire burneth, the fire causeth the waters to boil, to make thy name known to thine adversaries, that the nations may tremble at thy presence! When thou didst terrible things which we looked not for, thou cames down, the mountains flowed down at thy presence.*

Where God is, everything begins to melt. He touches the mountains, and makes them boil over with lava, like volcanoes in action ; at his touch the very sea begins to boil with the fervent heat of divine power. Then, when these wonderful results are perceived, even God's enemies are compelled to say, " This is the finger of God ;" and they tremble at his presence. We never know, brethren, what great things God will do, as we do not know all that he can do ; but we do believe that all things are possible to the Omnipotent Jehovah. When he brings his reserve forces into the field, the battle is a short one.

" When thou didst terrible things which we looked not for, thou camest down, the mountains flowed down at thy presence." It was so when Sennacherib, in Isaiah's day, besieged the city of Jerusalem. There was, apparently, no way of escape from the stupendous hordes of the mighty monarch ; but the angel of the Lord smote a hundred and eighty-five thousand of them in one night, and utterly overthrew them. God has but to appear in his terrible power, and his adversaries tremble at his presence, or are destoyed in an instant.

4. *For since the beginning of the world men have not heard, nor perceived by the ear, neither hath the eye seen, O God, beside thee, what he hath prepared for him that waiteth for him.*

The unexpected is always happening. God interposes in a way which we never thought of. Even if we have been listening for his footstep, we have not heard the sound of it ; if we have been watching for his coming, we have not seen his approach. God alone knows all that he will do.
"He in the thickest darkness dwells ; "
but out of that darkness he brings forth purposes of light and brightness to completely amaze his servants. " Ah! " says one, " but is he not long doing it ? " No, no ; it is our impatience that makes us think so, but the Lord never really delays.

5. *Thou meetest him that rejoiceth and worketh righteousness,*

God comes to meet us before we get to him, and then there is a blessed meeting: " Thou meetest him that rejoiceth and worketh righteousness." If you do right, God will meet you ; but he will meet you much sooner if you can rejoice at the same time, for there is no service for God that is so acceptable to him as the service that is done with delight: " Thou meetest him that rejoiceth and worketh righteousness." When we are glad to serve God, when we take a delight in suffering for his name's sake, then God will come and meet us for certain. We need not think that, under such circumstances, he will let us stand alone: " Thou meetest him that rejoiceth and worketh righteousness."

5. *Those that remember thee in thy ways:*

If you remember God, he will certainly remember you. The fact that you are thinking of him is proof positive that the Lord has thoughts of love towards you.

5. *Behold, thou art wroth ; for we have sinned: in those is continuance, and we shall be saved.*

God's wrath has no continuance in it towards his own people ; he soon makes it to pass away from them. His anger may endure for a night ; but his mercy cometh in the morning. His own word is, " For a small moment have I forsaken thee ; but with great mercies will I gather thee. In a little wrath I hid my face from thee for a moment ; but with everlasting kindness will I have mercy on thee, saith the Lord thy Redeemer." The Lord has a rod in his hand ; but the scourging of his own children does not last long. It is a rod, mark you, not an axe that brings death. But his mercy, his goodness, the purposes of his grace are perpetual: " In those is continuance, and we shall be saved."

Now comes a very mournful passage. You have read some of the lamentations of Jeremiah ; here is one of the lamentations of Isaiah. He lived to see his country in a very sad condition. Perhaps this was the state of affairs when Sennacherib invaded the land.

6. *But we are all as an unclean thing, and all our righteousnesses are as filthy rags ;*

If this is true of our righteousnesses, what must our sins be ? If even our righteousnesses are as filthy rags, where shall we find a metaphor to describe our sins ?

6. *And we all do fade as a leaf ; and our iniquities, like the wind, have taken us away.*

This does not allude to our mortality, but to our sin: " We all do fade as a leaf ; and our iniquities, like the wind, have taken us away." We are not like the green leaf on the tree ; we may seem to be so for a moment, but very soon our righteousness fades like a withered leaf ; and, in consequence, our iniquities, like the wind which bears the withered leaves from the bough, carry us away. This is what we all are by nature ; this is what the people were in Isaiah's day, the whole nation seemed to be unholy, its outwardly righteous men were not really righteous, its ministers were not truthful, its magistrates were not honest, and even the professors of purity were at heart immoral.

7. *And there is none that calleth upon thy name, that stirreth up himself to take hold of thee:*

We have not come quite to that condition yet ; there are still some who stir themselves up to take hold upon God, and who call upon his name. We are not left in so sad a state as the favoured nation was in Isaiah's days. It is a terrible thing when intercession fails ; perhaps the dark day that will mark the world's final doom will be a day unwhitened by prayer. Certainly, while prayer remains, the world is blessed ; but when prayer shall cease, when that divine disinfectant is taken away from this poor lazar-house, then the pestilence of sin will rage and destroy most terribly. It was so in the prophet's day: " There is none that calleth upon thy name, that stirreth up himself to take hold of thee."

7, 8. *For thou hast hid thy face from us, and hast consumed us, because of our iniquities. But now, O Lord, thou art our father ;*

The prophet himself begins to plead with God. Jehovah was known as the God of the children of Abraham ; he was not recognised as the God of the Assyrian, Sennacherib worshipped Nisroch as his god: " But now, O Jehovah, thou art our father."

8, 9. *We are the clay, and thou our potter ; and we all are the work of thy hand. Be not wroth very sore, O Lord, neither remember iniquity for ever: behold, see, we beseech thee, we, are all thy people.*

Isaiah could plead that, in a certain way, they were nominally the people of God ; but if we can plead this truly and spiritually on the behalf of any man, if we can plead it for ourselves, what a mighty plea it is! " Lord thou has made us, thou hast new-made us, and thou canst keep us. We are the clay, and thou art our potter ; we belong to thee. Oh, break not the vessels that thou hast made! Cast not away the people thou hast chosen. Be merciful to us, O God, for we are thy people! "

Then the prophet gives a pitiful description of the condition unto which the land of Judah was reduced.

10, 11. *Thy holy cities are a wilderness, Zion is a wilderness, Jerusalem a desolation. Our holy and our beautiful house, where our fathers praised thee, is burned up with fire: and all our pleasant things are laid waste.*

Their houses and God's house went together to destruction ; when their houses were burnt, God's house did not escape. This is the bitterest part of the trial to a genuine believer ; when his own estate is impoverished, he can bear it ; but when the kingdom of God suffers damage, this cuts him to the quick. God's house is our house ; the prophet thus speaks of it: " Our holy and beautiful house, where our fathers praised thee, is burned up with fire: and all our pleasant things are laid waste."

12. *Wilt thou refrain thyself for these things, O Lord ?*

" Canst thou stand still, and see all this ? " This is the kind of pleading for the people of God to use when sin abounds. When truth is trampled like mire in the street, we may come before the Lord, and say, " Wilt thou refrain thyself for these things, O Jehovah ? "

12. *Wilt thou hold thy peace, and afflict us very sore ?*

May God teach us how to plead for his people, and make us great intercessors on behalf of his Church and his cause in these evil days!

Amen.

FAMILY WORSHIP A COMMANDED DUTY

AN EXHORTATION TO HEADS OF FAMILIES

Oliver Heywood.

As no worship is to be observed that is not commanded in Scripture, so are no duties of worship and prayer commanded by God to be neglected or forsaken. That family worship is appointed and approved by God is demonstrated (1) *By his command, and design.* In the early ages of the world the church was limited to families, and this family religion did not cease when public assemblies were formed. Before the Mosaic Law, the first born of the family was priest to offer on the altar. Jacob was ordered by God to set up a family altar. Genesis 35 : 1-3. All believers are now made by Christ a holy priesthood to offer up spiritual sacrifices. Governors of families are still bound as priests to erect family altars for the worship of God. Altars in the New Testament signify the spiritual worship of God through Christ, Matt. 5 : 23-24 ; Rev. 11 : 1. If prayer is a great duty required at all times, in all places, 1 Tim. 2 : 8 " I will that men pray everywhere," then is family prayer a duty. Husbands and wives must pray together, 1 Pet. 3 : 7. (2) *By the practice of the servants of God.* Joshua resolves upon this, chapter 24 verse 15—" As for me and my house, we will serve the Lord." Worshipping God is serving Him. David a great king, in the midst of much political and ecclesiastical employment, returns to bless his house, which could be no other way but by prayer, and praising God for and with his family. 2 Sam. 6 : 20. Public duties must not hinder family worship. Job continually offered sacrifice on behalf of his family. Good expositors judge Daniel's prayers to have been of a family nature, being so obvious and discernible by his adversaries—Dan. 6 : 10. Devout Cornelius prayed to God with his family, Acts 10 : 2, which he declares, saying " I prayed in my house " verse 30. (3) *By the distinction made in Scripture between families which observe or neglect household worship.* Worship, like the altar Ed., testifies a solemn owning of the true God. On the contrary families which turn from God are judged as wicked. Deut. 29 : 18. This is what makes families evil, when instead of praying, reading Scriptures, singing psalms, there is mocking at serious godliness, vain talk, or only worldly discourse. (4) *By the account which heads of families must give for those under them.* Fathers must see that their children or servants obey God's commandments, teaching them to know and practise them, Deut. 6 : 6-7, duties which cannot be managed without prayer. You that have authority and influence over those who depend on you, if you improve not this talent, you will have a dreadful account to give ; especially as their blood will be required at your hands, because their sin will be charged on your neglect. (5) *By the blessing of God which usually attends family prayers.* " He will bless them that fear the Lord both small and great." How often have God's children met with God in their families ? Abraham had a promise of a child ; Cornelius had a glorious vision of a holy angel ; and our Lord came to Jairus's house, to raise his dead daughter. How often has God answered family prayer ? Polanus relates of an earthquake in the year 1584 in Berne, when a mountain violently hurried down in a land-slide, overturning a whole village of ninety houses and families, excepting half of one house, in which the father of the family, with his wife and children, were prostrate on their knees praying ! So true are the Scriptures, " The wicked are overthrown and are not, but the house of the righteous shall stand," Prov. 12 : 7. God blessed the habitation of the just. (6) *By the curse of God attending prayerless families.* That is a prophecy as well as a prayer, Jerem. 10 : 25, " Pour out thy fury upon the heathen that know thee not, and upon the families that call not on thy name." It is a dreadful prediction ; for the wrath threatened, is not ordinary displeasure, but fury. Dreadful in its measure, " Pour out thy fury," denotes plenty, an abundance of judgments, multitudes of plagues. Oh what would become of England if this fury were as universal as the neglect of family duty ! This great anger is not for murder or drunkenness, or blasphemy, no, it is for sins of omission, for not calling on God's name. Oh miserable families where religion is not exercised, there these threatenings must be executed ! Thus much for the reasons to prove that the erecting of family altars for God's worship is an important duty.

But there is no truth so plain, no duty so good, but Satan can find an argument against it. And it is strangs if men have not something to say against this duty, which apparently tends to under-mine Satan's kingdom.

Objection 1. Such kind of praying morning and evening is a con-fining of the Spirit, a limiting of God to man's time, when the Spirit moves not to it.

Answer. Christ and his apostles had set times for prayer ; Jesus often resorted to the garden, Judas knew his stated hour and place, John 18 : 2. And the apostles had an hour of prayer, Acts 3 : 1. Was this confining the Spirit ? God expects that men should stir up themselves to take hold of him.

Objection 2. I am poor, and we work hard and cannot spare the time.

Answer. Do you not and your family spend as much time in idle talk, needless visits, sitting by the fire, as you need for this duty ? None are so hard pressed in their calling, but they might redeem half an hour for God. Conscience will tell you, you spend much time, that might be better employed. Besides prayer gives success to worldly business, for it obtains a blessing of God. Eliezer, Abraham's servant prayed, and God prospered his journey.

F

Objection 3.   I have never practised family prayer and have been a housekeeper for 20, 30 or 40 years.   I am therefore hesitant to bring in a new practice, and condemn my former custom.

Answer.   I deny not but some godly persons may for a season live in the omission of some duties, either through want of information, or their own sloth, or through false teachers.   But such cannot plead custom to excuse their fault.   Will the thief say to the judge, my Lord, I have been so accustomed to stealing that I cannot leave it ?

What arguments more shall I use to persuade you of this duty of family worship ?   If your landlord should turn you out of your house, or your father should disinherit you, if you set not up this family altar, could you be content to suffer both, rather than do it ? And shall a threatening of your Father in Heaven, our great landlord, to reject or eject you out of Heaven avail nothing ?   If a law were imposed upon you to pay five shillings every time that you neglected prayer in your family, would you forfeit that sum as oft as you go prayerless to bed ; would you not fear it would bring poverty ?   And shall not greater losses and heavier penalties deter you from this omission ?   If a king or a nobleman should promise you five pounds every time that you call your family together, read a chapter, sing a psalm, kneel down and pray to God, would you not strive hard to procure that money ?   And will not a greater profit from Almighty God prevail with you to perform this exercise to obtain a reward ?   Suppose the next time you go prayerless to bed, your loveliest child should be snatched away by a sudden stroke of death, as it was in Egypt when the first born of Pharoah and others died.   Would not this move you into a better course ? Suppose, upon every omission of family prayer you should lose a limb, or member of your body, first one finger, then a toe should be cut off till all be gone, would not this force you to this duty ? And yet your precious souls, which are of ten thousand times more worth than a limb, yea, than the whole body, are in hazard by wilful neglect !   Is not the infinite God worthy of your love, fear, and worship ?   Are not the souls of your families precious ?

Oh ! you say, I would gladly set up an altar in my family to the Lord, but I know not how to set about it, or manage it in any way so that it may be acceptable to God, and profitable to my family.   I answer that I will willingly give you some directions.

1.   Begin in the name and strength of Christ.   See that your heads be well furnished with sound knowledge, and your hearts with saving grace.   You must find prayer in your heart, before you utter it with your lips.   Be sure you have a knowledge of God, of the Mediator, of the Holy Ghost that must help your infirmities, a knowledge of yourselves, of divine truths, commands, and promises ; " for that the soul be without knowledge it is not good," (Prov. 19 : 2).   Without this you will worship you know not what, or you care not how, or regard not why ; you will degenerate into formality.   " Search the Scriptures," these contain both the rule

and matter of prayer ; if you be mighty in the Scriptures, you will be mighty in prayer.

2. Rest not in the duty done without communion with God. Set your souls in God's presence : remember who it is you have to do with. Endeavour to affect your hearts with an awe of his divine majesty : consider his infinite perfections, and the great distance between the glorious God and poor worms. Oh that my soul were weighted with the glorious majesty of God !

3. Converse with God alone ; first pray in secret, or your family devotion will soon be a mere customary formality.

4. Value this duty as a great privilege. David thought it a great mercy that he and his people had anything to offer. 1 Chron. 29 : 9-14. Oh what an honour it is, that the King of Heaven gives you an admittance into his presence chamber with your families twice a day!

5. Observe regular times for family worship. If you promise to meet a person of quality at such an hour, when the clock strikes you would rise up and go. Oh take not more liberty with God than you would do with men ! Be sure to set aside the best time, and right season. Some spend all the evening in idle chat and vain discourse, and just when they are for going to bed, start up, and fall on their knees and rattle over a few words between sleeping and waking ; and most of the family fitter for their beds than for devotion. Alas ! sirs, does not God pronounce a curse upon such as do the work of the Lord negligently ? And does not God say, " Cursed be the deceiver that has in his flock a male, and voweth and sacrificeth to the Lord a corrupt thing ?" Mal. 1 : 14. Ah ! had you not a male, a better, fitter hour in your power, than a sleepy hour at bed-time ? Does not he that gives you all your time deserve the best ? Does not God bid you first seek his Kingdom ? And shall this be last ? Must the cream of your time be spent in vanity ? Some will not pray in their families, except a little on sabbath nights, when they have nothing else to do : as though all time were not God's, week-days as well as Lord's-days. Surely God is to be owned daily ; " I will," said David, " daily perform my vows," and " I cry unto thee daily." Psa. 61 : 8 ; Psa. 86 : 3.

6. Familiarize holy conversation with your families ; teach the members thereof the secret duties of prayer. If God be never in your thoughts all the day, you will but coldly pray at night. And if God be not in your thoughts, he will not be in your words. Tell your wife, and children, at due seasons, of the preciousness of souls, the necessity of grace, the excellency of Christ, the awfulness of eternity, the near approach of death, the great account of judgment, and the importance of watching and prayer.

7. Immediately commence this practice of family worship ; embrace the first conviction. Felix by delay lost his time and his soul. " I made haste," says David, " and delayed not to keep

thy commandments." He that is not fit to-day will be less fit tomorrow.

ADMONITION TO ENGLAND

John Knox.

" The eyes of the Lord are upon every sinful nation, to root it out of the earth."—(Amos 9).

For thy unthankfulness, O England, he suffereth false teachers to be a burden unto thee, whom if thou dost receive and allow their doctrine, be thou well assured his great wrath cometh shortly after to thy destruction. This is the accusomed order of God when he is minded to destroy. First he sendeth lying spirits in the mouths of their priests or prophets, which delighted in lies, then suffereth he them to be deceived by the same to their destruction. as he did with Ahab.

O England! now is God's wrath kindled against thee, now hath he begun to punish, as he hath threatened a long while, by his true prophets and messengers ; he hath taken from thee the crown of thy glory, and hath left thee without honour, as a body without a head ; and this appears to be only the beginning of sorrows, which appear to increase ; for I perceive, that the heart, the tongue, and hand of one Englishman is bent against another, and division to be in the whole realm, which is an assured sign of desolation to come.

O England, England! dost thou not consider, that the commonwealth is like a ship sailing on the sea ; if thy mariners and governors shall consume one another, shalt thou not suffer ship-wreck in a short process of time? O England, England! alas! these plagues are poured upon thee, for that thou wouldst not know the most happy time of thy gentle visitation. But wilt thou yet obey the voice of thy God, and submit thyself to his holy words ? Truly, if thou wilt, thou shalt find mercy in his sight, and the state of thy commonwealth shall be preserved.

But, O England, England! if thou obstinately wilt return into Egypt : that is, if thou returnest to thine old abominations, formerly used under the papistry, then assuredly, thou shalt be plagued and brought to desolation. Assuredly as my God liveth, and as those Israelites that obstinately returned into Egypt again were plagued to the death, so shall England taste what the Lord hath threatened by his prophets before.

" He, that being often reproved hardeneth his neck, shall suddenly be destroyed, and that without remedy." " The wicked shall be turned into hell, and all the nations that forget God." (Prov. 29 : 1 ; Psa. 9 : 17).

The Wickliffe Press, Finchley, N.3

THE
BANNER of TRUTH

(6th Issue)

Price 9d.

Subscription 5/6
for six issues.

EDITOR:

MR. IAIN MURRAY, B.A.,
65A BLENHEIM TERRACE, ST. JOHN'S WOOD,
LONDON, N.W. 8.

*   *   *

"Thou hast shewed thy people hard things;
Thou hast made us to drink the wine of
astonishment.   Thou hast given a banner to
them that fear Thee, that it may be displayed
because of the truth."   Psalm 60 : 3-4

*   *   *

CONTENTS

MAY, 1957
6th Issue

HYPER - EVANGELISM
'ANOTHER GOSPEL,' THOUGH A MIGHTY POWER
A Review of the Recent Religious Movement in Scotland

JOHN KENNEDY, D.D. OF DINGWALL.

John Kennedy was one of the foremost evangelical leaders in Scotland in the
last century. He was a contemporary and close friend of C. H. Spurgeon,
and was known by some as "the Spurgeon of the North." This review
is of D: L. Moody's campaigns.

When a movement is in progress in our land, during which
many are awakened to thought and feeling as to eternal things,
who were utterly unthinking and insensate before, when thousands
think that they have lately believed in Christ, and with the joy
of assurance profess that they have found Him, when from the
church are seen issuing many, who have enlisted as recruits, in a
crusade against the ungodliness and unbelief of the world, when
so many, who have a high position and commanding influence
in the church, declare that it is a gracious work of God by which
these results have been produced, and when many more, believing
this, are exceeding glad and abound in thanksgiving, sad, yea,
strained to breaking, must be the heart of one, who seeks the glory
of God and the salvation of souls, if he cannot share in the
prevalent hopefulness and joy. Being one of those, to whom the
present movement has hitherto yielded more grief than gladness,
I feel constrained to tell why I am a mourner and apart.

PRELIMINARY REMARKS

1. Those who, ere the movement had been developed into its
abiding fruits, hastened to declare it to be a gracious work of God,
must have laid claim to inspiration ; and only if that claim is
good can their judging be allowable. It may be legitimate to
form an *unfavourable* judgment, even at the outset of a religious
awakening, if the means employed in producing it are such as
the Lord cannot be expected to bless ; but a *favourable* verdict
at that stage, no man, not a prophet, has any right to pronounce.
Only He who "trieth the hearts and reins" can then judge.
He allows His disciples to try to know men only by their fruits
(Matt. vii. 20). Not at the outset, and not by the immediate
results, but by the fruits produced after trial, does He allow them
to form a favourable judgment regarding a religious movement
(John viii. 31). It is not enough to justify such a verdict, that
souls are anxious, that anxious souls attain to a faith that is
assured, and to a joy that is exceeding, and that a change of
conduct and zealous service are for a season the result. All this
was, once and again, under the ministry of Jesus Himself, without any lasting and saving result ; and men are sadly forgetful
and madly bold, who in the face of such a fact venture to trace

similar appearances at once to a gracious work of God (John vi. viii., xii).

2.   One is not compelled to affirm that a religious movement is not a work of grace, if he refrains from saying that it is.   This is a position into which some men, more zealous than discerning, seek to drive those who do not share their own blind sanguine-ness.   I am not to judge, at the outset, except of the means employed, and if these are unscriptural, I am forbidden to expect a good result (Isa. viii. 20).   If the means employed and the agents are unexceptionable, I can legimately form no decided opinion of the work, till its fruits are in due time developed.

3.   There is no necessity for regarding it as the great Deceiver's work, if it is considered not to be a gracious work of God.   There are impressions, which are not saving, produced by Divine influence in connection with the gospel (Heb. vi. 4-6).   The temporary impressions produced by the preaching of Christ are instances of this.   But that Satan can produce counterfeit, as surely as the Lord can make real, converts, I firmly believe.   And when he is at work, as " an angel of light," he best succeeds when men blindly accept, instead of wisely testing, the results.   There is, surely some reason to fear that his hand is on the agents as well as on the subjects of the work, when neither are careful to apply the test of truth (John iii. 20, 21 ; 1 John iv. 1).

4.   If I regard with little hopefulness a movement over which so many are chanting songs of joy, till all Christendom bends its ear to the voice of gladness that thrills from our land, my saying so will suffice to make some men decry me as opposed to a revival of the work of the Lord.   To this I lay my account.   If the Lord knows that I am not, I feel not very anxious as to the judgment of men.   But which of us incurs the greatest respon-sibility, you, who proclaim this movement to be a work of grace, or I, who cannot say that I as yet do so regard it ?   You commit the credit of true religion to cases which have not been proved—you point the attention of the ungodly to individuals whom you declare to be converts, and you call on them to judge of godliness by these ; you tell those, who are suddenly impressed, that they have been born again, when you know not whether they were or not ; you tell the Church to count on a great accession to her strength, when, so far as you know, only traitors may be added to her ranks ; you say, with the voice of thanksgiving to God, that He has done a work which you cannot know that He will acknowledge to be His.   Yours, at any rate, is a tremendous responsibility.   And if your estimate is false—and you cannot as yet prove it to be true—how fearful the results must be!   You will have hardened in ungodliness an unbelieving world ; you will have flattered into delusive security precious perishing souls ; you will have cheated the Church by inducing her to form a false

estimate of her strength ; and you will have dishonoured God by ascribing to Him work which His hand had never wrought. I merely refrain from judging anything "before the time." What I judge now, I am required to judge. I form an opinion, as one bound to "try the spirits" of the doctrines and modes of service which are the means of advancing the movement. If I do so fairly, I am so far free from blame. If my estimate is proved to be false as well as unfavourable, I am guilty, and if I formed it under the influence of prejudice, I am very guilty ; I suffer in the lack of the hope and gladness by which the hearts of others are so greatly stirred ; and I incur a woe, if, under the influence of a biassed opinion of the work, I refuse to take part in it, though called to do so by the Lord (Judges v. 23).

5. Of the means employed in promoting such a work, one is bound to judge. I am not to be blinded by dazzling results. A worthy end does not sanctify all the means that may be used in attaining it, nor does a seemingly good result justify all the means employed in producing it. Many seem to think that if they choose to call a religious movement a work of grace, no fault should be found with any instrumentality employed in advancing it. All must be right, they think, if the result is to be regarded as a revival of the work of God. To censure any doctrine preached or any mode of worship practised, seems to them to be opposition to the good work, and to tend to mar its progress. They may be of the same opinion, as to the impropriety of some of the means which are employed, with those who do not refrain from condemning them, but for the work's sake they tolerate them. As if the Lord's work could receive aid from aught that was unscriptural ! An enemy's hand is surely here. May it not be, that under cover such as this, the deceiver is introducing into the creed and worship of the Church what shall be statedly obstructive to a real work of grace ? Some there are who have this fear. It were well if all were careful lest this should be the result of acquiescence in unscriptural teaching and practices.

6. Some ministers, who took part with hesitation in the movement, justify their having done so by declaring their object to have been to check irregular tendencies, and to shape the development of the work. And what has been the issue of their prudence ? They merely serve to swell the volume, while utterly powerless to control the force, of the current. Hundreds of ministers have I seen, sitting as disciples at the feet of one, whose teaching only showed his ignorance even of "the principles of the doctrine of Christ" ; who, to their face, called the churches, which they represented, "first-class mobs" ; was organising before their eyes an association, for religious objects, outside the churches, which may yet prove as troublesome as the naked forces of the world ; was casting ridicule on their old forms of worship, which

they were sworn to uphold ; and was proposing to convert prayer-meetings into occasions of religious amusement, a change which he certainly did not ask them to approve, without giving them a specimen, which excited the laughter of thousands, and gave to themselves a sensation of merry-making in the house of the Lord.

7. I carefully refrain from forming an estimate of the results of this work, as these are to be found in individual cases. I confine myself to the general character of the movement, in so far as that is determined by the more prominent teaching under which it has advanced, and in connection with its bearing on the religious condition of the country. I most persistently continue to hope that good has been done ; for even were I persuaded that Satan was busy in forging counterfeits, I cannot conceive what would induce him to do so, unless he was provoked by a genuine work of grace which he was anxious to discredit and to mar.

There are two reasons why I cannot regard the present religious movement hopefully. 1. Because the doctrine which is the means of impression seems to me to be " another gospel," though a mighty influence.   Hyper-Evangelism I call it, because of the loud professions of evangelism made by those who preach it ; and because it is just an extreme application of some truths, to the neglect of others which are equally important parts of the great system of evangelic doctrine. 2. Because unscriptural practices are resorted to in order to advance the movement.

HYPER-EVANGELISM " ANOTHER GOSPEL."

In forming an estimate of the doctrine that was mainly effective in advancing the movement, I had sufficient materials at hand. I heard the leading teacher repeatedly, and I perused with care published specimens of his addresses. I have before me as I write what appears to me amply to justify all that I venture to affirm. Those who were present to hear, will recollect enough to enable them to judge of the correctness of my account of the kind of instruction by which such marked and frequent impressions were produced.

My objection, to the teaching to which I refer, is, that it ignores the supreme end of the gospel which is the manifestation of the Divine glory ; and misrepresents it as merely unfolding a scheme of salvation adapted to man's convenience. It drops the first note of the angel's song, in which the gospel is described as " glory to God in the highest, and on earth peace, good will toward men."   This objection has grown and has been confirmed in my mind, by considering, 1. That no pains are taken to present the character and claims of God as Lawgiver and Judge, and no indication given of a desire to bring souls, in self-condemnation, to " accept the punishment of their iniquity."   2. That it ignores the sovereignty and power of God in the dispensation of His grace.

3. That it affords no help to discover, in the light of the doctrine of the cross, how God is glorified in the salvation of the sinner that believeth in Jesus. 4. That it offers no precaution against tendencies to antinomianism on the part of those who profess to have believed.

I. *No pains are taken to present the character and claims of God as Lawgiver and Judge, and no indication given of a desire to bring souls in self-condemnation, to accept the punishment of their iniquity.*

The law of God has its place in the book, and its use in the work of God. " By the law is the knowledge of sin " ; and the Spirit, who convinces of sin, uses it in that department of His work. A due regard to the glory of God demands that it be so used. Sinners are not to be saved on a misunderstanding as to what they are, and as to what they merit. They must know Him against whom they have sinned. They must know what is justly due to Him from them as His creatures. They must be made acquainted with their iniquity as well as guilt, as sinners. And through the coming of the commandment sin must " revive " in their consciousness, so that they know that their are desperately wicked, as surely as that their persons are condemned to die. *Without this they can have no conception of gospel grace.* Any hope attained to without this, can only be based on a misunderstanding, and must involve dishonour to God. God is not to be conceived of as one who has to study man's convenience only, instead of supremely consulting His own glory. It should be an aim of preaching, therefore, to bring sinners to plead guilty before God ; to feel themselves, in excuseless guilt, shut up to the sovereign mercy of Him against whom they have sinned. The attainment of this may be the result of a moment's working of the power of God, or it may be reached only after a protracted process ; but to this all must come who are reconciled to God.

True, it cannot be expected that the operation of the applied law, on an unrenewed soul, can ever bring him to submit to God's claims as a Lawgiver, or to His terms as a Saviour. Subjection of the will to the law, is as impossible as submission to " the righteousness of God," on the part of an unregenerate sinner.

And this is one reason why this is not insisted on in ultra-evangelic teaching. To insist on God's claims—to consider what is due to God in the personal transaction between the sinner and Him as to peace—would bring the moral as well as the legal difficulty into view, and thus the necessity of the new birth would have to be faced as well as that of atonement. The latter cannot be passed over by any who profess to preach the gospel at all, though in the teaching referred to it is most perfunctorily dealt with ; but the former, as shutting up souls to repentance, to which only the renewed can attain, is most persistently ignored.

And this is done professedly in the interests of gospel grace. To require men to consider the claims of God as Lawgiver and Judge, in order that they may feel themselves shut up to His mercy as Sovereign, seems to such teachers to be raising an obstruction between sinners and the grace of the gospel. It seems hard to them that man's convenience should be interfered with by the claims of God. A call to repentance, therefore, never issues from their trumpet. In their view, there is no place for repentance either before or after conversion. A vague brief sense of danger is all that is required at the outset ; and converts are taught that, once they have believed, they are not to remember and mourn for their sins. " Why raise up your sins again, to think of and to confess them ? " their leading teacher said to them ; " for were they not disposed of nearly two thousand years ago ? Just believe this, and go home, and sing, and dance." It is no wonder, then, that they decry as not evangelical the preaching that does not ignore repentance. But they forget that, on the same ground, they might bring this charge against the Word of God itself ; and not only against the Book of Exodus, but against the Epistle to the Romans as well, the writer of which had not learned how to bring men to know the grace of the gospel, except by bringing them first to know God and His law, their sin and its demerit, and their hearts and their desperate wickedness. What a strange delusion men labour under who imagine that what is essential to any right appreciation of the grace of God and to an intelligent submission to it, must be dispensed with, in order to guard the freeness of the gospel ! By a " free gospel " they can only intend to indicate a gospel that suits a sinner's disposition, instead of being adapted to his state, that dispenses with all humbling of the soul before God, and of which man, unaided, can make use. Verily, for the defence of such a gospel, repentance must be excluded.

The favourite doctrine of sudden conversion is practically a complete evasion of the necessity of repentance. Suddenness is regarded as the rule, and not the exception, in order to get rid of any process preliminary to faith. And on what ground do they establish this rule ? Merely on the instances of sudden conversion recorded in Scripture. True, there are cases not a few of sudden conversion recorded in Scripture, and there have been such instances since the Book of God was sealed. There was a wise and gracious design in making them thus marked at the outset. They were intended, by their extraordinary suddenness, to show to all ages the wondrous power of God. But was their suddenness designed to indicate the rule of God's acting in all ages ? This it will be as difficult to establish, as that the miraculous circumstances attending some of them were intended to be perpetual. The work of conversion includes what we might expect to find detailed in a process. There can be no faith in

Christ without some sense of sin, some knowledge of Christ, such as never was possessed before, and willingness, resulting from renewal, to receive Him as a Saviour from sin. If a hearty intelligent turning to God in Christ be the result of conversion, it is utterly unwarrentable to expect that, as a rule, conversion shall be sudden. Indeed, the suddenness is rather a ground of suspicion than a reason for concluding that the work is God's The teaching of Christ, in the parable of the sower, warrants this suspicion. They who are represented as suddenly receiving the word with joy are those who, in time of temptation, fall away. Suddenness and superficiality are there associated, and with both ephemeralness. In the experience of some, whose conversion was sudden, there was, as in the case of the Apostle of the Gentiles, an after-process, intended to prepare them for useful service in the church. And is it not the fact, that those, who were most remarkable, in latter times, for their godliness and their usefulness, were the subjects of a detailed and extended process, before attaining to " peace and joy in believing ? "

The extremely unguarded use of the statement, that it is through faith, and not through feeling, salvation is attained, tends to the same effect. True, there is a danger of hampering oneself by the idea that, unless there is a certain state of conscious feeling, an effort to believe is vain. There is a danger, too, of substituting feeling for faith, and of resting on a certain experience, instead of on what is objectively presented in the Word, as a ground of hope. All earnest souls are apt, at a certain stage, to search for the warrant of faith in their own state of feeling, rather than in the written Word. True, reception of Christ is the immediate duty of all who hear the gospel ; and nought can excuse their not doing so. But is it not extremely dangerous even to appear to say that faith is the opposite of feeling ? Does not faith itself express a state of feeling ? Is it not an exercise of the heart as well as of the understanding ? Those who so thoroughly separate faith and feeling, are led to regard faith as merely the assent of the understanding to certain statements regarding the way of salvation. And is it not the practice of some evangelists to press men to believe certain propositions, while telling them that their state of feeling is to be made no account of, that they are just to receive these as true, and that, if they do so, they are to regard that belief as faith, and at once to conclude that they are saved because they have so believed. It seems to be imagined that, in order to have in faith the opposite of works, it is necessary to reduce it to mere belief. But in reality this is but to place it on the same footing with works. Faith, as mere belief, is considered to be something within the power of all ; and, by reducing it to a minimum of effort, both as to time and action, it is made to appear to be something different from protracted self-righteous labour. *But it is only different as an easier thing for men to do.* Never can faith be truly seen to be opposed to works, till it is considered as indicating a state of feeling—till it is seen to be a "believing with the heart"; for it is only when it is regarded as a hearty reception of Christ Himself as "all in all," that salvation through faith can be recognised as salvation by grace. To some minds the facility and the suddenness seem essential to the graciousness of faith. They reduce it to mere belief, that men may appear able to do it, and it must be done at once, that there may be no room for repentance, and that it may appear to be something else than a work. *But there never was more legal doctrine delivered, than that of those, who urge men to mere belief, in order to salvation.*

II. *It ignores the sovereignty and power of God in the dispensation of His grace.* This omission is usually justified on the ground, that references to these are apt to be abused or to give needless offence. If men are to be told that salvation is entirely at the disposal of God's sovereign will, and that sinners are so utterly lost that only the working of God's power can move them, either to will or to do, what is required by the claims of the law and by the call of the gospel, then the result will be, that some will be offended and go away, other fold their hands and sleep, and others still sink down into despair. Am I therefore to refrain from proclaiming Jehovah as King? Am I to be silenced by fear of the result of telling, that it is His right to regulate, by His own sovereign will, His own work of grace? Am I not rather very specially called to announce His sovereignty in connection with salvation? In no other sphere does he appear more gloriously kingly than in this. Did not the Divine preacher make the sovereignty of God the theme of His very first sermon, though His hearers were thereby so incensed, that only by a miracle could He preserve His life from their fury? (Luke iv.). And did He not, in all His preaching, ascribe salvation to the sovereign will of the Father who sent Him?

Men, anxious to secure a certain result, and determined to produce it, do not like to think of a controlling will, to whose sovereign behests they must submit, and of the necessity of almighty power being at work, whose action must be regulated by another will than theirs. Certain processes must lead to certain results. This selfish earnestness, this proud resolve to make a manageable business of conversion-work, is intolerant of any recognition of the sovereignty of God. "Go to the street," said the great American evangelist, to a group of young ladies, who were seated before him, "and lay your hand on the shoulder of every drunkard you meet, and tell him that God loves him, and that Christ died for him; and *if you do so, I see no reason why there should be an unconverted drunkard in Edinburgh for forty-eight hours.*"

There is of course frequent reference to the Spirit, and an acknowledgment of the necessity of His work, but there is, after all, very little allowed to Him to do ; and bustling men feel and act as if somehow His power was under their control. There is a prevalent notion, only in a few utterances assuming definite shape, that there is a pervading gracious presence of the Holy Spirit, requiring only, in order to its effective influence, a certain state of feeling and a certain amount of effort. There is prayer, but many who engage in it look around them for an overflowing, rather than upward for an outpouring, of the Spirit of promise. There is prayer, but it is rather to constitute a ground of hope, than the result of reaching that which is set before us in the gospel. Faith in the efficacy of prayer is far more common than faith in the Hearer of prayer. *Prayer, in order to produce expectation, may seem to be followed by an answer, when the susceptibility, caused by the hopefulness it engendered, accounts for all the result.*

It is true, that it is quite as unwarrantable, to expect the outpouring of the Spirit, without prayer for His coming, as it is to hope for His coming because this has been asked. There is a call and encouragement to ask, and those who ask in faith shall never ask in vain ; but the asking is under the sovereign control of God as surely as the giving. I believe, too, that men professing to ask for the coming of the Comforter, may really be asking something else, and may, in answer to their cry, be receiving as a judgment what they regard as a mercy. It is also true that, to pray for the Spirit's coming, and not to employ, in all earnestness, the means which He has been wont to acknowledge and to use, is nothing short of presumption. To wait for His coming is not to be idle till He comes. But it is also true, that those, who are blindly craving some excitement, may be preparing instruments to be used by some other power than that of the Spirit of the Lord. The prayers and the efforts, the asking and the preparation, may correspond, but the one may be directed towards something else than that which is presented in the promise of the Lord, and the other adapted for another hand than that by which the promise is fulfilled. It is true, besides, that the withholding of the Spirit, in His gacious influences, is a token of the Lord's anger provoked by iniquity, but it is terrible to think of an impenitent people, regarding as a gracious work of God that which is really not so, that, under covert of an imagined mercy, they may remain at ease in their sins, and congratulate themselves on having been favoured by the Lord, without having to part with their idols.

In the present movement, at any rate, there seems to be little that is allowed of work to the Spirit of the Lord. In the prominent teaching, there is no exposure of the total depravity and the utter spiritual impotence of souls " dead in trespasses and sins." To face this reality in the light of God's word, would be to discover the necessity of the Almighty agency of the Holy Ghost. This cannot be endured. But another reason must be assigned for

avoiding the doctrine of total depravity. To preach it is decried
as treating men as inert matter, to be wrought upon, but never
to be active. This must not be preached to sinners, it is said, lest
they fold their hands and sleep. They are intelligent and
responsible beings, and must be differently dealt with. And how
do you propose to treat them ? *Are you to hide from them what
they must know, ere they can ever act as intelligent beings in
dealing with their souls' condition* ? Are you to set them to work,
as if they were what they are not ? Is this your way of urging
them to act as becomes responsible beings ? You would hoodwink
their understandings, and misdirect the movements to which their
sense of responsibility urges them! But you hide the true state
of things from yourselves as well as from them. You do so that
you may have hope of success. You have no faith in the Spirit
as God. You cannot bear, therefore, to discover that there is a
great work for Him to do ; and you cannot endure to feel
dependent on His love, for you cannot trust in it as the love of
God ; and if you think of it as Divine, you know that you must
also think of it as sovereign. And you would fain account the
work to be done as not too much for your own power of persuasion ;
for you are ambitious of having it to do yourselves, as well as
hopeless of having it done by the Lord. And yet, forsooth, you
are the men who have faith, and those who differ from you are
the dupes of unbelief. Yes, you are men of faith, but yours is
faith in men. The man who can cry in faith for life, with a
valley of dry bones before him, is the man who has faith in God.

Sometimes, an address may be heard, in which the necessity
of regeneration is very strongly urged, but this is sure to be followed
by some statement that blunts the edge of all that was said before.
After some strong sayings about the necessity of regeneration,
in one of the leader's addresses, the question was put, " How is
this change to be attained ? " And the speaker answered the
question by saying, " You believe, and then you are regenerated " ;
and in confirmation, he referred to John i, 12, forgetting the verse
which follows! Faith regenerates! If it does so, as the act of a
living soul, then the soul could not have been dead in sins. If it
was, whence came the life put forth in believing ? If that
regenerating faith was the act of a dead soul, then a dead man,
by his own act, brings himself alive! The same teacher said on
another occasion, " God would not call men to believe, unless they
had the power to do so." I would like to hear his answer to the
question, Can natural men " love God with all their heart, and
soul, and mind, and strength," who yet are required by God to do
so ? And how would he expound the words, " The natural man
receiveth not the things of the Spirit of God ; for they are foolishness unto him ; *neither can he know them, because they are
spiritually discerned* " ; and the words of Jesus, " No man can
come unto me, except the Father who hath sent me, draw him."

There is a faith which can be exercised without the gracious aid of the Holy Ghost, but it cannot be the faith that is " to the saving of the soul." That is expressly declared to be " of the operation of God," and to require for its production " the working of His mighty power which He wrought in Christ, when He raised Him from the dead." *That faith stakes the eternal all of an immortal being, who is a lost sinner, on the truth of Divine testimony.* Can one do so who does not regard the testimony as Divine ? Can one so regard it who does not realise that God is, and that He speaks in that testimony to him ? Can a dead soul thus believe ? As well expect a sense of your presence, and a response to your words, from the bones that lie mouldering in the grave, beside which you stand and speak. True, there may be a persuasion of the truth, arising from its correspondence to the dictates of conscience, and because of evidence which has led to a rational conviction of its divinity ; for in the grave, in which lie the spiritually dead, there is still intellectual life and a moral faculty that may occasionally be very active. But this is something very different from the faith in God, which is the gift of God. *That faith, too, respects the person of Christ.* It does so, not merely as looking to the historical personage who appears in the inspired record, nearly two thousand years apart, in the hazy past from us, who has left a gospel and a salvation with us, with which, apart from His person, we can deal by faith. It not only realises Jesus of Nazareth as the Christ and the Son of God, but it apprehends Him as a living present Saviour in the testimony of God regarding Him. It actually receives Him as He is actually presented by God. It embraces Himself in order to finding all in Him. It is not merely belief in testimony, it is also trust in the person who is presented therein. It is the homage of confidence in and submission to the Son of God as Jesus the Christ of God. *That faith, besides, implies unreserved dependence on the grace of God.* It is not merely taking advantage of a convenient ground of hope. It is an acknowledgment, at the footstall of the Divine throne, of being justly condemned and of being utterly helpless,—It is the acceptance of salvation from the hands of the Sovereign in order " to the praise of His grace." *That faith is, moreover, the cordial reception of Christ in order to salvation from all sin.* It is not the mere appropriation of the boon of deliverance from death. This is all that is desired by those, who allow themselves to be hurried vaguely to believe in the love of God, and the substitutionary death of Jesus. *True faith is the act of a soul who, up to that hour, was a lover of sin and an enemy to holiness, but who now cordially receives the Saviour in order to the destruction of what he loved, and to the attainment of what he hated before. Can a man thus believe who has not been regenerated by the Holy Ghost ?* And why hide from sinners that they cannot ? Surely this cannot be wisely done

in order to make gospel grace more manifest. Which knows best
about the grace of the gospel, the man who thinks he is saved by
grace through a faith which he owes to himself alone, or the man
who has also learned that the faith, through which he is saved,
is not of himself, but " is the gift of God " ?   Did Jesus hide this
in His preaching from His hearers ?   Did He do so in His first
sermon (Luke iv.) ?   Did He do so in His first recorded dealing
with an inquirer (John iii.) ?   Did He not openly proclaim this
in His great gospel sermon addressed to a multitude by the sea
of Galilee (John vi.) ?   It was while preaching that sermon He
said, " No man can come unto me except the Father, which hath
sent me, draw Him."

It does raise one's indignation to hear some men speak of what
would conserve, to the Spirit of God, His place and His work, as
a mere obscuration of the grace of the gospel, and a fettering of
souls in bondage.   But it grieves one's heart to know that this
is tolerated, and even approved of, by some who ought to be more
zealous, for the grace and glory of the Lord, than to be able to
endure it.

III.   *No care is taken to show, in the light of the doctrine of
the cross, how God is glorified in the salvation of a sinner.*   The
designed overliness with which the doctrine of sin is stated,
necessarily leads to this.   The omission of any definite unfolding
of the law's claims, and of any distinct tracing of the sinner's relation
to it and to God—the lack of all that would raise the question,
" How can God be just in justifying the ungodly ? "—leaves the
anxious in such a state of mind and feeling, that all they require,
to satisfy them, is to discover that they have a convenient warrant
to hope.   Neither teacher nor disciple seems to desiderate aught
besides the assurance, that salvation can be reached through faith.
The gospel seems convenient for man, and that suffices.   How
salvation is to the praise of God's glory the one is not careful to
show, the other is not anxious to know.   To any unprejudiced
observer, this must have appeared a marked feature of revival
teaching.

True, much use is made of Christ's substitutionary death.   But
it is usually referred to only as disposing of sin, so that it no
longer endangers him, who believes that Christ died for him—who
accepts Christ as his substitute.   This use of the doctrine of substitution has been very frequent and very effective.   Christ, as
the substitute of sinners, is declared to be the object of faith.
But it is His substitution rather than Himself.   To believe in
the substitution is what produces the peace.   This serves to remove
the sense of danger.   There is no direct dealing with the person
who was the substitute.   There is no appreciation of the merit
of His sacrifice, because of the Divine glory of Him by whom it was
offered.   Faith, in the convenient arrangement for deliverance

from danger, is substituted for trust in the Person who glorified God on the earth, and " in whom " alone we can " have redemption through His blood." The blood of Jesus was referred to, and there was an oft-repeated " Bible-reading " on the subject of " the blood " ; but what approximation to any right idea regarding it could there be in the mind, and what but misleading in the teaching, of one who could say, " Jesus left His blood on earth to cleanse you, but He brought His flesh and bones to heaven."

Souls who have a vague sense of danger, excited by the sensational, instead of an intelligent conviction of sin, produced by the light and power of applied truth, are quite ready to be satisfied with such teaching as this. To these, such doctrine will bring all the peace they are anxious to obtain. But what is the value of that peace ? It is no more than the quiet of a dead soul, from whom has been removed an unintelligent sense of danger. A true sense of peace with God there cannot be, unless a sinner, assured that God was glorified by Him who died on the cross, can, with reverence of His glorious name, approach Him in the right of the crucified and exalted Jesus, having hope of acceptance in His sight. To this he cannot attain till, in the light of the Son's glory, he appreciates the merit of Jesus' blood, comes to Christ Himself to appropriate His blood in Him, approaches through Him to God, and receives, by the application of the promise of peace, a persuasion of acceptance, in faith, from the throne.

Where there is no wounding, there can be no healing, of conscience. The doctrine, that can do neither, can only do deceiver's work. A sinner, having peace without knowing, or caring to know, how the law, which he has transgressed, hath been magnified, how the justice, that demanded his death, hath been satisfied, how the name of God, which was by him dishonoured, has by Christ been glorified, and how what availed for these ends can be a ground of hope to him, in the presence of the God with whom he hath to do, may have enjoyment, may be zealous, may be active, but cannot have " a good hope through grace."

IV. *No precaution is offered against a tendency to antinomianism in those who profess to have believed.* Yea, this tendency must be fostered by the teaching given to them. If the law of God has not its own place accorded to it, in connection with the sinner's natural relation to God, and in order to conviction of sin, it is not likely to get it at a later stage. The man, who is disposed to think of his sin, as a great calamity, rather than as a heinous crime, is not likely either to reverence God or to respect His law. To his view, salvation is something which it would not be fair to withhold from him, rather than a gracious gift which a sovereign God is glorified in bestowing. The government under which he ventures to claim his salvation presents nothing venerable to his mind. He thinks of an easy reign of mercy, under which he

can be as imperious as if his own will were law. In his altered
position, it is easy for him to ignore the law of God. He never
had to face it ; and, if he has faith without life, there is nothing
in him to incline him to do so now. Not having respect to the
standard of God's law, it is easy for him to imagine that he is
without sin. He is taught that now he has nothing to do with
confession of sin, because his sins were long ago disposed of, and
that he should not now remember them. As for " the corruption
of his whole nature," it never was a trouble to him, and is less
likely to be so now than before, since a delusive peace has drugged
his soul to sleep. Antinomianism leading, in the first instance, to
perfectionism, must be the result of the teaching under which he
has been trained. In his leader's prayers he never hears any
confession of sin, and he is apt to think that, if he follows him,
he must be right. True, he is urged to work ; and there is no
service, however high, which, during his noviciate, he is not
directed to attempt. The work which he is disposed to choose,
and the first work he is instructed to engage in, is to preach to
others what he himself has found. Meetings are multiplied that
he may attend them, and crowds are gathered that he may address
them. The excitement of his first impressions is thus to be kept
up by the bustle of evangelistic service. And what kind of being
is he likely to become under such training as this ? A molluscous,
flabby creature, without pith or symmetry, breathing freely only
in the heated air of meetings, craving to be pampered with vapid
sentiment, and so puffed up by foolish flattery, as to be in a state
of chronic flatulency, requiring relief in frequent bursts of hymn-
singing, in spouting addresses as void of Scripture truth as of
common sense, and in belching flippant questions in the face of
all he meets. Self-examination he discards as a torture only meant
for slaves, humility and watchfulness as troublesome virtues which
the wise will eschew, secret communions with God as a relic of
less enlightened and less busy times, and the quiet habitual discharge of home duties, in the fear of God, as a tame routine for
legalists.

The doctrine of assurance, which is preached, tends to the
same effect. Assurance is regarded as the direct result of faith,
or as essential to its exercise. A consciousness of faith is of itself
deemed a sufficient ground of assurance. There is no place at
all allowed to an attestation of faith by works. True, faith does
often rise into assurance as to the sufficiency of Christ, as its
object, and of the Word of God, as its warrant. There is a hope
arising from the consciousness of this faith, as well as a hope
occasioned by it exercise. But there is also a place reserved by
God for the hope arising from the attestation of faith by works.
And the Lord calls the believer to examine himself, as to the
fruits which his faith produceth, in order to ascertain that his
faith is genuine, and that therefore Christ is already his. " Faith

without works is dead." Where there is a careful disallowing of self-examination, there is sufficient proof of the law being ignored, as the authoritative rule of the Christian's life. Suggestions, to this exercise, are not unfrequently decried as temptations of Satan, or as necessarily the result of backsliding. And why so ? Because it is imagined, that a man is not required to prove himself to be a genuine believer, by doing the will of Christ, in obedience to His law. And yet it will be on the ground of works, as evidence of true faith, that Christ Himself, on His great white throne, will justify the verdict which proclaims them blessed, who are heirs of the kingdom, prepared by His Father.

A religion without reverence and without contrition, can alone be fostered under such teaching as this. But now, as surely as of old, " Thus saith the Lord," " To this man will I look, even to him that is poor, and of contrite spirit, and trembleth at my word." Now, as of old, the heirs of the " kingdom which cannot be moved," " serve God acceptably with reverence and godly fear "; and only in that measure can they taste " the peace of God," and " rejoice with unspeakable and full of glory."

HYPER-EVANGELISM, A MIGHTY POWER.

I make no attempt to trace, to its source, the influence exerted in producing the marked effects resulting from the present religious movement. I confine my attention to the advantage, afforded by the state of feeling, which preceded that movement, and to certain elements of power in the means employed to advance it.

It was preceded by a very prevalent desire for a change. All classes of religious society seemed to be stirred by a wistful longing for something to break up the dead monotony, of which all were wearying. Some were actuated by genuine spiritual feeling. They felt that tokens of the Lord's absence abounded ; and turning to the Lord they cried for the manifestation of His power and glory. Others, strangers to stated spiritual enjoyment in the means of grace, were longing for some change—some excitement to lift them out of their dullness—and for some bustle in which they might take their share of service. Others, still, who knew no happiness in the house of God, and had no desire for His presence, would fain that something new were introduced into the mode of service which they felt so jading. The excitement of a revival would be to them a relief. " Special services " they strongly craved. Prayer for a revival was called for ; and many were ready to take part in the meetings convened for that purpose. These meetings resulted in the hope of an answer. Though but few truly appreciated what was needed, and really dealt with God, we cannot but hope that something was done by the Lord in answer to their cry. But many there were who merely craved a change—something to relieve them of the tedium of a routine, in which they found no enjoyment, because they were estranged from God—and who joined, in asking this, with those who were asking something better. These were the persons disposed to make much of their prayers, and who found it easy to hope just because they had chosen to ask ; and they may have received, though not in mercy, what they sought. The expectation of a change, at any rate, was general. There was an opening up of men's minds to an expected influence. This tended to affect even the Gallios who "cared for none of those things." A revival was talked of, prayed for, and expected, and thus a general susceptibility of impression was produced. Prayer meetings, fostering the desire and expectation of a change, were in all places the pioneers of the movement. Those who heard that a revival had taken place elsewhere, sought that it might reach their own locality. Many blindly asked for what was done in other places, instead of seeking the fulfilment of the Lord's promise.

In course of time, musical practisings were added to prayer meetings, as preparation for a revival ! From both the addresses and the music much was expected, when evangelistic deputies arrived.

What the effect would have been, had the awakened expectancy been left to be operated on by the stated ministrations of the sanctuary, or by extraordinary efforts, that introduced no departure from the usual mode of worship, no one can tell ; but I cannot refrain from expressing my persuasion, that the result would have been a healthier one than that which new appliances developed.

But on this wakeful state of mind, was brought to bear, a system of doctrine, that ignored those aspects of the truth, which are most offensive to "the natural man," and that, while offering something that seemed plausible to an unenlightened conscience, seemed to conserve the old heart's imagined independence of the sovereign and almighty grace of God, and by ignoring repentance preserved to it its idols. The gospel, modified to suit the taste of unrenewed men, was welcome. The recommendations of it, given by men of influence, tended to put down suspicion, and to induce the public to receive it as "the gospel of the grace of God." *The new style of teaching made it seem such an easy thing to be a Christian.* To find oneself easily persuaded to believe what was presented as the gospel, and to think that by this faith salvation was secured, and that all cause of anxiety was for ever gone, gave a new and pleasing sensation, which thousands were willing to share.

And once the movement had begun it could command an indefinite supply of agents. All who say they were converted are set to work. Any one, who can tongue it deftly, can take a part, —he requires neither knowledge nor experience. The excitement is kept up by the bustle of public service. No fear is felt of lifting up novices "lest they fall into the condemnation of the devil." That feeling may have been suitable in Paul's day, but it has now ceased to be so regarded. But there is a fear of converts ceasing to seem to be so, if they are not kept busy in religious service. A proselytising bustle must therefore be the outcome of their faith. There is an utter avoidance of *testing* work on the part of their instructors ; but *attesting* work enough is done. They have at once been proclaimed Christians in their own hearing, and in the presence of thousands ; and those, who presume to tell them this, are quite ready to join with themselves in thinking that they are fit for any service that they may choose to try. A season apart, to be alone with God, a solemn time for careful counting of the cost, has from Christ the double recommendation of His example and of His precept, but is desired neither by nor for these so-called converts.

To these advantages for effect were added various devices, which, though quite unscriptural, or rather, because they were so, were fraught with impressing power.

UNSCRIPTURAL DEVICES.

1. Excessive hymn-singing is one of these. The singing of uninspired hymns even in moderation, as a part of public worship, no one can prove to be scriptural ; but the excess and the misdirection of the singing in this movement were irrational as well. Singing ought to be to the Lord ; for singing is worship. But singing the gospel to men has taken the place of singing praise to God. This, at any rate, is something new—that indeed is its only recommendation—and when the singing is also good, its melody combines with its novelty to make an impression. The singing produced an effect. Many professed to have been converted by the hymns.

2. The use of instrumental music was an additional novelty, pleasing to the kind of feeling that finds pleasure in a concert. To introduce what is so gratifying there, into the service of the house of God, is to make the latter palatable to those to whom spiritual worship is an offence. The organ sounds effectively touch chords which nothing else would thrill. To Scottish Presbyterians is was something new ; but as their spiritual guides did not object to it, why should they ? Tided thus, by their pastors, over all difficulties, which their scruples might occasion, they found it pleasant to enjoy the new sensation. They could be at the concert and in church at the same time. They could get at once something for conscience and something for the flesh.

And yet it is not difficult to prove that the use of instrumental music, in the worship of God, is unscriptural, and that therefore all, who have subscribed the Confession of Faith, are under solemn vow against it. There was a thorough change, in the mode of worship, effected by the revolution, which introduced the New Testament dispensation. So thorough is this change, that no part of the old ritual can be a precedent to us. For all parts of the service of the house of God there must be New Testament precept or example. No one will pretend that for instrumental music, in the worship of God, there is any authority in New Testament Scripture. "The fruit of the lips," issuing from hearts that make "melody to the Lord," is the only form of praise it sanctions. The Church of Rome claims a right to introduce into the worship of God any innovation it lists ; the Church of England allows what is not expressly forbidden in Scripture ; but Scotch Presbyterians are bound, by the Confession of Faith, to disallow all that is not appointed in Scripture. (Conf. chap. xxi.) How those, who allow the use of instrumental music, in our Assembly Hall, can reconcile their doing so with their ordination vows, I cannot even conjecture.

It may seem strange, but it is quite as true as it is strange, that those who are ready to plead that principles and doctrine, inculcated under the former dispensation, are no longer entitled to our acceptance, unless re-delivered with New Testament sanctions, are just the parties who are also ready to go back to Old Testament antecedents in the mode of worship. What is eternally true is treated as if it were temporary, and that which has " vanished away " is regarded as perpetual. But if the ancient mode, of conducting the service of praise, furnishes an example for all times, on the self-same ground you are entitled to choose what you list out of the ceremonies of Old Testament worship. The altar and the sacrifice may be defended as surely as the organ.

" But we use the organ only as an aid," it is said. " It is right that we should do our best in serving the Lord ; and if the vocal music is improved by the instrumental accompaniment, then surely the organ may be used." On the same ground you might argue for the use of crucifixes and pictures, and for all the paraphenalia of the Popish ritual. " These," you might say, " make an impression on minds that would not otherwise be at all affected. They vividly present before worshippers the scenes described in Scripture, and if, as aids, they serve to do so, they surely cannot be wrong." To this, there are three replies, equally good against the argument for instrumental music. 1. They are not prescribed in New Testament Scripture, and therefore they must not be introduced into New Testament worship. 2. They are incongruous with the spirituality of the New Testament dispensation. 3. These additions but help to excite a state of feeling which militates against, instead of aiding, that which is produced by the word. An organ may make an impression, but what is it but such as may be made more thoroughly at the opera ? It may help to regulate the singing, but does God require this improvement ? And whence arises the taste for it ? It cannot be from the desire to make the praise more fevent and spiritual, for it only tends to take attention away from the heart, whose melody the Lord requires. It is the craving for pleasurable æsthetics, for the gratification of mere carnal feeling, that desires the thrill of organ sounds, to touch pleasingly the heart, that yields no response to what is spiritual. If the argument, against the use of the organ, in the service of praise, is good, it is, at least, equally so against its use in the service of preaching. If anything did " vanish away," it surely is the use of all such accessories in connection with the exhibition of Christ to men.

3. The novelty of the " inquiry room " was another effective aid in advancing this movement. It is declared to be desirable to come into close personal contact with the hearers of the gospel immediately after a sermon, in order to ascertain their state of feeling, to deepen impressions that may have been made, and to give a helping hand to the anxious. Such is the plea for " the inquiry room." In order that it may be supplied, hearers are strongly urged, after a sensational address, to take the position of converts or inquirers. They are pressed and hurried to a public confession. Strange means are resorted to, in order to commit them, by an open avowal of a certain state of feeling. But what right has any individual, not authorised by a Church of Christ, to do so,—to insist on a public confession on the part of any one ? Even the Church can admit to public confession only after trial. And the admission must be in connection with the dispensation of the appointed sealing ordinaces. But here is a stranger, who never saw their faces before, hurrying people, whom a sensational address has excited, to make public profession of faith, thus associating them, without possibility of trial, with the Christians of the locality, and involving the credit of religion in their future conduct before the world. This, surely, is both unwise and presumptuous. How unlike this to the Divine Teacher's way ! When a crowd of seemingly anxious souls gathered around Him, instead of urging them to confession, He tested them by searching doctrine, and the result was, that instead of crowding an inquiry room, they " went away and walked no more with Him." I feel persuaded that if an excited crowd, at a revival meeting, were to be addressed as were the multitude at the Sea of Galilee, the conductor would put the speaker down, denounce him for casting a gloom over the meeting, and give him no other opportunity of dealing with inquirers.

Why are men so anxious to keep the awakened in their own hands ? They, at any rate, seem to act as if conversion was all their own work. They began it, and they seem determined to finish it. If it is at all out of their hand, they seem to think that it will come to nothing. They must at once, and on the spot get these inquirers persuaded to believe, and get them also to say that they do. They may fall to pieces if they are not braced round by a band of profession. Their names or numbers must, ere the night passes, be added to the roll of converts. They are gathered into the inquiry room, to act in a scene, that looks more like a part of a stageplay, than aught more serious and solemn.

Oh, what trifling with souls goes on in these inquiry rooms, as class after class is dealt with in rude haste, very often by teachers who never " knew the grace of God in truth! " The inquiry room may be effective in securing a hasty profession of faith, but it is not an institution which the Church of Christ should adopt or countenance.

4. Even prayer-meetings are converted into factories of sensation. Brief prayers and brief addresses to the stroke of hammer, or the toll of bell, silent prayers, hymns, which often contain a considerable amount of nonsense, and occasionally of something worse, sung to the strains of an organ, and a chance to address or prayer given to any one who chooses to rise and speak, —such are the arrangements of the new prayer-meeting. The *silent prayer,* what is it ? It is secret prayer, and therefore ought to be prayer in secret. It must be *secret,* just because it is *silent.* And where is it engaged in ? In the closet ? No ; it was Christ who directed it to be there. There are other leaders now, and they direct that it should be in open assembly. Christ would have men, when they pray secretly, to enter their closet and shut the door. Now it must be done so that those who do it " may be seen of men." And this device, so directly opposed to the mind of Christ, is lauded as if nothing could be better. And it is becoming the habit now of worshippers as they enter the house of God. They assume, before the eyes of hundreds, the attitude of prayer, to do, in the public assembly, what Christ directed to be done in the closet. If they intend this as a public confession of their sin, in neglecting prayer in their closet, such confession would not be at all uncalled for, if duly made. They who forget to do it where Christ required it to be done, are the persons most likely to do it where it can only be a bit of will-worship and formality.

The device of " open meetings," what of it ? It is simply ceasing to take care that, in the worship of God, " all things be done decently and in order " ; and giving the place to those who have conceit and tongue, and nought beside, which ought to be filled by those who in honour prefer others to themselves, and who seek grace to " serve with reverence and godly fear."

I have had to endure the trial of watching over a darling child, during her dying hours. Spasm, succeeding spasm, was the only movement indicating life, each one, as it came, shattering the frame which it convulsed, and thus wearing out its strength. While the spasms lasted I knew there still was life, but I also knew that these must soon end in death. There was life, but it was dying, and the convulsions of life soon ended in the stillness of death. But after the double pain came the ecstacy of a resurrection hope, and my heart could sing beside the grave, that covered for a season my dead out of sight. With still greater grief, should I look on my Church, in a spasmodic state, subject to convulsions, which only indicate that her life is departing, the result of revivals gut up by men. It will be a sad day for our country, if the men, who luxuriate in the excitement of man-made revivals, shall with their one-sided views of truth, which have ever been the germs of serious errors, their lack of spiritual discernment, and their superficial experience, become the leaders of religious thought, and the conductors of religious movements. Already they have advanced as many, as inclined to follow them, far in the way to Arminianism in doctrine, and to Plymouthism in service. They may be successful in galvanising, by a succession of sensational shocks, a multitude of dead, till they seem to be alive, and they raise them from their crypts, to take a place amidst the living in the house of the Lord ; but far better would it be to leave the dead in the place of the dead, and to prophesy to them there, till the living God Himself shall quicken them. For death will soon resume its sway. Stillness will follow the temporary bustle, and the quiet will be more painful than the stir. But to whatever extent this may be realised in the future of the Church in Scotland, our country shall yet share, in common with all lands, in the great spiritual resurrection that will be the morning work of that day of glory, during which " the knowledge of the Lord shall cover the earth," and " all nations shall be blessed in Messiah, and shall call Him blessed." Meantime, were it not for the hope of this, it would be impossible to endure to think of the present, and of the immediate future, of the cause of true religion in our land. The dead, oh, how dead! the living, oh, how undiscerning! And if there continue to be progress in the direction, in which present religious activity is moving, a negative theology will soon supplant our Confession of Faith, the good old ways of worship will be forsaken for unscriptural inventions, and the tinsel of a superficial religiousness will take the place of genuine godliness.

*　　*　　*

" When a fire is kindled in a city we do not say coldly, ' Yonder is a great fire, I pray God it will do no harm.' In times of public defection we are not to preach tame lectures of contemplative divinity, or fight with ghosts of antiquated errors, but to oppose with all earnestness the growing evils of the world,whatever it may cost us." If men valued truth as they do their goods and their houses they would not regard error with such cool contentment. The cant of the present day is, ' Charity, Charity.' As if it were not the truest charity to grow indignant with that which ruins souls. It is not uncharitable to warn men against poisonous adulterations of their food, or invasions of their rights ; and surely it cannot be more uncharitable to put them upon their guard against that which will poison or rob their souls. Lukewarmness of love to truth is the real evil to be deprecated in these times. We have new doctrines among us, full of practical mischief, and against these there is need to cry out lest they gain so great a head that both church and state should be set on fire. Lord, arouse thy watchmen, and bid them arouse all thy saints, for the times are full of danger! "

C. H. SPURGEON. 1883.

THE FALSE CONVERT DETECTED

EXTRACTS FROM THOMAS SHEPARD (1605 - 1649).

' *Strait is the gate, and narrow is the way, which leadeth unto
life, and few there be that find it.*' Matt. 7 : 14. ' *They have
healed also the hurt of the daughter, of my people slightly, saying,
Peace, peace ; when there is no peace.*' Jerem. 6 : 14.

Look to all ages, and we shall find but a handful saved. As
soon as ever the Lord began to keep house, and there were but two
families in it, there was a bloody Cain living, and a good Abel
slain. And as the world increased in number, so in wickedness, Gen.
6 : 12. It is said, *All flesh had corrupted their ways,* and amongst
so many thousand men not one righteous but *Noah,* and his family ;
and yet in the Ark there crept in a cursed Ham. Afterwards, as
Abraham's posterity increased, so we see their sin abounded. When
his posterity was in Egypt, where, one would think, if ever men
were good, now it would appear, being so heavily afflicted by
Pharaoh, being by so many miracles miraculously delivered by the
hand of Moses, yet most of these *God was wrath* with, Heb. 3 : 11,
and only two of them, Caleb and Joshua, went into Canaan, a type
of Heaven. Look into Solomon's time : what glorious times ! what
great profession was there then ! Yet after his death *ten tribes*
fell to the odious sin of Idolatry. Look farther into Isaiah's time,
when there were multitudes of sacrifices and prayers, Isa. 1 : 11.
Yet then there was but a *remnant,* nay, a very little *remnant,* that
should be saved. And look to the time of Christ's coming in the
flesh (for I pick out the best time of all), when one would think
by such sermons he preached, such miracles he wrought, such a
life as he led, all the Jews would have entertained him ; yet it is
said, *He came unto his own, and they received him not.* John
1 : 11. In the Apostle's time many indeed were converted, but
few comparatively ; and amongst the best churches were many bad,
Philip. 3 : 18 ; Rev. 3 : 4. And presently after the Apostles time
Many grievous wolves came in and devoured the sheep, Acts 20 : 29.

Even amongst them that have the means of grace, but few
shall be saved. It's a strange speech of Chrysostom in his fourth
sermon to the people of Antioch, where he was much beloved,
and did much good ; ' How many do you think,' he says, ' shall
be saved in this city ? It will be an hard speech to you, but I will
speak it ; though here be so many thousands of you, yet there
cannot be found an hundred that shall be saved, and I doubt of
them too.' It may be sometimes amongst ninety-nine in a parish,
Christ sends a minister to call some *one* lost sheep among them,
Luke 15. Three grounds were bad where the seed was sown, and
only one ground good, Matt. 13. The number of them that shall
be saved is very small, Luke 13 : 24. . . . This ministers exhortation
to all confident people, that think they believe, and say they doubt

not but to be saved ; and hence do not much fear death. Oh, learn to suspect and fear your estate, and fear it so much that thou cannot be quiet until thou hast got some assurance thou shalt be saved. A confident opinion rages amongst divers sorts of people whom the Devil never troubles, because he is sure of them already, and therefore cries peace in their ears, whose conscience never troubles them, because it has shut its eyes : and hence they sleep, and sleeping dream that God is merciful unto them, and will be so ; yet never see. they are deceived, until they awake with the flames of Hell about their ears : and the world troubles them not, because they are friends to it, and so enemies to God. And ministers never trouble them, for they have none such as are fit for that work near them. And their friends never trouble them, because they are afraid to displease them. This one truth well thought on may damp thine heart. It may be there are better in Hell than thyself that art so confident ; and therefore tell me what thou hast to say for thyself, that thou shalt be saved ?

Thou wilt say probably, first, ' I have left my sins I once lived in, and am now no drunkard, no swearer, no liar, etc.'—I answer ; thou mayest be washed from thy mire (the pollution of the world), and yet be a swine in God's account, 2 Pet. 2 : 20. Thou mayest live a blameless, innocent, honest life, and yet be a miserable creature still, Philip. 3 : 6.

' But I pray, and that often.'—This thou mayest do, and yet never be saved, Isa. 1 : 11. ' *To what purpose is your multitude of sacrifices* ? ' Thou mayest pray with much affection, yet be a thousand miles off from being saved, Prov. 1 : 28.

' But I hear the Word of God, and like the best preachers.'— This thou mayest do too, and yet never be saved. Nay, thou mayest so hear, as to receive much *joy,* and comfort in hearing, nay, to believe and catch hold on Christ, and say and think he is thine, and yet not be saved, as the stony ground did, Matt. 13, who heard the word with *joy,* and for a *season believed.*

' I read the Scriptures often.'—This you may do too, and yet never be saved ; as the Pharisees, who were so perfect in reading the Bible, that Christ needed only to say, ' It hath been said of old times,' for they knew the text and place well enough without intimation.

' But I am grieved and sorrowful, and repent for my sins past.'—Judas did thus, Matt. 27 : 3, he repents himself with a legal repentance for fear of Hell, and with a natural sorrow for dealing so unkindly with Christ. True humiliation is ever accompanied with hearty reformation.

' I have very many good *desires* and *endeavours* to get to Heaven.'—These thou and thousands may have, and yet miss of Heaven, Luke 13 : 24.

These things thou may verily think of thyself, and yet be deceived, and damned at last. ' *There is a way that seemeth*

right to a man, but the end thereof is the way of death,' Prov.
14 : 12. Thou mayest go fairly, and live so honestly, that all the
best Christians about thee may think well of thee, and never suspect
thee ; and so mayest pass through the world, and die with a deluded
comfort, and never know thou art counterfeit, till the Lord brings
thee to thy strict and last examination, and so thou receivest that
dreadful sentence, *Go ye cursed.* So it was with the five foolish
virgins, that were never discovered by the wise, nor by themselves,
until the gate of grace was shut upon them, Matt. 25. If thou
hast therefore no better evidences to shew for thyseslf, that thine
estate is good, than these, I will not give a pin's point for all thy
flattering false hopes of being saved : but it may be thou hast never
yet come so far as this pitch ; and if not, Lord ! what will become
of thee ? Suspect thyself much, and when in this shipwreck of
souls thou seest so many thousands sink, cry out and conclude, It's
a wonder of wonders, and a thousand to one, if ever thou comest
safe to shore.

There are four strait gates which everyone must pass through
before he can enter into Heaven.

1. There is the strait gate of *Humiliation.* God saves none,
but first he humbles them. Now it is hard to pass through the
gates and flames of Hell ; hard to mourn not for one sin, but all
sins, and not for a season, but all a man's life-time. Oh, it is hard
for a man to suffer himself to be loaden with sin, and pressed to
death for sin, so as never to love sin more. It is easy to drop a
tear or two, and be sermon-sick : but to have a heart rent *for* sin
and *from* sin, this is true humiliation, and this is hard. If God
broke David's bones for his adultery, and the angels backs for their
pride ; the Lord, if ever he saves thee, will break thine heart too.

2. The strait gate of *Faith,* Eph. 1 : 19. It's an easy matter to
presume, but hard to believe in Christ. It is easy for man that was
never humbled to believe and say, *'Tis but believing ;* but it is an
hard matter for a man humbled, when he sees all his sins in order
before him, and crying out against him, and God frowning upon
him, now to call God Father. Judas had rather be hanged than
believe.

3. The strait gate of *Repentance.* It is an easy matter for a
man to confess himself to be a sinner, and to cry God forgiveness
until next time : but to have a bitter sorrow, and to turn from all
sin, and to return to God, and all the ways of God, which is true
repentance ; this is hard.

4. The strait gate of *Opposition of Devils,* the *World,* and a
man's own *Self,* who knock a man down when he begins to look
towards Christ and Heaven.

Hence learn, that every easy way to Heaven is a false way,
although ministers should preach it out of their pulpits, and angels
should publish it out of Heaven. There are easy ways to Heaven
(as men think), which all lead to Hell.

SOME COMMON CAUSES WHY SO MANY, BEING MISTAKEN IN THEIR HOPE OF SALVATION, ARE ETERNALLY RUINED

I. Error in the Understanding.

(1). The mind being ignorant of the height and excellency of true grace, imagines within itself such a measure of common grace to be true grace, which the soul easily having attained unto, conceives it is in the estate of grace, and so deceives itself miserably, Rom. 10 : 3. (By common grace is meant the possession of certain marks, such as are referred to in Heb. 6 ; Matt. 12 : 43 ; 2 Pet. 2 : 20, etc., which fall short of the true effects which always accompany regeneration). The mind comes to this position thus : The mind is haunted and pursued with troublesome fears of Hell, Conscience tells him he hath sinned, and the Law tells him he shall die, and Death appears and tells him he must shortly meet with him ; and if he be taken away in his sins, then comes a black day of reckoning, where no creature can comfort him. Hence, he says, Lord, keep my soul from these miseries ; he desires peace and ease, and to hear such sermons, and read such books, as may best satisfy him concerning the least measure of grace : for, sin only troubling him, grace only can comfort him soundly. And so grace, which is meat and drink to an holy heart, is but medicine to this kind of men, to ease them of their fears and troubles. Hereupon, being ignorant of the height of *true grace,* he fancies to himself such a measure of common grace to be true grace. As, if he feels himself ignorant of that which troubles him ; so much knowledge will I then get, he says. If some soul sins in his practice trouble him, these he will cast away, and so reforms. If omission of good duties molests him, he will hear better, and pray oftener. And now he is quieted.

When he has attained unto this pitch of his own, he thinks himself a young beginner, and a good one too. And now if he be pressed to get into the estate of grace, his answer is, *That is not to be done now, he thanks God ; that care is past.* The truth is, Beloved, 'tis too high for him ; all his grace coming by his own working, not by God Almighty's power. For the Lord's sake take heed of this deceit. True grace (I tell you), is a rare pearl, a glorious sun clouded from the eyes of all but them that have it, Rev. 2 : 17, a strange, admirable, almighty work of God upon the soul, which no created power can produce ; as far different, in the least measure of it, from the highest degree of common grace, as a Devil is from an Angel.

(2). In judging some trouble of mind, some light sorrows for sin, to be true repentance ; and so thinking they do repent, hope they shall be saved. Nay, it may be they will fast, and humble, and afflict their souls voluntarily for sin, Isa. 58 : 3. and hereupon when they hear that all that sin shall die, they grant this is true indeed, except a man repent ; and so they think *they have done already*. This is true, at what time soever a sinner repents, the Lord will blot out his iniquity : but this repentance is not when a man is troubled somewhat in mind for sin, but when he comes to mourn for sin *as his greatest evil ;* and that not for some sins, but all sins, little and great ; and that not for a time but always, like a spring, never dry, but ever running all a man's life time.

(3). In judging the striving of conscience against sin to be the striving of the flesh against the spirit, and hence they think being thus compounded of flesh and spirit, they are regenerate, and in no worse estate than the children of God themselves. So many among us know they should be better, and strive that they may grow better, but through the power of sin cannot ; conscience tells them they must not sin, their hearts and lusts say they must sin ; and here forsooth is flesh and spirit. Oh no, here is conscience and lust only together ; which striving Herod, Balaam, Pilate, or the vilest reprobate in the world may have. Know therefore that the striving of the spirit against the flesh is against sin *because it is sin ;* but the striving of thy conscience against sin, is only against sin because it is a troubling or a damning sin.

(4). In judging of the sincerity of the heart by some good affection in the heart. Hence many a deluded soul reasons the case out thus with himself : Either I must be a prophane man, or an hypocrite, or an upright man. Not prophane, for I am not given to drinking, swearing ; nor hypocrite, for I hate these outward shews, I cannot endure to appear better without than I am within : Therefore I am upright. Why ? Oh, because my heart is good ; my affections and desires within are better than my life without, I know mine own heart, and the heart is all God desires. And thus they fool themselves, Prov. 28 : 26. This is one of the greatest causes and grounds of mistake amongst men : they are not able to put a difference between good desires, and strong affections that arise from the love of Jesus Christ. Self-love will make a man seek his own good and safety : hence it will pull a man out of his bed betimes in the morning, and call him up to pray ; it will make him tug hard for pardon, for Christ, for mercy. But the love of Christ makes a man desire Christ and his honour for *himself,* and all other things for Christ.

(5). In judging of God's love to them, by aiming sometimes at the glory of God. Is this possible, that a man should aim at God's glory, and yet perish ? Yes, and ordinarily too, 2 Kings 10 : 18. But here's the difference, though a wicked man may make God's glory in some particular things his end, yet he never makes it *in his general practice his utmost and last end.* A subtle heart may

forsake all the world, as Judas did, may bind himself to all the
duties God requires outwardly at his hands, and so do good works ;
but what's his last end ?   It's that he might gain respect or place,
or that Christ may have some part of the glory, and he another.
There's many seek the honour of Christ, but do you seek his honour
only : Is it your last end, where you rest and seek no more but
that ?   Observe this rule ; If you are more grieved for the eclpse
of thine own honour, or for thine own losses, than for the loss of
God's honour ; it is an evident sign thou desirest it not in the prime
and chiefest place.   Sin troubled Paul more than all the plagues
and miseries of the world.   Indeed, if thy name be dashed with
disgrace, and thy will be crossed, thy heart is grieved and disquieted : but the Lord may lose his honour daily by thine own
sins, and those that be round about thee, but not a tear, nor a sigh,
nor a groan to behold such a spectacle.   As sure as the Lord lives,
thou seekest not the Lord's honour as thy greatest good.

(6).   In judging the power of sin to be but *infirmity*.   For if
any thing troubles an unregenerate man, and makes him call his
estate into question, it is sin, either in the being, or power of it.
Now sin in the being ought not, must not make a man question his
estate, because the best have that left in them that will humble
them, and make them live by Faith : therefore the power of sin
only can justly thus trouble a man.   (Which power reigns only in
the unregenerate).   Now if a man do judge of this to be only but
infirmity, which the best are compassed about with, he cannot but
think himself well.   And if this error be settled in one that lives
in no one known sin, it is very difficult to remove : for, let the
minister denounce the terror of God against them, they are never
stirred ; why ?   Because they think, *Here's for you tha' live in sin :*
but as for themselves, although they have sins, yet they strive
against them, and so cannot leave them ; for, say they,*we must have
sins so long as we live here.*   Now mark it, there's no surer sign of
a man under the dominion of his sins than this, that is, not to be
greatly troubled for sin (for they may be little troubled) because
they cannot overcome sin.   I deny not but the *best* do sin daily :
yet this is the disposition of Paul, and every child of God, he
mourns not the less, but the more for' sin.   This is the great
difference between a reigning sin and a sin of infirmity.   A sin of
infirmity is such a sin as a man would, but cannot, part with ; and
hence he mourns the more for it : a reigning sin is such a sin as a
man by virtue of his conscience would sometimes part with, but
cannot ; and hence mourns the less for it, and gives way to it.
Now for the Lord's sake take heed of this deceit ; for I tell you,
those sins you cannot part with, if you groan not day and night
under them (saying, O Lord, help me, for I am weary of myseslf),
will certainly undo you.   You say, you cannot but *speak idly,*
and *think vainly,* and *do ill,* as all do sometimes : I tell you, those sins

G

shall be everlasting chains to hold you fast in the power of the Devil.

And thus much of the understanding's corruption, whereby men are commonly deluded.

II. *Carnal Security, or False Peace.*

Now this false peace is begot in the heart by these three means :—

(1). *By Satan.* Luke 11 : 21. *'When the strong man keepeth the Palace, his goods are in peace'* :that is, when Satan armed with abundance of carnal reasonings possesses men's souls, they are at peace. As masters give their servants peace, even so the Devil. *a.* By removing those sins which trouble the conscience : for a man may live in a sin, and yet never be troubled for that sin ; for sin against the light of conscience only troubles the conscience. Mark the plot of the Devil : he will not suffer a man to live in any sin against conscience, whereby he should be troubled ; and so the poor deluded man himself goes up and down, not doubting but he shall be saved ; why ? because their conscience (they thank God) is clear, and they know of no one sin they live in. *b.* By giving the soul *liberty* to recreate itself in any sinful course, wherein the eye of conscience may not be pricked and wounded. To be pent up all the day long in doing God's work, *watching, praying, fighting* against every sin, this is a burden, this is too strict ; and because they cannot endure it, they think the Lord looks not for it at their hands. Now Satan gives men liberty to think thus ; and this liberty begets peace. and this peace makes them think well of themselves, 2 Pet. 2: 19. There are many rotten professors in these days that walk loosely. and take too much liberty in their speeches, liberty in their thoughts, liberty in their desires, in their pastimes, and that sometimes under a pretence of Christian liberty. Oh, this liberty that the Devil gives, and the world takes, besots most men with a foolish opinion that all is well with them. *c.* By giving the soul cessation sometimes from the act of sin : hence they are hardly persuaded that they live in sin, because they cease sometimes from the act of sin. Oh ! Satan will not always set men at his work. For if a man should never pray, never have good thoughts, never keep any Sabbath ; if a man should always speak idly, and never a good word drop from him ; a man's conscience would never be quiet, but shaking him up for what he does : but by giving him respite from sinning for a time, Satan gets stronger possession afterward, as Matt. 12 : 43. *d.* By giving the soul fair promises of heaven and eternal life, and fastening them upon the heart. Most men are confident their *estate is good.* Why ? Oh ! Satan bewitches them : for as he told Eve by the serpent, *she should not die ;* so he insinuates his persuasions to the soul.

(2). *By False Teachers,* partly by their loose examples, partly by their flattering doctrines, and their large charity, dawbing everyone up for honest and religious people ; and if they be but a little troubled, applying comfort presently, and so healing them that should be wounded. They say commonly, Thou hast sinned, but comfort thyself, despair not, Christ has suffered ; and thus skin over the wound, and let it fester within for want of cutting it deeper. I say therefore, because they want a faithful watchman to cry Fire, Fire, in that sleepy estate of sin and darkness, wherein they lie, therefore whole towns, parishes, generations of men are burnt up, and perish miserably, Lam. 2 : 14.

(3). *By a False Spirit,* this is a third cause that begets a false peace. As there is a true Spirit, *that witnesses to our spirits that we are the* sons of God, Rom. 8 : 16, so there is a false spirit, just like the true one, witnessing that they are the sons of God, 1 John 4 : 1. We are bid to *try the spirits* : Now if these spirits were not like God's true Spirit what need trial ? What need one try whether dirt be gold, which are so unlike each other ? And this spirit I take to be set down, Matt. 24 : 23. Mark this comparison. First, the Spirit of God humbles the soul : so before men have the witness of the *false spirit,* they are mightily cast down and dejected in spirit ; and hereupon they pray for ease, and purpose to lead new lives. Secondly, the Spirit of God in the Gospel reveals Jesus Christ and his willingness to save : so the false spirit discovers Christ's excellency, and willingness to receive him. It fares with this soul as with surveyors of lands, that take an exact compass of other men's grounds, of which they shall never enjoy a foot. So did Balaam, Num. 24 : 5, 9. This false spirit sheweth them the glory of heaven and God's people. Hereupon the soul comes to be affected, and to taste the goodness and sweetness of Jesus Christ, as those did, Heb. 6. The soul being comforted after it was wounded, now calls God *my* God, and Christ *my sweet Saviour* : and now it doubts not but it shall be saved, Hos. 8 : 2, 3, and *yet remains a deluded miserable creature still.* But here mark the difference between the witness of each spirit. The false spirit makes a man believe he is in the state of grace, and shall be saved, because he has tasted Christ, and so has been comforted, and that abundantly : But the true spirit persuades a man his estate is good and safe, because he has not only tasted but *bought* this Christ ; as the wise merchant in the Gospel who not only found *the pearl,* but sells away all to buy it. So a child of God tasting a little of God, and a little of Christ, at his first conversion, although he tastes not all the sweetness that is in God, yet he forsakes all for God, for Christ, and so takes them lawfully as his own. Again, the false spirit having given a man comfort and peace, suffers a man to rest in that estate : but the true Spirit having made the soul taste the love of the Lord, stirs up the soul to do and work mightily for the Lord.

III. Carnal Confidence.

Whereby men attempt to save themselves by their own duties and performances.

The paths to hell are but two. The first is the path of *Sin,* which is a dirty way. Secondly, the path of *Duties,* which (rested in) is but a cleaner way. But I think thou wilt object, 'No true Christian man hopes to be saved by his good works and duties, but only by the mercy of God, and merits of Christ.' I answer, it is one thing to trust to be saved by duties, another thing to *rest* in duties. A man rests in duties, when he is of this opinion that only Christ can save him, but in his practice he goes about to save himself . . . But because it is hard to know when a man rests in duties, and few men find themselves guilty of this sin, which ruins so many, I will shew some signs of a man's resting in duties.

(1) Those that never came to be sensible of their *poverty* and *utter emptiness* of all good rest in duties. Now did you ever feel thyself in this manner poor ? viz. I am as ignorant as any beast, as vile as any Devil : Oh Lord, what sin and rebellion lurks in my heart ! I once thought at least my heart and desires were good, but now I feel no spiritual life. Oh dead heart ! I am the poorest, vilest, blindest creature that ever lived. If thou dost not thus feel thyself poor, thou never came *out of thy duties ;* for when the Lord brings any man to Christ he brings him *empty.* (2) Those that gain no *Evangelical righteousness by duties* rest in *duties ;* I say, Evangelical righteousness, that is, more prizing of acquaintance with, desire after, loving and delighting in union with the Lord Jesus Christ. Now Jesus Christ is a Christian's gain, Philip. 1 : 21. and hence a child of God asks himself after sermon, after prayer, after sacraments, *What have I gained of Christ ? Have I got more knowledge of Christ, more admiring of the Lord Jesus ?* A carnal heart, that rests in his duties, asks only what he has done, as the Pharisee, 'I fast twice a week, I give alms,' and the like ; and thinks verily he shall be saved, because he *prays,* and because he *reforms,* and because he *sorrows* for his sins, that is *not* because of the gaining of Christ in a duty, but because of his naked performance of the duty. (3) Those that see little of their vile hearts in performing duties rest in their duties : for if a man be brought nearer to Christ, and to the light, by duties, he will spy out more moats ; for the more a man participates of Christ, his health and life, the more he feels the vileness and sickness of sin. As Paul, when he *rested in duties* before his conversion, before that the Law had humbled him, '*he was alive,*' Rom. 7, that is, he thought himself a sound man because his duties covered his sins, like fig leaves. Therefore ask thine own heart, if it be troubled sometimes for sin, and if after thy praying and sorrowing thou dost grow well, and think thyself safe, and feel not thyself more vile : If it be thus, I tell thee, thy duties be but fig-leaves to cover thy nakedness, and the Lord will unmask thee one day.

IV. Presumption, or False Faith.

This is the last and most dangerous rock that these times are split upon. When men see an insufficiency in all duties to help them, and themselves unworthy of mercy, they make a bridge of their own to carry them to Christ. I mean, they look not for faith wrought by an omnipotent power, which the eternal Spirit of the Lord Jesus must *work* in them ; but they content themselves with a faith of their own *forging* and *framing* : and hence they think and believe that Christ is their *sweet Saviour,* and so doubt not but they are safe, when there is no such matter. All men are of this opinion, that *there is no salvation but by the merits of Jesus Christ ;* and because they hold fast this opinion, therefore they think they hold fast Jesus Christ in the hand of faith, and so perish hanging on their own fancy and shadow. Some others catch hold of Christ before they come to feel the want of faith and ability to believe, and catching hold on him (like dust on a man's coat, whom God will shake off), now they say, they thank God they have got comfort by this means, and though God killeth them, yet they will trust unto him, Micah 3 : 11. This hope damns thousands.

Faith is ' *a precious faith,*' 2 Pet. 1 : 2. Precious things cost much, and we set them at a high rate : if thy faith be so, it has cost thee many a prayer, many a sob, many a tear. But ask most men how they came by their faith in Christ, the say, very easily. When the lion sleeps, a man may lie and sleep, by it ; but when it awakens, wo to that man : so while God is silent and patient, thou mayest befool thyself with thinking thou dost trust unto God ; but wo to thee when the Lord appears in his wrath ! Many of you trust to Christ, as the apricock-tree, that leans against the wall, but its fast rooted in the earth : so you lean upon Christ for salvation, but you are rooted in the world, rooted in your pride still. Wo to you if you perish in this estate, God will hew you down as fuel for his wrath. This therefore I proclaim from the God of heaven—

(1). You that never felt yourselves as unable to believe as a dead man to raise himself, you have as yet no faith at all.

(2). You that would get faith, first must feel your inability to believe : and fetch not this slip out of thine own garden ; it must come down from Heaven to thy soul, if ever thou partakest thereof.

*   *   *

"*He shall see of the travail of his soul, and shall be satisfied.*" (Isa. 53: 11). Christ will infallibly, and without miscarrying, obtain the end of his death. What was the end of his death ? The salvation of all such as belong to the election of grace. Christ died not at uncertainties, nor laid down his life at a venture, that some might be saved if they would ; but intention is fixed. He laid down his life ' for his sheep,' John x, 17 ; ' for his church,' Eph. v, 26 ; ' for his people,' Matt. i, 21. These expressions are exclusive ; these, and not all . . . —*T. Manton.*

TRUTH'S DEFENDERS VINDICATED
JOHN KENNEDY.

In times such as ours it is easy to seem a bigot, if one keeps a firm hold of truth, and is careful to have the seal of Heaven on his hope. No Christian can be true and faithful now-a-days on whose brow the world shall not brand the name of bigot. But let him bear it. It is a mark of honour, though intended to be a brand of shame. It proves him to be an associate of the men of whom the world was not worthy, but who, under the world's lash, did more for the world's good than all besides. The world ever *suffers* by the men it *honours*. The men of *mercy* to it are the men it *hates*. Ah, these old Covenanters of our native land were stern bigots in their day. It was well for Scotland that they were. They could part with their lives, but they could not sell the truth. They would yield all for conscience, but they would yield nought to despots. They could bear to suffer and to die, but they were afraid to sin. It was this bigotry which won its liberty for their native land. The legacy bequeathed to it by these men of faith, whose only home was oft the mountain cavern, and to whom the snow was oft the only winding-sheet which wrapped their bodies when they had given their lives for Christ, was a richer boon than all ever given to it by the kings who occupied its throne, and by all men of title and of wealth who owned its acres. Oh yes, they were bigots these, in the judgment of scoffing sceptics and of ruthless persecutors, and not all the piles they could kindle could burn their bigotry out of them.

And these were stern bigots, too, according to the world's estimate, who headed the crusade against Antichrist, when, at the era of the Reformation, a fire from Heaven had kindled in their hearts the love of truth. It was by unflinching resolution, induced by living faith, these men overcame in the times of stern trial in which they unfurled their banner in the name of God. A plaint Melanchthon would have bartered the gospel for peace—the stern courage of a Luther was needed to prevent the sacrifice. In every age, from the beginning, when the cause of truth emerged triumphant from the din and dust of controversy, the victory was won by a band of bigots who were sworn to its defence.

There is need now of the men whom the world calls bigots. Men of grasp less firm and of love less fervent will do little for the cause of truth and for the best interests of humanity. Other men than these will even barter their own eternal prospects for the honour which comes from men and for the ease which is won by compromise. How many such as these there are, even in the Churches, and even there in the van, who boast of a charity which is indiscriminate in its regards, of a sentiment that refuses the form which the truth imposes, and who have learned from the worldling his scorn of all seriousness, his contempt for all scrupulousness of conscience, and his sneers at the religion which is sustained by intercourse with Heaven! These have their followers. A widespread movement has begun away from vital religion, fixed beliefs, and holy living. The Churches are moving with the current.   The time may be fast approaching when the one alternative shall be living faith or open scepticism. A tide which few seem careful to resist is bearing us on to such a crisis. How the result may tell on Churches, communities, and individuals we cannot forecast, nor can we attempt to conjecture without sadness of feeling. But an assured victory is the destiny of the cause of truth. Till the hour of its triumph shall come, all who have linked their interests to the chariot of the gospel shall find themselves a diminishing band as they advance, their loneliness of feeling deepening as former friendships wane into neglect, coldness is changed into scorn, and contempt passes into bitter enmity ; and they can follow the cause of truth only amidst the scoffs of unbelievers and the shafts of persecutors.

But let no lover of the truth—let none whose eye ever rested on the hope of the gospel—turn craven-hearted back from trial. To fall in the cause of truth is but to rise in the kingdom of glory. To be trampled under foot till crushed dead by the heel of persecution is but to have the prison broken open, that the ransomed spirit may pass from bondage to a throne. And in his saddest hour let not the sufferer for truth refuse the joy which glimpses of prophetic light bring to his heart as they break through the clouds of present trial. His King shall triumph in His cause on earth, and His friends shall share His glory. All nations shall touch His sceptre. The old strongholds of unbelief shall be levelled in the dust. Iniquity shall hide its face ashamed. Truth, as revealed from Heaven, shall receive universal homage, and be glorious in the halo of its blissful triumphs before the eyes of all.

* * *

RECENT PUBLICATIONS OF THE SOVEREIGN GRACE BOOK CLUB. Publisher, Jay Green.

Thomas Manton (1620-1677). *Commentary on James.* pp.452 20/-.

In Manton's best style. An exhaustive work . . . Few such books are written now. Manton needs no praise from us. Whatever he does is done in a style worthy of a chief among theologians.—*C. H. Spurgeon.*

If anyone wants to buy a good specimen of a Puritan divine, my advice unhesitatingly is, " Let him buy Manton." *As a writer* Manton's chief excellence consists in the ease, perspicuousness, and clearness of his style. He sees his subject clearly, expresses himself clearly, and seldom fails in making you see clearly what he means. *As a theologian* I regard Manton as a divine of singularly well-balanced, well-proportioned, and scriptural views. He lived in a day when vague, indistinct, and indefinite statements of doctrine were not tolerated. The Christian Church was not regarded by any school as a kind of Pantheon, in which a man might believe and teach anything, everything, or nothing, so long as he was a clever and earnest man. Such views were reserved for our modern times. In the seventeenth century, every divine who would achieve a reputation and obtain influence, was obliged to hold distinct and sharply-cut opinions. A vague, colourless, boneless, undogmatic Christianity, supplying no clear comfort in life, and no clear hope in death, was a Christianity which found favour with none. Now, Manton was a Calvinist in his theology. He held the very doctrine which is so admirably set forth in the Seventeenth Article of the Church of England. He held the same views which were held by nine-tenths of the English Reformers, and four-fifths of all the leading divines of the Church of England down to the accession of James I. He was only one among hundreds of good men in England who all taught these truths.

As an expositor of Scripture, I regard Manton with unmingled admiration. Here, at any rate, he is *" facile princeps "* among the divines of the Puritan school. The end of all preaching is to bring men under the influence of God's Word ; and nothing seems so likely to make men understand and value the Word as lectures in which the Word is explained. It was so in Chrysostom's days ; it ought to be so again . . . The readers of Manton's works will find in them a very large supply of expository sermons. In all these they will find every verse and every sentence explained, expounded, and enforced, plainly, clearly, and usefully, and far more fully than in most commentaries. The value of these expository sermons is very great indeed. For my own part, I am painfully struck with the general neglect with which these expository works of Manton's have been treated of late. Modern commentators who are very familiar with German commentaries seem hardly to know of the existence of Manton's expositions . . . I rejoice to think that now at length these valuable works are about to become accessible to the general public. They have been too long buried, and it is high time they should be brought to light.

We have fallen upon evil days both for thinking and reading. Sermons which contain thought and matter are increasingly rare. The inexpressible shallowness, thinness, and superficiality of many popular sermons in this day is something lamentable and appalling. Readers of real books appear to become fewer every year. Newspapers, and magazines, and periodicals seem to absorb the whole reading powers of the rising generation. What it will all end in God only knows. The prospect before us is sorrowful and humiliating. In days like these, I am thankful that the publishers of Manton's works have boldly come forward to offer some real literary gold to the reading public. I earnestly trust that they will meet the success which they deserve.—*J. C. Ryle*, 1870.

Absolute Predestination by Jerome Zanchius (1516-1590). pp. 150.   **6s. 6d.**

No book can be more calculated to revive the spirit which animated the Reformers than this one, and never was the republication of this book more needed. Zanchius was one of the foremost Continental Reformers ; he was a close friend of several of the leading English Reformers, and his writings were deeply studied and valued by the English Puritans. " His clear insight into the truths of the gospel is wonderful," writes Toplady. " He was thoroughly experienced in the divine life of the soul, and a happy subject of that internal kingdom of God which lies in righteousness and peace, and joy in the Holy Ghost. This enabled him to sustain that impetus of opposition which he almost constantly met with. In him were happily centred all the meek benevolence of charity, and all the adamantine firmness of intrepidity ; qualities, alas! not constantly united in men of orthodoxy and learning." Matthew Poole, the famous English Puritan, terms him " A divine of the first class."

This work of Zanchius, translated by Toplady, gives the clearest, strongest, and most Scriptural presentation of the doctrine of predestination that we have seen, and we judge it to be the privilege and duty of every believer who is concerned to see the truth revived in these times to buy and read it. Toplady's words of 200 years ago are very applicable to the present—" Time has been, when Arianism was more generally predominant throughout the Christian Church, than even Arminianism is at present. The whole world, says history, wondered, to see itself become Arian. It was Athanasius against all the world, and all the world against Athanasius . . . Blessed be God, the doctrines of grace are again beginning to lift up their heads amongst us ; a sign, it is to be hoped, that the Holy Spirit hath not quite forsaken us, and that our redemption from the prevailing errors of the day draweth nigh. Now, if ever, is the time for all who love our Church and nation in sincerity to lend a helping hand to the ark, and contribute, though ever so little, to its return."

Readers in the Sterling area should order from THE SOVEREIGN GRACE BOOK CLUB OF ENGLAND, 48 Thorncliffe Road, Oxford.

Printed by the Wickliffe Press, 104 Hendon Lane, N. 3

THE
BANNER of TRUTH

(7th Issue)

Price 9d.

Subscription 5/6
for six issues.

EDITOR:

MR. IAIN MURRAY, B.A.,
65A BLENHEIM TERRACE, ST. JOHN'S WOOD,
LONDON, N.W. 8.

*   *   *

" Thou hast shewed thy people hard things ;
Thou hast made us to drink the wine of
astonishment. Thou hast given a banner to
them that fear Thee, that it may be displayed
because of the truth."   Psalm 60 : 3-4

*   *   *

CONTENTS

181

EDITORIAL

June, 1957

This is a special issue in regard to the formation of the contents. Hitherto our general policy (which we intend to maintain) has been to give first place to those doctrines and truths most needful for the times. In this issue, however, we are diverging from our general practice in order to hold before our readers one particular practical subject, namely, *the right instruction of children in the Gospel.* It is a subject of the utmost importance and significance. For the spiritual state of our children reveals much of the future prospects of the Church—they are expected to be the Church of tomorrow. The actions of to-day's guides of the young will have consequences which will long outlive their own generation. The effects, whether for harm or good, will endure. Errors in these matters will prove to be a flaw at the foundation, and will imperil the whole future structure of the Church. In the light of this, the absence of early piety in children, the neglect of household religion, and the prevalence of erroneous methods in child evangelism, are all to be viewed as alarming indications of a decaying Church.

How far Sunday schools have changed since their original institution readers of the article on page 26 will be able to judge. We include two of J. C. Ryle's sermons to children in order that the contrast between past and present might be still more plain. In those times all children's work proceeded from the conviction that children have immortal souls, that they are by nature equally as exposed to God's wrath as adults, and that the *same Gospel that saves grown-up people saves children.* Any watering down of the Apostle's definition of the Gospel—" The wages of sin is death but the gift of God is eternal life through Jesus Christ our Lord " (Rom. 6: 23); any failure to regard conviction of sin as the *first* part of conversion (Jn. 16: 9); any attempt to lay wisdom upon any other foundation than the fear of God (Ps. 111: 10), is a violation of the Scriptures. Robert McCheyne testifying to the effects of the awakening in Dundee (in 1839) upon children, records that the ministers, " believing that children are lost," spoke as plainly to them " as to grown persons ; and God has so greatly honoured their labours, that many children, from ten years old and upwards, have given full evidence of their being born again." " The reality of grace in a child," writes McCheyne, " *is best known by his sense of sin."* The change in the method of addressing children was beginning to become apparent towards the end of the last century, and Spurgeon had occasion to warn Sunday school teachers as follows—" I have noticed that children are often told, ' You must love Jesus, and then you will be saved.' Yes, *but that is not the Bible plan of salvation* . . . you were never sent to tell people, either old or young, that they would be saved by loving Christ ; you have altered your Master's commission, which you have no right to do."

We trust that our friends will circulate as many copies of this issue as possible, and to that end we have had a large quantity printed. A wide circulation is the best way to meet heavy costs. To none can such articles as the following be irrelevant. We all live in homes, and domestic religion is required from us all. We all have a responsibility to the rising generation, and in various degrees will all be held answerable for the state of posterity. We can all, by prayer, counsel, or example, do something to correct the fatal errors which prevail concerning the instruction of children. Oh that God might establish that promise to us—" The children of thy servants shall continue, and their seed shall be established before thee! " (Psa. 102: 28).

JUNE, 1957
7th Issue

CHRISTIAN HOMES

A. W. PINK.

Many of those who look no farther than the temporal happiness of individuals and the welfare of the State are not insensible of the importance and value of domestic relationships, realizing that the family is but the unit of the nation. No matter how excellent the constitution and laws of a country may be, or what its material resources, they are insufficient and ineffectual unless a sure foundation for social order and public virtue be laid in the healthy regulation and wise discipline of its families. The nation is but the aggregate of individuals comprising it, and unless there are good fathers and mothers, good sons and daughters, brothers and sisters, there will be no good citizens. It is because our home life has so sadly deteriorated that social decay is now so far advanced, nor can it be arrested until parents once again properly discharge their responsibility. We have no hesitation in saying that the future welfare of Britain (and the U.S.A. too) is more seriously menaced by the relaxation of family government and the breakdown of home life than by any governmental incompetence or foreign hostility.

Home! How much that one word used to convey! It is still one of the most precious in the English language unto some of us. Much more so when to all its natural attractions are added the hallowed associations which gather around a *Christian* home. Is not our favourite concept of heaven embodied in that blessed expression, " My Father's House " ? Because the Christian is not his own, but bought with a price, he is to aim at glorifying God in every relation of life. No matter what station he occupies, or wherever he be, he is to serve as a witness for Christ. Next to the church of God, his own home should be the sphere of his most manifest devotedness unto Him. All its arrangements should bear the stamp of his heavenly calling. All its affairs should be so ordered that everyone entering it should feel " God is here! " The supreme aim of family life should be *household piety,* everything else being subordinated thereto.

It is in the home our *real* characters are most manifested and best known. Out in the world a certain measure of restraint is placed upon both our corruptions and our graces, but in the home we are freer to act naturally, and it is there that our worst and best sides alike are exhibited the plainest. As a close observer and one of wide experience said, " I can never form a correct judgment of a man from seeing him in a religious meeting. He may seem a very spiritual person there, and say very beautiful things, but let me go home with him, and there I learn the actual state of the case." He may indeed pray like a saint in the church, but unless his home be governed according to the Word of God, and his own conduct be regulated by the spirit of Christ, he fails to witness for Him in that most important and influential sphere.

The reality and extent of " a work of grace " in the soul are most clearly revealed amid the petty trials of home life.   In the Scriptures we find some of its most eminent characters subjected to that severe test.   For example, the Lord gave as the reason for the intimate confidences He was about to make unto Abraham, " For I know that he will command his children and his household after him, and they shall keep the way of the Lord " (Gen xviii, 19) : thus his home life was as pleasing unto God as was his public. Nor are the Scriptures less explicit in showing us the disastrous consequences which attend a believer's unfaithfulness in this relation.   A notable case in point is the fearful ruin of Eli's family : " I will judge his house for ever for the iniquity which he knew, because his sons made themselves vile, and he restraned them not " (I Sam. iii, 13).   The state of a *preacher's home* is likewise made the test of his character : he is disqualified from the sacred office unless he be one who " ruleth well his own house, having his children in subjection with all gravity," adding, " if he know not how to rule his own house, how shall he take care of the church of God ? " (I Tim. iii, 4, 5).

"What have they seen in *thine* house ? (II Kings xx, 15). Have you observed, my reader, how much in the Scriptures is in the interrogatory form ?   How frequently the Lord used that method of teaching, both with His disciples, the masses, and His enemies !   It is a most definite and searching form of instruction. A considerable part of God's Word is made up of questions, and it is our wisdom not only to thoughtfully and prayerfully ponder them, but to regard the same as being addressed *to us* individually, and thereby bare our hearts to their penetrating power.   This we should do with the " Where art thou ? " of Genesis iii, 9, right through the Scriptures to the " Wherefore didst thou marvel " of Revelation xvii, 7.   The one now before us was uttered by way of *rebuke* unto Hezekiah's vanity, who in a spirit of pride and ostentation had shown the messengers from Babylon the treasures of his palace.

" What have they seen in *thine* house ? "   Let each of us take that inquiry home to himself and herself.   What do visitors, especially those who spend a night under your roof, behold in thy home ?   Do they see a household which is well ordered, everything regulated according to God's Word, or do they behold a scene of confusion and turmoil ?   Do the furnishings of your home bespeak a heart which is dead to the world ?   Is there a noticeable absence of the carnal luxury and fleshly display which mark those whose affections are set upon things below ?   On the other hand, is there that cleanliness and tidyness everywhere which honours the Lord ? Nothing is more incongruous for one who professes to be a " stranger and pilgrim " here than to behold him or her endeavouring to outshine their godless neighbours in that which ministers to " the lust of the flesh, and the lust of the eyes, and the pride of life." Equally so do neglect and dirt indicate that something is wrong with the heart, and mar a Christian's testimony.

" What have they seen in *thine* house ? " Do they behold a husband " under petticoat government," or one who takes his proper place at the head of the home ? The household must have a leader, and God has committed rule to the husband, and holds *him* responsible for its management. It is no valid excuse for him to say that he is the breadwinner, and therefore he leaves the wife to run the house. Not that he is to be a tyrant, but firm, asserting his authority, ruling in holy love. Yet unless the wife fully co-operates, much of his effort will be unavailing. Not only does God require her to be subject unto her husband's will (Eph. v, 22, 24), but to loyally support and further him—unless his requirements manifestly clash with the Bible. He is necessarily absent from the home most of the day, and therefore it largely devolves upon her to train up their children in the way they should go.

" *What* have they seen in thine house ? " Little or nothing to distinguish it from the worldlings ? or everything in it aiming at the glory of God ? The husband and wife conducting themselves as " being heirs together of the grace of life " (1 Peter iii, 7) ? The children brought up " in the nurture and admonition of the Lord " (Eph. vi, 3) and " in subjection, with all gravity " 1 Timothy iii, 4) ; or utterly spoiled, unruly, and a trial to those who have to endure their presence ? Do visitors behold an example of parental piety, of salutary discipline maintained, evidences on every side that their hearts are set upon something higher than the baubles of earth ? Do they behold the Sabbath day—duly honoured—all unnecessary cooking avoided ? If they do not, they will rightly suspect the genuineness of your Christian profession! If those things be absent, be not surprised if your children abandon religion as they grow older, having no confidence in what they were reared. God search every one of us with this important question.

For permission to reprint the above article we are indebted to The Bible Truth Depot, P.O. Box 86, Mifflinburg, Pa, U.S.A. These publishers are doing a fine work in making Mr. Pink's valuable writings available in book form: we hope to give readers a fuller account of this shortly.

A SERMON FOR PARENTS

By J. C. Ryle.

" Train up a child in the way he should go: and when he is old, he will not depart from it." Proverbs xxii, 6.

I suppose that most professing Christians are acquainted with this text. The sound of it is probably familiar to your ears, like an old tune. It is likely you have heard it, or read it, talked of it, or quoted it, many a time. Is it not so ?

But, after all, how little is the substance of this text regarded ! The doctrine it contains appears scarcely known ; the duty it puts before us seems fearfully seldom practised. Your own eyes are witnesses that I speak the truth. It cannot be said that the subject is a new one. The world is old, and we have the experience of nearly six thousand years to help us ; we live in days wherr there is a mighty zeal for education in every quarter ; we hear of new schools rising on all sides ; we are told of new systems and new books for the young, of every sort and description ; and still, for all this, the vast majority of children are manifestly not trained in the way they should go, for when they grow up to man's estate they do not walk with God.

The plain truth is this, the Lord's commandment in our text is not regarded ; and therefore, the Lord's promise in our text is not fulfilled.

My brethren, these things may well give rise to great searchings of heart. Suffer then a word of exhortation from your minister about the right training of children. Believe me, the subject is one that should come home to every conscience among you, and make you ask yourselves the question, " Am I in this matter doing what I can ? "

It is a subject that concerns almost all. There is hardly a household that it does not touch. Parents, nurses, teachers, uncles, aunts, brothers, sisters—all have an interest in it. Few can be found, I think, who might not influence some parent in the management of his family ; who might not affect the training of some child by suggestion or advice. All of us, I suspect, can do something here, either directly or indirectly, and I wish to stir up all to bear this in remembrance.

It is a subject too on which all concerned are in great danger of coming short of their duty. This is pre-eminently a point in which men can see the faults of their neighbours more clearly than their own. They will often bring up their children in the very path which they have denounced to their friends as unsafe. They will see motes in other men's families, and overlook beams in their own. They will be quick-sighted as eagles in detecting mistakes abroad, and yet blind as bats to fatal errors which are daily going on at home. They will be wise about their brother's house, but foolish about their own flesh and blood. Here, if any where, we have need to suspect our own judgment. This too you will do well to bear in mind.

Come now and let me place before you a few hints about right training. God the Father, God the Son, God the Holy Ghost, bless them and make them words in season to you all. Reject them not because they are blunt and simple ; despise them not because they contain nothing new. Be very sure, if you would train children for heaven, they are hints that ought not to be lightly set aside.

I. First then, if you would train your children rightly. *Train them in the way they should go, and not in the way that they would.*

Remember they are born with a decided bias towards evil, and therefore if you let them choose for themselves they are certain to choose wrong. The mother cannot tell what her tender infant may grow up to be—tall or short, weak or strong, wise or foolish ; he may be any of these things, or not—it is all uncertain. But one thing the mother can say with certainty, he will have a corrupt and sinful heart. " A child left to himself," says Solomon, " bringeth his mother to shame." It is the sin of man, says Isaiah, that " we have turned every one to his own way." It was an unsatisfactory state of things in Israel, when " every man did that which was right in own eyes." Then be merciful to your child, and leave him not to the guidance of his own will. Think for him, judge for him, act for him, just as you would for one weak and blind ; but for pity's sake, give him not up to his own wayward tastes and inclinations. It must not be his likings and wishes that are consulted : he knows not yet what is good for his body. You do not let him decide what he shall eat and what he shall drink, and how he shall be clothed. Be consistent, and deal with his mind in like manner. Train him in the way that is right, and not in the way that he fancies. Train him in the way that he should go, and not in the way that he would.

II. *Train up your child with all tenderness and affection.*

I do not mean that you are to spoil him, but I do mean that you should let him see that you love him.

Love should be the silver thread that runs through all your conduct. Kindness, gentleness, longsuffering, forbearance, patience, sympathy, a willingness to enter into childish troubles, a readiness to take part in childish joys—these are the cords by which a child may be led most easily—these are the clues you must follow if you would find the way to his heart. Few are to be found, even among grown-up people, who are not more easy to draw than to drive. There is that in all our minds which rises in arms against compulsion ; we set up our backs and stiffen our necks at the very idea

of a forced obedience.   We are like young horses in the hand of
a breaker—Handle them kindly and make much of them, bye and
bye you may guide them with a thread.   Use them roughly and
violently, and it will be many a month before you get the mastery
of them at all.   Children's minds are cast in much the same mould
as our own.   Sternness and severity of manner chill them and
throw them back ; it shuts up their hearts, and you will weary
yourself to find the door.   But let them only see that you have an
affectionate feeling towards them, that you are really desirous to
make them happy and do them good, that if you punish them it is
intended for their profit, and that, like the pelican, you would give
your heart's blood to nourish their souls—let them see this, I say,
and they will soon be all your own.   But they must be wooed
with kindness if their attention is ever to be won.

And surely reason itself might teach us this lesson.   Children
are weak and tender creatures, and, as such, they need patient
and considerate treatment.   We must handle them delicately, like
frail machines. lest by rough fingering we do more harm than good.
They are like young plants, and need gentle watering ; often, but
little at a time.   We must not expect all things at once.   We
must remember what they are and teach them as they are able
to bear.   Their minds are like a lump of metal ; not to be forged
and made useful at once, but only by a succession of little blows.
We must pour in the wine of knowledge gradually, or much of it
will be spilled and lost.   Line upon line, and precept upon precept,
here a little and there a little, must be our rule.   The whetstone
does its work slowly, but frequent rubbing will bring the scythe to
a fine edge.   Truly there is need of patience in training a child,
but without it nothing can be done.

Nothing will compensate for the absence of this tenderness and
love.   A minister may speak the truth as it is in Jesus, clearly,
forcibly, unanswerably ; but if he does not speak it in love, few
souls will be won.   Just so you may set before your children their
duty ; command, threaten, punish, reason—but if affection be
wanting in your treatment, your labour will be all in vain.

Love is the secret of successful training.   Anger and harshness
may frighten, but they will not persuade the child that you are
right ; and if he sees you often out of temper, you will soon cease
to have his respect.   A father who speaks to his son as Saul did
to Jonathan (I Sam. xx, 30), need not expect to retain his influence over that son's mind.   And it is a dangerous thing to make
your children afraid of you.   Anything almost is better than reserve
and constraint between your child and yourself, and that will come
in with fear.   Fear puts an end to openness of manner ; fear leads
to concealment ; fear sows the seed of hypocrisy, and leads to many
a lie.   There is a mine of truth in the Apostle's word to the

Colossians, "Fathers provoke not your children to anger, lest they be discouraged." Let not the advice it contains be overlooked.

III. *Train your children with abiding persuasion on your mind that much depends upon you.*

Grace is the strongest of all principles. See what a revolution grace effects when it comes into the heart of an old sinner ; how it overturns the strong-hold of Satan ; how its casts down mountains ; fills up valleys ; makes crooked things straight ; and new creates the whole man. Truly nothing is impossible to grace.

Nature too is very strong. See how it struggles against the things of the kingdom of God, how it fights against every attempt to be more holy ; how it keeps up an unceasing warfare within us to the last hour of life. Nature indeed is strong.

But after nature and grace undoubtedly there is nothing more powerful than education. Early habits (if I may so speak), are every thing with us, under God. We are made what we are by training. Our character takes the form of that mould into which our first years are cast. We depend in a vast measure on those who bring us up. We get from them a colour, a taste, a bias which clings to us more or less all our lives. We catch the language of our nurses and mothers, and learn to speak it almost insensibly, and unquestionably we catch something of their manners, ways, and mind, at the same time. Time only will show, I suspect, how much we all owe to early impressions and how many things in us may be traced up to seeds sown in the days of our very infancy by those who were about us. A very learned Englishman, Mr. Locke, has gone so far as to say, " That of all the men we meet with, nine parts out of ten are what they are, good or bad, useful or not, according to their education."

And all this is one of God's merciful arrangements. He gives your children a mind that will receive impressions like moist clay ; He gives them a disposition at the starting-point of life to believe what you tell them and to take for granted what you advise them, and to trust your word rather than a stranger's. He gives you in short a golden opportunity of doing them good. See that the opportunity be not neglected, and thrown away. Once let slip it is gone for ever.

Beware of that miserable delusion into which some have fallen :—that parents can do nothing for their children, that you must leave them alone, wait for grace, and sit still. These persons have wishes for their children in Baalam's fashion—they would like them to die the death of the righteous, but they go no further ; they desire much, and have nothing. And the devil rejoices to see such reasoning, just as he always does over anything which seems to excuse indolence, or to encourage neglect of means.

I know that you cannot convert your child ; I know well that they who are born again, are born not of the will of man, but of

God. But I know also that God says expressly, " Train up a child in the way he should go," and that He never laid a command on man which He would not give man grace to perform. And I know too that our duty is not to stand still and dispute, but to go forward and obey. It is just in the going forward that God will meet us ; the path of obedience is the way by which He gives the blessing. We have only to do as the servants were commanded at the marriage-feast in Cana, to fill the water-pots with water, and we may safely leave it to the Lord to turn that water into wine.

IV. *Train with this principle continually before your eyes, that the soul of your child is the first thing to be considered.*

Precious, no doubt, are these little ones in your eyes ; but if you love them, think often of their souls. No interest should weigh with you so much as their eternal interests. No part of them should be so dear to you as that part which will never die. The world, with all its glory, shall pass away; the hills shall melt; the heavens shall be wrapped together as a scroll ; and the sun shall cease to shine ; but the spirit which dwells in those little creatures whom you love so well, shall outlive them all, and whether in happiness or misery (to speak as a man), will depend on you.

This is the thought that should be uppermost in your mind, in all you do for your children. In every step you take about them, do not leave out that mighty question, " How will this affect their souls."

Soul love is the soul of all love. To pet and pamper, and indulge your child, as if this world was all he had to look to, and this life the only season for happiness ; to do this is not true love but cruelty. It is treating him like some beast of the earth, which has but one world to look to, and nothing after death. It is hiding from him that grand truth, which he ought to be made to learn from his very infancy, that the chief end of his life is the salvation of his soul.

A true Christian must be no slave to fashion, if he would train his children for heaven. He must not be content to do things merely because they are the custom of the world ; to teach them and instruct them in certain ways merely because it is usual ; to allow them to read books of a questionable sort, merely because everybody reads them ; to let them form habits of a doubtful tendency, merely because they are the habits of the day. He must train with an eye to his children's souls. He must not be ashamed to hear his training called singular and strange. What if it is ? The time is short—the fashion of this world passeth away. He that has trained his children for heaven, rather than for earth— for eternity, rather than for time—for God rather than for man, he is the parent that will be called wise at the last.

V. Train your children to a knowledge of the Bible.

You cannot make your children love the Bible, I allow. None but the Holy Ghost can give us a heart to delight in the Word. But you can make your children acquainted with the Bible ; and be sure they cannot be acquainted with that blessed Book too soon, or too well.

A thorough knowledge of the Bible is the foundation of all clear views of religion. He that is well-grounded in it will not, generally, be found a waverer, and carried about by every wind of new doctrine. Any system of training which does not make a knowledge of Scripture the first thing, is unsafe and unsound.

You have need to be careful on this point just now, for the devil is abroad, and error abounds. Some are to be found amongst us who give the Church the honour due to Jesus Christ. Some are to be found who make the Sacraments Saviours, and passports to eternal life. And some are found in like manner, who honour a Catechism more than the Bible ; or fill the minds of children with miserable little story books, instead of the Scripture of truth. But if you love your children, let the simple Bible be everything in training of their souls ; and let all other books go down and take the second place. This is the training, believe me, that God will honour. The Psalmist says of Him ; " Thou hast magnified Thy Word above all Thy name "; and I think that He gives an especial blessing to all who try to magnify it among men.

See that your children read the Bible *reverently.* Train them to look on it, not as the word of men, but as it is in truth, the Word of God, written by the Holy Ghost Himself ; all true, all profitable, and able to make us wise unto salvation, through faith which is in Christ Jesus.

See that they read it *regularly.* Train them to regard it as their souls' daily food—as a thing essential to their souls' daily health. I know well you cannot make this anything more than a form ; but there is no telling the amount of sin which a mere form may indirectly restrain.

See that they read it *all.* You need not shrink from bringing any doctrine before them. You need not fancy that the leading doctrines of Christianity are things which children cannot understand. Children understand far more of the Bible than we are apt to suppose. Tell them of sin, its guilt, its consequences, its power, its vileness—you will find they can comprehend something of this. Tell them of the Lord Jesus Christ, and His work for our salvation, the atonement, the cross, the blood, the sacrifice, the intercession—you will discover there is something not beyond them in all this. Tell them of the work of the Holy Spirit in man's heart, how He changes and renews, and sanctifies, and purifies—you will soon see they can go along with you in some measure in this. In short, I suspect we have no idea how much a little child can take in of

the length and the breadth of the glorious Gospel. They see far
more of these things than we suppose.

Fill their minds with Scripture. Let the word dwell in them
richly. Give them the Bible, the whole Bible, even while they are
young.

VI. *Train them to a habit of prayer.*

Prayer is the very breath of true religion. It is one of the
first evidences that a man is born again. " Behold," said the Lord,
of Saul, in the day he sent Ananias to him, " Behold he prayeth."
He had begun to pray, and that was proof enough. Prayer was the
distinguishing mark of the Lord's people in the day that there
began to be a separation between them and the world. " Then
began men to call upon the name of the Lord." Prayer is the
peculiarity of all real Christians now. They pray, for they tell
God their wants, their feelings, their desires, their fears, and mean
what they say. The nominal Christian may repeat prayers, and
good prayers too, but he goes no further. Prayer is the turning-
point in a man's soul. Our ministry is unprofitable, and our labour
is vain till you are brought to your knees.—Till then we have no
hope about you. Prayer is one great secret of spiritual prosperity.
When there is much private communion with God your souls will
grow like the grass after rain—when there is little, all will be at
a stand-still, you will barely keep your soul alive. Shew me a
growing Christian—a going forward Christian—a strong Christian
—a flourishing Christian— and sure am I, he is one that speaks
often with his Lord. He asks much, and he has much. He tells
Jesus everything, and so he always knows how to act.

Prayer is the mightiest engine God has placed in our hands.
It is the best weapon to use in every difficulty, and the surest
remedy in every trouble. It is the key that unlocks the treasure
of promises, and the hand that draws forth grace and help in time
of need. It is the silver trumpet God commands us to sound in
all our necessity, and it is the cry He has promised always to attend
to, even as a loving mother to the voice of her child.

Prayer is the simplest means that man can use in coming to
God. It is within reach of all—the sick, the aged, the infirm,
the paralytic, the blind, the poor, the unlearned—all can pray. It
avails you nothing to plead want of memory, and want of learning,
and want of books, and want of scholarship in this matter. So long
as you have a tongue to tell your soul's state, you may, and you
ought to, pray. Those words, " Ye have not because ye ask not,"
will be a fearful condemnation to many in the day of judgment.
Oh! that the prayerless among you would begin to pray. Oh!
that the prayerful would pray far more than they do.

Parents, if you love your children, do all that lies in your power
to train them up in a habit of prayer. Show them how to begin.

Tell them what to say. Encourage them to persevere. Remind them if they become careless and slack about it. Let it not be your fault, at any rate, if they never call on the name of the Lord.

This, remember, is the first step in religion which a child is able to take. Long before he can read you can teach him to kneel by his mother's side, and repeat the simple words of prayer and praise, which she puts in his mouth. And as the first steps in any undertaking are always most important, so is the manner in which your child's prayers are prayed, a point which deserves your closest attention. Few seem to know how much depends on this. You must beware lest they get into a way of saying them in a hasty, careless, and irreverent manner. You must beware of giving up the oversight of this matter to servants and nurses, or of trusting too much to your children doing it when left to themselves. I cannot praise that mother among you, who never looks after this most important part of her child's daily life herself. Surely if there be any habit which your own hand and eye should help in forming, it is the habit of prayer. Believe me, if you never hear your children pray yourself, you are much to blame. You are little wiser than the bird described in Job, " Which leaveth her eggs in the earth, and warmeth them in the dust, and forgetteth that the foot may crush them : or that the wild beast may break them. She is hardened against her young ones, as though they were not hers : her labour is in vain without fear." (Job xxxix, 14, 15, 16).

Prayer is, of all habits, the one which we recollect the longest. Many a grey-headed man could tell you how his mother used to make him pray in the days of his childhood. Other things have passed away from his mind perhaps.—The church where he was taken to worship—the minister whom he heard preach—the companions who used to play with him—all these, it may be, have passed from his memory, and left no mark behind. But you will often find it is far different with his first prayers. He will often be able to tell you where he knelt, and what he was taught to say, and even how his mother looked all the while. It will come up as fresh before his mind's eye, as if it was but yesterday.

Brethren, if you love your children, I charge you, do not let the seed-time of a prayerful habit pass away unimproved. If you train your children to anything, train them at least to a habit of prayer.

VII. Train them to habits of diligence, and regularity about public means of grace.

Tell them of the duty and privilege of going to the house of God, and joining in the prayers of the congregation. Tell them that wherever the Lord's people are gathered together, there the Lord Jesus is present in an especial manner, and that those who absent themselves must expect, like the apostle Thomas, to miss a

blessing.   Tell them of the importance of hearing the word
preached, and that it is God's ordinance for converting, sanctifying,
and building up the souls of men.   Tell them how the apostle Paul
enjoins us not to forsake the assembling of ourselves together, as
the manner of some is ; but to exhort one another, to stir one
another up to it, and so much the more as we see the great day
approaching.

Brethren, I call it a sad sight in a church, when nobody comes
up to the Lord's table but the elderly people, and the young men
and young women all turn away.   But I call it a sadder sight still,
when no children are to be seen in a church, except those who come
to the Sunday school and are obliged to attend.   Let none of this
guilt lie at your doors.   There are many boys and girls in every
parish, beside those who come to school, and you who are parents
and friends should see to it that they come with you to church.

Do not allow them to grow up with a habit of making vain
excuses for not coming.   Give them plainly to understand, that so
long as they are under your roof it is the rule of your house for
every one in health, to honour the Lord's house upon the Lord's
day, and that you reckon the Sabbath-breaker to be a murderer of
his own soul.

See to it too, if it can be so arranged, that your children go
with you to church, and sit near you when they are there.   To go
to church is one thing, but to behave well at church is quite another ; and, believe me, there is no security for good behaviour
like that of having them under your own eye.

The minds of young people are easily drawn aside, and their
attention lost, and every possible means should be used to counteract this.   I do not like to see them coming to church by themselves
—they often get into bad company by the way, and so learn more
evil on the Lord's day than in all the rest of the week.   Neither
do I like to see what I call a " young people's corner " in a church.
They often catch habits of inattention and irreverence there which
take years to unlearn, if ever they are unlearned at all.   What I
like to see is a whole family sitting together, old and young side
by side—men, women, and children, serving God according to
their households.

But there are some who say that it is useless to urge children
to attend means of grace, because they cannot understand them.
I would not have you listen to such reasoning.   I find no such
doctrine in the Old Testament.   When Moses goes before Pharaoh
(in Exodus x, 9.) I observe he says, " we will go with our young
and with our old, with our sons and with our daughters,—for we
must hold a feast unto the Lord."   When Joshua read the law
(in Josh. viii, 35) I observe " There was not a word of all
which Moses commanded, which Joshua read not before all
the congregation of Israel, with the women and the little ones,
and the strangers that were conversant among them."

" Thrice in the year " (says Exod. xxxiv, 23) " shall all your men children appear before the Lord God, the God of Israel." And when I turn to the New Testament, I find children mentioned there, as partaking in public acts of religion as well as in the Old. When Paul was leaving the disciples at Tyre for the last time, I find it said, (Acts xxi, 5) " They all brought us on our way, with wives and children, till we were out of the city : and we kneeled down on the shore and prayed."

Samuel, in the days of his childhood, appears to have ministered unto the Lord some time before he really knew him. (1 Sam. iii, 7). " Samuel did not yet know the Lord, neither was the word of the Lord yet revealed unto him." The apostles them-selves do not seem to have understood all that our Lord said at the time that it was spoken ; thus (John ii, 22), " When He was risen from the dead the disciples remembered that He had said this unto them." And (John xii, 16), " These things understood not His disciples at the first, but when Jesus was glorified then remembered they that these things were written of Him."

Parents, comfort your minds with these examples. Be not cast down because your children see not the full value of the means of grace now. Only train them up to a habit of regular attendance. Set it before their minds as a high, holy, and solemn duty, and believe me, the day will very likely come when they will bless you for your deed.

VIII. Train them to a habit of faith.

I mean by this, you should train them up to believe what you say. You should try to make them feel confidence in your judgment, and respect your opinions, as better than their own. You should accustom them to think that, when *you* say a thing is bad for them, it must be bad, and when *you* say it is good for them, it must be good ; that your knowledge, in short, is better than their own, and that they may rely implicitly upon your word. Teach them to feel that what they know not now, they will probably know hereafter, and to be satisfied there is a reason and a needs-be for everything you require them to do.

Who indeed can describe the blessedness of a real spirit of faith ? Or rather, who can tell the misery that unbelief has brought upon the world ? Unbelief made Eve eat the forbidden fruit ; she doubted the truth of God's Word, " Ye shall surely die." Unbelief made the old world reject Noah's warning, and so perish in sin. Unbelief kept Israel in the wilderness—it was the bar that kept them from entering the promised land. Unbelief made the Jews crucify the Lord of Glory—they believed not the voice of Moses and the Prophets, though read to them every day. And unbelief is the reigning sin of man's heart down to this very hour. Unbelief in God's promises—unbelief in God's threatenings—unbelief in our own sinfulness—unbelief in our own danger—unbelief in everything that runs counter to the pride and worldliness of our evil hearts. Brethren, you train your children to little purpose if you do not train them to a habit of implicit faith—faith in their parents' word, confidence that what their parents say must be right.

I have heard it said by some, that you should require nothing of children which they cannot understand ; that you should explain and give a reason of everything you desire them to do. I warn you solemnly against such a notion. I tell you plainly, I think it an unsound and rotten principle. No doubt it is absurd to make a mystery of everything you do, and there are many things which it is well to explain to them, in order that they may see they are reasonable and wise. But to bring them up with the idea that they must take nothing on trust ; that they with their weak and imperfect understandings, must have the why and the wherefore made clear to them at every step they take—this is indeed a fearful mistake, and likely to have the worst effect on their minds.

Reason with your child if you are so disposed, at certain times, but never forget to keep him in mind (if you really love him), that he is but a child after all ; that he thinks as a child, he understands as a child, and therefore must not expect to know the reason of everything at once. Set before him the example of Isaac, in the day when Abraham took him to offer him on Mount Moriah. He asked his father that single question, " Where is the lamb for a burnt offering ?" And he got no answer but this, " The Lord will provide himself a lamb." How, or where, or whence, or in what manner, or by what means, all this Isaac was not told : but the answer was enough. He believed that it would be well, because his father said so, and he was content. Tell them too, that we must all be learners in our beginnings ; that there is an alphabet to be mastered in every kind of knowledge ; that the best horse in the world had need once to be broken ; that a day will come when they will see the wisdom of all your training. But in the meantime if you say a thing is right, it must be enough for them—they must believe you and be content.

Brethren, if any point in training is important, it is this. I charge you by the affection you have for your children, use every means to train them up to a habit of faith.

IX. Train them to a habit of obedience.

This is an object which it is worth any labour to attain. No habit, I suspect, has such an influence over our lives as this. Parents, determine to make your children obey you, though it may cost you much trouble, and cost them many tears. Let there be no questioning, and reasoning, and disputing, and delaying, and answering again ; when you give them a command, let them see plainly that you will have it done.

Obedience is the only reality. It is faith visible, faith acting, and faith incarnate. It is the test of real dicipleship among the Lord's people, " Ye are my friends if ye do whatsoever I command you." It ought to be the mark of well-trained children—they do whatsoever their parents command them. Where indeed, is the honour which the fifth commandment enjoins, if fathers and mothers are not obeyed, cheerfully, willingly, and at once ?

Early obedience has all Scripture on its side. It is said in Abraham's praise, not merely he will *train* his family, but, " he will *command* his children, and his household after him." (Genesis xviii, 19). It is said of the Lord Jesus Christ Himself, that when " He was young He was *subject* to Mary and Joseph." Observe how implicitly Joseph obeyed the order of his father Jacob. See how Isaiah speaks of it as an evil thing when " the child shall speak proudly against the ancient." Mark how the apostle Paul names disobedience to parents as one of the bad signs of the latter days. (2 Tim. iii, 2). Mark how he singles out this *grace,* as one which should adorn a Christian minister, " A bishop must be one that ruleth well his own house, having his children in subjection with all gravity." And again, " Let the deacons rule their children and their own houses well." (1 Tim. iii, 4, 12). And again, an elder must be one " having faithful children," children " not accused of riot or unruly." (Titus i, 6).

Parents, do you wish to see your children happy ? Take care then that you train them to obey when they are spoken to—to do as they are bid. Believe me, we are not made for entire independence ; we are not fit for it. Even Christ's freemen have a yoke to wear—they serve the Lord Christ. Children cannot learn too soon, that this is a world in which we are not intended to rule, and that we are never in our right place, until we know how to obey. Teach them to obey while young, or else they will be fretting against God all their lives long, and wear themselves out with the vain idea of being independent of His control.

Brethren, this hint is only too much needed. You will see many in this day who allow their children to choose and think for themselves, long before they are able, and even make excuses for their disobedience, as if it were a thing not to be blamed. To my eyes a parent always yielding, and a child always having its own way, are a most painful sight :—painful, because I see God's appointed order of things inverted and turned upside down ; painful, because I feel sure the consequence to that child's character in the end will be self-will, pride and self-conceit. You must not wonder that men refuse to obey their Father which is in Heaven, if you will allow them, when children, to disobey their father who is upon earth.

Parents, if you love your children, let obedience be a motto and a watchword continually before their eyes.

197

X. Train them to a habit of always speaking the truth.

Truth speaking is far less common in the world than, at first
sight, we are disposed to think. The whole truth, and nothing
but the truth, is a golden rule which many would do well to bear
in mind. Lying and prevarication are old sins. The devil was
the father of them :—he deceived Eve by a bold lie ; and ever
since the fall it is a sin which all the children of Eve have need
to be on their guard. Only think how much falsehood and deceit
there is in the world, how much exaggeration, How many additions
are made to a simple story. How many things left out, if it does
not serve the speaker's interest to tell them. How few there are
about us of whom we can say, we put unhesitating trust in their
word. Verily the ancient Persians were wise in their generation :—
it was a leading point with them in educating their children, that
they should learn to speak the truth. What an awful proof it is
of man's natural sinfulness, that it should be needful to name such
a point at all.

Brethren, I would have you mark, how often God is spoken
of in the Old Testament, as the God of *truth*. Truth seems to be
especially set before us as a leading feature in the character of
Him with whom we have to do. He never swerves from the
straight line ;He abhors lying and hypocrisy. Try to keep this
continually before your children's minds. Press them at all times,
that less than the truth is a lie ; that evasion, excuse-making, and
exaggeration are all half-way houses towards what is false, and
ought to be avoided. Encourage them in any circumstances to be
straightforward, and, whatever it may cost them, to speak the truth.

I press this subject on your attention, not merely for the sake
of your children's character in the world—though I might dwell
much on this—I urge it rather for your own comfort and assistance
in all your dealings with them. You will find it a mighty help
indeed, to be able always to trust their word. It will go far to
prevent that habit of concealment, which so unhappily prevails
sometimes among children. Openness and straightforwardness
depend much upon a parent's treatment of this matter in the
days of our infancy.

XI. Train them to a habit of always redeeming the time.

Idleness is the devil's best friend. It is the surest way to
give him an opportunity of doing us harm. An idle mind is like
an open door and if Satan does not enter himself by it, it is
certain he will throw in something to raise bad thoughts in our souls.

No created being was ever meant to be idle. Service and
work is the appointed portion of every creature of God. The
angels in heaven work—they are the Lord's ministering servants,
ever doing His will. Adam, in paradise, had work, he was
appointed to dress the garden of Eden, and to keep it. **The**

redeemed saints in glory will have work—" They rest not day and night " singing praise and glory to Him who bought them. And man, weak sinful man, must have something to do, or else his soul will soon get into an unhealthy state. We must have our hands filled, and our minds occupied with something, or else our imaginations will soon ferment and breed mischief. And what is true of us, is true of our children too. Alas indeed for the man who has nothing to do. The Jews thought idleness a positive sin : it was a law of theirs that every man should bring up his son to some useful trade—and they were right. They knew the heart of man better than some of us appear to do.

Idleness made Sodom what she was. " This was the iniquity of thy sister Sodom ; pride, fulness of bread, and abundance of idleness was in her." (Ezekiel xvi, 49). Idleness had much to do with David's awful sin with the wife of Uriah ; I see (in 2 Sam. xi) that Joab went out to war against Ammon, " but David tarried still at Jerusalem." Was not that idle ? I see it goes on that " in an evening he arose from off his bed, and walked upon the roof of his house." Was not that idleness ? And then it was that he saw Bathsheba—and the next step we read of, is his fall.

Verily, I believe that idleness has led to more sin than almost any other habit that could be named. I suspect it is the mother of many a work of the flesh—the mother of adultery, fornication, drunkenness, and many other deeds of darkness, that I have not time to name. Let your conscience say whether I do not speak the truth. You were idle, and at once the devil knocked at the door and came in.

And indeed I do not wonder—everything in the world around us seems to teach the same lesson. It is the still water which becomes stagnant and impure : the running, moving streams are always clear. If you have steam machinery, you must work it, or it soon gets out of order. If you have a horse you must exercise him, he is never so well as when he has regular work. If you would have good bodily health yourself, you must take exercise. If you always sit still, your body is sure at length to complain. And just so is it with the soul. The active, moving mind, is a hard mark for the devil to shoot at. Try to be always full of useful employment, and thus your enemy will find it difficult to get room to sow tares.

Brethren, I ask you to set these things before the minds of your children. Teach them the value of time, and try to make them learn the habit of using it well. It pains me to see children idling over what they have in hand, whatever it may be. I love to see them active and industrious, and giving their whole heart to all they do—giving their whole heart to lessons, when they have to learn ; giving their whole heart to their amusements, when they go to play ; giving their whole heart even to sleep, when they go to rest, and sleeping sound.

But if you love them well, let idleness be counted a sin in your family.

XII.   Train them with a constant fear of over-indulgence.

This is the one point of all on which you have most need to be on your guard.   It is natural to be tender and affectionate towards your own flesh and blood, and it is the excess of this very tenderness and affection which you have to fear.   Take heed that it does not make you blind to your children's faults, and deaf to all advice about them.   Take heed lest it make you overlook bad conduct, rather than have the pain of inflicting punishment and correction.

I know well that punishment and correction are disagreeable things.   Nothing is more unpleasant than giving pain to those we love, and calling forth their tears.   But so long as hearts are what hearts are, it is vain to suppose, as a general rule, that children can ever be brought up without correction.

Spoiling is a very expressive word, and sadly full of meaning. Now it is the shortest way to spoil children to let them have their own way—to allow them to do wrong and not punish them for it. Believe me, you must not do it, whatever pain it may cost you, unless you wish to ruin your children's souls.

You cannot say that Scripture does not speak expressly on this subject.   " He that spareth his rod, hateth his son ; but he that loveth him, chasteneth him betimes." (Prov. xiii, 18). " Chasten thy son while there is hope, and let not thy soul spare for his crying." (Prov. xix, 18).   " Foolishness is bound in the heart of a child ; but the rod of correction shall drive it from him." (Prov. xxii, 15).   " Withhold not correction from the child, for if thou beatest him with the rod he shall not die.   Thou shalt beat him with the rod and deliver his soul from hell." (Prov. xxix, 15, 17).   How strong and forcible are these texts.   How melancholy is the fact, that in many Christian families they seem almost unknown.   Their children need reproof, but it is hardly ever given ; they need correction, but it is hardly ever employed.   And yet this book of Proverbs is not obsolete and unfit for Christians ; it is given by inspiration of God, and profitable ; it is given for our learning, even as the Epistles to the Romans and Ephesians.   Surely the believer who brings up his children without attention to its counsel, is making himself wise above that which is written, and greatly errs.

Fathers, and Mothers, I tell you plainly, if you never punish your children when they are in fault, you are doing them a grievous wrong.   I warn you, this is the rock on which the saints of God, in every age, have, only too frequently, made shipwreck.   I would fain persuade you to be wise in time, and keep clear of it.   See it in Eli's case.   His sons Hophni and Phinheas made themselves vile, and he restrained them not.   He gave them no more than a tame, and luke-warm reproof, when he ought to have rebuked them sharply. In one word, he honoured his sons above God. And what was the end of these things ? He lived to hear of the death of both his sons in battle, and his own grey hairs were brought down with sorrow to the grave. See too the case of David. Who can read, without pain, the history of his children, and their sins ? Amnon's incest—Absalom's murder, and proud rebellion—Adonijah's scheming ambition, truly these were grievous wounds for the man after God's own heart, to receive from his own house. But was there no fault on his side ? I fear there can be no doubt there was. I find a clue to it all in the account of Adonijah (in I Kings i, 6). " His father had not displeased him at any time in saying why hast thou done so ? " There was the foundation of all the mischief. David was an over-indulgent father—a father who let his children have their own way—and he reaped according as he had sowed.

Parents, I beseech you, for your children's sake beware of over-indulgence. I call on you to remember, it is your first duty to consult their real interest, and not their fancies and likings ; to train them, not to humour them ; to profit, not merely to please. You must not give way to every wish and caprice of your child's mind, however much you may love him ; you must not let him suppose his will is to be everything, and that he has only to desire a thing, and it will be done. Do not, I pray you, make your children idols, lest God should take away and break your idol just to convince you of your folly. Learn to say " No " to your children. Shew them that you are able to refuse whatever you think is not fit for them. Shew them that you are ready to punish disobedience, and that when you speak of it, you are not only ready to threaten, but also to perform. Do not threaten too much. Threatened folks, and threatened faults live long. Punish seldom, but really and in good earnest ; frequent and slight punishment is a wretched system indeed. Beware of letting small faults pass unnoticed, under the idea " it is a little one." There are no little things in training children ; all are important. Little weeds need plucking as much as any. Leave them alone, and they will soon be great.

Brethren, if there be any point which deserves your attention, believe me it is this one.

XIII. Train them, remembering continually how God trains His children.

I have told you often that God has an elect people—a family in this world. All poor sinners who have been convinced of sin, and fled to Jesus for refuge, make up that family. All of us who really believe on Christ for salvation are its members. And God the Father is ever training the members of this family for their everlasting abode with Him in heaven. He acts as a Husbandman purging his vines, that they may bear more fruit. He knows the character of each of us ; our besetting sins, our weaknesses, our peculiar infirmities ; our special wants. He knows our works and where we dwell, who are our companions in life, and what are our trials, what our temptations, and what are our privileges. He knows all these things,and is ever ordering all for our good, allotting to each of us, in His providence, the very things we need, in order to bear the most fruit ; as much sunshine as we can stand, and as much of rain ; as much of bitter things as we can bear, and as much of sweet. Brethren, if you would train your children wisely mark well how God the Father trains His. He doth all things well ; the plan which He adopts must be right.

See then how many things there are which God *withholds* from His children. Few could be found, I suspect, among them who have not had desires which He has never been pleased to fulfil. There has often been some one thing they wanted to attain, and yet there has been always some barrier to prevent attainment. It has been just as if God was placing it above our reach and saying, This is not good for you ; this must not be. Moses desired exceedingly to cross over Jordan,and see the goodly land of promise ; but you will remember his desire was never granted.

See, too, how often God *leads* His people by ways which seem dark and mysterious to our eyes. We cannot see the meaning of all His dealings with us ; we cannot see the reasonableness of the path in which our feet are treading.   Sometimes so many trials have assailed us—so many difficulties encompassed us, that we have not been able to discover the needs-be of it all. It has been just as if our Father was taking us by the hand into a dark place, and saying, Ask no questions, but follow me. There was a direct road from Egypt to Canaan, yet Israel was not led into it ; but round through the wilderness. And this seemed hard at the time. " The soul of the people," we are told, " was much discouraged because of the way."

See, also, how often God *chastens* His people with trial and affliction. He sends them crosses and disappointments ; He lays them low with sickness ; He strips them of their property and friends ; He changes them from one position to another ; He visits them with things most hard to flesh and blood ; and some of us have well nigh fainted under the burdens laid upon us. We have felt pressed beyond strength, and have been almost ready to murmur at the hand which chastened us. Paul the apostle had a thorn in the flesh appointed him, some bitter bodily trial, no doubt, though we know not exactly what it was. But this we know; he besought the Lord thrice that it might be removed ; yet it was not taken away.

Now, brethren, notwithstanding all these things, did you ever hear of a single child of God who thought his Father did not treat him wisely ? No, I am sure you never did. God's children would always tell you, in the long run, it was a blessed thing they

did not have their own way, and that God had done far better
for them than they could have done for themselves.   Yes, and they
would tell you too that God's dealings had provided more happiness
for them than they would ever have obtained themselves, and that
His way, however dark at times, was the way of pleasantness and
the path of peace.

Brethren, I ask you to lay to heart the lesson which God's
dealings with His people is meant to teach you.   Fear not to withhold from your child anything you think will do him harm,
whatever his own wishes may be.   *This is God's plan.*   Hesitate
not to lay on him commands, of which he may not at present see
the wisdom, and to guide him in ways which may not now seem
reasonable to his mind.   *This is God's plan.*   Shrink not from
chastising and correcting him whenever you see his soul's health
requires it, however painful it may be to your feelings ; and remember medicines must not be rejected because they are bitter.
This is God's plan.   And be not afraid, above all, that such a plan
of training will make your child unhappy.   I warn you against this
delusion ; depend on it, there is no surer road to unhappiness than
always having our own way.   To have our wills checked, and
denied is a blessed thing for us ; it makes us value enjoyments when
they come.   To be indulged perpetually is the way to be made
selfish ; and selfish people and spoiled children, believe me, are
seldom happy.

Brethren, be not wiser than God ; train your children as He
trains His.

*XIV.   Train them remembering continually the influence of
your own example.*

Instruction, and advice, and commands, will profit little unless
they are backed up by the pattern of your own life.   Your children
will never believe you are in earnest, and really wish them
to obey you, so long as your actions contradict your counsel.
Archbishop Tillotson made a wise remark, when he said, " To give
children good instruction, and a bad example, is but beckoning to
them with the head to shew them the way to heaven, while we
take them by the hand, and lead them in the way to Hell."

We little know the force and power of example.   No one of
us can live to himself in this world ; we are always influencing
those around us, in one way or another, either for good or for
evil, either for God or for sin.   They see our ways, they mark our
conduct, they observe our behaviour, and what they see us practise,
that they may fairly suppose we think right.   And never I believe
does example tell so powerfully as it does in the case of parents
and children.

Fathers and Mothers, do not forget that children learn more
by the eye than they do by the ear.   Imitation is a far stronger
principle with them than memory.   What they see has a much

stronger effect on their minds than what they are told. Take
care then what you do before a child. It is a true proverb, " Who
sins before a child sins double." Strive rather to be a living epistle
of Christ, such as your families can read, and that plainly too.
Be an example of reverence for the word of God, reverence in
prayer, reverence for means of grace, reverence for the Lord's
Day. Be an example in words, in temper, in diligence, in temperance, in faith, in charity, in kindness, in humility. Think not your
children will practise what they do not see you do. You are their
model picture, and they will copy what you are. Your reasoning
and your lecturing, your wise commands and your good advice ;
all this they may not understand, but they can understand your life.

Children are very quick observers, very quick in seeing
through some kinds of hypocrisy, very quick in finding out what
you really think and feel, very quick in adopting all your ways and
opinions, and you will generally find as the father is, so is the son.

Remember the word that the conqueror Cæsar always used
to his soldiers in a battle. He did not say " *Go* " forward but
" *Come*." So it must be with you in training your children. They
will seldom learn habits which they see you despise, or walk in
paths in which you do not walk yourself. He that preaches to his
children what he does not practise, is working a work that never
goes forward ; it is like the fabled web of Penelope of old, who
wove all day and unwove all night ; even so the parent who tries
to train without setting a good example, is building with one hand
and pulling down with the other.

XV.   Train them remembering continually the power of sin.

I name this shortly in order to guard you against unscriptural
expectations.

You must not expect to find your children's minds a sheet of
pure white paper, and to have no trouble if you only use right
means. I warn you plainly, you will find no such thing. It is
painful to see how much corruption and evil there is in a child's
heart, and how soon it begins to bear fruit. Violent tempers, envy,
sullenness, idleness, selfishness, deceit, cunning, falsehood, hypocrisy,
a terrible aptness to learn what is bad, a painful slowness to learn
what is good, a readiness to pretend anything in order to gain their
own ends—all these things, or some of them, you must be prepared
to see, even in your own flesh and blood. In little ways they will
creep out at a very early age ; it is almost startling to observe how
naturally they seem to spring up.

But you must not be discouraged and cast down by what you
see. You must not think it a strange and unusual thing, that little
hearts can be so full of sin. It is the only portion which our
father Adam left us ; it is that fallen nature with which we come
into this world ; it is that inheritance which belongs to us all. Let
it make you more and more careful, as far as in you lies, to keep

your children out of the way of temptation. Never listen to those who tell you your children are good, and well brought up, and can be trusted ; think rather that their hearts are always inflammable as tinder ; at their very best they only want a spark to set their corruptions alight. Parents are seldom too cautious. Remember the natural depravity of your children, and take care.

XVI. Train them remembering continually the promise of our text.

I name this also shortly, in order to guard you against discouragement.

You have a plain promise on your side. " Train up your child in the way he should go, and when he is old he shall not depart from it." Think what it is to have a promise like this. Promises were the only lamp of hope which cheered the hearts of the patriarchs before the Bible was written. Enoch, Noah, Abraham, Isaac, Jacob, Joseph—all lived on a few promises, and prospered in their souls. Promises are the cordials which in every age have supported and strengthened the believer. He that has got a plain text upon his side need never be cast down. Fathers and Mothers, when hearts are failing, and ready to halt, look at the word of our text and take comfort.

Think *Who it is that promises.* It is not the words of a man who may lie or repent, it is the word of the King of kings, who never changes. Hath He said a thing and shall He not do it ? Or hath He spoken and shall He not make good ? Neither is anything too hard for Him to perform ; the things that are impossible with men are possible with God. Brethren, if we get not the benefit of the promise we are dwelling upon, the fault is not in Him, but in ourselves.

Think too *what the promise contains,* before you refuse to take comfort from it. It speaks of a certain time when good training shall especially bear fruit, " when a child is old." Surely there is comfort in this. You may not see with your own eyes the result of careful training, but you know not what blessed fruits may spring from it, long after you are dead and gone. It is not God's way to give everything at once. " Afterwards " is the time when He often chooses to work, both in the things of nature and in the things of grace. " Afterwards " is the season when affliction bears the peaceable fruit of righteousness. " Afterwards " was the time when the son who refused to work in his father's vineyard, repented and went. And " Afterwards " is the time to which parents must look forward if they see not success at once—you must sow in hope and plant in hope—" Cast thy seed upon the waters " saith the Spirit, " and thou shalt find it after many days." Many children, I doubt not, shall rise up in the day of judgment and bless their parents for good training, who never gave any signs of having profited by it during their parents' lives. Go for-

H

ward then in faith, and be sure that your labour shall not be
altogether thrown away. Three times did Elijah stretch himself
upon the widow's child before it revived. Take example from him
and persevere.

*XVII. Train them, lastly, with continual prayer for a blessing
on all you do.*

Without the blessing of the Lord, your best endeavours will
do no good. He has the hearts of all men in His hands, and except
He touch the hearts of your children by His Spirit, you will weary
yourself, to no purpose. Water, therefore, the seed you sow in
their minds with unceasing prayer. The Lord is far more willing
to hear than we are to pray ; far more ready to give blessings than
we are to ask them ; but He loves to be entreated for them. And I
set this matter of prayer before you, as the topstone and seal of all
you do. I suspect the child of many prayers is seldom cast away.

Look upon your children as Jacob did on his ; he tells Esau,
they are "The children which God hath graciously given thy
servant." Look upon them as Joseph did on his ; he told his father,
" They are the sons whom God hath given me." Count them, with
the Psalmist to be " An heritage and reward from the Lord." And
then ask the Lord with a holy boldness to be gracious and merciful
to His own gifts. Mark how Abraham intercedes for Ishmael
because he loved him. " Oh, that Ishmael might live before Thee."
See how Manoah speaks to the angel about Sampson, " How shall
we order the child, and how shall we do unto him." Observe how
tenderly Job cared for his children's souls, " He offered burnt
offerings according to the number of them all, for he said, it may
be my sons have sinned and cursed God in their hearts. Thus did
Job continually." Parents, if you love your children, go and do
likewise. You cannot name their names before the mercy-seat
too often.

And now, dear Brethren, in conclusion let me once more
press upon you all the necessity and importance of using every single
means in your power, if you would train children for heaven.

I know well that God is a sovereign God, and doeth all things
according to the counsel of His own will. I know that Rehoboam
was the son of Solomon, and Manasseh the son of Hezekiah and
that you do not always see godly parents having a godly seed.
But I know also that God is a God who works by means, and sure am
I, if you make light of such means as I have mentioned, your
children are not likely to turn out well.

Fathers and Mothers, you may take your children to be
baptized, and have them enrolled in the ranks of Christ's Church ;
you may get godly sponsors to answer for them and help you by
their prayers ; you may send them to the best of schools, and give
them Bibles and Prayer Books, and fill them with head knowledge,
but if all this time there is no regular training at home, I tell you

plainly, I fear it will go hard in the end with your children's souls. Home is the place where habits are formed—home is the place where the foundations of character are laid—home gives the bias to our tastes, and likings, and opinions. See then, I pray you, that there be careful training at home. Happy indeed is the man who can say as Bolton did upon his dying bed to his children, " I do believe not one of you will dare meet me before the tribunal of Christ in an unregenerate state."

Fathers and Mothers, I charge you solemnly before God and the Lord Jesus Christ, take every pains to train your children in the way they should go. I charge you, not merely for the sake of your children's souls ; I charge you for the sake of your own future comfort and peace. Truly it is your interest to do so. Truly your own happiness in great measure depends on it. Children have ever been the bow from which the sharpest arrows have pierced man's heart. Children have mixed the bitterest cups that man has ever had to drink. Children have caused the saddest tears that man has ever had to shed. Adam could tell you so ; Jacob could tell you so ; David could tell you so. There are no sorrows on earth like those which children have brought upon their parents. Oh, take heed lest your own neglect should lay up misery for you in your old age ; take heed lest you weep under the ill treatment of a thankless child, in the days when your eye is dim and your natural force abated.

If ever you wish your children to be the restorers of your life and the nourishers of your old age ; if you would have them blessings and not curses ; joys and not sorrows ; Judahs and not Reubens ; Ruths and not Orpahs—if you would not, like Noah, be ashamed of their deeds, and, like Rebekah, be made weary of your life by them—if this be your wish, remember my advice betimes, train them while young in the right way.

And as for me, I will conclude by putting up my prayer to God for you all, that you may all be taught of God to feel the value of our own souls. This is one reason why baptism is too often a mere form, and christian training despised and disregarded ; you feel not for yourselves, and so you feel not for your children. You do not realise the tremendous difference between a state of nature and a state of grace, and therefore you are content to let them alone.

Now the Lord teach you all that sin is that abominable thing which God hateth. *Then,* I know you will mourn over the sins of your children, and strive to pluck them out as brands from the fire.

The Lord teach you all how precious Christ is, and what a mighty and complete work He hath done for your salvation. *Then,* I feel confident you will use every means to bring your children to Jesus, that they may live through Him.

The Lord teach you all your need of the Holy Spirit, to renew, sanctify, and quicken your souls. *Then* I feel sure you will urge your children to pray for Him without ceasing, and never rest till He has come down into their hearts with power, and made them new creatures.

The Lord grant this, and then I have a good hope that you will indeed train up your children well—train well for this life and train well for the life to come ; train well for earth and train well for heaven ; train them for God, for Christ and for eternity.

*   *   *

SCRIPTURAL SUNDAY SCHOOLS—THEN OR NOW ?

It was in 1789 that the Sunday Schools began to be systematically carried on. They were set on foot first in Wales by Mr. Charles and increased rapidly. The success of these schools, and the manner of conducting them, will be seen by the following extracts from Mr. Charles's letters. " Here at Bala we have had a very great, powerful, and glorious outpouring of the Spirit . . . *especially on the children and young people* . . . Children that were afore time like jewels buried in rubbish, now appear with divine lustre and transcendent beauty. Little children from six to twelve years of age, are affected, astonished, and overpowered. Their young minds, day and night, are filled with nothing but soul-concerns. The Lord hath done great things for us, and to Him be the praise." May, 1792—" That it was the work of God I am not left in doubt in the least degree. It carries along with it every scriptural satisfactory evidence ; such as *deep conviction of sin,* of righteousness, and judgment—great reformation of manners—great delight in the word of God and prayer. These, *even in young persons,* occupy the place and employ the time that was spent in vain diversions and amusements." " Thousands of young people all over the country, have at this time their attention engaged upon divine things . . . Boys and girls, from eight to sixteen, learn whole books of the Scriptures, and repeat what time permits us to hear ; such as the whole epistle to the Ephesians, Hebrews, etc. Others learn selected chapters, to an astonishing number ; such as ten, twenty, thirty, etc. One little girl learnt seventy-two psalms and chapters ; another, the astonishing number of ninety-two ; the list of which I have in my possession." In these Sunday schools, which were largely instrumental in the great religious awakening of this period, the children were instructed in the following truths—" The being of God—the doctrine of the Trinity—the inspiration of the Scriptures—the Person of Christ as God-man—the Person, titles and work of the Spirit—the corruption and renewal of the powers of man's soul—the necessity, nature and effects of regeneration—the privileges of believers—justification—redemption, that is, the necessity of it—the names given in Scripture to heaven and hell, with the names of the two roads which lead to these two places—the names given to Christ—the sin of sloth and idleness, etc." " In my opinion," writes Mr. Charles, " in the education of children, it is of the utmost importance, *in the first place,* to impress their minds with a knowledge that they are candidates for another world, and that things pertaining to their eternal felicity there, are of infinitely greater importance to them, than the little concerns which belong to our short existence here. The neglect of this is, I apprehend, a very great defect in the education of children."

—From Morgan's Life of Thomas Charles of Bala.

TWO SERMONS FOR CHILDREN

By J. C. Ryle.

" THE TWO BEARS "

*" He went up from thence unto Bethel: and as he was going up by
the way, there came forth little children out of the city, and
mocked him and said unto him, Go up, thou bald head, go up
thou bald head.*
*" And he turned back, and looked on them, and cursed them in
the name of the Lord. And there came forth two she bears out
of the wood, and tare forty and two children of them."*
—2 Kings ii, 23, 24.

Dear Children, Did you ever see a bear ?   Perhaps not.
There are no wild bears in this country now.   There are some
kept fastened up in wild-beast shows, or carried about in cages.
But there are none loose in the woods and fields.   So perhaps you
never saw a bear.

A bear is a large, shaggy, savage wild beast, with great teeth
and claws, and very strong.   It will kill sheep, and lambs, and
calves, and goats, and eat them.   When it is very hungry it will
attack men, women, or children, and tear them to pieces.   She-
bears that have little cubs are particularly fierce and cruel.   How
thankful we ought to be, that we can walk about in England
without fear of being caught by a bear !

Now I am going to tell you a story about a good man, two
bears and some children.   It is a story out of the Bible, and so you
may be sure it is all true.   Stories in other books are often only
" make-believe," and tell us things that never really happened.
Stories out of the Bible, you must always remember, are true,
every word.   Never forget that !

Once on a time, about twenty-seven hundred years ago, there
lived a good man whose name was Elisha.   He was at first servant
to a famous prophet of God named Elijah.   After Elijah was taken
up to heaven in a chariot of fire, Elisha was appointed to be prophet
in his place.   From that time to his death he was a very great and
a very useful man.   He did many miracles.   He used to go up and
down the land of Israel, teaching people how to serve God, and
reproving sinners.   In some places he kept up schools, called
" schools of the prophets."   In this way he became famous all over
the country.   All people knew Elisha, and all good people
loved him.

One day, not long after Elijah had been taken up to heaven,
Elisha went to a place called Bethel, where there was a school.
I dare say he went to see how the school was getting on, and
whether it was doing any good.   All schools need looking after
and examining ; and it does them good to be examined.   It is only
bad boys and girls who dislike being asked what they have learned.

Now as this good old man Elisha got near Bethel, a very sad thing happened. A great number of little children came out of the town, and behaved extremely ill. They began to mock Elisha, and call him names. Instead of respecting him, and bowing to him, like good children, they made game of him, and said silly things—"Go up, thou bald head," they cried, "go up, thou bald head." They called him "bald head" I have no doubt, because the good prophet was bald with age, and had no hair on his head. They said, "Go up," I suspect, because his master Elijah had lately gone up to heaven, as everybody knew. And they meant that Elisha had better go away after his master, and not trouble them any more with his teaching. It was as much as saying. "Be off and begone! It is high time for you to go up, as well as your master."

Just think for a moment how wicked these children were! They lived in a town where they might have learned better things. There was a school of prophets at Bethel. But I am afraid they had not used their opportunities, and had loved play better than lessons. They had no business to mock Elisha, and treat him so badly. He had done them no harm, and had never been unkind to them. He was a good man, and one who was their best friend. Above all, they ought not to have said, "Go up, and get away." They ought rather to have said, "Stay with us, and teach us the way to heaven." Truly it is sad to see what lengths of wickedness even little children may go. It is sad to see how corrupt boys and girls may become, and what naughty things they will say, even when they live close to a school!

But what did Elisha do when these children behaved so ill? We are told that he "turned back and looked on them" with sorrow and displeasure. They had probably often done the same thing before. It had become a habit with them which could not be cured. The time had come when they must be punished. And then we are told that "he cursed them in the name of the Lord." That does not mean, you may be sure, that Elisha flew into a passion, and swore at the children, as some bad old men might have done. He was not the man to do that! It only means that he solemnly pronounced God's anger and displeasure against them. He gravely told them, "in the name of the Lord," that God would certainly punish them, and that it was his duty as God's servant to say so. No indeed! Elisha did not speak in passion or ill-temper. The Judge at the Assizes is not angry with the prisoner when he sentences him to be put in prison. When Elisha pronounced God's curse on these wicked children, he did it as God's appointed servant, firmly and faithfully, but in sorrow. God told him no doubt what to do, and like an obedient servant, he did it.

And what happened as soon as Elisha had spoken? At once there came forth out of a wood close by, two she-bears, which rushed upon these wicked children, tearing and killing all they caught. Think what an awful surprise that must have been! How dreadfully frightened these children must have felt! What running, and screaming, and tumbling over one another, and crying for help, there must have been! How sorry and ashamed of themselves they must have felt! But with many it was too late. Before they could get within the walls of Bethel the bears had caught and killed no less than forty-two children. Forty and two little boys and girls that night never came home to Bethel alive. Forty and two little suppers were not eaten! Forty and two little beds were not slept in! Forty and two little funerals took place next day! Many children, I cannot help hoping, got home safe, and were not hurt. But I am sure they would never forget what they had seen. They would remember the two bears as long as they lived.

Now, dear children, this is a sad story. But it is a very useful and instructive one. Like everything else in the Bible, it was written for your good. It teaches lessons which boys and girls ought never to forget. Let me tell your what those lessons are.

(1). Learn, for one thing, that *God takes notice of what children do.* He took notice of the " little children " at Bethel, and punished them for their wickedness. Remember, I beg of you, that God is not altered. He is still the same. He is every day taking notice of you.

I believe some people fancy that it does not matter how children behave, because God only notices grown-up men and women. This is a very great mistake. The eyes of God are upon boys and girls, and He marks all they do. When they do right He is pleased, and when they do wrong He is displeased. Dear children, never forget this.

Let no one make you think that you are too young to serve God, and that you may safely wait till you are men and women. This is not true. It is never too soon to take up religion. As soon as you know right from wrong, you are old enough to begin taking the right way. As soon as you are old enough to be punished for doing wrong, you are old enough to give your heart to God, and to follow Christ. The child that is old enough to be chastised for swearing and telling lies, is not too young to be taught to pray and read the Bible. The child that is big enough to displease God, is also big enough to please Him. The child that is old enough to be tempted by the devil, is not too young to have the grace of the Holy Spirit in his heart.

Children, however little and young you are, God is always noticing you. He notices how you behave at home, how you behave at school, and how you behave at play. He notices whether you say your prayers or not, and how you say them. He notices whether you mind what your mother tells you, and how you go on when you are out of your mother's sight. He notices whether you are greedy, or selfish, or cross, or tell lies, or take what is not your own. In short, there is nothing about children that God does not notice.

I read in the Bible, that when little Ishmael was almost dead with thirst in the wilderness, "God heard the voice of the lad." (Gen. xxi, 17). Mark that, He listened to the child's prayer. I read that when Samuel was only a little boy, God spoke to him. (1 Sam. iii, 10). I read that when Abijah, the child of Jeroboam, was sick and dying, God said by the mouth of His prophet, " there is some good thing found in him towards the Lord God of Israel." (1 Kings xiv, 13). Children, these things were written for your learning.

Now I will give you a piece of advice. Say to yourselves every morning when you get up—" God sees me. Let me live as in God's sight." God is always looking at what you do, and hearing what you say. All is put down in His great books, and all must be reckoned for at the last day. It is written in the Bible—" Even a child is known by his doings." (Pro. xx, 11).

(2). Learn, for another thing that it is *very wrong to mock at good people, and despise religion.* The little children of Bethel mocked at Elisha, and called him " bald-head." For so doing they were terribly punished.

Dear children, as long as you live, make it a rule never to laugh at religion, or to mock anybody who is religious. This is one of the wickedest things you can do. It is pleasant to see boys and girls merry and happy. Youth is the time for laughter and merriment. But take care never to laugh at anything belonging to God. Whatever you laugh at, do not laugh at religion.

Some boys and girls, I am sorry to say, are very thoughtless about this. They think it clever to make game of those who read their Bibles, and say their prayers, and keep their Sundays properly, and attend to what is said at Church. They laugh at other boys and girls who mind what their mothers say, and try to corrupt them. Some, indeed, are so wicked that when they see other children trying to do what pleases God, they will point their fingers at them, and cry—" There goes a little *saint.*"

Now, all this is very wrong, and offends God exceedingly. There sits One in heaven who see these wicked children, and when He sees them He is greatly displeased. We cannot wonder if such children come to trouble, or turn out badly. All who despise God's people, despise God Himself. It is written, " Them that honour Me I will honour and they that despise Me shall be lightly esteemed." (1 Sam. ii, 30).

I read in the Bible that Ishmael was turned out of Abraham's house because he mocked his little brother Isaac. St. Paul tells us about this, that "he persecuted him." (Gen. xxi, 9 ; Gal. iv, 22). At the time when Ishmael did this he was only a boy. But, boy as he was, he was old enough to offend God by mocking, and to bring himself and his mother into great trouble.

Dear children, some of you have good fathers and mothers, who tell you to read your Bibles and say your prayers. I hope that you never laugh at them behind their backs, and mock at what they tell you about religion. Be sure, if you do this, that you commit a great sin. It is written—"The eye that mocketh at his father, and despiseth to obey his mother, the ravens of the valley shall pick it out, and the young eagles shall eat it." (Prov. xxx, 17).

(3). Learn, in the last place, that *sin is sure to bring sorrow at last*. It brought wounds and death on the little children of Bethel. It brought weeping and crying to the homes of their parents. If these wicked boys and girls had not displeased God, they would not have been torn by the bears.

Dear children, as long as you live, you will always see the same thing. Those who will have their own way and run into sin, are sure, sooner or later, to find themselves in trouble. This trouble may not come at once. It may even be kept off for many long years. But sooner or later it is sure to come. There is a dreadful hell at last, and those who will go on sowing sin, are sure at last to reap sorrow.

Adam and Eve would eat the forbidden fruit in Eden, and what was the consequence ? Sorrow. They were cast out of the garden with shame.

The people before the flood would go on eating, and drinking, and despising Noah's advice about the flood. And what was the consequence ? Sorrow. The flood came, and they were all drowned.

The people of Sodom and Gomorrah would go on sinning in spite of Lot's warnings. And what was the consequence ? Sorrow. The fire fell from heaven, and they were all burned.

Esau would have the mess of pottage, and despised his birthright. And what was the consequence ? Sorrow. He sought it afterward too late, with many tears.

The children of Israel would not obey God's command, and go up into the land of Canaan, when He commanded them. And what was the consequence ? Sorrow. They wandered forty years in the wilderness.

Achan, when Jericho was taken, would not obey the command of Joshua, but took money, and hid it under his tent. And what was the consequence ? Sorrow. He was found out, and publicly stoned.

Judas Iscariot, one of the twelve apostles, would not give his whole heart to Christ, but coveted money and betrayed his Master. And what was the consequence ? Sorrow. The money did him no good, and did not make him happy, and he hanged himself.

Ananias and Sapphira told a great lie to Peter and the Apostles, in order to be thought good, and yet keep hold of their riches at the same time. And what was the consequence ? Sorrow. They were both struck dead in one day.

Dear children, remember these things to the end of your lives. The wages of sin is death. The fruit of sin at last is trouble. Those who tell lies, or steal, or get drunk, or break the Sabbath, may not suffer for it at first. But their sin will find them out. Sooner or later, in this world or the next, those that sow sin, like the children of Bethel, are sure to reap sorrow. The way of transgressors is hard.

And now I will finish all I have been saying with three parting counsels. Consider them well, and lay them to heart.

(1). In the first place, settle in your minds, that the way to be happy is to be really good in the sight of God. If you will have your own way, and follow sin, you are sure to have trouble and sorrow.

(2). In the second place, if you want to be really good, ask the Lord Jesus Christ to make you good, and to put His Spirit into your hearts. You cannot make yourselves good, I know. Your hearts are too weak, and the world and the devil are too strong. But Jesus Christ can make you good, and is ready and willing to do so. He can give you new hearts, and power to overcome sin. Then take Jesus Christ for your Shepherd and Friend. Cast your souls upon Him. Jesus, who died on the cross to save us, has a special care for little children. He says, " I love them that love Me, and them that seek Me early shall find Me." "Suffer the little children to come unto Me, and forbid them not, for of such is the kingdom of God." (Prov. viii, 17 ; Matt. xix, 14).

(3). In the last place, if you want to be kept from the evil that is in the world, remember daily that God sees you, and live as in God's sight. Never mock at good people, or make game of religion. Love those most who love God most, and choose for friends those who are God's friends. Hate sin of all sorts. When sinners entice you, do not consent. Abhor that which is evil. Cleave to that which is good.

Dear children, if you live in this way, God will bless you, and you will find that you have " chosen the good part which cannot be taken from you." (Luke x, 42).

Remember these things, and you will have learned something from the " TWO BEARS."

NO MORE CRYING!

*" God shall wipe away all tears from their eyes; and there shall
be no more death, neither sorrow nor crying, neither shall there be
any more pain."*—Rev. xxi, 4.

Beloved Children, a Bible text stands at the top of this page.
I should like you to read it twice over. I am going to tell you
something which, I hope, will make you remember that text as
long as you live.

I am going to tell you about three places of which the Bible
says a great deal. It matters little what we know about some
places ; but it matters much to know something about the three
places of which I am now going to speak.

I.　Firstly :　There is a place where there is a great deal of
crying.

II.　Secondly :　There is a place where there nothing else
but crying.

III,　Thirdly :　There is a place where there no crying at all.

Now attend to me, and I will tell you a few things worth knowing.

I.　First of all. *There is a place where there is a great deal of
crying.*

What is that place ?　It is the world in which you and I live.
It is a world full of beautiful and pleasant things. The sun shining
by day and the stars by night : the hills looking up to heaven, and
the rolling sea ebbing and flowing ; the broad quiet lakes, and the
rushing restless rivers : the flowers blooming in the Spring, and the
fields full of corn in Autumn ; the birds singing in the woods, and
the lambs playing in the meadows—all, all are beautiful things.
I could look at them for hours and say, " what a beautiful world
it is ! "　But still it is a world where there is a great deal of crying.
It is a world where there are many tears.

There was " crying " in Bible times, Hagar wept when she
thought Ishmael was dying ; Abraham mourned when Sarah dies ;
Joseph wept when his brothers sold him into Egypt : David wept
when Absalom was killed. There was weeping in Bethlehem when
Herod killed all the little children who were two years old. These
things, and many like them you will find in your Bible.

There is " crying " now all over the world. Little babies cry
when they want anything, or feel pain, Boys and girls cry when
they are hurt or frightened, or corrected. Grown up people cry
sometimes when they are in trouble, or when they see those die
whom they love. In short, whenever there is sorrow and pain,
there is " crying."

I dare say you have seen some people come to Church all
dressed in black. That is called being in mourning. Some relation
or friend of these people is dead, and therefore they dress in black.

Well! remember when you see people in mourning, somebody has been " crying."

I dare say you have seen graves in churchyards and have heard that when people die, they are buried there. Some of them are very little graves, no longer than you are. Well! remember that when those graves were made, and little coffins were let down into them, there was " crying."

Children, did you ever think what all this crying came from ? Did you ever hear how weeping and tears came into the World ? God did not make crying :—that is certain. All that God made was " very good." Listen to me, and I will tell you how " crying " began.

Crying came into the World by reason of sin. Sin is the cause of all the weeping, and tears, and sorrow, and pain, which there are upon earth. All the crying began when Adam and Eve ate the forbidden fruit and became sinners.

It was sin which brought into the World pain and sickness and death. It was sin which brought into the World selfishness, and ill nature, and unkindness, and quarrelling, and stealing, and fighting. If there had been no wickedness, there would have been no weeping.

If there had been no sin, there would have been no " crying."

See now, my beloved children, how much you ought to hate sin. All the unhappiness in the World came from sin. How strange and wonderful it is that anyone can take pleasure in sin! Do not let that be the case with you. Watch against sin. Fight with it. Avoid it. Listen not to it. Take the advice of St. Paul : " Abhor that which is evil." Take the advice of Solomon : " When sinners entice thee, consent thou not." Say to yourself every morning, " Sin caused crying, and so I will hate sin."

See again, my beloved children, how foolish it is to expect perfect happiness in this World. It is expecting what you will not find. The World is a place where there is much " crying " and where things do not always go on pleasantly. I hear many boys and girls talking of pleasures they will have when they are men and women. I am sorry for them when I hear them talking in this way. I know they are mistaken. I know they will be disappointed.

They will find when they grow up, that they cannot get through the world without many troubles and cares. There are no roses without thorns. There are no years without dark and rainy days. There is no living on earth without " crying " and tears.

II. I will now speak of the second place about which I promised to tell you something. *There is a place where there is nothing else but " crying."*

What is this place ? It is the place to which all bad people go when they are dead. It is the place which the Bible calls hell.

In hell there is nothing but "weeping and gnashing of teeth." In hell there is no laughter and smiling.

In hell there is no happiness. Those who go there cry on night and day without stopping. They have no rest. They never go to sleep and wake up happy. They never stop crying in hell.

Beloved children, I am sorry to tell you that there are many people going to hell. "Broad is the way that leadeth unto destruction and many there be which go in it." I am afraid that many children are going to hell. I see many boys and girls who are so naughty and ill-behaved, that I am sure they are not fit for heaven. And if they are not fit for heaven, where will they go if they die ? There is only one other place to which they can go. *They must go to Hell.*

Dear Children, it makes me sad to say these things. I cannot bear the thought of boys and girls going to that dreadful place where there is nothing but crying. My heart's desire and prayer to God for you is, that you may not go to hell. But I want you to know some things which you must mind if you would not go to hell. Listen to me now while I ask you a few questions.

For one thing, I will ask you—Do you love Jesus Christ ? You ought to love Him. He died for your sins upon the cross, that he might save you from hell. He allowed Himself to be shut up in the dark prison of the grave, that your sins might be forgiven, and that you might not be chained in hell for ever. Dear children, think about this ! If you love nothing but play and eating and drinking and fine clothes and stamp-books and do not love Christ, you are not in the right way. Take care. If you do not mind, you will go at last to the place where there is *nothing but " crying."*

I will ask you another thing—Do you say your prayers ? You ought to do so. God will never be a friend to you if you do not speak to Him, and ask Him to take care of your soul and make you good. If you never pray, or say your prayers without thinking, your heart will soon be full of mischief and sin. It will never be empty for a day. I once heard of a boy who had a little garden given to him all full of flowers. But he did nothing for it. He never raked it or weeded it. And after a few weeks, the weeds came up so thick that the flowers died. Dear children, think of this ! If you do not ask God to put the Holy Spirit in your hearts the devil will soon fill them with sin. Take care. If you do not mind you will go at last to the place where there is *nothing but " crying."*

I will ask you one more question—Do you read your Bible ? You ought to do so. That beautiful book is able to keep you from hell and save your soul. If you use the Bible rightly you will not be hurt by the devil. I once heard of a little boy in Africa, who was sleeping with his father in the open air, near a fire. He woke in the middle of the night and saw a great lion close to him, looking as if he was going to seize him. The little boy took up a lighted stick out of the fire, and put it in the lion's face, and drove him away. Dear children, think of this! The devil is "a roaring lion seeking whom he may devour." But he cannot harm you if you make a right use of the Bible. If you would drive him from you you must read your Bible. If you can read, and yet neglect your Bible, you are in great danger. Take care. If you do not mind the devil will carry you off to the place where there is *nothing but " crying."*

Beloved children, remember my three questions. Think of them often, and try your own hearts by them. I am not afraid about children who love Jesus, and try to please Him, and keep the Sunday holy, and pray and read their Bibles. I am not afraid that they will go to hell if they die. But I am afraid about children who care nothing about these things. I think they are in great danger.

III. I will now speak of the third place about which I promised to tell you something. *There is a place where there is no crying at all.*

What is this place ? It is heaven. It is the place to which all good people go when they are dead. There all is joy and happiness. There no tears are shed. There sorrow and pain and sickness and death can never enter in. There can be no crying in heaven, because there is nothing that can cause grief.

Dear children, there will be no more lessons in heaven. All will have been learned. The school will be closed. The rod of correction will be laid aside for ever. There will be an eternal holiday.

There will be no work in heaven. Man will no longer need to labour for his bread. The head will no longer have to ache with thinking. The hands will no longer be stiff and brown with toiling. There will be an eternal rest for the people of God.

There will be no sickness in heaven. Pain and disease and weakness and death will not be known. The people who dwell there shall no more say, " I am sick." They will be always well. There will be nothing but health and strength for evermore.

There will be no sin in heaven. There will be no bad tempers, no unkind words, no spiteful actions. The great tempter, the devil, will not be allowed to come in and spoil the happiness. There shall be nothing but holiness and love for evermore.

Best of all the Lord Jesus Himself will be in the midst of heaven. His people shall at last see Him face to face, and go out from His presence no more. He shall gather His lambs into His bosom, and wipe away all tears from all eyes. Where He is will be fulness of joy, and at His right hand shall be pleasures for evermore.

Dear Children, would you not like to go to heaven ? We cannot live always in this world. One day will come when we must die, like the old people who have died already. Children, would you not like to go to heaven when you die ? Listen to me, and I will tell you something about the way by which you must go.

If you would go to heaven, you must have your sins forgiven, and your hearts made new and good. There is only One who can do this for you. That One is the Lord Jesus Christ. God has appointed Him to be the friend of sinners. He can wash away your sins in His own precious blood. He can make your hearts new by putting the Holy Spirit in them. He is the Way and the door into heaven. He has the keys in His hands. Children, if you want to go to heaven, you must ask Jesus Christ to let you in. Ask Jesus in prayer to get ready a place for you in that world where there is no " crying." Ask Him to put your name in His book of life, and to make you one of His people. Ask Him to cleanse you from all your sins, and to put the Holy Ghost in your heart. Ask Him to give you power to fight His battle against sin, the world and the devil. Ask Him to give you grace to make you good while you are young, and good when you are grown up, that so you may be safe while you live, and happy for ever when you die.

Children, Jesus Christ is ready to do all this, if you will only ask Him. He has done it for many people already. He is waiting to do it for you at this very time. Do not be afraid to ask Him. Tell Him you have heard that He was very kind to people when He was on earth, and ask Him to be kind to you. Remind Him how kind He was to the poor dying thief on the cross. Say to Him, " Lord Jesus, remember me ; I want to go to heaven. Lord, think upon me. Lord, give me the Holy Spirit. Lord, pardon my sins, and give me a new heart. Lord Jesus, save me."

And now, children, I have kept my word. I have told you of three places. I have told you of a place where there is nothing but crying. I hope none of you will go there—I have told you of a place where there is no crying. I hope you will all go there. I have told you of a place where there is a great deal of crying. That place is the world in which you are living. Would you like, last of all, to know the best way to be happy in this world ? Listen to me, and I will tell you.

The happiest people in this world are those who make the Bible the rule of their lives. They read their Bibles often. They believe what the Bible says. They love that Saviour Jesus Christ of whom the Bible speaks. They try to obey what the Bible commands. None are so happy as these people. They cannot prevent sickness and trouble coming to them sometimes. But they learn from the Bible to bear them patiently. Children, if you would get through the world happily, make the Bible your best friend.

Shall I tell you a story that I once heard about a little boy and the Bible ? Perhaps it will help you to remember what I have just been saying. I want the words I have just written to stick for ever in your minds.

219

"Father," said this little boy one day, "I do not see any use in reading the Bible. I do not see that it does any good."—Little Johnny said this in a rather cross and pettish way, and his father thought it best not to begin reasoning with him. "Johnny," he said, "put on your hat and come out, and take a walk with me."

Johnny's father took him first to a house where there was an old woman who was very poor, and he talked to her about her poverty.—"Sir," said the old woman, "I do not complain. I have read in the Bible these words, 'I have learned in whatsoever state I am therewith to be content.'" "Johnny," said the little boy's father, "hear what the old woman says."

They went on to another house, where was a young woman who was very ill, and never likely to get better. Johnny's father asked her if she felt afraid to die—"No!" she said, "I find it written in the Bible 'Though I walk through the valley of the shadow of death I will fear no evil, for Thou art with me.'" " Johnny," said the little boy's father again, "hear what the young woman says."

Children, when Johnny and his father came home that afternoon from their walk his father asked him one question. "Johnny," he said, "do you think it is of any use to read the Bible ? Do you think reading the Bible does people any good ?"

And now what do you think Johnny said ? I will tell you. He held down his head, and said nothing. But his face got very red, and he looked very much ashamed.

Children, from that very day Johnny was never heard again to say, "It is of no use reading the Bible."

Beloved children, remember my parting words. The way to get through the world with the least possible crying, is to read the Bible, believe the Bible, pray over the Bible, live by the Bible.

He that goes through life in this way will have the least "crying" in this world. And best of all, he will have *no crying at all in the world to come.*

A CONSIDERATION OF PARENTAL DUTIES

Extracts abridged from Edward Payson's Sermons.

It may perhaps appear strange to some of you that we have chosen such a subject as this for a day of public fasting and prayer. But we are not without hopes that, before we have done with the subject, you will be convinced that we could not have chosen one more important, nor more suitable to the present occasion. We are assembled this day for the purpose of humbling ourselves before God, for our personal and national sins, and praying for public and private prosperity. Now I firmly believe, that no sin is more prevalent among us, more provoking to God, or more destructive of individual, domestic, and national happiness, than that to which we propose to call your attention. Could we trace the public and private evils, which infect our country, to their source, I doubt not we should find that most of them proceed from a general neglect of the moral and religious education of children. I am more and more persuaded that this is one of the most crying sins of which we are guilty as a people. And if our civil and religious institutions should ever be subverted ; and this nation should share the fate of many other once flourishing nations of the earth, our destruction, like that of the house of Eli (1 Sam. 3 : 13, 14), will have been occasioned by this very sin ; a sin, which is the parent of innumerable others sins, and which, consequently, directly tends to draw down upon those nations, among whom it prevails, the judgments of offended heaven. My friends, this subject calls loudly for our attention, as citizens, as parents, as Christians ; and if we have any love either for our country, our children, our God, or ourselves, we shall learn to give it that attention which it deserves.

Children to be educated for God.

In the first place, in order to qualify yourselves for instructing and preparing your children for God's service, you diligently study His Word, to ascertain what He requires of them, and frequently pray for the assistance of His Spirit, both for them and yourselves. In the next place, as soon as they arrive at a suitable age, *which is much earlier than is generally supposed,* you will begin to tell them of your own inability to preserve them from misery, and render them happy either in this world or the next ; of their indispensable need of some other friend and protector, of the gracious invitations of their heavenly Father, of the infinite importance of securing His favour, and the inconceivably dreadful consequences of incurring his displeasure. You will also early begin to teach them the language of heaven, the dispositions, employments and enjoyments of its inhabitants, and the qualifications which are necessary to prepare them for it. You will tell them that God is able and willing to impart these qualifications to all who come to Him in the name of Christ ; that He has already conferred on them ten thousand favours ; that He is the greatest, wisest, and best of beings, and that His Son Jesus Christ is the friend of children, and the Saviour of sinners. You will diligently caution them against all those sinful tempers and practices which are inconsistent with the favour of God, and prevent them so far as possible, from associating with companions who might weaken their sense of the infinite importance of religion. In a word, you will carefully guard against saying or doing anything which may, either directly or indirectly, lead them to consider religion as an object of secondary importance ; on the contrary you will constantly labour to impress upon their minds a conviction, that you consider religion as the great business of life ; the favour of God, as the only proper object of pursuit, and the enjoyment of Him hereafter, as the only happiness ; while everything else is comparatively of no consequence, however important it may otherwise be.

To educate children for God implies, *That we pay more attention to the soul than the body.* We do not mean that the body is to be neglected ; but the soul must be considered as the superior part, and the body merely as its servant. In this respect multitudes of parents fail. They are extremely attentive to the bodies of their children, their health, their beauty, and the gracefulness of their deportment ; but seem entirely to forget that they have a soul, a mind, a heart, that deserves attention. If the slightest illness affects their children, they are alarmed ; but they feel neither concern nor anxiety on account of the diseases of their minds. They would be unspeakably distressed should their children be distorted or deformed, and would use every possible means to correct or remove the deformity ; but their minds may be deformed by a thousand evil passions, without giving them any disturbance. They would be extremely mortified to see their children awkward, rude and unpolished in their behaviour to their fellow-creatures ; but seem to think it of no consequence with how much indecent rudeness and impiety, they treat their Creator. But surely this is not educating children for God.

Educating children for the service of God implies, *that we educate them for eternity, rather than for time ; for a future world, rather than this.* You need not be told, my friends, that a different education is necessary to prepare us for different situations. For instance, if a parent designs one of his children for the navy, another for the bar, a third for the desk, he will give them in some respects a different education ; an education suited to their respective destined employments. So he who educates his children for this world, will, in many respects, educate them very differently from one who educates them for the next. The first will confine his views to the present life, and be anxious to teach his children only those things which are necessary to qualify them for acquiring riches, or honours, or applauses here. But the other will extend his views to eternity, and be principally, though not entirely concerned, to give his children that knowledge which will be useful to them beyond the grave. Here, again, multitudes fail. How few parents educate their children in such a manner as would lead a stranger to conclude that they believed in God, or a future state ; that they viewed their children as immortal beings, in a state of probation for eternity, and candidates for everlasting happiness or misery. He would see many anxious for the success of their children here, rising early, and taking rest late, and eating the bread of carefulness, to promote their temporal welfare ; while no anxiety is manifested respecting the destiny of their undying souls.

The guilt of preventing children from coming to Christ,
Mark 10 : 14.

Who are guilty of preventing or discouraging children from
coming to Christ ? To assist you in answering this question,
permit me to remind you, that in this, as in other respects, he that
is not with Christ is against Him. Your example must be either
positively good or positively bad ; every one, who does not encourage children in coming to Christ, is guilty of indirectly preventing it ; and his negligence leads them to suppose that to come
is of no consequence . . . Those are indirectly guilty of preventing
their children from coming to Christ, who employ no means to
bring them to him, who are careful to educate them for this world
but not for the next. Children are prone to imbibe the opinions
and imitate the conduct of others, especially of their parents. They
receive impressions from conversation at a much earlier age than
is commonly supposed ; and their first impressions are not only
most easily made, but are generally most deep and lasting. Almost
every seed, which is then sown in the mind, will take root and produce fruit in abundance through life and often through eternity . . .
Especially do children learn from parents how to estimate the value
of different objects. If they perceive that their parents and others,
who are entrusted with their education, are more solicitous to
educate them for this world than for the next ; more anxious for
their present than their future welfare ; more desirous to see them
prosperous than pious, and more concerned for the health of their
bodies than the salvation of their souls, they will inevitably be led
to conclude that religion is of little consequence ; and that to
obtain learning, riches, honour and applause, are the great objects
for which men were created. All parents therefore who thus
educate their children take the most effectual means to prevent
them from coming to Christ, and to cultivate that worldly-minded-
ness which is directly opposed to the love of God.

From this subject parents may learn the awful responsibility
which rests upon them. Were the guidance and direction of one,
two, or more worlds entrusted to you would you not feel that yours
was a most important and awfully responsible situation ? My
friends, if you are parents, something infinitly more important than
worlds is committed to your care. You have the charge of immortal
souls ; souls, which our Saviour has taught us are each of them
worth more than whole worlds. This charge is committed to you,
that you may bring them up in the nurture and admonition of the
Lord. And God considers you as answerable for the performance
of this duty, and in some measure for the salvation of your children.
At least He will consider you as answerable for their destruction,
should they perish, unless you do all in your power to prevent it.
If you doubt this, hear what He says to His ministers. Son of man
I have made thee a watchman, hear the word at my mouth, and

give them warning from me. When I say unto the wicked, Thou shalt surely die ; and thou givest him not warning, he shall die in his iniquity, but his blood will I require at thy hand. But, my friends, parents are at least as much appointed by God to be watchmen over their children, as ministers are to be watchmen over their people. Therefore if parents prove unfaithful, the blood of their children will be required at their hands. How much reason have many parents to cry, Deliver us from blood guiltiness. How dreadfully is our whole land stained and polluted by their blood, and how loudly does it call for vengeance ! What multitudes of parents and children go on together, hand in hand, to eternal ruin, without once pausing to inquire or reflect, whither they are going. My friends, of all the melancholy, heart-rending spectacles, which this lost world affords, this is perhaps the worst ; and of all the sins which exist among us, none is more prevalent or destroys more immortal souls, than the neglect of educating children for God. It involves the souls both of parents and children in one common ruin. Nor is any sin more destructive to a nation, or detrimental to the peace of society. How can it be expected that children, who were never governed or restrained while young, should prove friends of good order, or useful members of society when old ?

The consequences of parental unfaithfulness.

" For I have told him, that I will judge his house forever, for the iniquity which he knoweth : because his sons made themselves vile, and he restrained them not. And therefore I have sworn unto the house of Eli, that the iniquity of Eli's house shall not be purged with sacrifice nor offering forever."—1 Sam. 3 : 13, 14. Samuel was directed to begin his ministry by denouncing God's judgments against a sin which, it seems, was but too common then, as it is now ; the sin of neglecting the moral and religious education of children. It was this sin which drew down the most awful threatenings upon the house of Eli. His sons made themselves vile, and he restrained them not. We may be ready to think this a small and pardonable offence ; but God thought otherwise, and He made Eli to know that He did so in a most awful manner.

Consider the sin here mentioned. It is not said that Eli set them a bad example. It is evident, on the contrary, that his example was good. Nor is he accused of neglecting to admonish them ; for we are told that he reproved them in a solemn and affectionate manner, and warned them of the danger of continuing to pursue vicious courses. In this respect he was much less culpable than many parents at the present day ; for not a few set before their children an example positively bad ; and still more entirely neglect to admonish and reprove them. But though Eli admonished, he did not restrain his children. He did not employ the authority with which he was clothed, as a parent, to prevent them from indulging their depraved inclinations. This is the only sin of which he is accused ; and yet this was sufficient to bring guilt and misery upon himself, and entail ruin upon his posterity.

Of the same sin those parents are now guilty, who suffer their children to indulge, without restraint, those sinful propensities to which childhood and youth are but too subject ; and which, when indulged, render them vile in the sight of God. Among the practices which thus render children vile, are a quarrelsome, malicious disposition, disregard to truth, excessive indulgence of their appetites, neglect of the Bible, profanation of the Sabbath, profane language, wilful disobedience, and idleness which naturally leads to everything bad. From all these practices it is in the power of parents to restrain their children in a very considerable degree, if they steadily and perseveringly employ the proper means ; and those who neglect to do this are guilty of the sin mentioned in the text. Nor will a few occasional reproofs and admonitions, given to children, free parents from the guilt of partaking in their sins. No, they must be restrained ; restrained with a mild and prudent, but firm and steady hand ; restrained early, while they may be formed to habits of submission, obedience, and diligence ; and the reins of government must never, for a moment, be slackened, much less given up into their hands, as is too often the case.

My friends, the terrible punishments denounced against this sin sufficiently show that it is exceedingly displeasing in the sight of God. Eli's sons were given up to a hard heart and reprobate mind. They could not now be brought to repentance ; and, of course, no sacrifice or offering could purge away their sins. It is still the same, and there can be no room to doubt, that there are thousands now in the regions of despair, and thousands more on their way to join them, who will forever curse their parents, as the authors of their misery. Let us then inquire the reasons why this sin is so provoking to God, as it evidently is. Why is it so ? To this we answer, it is so,

(1). Because it proceeds from very wicked and hateful principles. Actions take their character in the sight of God principally from the motives and dispositions in which they originate. Now there is scarcely any sin which proceeds from worse principles than this . . . In religious parents, this sin almost invariably proceeds from indolence and selfishness. They love their own ease to well to employ that constant care and exertion, which are necessary to restrain their children, and educate them as they ought. They cannot bear to correct them, or put them to pain ; not because they love their children, but because they love themselves, and are unwilling to endure the pain of inflicting punishment, and of seeing their children suffer ; though they cannot but be sensible, that their happiness requires it. There is also much unbelief, much contempt of God, and much positive disobedience in this sin. Parents are as expressly and as frequently commanded to restrain, to correct, and instruct their children, as to perform any other duty whatever.

Great promises are made to the performance of this duty ; awful threatenings are denounced against the neglect of it.   Yet all these motives prove ineffectual.   The commands are disobeyed, the promises and threatenings are disbelieved and disregarded, and thus parents honour their children more than God, and seek their own ease rather than His pleasure, as Eli is said to have done. Now these are some of the worst principles of our depraved nature ; and therefore we need not wonder that a sin, which proceeds from such sources, is exceedingly displeasing to God.

(2).   This sin is exceedingly displeasing to God, because, so far as it prevails, it entirely frustrates His design in establishing the family state.   We are taught, that He at first formed one man and one woman, and united them in marriage, that He might seek a Godly seed.   But this important design is entirely frustrated by those parents who neglect the moral and religious education of their children ; and therefore God cannot but be greatly displeased with a sin which renders His benevolent measures for our happiness unavailing.

(3).   God is greatly displeased with this sin on account of the good which it prevents, and the infinite evil which it produces. He has taught us, that children properly educated will be good and happy, both here and hereafter.   He has also taught us that children, whose education is neglected, will probably be temporally and eternally miserable.   At least, it will not be owing to their parents, if they are not.   He also compels us to learn from obser-vation and experience, that innumerable evils and miseries do evidently result from this sin ; that the happiness of families is destroyed ; that the peace of society is disturbed ; that the pros-perity of nations is subverted, and that immortal souls are ruined by its effects.   Now the anger of God against any sin, is in pro-portion to the evils and the misery which it tends to produce.   But it is evident that no sin tends to produce more evils, or greater misery than this.   It is the fruitful parent of thousands of other sins, and entails ruin upon our descendants to the third and fourth generation—Exod. 34 : 37.   We often speak of acting for our posterity, of providing for their happiness ; but in no way can we promote their happiness so effectually, as by abstaining from sin ; and no way can we do more to destroy it, than by continuing in sin.   A measure of iniquity nearly full is a terrible inheritance to bequeath to posterity !   Yet such an inheritance we shall certainly transmit to them, unless a more general reformation, than there seems any reason to expect, should prevent.   May God have mercy upon our posterity, for I fear we shall have none !

If there are any children or youth now present, whose parents do not restrain them, and who make themselves vile by indulging in sinful practices, they may learn from this subject, what will be their fate, unless repentance prevent.   Children and youth, I am now speaking to you.   You are deeply interested in this subject.

Remember the character and the fate of Eli's sons. They made themselves vile, and God slew them. Remember that a quarrelsome temper, disobedience to parents, idleness, neglect of the Sabbath, and the Bible, profane and indecent language, and falsehood, render you vile in the sight of God, and are the high road to poverty and contempt in this world, and everlasting wretchedness in the next. Remember too that, if your parents do not forbid, and punish you for these sins, that will not excuse you in the sight of God. Eli did not restrain his sons, and yet God destroyed them. But if any of you, who have religious parents, pursue such courses in defiance of their admonitions, your doom will be still worse. There is no more certain forerunner of ruin in this world and the next, than habitual disregard to the counsels and warnings of such parents. We are told that Eli's sons hearkened not to their father, because the Lord would slay them ; and if any children present refuse to obey their parents, it gives reason to fear that God intends, in like manner, to destroy them.

The reward of parental faithfulness.

Part of the reward which God bestows on those who educate their children for Him, is the happiness which they enjoy, when they see their labours crowned with success. This happiness will usually, if not always, be enjoyed by those who seek with proper earnestness and perseverance the blessing of God to render their exertions effectual. I am warranted to make this assertion by the authority of Scripture. We are there expressly assured, that if we train up a child in the way he should go, when he is old, he will not depart from it. In addition to this, God's language to every believing parent, to every child of Abraham is, I will be a God to thee and to thy seed after thee. These passages are abundantly sufficient to warrant a belief, that God will save, at least, some of the seed of every believer, who, like Abraham, teaches and commands his children and his household after him . . . We dare challenge any person to produce a single instance, in which all the offspring of believing parents who educate their children for God, in the manner above described, died without giving evidence of hopeful piety. We know, indeed, that many children of parents undoubtedly pious, far from imitating their example, have been notoriously wicked ; but we know also that many parents, really pious, do not educate their children, by any means as they ought. We know also that all the means and endeavours which parents can use, will avail nothing, without the sovereign grace of God ; but we likewise know that God usually works by means, and converts those children whose parents labour and pray most earnestly for their conversion. The labours of ministers for their people are no more effectual without the grace of God, than those of parents for their children ; yet St. Paul assures Timothy, that if he took heed to himself and to his doctrine, and continued in them, he should in

so doing, both save himself, and them that heard him.   Why then
may we not with equal reason conclude, that if parents take heed
to themselves, to their conduct, and the doctrines of Christ, and
continue in them, they shall save, not only themselves, but their
children ?

My friends, what a reward is this!   What music can be more
sweet to a parent's ear, than the accents of a beloved child exulting
in hope of the glory of God, and gratefully declaring that to the
prayers, labours and pious example of his parents, he is indebted,
under God, for all his present happiness and future hopes.   How
must it alleviate the pangs of separation, when death arrives, to
know that we leave our children under the care of an infinitely
good, wise, and powerful being, who will do for them all that they
need to have done, and watch over them with more than parental
tenderness.   And hereafter, when we meet them in the abodes of
the blessed, when we see them praising God, for giving them such
parents, and hear Him greet us with, Well done, good and faithful
servants, enter ye into the joy of your Lord—what will be our
feelings ?   How inconceivable our happiness!   How great the
reward of educating children for God!

*   *   *

CHILDREN CALLED TO CHRIST

Like mist on the mountain,
   Like ships on the sea,
So swiftly the years
   Of our pilgrimage flee ;
In the grave of our fathers
   How soon we shall lie!
Dear children, to-day
   To a Saviour fly.

When Samuel was young,
   He first knew the Lord,
He slept in His smile
   And rejoiced in His word:
So most of God's children
   Are early brought nigh:
Oh, seek Him in youth—
   To a Saviour fly.

How sweet are the flowerets
   In April and May!
But often the frost makes
   Them wither away.
Like flowers you may fade:
   Are you ready to die ?
While " yet there is room,"
   To a Saviour to fly.

Do you ask me for pleasure ?
   Then lean on His breast,
For there the sin-laden
   And weary find rest.
In the valley of death
   You will triumphing cry—
" If this be called dying,
   'Tis pleasant to die! "

R. M. McCheyne, 1831.

Wickliffe Press, 104 Hendon Lane, N.3

THE
BANNER of TRUTH

(8th Issue)

Price 9d.

Subscription 5/6
for six issues.

EDITOR:

MR. IAIN MURRAY, B.A.,
65A BLENHEIM TERRACE, ST. JOHN'S WOOD,
LONDON, N.W. 8.

●　　●　　●

"Thou hast shewed thy people hard things;
Thou hast made us to drink the wine of
astonishment.　Thou hast given a banner to
them that fear Thee, that it may be displayed
because of the truth."　　Psalm 60 : 3-4

●　　●　　●

CONTENTS

229

1. Rejoice not, O Israel, for joy, as other people: for thou hast gone a whoring from thy God, thou hast loved a reward upon every cornfloor.

2. The floor and the winepress shall not feed them, and the new wine shall fail in her.

3. They shall not dwell in the Lord's land; but Ephraim shall return to Egypt, and they shall eat unclean things in Assyria.

4. They shall not offer wine offerings to the Lord, neither shall they be pleasing unto him: their sacrifices shall be unto them as the bread of mourners; all that eat thereof shall be polluted: for their bread for their soul shall not come into the house of the Lord.

5. What will ye do in the solemn day, and in the day of the feast of the Lord ?

6. For, lo, they are gone because of destruction: Egypt shall gather them up, Memphis shall bury them: the pleasant places for their silver, nettles shall possess them: thorns shall be in their tabernacles.

7. The days of visitation are come, the days of recompence are come; Israel shall know it: the prophet is a fool, the spiritual man is mad, for the multitude of thine iniquity, and the great hatred.

8. The watchman of Ephraim was with my God: but the prophet is a snare of a fowler in all his ways, and hatred in the house of his God.

Hosea 9 : 1-8.

Special Issue.

THE FAITHFUL MINISTER
HIS CHARACTER AND CALLING

EIGHTH ISSUE

AUGUST, 1957

EDITORIAL

A comment on the passage of Scripture on the adjoining page will show us something of the significance of the subject with which this issue is largely concerned. The prophet's first purpose is to overthrow the carnal joy and confidence of the Israelites by giving them a description of the judgments which were to come upon them for their sins—famine, v. 2, exile, v. 3, the removal of public ordinances, v. 4, and of solemn festivals, v. 5, in which condition they would miserably perish, v. 6. He declares that the failure of their material provisions and the ejection from their own homes and land was to be followed by something more dreadful, " *They shall not offer wine offerings to the Lord* . . . " The meaning is that God would remove from them His visible ordinances, the offerings and sacrifices, which they could once present acceptably in the place where God had revealed Himself, would no longer be possible, and any acts of worship which they might seek to offer would all be rejected. The question then follows, " *What will ye do in the solemn day, and in the day of the feast of the Lord?* " Solemn days and feast days were those times fixed by God, days such as the Sabbath, and times such as the passover, pentecost, and feast of tabernacles, when holy meetings were to be held, and when generally trumpets representing, as it were, the voice of God sounding from heaven, summoned the people to the temple. But in exile, as the temple and outward ordinances would all be missing, they would be unable to observe any of the feast days and their recurrence would therefore bring them nothing save a bitter realisation of what their sins had procured for them. When the trumpets ceased to call them to public worship, comments Calvin, " it was the same as if the Lord, by commanding silence, had proved that He no longer cared for the people. Something worse than exile is threatened. ' The Lord will take away the whole of your worship, and will deprive you of all evidences of His presence. What then will you do ? But if a brutish stupor should so occupy your minds, that this should not recur to your thoughts daily, the solemn and festival days will at least constrain you to think how dreadful it is, that you have nothing remaining among you, which may offer you a hope of God's favour.' We hence learn," continues Calvin, " that nothing worse can happen to us in this world, than to be scattered without any order. It would be better for us to be deprived of meat and drink, and to go naked, and to perish at last through want, than that the ordinances of religion should be taken away from us. Let us then learn to fear lest the Lord should deprive us of our festal-days ; that is, take away all the aids of religion by which He shows us to be a part of His Church."

In verse 6 Hosea rejects the false hope of the Israelites that Egypt and Memphis would provide a temporary shelter and refuge from Assyrian oppression. *"Lo, they are gone because of destruction"*—that is, to escape from the devastation of their country. The present tense is used, as in the following verse, to set out the certainty of the exile which was yet future. But instead of finding shelter in Egypt, they would be gathered, shut up, and buried—it would prove a grave—and their own homes would be left uninhabited so long that they would become neglected ruins—*" nettles shall possess them."*

"The days of visitation are come !" Because they had not been immediately punished for their sins, they thought they had escaped and forgot that God has certain fixed days of visitation and retribution. Their affliction would enforce the instruction they had hitherto neglected—*" Israel shall know,"* too late, by experience, the greatness of the God with whom they dealt, the vileness of sin, and the dreadfulness of divine wrath. But this experimental knowledge relates especially to what follows. Israel shall then know that *" the prophet is a fool, the spiritual man is mad."* Those whom they had regarded as prophets and men possessing the Spirit of God they would now see to be " fools " who had deluded and flattered them with promises of God's favour and blessing, and led them blindfold into ruin and error. Yet, although false prophets had thus deceived them, this would in no way excuse their fault ; God had given them over to " a reprobate mind " (Rom. 1 : 28), *" for the multitude of thine iniquity, and the great hatred."* That is to say, their teachers were a punishment for their guilt and hatred of God and His truth. It is one of God's common providences towards a people who have no love for His Word to give them ministers according to their own likings and opinions— " There shall be like people, like priest : and I will punish them for their ways " (Hos. 4 : 9). Burroughs comments on this solemn fact as follows, " When people dislike the powerful ministry of the word, and their hearts cannot bear its spirituality and force, God, in just judgment, sends unto them ministers according to their very lusts, ministers that shall be suitable to harden them in that very disposition of their hearts. And this is a fearful judgment on a people. They may rejoice, and bless themselves in it, and think themselves now quiet and secure, and say they have got a very honest and peaceable man amongst them ; but while they are rejoicing, the wrath of God is in a most dreadful manner let out against them, in sending them a minister according to their lusts. As God threatens in Ezek. 14 : 4, " If a man set up an idol in his heart, God will answer him according to his idol "; so, when people set up idols in their hearts, God, in His just judgment, will answer them according to their own heart's lusts, and they shall have such ministers sent amongst them as will harden them in their wickedness."

"The watchman of Ephraim was with my God," v. 8. The force

of this verse as it stands in our English A.V. translation is to point out the sad contrast between the old prophets who formerly stood like watchmen and knew the mind of God, and those so-called prophets who now pretended to the office yet who did nothing but ensnare and ruin the people with their errors. A deplorable change had taken place! But this interpretation though containing a striking truth, is not the most satisfactory and is based largely on the insertion.of the words " was " and " but," which are not in the Hebrew text, and upon the English punctuation. An alternative translation is therefore quite permissible—" *The watchman of Ephraim, before his God a prophet, is a snare of a fowler in all his ways, and hateful in the house of his God.*" Taken like this, the first part of the sentence is now a statement of the purpose and function of the prophet's calling, to maintain a vigilant watchfulness over the safety of the people and to convey the mind of God to them ; the second part is a description of what was in reality their character and practice—their conduct was wholly at variance with their office, and instead of having the approbation of God they were in fact an effect of His hatred and a procuring cause of further wrath.

We are now in a position to consider some of the truths which arise out of this passage.

I. The fact that Israel was rejoicing (v.1) when judgment was about to fall on her shows us how far error is able to blind people to realities. These verses moreover indicate that the success and strength of error lies in its disguised and plausible character. It appears in such a way that few recognise its real nature and consequences. Those who propagate it generally seem to be prophets and spiritual men, their doctrine like the bait of a birdcatcher—" a snare of a fowler "—is designed to appear pleasing, harmless, and attractive. Men may appear as "the apostles of Christ," preaching in His name and displaying an apparent likeness to His character, so that they are viewed by many as " ministers of righteousness " (2 Cor. 11 : 13-15 ; Matt. 24 : 24), but they will at the last day cause multitudes to exclaim " *the prophet is a fool, the spiritual man is mad.*" Spurious spirituality has always deceived many. Athanasius alone in the 4th century could see through Arianism when he declared, " It professes the Saviour's name, which is excellent and transcends all, and is disguised under Scripture expressions." None could detect any error in that ' holy ' monk Pelagius till God raised up Augustine. Those fatal errors which deceived almost the whole of Europe throughout the long middle ages were not easily discovered. " The canonists, the popish dissemblers, and other heretics," writes Luther, " are right chimaeras ; in the face resembling a fair virgin but in the tail like a snake. Even so is it with.their doctrine ; it glitters, and has a fair aspect, and what they teach is agreeable to mortal wisdom and appreciation, and acquires repute ; but in the end, it shows itself a slippery doctrine, having, like a snake, a smooth skin, sliding through the hand." Let us learn from this that the most dangerous errors have never been obvious, and they are not so to-day.

II. The Lord's giving up a Church to the delusions of false teachers is a fruit of their sins and an evidence of His wrath. It is one of the most solemn threatenings in Scripture, " The Lord shall smite thee with madness, and blindness, and astonishment of heart." Deut. 28 : 28. Although error come immediately from the devil, yet it is governed and directed by God for righteous ends. So in 1 Kings 22 : 22, the evil spirit had a commission from God to be a lying spirit in Ahab's prophets—" Go forth and do so, and thou shalt prevail with him." Likewise Ezekiel 14 : 9, " If the prophet be deceived when he hath spoken a thing, I the Lord have deceived that prophet." " The deceived and the deceiver are his," Job 12 : 16, that is to say, deceivers are subject to the government and disposal of God's providence, how and whom they shall deceive, and how far they shall deceive. Jeremiah understood this when he cried, " Ah, Lord God ! surely thou hast greatly deceived this people and Jerusalem, saying (by the false prophets) Ye shall have peace ; whereas the sword reacheth unto the soul." Jerem. 4 : 10. This truth is equally plain in the New Testament. Upon those that receive not the love of the truth " God shall send strong delusion, that they should believe a lie." 2 Thess. 2 : 11.

> " They trifle with the truth, until, at last,
> Delusions strong as Hell shall bind them fast."

" False teachers," says Luther, are marks of " God's greatest anger and displeasure, and are punishments for evil times. When God wills to punish a people or a kingdom, He takes away from it godly teachers and preachers. Then are the common people secure and merry ; they go on in all wilfulness, they care no longer for the truth and for divine doctrine ; nay, they despise it, and fall into blindness."

III. The removal of ordinances is to be regarded as the saddest calamity which a visible church can suffer, this is conveyed to us by the question " *What will ye do in the solemn day* ? " The chief ordinances granted to the visible church in the Old Testament were the Levitical offerings and priesthood, but the primary ordinance in the New Testament is the preaching of the Word and the office of the ministry. If we understand this, then we are in a position to appreciate the subsequent article in this issue on " The Puritan View of the Ministry and Its Relation to Church Government." The Puritans laid great stress on maintaining the purity and order of the visible church ; they did so because they were aware that it is the responsibility of the church to safeguard the entrance into the ministry and to appoint only those who manifest the scriptural qualifications necessary for the ministerial office.

If the visible church degenerate, then they clearly saw that the ministry would be thrown open to all, and confusion and error inevitably follow.

How few consider the relevance of these matters to the contemporary situation in England! May God enable us to read the rest of the issue in the light of these Scriptures, and to lay this question deeply upon our hearts—" *What will ye do in the solemn day, and in the day of the feast of the Lord ?* "

□　　□　　□

IMPORTANCE OF SERIOUSNESS TO THE CHRISTIAN MINISTER

DANIEL DANA, D.D.

A minister, if he is not one of the most inconsistent and wretched of human beings, is a Christian. In other words, he is a professed follower, and humble representative, of the Son of God. And how shall this sublime character be maintained and exhibited ? Not surely by a levity of spirit, nor by a trifling demeanour. Nothing could be more palpably the reverse of his divine Exemplar. The Saviour's mind was invariably occupied with objects of infinite interest and moment ; objects which, no doubt, diffused their own unearthly character over his countenance, his deportment, and every action of his life. Some portion of these characteristics will then be visible in all his real followers. A gay, volatile, trifling Christian is scarcely less a solecism, than a profane or prayerless Christian.

Every Christian was once a child of wrath ; a borderer on the world of despair. And must not every recurrence of this thought bring with it a variety of humbling, heart-felt sensations ? True, he is delivered from this condition ; and well may this deliverance inspire a joy which no words can express. But this joy is a mingled and a chastened sensation. It is as far removed from gaiety, as from despondence itself. Especially when the Christian recollects who was his Deliverer, and through what seas of blood and suffering his redemption was reached ; his gratitude, and even his grief, is everything but overwhelming. Nor should these tender thoughts be mere casual visitors. Is not the day, is not even the hour, from which they are wholly banished, a guilty day or hour ?

A Christian is a servant of the living God. And he is more— a friend, a favourite, a son. He has daily and familiar access to the presence-chamber of the King of Kings. By the advocates of royalty it has been contended, that in a court the style of manners is altogether peculiar and superior ; and that even in the aspect

235

and mien of its frequenters, there is a dignity and grace which distinguish them from all others. This is a question which we need not discuss. But of this we are sure, that the frequenters of a heavenly court cannot fail to acquire something of its sublime spirit and air. It cannot but impart to their sentiments and demeanour an exalting, hallowing influence—an influence placing them aloof from the vanities of the world, and destroying the relish for its follies and trifles.

In a word, the Christian is on earth a pilgrim and a stranger. His heart, his hopes, and his favourite enjoyments, are in heaven. In some bright and privileged moments, he dares anticipate the perfect, unmingled blessedness of that world. There are seasons, too, in which a sense of unworthiness and guilt comes over him like a cloud, veiling every prospect, and almost extinguishing every hope. Here, then, let the question be asked, In which of these two widely different states can he find time or heart for levity ? Must not even a momentary uncertainty on the subject of his immortal destiny burden his mind with solicitude inexpressibly painful ? And must not every hope he entertains of the joys of heaven fill him with emotions as solemn as delightful, and thus render the follies of the present scene insipid and disgusting ?

It appears, then, plain to demonstration, that the spirit of levity and the spirit of religion are opposites ; that their habitual predominence in the same subject is impossible ; that the true Christian is a truly serious man ; and that the comforts and distresses of his spiritual course are equally fitted to increase his seriousness of mind, and to put the opposite dispositions to flight.

But with what superior force do these considerations apply to the minister of the gospel ! If a vain, trifling Christian is a contradiction, a vain, trifling minister is a most disgusting absurdity.

To the private Christian are intrusted the concerns of a single soul. And when he reflects that his little moment of life will give complexion to his whole eternity, and that he is continually a borderer on unending joys or miseries ; the thought must press upon his inmost spirit. But to the minister is committed the care of hundreds of souls. Indeed, thousands, and tens of thousands of immortal beings, either near or remote, either existing or unborn, may receive their stamp for eternity under his influence ! What overwhelming considerations are these ! How adapted to crush a tender spirit ! Yet the minister from whose mind they are banished has not learned the first lesson of his vocation ; while he to whose mind they are familiar cannot fail to find their resistless influence, putting to flight the spirit of worldliness and levity, and filling the heart with the deepest emotions and solicitudes.

It is a constantly recurring duty of the Christian minister to converse with the sublimities of the gospel ; to meditate its profound and unsearchable mysteries. These are the subjects which occupied from eternity the mind of the Infinite God. These are themes in which angelic minds are lost. Here are embraced at once, the glories of the Deity and the everlasting destinies of millions on millions of created beings. And what is the spirit in which themes like these are to be approached? And what is the influence which their contemplation is fitted to exert on the mind ? Reason and common sense give the answer. None but a mind deeply serious is prepared to enter this hallowed enclosure. Nor can any mind, not awfully insensible, retire from it without the profoundest awe and solemnity. The minister who converses much with the glories of the gospel, ascends to a superior region, and breathes in a purer atmosphere. To him the very gravest schemes and employments of earth be like the playthings of children. What then must be its amusements and frivolities ?

But in the sacred volume other themes present. It portrays the guilt, the ruin, and the wretchedness of man. It reveals the terrors of the Holy One, and the awful doom of the wicked. It uncovers the pit of despair. It imparts vivid views of the ever-enduring, ever-increasing woes of the rejectors of gospel mercy. And these are themes from which, however painful, the minister may not turn away. He must even be familiar with them ; or how can he, with due solemity and feeling, dispense the warnings of the gospel ? Nor is it possible that, with a mind and heart occupied with these things, he should not be habitually and deeply serious.

It is one of the first duties of the minister to bring his people daily to the throne of God ; to pour their sins, their sorrows, their wants, their dangers, into the ear of the Eternal. It is his duty to plead, to wrestle, to agonize, for their salvation. Will not such duties, thus performed, leave an influence behind them ? Must not the minister who daily bears his people to the throne of grace, habitually bear them on his heart ? Will not the great concern of their salvation, while it fills his mind with tender solicitudes and fears, effectually exclude every species of levity ?

It is a fine remark of Thomsom,

> Ah, little think the gay, licentious crowd,
> How many feel this very moment death,
> And all the sad variety of pain.

The implication is that habitual gaiety is a species of moral delinquency, a wrong to suffering humanity. It is not fit that while one portion of the human family is plunged in the depths of distress, the other portion should be sporting in thoughtless merriment. And the sentiment is supported by more than poetical truth. Who, then, is more deeply dipped in this offence than the light-minded minister ? For who is more frequently summoned to scenes of distress ; and who can be more strongly bound to sympathise with the sufferers ? And shall this sympathy be a mere

I

thing of the moment ? Shall he hasten from the sick bed, or from the dying bed, to participate, perhaps to increase, the merriment of a convivial circle ?

But the miseries of the present scene are short-lived and evanescent. The true minister looks beyond. He is surrounded by immortal beings, who forget their immortality ; with dying creatures, who live only for this world ; with sinners who, unconscious of their depravity and guilt, neglect their souls and their Saviour . . . The true minister lives less for the present than the future. He has eternity in his eye. The celebrated remark of an ancient painter, " I paint for eternity," has more of the shadow than the substance. But on the lips of a Christian minister, a similar sentiment has all the beauty and grace of simple truth. He lives and acts, he preaches and prays, for eternity. And millions of ages hence, his life and actions, his sermons and his prayers, may be remembered by millions of beings beside himself, with unutterable joy or grief. This is enough. The minister who forgets this may be a trifler, and will be a trifler. The minister to whom this single vast idea is habitually present, and present as a reality, may trifle if he can. But it is impossible. He will be serious, engaged, devoted, absorbed—absorbed in the great object of meeting with joy his final Judge, and meeting with joy the favoured happy beings whom his fidelity has instrumentally saved.

Such are some of the considerations which show that the Christian minister, if worthy of the name, will be a man distinguished for seriousness. Let us now spend a few thoughts on the happy influence and effect of this spirit, both on himself and on others.

It will exert a most salutary influence on his studies. One of the first and most important duties of a gospel minister, is the investigation of truth. If he fails here he fails everywhere. And truth, gospel truth, is of a very peculiar character. It is not the result of cold and heartless speculation. It is not discovered by the mere power of intellect. It mocks the pride of the philosopher. But to the meek, humble, subdued mind of the sincere Christian, it spontaneously unveils its charms, and imparts its treasures. In a word, to the discovery of gospel truth, the chief requisite, the grand desideratum, is seriousness. It is itself the surest, safest guide. And it has the promise of divine, infallible teaching. " The secret of the Lord is with them that fear him ; and he will show them his covenant."

The importance of the same seriousness of spirit may be eminently seen as it regards *prayer*. Without it, neither will the necessity of this precious exercise be felt, nor its sweetness tasted, nor its advantages enjoyed. Where is the Christian, and where the Christian minister, who has not found that much in *proportion* to the spirituality of his frame, has been his nearness to God in prayer, and the satisfying sense of a real communion with the Father of his spirit ?   The minister who has feeble impressions of eternal things, and of the greatness of his charge, will find many temptations to estrange himself from the mercy seat.   And while he is there, his supplications will be comparatively formal and heartless. While to the serious minister, the duty of prayer will be full of attraction, of delight and profit.

It scarcely needs be stated, that that style of *preaching* which is most strongly marked with seriousness, has a vast advantage over every other.   Who expects an unimpressed preacher to make a deep impression on an audience ?   Who expects to find a seriousness in the pew, of which there is no example in the pulpit ?   It was said by Calamy of Baxter, that " he talked in the pulpit about another world, like one who had been there, and was come as a sort of express to make a report concerning it."   It was remarked by James the Sixth of a certain minister, that he always preached before him *as if death stood at his elbow.*   These are but samples of the very style in which *every* minster should aim to preach.   If preaching of this stamp were more common, can it be doubted, whether correspondent effects would attend it ?   It may be propounded as a general fact, to which there are few exceptions, that the success of ministers in converting and saving souls, has been far less in proportion to their genius, or eloquence, than to their seriousness and piety.

Most men, it is certain, see religion chiefly through the medium of its ministers, and form their judgment accordingly.   True, they are apt to be blind to what is excellent.   But their eyes are wide open to all that is inconsistent and defective.   Let ministers, then, beware.   Let them dread, as death, the thought of dishonouring religion, or of exhibiting it before their fellow men in a false aspect. We plead not for needless austerities, nor for affected singularities. We ask only that the ministers of Christ be true to their Master, and true to the religion they preach—a religion which bears inscribed on its front, " Be not conformed to this world "—a religion not more irreconcilably hostile to the world's vices, than to its thoughtlessness and gaiety.   What shall repress this thoughtlessness and gaiety, if ministers themselves, instead of stemming the torrent, are carried away with it ?

This is an affair of immense consequence.   There are thousands at the present day—and the number is rapidly increasing—who have settled it with themselves, that the religion of former times is a factitious and needless thing.   They view it as superstition, or gross hypocrisy ; at best, as mere enthusiasm and delusion.   And they are confirmed in these pernicious views by what they see, or think they see, in the professors of religion, and even in its ministers. " These preachers," they are ready to say, " are very solemn and starched in the pulpit ; but out of it, they are very free and easy. Their discourses are sometimes very alarming ; but it is evident they are not greatly disquieted themselves. Why should *we* be much disturbed with that which gives *them* so little trouble, and which they appear scarcely to believe ? "

Is it not a matter of the deepest regret that such things should be said ; and still more, that they should be said with any shadow of reason ? And is it not time for ministers to ponder the serious, mortifying question, how far they themselves may have given occasion and countenance to the wide spread and still extending infidelity of the day ? It is an undeniable fact, that the lives of ministers preach even more loudly than their sermons, and that if their sermons find a contradiction in their lives, they lose all their force and efficiency. It was said of one of the ancient fathers, that he *thundered* in his preaching, and *lightened* in his life. Something like this should be the aim of every minister. And he may be assured that if the lightning be absent, the thunder will pass over the heads of his hearers, harmless and useless.

In every view, then, it appears important that ministers should be eminently serious, spiritual, and holy. It is the just expectation of heaven and earth concerning them. An indiscreet, light-minded minister is the opprobium of religion, the grief of the pious, the scorn even of the ungodly, and the stumbling-block of thousands around him. While the devout, engaged minister is a " living epistle of Christ, known and read of all men." His life at once explains, defends, enforces, and adorns the religion of the gospel. Ministers of this description have been, for a long series of years, the glory of our land. If, in this grand point, we shall continue to be favoured of Heaven, the brightest hopes may be indulged. Our churches will be purified and replenished. Religion will rise from the dust ; will shed her countless blessings on the present age, and will be transmitted, a fair and unpolluted inheritance, to distant posterity. Should there be, in this regard, a degeneracy ; should the clergy of the present and the coming age lose that spirit of exalted and serious piety, which distinguished their predecessors, the prospect will be dark and mournful indeed. Infidelity and scepticism, now but too prevalent, will increase their ravages, and multiply their victims. Error, irreligion, and false religion, will gather strength, and advance to new triumphs. The church will languish and decay ; and all the great interests of our country will suffer vital and irreparable injury.

*   *   *

How sweet to feel dead to all below; to live only for eternity; to forget the short interval that lies between us and the spiritual world; and to live always *seriously*. *The seriousness* which this sorrow produces, is indescribably precious; O that I could always retain it, when these impressions shall be worn away!

—*A note in Henry Martyn's diary occasioned by the death of his sister. Sargent's Life of Martyn is a most valuable biography.*

MINISTERIAL STUDY

Notes from Dr. J. W. Alexander's Letters to Young Ministers.

We are persuaded that grave errors prevail in respect to what should be the aim of the pastor, in his parochial studies and discipline. Looking at the greatness of the harvest, and the shortness of life, one is tempted at the first blush to say, " Let the study alone ; go forth and save souls." When learning in the ministry is mentioned, some are ready to think of a purely secular erudition, such as withdraws a man from his duty, or unfits him for it. I beg you to observe that the ministerial learning which I am recommending is solely the discipline and accomplishment whereby you shall be better fitted for your work. The study is not a place for lettered luxury, but the sacred palaestra in which Christ's soldier is supposed to be forging his armour, and hardening his muscle, and training his agility, for the actual combat of the ministry. If, in the daily pursuit of knowledge, you keep constantly before your mind the end for which you seek it, there need be no fear of excess. To the last day of life, regard your mental powers as given you to be kept in continual working order, and continual improvement, and this with reference to the work of preaching and teaching. You will find all great preachers to have lived thus. I earnestly charge you to hold all studies as only means to this end, the glory of God in the salvation of souls. The day is near when your whole ministerial life will seem to you very short in retrospect.

You must allow me to tell you plainly, that the danger is not that you will have too much of this preparation, that you will be over-educated, or extravagantly learned, but all the reverse. You may get great learning, with a bad motive ; you may get little, with same : but all you will ever get, multiplied ten times, will not be too much for your work, or more than the Church and the times demand. Neither devotion, nor active labour, will furnish you an excuse for the neglect of knowledge. This is a question where examples are worth more than reasons. Look at Luther. Who was more devout ? Who was more active ? Yet who was more devoted to learning, or more profoundly anxious, to the very close of life, that literature and religion should never be divorced, in the ministry of the Protestant Churches ? " There be some," he says, " who think that the writer's office is a light trifling office, but that to ride in armour, and bear heat, cold, dust, drought, and the like, is labour indeed. I would fain see the knight who could join me in sitting still all day, looking on a book ! " John Owen and Richard Baxter, whose works by themselves make a library, were working pastors, through as much of their life as was allowed to them from persecution. Edmund Calamy is famous, as one of the authors of Smectymnuus, written in answer to Bishop Hall's

Divine Right of Episcopacy. No London preacher was favoured by greater crowds, and that for twenty years. But he had not attained his fulness of preparation without some pains. While a chaplain, he studied sixteen hours a day. Need I assert the diligence or erudition of Matthew Pool ? Look at his tall folios, especially his Synopsis Criticorum, the fruit of ten years' toil, during which he used to rise at three and four o'clock. He was pastor of St. Michael's, London, fourteen years, till the Bartholomew's Day, and was a laborious preacher. Tuckney is memorable as the principal writer of the Shorter Catechism. Calamy relates, in regards to the college elections, that Tuckney used to say, " No one shall have greater regard to the truly godly than I ; but I am determined to choose none but *scholars* : they may deceive me in their godliness, but in their scholarship they cannot." The grace of God did not leave our Scottish forefathers without some striking examples of parochial studies and successes. The value which they set upon ministerial learning is inscribed on the constitution of our Church. It could not be otherwise, where the foundations were laid by such hands as those of Knox, Buchanan, and the Melvills. Robert Bruce, that saintly preacher, favoured beyond most with near approaches to God in prayer, and marvellous power in awakening sinners ; and whose life you ought to examine in detail, thus speaks of himself in old age :—" I have been a continued student, and I hope I may say it without offence, that he is not within the isle of Britain, of my age, that takes greater pains upon his Bible." David Dickson's name is a precious ointment in Scotland. He was exceedingly blessed in an age of wonderful revivals. Multitudes were convinced and converted by his means, yet Dickson was the author of several learned works and in his latter years professor of theology in Glasgow. I must mention Samuel Rutherford. Christians of the present day, knowing him chiefly by his letters, scarcely remember that he was one of the most learned men of his age. He was professor as well as preacher. He commonly rose about three in the morning. He spent all his time either in prayer, or reading and writing, or visiting families. Read his Letters ; they will prove to you that great study need not quench the flame of devotion. I could easily record the names of clergymen still living, who add to the constant labours of the ministry, regular and persistent efforts to discipline the understanding and enrich the heart by private study.

Engrave it upon your souls, that the whole business of your life is to prepare yourself for the work, and that no concentration of powers can be too great. *Ministerial study is a sine qua non of success.* There is such a thing as maintaining a transient popularity, and having a little usefulness, without any deep study ; but this fire of straw soon burns out, this cistern soon fails. The preacher who is constantly pouring out, and seldom pouring in, can pour but a little while. The crying evil of our sermons is *want of matter;* we try to remedy this evil, and that evil, when the thing we should do is to get something to say. The grand point is this : there must be perpetual acquisition. This is the secret of preaching.

Ministerial study is twofold—special and general. By special study, I mean that preparation for a given sermon ; by general study that preparation which a liberal mind is perpetually making, by reading, writing, and thinking over and above the sermonizing, and without any direct reference to preaching. What theologians say of preparation for death, may be said of preparation for preaching; there is habitual and there is actual preparation : the current of daily study, and the gathering of material for a given task. The clerical scholar, however, diligent, punctual, and persistent, who throws his whole strength into the preparation of sermons, and never rises to higher views, or takes a larger career through the wide expanse of methodized truth, must infallibly grow up cramped, lopsided, and defective. His scheme of preaching may never take him through the entire curve of theology and Scripture ; or the providential leadings of his ministry may bring him again and again over the same portions. These are evils which can be prevented only by the resolute pursuit of general studies, irrespectively of special pulpit performance. Such habits will tend to keep a man always prepared ; and instead of getting to the bottom of his barrel as he grows older, he will be more and more prepared.

The objection to regular studies which meet us most frequently is, that there is no time for labour in the closet, from the pressure of parochial cares. Indeed, I fancy I hear you exclaiming, How is it possible for one situated as I am, to find hours for learning ? I desire to suggest a few considerations which will, perhaps, clear the path, and open some light through the seeming forest.

1. Maintain a reverential love for Holy Scripture. Keep one sacred object in view in every study you undertake. All your discipline and your acquisition are only so many means for learning God's Word, and for teaching it. Devote the first and last part of every day to the perusal of the Bible in the original tongues.

It is a source of deep regret to many in review of life, that they have scattered themselves over too many fields; let me entreat of you to spend your strength on one.

2. From what has been said, you will deduce the all important rule, to lop off all irrelevant studies. If you mean to succeed, and to save precious time, see to it that you rid yourself of all impertinent matters. Be determined to be ignorant of many things in which men take pride. Read solid literature. Familiarize

yourself with masterpieces, and disregard the perishing nothings of the hour.

3. Observe the evils which attend the lack of thorough preparation. Of all the ways of preaching God's Word, the worst is the purely extemporaneous—where a man arises to speak in God's name without any solid material, and without any studious preparation. As all men dislike labour in itself considered, the majority will perform any task in the easiest way which is acceptable. And as most hearers unfortunately judge more by external than internal qualities, they will be, for a certain time, satisfied with this ready but superficial preaching. The resulting fact is, that in numberless instances, the extemporaneous preacher neglects his preparation. If he has begun in this slovenly way while still young, and before he has laid up stores of knowledge, he will, in nine cases out of ten, be a shallow, rambling sermonizer as long as he lives.

4. You cannot well overrate the benefit to be derived from carrying always with you a high estimate of your study-labours. The clergyman's study, which some people regard as they would a pantry, is the main room in the house. It is the place where you speak to God, and where God speaks to you ; where the oil is beaten for the sanctuary ; where you sit between the two olive-trees, Zech. 4 : 3 ; where you wear the linen ephod, and consult Urim and Thummim. As you are there, so will you be in the house of the Lord. A prevalent sense of this will do more than anything to procure and redeem time for research, and will cause you to learn more in an hour, than otherwise in a day.

5. Practise an economy of time in punctuality and order : as Hannah More says, " It is just as in packing a trunk ; a good packer will get twice as much in as a bungler." Follow a plan. Propose questions to yourself—What part of the week do I devote to study ? What head of theology has lately been under investigation ? What is my plan of study for the coming day ? Cover the majority of the day's study as early as possible. Tell me how you spend your forenoon in your early ministry, and I shall be better able to predict how you will preach.

But after all, it cannot be concealed that there will be need of vigorous and unceasing efforts, to secure time for application, and to cut off all occasions of sloth and waste. You will be under a perpetual attraction to leave your study. There is constant need of decision, self-denial, and self-control. Read a book as itinerants do finding one in their chamber windows, as though you should never see it again. He grossly errs who considers the life of an evangelist as other than a conflict. Yet it is happy ; indeed

I hesitate not to express my conviction, that the life of a faithful minister is the happiest on earth. To declare God's truth so as to save souls, is a business which angels might covet : acquire the habit of regarding your work in this light. Such views will lighten the severest burdens and dignify the humblest labour. Think more of the treasure you carry, the message you proclaim, and the heaven to which you invite. Such are the considerations which may well serve to awaken true ministerial zeal.

We must take heed that we do not neglect our pulpit preparation. The matter and style of our sermons must be equal to the demands of the times. Some may be ready to say at the end of the week, " I have been working for God the whole of the week.—I have been attending the school, visiting from house to house, distributing tracts, making speeches ; and if my sermons on Sunday are not quite what they might be, at any rate I have not been idle."—We should remember, that all work of this description, if it trenches on the preparation of our sermons, *is work ill-spent.* It is no excuse in the sight of God, if our sermons on Sundays are poor, because we have been working so hard all the week. What costs little is worth little. If a man comes to his Bible on the Saturday, takes the first text that occurs to him, puts a few thoughts together, and then, trusting to his extempore powers, goes with that preparation only into the pulpit the next morning, we must not be surprised if the people complain of sameness in their pastor's ministrations. There never was a period when the pulpit demanded more preparation, more serious, hearty, studious preparation, at the hand of all God's faithful ministers. I must plainly give it as my opinion that clergymen who think there is no occasion for reading and study make a great mistake, and are likely to bring the ministry into great contempt.—*J. C. Ryle,* from an address to a large minister's meeting, held at Weston-Super-Mare in 1858.

If *you* must take heed how you hear, then *we* must take heed how we preach ; for you hear that which we preach. Therefore Paul putteth none among the number of preachers, but they which ' cut the word aright ' 2 Tim. 2: 15 ; that is, in right words, in right sense, and in right method ; and because none can do this without study and meditation, therefore he teacheth Timothy to ' give attendance to doctrine '; that is, to make a study and labour of it ; for as Saint Peter saith, that in Paul's epistles ' there be many things hard to understand,' 2 Pet. 3: 16 ; so in Peter's epistles, and John's epistles, and James's epistle, there be many things too which David before called, ' the wonders of the law ' Psa. 119: 18, and Paul calleth ' the mystery of salvation,' Eph. 3:3, and Christ calleth, ' a treasure hid in the ground.' Therefore Solomon confessed that he studied for his doctrines, Eccles. 12:10. Although he was the wisest and learnedest man that ever was, yet he thought that without study he could not do so much good. Daniel was a prophet, and yet he desired respite to interpret Nebuchadnezzar's dream, Dan. 2: 16. Is the Scripture lighter than a dream, that we should interpret it without meditation ? It seems that Solomon and Daniel would not count them sermons which come forth, like untimely births, from uncircumcised lips, and unwashed hands, as though they had the Spirit at commandment. Wheat is good, but they which sell the refuse thereof are reproved, Amos 8: 6. So preaching is good, but this refuse of preaching is but like swearing ; for one takes the name of God in vain, and the other takes the Word of God in vain. As every sound is not music, so every sermon is not preaching, but worse than if he read an homily. For if James would have us consider what we ask before we come to pray, much more should we consider before we come to preach; for it is harder to speak God's Word, than to speak to God; yet there are preachers risen lately up, which shroud every absurd sermon under the name of the simple kind of teaching, like the popish priests, which made ignorance the mother of devotion: but, indeed, to preach simply, is not to preach unlearnedly, nor confusedly, but plainly and perspicuously, that the simplest which doth hear, may understand what is taught.—*Henry Smith (1560-1591). Lecturer at St. Clement Danes, London.*

□   □   □

THE CHARACTER OF A COMPLETE EVANGELICAL PASTOR DRAWN BY CHRIST

Notes of a sermon delivered to an assembly of ministers by John Flavel, on the occasion of the restoration of their liberty to preach, following the nation's deliverance from Popery in 1688.

Who then is a faithful and wise servant, whom the Lord hath made ruler over his household, to give them meat in due season? Blessed is that servant, whom his Lord, when he cometh, shall find so doing. Verily, I say unto you, that he shall make him ruler over all his goods.—Matt. 24 : 45-47.

We are met this day to review and consider the cases of our respective congregations; which I doubt we shall find too like that description, Prov. 24 : 31, all over-grown with thorns and nettles, and the stone-wall broken down. Thus ignorance and error have overspread the people, and the wall of discipline greatly decayed. Our business is to cleanse our churches, and repair their walls; that so they may become gardens of delight, and beds of spices, for Christ to walk and take pleasure in.

Not to spend much time about the order and relation of the text; Christ had been solemnly warning the disciples, and all the Christian world, of his most certain coming to judgment; and therefore to beware of luxury, idleness, and security, the sins of the world; and that all be found at his coming, watchful and diligent in their proper places of duty. This exhortation he infers, from what common prudence would teach any servant, especially any steward of an house to do, to whom his Lord hath committed the care of his family. It is agreed by all, that the words have a special and immediate respect to gospel-ministers, the stewards of Christ's house, or church, to whom Christ hath trusted the care and dispensation of the affairs thereof. So speaks the apostle,

1 Cor. 4 : 1. 'Let a man account of us, as the ministers of Christ, and stewards of the mysteries of God.' To them he hath committed the dispensation of the word and sacraments.

Every private person, who hath received any talent from God, is a steward, and will be called to account for the employment, or non-employment of that talent in the audit-day. But ministers are stewards in the strict and special sense : Christ distinguishes them from the others, as porters from the rest of the servants, Mark 13 : 34. Nor may any assume that office, but by order from Christ the Master of the family.

In these words we find, I. An evangelical pastor described. II. The reward of such as answer that description, propounded, 'Blessed is that servant.'

I. Christ's description of an evangelical pastor, ver. 45, which he doth by two excellent and essential properties, or qualifications, *faithful* and *wise ;* both which make up the character of a complete gospel-minister : for if he be faithful, he deceives not others ; and if wise, or prudent, he is not apt to be deceived himself. His prudence will enable him to discern, and his faithfulness oblige him to distribute wholesome food to his flock. These two therefore meeting together, make a pastor *after God's own heart,* according to Jer. 3 : 15.

Faithfulness is an essential requisite to a steward, 1 Cor. 4 : 2. What ground is there for *trust,* where there is no *truth* ? Hence is that solemn charge, 2 Tim. 2 : 2, to commit that great trust of the ministry to *faithful* men. This *faithfulness,* as it respects God, ourselves, and the flocks committed to us, includes, (1) *Pure and spiritual aims and intentions for God.* A servant must aim at his master's honour, and interest, not his own. Fidelity will not endure self-ends, disguised with a pretence of zeal for Christ. Pure *ends* in our service, will give abundant comfort *at the end* of our service. Have a care, brethren, of all designs to accommodate carnal interests, under a shew of devotion to God. (2). *Personal sincerity.* It is said of Abraham, that God found his heart faithful ; that is, sincere before him. Neh. 9 : 8. Let this be our 'rejoicing, that in all sincerity, and godly simplicity, we have had our conversation in this world,' 2 Cor. 1 : 12. We of all men, are most in danger to be deceived by hypocrisy : For our employment lying in, and about spiritual things, we are, on that account, stiled spiritual men, Hos. 9 : 7. But it is plain, from that very place, that a man may be objectively a spiritual, and all the while subjectively a carnal man. Brethren, it is easier to declaim against a thousand sins of others, than to mortify one sin in ourselves ; to be more industrious in our pulpits, than in our closets. Believe it, sirs, all our reading, studying, and preaching, is but trifling hypocrisy, till the the things read, studied, and preached, be felt in some degree upon our own heart. (3). *Diligence.* A slothful cannot be a faithful servant. Matt. 25 : 26, 'His Lord answered, and said unto him, Thou wicked and slothful servant,' etc. The labours of the ministry are fitly compared to the toil of men in harvest, to the labours of a woman in travail, and to the agonies of soldiers in the extremity of a battle. We must watch when others sleep. And indeed it is not so much the expense of our labours, as the loss of them, that kills us. It is not with us, as with other labourers : They find their work as they leave it, so do not we. Sin and Satan unravel almost all we do, the impressions we make on our people's souls in one sermon, vanish before the next. How many truths have we to study! How many wiles of Satan, and mysteries of corruption, to detect! How many cases of conscience to resolve! Yea, we must fight in defence of the truths we preach, as well as study them to paleness, and preach them unto faintness. (4) *Impartiality in all the administrations of Christ's house.* He that is partial, cannot be faithful. O with what extraordinary solemnity doth Paul set on this exhortation upon Timothy! 1 Tim. 5 : 21. Brethren, you will shortly appear before an *impartial* God, see that ye be *impartial stewards.* Remember all souls are rated at one value in your Master's book, and your Redeemer paid as much for the one as for the other. Take the same care, manifest the same love, attend with the same diligence, the poorest and weakest souls that are committed to your care, as you do the rich, the great, and honourable. (5) *Stedfastness.* Ministerial faithfulness includes constancy : Not a backsliding, or flinching servant, Rev. 2 : 10. 'Be thou faithful (i.e. fixed and constant), to the death, and I will give thee a crown of life.' Many of us have cause to bless the Lord, who enabled us to be stedfast and unmovable in the trials that have passed over us. But our warfare is not yet ended. Our faithfulness is not yet faithfulness to the death ; we hope it will shortly be called so, whilst it thus involves our self-denial, sincerity, diligence, impartiality, and constancy.

The second qualification in the text is *ministerial prudence.* The Lord's servant must not only be faithful, but prudent, discreet, and wise. Faithfulness will fix the eye upon the right end ; but it is prudence that must direct to the proper means of attaining it. The use of prudence to a minister of Christ is unspeakably great ; it not only gives clearness to the mind, by freeing it from passions, enabling it thereby to apprehend what is best to be done ; but enables it in its deliberations, about the means, to make choice of the season, without precipitation, by too much haste ; or hazard, by too tedious delay.

I know there is a carnal policy, an unworthy pusillanimity, that often show themselves under the name of prudence ; I have nothing to do with mock graces here : My business is to shew you, in what particulars true ministerial prudence is highly serviceable to the affairs of Christ's house or kingdom.

(1) *Prudence will direct us, to lay a good foundation of knowledge in our people's souls, by catechizing and instructing them in the principles of Christianity, without which we labour in vain.* Except you have a knowing people, you are not like to have a gracious people. St. Paul's prudentials lay much in this, 1 Cor. 3 : 10, ' As a wise master-builder, I have laid the foundation.' You can never pitch upon a better project, to promote and secure the success of your labours, than catechizing. What age of Christianity ever produced more lively and stedfast Christians, than the first ages ? And then the care of this duty most eminently flourished in the churches. We that live in this age, have as much obligation as they, and God hath furnished to our hands the best help for it, that ever any age since Christ enjoyed. Our venerable assembly (lately sitting at Westminster, now in glory) composed for us the most judicious and compendious system.

(2) *Prudence discovers itself in the choice of such subjects, as the needs of our people's souls do most require, and call for.* A prudent minister will study the souls of his people, more than the best human books in his library ; and not chuse what is easiest for him, but what is most necessary for them. Ministers that are acquainted with the state of their flocks, as they ought to be, will be seldom at a loss in the choice of the next subject : Their people's wants will chuse their text, from time to time, for them. The greatest part of our congregations are poor, ignorant, and unregenerated people. This will direct us to the great doctrines of *conviction, regeneration,* and *faith.* Others are withering and decaying in their affections, or staggering and floating in their judgments : Prudence will enable the man of God to give to every one his proper food, or physic, in due season. This will make us spend more hours in our studies, and set to it with all our might and skill, that thereby we may both save ourselves, and them that hear us.

(3) *Ministerial prudence will shew us, of what great use our own affections are, for moving of others ;* and therefore advise us, that, as ever we expect the truths we preach shall operate upon the hearts of others, we first labour to work them in upon our own hearts. Such a preacher was St. Paul ; he preached with tears accompanying his words, Phil. 3 : 18. An hot iron, though blunt, will pierce sooner than a cold one, though sharper.

(4) Prudence will direct the servants of Christ (who highly value, and earnestly long for the success of their labours) to be careful, *by the strictness and gravity of their deportment, to maintain their esteem in the consciences of their people.* In your pulpits, you are carrying on a treaty of peace betwixt God and them ; and therefore it will not allow you to do anything out of your pulpits, to make the breach wider, or hinder the happy close between him and them. Remember that of Solomon, Prov. 11 : 30

'He that winneth souls is wise.' Prudence will not allow the ministers of Christ to intermix themselves with vain company, and take the same liberty they do in vain jests, and idle stories. To you that are juniors and candidates for the ministry, I will assume the boldness to address you with one seasonable word of advice ; and it is this : Have a care of that light and airy spirit, which so much obtains every where in this unserious age. It was the charge of God against some ministers of old, that they were light persons, and yet I cannot but think, comparatively speaking, with some of our times, they might pass for grave and serious. The people have eyes to see how we walk, as well as ears to hear what we say. It will be our wisdom and great advantage, to be able to say, as St. Paul did, Phil. 4 : 9, ' The things which you have both heard and seen in me do.'

(5) *Ministerial prudence will send you often to your knees,* to seek a blessing from God upon your studies and labours, as knowing all your ministerial success entirely depends thereupon, 1 Cor 3 : 7. Those are the best sermons, that are obtained by prayer. Blessed Bradford studied upon his knees. Luther obtained more this way, than by all his studies. If an honest husbandman could tell his neighbour, that the reason why his corn prospered better than his, was, because he steeped the seed in prayer, before he sowed it in the field ; we may blush to think, how much more precious seed we have sown dry, and unsteeped in prayer, and by this neglect have frustrated our own expectations. Thus laying our foundations in the knowledge of principles, chusing our subjects by the people's necessities ; working them first upon our own affections, enforcing them by strict conversation, and steeping this holy seed in prayer ; we shall approve ourselves the prudent ministers of Christ.

II. The reward of those that answer these characters, is propounded (1) *In proper terms ; Blessed is that servant,* ver 46, he is certainly blessed of God, whatever his usage be from men. If he be *faithful,* all his *prudence* will not secure him from the hatred and persecution of men, but it is enough that Christ calls and counts him blessed ; and those whom he blesseth, are truly and eternally blessed. (2) *In metaphorical terms ;* ver. 47, ' Verily, I say unto you, that he shall make him ruler over all his goods.' In allusion to the custom of great kings and generals who use to prefer and advance faithful servants to places of eminent trust, profit, and honour. The sense thus cleared, runs naturally and easily into this doctrine, That our Lord Jesus Christ will amply reward the faithful and prudent stewards of his house, in the day of their account. The glory prepared for, and promised to such servants of Christ, is elegantly laid out, in shining terms, by the prophet Daniel, Dan. 12 : 3, " And they that be wise, shall shine as the brightness of the firmament ; and they that turn many to righteousness, as the stars for ever and ever.' A promise which points directly to faithful and wise ministers. The question about degrees of glory in heaven is not necessary, but problematical. Nor is it questioned, among the orthodox, whether there be an equality of glory, as to the essentials ; but only in respect to the accidentals, and concomitants : Amongst which, they place the additional glory and joy of such ministers. And of this the apostle speaks, 1 Thess. 2 : 19-20, ' For what is our hope, or joy, or crown of rejoicing ? Are not even ye, in the presence of our Lord Jesus Christ at his coming? For ye are our glory and joy.' Where we find a very remarkable gradation. He calls his Thessalonian converts, *His hope,* that is, the matter of his hope, that they should be saved. *His joy,* as they had already given him abundant cause of joy, in their conversion to Christ by his ministry. And the " crown of his rejoicing . . . at his coming." This is an high strain indeed ! The meaning, I suppose, is that the fruit and success of his ministry among them, would add to his crown, and redound to his glory in the day of Christ.

O brethren ! who would not study and pray, spend and be spent, in the service of such a bountiful Master ! Is it not worth all our labours and sufferings, to come with all those souls we instrumentally begat to Christ : and all that we edified, confirmed, and comforted in the way to heaven ; and say, *Lord, here am I, and the children thou hast given me ?* O sirs ! we serve a good Master. He keeps an exact account of all your fervent prayers, of all your instructive and persuasive sermons ; and all your sighs, groans, and pantings, with every tear and drop of sweat, are placed like marginal notes against your labours in his book, in order to a full reward.

I consider to whom I speak, and shall be the shorter in the application ; which I shall dispatch apace, in three uses.

Use I. First for our information. By this it appears, *Christ hath established an order and government in his house, which none must violate.* The church is a well ordered family, or household, whereof Christ is the Head, Christians members, ministers stewards, the ordinances food to be dispensed by them in season. Every one is to keep his own place and station. Pastors must faithfully feed and govern the flocks of Christ, Acts 20 : 28. People must know, honour, and obey those that are over them in the Lord, 1 Thess. 5 : 12. Heb. 13 : 17, the one must not impose, nor the other usurp ! but each walk according to the rule of Christ, with a right foot, ordinately and comely. This order is the Church's beauty, Col. 2 : 5, and truly we may expect so much of Christ's presence, as we have of his rule and order amongst us, and no more. O that the rules and orders of his house were better known, and observed !

In the light of this truth, we may also read our duty, how we ought to govern ourselves in the ordination of men to the ministerial office. This office is to be committed unto faithful and able men, 2 Tim. 2 : 2, not to novices, 1 Tim. 3 : 6. I know the necessities of the churches are great, but no more haste (I beseech you) to supply their wants, than good speed. It is a less hazard, to put an ignorant rustic into a chemist's shop, to compound and prepare medicines for men's bodies, than to trust a man, destitute both of faithfulness and prudence, with the dispensation of Christ's ordinances to men's souls. Some men are moved by pitiful low ends. 1 Sam. 2 : 36, 'Put me into the priest's office, that I may eat a piece of bread.' Some by ambition, conceiting themselves as able and holy as the best, Numb. 16 : 3. What men's secret ends are, we cannot know ; but their qualifications for that work we may, and ought to know. We are solemnly charged, to 'lay hands suddenly upon no man,' 1 Tim. 5 : 22.

Use II. This point casts an ireful countenance upon all unfaithful and imprudent ministers, who give their people the chaff for the wheat, and stones for bread. They preach, they pray, because they must do so ; but none are the better for their prayers, or preaching. They seem to labour an hour or two in a week, but their labours turn to no account. I came not hither to deal with this sort of men ; and therefore shall leave them to consider the words immediately following my text, which like a thunder-clap from the mouth of Christ, discharges woes and threatenings upon them ; ver 48, to the end : 'The Lord of that servant shall come in a day that he looketh not for him, and in an hour that he is not aware of ; and shall cut him asunder, and appoint him his portion with hypocrites. There shall be weeping, and gnashing of teeth.'

Use III. I am principally concerned at this time about our own defects, both in faithfulness, and in prudence. Our vain expense of much precious time, our shuffling haste in so weighty a study as the salvation of our people is ; our sinful silence, when conscience saith, reprove ; our coldness and dead-heartedness ; our unserious and unprofitable converses ; our pride and ostentation of gifts ; our neglect and personal conferences : all these evidently discover that both our brains and hearts need more strength and tenderness.

Are faithfulness and prudence the essential requisites of the servants and stewards of Christ's house? And will he so amply reward them in whomsoever he finds them ? Then let it be our care and study to approve ourselves to him, such as he here describes and encourages.

But who am I, to manage such a work as this, among men every way above me ! However, you have called me to this service, and Christ hath directed me to this subject. I despair of ever having such another opportunity ; I see many faces in this assembly, whom I shall never see any more in this world. I speak to the ministers of Christ, the guides and pastors of so many flocks. My brethren, this is the day I have often wished for, when in the sad and silent years that are past, I have been searching my own heart, and enquiring into the causes of God's indignation. And now I am where my soul hath long desired to be, and the vows of God are upon me ; suffer therefore (dear brethren) this word of exhortation :*Take heed to your ministry that you fulfil it* : *Take heed to yourselves, and to the flocks over which the Holy Ghost hath made you overseers.* Let us so study and preach, let us so pray and converse among our people, that we may both save ourselves, and them that hear us ; let us frugally and industriously husband our time and talents for Christ ; let us prudently contrive, zealously and unanimously execute our holy contrivances for the advancement of his kingdom. Let us redeem our many silent Sabbaths, by double and triple improvements of those we enjoy : Let none of us dare to bring our old sins into our new pulpits. I suspect our greatest danger will be in the sunshine of liberty.

We have a solemn charge given us by Christ, 2 Tim. 4 : 1-1. ' I charge thee therefore before God, and the Lord Jesus Christ, who shall judge the quick and the dead at his appearing, and his kingdom ; preach the word, be instant in season, and out of season ; reprove, rebuke, exhort with all long-suffering and doctrine.' It must be a powerful opiate indeed, that can so benumb and stupify the conscience of a minister, as that he shall not feel the awful authority of such a charge. The precious and immortal souls of men are committed to us ; souls, about which God hath concerned his thoughts from eternity ; for the purchase of which Christ hath shed his own blood ; for the winning of which he hath put you into this office ; at whose hands he will also require an account of them in the great day. ' We watch for their souls, as those that must give account,' Heb. 13 : 17. And what can more powerfully excite to faithful diligence in the discharge of duty, than the consideration of that day! When the apostle had mentioned, in 2 Cor. 5 : 10, this awful appearance before the judgment-seat of Christ ; he immediately infers, ver. 11, ' Knowing therefore the terror of the Lord, we persuade men.' O brethren ! let us beware of committing, or of neglecting anything, that may bring us within the compass of the terrors of that day. Let our painfulness and faithfulness, our constancy and seriousness, compel a testimony from our congregations, as the apostle did from his, Acts 20 : 26 ' That we are pure from the blood of all men.' We have a great opportunity to improve for Christ ; which if we do, we shall fulfil his charge, and escape the terrors of his judgment in that great day. We have now the fairest season we ever enjoyed, since we first preached Christ ; if this be lost, I question whether we may ever expect the like.

THE PURITAN VIEW OF THE MINISTRY, AND ITS
RELATION TO CHURCH GOVERNMENT

" I know I have writ in a perilous time, and at a great disadvantage, what the father complained, that the whole World was turned Arian may be turned upon us. This ordinance (of the Ministry) is everywhere spoken against . . . the cry of our age is for liberty so much, that the most are for God's inclosures to be made commons . . . If the ministry falls Christ must fall too, and his Word, and Kingdom must fall. I had rather perish with Christ than outlive the Kingdom of Christ in England."

> *Jn. Collings,* Vindicae Ministerii Evangelici, A Vindication of the great ordinance of God, A Gospel Ministry, 1651.

It is impossible to understand the rise of the great Puritan movement, and its subsequent history, without knowing the position they held on matters of church govenment and order. The term ' Puritan ' was first used early in the reign of Elizabeth (1558-1603) as a label of reproach for those who were judged overscrupulous in their concern for the purity of the visible church. The Puritans regarded the religious settlement of Edward VI (1547-1553) as incomplete, for while it had reformed the church in matters of doctrine there was much left in its government and practice for which no Scriptural warrant could be found. Their dissatisfaction was the natural outcome of their conviction that the Scriptures are the only standard for practice as well as doctrine, that they contain the standing rules for the ordering of churches in every age, and that these rules are as equally binding in their authority as the doctrinal parts of Scripture. The importance which the Puritans —and their Scottish contemporaries—attached to these principles is forcibly illustrated by the manner in which they suffered for them. Why did thousands between 1620 and 1640 endure such severe hardships in leaving their native shores to cross to the howling wastes of New England ? Why were some two thousand Puritan ministers ejected from their churches in 1662 and cast into extremity and poverty ? Why in Scotland between 1660 and 1668 did 18,000 men and women suffer death or extreme punishments ? The answer to all these questions is that they could not conform to any government of the visible church which they held to be unscriptural. Many detailed examples of their resolution on these points could be given. After the restoration of the Stuarts, and the return of episcopacy to Scotland, the Archbishop of Glasgow maintained that there would not be ten ministers in all his diocese who would refuse to conform. " Middleton (one of the King's Courtiers), who had no idea of men throwing themselves and their families on the wide world, for the sake of a good conscience, sneered at the bare supposition. To his utter amazement, and to the unspeakable mortification of the bishops, nearly *four-hundred* ministers chose to be ejected from their charges rather than comply. Turned out of their homes in the depth of winter, and deprived of all maintenance, they exhibited to their congregations a firmness of principle which elevated and endeared them more than ever." —(T. McCrie. Sketches of Scottish Church Hist., vol 2, p. 90).

These are startling facts for they immediately teach us that either we or the Puritans have seriously misunderstood the importance of this subject of church government. The Puritans would have been utterly at a loss to understand the views of evangelicals to-day on these matters, while we, for our part, find their attitude strange and new to our conceptions. An enquiry into this neglected subject is long overdue ; if the Puritans were right we will surely be led to see that in a departure from these principles which they asserted, we have one of the truest explanations of the low state of the church to-day.

For the preservation and continuance of the church in a prosperous condition, the Puritans taught, Christ has appointed two principal means.

(1) He instituted the means of grace which the church must administer—the preaching of the Word, and the sacraments. (2) He gave to the church its form of government and officers, and clothed them with divine authority so that they can speak and act in His name. Matt. 10 : 1 ; 16 : 19 ; Jn. 20 : 21-23 ; Eph. 4 : 11-12. Now these two means are essentially and vitally connected. The preaching of the Word, and administration of sacraments have been entrusted to the officers of the church. (2 Tim. 2 : 2 ; 1 Cor. 4 : 1). So if the offices in the church are corrupted, or if men undertake these offices without being lawfully appointed by God, the result will certainly be that the Word is no longer purely preached, and error and confusion will spread in the visible church. Calvin saw this more clearly than any of the other reformers and he had a profound influence on the Puritans. In his great chapter " Of the teachers and ministers of the Church " (Institutes. Book IV. Ch. III) he comments on Eph. 4 : 8-13 as follows :—" By these words he shows that the ministry of men, which God employs in governing the church, is a principal bond by which believers are kept in one body. He also intimates, that the Church cannot be kept safe, unless supported by those guards to which the Lord has been pleased to commit its safety. Whoever, therefore, studies to abolish this order and kind of government of which we speak, or disparages it as of minor importance, plots the devastation, or rather the ruin and destruction of the church. For neither are the light and heat of the sun, nor meat and drink, so necessary to sustain and cherish the present life, as is the apostolical and pastoral office to preserve a Church in the earth."

(Clarkes edit. 1949, vol. 2, p. 317). Although the Church, the Puritans would agree, can exist and has existed, without observing the Scriptural form of government, *it can never continue in a spiritually prosperous and powerful state without it.* When Scripturally governed " the church is then truly visibly militant, becomes terrible like a well ordered army with banners. But when you loose the ranks, and rout the company, by disorderly administrations, it is the overthrow of the army, and so of the church." (Thos, Hooker. Survey of the Summe of Church Discipline, 1648. Part 1, p. 2). A matter so closely affecting the welfare of the church could therefore by no means be a subject of indifference to the Puritans.

The officers to whom Christ committed the government of the visible church after his ascension were apostles, prophets, evangelists, elders and deacons. The Reformers and Puritans were all agreed that of these five classes of officers, the first three were extraordinary and confined to the New Testament period. Apostles had an immediate call from Christ, they could raise the dead, convey the Holy Ghost, and speak infallibly in doctrine. Prophets could give information of the will of God which was not contained in Scripture. Evangelists travelled with the apostles, and were their deputies and substitutes. An ignorance or denial of the cessation of these offices has led to many of the abuses which have appeared during the history of the Christian Church. On the other hand serious evils have resulted from the failure to realise the permanence of the office of the eldership, and its authority. Elders are to be divided into two groups (1 Tim. 5 : 17), those who preach and expound " the word and doctrine," and those whose function it is to assist the first group in ruling and ordering the church (" he that ruleth," Rom. 12 : 8, who has the gift of " government," 1 Cor. 12 : 28). It is with the first group that we are concerned, the preaching elders, who are sometimes referred to as " pastors and teachers " (Eph. 4 : 11), sometimes as " bishops " (=" overseers," Acts 20 : 28 ; Philip. 1 : 1 ; Titus 1 : 5, 7, etc.) and who are commonly known by the term " ministers." The practical consequences of a neglect of Scriptural government are nowhere more dangerous than here. Two proofs that this office is of a permanent nature ought to be sufficient. (1) While other offices in the New Testament are indicated as temporary, there is no such indication regarding the eldership. There are no instructions concerning the appointment or qualifications of new apostles, prophets, or evangelists, they would have been useless and unnecessary as no successors were intended for these offices. But we have clear teaching on the appointment of further elders, and the qualifications required in them (1 Tim. 3 ; Titus 1). Timothy was to ordain, " lay hands on," " faithful men, who shall be able to teach others also." (Tim. 5 : 22 ; 2 Tim. 2 : 2). (2) Pastors and teachers were given " for the

edifying of the body of Christ : *till* we all come in the unity of the
faith . . . unto a perfect man," that is till the whole church is
complete, an event still future, therefore the need for this office
still remains.   If ministers were required while the apostles were
still alive how much more now ?

*How then are men to be appointed to the office of the ministry in
the church ?*   William Perkins (1558-1603), one of the most powerful preachers and one of the ablest writers of the Puritan period,
is well fitted to be their spokesman here.   In his valuable sermons
"Of the Calling of The Ministry" (Perkins works. vol 3, p. 429.
1609 edit.) he comments on the words "Whom shall I send" (Isa.
6 : 8) as follows—"The Lord would teach us, that no man is to
undertake this function, unless God call and send him : therefore
here are condemned the profane fancies of the Anabaptists, and all
like them, who think that any man upon a private motion (desire),
may step forth and undertake the duties of a prophet, to preach
and expound . . .   Oh but, say they, these motions are from God's
spirit : but that cannot serve their turn : for if we say, contrariwise
nay, but they are from the devil, or at least from your own vanity
and pride, how can they disprove it? . . .   If any ask, how he shall
know when God calls him? I answer, God calleth ordinarily by his
church, her voice is his : therefore whensoever the Church of God
saith unto thee, thou shalt be sent, and thou shalt go for us, even
then doth the Lord call us out to this holy function." (p. 459).   Then
again on the verse "Go, and speak unto this people"—"God both
gives him leave to go, and further doth furnish him with authority,
both to go and speak.   Wherein the principal point is, that the
authority of the prophets calling is derived from God himself.   So
in the New Testament the Apostles went not into the world to
preach till they had their commission, "Go and teach all nations"
. . . In all which is discovered and condemned the pride and presumption of those who dare run on their own heads and will not
stay till the Lord say unto them, "Go and speak."

   "But it will then be demanded, how may I know if God bid me
go ?   For God speaks not now from heaven as in old time, and
as to this prophet : I answer, it is true, we are to look for no such
visions, nor apparitions from heaven . . . for now ordinarily, God
speaketh in another manner to his church : for in general duties
God speaketh to us out of His word, and in particular and personal
duties (where the Word in plain terms serveth not) he speaketh
to a man by his own conscience, and by the voice of his church . . .
Wouldest thou know whether God would have thee to go or no ?
then thou must ask thy own conscience, and ask the Church.   Thy
conscience must judge of thy willingness, and the Church of thy
ability : and as thou mayest not trust other men, to judge of thy
inclination or affection, so thou mayest not trust thy own judgment,
to judge of thy worthiness or sufficiency . . . If thy conscience do

truly testify unto thee, that thou desirest to do service to God and his Church, in this calling above any other : And if withall, upon signification hereof to the Church, and upon trial made of thy gifts and learning, the Church (that is, many learned, wise, and godly, and such as the Church hath publikely appointed for that purpose) do approve of that thy desire, and of thy sufficiency to do God service in his ministry, and thereupon by a publick calling, bid thee go, then assuredly God himself hath bid thee go.   And it is as effectual a calling, as if thou heardest the voice of God from heaven." (p. 462).   Richard Bernard in his treatise on the ministry, famous in its day, entitled " The Faithful Shepherd," lays down the manner of entrance into the ministry in the same way—" He must come with the authority of the Church, else it is presumption in him, contempt of superiority, breach of order, the nurse of confusion, the mother of schism, and the bane of the Churches peace." (1621 edition. p. 93-94).   The Puritans were all fully agreed on this matter, it is not enough for a man to have an inward call, *he must have an external call by the church, before he can undertake the office of the ministry.*

" The inward call," asserts Thomas Manton, " is not enough ; to preserve order in the church, an outward call is necessary.   As Peter, Acts 10, was called of God to go to Cornelius ; and then, besides that, he had a call from Cornelius himself.   So must we, having an inward call from the Spirit, expect an outward calling from the church, otherwise we cannot lawfully be admitted to the exercise of such an office and function.   As in the Old Testament, the tribe of Levi and house Aaron were by God appointed to the service of the altar, yet none could exercise the calling of a Levite, or serve as a high priest, till he was anointed and purified by the church, Exod. 28 : 3.   The like is repeated, Num. 3 : 3.   So the ministers of the gospel though called by God, must have their external separation, and setting apart to that work by the church ; as the Holy Ghost saith, Acts 13 : 2, ' Separate me Barnabas and Saul for the work whereunto I have called them.'   Mark, the Spirit of God had chosen them, and yet calls upon the church, the elders of Antioch, to separate them for the work of the ministry."

The important question now to be faced is this.   *Can any publicly teach or expound Scripture without being thus ordained by the Church ?*   This question must be rightly understood before it is answered.   It does not ask what a man ought to do within the confines of his own family.   It is not speaking of extraordinary circumstances, of times of persecution when settled churches are scattered, or of places where there are no lawful ministers—God may then permit unusual liberty. (2 Chron. 29 : 34).   It does not mean that a Christian may not exhort his brother, nor does it question whether private Christians may meet together, confer, relate experiences, or repeat sermons. The question is whether private persons may teach or expound, without a solemn setting apart to the office ?

To this question the Puritans were strongly united in returning a negative answer. Their reasons for this conviction we will now consider.

First, Their general and principal argument is that it is contrary to the Scripture. Here I shall quote somewhat extensively from John Collings, an eminent Puritan divine, whose treatise mentioned above is largely devoted to this subject. John Downam in a preface to this work, expresses his opinion that " This polemical treatise, is in my judgment so impregnable (as tending to correct the shameful abuse of these times, wherein men having no calling, presumptuously take upon them the office of God's ministers, and to preach publiquely unto the people) . . . that I approve it worthy to be printed and published." Collings argues " not to observe Gospel order in acts of instituted worship is sinful, and unlawful." For any to take upon them acts of office being no officers is a breach of that order. " Ordinary preaching, interpreting, and applying Scriptures, are acts of office. ' If any desire the office of a bishop he desires a good thing.' 1 Tim. 3 : 1. Preaching is the main and chief act and end for which God set up the office. It is the ordinance of God that those that take upon them to preach should not only be gifted, and desired (by the people), but solemnly set apart by fasting and prayer, and laying on of hands . . . In things relating to the worship of God it is a general rule that nothing ought to be done without an express warrant in the Gospel. Let any example in the New Testament be given where any in an orderly Gospel-Church undertook the work of opening and applying Scripture, being neither apostle, evangelist, prophet, pastor or teacher . . . Gospel examples prove, that such as preached the Gospel had beside their inward gifts and graces, a solemn setting apart to that great work. Titus is commanded ' to ordain elders in every city ' (Tit. 1 : 5). If St. Paul had thought gifts enough to make a preacher, it had been enough for him to have sent Titus, to give order that all that had gifts should exhort and convince gainsayers, but here is another act required of Titus. The original word ' ordain ' signifies to appoint, set some over others, plainly Paul means that he should set some over others—those whom he ordains are called bishops, v. 7, a name of office and authority."

Secondly, They denied the lawfulness of unordained preachers because such persons could speak with no authority. A minister's authority derives from his office. " Ministers are angels (messengers) in the very institution of their calling. Therefore thou must preach God's word, *as God's word*, and deliver it, as thou receivest it,

ambassadors and messengers carry not their own message, but the
message of their Lord and Master who sent them, and ministers
carry the message of the Lord of hosts, therefore they are bound
to deliver it *as the Lord's,* and not their own (1 Pet 4 : 11 . . .
Hearers are here taught that if their ministers be angels sent them
from God then they are to hear them gladly, willingly, reverently,
obediently : gladly and willingly, because they are ambassadors ;
reverently and obediently because they are sent from the high God,
the King of Kings, and do deliver his embassage." (Perkins, vol 2,
429-30). " A minister in the execution of his office, let him preach
Christ's eternal truth, deliver it and prove it ; whatever humane
weakness there be in him, whatever darkness there is in others, yet
he is therein above churches, kings or angels, and they shall
answer it at the great day, that do not submit." (Tho. Shepard).
This authority belongs only to ministers.   Collings writes " The
authority of him who preacheth is that which makes the action of
him that heareth a duty . . .   God's law hath not commanded me
to hear everyone that speaketh a good discourse or reads a chapter,
he must be specially authorised to preach, or I shall not be specially
obliged to hear."   None can preach with authority " but who is
in office.   The authority of this preacher doth two things.   1.   *It
obligeth him to preach.   Woe to me (saith Paul) if I do not preach
the Gospel.*   2.   *It obligeth people to hear,* for the preacher is to
that purpose sent.   The unordained, " 1.   *May hold his peace if
he please,* for who hath required this service at his hands ?   Christ
hath not by his Church said to him go and preach, much less
immediately sent him.   2.   *He may preach,* but he may preach
to the walls too if people please ; no soul sinneth in neglecting to
hear him . . .   On the contrary, he that preacheth authoritatively,
1.   Is bound to preach, if God gives him opportunity.   2.   If
upon the Lord dayes he preacheth and people will not hear, he
may shake off the dust of his feet against them, and it shall be more
tolerable in the great day for Sodom than for that people.
3.   People may and ought to go out to hear him *in faith,* believing
*that his preaching is the publike ordinance of Christ for the saving
of their souls.*   We say, and say again, that all the gifted men in
the world cannot make one such Sermon ; they may begg but cannot command either auditory or attention." (Vindiciae Ministerii
Evangelici Revindicatae, 35-45, 1658).
*Thirdly, The Puritans asserted that unordained preachers were
a primary cause of error and confusion in the visible church.*
Perhaps no Puritan treatise is more relevant to our present times
than John Flavel's " The Causes and Cure of Mental Errors."
The proper course for preventing the spread of error, he writes,
" is by labouring to bound and contain Christians within those
limits Christ himself has set.   *Limitation* 1.   Though Christ hath
indulged to the meanest and weakest Christian, a liberty to read

and judge of the Scriptures for himself ; yet he hath neither thereby
nor therewith granted him a liberty publicly to expound and preach
the word to others : That is quite another thing. Every man that
can read the scriptures, and judge of their sense, is not thereby
presently made Christ's commission-officer, publicly and authoritatively to preach and inculate the same to others : Two things
are requisite to such an employment, viz : *Proper qualifications.*
2 Tim. 3. *And a solemn call or designation.* Rom. 10 : 14, 15.
The ministry is a distinct office, Acts 20 : 17-28. 1 Thess. 5 : 12.
and none but qualified and ordained persons can authoritatively
preach the Word, 2 Tim. 1 : 16 ; 1Tim. 4 : 14 and 5 : 22.

" Christians may privately edify one another by reading the
scriptures, communicating their sense one to another of them,
admonishing, counselling, reproving one another in a private,
fraternal way, at seasons wherein they interfere not with more
public duties : But for every one that hath confidence enough (and
the ignorant usually are best stocked with it) to assume a liberty
without due qualification or call to expound and give the sense of
scripture, and pour forth his crude and unstudied notions, as the
pure sense and meaning of God's spirit in the scriptures ; this is
what Christ never allowed, and through this flood-gate errors have
broken in, and over-flowed the church of God, to the great scandal
of religion, and confirmation of Popish enemies." (Flavel's works
1820 edit. vol. 3, p. 448). " Satan will soon spy out and make use
of the want of proper calling," writes Manton, " as he did in the
sons of Sceva : Acts 14 : 14-15, ' Jesus I know, and Paul I know ;
but who are ye ? ' I know Jesus as the Lord, Paul as an authorised
minister, one that had a lawful commission, ' But who are ye ? '
And then the devil fell upon them, and wounded them, ver. 16.
It is true, we have not such visible instances of the devil's power
now as then, because God rules the world now by wisdom, not by
power ; but yet we may observe the secret power of the devil upon
those that run of their own accord, and venture upon the office
of the ministry without a call. *None are more apt to be led aside
into errors, and those of the grossest nature, than those that venture
upon this office without a call.* Origen's errors are by many ascribed to his neglect or want of ordination. And the Arians, saith
the synod of Alexandria, were infamous for want of a right call
to the ministry, and therefore fell into that damnable error."
*Fourthly, The danger involved in doing the work of the Ministry
(that is preaching) without holding the office is a warrant against it.*
" Consider how dangerous a thing it is to usurp an office. How
dreadfully did the Lord witness against Korah, Dathan, and
Abiram for attempting this violation of his orders ? (Numbers 16).
The instances of Saul and Uzzah for usurping the priests office
are such as may make tender spirited Christians tremble . . . Uzzah
was cut off for touching the ark and carrying it on a cart. 1 Chron.

13 : 10.   What matter whether it was carried on a cart, or on their
shoulders ?   Whether they touched it or the priests only ? 1 Chron.
15 : 2.   *God will have his ends done by his means and in his order.*
It is a dangerous thing for us when God hath prescribed us an
order for his worship to make ourselves wiser than God, by arguing
from carnal reason a needlessness of observing details . . .   If I
have made it good that the preaching of those that have only gifts,
is a sin, and warrantable by no Scripture ; then let Socinians and
Erastians do it, and Arminians and Socinians, but surely none that
fear the Lord will presume to do it." (Collings).

*Fifthly, The very nature of preaching, its difficulty and solemn
responsibility, excludes those who are not qualiced by Scriptural
rules.*   "Many weak and slight spirits in these days think that it
is as easy to preach as to play, and so they hop from one thing to
another, and those that are not qualified nor fit for the least and
lowest employment, yet judge themselves fit enough for the greatest
and weightiest employment in the world, and that which would
certainly break the backs, not only of the best and strongest men,
but even of the very angels, should not God put under his ' everlasting arms.'   ' Who is sufficient for these things ? '   2 Cor. 2 : 12.
Almost every upstart in these days thinks himself sufficient.   ' Who
am I ? ' says Moses.   Who am I not ? saith every green-head in
these days."   (Thos Brooks, vol. 3, 210-11, Nichol's series).

The difficulty of preaching.   The work of the preacher, says
Perkins, is " to stand in God's presence, to enter into the holy of
the holiest, to go betwixt God and his people, to be God's mouth
to the people, and the peoples to God : to be the interpreter of the
eternal law of the Old Testament, and the everlasting Gospel of
the New : to stand in the room, and to beare the office of Christ
himself, to take the care and charge of souls : these considerations
are so many amazements to the consciences of such men, who do
with reverence approach, and not with rashness rush into this
sacred seat."   (Works, vol. 3, 432).   " Is it not hard to teach? "
asks Collings.   " My beloved friends ! we are with you in much
fear and trembling ; and when we have consulted the original,
weighed the coherence of a text, compared our thoughts with the
thoughts of many other divines, and chiefly compared Scripture with
other Scripture, yet are we trembling, and see cause to cry unto the
Lord with St. Augustine (before our interpretations of Scripture)
'Grant Lord that we may neither be deceived ourselves in the understanding of thy will, nor deceive others by a false interpretation.'
It is one of the greatest pieces of High Treason against the Almighty
to adulterate the coin of his Word, and wrest the meaning :
If we had nothing else to do but to consult the original, to compare
Scripture with Scripture, and to consider the coherence (which
are necessary to any true interpretation of Scripture) and then to
cast our thoughts into order, that we might communicate them to

you, we shall yet find it a work impossible to be dispatched in so little time as we know is the *all* you can spare from your necessary callings, especially considering there lies a duty upon you towards your families that they may not be ignorant while you are teachers of others, lest you prove worse than infidels."

The responsibility of preaching. No one is in a more solemn position than the minister of the Gospel. No one will have to give an account of so much at the last day (Heb. 13 : 17, a verse which Chrysostom said shook him like an earthquake). If he fails to rightly divide the word of truth (2 Tim. 2 : 15), if he doesn't preach every doctrine in its Scriptural proportion, if he doesn't place a true emphasis on each of the revealed attributes of God, his failure may have eternal consequences. "Our whole preaching must be Scripture proof, or we and our works must burn together," says Brooks. More terrible even than that, an incapable preacher may become guilty of the blood of souls. "Now, a man were better to have all the blood of the world upon him than the blood of one soul. The blood of souls, of all blood, cries loudest and wounds deepest. The lowest, the darkest, and the hottest place in hell will be the sad and dreadful portion of such upon whose skirts the blood of souls shall be found at last. Hence that passage of Paul in 1 Cor. 9 : 16. 'Woe unto me if I preach not the gospel.' The motto that should be writ upon preachers' study-doors, and on their walls, and on all the books they look on, on the beds they lie on, and on the seats they sit on, etc., should be this, '*The blood of souls, the blood of souls.*' The soul is the better, the nobler part of man ; it bears most of the image of God ; it is capable of union and communion with God. Christ sweat for it, and bled for it ; and therefore woe to those merchants that make merchandise of the souls of men. This was a comfort and honour to Paul, that he kept himself from the blood of souls, Acts 20 : 25, 27." (Brooks vol. 3, 209-10).

All these statements which we have considered lead to one profound impression, that is the serious and high view the Puritans had of the ministry. It was a life which filled them with awe. They were of the same spirit as Luther who was wont to say that if he were again to choose his calling, he would dig, or do anything, rather than take upon him the office of minister. Calvin, even after he had written his mighty 'Institutes,' judged himself insufficient to undertake the weight of the ministerial function. Knox, even at the age of forty-two, was so deeply affected with the awful responsibility of the office that it was only with great difficulty that he could be induced to begin his preaching ministry. William Jenkyn in his funeral sermon on the death of that great Puritan William Gouge—who always rose to study at five in the morning in winter and at four in summer—tells us that Gouge entered the ministry in his thirty-second year " an age suitable to that calling which being so weighty, he durst not undertake rashly, and un-advisedly (I wish all those whom it concerns would take notice of it and example by him herein) : he *laid up,* before he *laid out,* he first laboured to fit himself with endowments, and not till then did he put himself upon employment." So great was James Durham's concern to rightly divide the Word, that towards the end of his famous ministry in Scotland he declared that if he were to live ten years longer, he would choose to live nine years in study for preaching the tenth. William Perkins was so impressed by the charge he was under that he would write on the title page of all his books, " Thou art a minister of the Word, Mind thy business.." Thomas Shepard addressed several young ministers who called to see him on his deathbed as follows : " Your work is great, and requires great seriousness. For my own part, I never preached a sermon which, in the composing, did not cost me prayers, with strong cries and tears. I never went up into the pulpit but as if I were going to give an account of myself to God."

We believe that the Puritan standard is nothing less than the standard required by the Word of God for ministers. The practical implications of this for our time are very grave. Nothing more provokes the wrath of God against nations or churches than the lowering of this standard. When Jeroboam appointed unqualified and incapable men to the office of the priesthood " *this thing became sin unto the house of Jeroboam, even to cut it off, and to destroy it from off the face of the earth.*" (1 Kings 13 : 34). " A whirlwind of the Lord is gone forth in fury " to fall on the heads of such men (Jerem. 23 : 19). Error, blindness, and corrupt minds are the punishments God sends upon churches for such offences. The absence of faithful ministers, a famine for the word in its purity, and an ignorance of the true cause of these evils, are the judgments which have overtaken us as a nation. Whether or not such a desperate situation can yet be remedied may well depend on our readiness to re-examine the subject of this article. Cotton Mather tells us that when that mighty New England Puritan John Wilson lay dying in Boston, many ministers who had assembled in his home from all parts of the colony " asked him to declare solemnly what he thought might be the sins which provoked the displeasure of God against the country. Whereto his answer was, ' I have long feared several sins ' whereof, one, he said, was *Korahism* (Num. 16). ' That is, when people rise up as Korah against their ministers, as if they took too much upon them, when indeed they do but rule for Christ, and according to Christ.' " Is not Korahism a sin very much alive in the evangelical world to-day ? Are its consequences any less than John Wilson and the Puritans feared ? These are questions which very seriously need to be faced.

EXPOSITORY PREACHING. " The expository method affords inducement and occasion to the preacher to declare the whole counsel of God. Holy Scripture cannot make its true impression unless it be read in continuity ; a whole epistle, a whole gospel, a whole prophecy at once ; but this is altogether incompatible with the piecemeal method. No man, who selects his insulated texts at random, has any good reason to be satisfied that he is not neglecting the inculcation of many important doctrines or duties. Usually the indolence or caprice which renders anyone averse to the expository method will likewise withhold him from methodical series of any kind in his discourses. There is perhaps no man who has not an undue fondness for some one circle of subjects : and this does not always comprise the whole of what he is bound to declare. But the regular exposition of a few entire books, well selected, would go far to supply every defect of this nature."—J. W. Alexander.

*　　*　　*

NOT CORRUPTING THE WORD. ' For we are not as many, which corrupt the Word of God.' 2 Cor. 2 : 17. " When can it be said of us, that we corrupt the Word of God in the present day ? What are the rocks and shoals which we ought to shun, if we would not be of the ' many ' who deal deceitfully with God's truth ? A few suggestions on this head may not be without use

We corrupt the Word of God most dangerously, when we throw any doubt on the plenary inspiration of any part of Holy Scripture. This is not merely corrupting the bucket of living water, which we profess to present to our people, but poisoning the whole well. Once wrong on this point, the whole substance of our religion is in danger. It is flaw in the foundation. It is a worm at the root of our theology. Secondly, we corrupt the Word of God when we make defective statements of doctrine. We do so when we take away from the Bible, for the sake of pleasing men ; or, from a feeling of false liberality, keep back any statement which seems narrow, and harsh, or hard. We do so when we try to soften down anything that is taught about eternal punishment, or the reality of hell. We do so when we bring forward doctrines in their wrong proportions. We do so when we exhibit an excessive anxiety to fence, and guard, and qualify such doctrines as justification by faith without the deeds of the law, for fear of the charge of antinomianism. We do so, not least, when we shrink from the use of Bible language in giving an account of doctrines. We are apt to keep back such expressions as ' born again,' ' election,' ' adoption,' ' conversion,' ' assurance,' and to use a roundabout phraseology, as if we were ashamed of plain Bible words. I cannot expand these statements, for want of time, but leave them to your private thought." —J. C. Ryle.

*　　*　　*

NEGLIGENT PREACHERS. " God commandeth thee to preach, ' If thou warn not the wicked he shall die in his wickedness, but I will require his blood at thy hand.' Hearken well to this, mark it well, you curates— ' I will ask his blood at thy hand.' If you do not your office, if you teach not the people, and warn them not, you shall be damned for it ! Many make a mingling of the way of God and man's way, Christ did not so, He taught the way of God truly . . . Oh that a man might have the contemplation of hell; that the devil would allow a man to look into it, and see its state, as he shewed all the world, when he tempted Christ in the wilderness. On yonder side, would the devil say, are punished unpreaching prelates. I think verily a man might see as far as a kenning, as far as from Calais to Dover I warrant you, and see nothing but unpreaching prelates ! " —*Hugh Latimer, martyr, 1555.*

MINISTERIAL BOLDNESS

What kind of boldness must the minister's be? First, a *convincing* boldness. How forcible are right words, saith Job; and how feeble are empty words, though shot with a thundering voice. Great words in reproving an error or sin, but weak arguments, produce laughter oftener than tears . . . Secondly, a *wise* boldness. The minister is to reprove the sins of all, but to name none. Paul, being to preach before a lascivious and unrighteous prince, touched him to the quick, but did not name him in his sermon. Felix' conscience saved Paul that labour . . . Thirdly, a *meek* boldness . . . Let the reproof be as sharp as thou wilt; but thy spirit must be meek. Passion raiseth the blood of him that is reproved; but compassion breaks his heart. We must not denounce wrath in wrath, lest sinners think we wish their misery; but rather with such tenderness, that they may see it is no pleasing work to us, but we do it that we might not, by a cruel silence, be accessory to their ruin, which we deire to prevent . . . Fourth, an *humble* boldness; such a boldness as is raised from a confidence in God, and not from ourselves, our own gifts or ability, courage or stoutness . . . Fifthly, a *zealous* boldness. Our reproofs of sin must come from a warm heart. Paul's spirit was stirred within him when he saw the city given to idolatry. Jeremiah tells us the word of God was a fire in his bones; it broke out of his mouth like a flame out of a furnace. The word is a hammer; but it breaks not the stony heart when lightly laid on. King James said of a minister in his time, that he preached as if death were at his back. Ministers should set forth judgment as if it were at the sinner's back to take hold of him. Cold reproofs or threatenings are like the rumble of thunder afar off, which affrights not as a clap over our head. I told you the minister's boldness must be meek and merciful; but not to prejudice zeal . . .

Some helps to produce this boldness. First, *a holy fear of God*. We fear man so much, because we fear God so little. One fear cures another. When man's terror scares you, turn your thoughts to the wrath of God; this is the way Jeremiah was cured of his aguish distemper, fearing man: Jer. 1: 17 . . . Secondly, castle thyself within *the power and promise of God* for thy assistance and protection . . . Our eye, alas! is on our danger, but not on the invincible walls and bulwarks which God has promised to set about us. The prophet's servant that saw the enemy army approaching, was in a panic; but the prophet that saw the heavenly host for his life-guard about him, cared not a straw for them all . . . Thirdly, *keep a clear conscience*: he cannot be a bold reprover, that is not a conscientious liver; such a one must speak softly, for fear of waking his own guilty conscience . . . Unholiness in a preacher's life will either stop his mouth from reproving, or the people's ears from receiving. O how harsh a sound does such a cracked bell make in the ears of his audience! . . .Good counsel from a wicked man produces no effect . . . Fifthly, consider, if thou be not now bold for Christ in thy ministry, *thou canst not be bold before Christ at His judgment;* he that is afraid to speak for Christ, will certainly be ashamed to look on His face then. 'We must all appear before the judgment-seat of Christ ' 2 Cor. 5: 10. Now what use doth Paul make of this solemn meditation? ' Knowing therefore the terror of the Lord, we persuade men.' . . . A serious thought of that day, as we are going to preach, would shut all base fear out of the pulpit. It is a very small thing to be judged by men now for our boldness, but dismal to be condemned by Christ for our cowardice . . . Sixthly, *consider how bold Christ was in His ministry* . . . 1 Tim. 6: 13 Seventhly, *pray for this holy boldness*. Thus did the apostles come by it . . . it was the child of prayer, Acts 4: 29 f . . . Mark, they do not pray to be excused the battle, but to be armed with courage to stand in it; they had rather be lifted above the fear of suffering, than have immunity from the suffering . . . If this be thy sincere request, God will not deny it. WILLIAM GURNALL, 1616-1679.

PAST & PRESENT MINISTERS COMPARED
J. C. RYLE, 1816 - 1900.

Would we know why the ministers who profess to follow the evangelical fathers are so much less successful than they were? The question is a delicate and interesting one, and ought not to be shelved. The suspicion naturally crosses some minds, that the doctrines which won victories a hundred years ago are worn out, and have lost their power. I believe that theory to be an entire mistake. The answer which I give to the enquiry is one of a very different kind. I am obliged to say plainly, that, in my judgment, we have among us neither the men nor the doctrines of the days gone by. It is a humbling conclusion; but I have long felt that it is the truth. Give us like men and a like message, and I have no fear that the Holy Ghost would grant us like results.

Wherein do evangelical Churchmen fall short of their great predecessors? Let us look this question fairly in the face. Let us come to particulars. They fall short *in doctrine*. They are neither so full nor so distinct, nor so bold, nor so uncompromising. They are afraid of strong statements. They are too ready to fence, and guard, and qualify all their teaching, as if Christ's Gospel was a little baby, and could not be trusted to walk alone. They fall short *as preachers*. They have neither the fervour, nor fire, nor thought, nor illustration, nor directness, nor boldness, nor grand simplicity of language which characterized the last century. Above all, they fall short *in life*. They are not men of one thing, separate from the world, unmistakable men of God, ministers of Christ everywhere, indifferent to man's opinion, regardless who is offended, if they only preach the truth. They do not make the world feel that a prophet is among them, and carry about with them their Master's presence, as Moses when he came down from the mount. I write these things with sorrow. I desire to take my full share of blame. But I do believe I am speaking the truth.

It is no use trying to evade the truth on this subject. I fear that, as a general rule, the evangelical ministry in England has fallen far below the standard of the last century, and that the simple account of the want of success to which so many point is, the low standard both of doctrine and life which prevails. Ease and popularity, and the absence of persecution, are ruinous to some. An extravagant and excessive attention to petty details withers up the ministry of others. An absurd straining after the reputation of being "intellectual" and original is the curse of others. A desire to seem charitable and liberal, and keep in with everybody, paralyzes the ministry of others. The plague is abroad. We want a revival among evangelical ministers. We are where we are, because we have come short of our fathers.

I repeat it emphatically, for I believe it sincerely. The first want of our day is a return to the old, simple, and sharply-cut doctrines of our fathers; and the second want is a generation of like-minded and like-gifted men to preach them.   Give me in any county of England and Wales a man like Grimshaw or Rowlands, or Whitefield, and there is nothing in the present day which would make me afraid.   Let us ask Him who holds the stars in His right hand to revive His work among our ministers, and to raise up men for our times.   He can do it.   He waits to be entreated.   Then let all who pray cry night and day to the Lord of the harvest, " Lord, send forth more labourers into Thy harvest."

*   *   *

DIRECTIONS FOR MINISTERS.   " 1.   Be much in prayer to God: thereby you shall find more succour and success in your ministry, than by all your study.

2.   Preach much about the misery of the state of nature, the preparatives to conversion; the nature of conversion, or effectual calling; the necessity of union and communion with Christ; the nature of saving and justifying faith, and the fruits thereof—love and good works, and sanctification.

3.   Explain the words of your text clearly; bring clear proof of parallel Scriptures; let your reasons be Scripture-reasons; but be most in application; which is spent in five uses, refutation of error, information of the truth, correction of manners, exhortation and instruction in righteousness. All which you find in 2 Tim. 3: 16, 17.   And there is a fifth use, viz.: of comfort, 1 Cor. 14: 3.

4.   I advise you being in office to catechise every Lord's Day in the afternoon, so as to go through the catechism once in a year.

Finally, be very careful of Scriptural rules to God's ministers, to divide rightly the Word, to walk uprightly, and be instant in prayer."

—*Charles Chancey,* 1589-1671, *President of Harvard College, New England.*

*   *   *

A SHORT BIBLIOGRAPHY FOR MINISTERS

Student and Preacher, Cotton Mather.   *Thoughts on Preaching,* J. W. Alexander.   *The Student's Manual,* John Todd.   These three writers were American divines of the first class.   *The Reformed Pastor,* Richard Baxter. *The Christian Ministry,* with an inquiry into the causes of its inefficiency, Charles Bridges.   *An All-Round Ministry, Lectures to my Students* (2 vols.), *Commenting and Commentaries,* C. H. Spurgeon.   *An Earnest Ministry,* the want of the times, J. A. James.   *The Minister's Duty and Dignity,* Thomas Brooks, (Works, vol. III, p. 207-232).

Wickliffe Press, Finchley, N. 3.

THE
BANNER of TRUTH

(9th Issue)

Price 9d.

Subscription for six
issues, 6/6 or $1.25

EDITOR:

MR. IAIN MURRAY, B.A.,
65A BLENHEIM TERRACE, ST. JOHN'S WOOD,
LONDON, N.W. 8.

ASSISTANT EDITOR:
MR. ERROLL HULSE.

•   •   •

"Thou hast shewed thy people hard things;
Thou hast made us to drink the wine of
astonishment.   Thou hast given a banner to
them that fear Thee, that it may be displayed
because of the truth."   Psalm 60 : 3-4

•   •   •

CONTENTS

K

INFORMATION FOR READERS

This magazine is not a periodical, published at fixed intervals, but is designed rather as a booklet which can be of permanent usefulness and reference. The time of publication is therefore determined by the amount of edifying material which we have available for printing and not by our committal to any particular dates. We trust this will help to preserve the quality of the contents. Five issues have now been published during this year and it is hoped that at least the same number will appear in 1958. Back numbers are available. Subscribers to the magazine will, from time to time, be freely sent news of books published by The Banner of Truth Trust.

Subscription for 6 issues 6/6 including postage.
U.S. price   „   „ $1.25   „   „

A sample copy will gladly be sent to any of your friends whom you believe would be interested. All money received is put to the cause of spreading the truth. We gratefully acknowledge the assistance given to date in this respect by our subscribers.

NOVEMBER, 1957

EDITORIAL

"Good Reader, Solomon tells us long since, that there is no end to many books, Eccles. 12: 12. Writing (it seemeth) is no novel humour, but abounded then, even when the means of transmitting knowledge were more difficult ; if there was cause for the complaint then, there is much more now ; since the Presse has helped the Penne, every one will be scribbling, and so better books are neglected, and lie like a few grains of corn under an heap of chaff and dust: Usually books are received as fashions ; the newest, not the best and most profitable, are most in esteem ; insomuch as really learned and sober men have been afraid to publish their labours, lest they should divert the world from reading the useful works of others that wrote before them . . . Certainly reader 'tis for thy profit sometimes to look back and consult with them that first laboured in the mines of knowledge, and not always to take up what cometh next to hand."

THOMAS MANTON, 1669.

In our first issue, published in September, 1955, we expressed the desire " to propagate the truth as fully, widely, and often as possible." Since that time we have occasionally briefly recorded for the benefit of our subscribers and friends the increase of this work from its small beginnings. In recent months this development has so progressed that it is necessary to inform our readers of the encouraging position that has now been reached. The support we have received is such that the magazine has been legally incorporated into a Trust—The Banner of Truth Trust—which is committed to the publication of Reformed literature in this country. Our intention is the same as at the start but now the means to carry it out have been greatly enlarged. We have therefore some half-dozen books at the printers and are hoping to carry out a larger re-publishing programme next year. In this November issue selections will be found from three of the first books that will appear and their character will indicate something of the range and type of book we hope to make available.

Priority will be given to commentaries and *Burrowes* on " *The Song of Solomon* " is the first of an expository series of reprints on Old and New Testament books. *Watson's " Body of Divinity "* contains some of the richest doctrinal and experimental material to be found anywhere amongst the Puritans. Who can estimate how much we have suffered individually and as a nation for neglecting our unsurpassed seventeenth century literature ! *George Whitefield's Select Sermons,* with an account of his life by J. C. Ryle, is the first of a class of books which are intended to convey biographical accounts of Christian Leaders with selections from their sermons or writings. Whitefield's ministry has an unusual relevance at the present time, for there is not only a widespread misconception of the nature of a true revival, but also a common misunderstanding of the very Gospel that was preached in former times. This book presents some forgotten truths and facts in a very powerful manner. We will later notify subscribers of the publishing date of these three books and of the means of obtaining them.

Continued on page 31.

ANOTHER LILY GATHERED

" My beloved is gone down into his garden to gather lilies."
—Song VI, 2.

EDITOR'S NOTE :

The following is an account, abridged from a children's tract by R. M. McCheyne, of the conversion of a boy who died at the age of thirteen. We judge this to be one of the most important articles we have re-printed. Surely the disappearance amongst our children of the experiences known by this little boy should awaken us to the fact that God in His saving power is a stranger in the land today. The modern spiritual approach to children's work, based on Arminian principles, is reaping its sad consequences. Our seventh issue was largely devoted to this subject. Copies of this issue are still available.

GOD loves His mighty works to be remembered. He has done great things for us in this corner of His vineyard, whereof we are glad. In this little narrative we would raise up an humble stone to the memory of a dear boy who now sleeps in Jesus, and to the praise of that God and Saviour who planted, watered, and gathered His own lily.

JAMES LAING was born on 28th July, 1828, and lost his mother before he was eight years old. James was seized with the same fever as that of which his mother died, and hd never enjoyed good health afterwards.

The first time that he showed any concern for his soul was in the autumn of 1839. His elder brother, Alexander, a sailor boy, was at that time awakened, and the same glorious Spirit seemed to visit James for a time. One evening their sister Margaret, returning home from a meeting, found her two brothers on their knees earnestly crying for mercy. She did not interrupt them, but Alexander afterwards said to her, " Jamie feels that he needs Christ too. We will easily know if he be in earnest, for then he will not need to be bidden to pray." The test was a trying one ; James soon gave up secret prayer, and proved that his goodness was like a morning cloud and the early dew which goeth away. This is the mark of the hypocrite laid down by Job, " Will he always call upon God ? " —Job xxvii. 10.

Another night Margaret observed James coming from the prayer-meeting in the school in great distress. He kept close by the wall of the church that he might escape observation. He was much concerned that night, and, after retiring to rest, said to his sister, in his own Scottish dialect, " There's me come awa' *without Christ* to-night again."

One Thursday evening he attended the weekly meeting held in the church. The passage explained was Romans iv. 4-6, and sinners were urged to receive the " righteousness without works." Many were deeply affected, and would not go away even after the blessing. James was one of those who remained, and when I came to him he was weeping bitterly. I asked him if he cared for his soul: he said, " Whiles." I asked if he prayed: he said, " Yes." He was much concerned on his return home that night both for others and for his own soul. But these dew drops were soon dried up again.

He attended the Sabbath-school in the lane where their cottage stands. Often when the teacher was reading the Bible, or some awakening anecdote, the tears flowed down his cheeks; but· he tried to conceal his emotion from the other boys lest they should laugh at him. He afterwards said in his last illness, "O that I had just another night of the Sabbath-school! I would not care though they should laugh at me now." Sometimes during the reading and prayer in the family, the word of God was like a fire to him, so that he could not bear it, and after it was over he would run to his wild companions in order to drown the cries of his awakened conscience.

In July 1841 he went up to Glammiss for his health. I was preaching in the neighbourhood, and he wished much to go and hear, but was not able to walk the distance. One night he heard Mr. Cormick of Kirriemuir preach in a cottage on John vii, 37. He felt it deeply, and wept bitterly, but he remarked that none of the people wept. He knew well when people showed any concern for their soul; and he often remarked that to be anxious is not to be *in Christ*. When he came home he spoke much of the carelessness of the people where he had been. "Ah! Margaret, there was no Bible read yonder. The people a' went to their bed just as if there had not been a God." What a faithful picture is this of the state of many of our country parishes!

The day of Immanuel's power, and the time of love, was near at hand. As the cold winds of October set in, his sickly frame was much affected: he became weak and breathless. One Tuesday, in the end of October, he turned decidedly worse, and became intensely anxious about the salvation of his soul. His lamentable cry was, "Oh, Jesus save me—save me!" Margaret asked if his concern was real, for he had often deceived her hopes before. He wept, and said "Yes." His body was greatly pained, but he forgot all in the intense anxiety for his precious never-dying soul. On the Saturday I paid a visit to their humble cottage, and found the little sufferer sitting by the fire. He began to weep bitterly while I spoke to him of Jesus having come into the world *to save sinners.* I was enabled in a simple manner to answer the objections that sinners make to an immediate closing with Christ. Margaret wondered; for the minister could not have spoken more to the case of her brother if he had known it; and she inwardly thanked God, for she saw that He was directing it. James spent the rest of the day on his knees in evident distress of soul. O how little the most of those called Christians know what it is to pass through such deep waters! Margaret asked him if he was seeking Jesus: he said, "Yes." She asked, "If he would like anything—a bit of bread?" he said, "No; but I would take a bit of the bread of life if you would give it me." She replied, "I cannot give you that; but if you seek it you will get it." He remained alone till evening, and was never off his knees. Towards night he came to the other end of the cottage, and put this question—"Have I only to believe that Jesus died for sinners? Is that all?" He was told, "Yes." "Well, I believe that Jesus died for me, for I am a poor hell-deserving sinner. I have been praying all this afternoon, that when Jesus shed His blood for sinners, He would sprinkle some of it upon me and *He did it.* He then turned up Rom. v. 8, and read these words, "While we were yet sinners Christ died for us." His sister wept for joy, and James added, "I am not afraid to die now, for Jesus has died for me." Often after this he bade his sister read to him Rom. v., Psa. ciii., and Psa. cxvi. These were favourite portions with him.

From that day it was a pleasant duty indeed to visit the cottage of this youthful inquirer. Many a happy hour have I spent beneath that humble roof. Instead of dropping passing remarks, I used generally to open up a passage of the Word, that he might grow in knowledge. I fear that, in general, we are not sufficiently careful in *regularly instructing* the sick and dying. A pious expression and a fervent prayer are not enough to feed the soul that is passing through the dark valley. Surely if sound and spiritual nourishment is needed by the soul at any time, it is in such an hour when Satan uses all his arts to disturb and destroy.

One Thursday afternoon I spoke to him on Matt. xxiii. 37, " How often would I have gathered your children." He was in great darkness that day, and, weeping bitterly, said, " I fear I have never been gathered to Christ ; but if I have never been gathered, O that I were gathered to Christ *now* !" After I was gone he said, " It would give me no peace though the minister and everybody said I was a Christian, if I had not *the sense* of it between God and myself."

He was very fond of the Song of Solomon, and many parts of it were opened up to him. One day I spoke on Song v. 13, " His lips are like lilies, dropping sweet-smelling myrrh." I told him that these were some of the drops that fell from the lips of Jesus—" If any man thirst, let him come to Me and drink." " I came to seek and to save that which was lost." " Wilt thou be made whole ? " " I give unto them eternal life." He said solemnly, " That's fine."

One Sabbath I had been preaching on Caleb following the Lord fully (Numb. xiv. 24), and had stated that every sin, committed after conversion, would take away something from the believer's weight of eternal glory. Alexander, his brother, was present, it being his only Sabbath on shore. He was much troubled, and said, " Ah, I fear mine will be all lost." He told the statement to James, who was also troubled. Alexander said, " You don't need to be troubled, Jamie ; you are holy." James wept, and said, " I wonder to hear you speak." Alexander said, " Ah, but you are holier than me."

In the same sermon, I had said, that if believers did nothing for Christ, they would get in at the door of heaven, but nothing more. The sailor-boy told this to his brother, who wept again, saying, " I have done nothing for Christ." Alexander said he had done less. James added, " I would like to be *near* Jesus. I could not be happy, unless I was near Him."

How lovely this simple domestic scene ! Happy families ; but, ah ! how few where the children fear the Lord, and speak often one to another. Surely the Lord stands behind the wall hearkening, and He will write their words in His book of remembrance. " And they shall be Mine, saith the Lord of Hosts, in that day when I make up My jewels."

Some of my dear brethren in the ministry visited this little boy, to see God's wonderful works in him, and to be helpers of his joy. It is often of great importance in visiting the dying, to call in the aid of a fellow-labourer. Different lines of testimony to the same Saviour are thus brought to meet in the chamber of sorrow. In the mouth of two or three witnesses shall every word be established. Mr. Cumming of Dumbarney, visiting him one day, asked him if he suffered much pain. *James* " Sometimes." *Mr. C.*—" When you are in much pain, can you think on the sufferings of the Lord Jesus ? " *James*—" When I see what Jesus suffered for me it takes away my pain. Mine is nothing to what He suffered." He often repeated these words, " My light affliction, which is but for a moment."

At another time Mr. Miller of Wallacetown called with me and our little sufferer spoke very sweetly on eternal things. *Mr. M.*—" Would you like to get better ? " *James*—" I would like the will of God." *Mr. M.*— " But if you were getting better, would you just live as you did before ? " *James*—" If God did not give me grace I would." During the same visit I was asking Margaret when he was first awakened. She told me of his first concern, and then of the first day I had called. James broke in, and said, " Ah, but we must not lean upon that." His meaning was, that past experiences are not the foundation of a sinner's peace. I never met with any boy who had so clear a discovery of the way of pardon and acceptance through the doing and dying of the Lord Jesus, laid to our account.

One of the loveliest features in the character of this little boy was his intense love to the souls of men. He often spoke with me on the folly of men living without Christ in the world. I shall never forget the compassionate glance of his clear blue eye as he said, " What a pity it is that they do not a' come to Christ—they would be sic happy." He often reminded me of the verse, " Love is of God, and every one that loveth is born of God."—1 John iv. 7.

One Sabbath evening I spoke to the scholars in the Sabbath-school about him. When the school was over, they all came into his cottage to see him. The little throng stood silent round his bed, while he spoke to them with great solemnity. " You all know what I was ; I was no better than you ; but the Holy Spirit opened my eyes, and I saw that I was on the very brink of hell. Then I cried to Jesus to save me, and give me a new heart ; I put my finger on the promise, and would not come away without it and He gave me a new heart ; and He is as willing to give you all a new heart. I have sinned with you, now I would like you to come to Christ with me. You would be far happier in Christ than at your play. There are sweeter pleasures in Christ. Here are two awful verses to me :—

> ' There is a dreadful hell,
>   And everlasting pains ;
> There sinners must with devils dwell
>   In darkness, fire, and chains.
>
> Can such a wretch as I
>   Escape this cursed end ?
> And may I hope, whene'er I die,
>   I shall to heaven ascend ! ' "

Then, pointing to the fire, he said, " You could not keep your finger long there, but remember hell is a *lake of fire*. I would give you all a prayer to pray to-night. Go and tell Jesus that you are poor, lost, hell-deserving sinners, and tell Him to give you a new heart. Mind, He's willing, and oh, be earnest—ye'll no get it unless ye be earnest."

These were nearly his very words. Strange scene ! a dying boy speaking to his fellows. They were impressed for a time, but it soon wore away. Several Sabbath evenings the same scene was renewed. The substance of all his warnings was, " Come to Christ and get a new heart." He often told me afterwards that he had been inviting them to Christ, but (he added) *they'll no come*."

One day, during his illness, his sister found him crying very bitterly. She asked him what ailed him. He said, " Do you remember when I was at the day-school at the time of the Revival ? One day when we were writing our copies, one of the boys had been *some anxious* about his soul ; he wrote a line to me on a slip of paper, ' *Ezek.* xxxvi. 26. *To James Laing. Pray over it.*' I took the paper, read it, and tore it, and threw it on the floor, and laughed at the boy. O Margaret, if I hadna laughed at him, maybe he would have sought Christ until he had *found* Him. Maybe I have been the means of ruining his soul to all eternity." In how touching a manner this shows the tenderness of his care for the souls of others; and also how a rash word or deed, little thought of at the time, may plant a sting in the dying pillow.

One night I went with my little cousin to see James. I said, "I have brought my Jamie to see you." He took him kindly by the hand, and said, "We're twa Jamies thegither. May we both meet in heaven. Be earnest to get Christ. You'll no get Christ unless you are earnest." When we were gone, he said to his sister, "Although Jamie bides with the minister, unless the Spirit open his eyes, he canna get Christ."

His knowledge of the peculiar doctrines of the Gospel was very wonderful. It was not mere *head knowledge*—it came fresh and clear from the heart, like spring water welling up from a great depth. He felt the *sovereignty* of God very deeply. Once I quoted to him the hymn,

"Chosen not for good in me."

He said, "I am sure it was for naething in me. I am a hell-deserving sinner." Often when speaking of the great things God had done for their family, he would say, "Ah, Margaret, I wonder that Christ would look in here and take us." Once he said, "I wonder how Jesus died for such a sinner as me. Why me, Lord, why me?"

The greatest want in the religion of children is generally *sense of sin.* Artless simplicity and confidence in what is told, are in some respects natural to children; and this is the reason why we are so often deceived by promising appearances in childhood. The reality of grace in a child is best known by his sense of sin. Little James often wondered "how God sent His servant sic often to him, such a hell-deserving sinner." This was a common expression of his. On one occasion, he said, "I have a wicked, wicked heart, and a tempting devil. He'll not let me alone, but this is all the hell that I'll get. Jesus bore my hell already. O Margaret, this wicked heart of mine would be hell enough for me though there was no other. But there are no wicked hearts in heaven." Often he prayed, "Come, Holy Spirit, and make me holy—make me like Jesus."

The way of salvation through *the righteousness of Christ* was always sweet to him. He had an uncommon grasp of it; Christ crucified was all his salvation and all his desire. One day his sister said to him, "You must meet death in Jesus, and go to the judgment-seat in Jesus, and spend eternity in Jesus. You will be as hell-deserving in yourself when you stand before the throne as now." He smiled sweetly, and said, "Margaret, I see it must be all Jesus from beginning to end."

He had a very clear discovery of the dead and helpless condition of the carnal mind, and of the *need of the Holy Spirit* to convert the soul. Telling me once of a boy under concern, and of what he had been saying to him, he added, "But it is nonsense to speak of these things without the Holy Spirit." At another time I was speaking on John xiv. 1. He seemed to be thinking about something else, and suddenly said, "When we lose our first love, it's no easy getting our second love; only the Spirit of God can give it."

Often when he saw the family preparing to go to church, he would pray that I might be filled with the Holy Spirit in speaking, so that some sinners might be caught. "I mind often sitting on the pulpit stairs careless; I would like if I had that place again. If I had but one sermon I would not be so careless now." He often wished to be carried to the church, but was never able to bear the exertion."

He was no stranger to *temptations* from the wicked one. I scarcely ever visited him but he spoke to me of these.

Once I found him kneeling on a pillow by the fire ; he complained of great darkness, and doubted his interest in Christ. I told him that we must not close with Christ because we feel Him, but because God has said it, and that we must take God's word even in the dark. After that he always seemed to trust God in the dark, even at times when he had no inward evidence of being Christ's. At one of these times, a believer, who is often in great darkness, came in, and asked him, " When you are in darkness, Jamie, how do you do ? Can you go to Jesus ? " He answered, in his own pointed manner, " Annie, woman, *I have no ither ge: to gang.*"

A dear Christian lady used to bring him flowers. She spoke to him of Christ being the " lily of the valley," and on one occasion brought him one. He asked her to pick it out from the rest, and give it into his hand Holding the gentle flower in his pale wasted fingers, he looked at it, and said, " This might convince the world that there is a God, though there were nothing else. Aye, there is a God—there is a heaven—there is a hell—and there is a judgment-seat—whether they will believe it or no." He said this in a very solemn way, pausing between every member of the sentence.

He delighted in *secret prayer*. In weakness and pain, yet he spent hours upon his knees, communing with an unseen God. When unable for the outward part of the exercise, he said, " Margaret, I prayed to Jesus as long as I was able ; but now I'm not able, and He does not want it from me ; but I'm just always giving Him my heart." Many a night he got no sleep. I asked him if he wearied during the silent watches. He said, " No ; His left hand is under my head, and His right hand doth embrace me." God gave this dear boy a very *calm and cheerful spirit* in the midst of all his trials. Neither bodily pain nor the assaults of the devil could sour his temper, or ruffle his placid brow. At any time when his pain increased, he would say, " It is the Lord, let Him do what seemeth Him good." One time in darkness, he cried out, " Though He slay me, yet will I trust in Him."

On the last day of 1841 he said to his sister, " I will tell you what I would like for my New Year (Gift). I would like a praying heart, and a heart to love Christ more." Next day a woman came in, and said, " Poor Jamie ! you'll get no fun this New Year's Day." James said, " Poor body, she thinks like as I care for the New Year. I have far better than you have, though you had the whole world. This is the happiest New Year's Day that ever I had, for I have Christ." She was very deaf, and did not hear what he said ; but he often pitied that woman and prayed for her.

A little after the New Year, he said, " Margaret, I am not to die yet, for I have mair to suffer ; but I am willing, though it should be years." On one occasion when he was suffering much pain, he said, " Five minutes in glory will make up for all this suffering."

In a season of great darkness, he said, " Margaret, give me my Bible " (meaning a little book of texts, called *Dew Drops*) ; when he had got it, he sought out the verse, " The Lord is a stronghold in the day of trouble, and He knoweth them that trust in Him." He said, " Margaret, I'll trust in Him, though I cannot see Him. I will lie down upon that verse." When his bed was made at night, he would take another verse to *lie down upon,* as he called it ; so he was fed by the dew of the word.

In the latter part of his illness he was used as an instrument in awakening another boy, whose impressions I earnestly hope may never wear away. D. G. had been a very wild boy—so much so, that he was expelled from the Sabbath-school. He found his way into James' cottage, and there saw exemplified the truths he would not listen to in school. From that day till James died, David regularly visited him, and learned from him with deepest interest the things that belonged to his peace. James often prayed with him alone.

The last visit I paid to this young Christian was on the Tuesday before he died, in company with Mr. Miller of Wallacetown, and Mr. Smith, one of our Jewish missionaries at Pesth, who was that same day to sail for his native land. After speaking a little we prayed, and I asked what I would pray for him. James said, " Dying grace." He shook hands with us all. When the missionary held his hand, he said, " God's people have much need to pray for you, and for them there." When we had gone out he said, " Maybe I'll never see the minister again."

On the Thursday he said, " Ah! Margaret, mind it's no easy to die. You know nothing about it. Even though you have Christ, it is dark." The same day he bade her give D. G. his Sunday trowsers, and new boots, that he might go to the church. He gave his father *The Dying Thief* ; and said, " I am going to give Alick my Bible " (meaning *Dew Drops*). There was a piece of money under his pillow. He said it was to buy Bibles for them that never heard of Jesus.

His aunt came in on the Friday morning. He said, " Oh, aunt, don't put off Christ to a death-bed, for if I had Christ to seek to-day, what would have become of me ; but I have given my heart to Christ."

All that day he spoke very little. In the evening he grew much worse. His sister wished to sit up with him that night, but he would not allow her. She said, " These eyes will soon see Him whom your soul loves." James said, " Aye." After midnight Margaret, seeing him worse, arose and woke her father. She tried to conceal her tears ; but James saw them, and said, with a look of solemn earnestness, " O woman, I wonder to see you do the like of that." He spoke little after this, and about one o'clock on the Saturday morning, 11th June, 1842, fell asleep in Jesus.

From this affecting history, *all children* should learn an impressive lesson. What is said of Abel is true of this dear boy. " He being dead yet speaketh." You see here that you are not too young to have the Holy Spirit striving with you. You are not too young to resist the Holy Ghost. You are not too young to be converted and brought to Christ. If you die without Christ, you will surely perish. The most of you are wicked, idle, profane, prayerless, ungodly children. Many of you are open Sabbath-breakers, liars, and swearers. If you die thus, you will have your part in that lake that burneth with fire and brimstone. You will see this little boy in the kingdom of God, and you yourselves thrust out. O repent and be converted, that your sins may be blotted out. You may die very soon. O that your latter end may be like his!

Parents also may learn from this to seek the salvation of their children. Alas! most parents are like the cruel ostrich in the wilderness, " which leaveth her eggs in the earth, and warmeth them in the dust ; and forgetteth that the foot may crush them, or that the wild beast may break them ; She is hardened against her young ones as though they were not hers."— Job xxxix. 14-16. Alas, are not the family altars of Scotland for the most part broken down, and lying desolate ? Is not family government in most of your houses an empty name ? Do not family quarrels, and unholy companies, and profane jests, and sordid worldliness, prevail in most of your tabernacles ? What can you expect but that your children shall grow up in your image, formalists, lovers of pleasure more than lovers of

God ? O that God would touch your hearts by such a tale as this, that you may repent and turn to the Lord, and yearn over your children in the bowels of Jesus Christ. Would you not love to see them fall asleep in Jesus ? Would you not love to meet them at the right hand of the Judge ? Seek their conversion *now*, if you would meet them in glory *hereafter*. How will you bear to hear their young voices in the judgment, saying, " This father never prayed for me ; this mother never warned me to flee from the wrath to come ? "

Dear brethren in the ministry and labourers in the Sabbath-school, suffer the word of exhortation from one who is " your brother and companion in tribulation." May we not learn from this to be more earnest both in prayers and labours, in seeking the salvation of little children ? We have here one bright example more in addition to all those who have been recorded before, that God can convert and edify a child with the same ease with which He can change the hearts of a grown man. I have with religious care refrained from embellishing, or in any way exaggerating, the simple record of God's dealings with this boy. We must not " speak wickedly for God, nor talk deceitfully for Him."

How evident is it, then, that God is willing and able to convert the young ! How plain that if God gives grace, they can understand and relish divine things as fully as those of mature age ! A carnal mind of the first order will evermore despise and reject the way of salvation by Christ ; but the mind of a child, quickened by the Holy Spirit, will evermore realize and delight in the rich and glorious mystery of the gospel. " I thank thee, O Father, Lord of heaven and earth, because thou hast hid these things from the wise and prudent, and hast revealed them unto babes. Even so, Father, for so it seemed good in thy sight." Let us awake from an unbelieving dream. Let us no more be content to labour without fruit. Let us seek the *present* conversion to Christ of our little children. Jesus has reason to complain of us that He can do no mighty works in our Sabbath-schools because of our unbelief.

" Now unto the King eternal, immortal, invisible, the only wise God, be honour and glory for ever and ever. Amen."

*   *   *

SELECTIONS FROM THOMAS WATSON'S BODY OF DIVINITY*

Although Thomas Watson was one of the leading Puritan divines of the seventeenth century there are few facts known about his life. After a training at Emmanuel College, Cambridge, he became rector of St. Stephen's, Walbrook, where in the very heart of London he exercised a powerful and popular ministry for nearly sixteen years. At the end of the Commonwealth period and at the accession of Charles II, Watson was ejected from his church and living, along with 2,000 other Puritan ministers, by the Act of Uniformity, August, 1662. Thereafter, despite the liability to fines and imprisonment, he continued to preach as much as circumstances allowed. Upon the Indulgence, in 1672, he licensed a large hall in the city where he preached for several years.

★ *A Body of Divinity,* by Thomas Watson. pp. 226, 8/-. U.S. price pending.

Stephen Charnock was joint pastor with him from 1675 till his death in 1680. Watson at length removed to Essex, and died suddenly while in secret prayer, about 1689 or 1690. "He was so well known for his piety and usefulness," wrote a contemporary, "that he carried a general respect from all sober persons along with him to his grave."

Watson's sermons on the Assembly's Catechism were first published in 1692, and they at once became one of the most esteemed of all the Puritan writings. The sermons cover practically the whole range of doctrinal and experimental truth, and are written in such a clear, vigorous, and arresting style that the book long remained a favourite amongst the common people. Never was profound theology presented in a more lively manner. His general method is to propose the question, summarize, expand and prove the answer from Scripture, deal with objections, then, having informed the understanding, he applies each question powerfully to the heart and conscience in a series of "Uses." We will now let the book speak for itself in the following variety of quotations :—

One Proof That The Scriptures Are The Word of God :

As the matter of Scripture is so full of goodness, justice and sanctity, that it could be breathed from none but God ; so the holiness of it shows it to be of God. Scripture is compared to silver refined seven times. Psa. xii. 6. The Book of God has no errata in it ; it is a beam of the Sun of Righteousness, a crystal stream flowing from the fountain of life. All laws and edicts of men have had their corruptions, but the Word of God has not the least tincture, it is of meridian splendour. Psa. cxix. 140. "Thy word is very pure," like wine that comes from the grape, which is not mixed or adulterated. It is so pure that it purifies everything else. John xvii. 17. "Sanctify them through thy truth." The Scripture presses holiness, so as no other book ever did : it bids us live "soberly, righteously, and godly ;" Titus ii. 12 ; soberly, in acts of temperance ; righteously, in acts of justice ; godly, in acts of zeal and devotion. It commends to us, whatever is "just, lovely, and of good report." Phil. iv. 8. This sword of the Spirit can cut down vice. Eph. vi. 17. Out of this tower of Scripture is thrown a millstone upon the head of sin. The Scripture is the royal law which commands not only the actions, but affections ; it binds the heart to good behaviour. Where is there such holiness to be found, as is digged out of this sacred mine ? Who could be the author of such a book but God himself ?

The Effects of Sin On Man's Nature :

(1). Original sin has depraved the intellectual part. As in the creation "darkness was upon the face of the deep," Gen. i. 2, so it is with the understanding ; darkness is upon the face of this deep. As there is salt in every drop of the sea, bitterness in every branch of wormwood, so there is sin in every faculty. The mind is darkened, we know little of God. Ever since Adam did eat of the tree of knowledge, and his eyes were opened, we lost our eye-sight. Besides ignorance in the mind, there is error and mistake ; we do not judge rightly of things, we put bitter for sweet, and sweet for bitter. Isa. v. 20. Besides this, there is much pride, superciliousness and prejudice, and many fleshly reasonings. "How long shall thy vain thoughts lodge within thee ?" Jer. iv. 14.

(2). Original sin has defiled the heart. The heart is deadly wicked. Jer. xvii. 9. It is a lesser hell. In the heart are legions of lust, obdurateness, infidelity, hypocrisy, sinful estuations ; it boils as the sea with passion and revenge. Madness is in their heart while they live. Eccl. ix. 3. The heart is, *Officina diaboli,* the devil's shop or workhouse, where all mischief is framed.

(3). The will. Contumacy is the seat of rebellion. The sinner crosses God's will to fulfil his own. " We will burn incense to the queen of heaven." Jer. xliv. 18. There is a rooted enmity in the will against holiness ; it like an iron sinew, it refuses to bend to God. Where is then the freedom of the will, when it is so full not only of indisposition, but opposition to what is spiritual ?

(4). The affections. These, as the strings of a viol, are out of tune. They are the lesser wheels, which are strongly carried by the will, the master-wheel. Our affections are set on wrong objects. Our love is set on sin, our joy on the creature. Our affections are naturally as a sick man's appetite, who desires things which are noxious and hurtful to him ; he calls for wine in a fever. So we have impure lustings instead of holy longings.

What Is Effectual Calling ? *" Them he also called."* Rom. viii. 30.

Ans. It is a gracious work of the Spirit, whereby he causes us to embrace Christ freely, as he is offered to us in the gospel.

In this verse is the golden chain of salvation, made up of four links, of which one is vocation. " Them he also called." Calling is *nova creatio,* a new creation, the first resurrection. There is a two-fold call: 1. An outward call: 2. An inward call.

1. An outward call, which is God's offer of grace to sinners, inviting them to come and accept of Christ and salvation. " Many are called, but few chosen." Matt. xx. 16. This call shows men what they ought to do in order to salvation, and renders them inexcusable in case of disobedience.

2. There is an inward call, when God with the offer of grace works grace. By this call the heart is renewed, and the will is effectually drawn to embrace Christ. The outward call brings men to a profession of Christ, the inward to a possession of Christ.

Q. What are the means of this effectual call ?

Ans. Every creature has a voice to call us. The heavens call to us to behold God's glory. Psalm xix, 1. Conscience calls to us. God's judgments call us to repent. " Hear ye the rod." Mic. vi. 9. But every voice does not convert. There are two means of our effectual call :

1. The " preaching of the word," which is the sounding of God's silver trumpet in men's ears. God speaks not by an oracle, he calls by his ministers. Samuel thought it had been the voice of Eli only that called him ; but it was God's voice. 1 Sam. iii. 6. So, perhaps, you think it is only the minister that speaks to you in the word, but it is God himself who speaks. Therefore Christ is said to speak to us from heaven. Heb. xii. 25. How does he speak but by his ministers ? as a king speaks by his ambassadors. Know, that in every sermon preached, God calls to you ; and to refuse the message we bring, is to refuse God himself.

2. The other means of our effectual call is the Holy Spirit. The ministry of the word is the pipe or organ ; the Spirit of God blowing in it, effectually changes men's hearts. " While Peter spake, the Holy Ghost fell on all them that heard the word of God." Acts x. 44. Ministers knock at the door of men's hearts, the Spirit comes with a key and opens the door. " A certain woman named Lydia, whose heart the Lord opened." Acts xvi. 14.

Q. What is the cause of the effectual call ?

Ans. God's electing love. " Whom he predestined, them he also called." Rom. viii. 30. Election is the fountain-cause of our vocation. It is not because some are more worthy to partake of the heavenly calling than others, for we were " all in our blood." Ezek. xvi. 6. What worthiness is in us ? What worthiness was there in Mary Magdalene, out of

whom seven devils were cast ?   What worthiness in the Corinthians, when
God began to call them by his gospel ?   They were fornicators, effeminate,
idolaters.   " Such were some of you, but ye are washed," etc. 1 Cor. vi. 11.
Before effecctual calling, we are not only " without strength, Rom. v. 6,
but " enemies," Col. i. 21.   So that the foundation of vocation is election.
    Q. *What are the qualifications of this call ?*
    Ans. 1st. It is a powerful call. *Verba Dei sunt opera.* Luther. God
puts forth infinite power in calling home a sinner to himself: he not
only puts forth his voice but his arm.   The apostle speaks of " the exceeding greatness of his power, which he exercises towards them that
believe." Eph. i. 19.   God rides forth conquering in the chariot of his
gospel ; he conquers the pride of heart, and makes the will, which stood
out as a fort-royal, to yield and stoop to his grace ; he makes the stony
heart bleed.   Oh, it is a mighty call!   Why then do the Arminians seem
to talk of a moral persuasion, that God in the conversion of a sinner only
morally persuades and no more ; sets his promises before men to allure
them to good, and his threatenings to deter them from evil ; and that
is all he does ?   But surely moral persuasion alone are insufficient to the
effectual call.   How can the bare proposal of promises and threatenings
convert a soul ?   This amount not to a new creation, or that power which
raised Christ from the dead.   God not only persuades, but enables. Ezek.
xxxvii. 27.   If God, in conversion, should only morally persuade, that is,
set good and evil before men, then he does not put forth so much power
in saving men as the devil does in destroying them.   Satan not only pro-
pounds tempting objects to men, but concurs with his temptations : therefore he is said to " work in the children of disobedience." Eph. ii. 2.
The Greek word, to work, signifies *imperii vim,* Camer., the power Satan
has in carrying men to sin.   And shall not God's power in converting be
greater than Satan's power in seducing ?   The effectual call is mighty and
powerful.   God puts forth a divine energy, nay, a kind of omnipotence ;
it is such a powerful call, that the will of man has no power effectually
to resist.
    Use 1. See the necessity of the effectual call.   A man cannot go
to heaven without it.   First, we must be called before we are glorified.
Rom. viii. 30.   A man uncalled can lay claim to nothing in the Bible
but threatenings : a man in the state of nature is not fit for heaven, no
more than a man in his filth and his rags is fit to come into a king's
presence.   A man in his natural state is a God-hater, and is he fit for
heaven ?   Rom. i. 30.   Will God lay his enemy in his bosom ?
    Use 2. *Of trial.*   Whether we are effectually called ?   This we may
know by its antecedent and consequent.
    1. By the antecedent.   Before this effectual call, a humbling work
passes upon the soul.   A man is convinced of sin, he sees he is a sinner
and nothing but a sinner ; the fallow ground of his heart is broken up.
Jer. iv. 3.   As the husbandman breaks the clods, then casts in the seed ;
so God, by the convincing work of the law, breaks a sinner's heart, and
makes it fit to receive the seeds of grace.   Such as were never convinced
are never called.   " He shall convince the world of sin." John xvi. 8.
Convict on is the first step in conversion.
    2. By the consequents, which are two.   (1.) He who is savingly called
answers to God's call.   When God called Samuel, he answered, " Speak,
Lord, thy servant heareth." 1 Sam. iii. 10.   When God calls thee to an
act of religion, dost thou run at God's call ?   " I was not disobdieent to
the heavenly vision." Acts xxvi. 19.   If God calls to duties contrary to
flesh and blood, we obey his voice in everything ; true obedience is like
the needle, which points that way which the loadstone draws.   Such as
are deaf to God's call show they are not called by grace.   (2.) He who
is effectually called stops his ears to all other calls which would call
him off from God.   As God has his call, so there are other contrary calls.
Satan calls by temptation, lust calls, evil company calls ; but as the

adder stops its ear against the voice of the charmer, so he who is effectually called stops his ear against all the charms of the flesh and the devil.

What Is Justification ?

Ans. It is an act of God's free grace, whereby he pardons all our sins, and accepts us as righteous in his sight, for the righteousness of Christ only, imputed to us, and received by faith alone.

Justification is the very hinge and pillar of Christianity. An error about justification is dangerous, like a defect in a foundation. Justification by Christ is a spring of the water of life. To have the poison of corrupt doctrine cast into this spring is damnable. It was a saying of Luther, " that after his death the doctrine of justification would be corrupted." In these latter times, the Arminians and Socinians have cast a dead fly into this box of precious ointment.

I shall endeavour to follow the star of Scripture to light me through this mysterious point.

Q. *What is meant by justification ?*

Ans. It is *verbum forense,* a word borrowed from law-courts, wherein a person arraigned is pronounced righteous, and is openly absolved. God, in justifying a person, pronounces him to be righteous, and looks upon him as if he had not sinned.

Q. *What is the source of justification ?*

Ans. The *causa,* the inward impellant motive or ground of justification, is the free grace of God : " being justified freely by his grace." Ambrose expounds this, as " not of the grace wrought within us, but the free grace of God." The first wheel that sets all the rest running, is the love and favour of God ; as a king freely pardons a delinquent. Justification is a mercy spun out of the bowels of free grace. God does not justify us because we are worthy, but by justifying us makes us worthy.

Q. *What is the ground, or that by which a sinner is justified ?*

Ans. The ground of our justification is Christ's satisfaction made to his Father. If it be asked, how can it stand with God's justice and holiness to pronounce us innocent when we are guilty ? The answer is, that Christ having made satisfaction for our fault, God may, in equity and justice, pronounce us righteous. It is a just thing for a creditor to discharge a debtor of the debt, when a satisfaction is made by the surety.

Q. *But how was Christ's satisfaction meritorious, and so sufficient to justify ?*

Ans. In respect of the divine nature. As he was man he suffered, as God he satisfied. By Christ's death and merits, God's justice is more abundantly satisfied than if we had suffered the pains of hell for ever.

Q. *Wherein lies the method of our justification ?*

Ans. In the imputation of Christ's righteousness to us. " This is the name whereby he shall be called," *Jehovah Tzidkennu,* " THE LORD OUR RIGHTEOUSNESS." Jer. xxiii. 6. " He is made to us righteousness." 1 Cor. i. 30. This righteousness of Christ, which justifies us, is a better righteousness than the angels'; for theirs is the righteousness of creatures, this of God.

Q. *What is the means or instrument of our justification ?*

Ans. Faith. " Being justified by faith." Rom. v. 1. The dignity is not in faith as a grace, but relatively, as it lays hold on Christ's merits.

Faith :

The Spirit applies to us the redemption purchased by Christ, by working faith in us.

Christ is the glory, and faith in Christ the comfort, of the gospel.

Q. *What are the kinds of faith ?*

Ans. Fourfold: 1. An historical or dogmatic faith, which is believing the truths revealed in the Word, because of divine authority.

2. There is a temporary faith, which lasts for a time, and then vanishes.

"Yet hath he no root in himself, but dureth for a while " Matt. xiii. 21.
A temporary faith is like Jonah's gourd, which came up in a night and
withered. Chap. iv. 10.

3. A miraculous faith, which was granted to the apostles, to work
miracles for the confirmation of the gospel. This Judas had ; he cast out
devils, yet was cast out to the devil.

4. A true justifying faith, which is called "A faith of the operation
of God," and is a jewel hung only upon the elect. Col. ii. 12.

Q. *What is justifying faith* ?

Ans. I shall show, (1.) *What it is not.* It is not a bare acknowledgment
that Christ is a Saviour. There must be an acknowledgment, but that is
not sufficient to justify. The devils acknowledged Christ's Godhead.
"Jesus the Son of God." Matt. viii. 29. There may be an assent to divine
truth, and yet no work of grace on the heart. Many assent in their
judgments, that sin is an evil thing, but they go on in sin, whose corruptions
are stronger than their convictions ; and that Christ is excellent ; they
cheapen the pearl, but do not buy.

(2.) *What justifying faith is* ? True justifying faith consists in three
things :

1. Self-renunciation. Faith is going out of one's self, being taken
off from our own merits, and seeing we have no righteousness of our own.
" Not having mine own righteousness." Phil. iii. 9. Self-righteousness is
a broken reed, which the soul dares not lean on. Repentance and faith
are both humbling graces ; by repentance a man abhors himself ; by faith
he goes out of himself.

2. Reliance. The soul casts itself upon Jesus Christ ; faith rests on
Christ's person. Faith believes the promise ; but that which faith rests
upon in the promise is the person of Christ : therefore the spouse is said
to " lean upon her Beloved." Cant. viii. 5. Faith is described to be
" believing on the name of the Son of God," 1 John iii. 23, viz., on his
person.

3. Appropriation, or applying Christ to ourselves.

Uses of the Unchangeableness of God's Decree :

Use 1. If God's decree be eternal and unchangeable, then God does
not elect upon faith foreseen, as the Arminians maintain. "The children
being not yet born, that the purpose of God according to election might
stand, it was said, Jacob have I loved, Esau have I hated." Rom. ix. 11,
14. We are not elected for holiness, but to holiness. Eph. i. 4. If we
are not justified for our faith, much less are we elected for our faith ; but
we are not justified for it. We are said to be justified through faith as
an instrument in Eph. ii. 8, but not for faith as a cause ; and, if not
justified for faith, then much less elected. God's decree of election is
eternal and unchangeable, and therefore depends not upon faith foreseen.
" As many as were ordained to eternal life, believed." Acts xiii. 48.
They were not elected because they believed, but they believed because
they were elected.

Use 2. If God's decree be unchangeable, it gives comfort in two
cases. 1. Concerning God's providence towards his church. We are
ready to quarrel with Providence, if everything does not accord with our
desire. Remember God's work goes on, and nothing falls out but what
he has decreed from from eternity. 2. God has decreed troubles for the
church's good. The troubles of God's church is like the angel's troubling
the water, which made way for healing his people. John v. 4. He has
decreed troubles in the church. " His fire is in Sion, and his furnace in
Jerusalem." Isa. xxxi. 9. The wheels in a watch move cross one to
another, but they all carry on the motion of the watch ; so the wheels of
Providence often move cross to our desires, but still they carry on God's
unchangeable decree. " Many shall be made white." Dan. xii. 10. God
lets the waters of affliction be poured on his people to make them white.
Therefore murmur not at God's dealings ; his work goes on, nothing falls

out but what he has wisely decreed from eternity; everything shall promote God's design, and fulfil his decree.

Use 3. Comfort to the godly in regard of their salvation. 2 Tim. ii. 19. " The foundation of God standeth sure, having this seal, The Lord knoweth them that are his." God's counsel of election is unchangeable. Once elected, for ever elected. " I will not blot his name out of the book of life." Rev. iii. 5. The book of God's decree has no errata in it, no blottings out. Once justified, never unjustified. " Repentance shall be hid from mine eyes." Hos xiii. 14. God never repents of his electing love. " He loved them to the end." John xiii. 1. Therefore, if thou art a believer, comfort thyself with this, the immutability of God's decree.

Objection.   If God's decree be unchangeable, and cannot be reversed, to what purpose should we use means ?   Our endeavours towards salvation cannot alter His decree :

Ans. The decree of God does not affect my endeavour; for he that decreed my salvation decreed it in the use of means, and if I neglect the means I reprobate myself. No man argues thus: God has decreed how long I shall live, therefore I will not use means to preserve my life, I will not eat and drink. God has decreed the time of my life in the use of means; so God has decreed my salvation in the use of the Word and of prayer. As a man who refuses food murders himself, so he that refuses to work out his salvation destroys himself. The vessels of mercy are said to be prepared unto glory. Rom. ix. 23. How are they prepared but by being sanctified ? and that cannot be but in the use of means ; therefore let not God's decree take thee off from holy endeavours. It is a good saying of Dr. Preston, " Hast thou a heart to pray to God ? it is a sign no decree of wrath hath passed against thee.

What Shall We Do To Obtain Spiritual Joy ?

Ans. Walk consistently and spiritually. God gives joy after long and close walking with him. (1.) Observe your hours. Set time every day apart for God. (2.) Mourn for sin. Mourning is the seed, as Basil says, out of which the flower of spiritual joy grows. " I will restore comfort to his mourners." Isa. lvii. 18. (3.) Keep the book of conscience well written. Do not by presumptuous sins blur your evidences. A good conscience is the ark in which God put the hidden manna. (4.) Be often upon your knees, pray with life and fervency. The same spirit that fills the heart with sighs fills it with joys. The same Spirit that indites the prayer, seals it. When Hannah had prayed, her countenance was no more sad. 1 Sam. i. 18. Praying Christians have much intercourse with God ; and none are so like to have the secrets of his love imparted, as those who hold correspondence with him. By close walking with God we get bunches of grapes by the way, which are an earnest of future happiness.

How Shall We Know Whether We Grow In Grace ? :

Ans. For deciding this question I shall,

First, Show the signs of our not growing ; Secondly, of our growing.

1st. The signs of our not growing in grace, but rather falling into a spiritual consumption.

1. When we have lost our spiritual appetite. A consumptive person has not the stomach to his meat as formerly. Perhaps, Christian, thou canst remember the time when thou didst hunger and thirst after righteousness, thou didst come to the ordinances with such a stomach as to a feast ; but now it is otherwise, Christ is not so prized, nor his ordinances so loved. This is a sad presage that grace is on the declining hand ; and thou art in deep consumption. It was a sign that David was near his grave when they covered him with clothes, and he got no heat (1 Kings i. 1); so, when a person is covered with the warm clothes of ordinances, and yet has no heat of affection to spiritual things, it is a sign that he is declining in grace.

2. When we grow more worldly. Perhaps we once mounted into higher orbs, we set our hearts on things above, and spake the language of Canaan ; but now our minds are taken off from heaven, we dig our comfort out of the lower mines, and with Satan compass the earth. This is a sign we are going down the hill apace, and our grace is in a consumption. It is observable when nature decays, and people are near dying, they grow more stooping ; and truly, when men's hearts grow more stooping to the earth, and they can hardly lift up themselves to a heavenly thought, if grace be not dead, yet it is ready to die. Rev. iii. 2.

3. When we are less troubled about sin. Time was when the least sin grieved us, as the least hair makes the eye weep ; but now we can diges. sin without remorse. Time was when we were troubled if we neglected closet prayer ; now we can omit family-prayer. Time was when vain thoughts troubled us ; now we are not troubled for loose practices. Here is a sad declension in religion ; and truly grace is so far from growing that we can hardly perceive its pulse to beat.

2ndly. The signs of our growing in grace.

1. The first sign of our growing, is, when we have got beyond our former measures of grace. It is a sign a child thrives when he has outgrown his clothes. That knowledge which would serve us before will not serve us now ; we have a deeper insight into religion, our light is clearer, our spark of love is increased into a flame ; there is a sign of growth. That competency of grace we once had is too scanty for us now ; we have outgrown ourselves.

2. When we are more firmly rooted in religion. " Rooted in him, and established:" the spreading of the root shows the growth of the tree. Col. ii. 7. When we are so strongly fastened on Christ, that we cannot be blown down by the breath of heretics, it is a blessed sign of growth. Athansius was called *Adamas ecclesiae,* an adament that could not be moved from the love of the tree.

3. When we have a more spiritual frame of heart. 1st. When we are more spiritual in our principles ; when we oppose sin out of love to God, and because it strikes at his holiness. 2ndly. When we are more spiritual in our affections. We grieve for the first rising of corruption, for the bubbling up of vain thoughts, and for the spring that runs underground. We mourn not only for the penalty of sin, but for its pollution. It is not a coal only that burns, but blacks. 3rdly. When we are spiritual in the performance of duty. We are more serious, reverent, fervent ; we have more life in prayer, we put fire to the sacrifice. " Fervent in spirit." Rom. xii. We serve God with more love, which ripens and mellows our duty, and makes it come off with a better relish.

How May We Comfort Such as Complain They Do Not Grow In Grace ?

Ans. They may mistake ; for they may grow, when they think they do not, " There is that maketh himself poor, yet hath great riches." Prov. xiii. 7. The sight Christians have of their defects in grace, and their thirst after greater measures of grace, make them think they do not grow when they do. He who covets a great estate, because he has not so much as he desires, thinks himself to be poor. Indeed Christians should seek after the grace they want, but they must not therefore overlook the grace they have. Let Christians be thankful for the least growth. If you do not grow so much in assurance, bless God if you grow in sincerity ; if you do not grow so much in knowledge, bless God if you grow in humility. If a tree grows in the root, it is a true growth ; so if you grow in the root-grace of humility, it is as needful for you as any other growth.

A Believer's Privilege At Death :

To a believer death is great gain. A saint can tell what his losses for Christ are here, but he cannot tell how great his gains are at death. " To me to die is gain." Death to a believer is *crepusculum gloriae*, the daybreak of eternal brightness. To show fully what a believer's gains are at death were a task too great for an angel ; all hyperboles fall short of it ; the reward of glory exceeds our very faith. Let me give you some dark views and imperfect lineaments only of that infinite glory the saints shall gain at the hour of death. " To me to die is gain."

1. Believers at death shall gain a writ of ease from all sins and troubles ; they shall be in a state of impeccability : sin expires with their life. At death all troubles die.

2. They shall behold the glorified body of Jesus Christ ; and if it be pleasant to behold the sun, how blessed a sight will it be to see Christ, the Sun of Righteousness, clothed with. our human nature, shining in glory above the angels !

3. The saints at death shall not only have a sight of God, but shall enjoy his love. There shall be no more a vail on God's face, nor shall his smiles be chequered with frowns, but his love shall discover itself in all its orient beauty and fragrant sweetness. Here the saints pray for his love, and they have a few drops ; but there they shall have as much as their vessels can receive.

4. Believers at death shall gain a celestial palace, a house not made with hands. 2 Cor. v. 1. Here the saints are straitened for room ; they have but mean cottages to live in ; but they shall have a royal palace to live in hereafter.

5. Believers at death shall gain the sweet society of glorified saints and angels ; which will add to the felicity of heaven, as every star adds some lustre to the firmament.

6. Believers at death shall gain perfection of holiness. Here grace is but *in cunabulis*, in its cradle, very imperfect ; so that we cannot write a copy of holiness without blotting : here believers receive but *primitias Spiritus,* the first-fruits of the Spirit. Rom. viii. 23. At death the saints will arrive at perfection ; their knowledge will be clear ; their sanctity perfect ; their sun will be in its full meridian splendour. They need not then pray for increase of grace ; for they shall love God as much as they would love him, and as much as he desires to have them love him. They shall be in respect of holiness as the angels of God.

7. At death, the saints will gain a royal magnificent feast.

8. Believers at death shall gain honour and dignity ; they shall reign as kings. When all worldly honour shall lie in the dust, the mace, the star, the robe of ermine, the imperial diadem, then shall the saints' honour remain ; not one jewel shall be plucked out of their crown. At death they shall gain a blessed eternity. If the saints could have the least suspicion or fear of losing their glory, it would cool and imbitter their joy ; but their crown fadeth not away. 1 Pet. v. 4. As the wicked have a worm that never dies, so the elect have a crown that never fades. Ever, is a short word, but it has no end. " The things which are not seen are eternal." 2 Cor. iv. 18. " At thy right hand are pleasures for evermore." Psa. xvi. 11. Who can span eternity ? Millions of ages stand but for ciphers in eternity. Ever in Christ's bosom is the *elah*, or highest strain of the saint's glory.

Q. *How come the saints to have all this gain ?*

Ans. They have a right to all this gain at death upon several accounts, as by virtue of the Father's donation, the Son's purchase, the Holy Ghost's earnest and faith's acceptance. Therefore. the state of future glory is called the saint's proper inheritance. Col. i. 12. They are heirs of God and have a right to inherit.

Use 1. See the great difference between the death of the godly and the wicked. The godly are great gainers, but the wicked are great losers at death. They lose four things : —

1. They lose the world ; and that is a great loss to the wicked. They laid up their treasures upon earth. and to be turned out of it all at once is a great loss.

2. They lose their souls. Matt. xvi. 26, 27. The soul was at first a noble piece of coin, upon which God stamped his own image. This celestial spark is more precious than the whole globe of the world ; but the sinner's soul is lost: not that the souls of the wicked are annihilated at death, but tormented:

3. They lose heaven. Heaven is *sedes beatorum,* the royal seat of the blessed ; it is the region of happiness, the map of perfection. There is the manna which is angel's food ;' there is the garden of spices, the bed of perfumes, the river of pleasure. Sinners at death, lose all these.

4. They lose all hope. Though they lived wickedly, they hoped God would be merciful, and they hoped they should go to heaven. Their hope was not an anchor, but a spider's web. At death they lose their hopes, and see they did but flatter themselves into hell. " Whose hope shall be cut off." Job. viii. 14. It is sad to have life and hope cut off together.

Use 2. If saints gain such glorious things at death, well may they desire it. Does not every one desire preferment ? Faith gives a title to heaven: death gives the possession. Though we should be desirous of doing service here, yet we should be ambitious of being with Christ. Phil. i. 23. We should be content to live, but willing to die. Is it not a blessed thing to be freed from sin, and to lie for ever in the bosom of divine love ? Is it not a blessed thing to meet our godly relations in heaven, and to be singing divine anthems of praise among the angels ? Does not the bride desire the marriage day, especially if she has the prospect of a crown ? What is the place we now live in, but a place of banishment from God ? We are in a wilderness, while angels live at court. Here we are combating with Satan, and should we not desire to be out of the bloody field, where the bullets of temptation fly fast, and receive a victorious crown ? Think what it will be to have always a smiling look from Christ's face ! to be brought into the banquet-house, and have the banner of love displayed over us ! O ye saints, desire death ; it is your ascension-day to heaven. *Egredere, anima, egredere* ! said Hilarion on his death-bed, " Go forth, my soul, Go forth!" Another holy man said, " Lord, lead me to that glory which I have seen though a glass ; haste, Lord, and do not tarry." Some plants thrive best when they are transplanted ; so believers, when transplanted by death, cannot but thrive, because they have Christ's sunbeams shining upon them. What though the passage through the valley of the shadow of death be troublesome ! who would not be willing to pass a tempestuous sea, if he were sure to be crowned so soon as he came to shore.

The above abridged quotations illustrate something of what will be found in full throughout the whole 221 pages of this work. We judge that the reader will not be long in coming to agree with Spurgeon's opinion—" Thomas Watson's ' *Body of Practical Divinity* ' is one of the most precious of the peerless works of the Puritans ; and those best acquainted with it prize it most. Watson was one of the most concise, racy, illustrative, and suggestive of those eminent divines who made the Puritan age the Augustine period of evangelical literature."

GEORGE WHITEFIELD AND HIS MINISTRY*

J. C. RYLE.

Who were the men that revived religion in England in the 18th century ? Where were they born ? How were they educated ? What are the leading facts in their lives ? The instruments that God employs to do His work in the world deserve a close inspection.

The first and foremost whom I will name is the well-known George Whitefield. I place him first in the order of merit, without any hesitation. Of all the spiritual heroes of this dark period none saw so soon as Whitefield what the times demanded, and none were so forward in the great work of spiritual aggression. I should think I committed an act of injustice if I placed any name before his.

Whitefield was born at Gloucester in the year 1714. That venerable county-town, which was his birth-place, is connected with more than one name which ought to be dear to every lover of Protestant truth. Tyndale, one of the first and ablest translator of the English Bible, was a Gloucestershire man. Hooper, one of the greatest and best of our English reformers, was Bishop of Gloucester, and was burned at the stake for Christ's truth, within view of his own cathedral, in Queen Mary's reign. The city where Hooper preached and prayed, was the place where the greatest preacher of the gospel England has ever seen was born.

Like many other famous men, Whitefield was of humble origin, and had no rich or noble connections to help him forward in the world. His mother kept the Bell Inn at Gloucester, and appears not to have prospered in business.

Whitefield's early life, according to his own account, was anything but religious ; though, like many boys, he had occasional prickings of conscience and spasmodic fits of devout feeling. But habits and general tastes are the only true test of young people's characters. He confesses that he was " addicted to lying, filthy talking, and foolish jesting," and that he was a " Sabbath-breaker, a theatre-goer, a card-player, and a romance-reader." All this, he says, went on till he was fifteen years old.

The only known fact about his schooldays is this curious one, that even then he was remarkable for his good elocution and memory, and was selected to recite speeches before the Corporation of Gloucester at their annual visitation of the Grammar School.

★ This is an abridged version of Ryle's famous essay on Whitefield. A fuller account is contained in the volume we are now reprinting entitled "The Select Sermons of George Whitefield." This book contains six of Whitefield's best sermons, together with a Funeral Sermon preached at his death by R. Elliot. A.B. Elliot gives the clearest and strongest description of Whitefield's doctrine that we have seen and presents the doctrines of grace in their most definite form. The Foreword to this reprint is by Dr. Lloyd-Jones. Price 6/. U.S. price pending.

At the age of fifteen Whitefield appears to have left school, and to have given up Latin and Greek for a season. In all probability, his mother's straitened circumstances made it absolutely necessary for him to do something to assist her in business and to get his own living. He began, therefore, to help her in the daily work of the Bell Inn. "At length," he says, "I put on my blue apron, washed cups, cleaned rooms, and, in one word, became a professed common drawer for nigh a year and a half."

This state of things, however, did not last long. His mother's business at the Bell did not flourish, and she finally retired from it altogether. An old school-fellow revived in his mind the idea of going to Oxford, and he went back to the Grammar School and renewed his studies. Friends were raised up who made interest for him at Pembroke College, Oxford, where the Grammar School of Gloucester held two exhibitions. And at length, after several providential circumstances had smoothed the way, he entered Oxford as a servitor at Pembroke at the age of eighteen.

Whitefield's residence at Oxford was the great turning-point in his life. For two or three years before he went to the University his journal tells us that he had not been without religious convictions. But from the time of his entering Pembroke College these convictions fast ripened into decided Christianity. He diligently attended all means of grace within his reach. He spent his leisure time in visiting the city prison, reading to the prisoners and trying to do good. He became acquainted with the famous John Wesley and his brother Charles, and a little band of like-minded young men, including the well-known author of "*Theron and Aspasio*," James Hervey. These were the devoted party to whom the name "Methodists" was first applied, on account of their strict "method" of living.

He says in his Journal, "I always chose the worst sort of food. I fasted twice a week. My apparel was mean. I thought it unbecoming a penitent to have his hair powdered. I wore woollen gloves, a patched gown, and dirty shoes; and though I was convinced that the kingdom of God did not consist in meat and drink, yet I resolutely persisted in these voluntary acts of self-denial, because I found in them great promotion of the spiritual life." Out of all this darkness he was gradually delivered, partly by the advice of one or two experienced Christians, and partly by reading such books as Scougal's "*Life of God in the Heart of Man*," Law's "*Serious Call*," Baxter's "*Call to the Unconverted*," Alleine's "*Alarm to Unconverted Sinners*," and Matthew Henry's "*Commentary*." "Above all," he says, "my mind being now more opened and enlarged, I began to read the Holy Scriptures upon my knees, laying aside all other books, and praying over, if possible, every line and word."

Once taught to understand the glorious liberty of Christ's

gospel, Whitefield never turned again to asceticism, legalism, mysticism, or strange views of Christian perfection. The experience received by bitter conflict was most valuable to him. The doctrines of free grace, once thoroughly grasped, took deep root in his heart, and became, as it were, bone of his bone and flesh of his flesh. Of all the little band of Oxford methodists, none seem to have got hold so soon of clear views of Christ's gospel as he did, and none kept it so unwaveringly to the end.

At the early age of twenty-two Whitefield was admitted to holy orders by Bishop Benson of Gloucester, on Trinity Sunday, 1736. His ordination was not of his own seeking. The bishop heard of his character from Lady Selwyn and others, sent for him, gave him five guineas to buy books, and offered to ordain him, though only twenty-two years old, whenever he wished. This unexpected offer came to him when he was full of scuples about his own fitness for the ministry.

Whitefield's first sermon was preached in the very town where he was born, at the church of St. Mary-le-Crypt, Gloucester. His own description of it is the best account that can be given :— " Last Sunday, in the afternoon, I preached my first sermon in the church of St. Mary-le-Crypt, where I was baptized, and also first received the sacrament of the Lord's Supper. Curiosity, as you may easily guess, drew a large congregation together upon this occasion. The sight at first a little awed me. But I was comforted with a heartfelt sense of the divine presence. I trust I was enabled to speak with some degree of gospel authority. Some few mocked, but most seemed for the present struck ; and I have since heard that a complaint was made to the bishop that I drove fifteen mad the first sermon ! The worthy prelate wished that the madness might not be forgotten before next Sunday."

Almost immediately after his ordination, Whitefield went to Oxford and took his degree as Bachelor of Arts. He then commenced his regular ministerial life by undertaking temporary duty at the Tower Chapel, London, for two months. While engaged there he preached continually in many London churches.

From the very first he obtained a decree of popularity such as no preacher, before or since, has probably ever reached. Whether on week-days or Sundays, wherever he preached, the churches were crowded, and an immense sensation was produced.

From London he removed for two months to Dummer, a little rural parish in Hampshire, near Basingstoke. From Dummer he accepted an invitation to visit the colony of Georgia in North America. He sailed for America in the latter part of 1737, and continued there about a year.

Whitefield returned from Georgia at the latter part of the year 1738. He soon discovered that his position was no longer what it was before he sailed for Georgia. The bulk of the clergy were no longer favourable to him, and regarded him with suspicion

as an enthusiast and a fanatic.   They were especially scandalized
by his preaching the doctrine of regeneration or the new birth,
as a thing which many baptized persons greatly needed!   The
number of pulpits to which he had access rapidly diminished.

The step which at this juncture gave a turn to the whole
current of Whitefield's ministry was his adoption of the system of
open-air preaching.   Seeing that thousands everywhere would
attend no place of worship, spent their Sundays in idleness or sin,
and were not to be reached by sermons within walls, he resolved,
in the spirit of holy aggression, to go out after them " into the
highways and hedges," on his Master's principle, and " compel
them to come in."   His first attempt to do this was among the
colliers at Kingswood near Bristol, in February, 1739.   After much
prayer, he one day went to Hannam Mount, and standing upon a
hill began to preach to about a hundred colliers upon Matt. v. 1-3.
The thing soon became known.   The number of hearers rapidly
increased, till the congregation amounted to many thousands.   His
own account of the behaviour of these neglected colliers, who had
never been in a church in their lives, is deeply affecting :—
" Having," he writes to a friend, " no righteousness of their own
to renounce, they were glad to hear of a Jesus who was a friend to
publicans, and came not to call the righteous, but sinners to repentance.   The first discovery of their being affected was the sight
of the white gutters made by their tears, which plentifully fell
down their black cheeks as they came out of their coal-pits.
Hundreds of them were soon brought under deep conviction,
which, as the event proved, happily ended in a sound and thorough
conversion."

Two months after this Whitefield began the practice of open-
air preaching in London, on April 27, 1739.   The circumstances
under which this happened were curious.   The upshot of the
matter was, that being forbidden by the churchwardens to occupy
the pulpit in a church where he was due to preach, he went outside
after the communion-service, and preached in the churchyard.
" And," says he, " God was pleased so to assist me in preaching,
and so wonderfully to affect the hearers, that I believe we could
have gone singing hymns to prison."

From that day forward he became a constant field-preacher,
whenever weather and the season of the year made it possible.
Two days afterwards, on Sunday, April 29, he records :—" I
preached in Moorfields to an exceeding great multitude.   Being
weakened by my morning's preaching, I refreshed myself in the
afternoon by a little sleep, and at five went and preached at
Kennington Common, about two miles from London, when no
less than thirty thousand people were supposed to be present."
Henceforth, wherever there were large open spaces round London,
wherever there were large bands of idle, godless, Sabbath-breaking
people gathered together, in Hackney Fields, Mary-le-bonne Fields,

May Fair, Smithfield, Blackheath, Moorfields, and Kennington Common, there went Whitefield and lifted up his voice for Christ. (The reader will remember that all this happened when London was a comparatively small place). The gospel proclaimed was listened to and greedily received by hundreds who never dreamed of going to a place of worship. But it was going much too fast for the Church of those days. The clergy, with a few honourable exceptions, refused entirely to countenance this strange preacher. He loved the Church in which he had been ordained ; he gloried in her Articles ; he used her Prayer-book with pleasure. But the Church did not love him, and so lost the use of his services.

The facts of Whitefield's history from this period to the day of his death are almost entirely of one complexion. From 1739 to the year of his death 1770, a period of thirty-one years, his life was one uniform employment. He was eminently a man of one thing, and always about his Master's business. From Sunday mornings to Saturday nights, from the 1st of January to the 31st of December, excepting when laid aside by illness, he was almost incessantly preaching Christ, and going about the world entreating men to repent and come to Christ and be saved. There was hardly a considerable town in England, Scotland, or Wales, that he did not visit as an evangelist. For thirty-one years he laboured in this way, always proclaiming the same glorious gospel, and always, as far as man's eye can judge, with immense effect. In one single Whitsuntide week, after preaching in Moorfields, he received one thousand letters from people under spiritual concern, and admitted to the Lord's table three hundred and fifty persons. In the thirty-four years of his ministry it is reckoned that he preached publicly eighteen thousand times.

His journeyings were prodigious, when the roads and conveyances of his time are considered. He was familiar with " perils in the wilderness and perils in the seas." He visited Scotland fourteen times, and was nowhere more acceptable or useful than he was in that Bible-loving country. He crossed the Atlantic seven times, backward and forward, in miserable slow sailing ships, and arrested the attention of thousands in Boston, New York, and Philadelphia. He went over to Ireland twice, and on one occasion was almost murdered by an ignorant Popish mob in Dublin.

His regular ministerial work in London for the winter season, when field-preaching was necessarily suspended, was something prodigious. His weekly engagements at the Tabernacle in Tottenham Court Road, which was built for him when the pulpits of the Established Church were closed, comprised the following work :—Every Sunday morning he administered the Lord's Supper to several hundred communicants at half-past six. After this he read prayers, and preached both morning and afternoon. Then he preached again in the evening at half-past five, and concluded by addressing a large society of widows, married people, young men and spinsters, all sitting separately in the area of the Tabernacle, with exhortations suitable to the respective stations. On Monday, Tuesday, Wednesday and Thursday mornings, he preached regularly at six. On Monday, Tuesday, Wednesday, Thursday and Saturday evenings, he delivered lectures. This, it will be observed, made thirteen sermons a week! And all this time he was carrying on a large correspondence with people in almost every part of the world.

That any human frame could so long endure the labours that Whitefield went through does indeed seem wonderful. That his life was not cut short by violence, to which he was frequently exposed, is no less wonderful. But he was immortal till his work was done. He died at last very suddenly at Newbury Port, in North America, on Sunday, September the 29th, 1770, at the comparatively early age of fifty-six.

Having felt ill one day in September, 1770, he had nevertheless felt constrained to deliver a sermon to a very great multitude assembled in the fields near Exeter. Preaching on II Corinthians 13 : 5, he preached for nearly two hours. After the Sermon was over, Whitefield dined with a friend, and then rode on to Newbury Port, though greatly fatigued. On arriving there he supped early, and retired to bed. Tradition says, that as he went upstairs, with a lighted candle in his hand, he could not resist the inclination to turn round at the head of the stair, and speak to the friends who were assembled to meet him. As he spoke the fire kindled within him, and before he could conclude, the candle which he held in his hand had actually burned down to the socket. He retired to his bedroom, to come out no more alive. A violent fit of spasmodic asthma seized him soon after he got into bed, and before six o'clock the next morning the great preacher was dead. Where he died there he was buried, in a vault beneath the pulpit of the church where he had engaged to preach.

GEORGE WHITEFIELD, in my judgment, was so entirely chief and first among the English Reformers of the 18th century, that I make no apology for offering some further information about him. The real amount of good he did and the peculiar character of his preaching are points that deserve consideration. They are points, I may add, about which there is a vast amount of misconception.

This misconception perhaps is unavoidable, and ought not to surprise us. The materials for forming a correct opinion about such a man as Whitefield are necessarily very scanty. He wrote no book for the million, of world-wide fame, like Bunyan's *"Pilgrim's Progress."* He headed no crusade against an apostate Church, with a nation at his back, and princes on his side, like Martin Luther. He founded no religious denomination, which pinned its faith on his writings and carefully embalmed his best acts and words, like John Wesley. There are Lutherans and Wesleyans in the present day, but there are no Whitefieldites. The records of such a man are large and full in heaven, I have no doubt. But they are few and scanty upon earth.

The question, " What good did Whitefield do ? " is one which I answer without the least hesitation. I believe that the *direct good* which he did to immortal souls was enormous. I will go further—I believe it is incalculable. Credible witnesses in England, Scotland, and America, have placed on record their conviction that he was the means of converting thousands of people. Many, wherever he preached, were not merely pleased, excited, and arrested, but positively turned from sin, and made thorough servants of God. "Numbering the people," I do not forget, is at all times an objectionable practice. God alone can read hearts and discern the wheat from the tares. Many, no doubt, in days of religious excitement, are set down as converted who are not converted at all. But I wish my readers to understand that my estimate of Whitefield's usefulness is based on a solid foundation.

He was among the first in the eighteenth century who revived attention to the old truths which produced the Protestant Reformation. His constant assertion of the doctrines taught by the Reformers, his repeated reference to the Articles and Homilies, and the divinity of the best English theologians, obliged many to think, and roused them to examine their own principles.

The peculiar *character of Whitefield's preaching* is the subject which next demands some consideration. To command the ear of " the masses " for a quarter of a century, and to be preaching incessantly the whole time, is an evidence of no common power.

For one thing, Whitefield preached a *singularly pure gospel*. Few men, perhaps, ever gave their hearers so much wheat and so little chaff. He did not get up to talk about his party, his cause, his interests, or his office. He was perpetually telling you about your sins, your heart, Jesus Christ, the Holy Ghost, the absolute need of repentance, faith and holiness, in the way that the Bible presents these mighty subjects. "Oh, the righteousness of Jesus Christ ! " he would often say ; " I must be excused if I mention it in almost all my sermons." Preaching of this kind is the preaching that God delights to honour. It must be pre-eminently a *manifestation of truth*.

Another leading characteristic of Whitefield's preaching was his *tremendous earnestness*. One poor uneducated man said of him, that " he preached like a lion." His sermons were not like the morning and evening gun at Portsmouth, a formal discharge, fired off as a matter of course, that disturbs nobody. They were all life and fire. There was no getting away from them. Sleep was next to impossible. You must listen whether you liked it or not. There was a holy violence about him which firmly took your attention by storm. You were fairly carried off your legs by his energy before you had time to consider what you would do.

One more feature in Whitefield's preaching deserves special notice ; and that is, the *immense amount of pathos and feeling* which it always contained. It was no uncommon thing with him to weep profusely in the pulpit. Cornelius Winter, who often accompanied him in his latter journeys, went so far as to say that he hardly ever knew him get through a sermon without tears. He felt intensely for the souls before him, and his feelings found an outlet in tears. " I came to hear you," said one to him, " with my pocket full of stones, intending to break your head ; but your sermon got the better of me, and broke my heart."

Whitefield possessed *singular power of description*. He used to draw such vivid pictures of the things he was handling, that his hearers could believe they actually saw and heard them. " On one occasion," says one of his biographers, " Lord Chesterfield was among his hearers. The great preacher, in describing the miserable condition of an unconverted sinner, illustrated the subject by describing a blind beggar. The night was dark, and the road dangerous. The poor mendicant was deserted by his dog near the edge of a precipice, and had nothing to aid him in groping his way but his staff. Whitefield so warmed with his subject, and enforced it with such graphic power, that the whole auditory was kept in breathless silence, as if it saw the movements of the poor old man ; and at length, when the beggar was about to take the fatal step which would have hurled him down the precipice to certain destruction, Lord Chesterfield actually made a rush forward to save him, exclaiming aloud, ' He is gone ! he is gone ! ' The noble lord had been so entirely carried away by the preacher, that he forgot the whole was a picture."

For my own part, I have no hesitation in saying that I believe no English preacher has ever possessed such a combination of excellent qualifications as Whitefield. Some, no doubt, have surpassed him in some of his gifts ; others, perhaps, have equalled him in others. But for a well-balanced combination of some of the finest gifts that a preacher can possess, united with an unrivalled voice, manner, delivery, action, and command of words, Whitefield, I repeat my opinion, stands alone. No Englishman, I believe, dead or alive, has ever equalled him.

GEORGE BURROWES ON THE SONG OF SOLOMON*

George Burrowes, a prominent American minister of the last century, was born at Trenton, New Jersey, on April 3, 1811. He was educated at Princeton College where he graduated in 1832. Like so many others who became leaders in the North American churches he took his ministerial training at Princeton Theological Seminary, under the supervision of such distinguished teachers as Archibald Alexander and Charles Hodge. After leaving the Seminary in 1835 he entered his first pastorate at West Nottingham, Md., where he remained till 1850. In that year he was appointed professor of Latin and Greek at Lafayette College, Easton, Penn. From 1857 to 1859 Burrowes was pastor of Newtown Presbyterian Church, Penn. In 1859 he was called to the west coast of America, and there he appears to have spent the remainder of his life being principally occupied with the training of men for the ministry.

Burrowes' once famous commentary was first published in 1853, and by 1861 it had passed into a third edition. Dr. D. M. Lloyd-Jones in his Foreword to this present British reprint of the work, after indicating the neglect into which this valuable book of Scripture has fallen and the evident need which the average Christian has for help in understanding its meaning, continues, " It is because I know of nothing which in any way approaches this commentary in that respect that I am glad that it is being reprinted and made available. It has everything that should characterise a good commentary—learning and scholarship, accuracy and carefulness, but, above all, and more important than all else, true spiritual insight and understanding. It provides a key to the understanding of the whole, and of every verse which the humblest spirit can easily follow. I predict that all who read it and study it will agree with me in saying that they have never read anything more uplifting and heart-warming. It will lead them to their Lord and enable them to know and to realize His love as they have never done before."

Before beginning his verse by verse commentary, Burrowes gives a summary of the book which we now re-produce in full, and a more detailed analysis of the chapters from which we will give his analysis of Ch. 5. These extracts will provide some indication of the way in which he expounds this fragrant book of Scripture.

A Summary of The Song

This Book consists of three parts : The first includes Ch. 1, verse 1 ; Ch. 2, verse 7. The second extends from Ch. 2, verse 8

* A Commentary on The Song of Solomon, by George Burrowes. pp. 456, 10/6. U.S. price pending.

to Ch. 7, verse 9. The third includes the remainder of the book,
Ch. 7, verse 10, to Ch. 8, verse 14.

I.   The way in which the soul longing for the manifestation
of the love of Christ is led along in the gratification of that desire,
from one degree to another of pious enjoyment, until attaining
the greatest delight possible for the saint in the present world.
Ch. 1 : 1 ; Ch. 2 : 7.

These periods of enjoyment are separated by vicissitudes
of fortune and diversity of feeling, through which the believer is
brought to those more cheering scenes in his progress to heaven.
These seasons may be repeated in our experience, some of them
more than once, before we attain those which succeed. 1. · We
enjoy the love of Jesus, as manifested in private communion, in
" his chambers." Ch. 1 : 4.   2. In the way of duty and self-
denial. Ch. 1 : 7-11.   3.   In sitting with the King in the circle
of his friends, and enjoying, as one of them, the delights of social
communion with him. Ch. 1 :12-14.   4.   In delightful repose
with him amid enlarged prospects of spiritual beauty. Ch. 1 :
15-17.   5.   In the protection and delights set forth in Ch. 2 : 1-3.
6.   And in enjoying, at last, the pleasures mentioned in Ch. 2 : 4-7,
the greatest possible on earth.

II.   An exhibition of motives by which the Lord Jesus would
allure such a soul away from the present world, for being with him
in glory.   Ch. 2 : 8 ; Ch. 7 : 9.

As we are treated throughout our redemption and discipline
here, like beings possessing a will, the spiritual decays and sluggishness into which we are liable to fall, must be counteracted by the
presentation of powerful motives to the mind ; and our faith can
be best matured by strengthening the soul, as is done in these
periods of great enjoyment, and then leaving us in that strength,
without such sensible pleasures, to manifest our steadfastness by
struggling against difficulty and the absence of Jesus, by dependence
upon his word and promises and love.   Hence our Lord allures us—

1.   By the beauty of heaven, as a place he has prepared for
us, and where he is awaiting us.   Ch. 2 : 8-17.

2.   By the splendour of the reception awaiting us there, no
less than by the security and grandeur of our conveyance towards
glory.   Ch. 3 : 1-11.

3.   By his great love for us—an affection so intense as to be
incapable of being fully expressed by the strongest illustrations,
and so strong as to remain constant even amid our neglect.   Ch. 4 :
1 ; Ch. 7 : 9.

III.   The effect produced on the heart of the saint by these
manifestations of love, and by these motives.   Ch. 7 : 10 ; Ch. 8 :
14.   1. Assurance of hope.   Ch. 7 : 10.   2. Desire to be much
alone in communion with Christ.   Ch. 7 : 11.   3. Willingness to
engage in labours of holiness and love.   Ch. 7 : 12.   4. Consecration to him of our best and most valued gifts and possessions.

Ch. 7 : 13.   5. Desire that everything hindering the full inter-change of affection between Jesus and our soul be removed. Ch. 8 : 1, 2.   6. The desire to guard against every sin and every act at all likely to cause the withdrawal of Jesus' love. Ch. 8 : 3, 4. 7. The pleasing consciousness of leaning on Jesus, and of being upheld by his everlasting arms. Ch. 8 : 5.   8. Desire to lie con-tinually near the heart of Jesus, and to be sustained by his power. Ch. 8 : 6.   9. Willingness to sacrifice everything coming between us and Christ. Ch. 8 : 6.   10. A conviction of the meanness of everything the world could offer for bribing us to renounce Christ. Ch. 8 : 7.   11. An interest for the salvation of the impenitent. Ch. 8 : 8-10.   12. A sense of our accountability as stewards of God, holding our property and our all in trust. Ch. 8 : 12. 13. The privilege of access continually to the throne of grace, with full encouragement from our Lord for addressing to him our voices in prayer and praise. Ch. 8 : 13.   14. The desire for the com-pletion of our redemption, and for the perfecting of his love to us and of our love to him, by the second coming of our Lord. Verse 14.

An Analysis of Ch. 5

In chapter 5 (as well as in 6 and 7), we have. 1. The effect of sluggishness and indifference when the Lord Jesus draws near to the soul ; viz. the loss of his presence and favour : verses 2-6. 2. The anxiety, labour, and trouble to which this neglect gives rise, in our efforts for seeking him : verses 7, 8.   3. The answers given to the questions put by those who witness our anxiety and sorrow at such times—viz. What is the character of him who is so anxiously sought? verse 9, and, Where has he gone, where may he be found ? chapter 6 : 1.   4. The willingness of Jesus, even when he has been forced from us by our own sins, to receive his people who seek for him in sincerity and truth, as shown by the address of the beloved to the spouse, ch. 6 : 4 ; 7 : 9.   5. The feelings towards our Lord by the soul thus kindly received into his love, expressed in the wish to enjoy retirement with him, and to offer him our best gifts, ch. 7 : 10-13 and to the end of ch. 8.

After the most glorious displays to us of the love of Jesus, we may soon sink into indifference, our perceptions being allowed to close against these manifestations of grace through our own apathy and sluggishness.   But while at such time, the flesh may be weak, the spirit remains willing—we sleep but our heart waketh ; though there is a law in our members, waring against the law of our mind and bringing us into captivity to the law of sin, we do yet delight in the law of God after the inward man, Rom. 7 : 22. Though the outward evidences of love to Christ have very much disappeared under the pressure of spiritual sloth and decay, grace is still in the heart with its glimmerings ; the heart is awake, but not in sufficient strength to counteract the pressure of carnality and control the doings of the body. So far from fulfilling his wishes and coming away from Lebanon, etc., ch. 4 : 8, to the mountain of myrrh, there to meet with him, we prefer the indulgence of our fleshly, carnal inclinations—sleep—to all the attractions of his loveliness and society.   Verse 2.

But so strong is his love, that when he does not find us meeting him at the appointed place, he graciously comes to seek us, even in our sloth, and tries to allure us away, by considerations the most endearing and affecting : " Open to me, etc." Rev. 3 : 20.   Unmoved by these, we content ourselves in our apathy, by excuses the most frivolous.   The love of our Lord does then prompt him to go further than entreaty, to use exertions, for finding his way into our heart : " My beloved, etc." Verse 4.

At length, moved by his tender addresses to us, and by the measures of mercy used by him for reviving our love, the affections begin to move, and we arise to meet him.   Instead, however, of running at once to meet him, and opening our soul to him, just as it is, we delay in order to prepare ourselves to see him ; and the consequence of this delay is, that although we bring with us the best of our acts and endeavours, our hands dropping with myrrh, etc., he is gone.   Nothing of our own, however costly, as duty and self denial, and mortification, can excuse us for hesitating to rush into his arms ; and as many a repenting sinner loses all interest in him, and also the soul, by delaying in order to make himself fit to come, so does many a saint often lose precious interviews with the Lord.   Verses 5 and 6.

Her soul had been deeply moved under the language of the beloved standing at the door ; and thus moved, does now impel her to seek him.   While the withdrawals of Jesus are a just recompense for our sluggishness, they give occasion for calling into exercise our love, and for showing its strength.   What was lost by indifference, can now be got only by great exertion ; we seek him ; we call on him without receiving an answer ; we have to suffer reproach and ill-treatment from the watchmen of Zion, who, instead of helping us in our zeal, view our love and devotion as fanaticism, and both misuse us and expose us to shame ; " Took away my vail, etc. . . . "   The sympathy that is often denied to the devoted heart by those high in office in the Church, may be found among our pious equals ; and seeking an interest in their prayers, Eph. 6 : 19 ; II Thess. 3 : 1 ; we entreat their aid, serving, seeking and following our Lord.   Verses 7-8.

This earnestness and zeal is not without its effect on others before whom the light of the believer is thus made to shine.   Seeing the manifestations in various ways, of such intense love to Christ, a love that will be satisfied with nothing short of himself, and which is willing, for the enjoyment of his presence, to incur any self-denial and any humiliation, they naturally inquire, what there is in Christ above others, that so strongly affects us ?   The illustration or setting forth of his beauty, that follows in verses 10-16, is unequalled for beauty and richness. It is the Holy Spirit, by the mouth of an inspired saint, illustrating the beauty of Christ by language, through the same means used in creation, drawn from the beauties of the world. The most fine gold, the raven's blackness, the eyes of doves, the beds of spices, the lilies dropping sweet-smelling myrrh, etc. ; all these, as works of Christ, show his excellence. But when we would understand the loveliness of the human person through which the Son of God, the eternal Creator, manifests himself as Redeemer, these separate clusters, radiant with his glory, and scattered at large in his works, must be gathered into the form of the man Christ Jesus ; and we are told that, just as beautiful as a person must be, whose appearance would impress us with all the ideas of loveliness got from the most fine gold, the beds of spices, , the majesty of Lebanon, etc., etc. ; so beautiful is Christ. Yes, though even in a case like this, there would still be something wanting ; in Jesus there is everything that can be desired; he is altogether lovely. This person combining beauties beyond what man may possess, or the mind of man in the farthest stretch of his imagination, unaided by the Spirit of God, could conceive—" This is my beloved, and this is my friend." Verses 9-16.

*　　*　　*

Continued from page 1.

In some ways this is not a promising hour for such a venture. We are not living in Reformation times when men would sell their possessions to buy the truth and were ready to purchase the works of the Reformers sometimes at the penalty of their lives. In those tumultuous days many would give even the night watches to study if they could find no other time. No such value is put on the Word of God today and the fact that Christians are generally no longer a studying people is one of the truest explanations of our present condition. Errors and practices which would have received no quarter from our forefathers are allowed to go unchallenged, the great facts of God's past dealings with us as a church and nation are forgotten and the consequences of all this have gone so far that unless they are soon averted a final downfall must speedily overtake us. Many sad years have passed since J. C. Ryle wrote, " My wish is that men may write on their hearts that the well-being of England depends not on commerce, or clever politicians, or armies, or navies, or gold, or iron, but on the maintenance of the principles of the English Reformation . . . *The maintenance of them is rapidly becoming a matter of life or death.*" If anything is to be done it is to be done now, there are still great opportunities open to us, " with God nothing shall be impossible," and if He will grant us all the earnest intention to stand by the truth in this dark time, we may yet see a glorious re-awakening.

L

BOOK REVIEWS

"*The Sovereignty of God*" by A. W. Pink. (320 pp. $3. 18/6. Publishers: Bible Truth Depot, P.O. Box 86, Mifflingburg, Penna. U.S.A.).

" I am glad to welcome this new edition of '*The Sovereignty of God*' by A. W. Pink and to know that arrangements have been made to make it more easily accessible to British readers. It is one of the most notable of his works that I have read, characterized by his customary clarity and forcefulness of presentation. At such a time as this nothing is more calculated to strengthen the faith of believers, indeed it will give them a sense of triumph and glory."   D. M. LLOYD-JONES.

"*The Life of Elijah*" by A. W. Pink. (314 pp. $4.95. Publishers: The Bible Truth Depot).

Reading Mr. Pink's book, "*The Life of Elijah*" is like opening up a chest filled with good things. The pages abound with instruction and sound doctrine as well as original and elucidating exposition. Digressing pleasantries, vain sentimentalities and unnecessarily long descriptions are happily absent.

The book is essentially for our times. To use the words of the author himself: " A study of the life of Elijah is particularly pertinent today, for our lot is cast in times which closely resemble those which the prophet encountered." The manner in which Mr. Pink deals with the contemporary scene is most out-spoken and direct, for example we have the following typical comments: —

" There is no surer and more solemn proof that God is hiding His face from a people or nation than for Him to deprive them of the inestimable blessing of those who faithfully minister His Holy Word to them, for as far as heavenly mercies excel earthly so much more dreadful are spiritual calamities than material ones." p. 37.

" Truth cannot be judged by the numbers who avow and support it: the Devil has ever had the vast majority on his side. And is it any otherwise today ? What percentage of present-day preachers are uncompromisingly proclaiming the Truth, and among them how many practice what they preach ? " p.133.

" Many today talk about their service *for* Christ, as though He needed their assistance, as though His cause would not prosper unless they patronized and furthered it—as though the holy ark must inevitably fall to the ground unless their unholy hands uphold it. This is all wrong, seriously wrong—the product of Satan-fed pride. What is so much needed (by us !) is service *to* Christ—submission to His yoke, surrender to His will, subjection to His commandments. Any " Christian service " other than walking in His precepts is a human invention, fleshly energy, ' strange fire.' " p. 61.

In the course of his expositions, the author does not hesitate to differ with popular commentators. Where he does differ, he establishes his arguments upon the solid foundations of Scripture. His expositions of the texts:

" Hide (absent) thyself by the brook Cherith." 1 Kings 17: 3,
" And when he saw that, he went for his life." 1 Kings 19: 3.
" I have left me seven thousand in Israel." 1 Kings 19: 18,
are of singular interest and profit.

Mr. Pink is prolific in his quotation of Scripture, yet is seldom laborious. Note the instruction contained in the description of Elijah meeting the widow Zarephath:

" Behold! here she comes forth as if on purpose to meet him: yet he did not know her, nor she him. It had all the appearance of being accidental, and yet it was decreed and arranged by God so as to make good His word to the prophet. Ah, my reader, there is no event in this world, however great or however small, which happens by chance. ' Oh Lord, I know that the way of man is not in himself: it is not in man that walketh to direct his steps ' (Jer. 10: 23). How blessed to be assured that ' the steps of a good man are ordered by the Lord ' (Psa. 37: 23). It is sheer unbelief which disconnects the ordinary things of life from God. All our circumstances and experiences are directed by the Lord, for ' of Him, and through Him, and to Him, are all things: to whom be glory for ever ' (Rom. 11: 36)."

We recommend this book to both general reader and student, but particularly to those who, discouraged by the unmitigating scene of apostasy feel the situation today to be a hopeless one. This account of the life of the lonesome prophet will not fail to stimulate you and renew your hope.

E.H.

A Catalogue of books and pamphlets by A. W. Pink, now available, can be obtained from The Bible Truth Depot.

" Redemption Accomplished and Applied " by Professor John Murray. (Publishers: Eerdmans Publishing Company, Grand Rapids 3, Michigan, U.S.A. 22/6. Approx. 200 pages).

This book by Prof. Murray, who is professor of Systematic Theology at the Westminster Theological Seminary, Philadelphia, deserves to be regarded as a standard work. It is suitable for all; ministers, students and laymen. It is compact, fluent and lucid in style and full of valuable exposition of the highest quality. Prof. Murray is a master of definition and this perhaps accounts for his ability to comfortably accommodate a great deal of teaching in relatively few pages.

Redemption involves the very heart of Christianity and every Christian should endeavour by all means to be well instructed on this subject. In part one of the book, titled " Redemption Accomplished," the author sets out the subject of the Atonement explaining its necessity, its nature, its perfection and its extent. Under the heading " The Nature of the Atonement," he systematically defines the meaning of the terms Sacrifice, Propitiation, Reconciliation and Redemption. The pages on Reconciliation are particularly edifying.

The mistaken concept of Universal Atonement is the pivotal point from which has developed the main line of Evangelical appeal today and which is so vastly different from Reformed doctrine, hence the chapter entitled " The Extent of the Atonement " is particularly relevant to the times and worthy of close attention. We are not to think, declares the author, that the quotation of a few texts like 1 John 2: 2, Heb. 2: 9 and Isa. 53: 6, determines the question of Atonement. From beginning to end, the Bible uses expressions that are universal in form but cannot be interpreted as meaning all men distributively and inclusively. He then goes on to quote examples of this before proceeding in a most positive and convincing manner to prove from the Scriptures that Christ did not come merely to put men into a redeemable position, nor merely to make the human race salvable ; but, that He came with the purpose of effectually and infallibly redeeming every one whom the Father had given Him.

In part two, " Redemption Applied," Prof. Murray begins with a short chapter giving his reasons for the order of the application of redemption which he is about to systematically expose, and which he sets forth under the following headings:—Effectual calling, Regeneration, Faith and Repentance, Justification, Adoption, Sanctification, Perseverance, Union with Christ and Glorification.

Part two is particularly concise and full of Scriptural definition. For instance on p. 127 we find this assertion: " we are not born again by faith, or repentance or conversion ; we repent and believe because we have been regenerated." Those who disagree with this will find it most difficult to refute the author's Scriptural arguments. He goes on to allege that far too frequently, the conception of conversion is so superficial and beggarly that it completely fails to take account of the momentous change (regeneration) of which conversion is the fruit. He ends this section by asseverating the need of again thinking in terms of the Gospel as the POWER OF GOD unto salvation.

The author's approach in dealing with the doctrine of the perseverance of the saints is most refreshing. Instead of beginning with positive Scriptural assertions such as John 10: 28, he begins with the texts that appear to many to deny the doctrine. So skilfully does he proceed to expose text by text, that by the time he comes to deal with the positive assertion at the end, one feels it is hardly necessary to continue since the preliminary arguments are so thoroughly clear and convincing.

There are useful indexes at the back of the book on the Scripture texts used and the subjects embraced. There are not many quotations from other writers, but occasional references are made to R. M. Baillie, Calvin, T. J. Crawford, A. A. Hodge, Hugh Martin, George Smeaton, B. B. Warfield and others.

Rev. W. J. Grier, in his review of this book in " The Irish Evangelical," declares that every chapter is worth reading and re-reading. We heartily endorse his sentiments.   E.H.

The above books may be ordered from The Westminster Chapel Book Room, Buckingham Gate, London, S.W. 1.

" The Wisdom of Our Fathers."

Under this title the six addresses delivered at last year's Puritan Conference can be obtained in booklet form. Mimeographed, pp. 69, 2/- or 2/6 by post. These addresses are on various doctrinal and practical subjects such as, " The Witness Of The Spirit ; The Puritan Teaching ": " The Puritans' Dealings With Troubled Souls ": " Richard Greenham and The Trials Of A Christian." Copies of these papers, together with information about the Puritan Conference which is held annually at Westminster Chapel, may be obtained from *Mr. David Fountain,* 275 Spring Road, Southampton. The next Conference is on Dec. 17th and 18th, 1957.

Publications of The Sovereign Grace Book Club

Jay Green, 1124 S.E. First Street, Evansville, Indiana, U.S.A.

1. *Keeping the Heart* by John Flavel (3/6).
2. *Prayer* by John Bunyan & *Return of Prayers* by Thomas Goodwin (4/6).
3. *Exposition of Romans* by Robert Haldane (3 vols. at 50/-).
4. *Exposition of First Peter* by John Brown (3 vols. at 47/6).
5. *Exposition* of James by Thomas Manton (20/-).
6. *Saints Everlasting Rest* by Richard Baxter (2 vols. at 27/-).
7. *A Mute Christian Under the Smarting Rod* by T. Brooks (15/-).
8. *Absolute Predestination* by Jerome Zanchius (Pp. 6/6, Cloth 10/6).
9. *The Cause of God and Truth* by John Gill (16/6).
10. *Multilinear Translation of Hebrews* (3/6).

The *new address* of the English branch of the Sovereign Grace Book Club is 1 Cliff House, Weston Lane, Southampton. Cheques and postal orders payable to T. E. Watson.

Jay Green's bi-monthly magazine " *The Way, The Truth, and The Life,*" can be obtained by ordering direct from the U.S., price 8/- per year.

Wickliffe Press, Wickliffe Avenue, 104 Hendon Lane, Finchley, N.3.

THE
BANNER of TRUTH

(10th Issue)

Price 9d.

Subscription for six
issues, 6/6.

EDITOR:

IAIN MURRAY, B.A.
65A Blenheim Terrace, St. John's Wood,
London, N.W. 8.

ASSISTANT EDITOR:
ERROLL HULSE.

*   *   *

"Thou hast shewed thy people hard things;
Thou hast made us to drink the wine of
astonishment.   Thou hast given a banner to
them that fear Thee, that it may be displayed
because of the truth."   Psalm 60 : 3-4.

*   *   *

CONTENTS

INFORMATION FOR READERS

This magazine is not a periodical, published at fixed intervals, but is designed rather as a booklet which can be of permanent usefulness and reference. The time of publication is therefore determined by the amount of edifying material which we have available for printing and not by our committal to any particular dates. We trust this will help to preserve the quality of the contents. Five issues were published during 1957 and it is hoped that at least the same number will appear this year. Back numbers are available. Subscribers to the magazine will, from time to time, be freely sent news of books published by The Banner of Truth Trust.

Subscription for 6 issues 6/6 including postage.

FEBRUARY, · 1958

EDITORIAL

"Men print, in a sense, for eternity. Sermons preached, or men's words, pass away with many like wind — how soon are they buried in the grave of oblivion! but sermons printed are men's works, live when they are dead, and become an image of eternity: 'This shall be written for the generation to come: and the people which shall be created shall praise the Lord.'"

George Swinnock, 1627-1673.

The reader will find enclosed with this issue a statement of the first of our book publications. To those previously familiar with the contents of this magazine the character of these books will not be unexpected, but to all of us, perhaps, the formation of such a project at the present time will come as a matter of surprise. It may come as a surprise to some that the very books which only thirty years ago were often unwanted and thrown out as useless are now being republished. To others the surprise may be that these books are advocating doctrines and principles which they thought were worn out with age and neglect. But to us the surprise is rather at the sudden appearance of such great possibilities. The Lord can make the sun rise at mid-night as well as make it "go down at noon" (Amos 8 : 9). The disappearance of our great Reformed and Puritan literature over the past fifty years was no accident—it was the hand of God removing means of grace which had been despised. The present dying condition of our nation is a terrible proof of the efficacy of that punishment. But when God wills to make His Name glorious in mercy He can bring back His Word as surely as He brought back the Jews from Egypt and Babylon. *Post Tenebras Lux, After Darkness, Light*! was the motto written in letters of gold in the old town hall at Geneva. May it prove our motto in this coming year!

THE REPUBLICATION OF JONATHAN EDWARDS' WORKS

There will be available next month the first of what is hoped to be a series of volumes containing the best works of this great New England divine. This republication marks the bi-centenary of Edwards' death on March 22nd, 1758. Volume I of this British edition contains a new and full account of Jonathan Edwards' life and ministry in five chapters, drawn from his diary, letters and early biographers. The first of Edwards' works ever to be published in England, his "Narrative of Surprising Conversions," follows this introductory biography. This describes the 1735 Revival at Northampton. Three of his most notable sermons complete the book. This *Banner of Truth Publication* will sell at 8/-. The following article will indicate some of the facts which make a consideration of Jonathan Edwards so important and relevant at the present time.

AN INTRODUCTION TO
JONATHAN EDWARDS (1703-1758)

In 1694 Mr. Timothy Edwards became the first minister of the Church at East Windsor, on the Connecticut river, and married Esther Stoddard, a daughter of the Rev. Solomon Stoddard the famous minister of Northampton. His father, a prosperous merchant in Hartford, purchased a farm of moderate extent for them and erected a pleasant building for their new home. " It was," we are told, " a solid substantial house of moderate dimensions, had one chimney in the middle, and was entered, like all other houses at that period, by stepping over the sill." Here at East Windsor, their only son, Jonathan, was born on the 5th of October, 1703.

We know very little of how Jonathan Edwards and his ten sisters spent their childhood days at the farm in East Windsor. The fertile fields and beautiful scenery would provide much to delight the hearts of children, and the enlightened piety of their home would not frown on such joys. Nevertheless the Puritan spirit of the Edwards parents was constantly calculated to raise the attention of their children to higher pleasures and spiritual concerns. The daily necessity of searching the Scriptures and of secret prayer, the preciousness of time and the duty of developing all their faculties to the glory of God were lessons which grew up with them from their earliest years.

Edwards entered Yale College in New-Haven, in September, 1716. Hitherto he had been educated at home, where his father apparently kept a small school. When only six he had begun the study of Latin, and by the time of his entrance into college the foundations of his mental powers were well laid. In his six years at Yale he was to learn those habits of disciplined study which were later to contribute so much to the power of his preaching and writing. The Puritans, like the Reformers, had no doubts about the unity between the Gospel and sound learning. The class, of which Edwards was a member, finished their degree course in September, 1720, before he was seventeen years old, but he resided at college a further two years preparing himself for the work of the ministry. It was to these two years that Edwards later dated his conversion experience" Towards the latter part of my time at college," he writes, " when it pleased God to seize me with a pleurisy ; in which He brought me nigh to the grave, and shook me over the pit of hell . . . I was brought to seek salvation, in a manner that I never was before ; I felt a spirit to part with all things in the world, for an interest in Christ ; I made seeking my salvation the main business of my life.

" From my childhood up, my mind had been full of objections against the doctrine of God's sovereignty, in choosing whom He would to eternal life ; and rejecting whom He pleased ; leaving them eternally to perish, and be everlastingly tormented in hell. It used to appear like a horrible doctrine to me. But I remember the time very well when I seemed to be convinced, and fully satisfied, as to this sovereignty of God, and His pleasure. . . .

" From about that time I began to have a new kind of apprehension and idea of Christ, and the work of redemption, and the glorious way of salvation by Him. An inward, sweet sense of these things, at times, came into my heart ; and my soul was led away in pleasant views and contemplations of them. And my mind was greatly engaged to spend my time in reading and meditating on Christ, on the beauty and excellency of His person, and the lovely way of salvation by free grace in Him. I found no books so delightful to me, as those that treated of these subjects. Those words Cant. 2 : 1, used to be abundantly with me, ' I am the rose of Sharon, and the lily of the valley.' The words seemed to me sweetly to represent the loveliness and beauty of Jesus Christ . . . I felt then great satisfaction as to my good estate ; but that did not content me. I had vehement longings of soul after God and Christ, and after more holiness, wherewith my heart seemed to be full, and ready to break ; which often brought to my mind the words of the psalmist, Psa. 119 : 28, ' My soul breaketh for the longing it hath.' "

Thus prepared in mind and soul Edwards was licensed to preach the Gospel in the nineteenth year of his age. His first charge was to a Presbyterian congregation in New York, where he went in the beginning of August, 1722.

His preachings soon won the earnest attention and affection of the New York congregation and they warmly solicited him to remain with them for life. But although he became greatly attached to the people and the place, a variety of circumstances pointed to the limitations of his usefulness in this sphere, and so, after a period of eight memorable months, he returned home at the end of April, 1723. The summer was spent at East Windsor in close study. In September, 1723, Edwards re-visited his old college at New-Haven to receive his degree of Master of Arts, and he was at the same time elected a tutor in the college. Although he was now receiving several invitations to various congregations, he was conscious of his need of further study before he could attain those high qualifications which the Scriptures require of ministers, and therefore gladly accepted the proposal that he should spend a further period at Yale.

Edwards had continued in the office of tutor at Yale for just over two years, when he received an invitation from the church at Northampton to join his grandfather, Mr. Stoddard, in the ministry there. Many factors conspired to prompt his acceptance. Northampton was the shire town town of Hampshire—a county which embraced nearly one half of the area of the colony—and its strong and united church had long held considerable influence among the churches of New England.   It was thus a situation which afforded opportunities for extensive usefulness.   Moreover, his grandfather, now in his eighty-fourth year, stood in need of assistance, and wished him to be his successor.

Great changes had taken place in New England since Solomon Stoddard had begun preaching in Northampton in 1669.   It is true he had witnessed five powerful revivals at Northampton during his long ministry.   Indeed Whitefield tells us that on one occasion as many as two or three hundred souls were awakened by a sermon of Stoddard's on the text, " But ye believe not, because ye are not my sheep."   Nevertheless it is evident that towns such as Northampton were exceptions to the general condition of the colony, and that men of Stoddard's age had lived to see a great decline in the power and life of the churches at large.   Few had arisen to succeed the spiritual giants who had led the first generation of Puritan settlers ; growing material prosperity displaced spiritual concerns ; preaching lost first its unction, then, in some places, its orthodoxy , morality became confused with godliness ; and the old practices of secret prayer, family government and sabbath observance began to fall into disuse.

The condition of New England about the commencement of Edwards' ministry at Northampton is clearly described in a letter recorded in Gillies' valuable " Historical Collections."   " A very lamentable ignorance of the main essentials of true practical religion, and the doctrines nextly relating thereunto, very generally prevailed.   The nature and necessity of the new birth was but little known or thought of.   The necessity of a conviction of sin and misery, by the Holy Spirit opening and applying the law to the conscience, in order to a saving closure with Christ, was hardly known at all to the most.   It was thought that if there was any need of a heart-distressing sight of the soul's danger, and fear of Divine wrath, it was only needful for the grosser sort of sinners . . . According to these principles, and this ignorance of some of the most soul-concerning truths of the Gospel, people were very generally thro' the land careless at heart, and stupidly indifferent about the great concerns of eternity ; and indeed the wise, for the most part, were in a great degree asleep with the foolish."

It was in July, 1731, that the young minister of Northampton began to become widely known.   In that month he had the honour of being invited to preach the " public lecture " at Boston.   Edwards took for his subject the absolute dependence of man upon God in all parts of his salvation, expounding the text 1 Cor. 29. 30, " That no flesh should glory in his presence . . . "   It was a doctrine that had been ordinary enough to Puritan congregations, but the power and clarity of his presentation was novel for his times, and it produced a profound impression. This event was a land-mark not only in Edwards' life, but in the history of New England theology. It was an uncompromising declaration of the faith of their fathers and a clarion call to return to the doctrines of the previous century.

The events leading up to the unforgettable winter of 1734-5 are detailed by Edwards in his "Narrative of Surprising Conversions." "About this time," he writes, referring to the winter of 1734, "began the great noise, in this part of the country, about Arminianism, which seemed to appear with a very threatening aspect upon the interests of religion here. The friends of vital piety trembled for fear of the issue. Many who looked on themselves as in a Christless condition, seemed to be awakened by it, with fear that God was about to withdraw from the land, and that we should be given up to heterodoxy and corrupt principles ; and that then their opportunity for obtaining salvation would be past." Edwards, "well-knowing that the points at issue had an immediate bearing on the great subject of salvation," determined, in opposition to the fears and counsels of many of his friends, to deal with the various Arminian errors in a series of sermons. He had already spoken on this heresy in his famous Boston sermon in 1731, but now he was convinced of the necessity of dealing with it at much greater length. The discourses which were thus occasioned by this controversy led to one of the greatest awakenings since the time of the apostles. "Although great fault was found with meddling with the controversy in the pulpit," Edwards' narrative continues, "yet it proved a word spoken in season here ; and was most evidently attended with a very remarkable blessing of heaven to the souls of the people in this town. *Then* it was, in the latter part of December, *that the Spirit of God* began extraordinarily to set in, and wonderfully to work amongst us."

When the year 1735 opened, deep and solemn attention to the great truths of the Gospel prevailed in Northampton. "A great and earnest concern about the great things of religion, and the eternal world, became universal in all parts of the town, and among persons of all degrees, and all ages . . . religion was with all sorts the great concern, and the world was a thing only by the bye. The only thing in their view was to get the Kingdom of Heaven, and every one appeared pressing into it. It then was a dreadful thing amongst us to lie out of Christ, in danger every day of dropping into hell ; and what persons' minds were intent upon, was to escape for their lives, and to *fly from wrath to come* . . . This work of God, as it was carried on, and the number of true saints multiplied, soon made a glorious alteration in the town ; so that in the spring and summer following, anno 1735, the town seemed to be full of the presence of God : it never was so full of love, nor of joy, and yet so full of distress, as it was then . . . Our young people, when they met, were wont to spend the time in talking of the *excellency* and dying *love* of Jesus Christ, the glory of the way of *salvation,* the wonderful, free, and sovereign grace of God, His glorious work in the *conversion* of a soul, the *truth* and certainty of the great things of God's Word, the sweetness of the views of His perfections, etc.   And even at weddings, which formerly were mere occasions of mirth and jollity, there was now no discourse of anything but religion, and no appearance of any but spiritual mirth."

"It will not be easy to find discourses in any language," says Edwards' biographer, "more solemn, spiritual, or powerful, than many of those which he now delivered."   While he urged repentance on every sinner, as his immediate duty, he also strongly insisted that God is under no manner of obligation to any natural man, and can justly give or withhold grace according to His sovereign pleasure.   The discourses, which, beyond measure more than any others which he preached, "had an immediate saving effect," were several from Rom. 3 : 19—"That every mouth may be stopped" —in which he endeavoured to show that it would be just with God, for ever to reject, and cast off, mere natural men.

Concerning the extent of this awakening, while mindful that appearances are not always realities, Edwards gives us some figures. In the months of March and April, when the work of God was carried on with the greatest power, he supposes the number of genuine conversions, to have been at least four a day, or nearly thirty a week, for five or six successive weeks.   More than three hundred persons, in half a year, and about as many of them males as females, appeared to have become Christians.   When it is realized that the total population of Northampton consisted of only two hundred families, then the extent of his work is very striking. "There were remarkable tokens of God's presence in almost every house," writes Edwards.   In the spring of 1735, the revival spread to other towns and villages in New Hampshire, until, Edwards asserts, it "extended from one end to the other of this county," and also to "many places in Connecticut."

In the summer of 1735 a short account of the work of God at Northampton was published in Boston, and this, being forwarded to London, arrested the attention of Drs. Watts and Guyse and prompted them to write to Edwards for a fuller account.   Edwards was thus induced to prepare a longer statement, and this he dispatched to these two English Nonconformist leaders in the form of a letter, dated November 6, 1736.   It was then published in London, under the title of "Narrative of Surprising Conversions."

Dwight, Edwards' biographer, after stating that Edwards' intention in publishing the "Narrative" was to explain the nature of a true saving conversion and of a genuine work of the Spirit in revival, summarizes the importance of this publication : "For a long period, revivals of religion had been chiefly unknown, both

312

in Great Britain and on the Continent of Europe.   The church at large had generally ceased to expect events of this nature ; and appear to have entertained very imperfect views of their causes, their nature, and the manner in which they ought to be regarded. In no previous publication had these important subjects been adequately explained . . . By the astonishing work of grace at Northampton, an impulse had been given to the church of this whole western world, which could not soon be lost.   The history of that event, having been extensively circulated, produced a general conviction in the minds of Christians, that the preaching of the Gospel might be attended by effects, not less surprising, than those which followed it in apostolic times.   This conviction produced an important change in the views, and conduct, both of ministers and churches."

Having now considered something of the outward effects of Edwards' early ministry, it will be of profit to us to consider something of his normal life during this period.   Edwards followed the great Puritan tradition of living " by rule," that is to say his everyday life was governed by such definite plans and methods as were most conducive to the redeeming of time and to the greatest spiritual usefulness.   By exercising constant discipline and attention to such matters as sleep, diet, and exercise, Edwards was able to do more in a few years than many ministers do in a lifetime.   He commonly rose between four and five in the morning and spent thirteen hours every day in his study.   " I think," he notes in his diary, " Christ has recommended rising early in the morning, by His rising from the grave very early."   If it be asked what duties detained him so long in solitude, the answer is those two apostolic duties of attendance to the Word of God and prayer, Acts 6 : 4. " There is much evidence," writes his biographer, " that he was punctual, constant, and frequent in secret prayer, and often kept days of fasting and prayer in secret.   It appears from his diary, that his stated seasons of secret prayer were, from his youth, three times a day—in his journeys, as well as at home.   He was, so far as can be known, much on his knees in secret, and in devout reading of God's word, and meditation upon it."   Edwards was deeply conscious that the power of a man's ministry was not in proportion to his activity, but rather in proportion to his communion with God and to his spiritual understanding of the truth.   Let those who doubt whether such ministerial habits as these are practical remember the practical effects which accompanied such a course of living !   Is not the absence of such practices among ministers today a sign of our underestimating the necessity of being deeply familiar with the whole of the oracles of God ?

The following brief extracts from his account of his spiritual experiences give some idea of their nature :

" Once, as I rode into the woods for my health, in 1737, having alighted from my horse in a retired place, as my manner commonly has been, to walk for divine contemplation and prayer, I had a view that for me was extraordinary, of the glory of the Son of God, as Mediator between God and man, and His wonderful, great, full, pure and sweet grace and love, and meek and gentle condescension. This grace that appeared so calm and sweet, appeared also great above the heavens. The person of Christ ineffably excellent with an excellency great enough to swallow up all thought and conception—which continued, as near as I can judge, about an hour ; which kept me the greater part of the time in a flood of tears, and weeping aloud. I felt an ardency of soul to be, what I know not otherwise how to express, emptied and annihilated ; to lie in the dust, and to be full of Christ alone ; to love Him with a holy and pure love ; to trust in Him ; to live upon Him ; to serve and follow Him ; and to be perfectly sanctified and made pure, with a divine and heavenly purity. I have, several other times, had views very much of the same nature, and which have had the effects . . .

"Often, since I lived in this town, I have had very affecting views of my own sinfulness and vileness ; very frequently to such a degree as to hold me in a kind of loud weeping, sometimes for a considerable time together ; so that I have often been forced to shut myself up. I have had a vastly greater sense of my own wickedness, and the badness of my heart, than ever I had before my conversion. It has often appeared to me, that if God should mark iniquity against me, I should appear the very worst of all mankind.

"My wickedness, as I am in myself, has long appeared to me perfectly ineffable, and swallowing up all thought and imagination ; like an infinite deluge, or mountains over my head. I know not how to express better what my sins appear to me to be, than by heaping infinite upon infinite, and multiplying infinite by infinite. Very often, for these many years, these expressions are in my mind, and in my mouth, 'Infinite upon infinite —Infinite upon infinite !' When I look into my heart, and take a view of my wickedness, it looks like an abyss infinitely deeper than hell. And it appears to me, that were it not for free grace, exalted and raised up to the infinite height of all the fullness and glory of the great Jehovah, and the arm of His power and grace stretched forth in all the majesty of His power, and in all the glory of His sovereignty, I should appear sunk down in my sins below hell itself ; far beyond the sight of everything, but the eye of sovereign grace, that can pierce down to such a depth. And yet it seems to me, that my conviction of sin is exceeding small, and faint ; it is enough to amaze me, that I have no more sense of my sin. I know certainly, that I have very little sense of my sinfulness. When I have had turns of weeping for my sins I thought I knew at the time, that my repentance was nothing to my sin."

EDWARDS' FORMER INFLUENCE AND CONTEMPORARY RELEVANCE

Edwards' direct usefulness to his own generation was very great, and the visible effects of his preaching were such as were never paralleled in New England. There are many testimonies to the immediate influence wrought by his sermons upon immortal souls. One hearer, who heard him describe the day of judgment, declared " that so vivid and solemn was the impression made on his own mind, that he fully supposed, that as soon as Mr. Edwards should close his discourse, the Judge would descend, and the final separation take place." Another, who was still a child during Edwards' ministry, remembered how the congregation would sit fixed and motionless for over two hours under his preaching, the truth bearing down upon their minds with irresistible power, and at the close would seem disappointed that it had terminated so soon. The same effects accompanied the occasional sermons Edwards preached in other places. His visit to Enfield, for instance, at a time of great religious indifference, is related by one eye-witness in the following words : " When they went into the meeting-house, the appearance of the assembly was thoughtless and vain. The Rev. Mr. Edwards, of Northampton, preached ; and before the sermon was ended, the assembly appeared deeply impressed, and bowed down with an awful conviction of their sin and danger. There was such a breathing of distress and weeping, that the preacher was obliged to speak to the people and desire silence, that he might be heard." Bancroft, the great American historian, sums up the deep impact Edwards made upon his times in the following words : " He that would know the workings of the New England mind in the middle of the last century and the throbbings of its heart, must give his days and nights to the study of Jonathan Edwards."

But great as the direct effects of his labours were, the indirect effects were even greater. His written works and printed sermons were to influence thousands who never saw or heard him. None were more qualified to speak on revivals than Edwards, and his writings on this subject became regarded as standard text-books. His sermons became to many " the models of a style of preaching, which has been most signally blessed by God to the conversion of sinners, and which should be looked to as a standard, by those who wish, like him, to turn many to righteousness, that with him they may shine, as the stars for ever."

There are many testimonies to Edwards' worth by men who only knew him by his writings. The famous John Newton was once asked who he thought was the greatest preacher he ever heard. " Whitefield," he replied. And who was the greatest divine ? " Edwards," was the answer. Robert Hall, the English Baptist leader, declared, " I regard Edwards as the greatest of the sons of men." The foremost evangelical leaders in Wales and Scotland in the early nineteenth century, ministers like John Elias and Thomas Chalmers, were deeply read in and influenced by his works. Owen Jones refers to Edwards as one of the three chief authors whom Elias studied. " I have long esteemed him," said Dr. Chalmers, " as the greatest of theologians, combining in a degree that is quite unexampled the profoundly intellectual with the devotedly spiritual and sacred." Chalmers' pupils in the Divinity Hall at Edinburgh, young men such as Robert Murray McCheyne, who themselves were to be greatly used in revival, learned by experience the truth of their professor's opinion. Probably no other uninspired writer had such a formative influence on McCheyne's life and ministry as Jonathan Edwards. We may confidently anticipate that Edwards' indirect usefulness is by no means ended, and that wherever there is a revival of spiritual Christianity there will be a return to the sermons and writings of the faithful pastor of Northampton.

Two hundred years have now passed since Jonathan Edwards' death and great changes have been seen in the church of God. What bearing then can his life have upon us ?   What relevance has his ministry to our times ?   Is his theology as out of date as eighteenth century spinning wheels and oil lamps ?   Are the truths and methods he used to promote the kingdom of God to be viewed like some rusty and antique armour, suitable as interesting ornaments, but unfit for further battles ?   These are the final considerations with which we must close.

Many are the neglected lessons forcibly presented to us by the history of Edwards' life and ministry.   The connection between holiness and the blessing of God, between deep study and powerful preaching, between doctrine and practice, these are all matters that need to be re-learned today.   That a minister's usefulness is not in proportion to his outward activity but to his inner life, that the greatest successes of the Gospel have not been achieved by organisation, advertisement, or campaigns, these are facts which are widely forgotten.

But one supreme lesson emerges beyond all others.   Edwards was as far from the Reformers in time as we are from him.   By his day the doctrines, which had been so widely recognised a century and two centuries before, had fallen from their prominence : a general suspicion was abroad that although they may have won victories in the days of the forefathers they were now worn out, and had lost their power—or at least that they needed modifying and softening down to suit the taste of the eighteenth century.   The successors of the Puritans seemed ashamed of their cause, and even good men like Doddridge and Watts made no attempt to defend the truths which their predecessors held so dear.   Arminian theology was widely prevalent ; divine sovereignty was denied or ignored, and the work of the Holy Ghost in regeneration had been replaced by man's alleged power of choice.   When therefore Edwards preached his first sermon to the outside world, at the public lecture in Boston in 1731 and took for his subject " God glorified in Man's Dependence," it was an epochal event.   The young preacher had laid down a challenge to the age.   It was evident to all that a great champion had arisen to defend the old discredited theology, and to point men back to old paths.   With an emphasis of certainty and an intensity of tone, the doctrines of Scripture and the faith of the Reformers had been reasserted.   The conviction Edwards had expressed at the close of that memorable sermon never left him and it was soon to be impressed on a great part of the religious world : —

"Those doctrines and schemes of divinity that are in any respect opposite to such an absolute and universal·dependence on God, do derogate from God's glory, and thwart the design of the contrivance for our redemption. Those schemes that exalt man into the place of either Father, Son, or Holy Ghost, in anything pertaining to our redemption ; that own that we depend on God for the gift of a Redeemer, but deny so absolute a dependence on Him for the obtaining of an interest in the Redeemer ; that own an absolute dependence on the Son for working our redemption, but not so entire a dependence on the Holy Ghost for conversion ; that own a dependence on God for means of grace, but not absolutely for the success of those means ; that own a partial dependence on the power of God, for the obtaining and excercising holiness, but not a mere dependence on the arbitrary and sovereign grace of God ; and whatever other way any scheme is inconsistent with our entire dependence on God for all, *it is repugnant to the design and tenor of the gospel, and robs it of that which God accounts its lustre and glory.*

The application of all this to our generation should be very obvious. Why has the converting power of the Gospel largely disappeared in our churches ? Why is it we see no awakenings or congregations broken down under conviction of sin ? Let not the unexpectedness of the answer cause us to reject it. We have offended the God who is jealous for the glory of His truth. Those errors which are so harmonious with man's fallen nature have again overspread the visible church. Arminianism is again the fashionable theology, and we may cease to expect any revival until this is recognised. For, as Edwards truly asserts, " It is the manner of God before He removes any awful judgments which He has brought upon a people for their sins, first to cause them to forsake those sins which procure those judgments." A call to return to the God of our fathers and to the Word of God in its purity is the supreme lesson which Edwards' works should leave upon our soul. Let the example of his firm and fearless defence of the truth—at a time when it had almost fallen to the ground—and the remembrance of the approbation of God which accompanied his ministry, remain on our hearts. It is to the truth, not to numbers, or talents, or activity, that we must look for success. It is faithfulness to His Word that God will bless. If this is realised then there is nothing in the present or future that we need fear, for " The lip of truth shall be established for ever : but a lying tongue is but for a moment." Prov. 12 : 19.

" The greatest loss I feel is that of the Spirit, and earnestness of secret prayer . . . Oh, that we might have more communion and fellowship with the Holy Ghost! Let us pray more for it, and may we sincerely shun those things that grieve Him. Many are content without the Spirit's influences, and thus grieve the Holy Ghost by this indifference to His operations, being willing to go on without Him ! "   —(*John Elias*),

CHARLES HODGE (1797-1878)*

In the pleasant little town of Princeton, situated on the fertile slopes of New Jersey, a theological seminary was founded in 1812. From here were to go forth a long line of distinguished ministers and missionaries who made the name of their seminary revered throughout the English-speaking world. For over a hundred years, while great and sad changes were taking place within the Protestant churches, " Princeton theology " was to remain a synonym for orthodoxy and, long after other colleges had gone down before the inroads of error, Princeton was to stand firm in its reverent and faithful allegiance to the Word of God.

At the inaugural service, held in the old Presbyterian church, a youthful figure could be seen, leaning against the rail of the gallery, listening with rapt attention to the address of Dr. Archibald Alexander, one of the senior professors of the new seminary. It was an event which fourteen year old Charles Hodge was never to forget. That same year he had left his home in Philadelphia and entered Princeton College, one of the old American seats of learning —associated with the names of such men as Jonathan Edwards. As it provided a general education, the College remained distinct from the Seminary which was specifically theological, but it quickly became the custom for students entering the ministry to pass from one to the other. Thus, after graduating from the College in 1815, Hodge enrolled his name, on 9th November, 1816, as one of the twenty-six students attending the Seminary.

From his childhood Hodge had never wavered in his sense of a call to the ministry, though the profession did not run in his family. His grandfather, an emigrant from Northern Ireland in 1730, had been a successful merchant, and his father—who died only six months after his birth— had been a medical practitioner. It was to his mother, Hodge used later to say, that, under God, he owed everything. Before her marriage in 1790, she had been known as " the beautiful Mary Blanchard of Boston "; her family were of Huguenot extraction, and she inherited their strong character and earnest piety. Left a widow at an early age, Mrs. Hodge by her example brought her youngest son, Charles, under the power of godliness from his infancy and by self-denying economy she was able to give him a first class education. Hodge later wrote concerning the influence of his home : " I think that in my childhood I came nearer to conforming to the apostle's injunction, ' Pray without ceasing,' than in any other period of my life. As far back as I can remember, I had the habit of thanking God for everything

---

* As we are re-publishing more than one work by Dr. Hodge we felt that a sketch of his life would be of particular interest to readers. The reprint of his "Princeton Sermons " (pp. 400, 13/6.) is now available, this will be followed in April, 1958, by his commentary on I Corinthians (11/-).

I received, and asking him for everything I wanted. If I lost a book, or any of my playthings, I prayed that I might find it. I prayed walking along the streets, in school and out of school, whether playing or studying. I did not do this in obedience to any prescibed rule. It seemed natural. I thought of God as an everywhere-present Being, full of kindness and love, who would not be offended if children talked to Him. I knew He cared for sparrows. I was as cheerful and happy as the birds, and acted as they did."

At Princeton Seminary Hodge showed himself an earnest and successful student, diligent at his books, ardently devoted to his professors (then two in number), and warmly attached to his friends. He graduated on 28th September, 1819, and a month later the presbytery of Philadelphia licensed him to preach the Gospel. Missionary zeal was already a marked characteristic in his life ; " I would give the world," he recorded, "were my desire of honouring Christ and of saving souls so strong that I should be indifferent to what related merely to myself." When, therefore, he received a proposal about this time to become an assistant-teacher of Biblical literature and exegesis in his former seminary, we find him writing : "Did the duties of the contemplated office require me to give up the prospect of preaching altogether, I think I should not hesitate in declining it ; for I believe that preaching the Gospel is a privilege superior to any other entrusted to men." The office did not call for the relinquishment of any directly spiritual duties, and Hodge, well aware of the intimate connection between the prosperity of the Church and the propagation of sound theology, accepted the appointment in 1820. After two years his two senior professors, Dr. Alexander and Dr. Samuel Miller, were so satisfied with his abilities that they successfully recommended to the Assembly his appointment to a regular professorial chair. A month later he married Sarah Bache, a young lady of unusual beauty both of person and character who attributed her conversion to his instrumentality. A new house was built for them near the Seminary and it became the scene of Hodge's life and labours for more than half a century to come. Here his eight children, except the eldest, were born, and here his loved partner was reft from him by death in 1849. His two sons, A. A. Hodge, and Caspar Wistar Hodge, and his grandson, Caspar Wistar Hodge Junr., were themselves later to become professors in the Seminary and his eminent successors.

From this early period in Hodge's life till the day of his death his activities were almost entirely of the same character. Year after year his life was one of uniform devotion to the training of men to preach the glorious gospel of the grace of God. Some 3,000 students passed through his classes, and for over fifty years he continued to mould the current opinions of his Church and country. Hodge was a man of wide outlook ; at an early period in his life he spent two years at German Universities listening to men of very different views from his own, yet he never faltered in his conviction that historic Calvinism provides the only sound basis for true exposition and evangelical preaching. By deep study he arrived at the settled conclusion that the doctrinal standards of the Reformers and Puritans were the truth, and in 1872 at his jubilee, when multitudes were elsewhere confounding novelty with truth, he boldly declared—" I am not afraid to say, that a new idea never originated in this seminary." Strife was not congenial to his nature, but he could not, and did not shun controversy on these doctrinal principles. In an age of increasing uncertainty, compromise and confusion, he saw clearly, in the words of his son, that " The last issue must be between Atheism, and its countless forms, and Calvinism. The other systems will be crushed as the half-rotten ice between two great bergs." Dr. Shedd spoke the truth when he said, " Dr. Hodge has done more for Calvinism than any other man in America." It was a fact which his opponents unconsciously recognised when they referred to him as the greatest hindrance on theological " progress " that the century had seen!

Hodge's life is itself the best answer to those who have wrongly deemed narrowness and coldness to be the necessary accompaniments of the Reformed Faith. He was no abstract systematizer, but ever concerned with the living application of the great truths of Scripture to men's spiritual experience. He did not forget the the warning of an old Puritan divine, " Beware of a strong head and a cold heart." The mention of the love of Christ would sometimes, even in the classroom, affect him to tears, and in no spirit of exaggeration a life-long friend testified—" Not Rutherford himself was more absorbed with the love of Christ." Professor B. B. Warfield, who later succeeded to Hodge's theological chair, gives the following description of his manner of teaching : " After his always striking appropriate prayer had been offered, and we were settled back into our seats, he would open his well-thumbed Greek Testament—on which it was plain that there was not a single marginal note—look at the passage for a second, and then, throwing his head back and closing his eyes, begin his exposition. He scarcely again glanced at the Testament during the hour : the text was evidently before his mind, verbally, and the matter of his exposition thoroughly at his command. In an unbroken stream it flowed from subject to subject, simple, clear, cogent, unfailingly reverent. Now and then he would pause a moment, to insert an illustrative anecdote—now and then lean forward suddenly with tearful, wide-open eyes to press home a quick-risen inference of the love of God to lost sinners."

In his home Hodge was ever found to be a humble, lovable Christian. " Clear light did not interfere with warm love in good old Dr. Hodge," declared one visitor. " I remember his parlour-study as one of the cheeriest glimpses I had of an American interior." His study was in fact the family thoroughfare through which the children, boys and girls, went in and out for work and play. Often if too busy to rise and open his door, he would leave it off the latch " so that the least child might toddle in at will unhindered."

Charles Hodge finally bade farewell to his beloved Princeton and entered his eternal rest on the 19th of June, 1878. The last consecutive utterance of his expiring moments was " To be absent from the body is to be present with the Lord ; to be present with the Lord is to see Him ; to see Him is to be like Him." A great life's work was done, but behind him in his books he left a legacy to enrich the Church of God till the end of time. He was a great writer and his pen seems never to have been idle. For over forty years he had been the editor of and chief contributor to the " Biblical Repertory and Princeton Review," and through its pages he had exerted a very weighty influence. In 1835 he issued his great commentary on Romans which was followed later by his fine expositions on I and II Corinthians and Ephesians. " The more we use Hodge, the more we value him. This applies to all his commentaries," wrote Spurgeon. At length, after his sixty-ninth birthday, his masterpiece and " magnum opus " on " Systematic Theology " was written and published.

After Hodge's death there was found in the drawers of his study a " large accumulation of careful preparations " for the memorable sermons which he had preached to the students on Sabbath afternoons over a period of many years. It had been his custom to write out fully a careful analysis of every sermon. These were edited by his son, A. A. Hodge and published in 1879 under the title of " *Princeton Sermons.*" This long out-of-print volume we have now re-published with a Foreword by Professor John Murray, Professor of Systematic Theology at Westminster Seminary, Philadelphia.

The work contains 249 sermon outlines, they are classified into 10 sections—God and His Attributes ; Christ, His Person and Offices ; The Holy Spirit and His Offices ; Satan and His Influence —Sin and Sins ; Conversion—Entrance Upon The Christian Life ; Christian Experiences, Characteristics and Privileges ; Christian Responsibilities and Duties ; The Means of Grace—The Scriptures, Ministry, Sacraments, etc. ; Death, and the Consummation of Redemption ; Last Words—Papers Prepared During The Last Year Of His Life. These outlines though lacking the full expansion Hodge gave them in delivery ' yet remain in themselves,' says A. A. Hodge, ' very remarkable examples of that analysis, that logical grouping and perspicuous exhibition of truth which is an essential faculty of the effective preacher. They present in this analytic form an amount and quality of homiletical example and suggestion probably not surpassed in the same number of pages in the English language."

" Hodge's ' Princeton Sermons ' offer his mature thoughts on a great many subjects," writes Professor John Murray, " and they breathe the warmth of devotional fervour. Here is a fund of succinct definition on the great themes of theology as they are related to the most practical concerns of the Christian and of the pastor . . . The masterful survey provided by this volume is calculated to re-habilitate in the thinking and practice of the present day those very patterns which are largely lost and which are our clamant need. May it be that by God's grace this may be the fruit."

One of Hodge's sermons outlines is appended to this article to give an example of their character.

THE OUTLINE OF A SERMON BY CHARLES HODGE

" Who will have all men to be saved and to come unto the knowledge of the truth." 1 Tim. 2 : 4.

There are two principles which must control the interpretation of the Scriptures. That is, when a passage admits of two inter-pretations, the choice between them is to be determined, first, by the analogy of Scripture. If one interpretation contradicts what the Bible elsewhere teaches and another accords with it, then we are bound to accept the latter. Or, secondly, the interpretation must be decided by established facts. That is, if one interpretation agrees with such facts and another contradicts them, then the former must be true.

This passage admits of two interpretations so far as the signific-ation of the words are concerned. *First,* that God *wills,* in the sense of purposing or intending, the salvation of all men. This cannot be true, first, because it contradicts the Scriptures. The Scriptures teach 1st, that the purposes of God are immutable, and that they cannot fail of their accomplishment. 2nd. That all men are not to be saved. It is clearly taught that multitudes of the human race have perished, are now perishing, and will hereafter perish. That God intends and purposes what he knows is not to happen, is a contradiction. It contradicts the very idea of God, and is an impossibility, Secondly, this interpretation contradicts admitted facts as well as the explicit statements of the Bible.

1. It is a fact that God does not give saving grace to all men. 2. It is a fact that he does not and never has brought all men to the knowledge of the truth. Multitudes of men are destitute of that knowledge, and ever have been. By truth it is clear the apostle means saving truth, the truth as revealed in the gospel, and not merely the truth as revealed by things that are made. This inter-pretation therefore cannot be correct.

The *second* interpretation is that God desires the salvation of all men. This means 1st, just what is said when the Scriptures declare that God is good ; that he is merciful and gracious, and ready to forgive ; that he is good to all, and his tender mercies over all his works. He is kind to the unthankful and to the evil. This goodness or benevolence of God is not only declared but revealed in his works, in his providence, and in the work of redemption. 2nd, It means what is said in Ezek. xxxiii, 11. " As I live, saith the Lord God, I have no pleasure in the death of the wicked," and in Ezek. xviii, 23," Have I any pleasure at all that the wicked should die, saith the Lord God, and not that he should return from his ways and live ? " Also Lam. iii, 33, " For he doth not afflict willingly nor grieve the children of men." It means what Christ taught in the parable of the prodigal son, and of the lost sheep and the lost piece of money ; and is taught by his lament over Jerusalem.

All these passages teach that God delights in the happiness of his creatures, and that when he permits them to perish, or inflicts evil upon them, it is from some inexorable necessity ; that is, because it would be unwise and wrong to do otherwise. His relation is that of a benevolent sovereign in punishing crime, or of a tender judge in passing sentence on offenders, or, what is the familiar representation of Scripture, that of a father who deals with his children with tenderness, yet with wisdom and according to the dictates of right.

This is the meaning of the passage. That it is the correct one is plain, 1. Because it is agreeable to the meaning of the word *thelein*. In innumerable cases it means to love, delight in, to regard with satisfaction as a thing desirable. " Sacrifice and offerings thou wouldst not," " neither hadst pleasure therein." " Ye cannot do the things that ye would." " For what I would, that do I not, but what I hate, that I do." " We would see a sign from thee.' " Be it unto thee even as thou wilt." " If he delight in him " is *ei thelei auton*. 2. This passage thus interpreted teaches just what the Scriptures elsewhere teach of the goodness of God. 3. It does not contradict the Scriptures as the other does, or make God mutable or impotent. 4. It is accordant with all known facts. It agrees with the fact, that God is benevolent, as shown in his works, and yet that he permits many to perish.

This truth is of great importance, 1. Because all religion is founded on the knowledge of God and on the proper apprehensions of his character. We should err fatally if we conceived of God as malevolent.

2. The conviction that God is love, that he is a kind Father, is necessary to encourage sinners to repent. The prodigal hesitated because he doubted his father's love. It was his hope that encouraged him to return.

3. This truth is necessary to our confidence in God. It is the source of gratitude and love.

4. It is to be held fast to under all circumstances. We are to believe though so much sin and misery are allowed to prevail. We

are not to resort to false solutions of this difficulty, to assume that
God cannot prevent sin, or that he wills it as a means to happiness.
He allows it because it seems good in his sight to do so, and this is
the highest and the last solution of the problem of evil.

SAYINGS OF GEORGE WHITEFIELD*

" As God can send a nation or people no greater blessing than to give
them faithful, sincere, and upright ministers, so the greatest curse that God
can possibly send upon a people in this world, is to give them over to
blind, unregenerate, carnal, lukewarm, and unskilful guides."

" We cry out against popery, and that very justly ; but we are all
Papists ; at least, I am sure, we are all Arminians by nature ; and,
therefore, no wonder so many natural men embrace that scheme."

" God the Father and God the Son entered into a covenant concerning
the salvation of the elect from all eternity, wherein God the Father
promised, that, if the Son would offer his soul a sacrifice for sin, he should
see his seed. God, as a reward of Christ's sufferings, promised to give
the elect faith and repentance : and both these, and every thing else
necessary for their everlasting happiness, are infallibly secured to them in
this promise . . . Would to God this point of doctrine was considered more,
and people were more studious of the covenant of redemption between
the Father and the Son ! we should not then have so much disputing against
the doctrine of election. For my own part, I cannot see how true humble-
ness of mind can be attained without a knowledge of it ; and though I
will not say, that every one who denies election is a bad man, yet I will
say, it is a very bad sign . . . redemption is so ordered, that no flesh should
glory in the Divine presence ; and hence it is, that the pride of man opposes
this doctrine, because, according to this doctrine, and no other, ' he that
glories, must glory only in the Lord.' "

" One reason among many others why I admire the doctrine of election,
and am convinced that it should have a place in a gospel ministry is that
it has a natural tendency to rouse the soul out of its carnal security, and
therefoie many carnal men cry out against it: whereas universal redemption
is a notion sadly adapted to keep the soul in its lethargic sleepy condition,
and therefore so many natural men admire and applaud it."

" It is the doctrine of election that mostly presses me to abound in
good works. I am made willing to suffer all things for the elect's sake. This
makes me preach with comfort, because I know salvation doth not depend
on man's free-will, but the Lord makes them willing in the day of his
power, and can make use of me to bring some of his elect home, when
and where he pleases."

" I go ; I go to a rest prepared : my sun has given light to many, but
now it is about to set—no, to rise to the zenith of immortal glory. . have
outlived many on earth, but they cannot outlive me in heaven. Many
shall outlive me on earth and live when this body is no more, but there—
oh, thought divine !—I shall be in a world where time, age, sickness, and
sorrow are unknown. My body fails, but my spirit expands. How willingly
would I live for ever to preach Christ. But I die to be with him . . . "
(Extracts from Whitefield's last sermon before his death).

*The following are extracts from ' The Select Sermons of George Whitefield.'
This book is now available at 6/-.*

THOMAS V. MOORE ON ZECHARIAH*

The seventy years preceding the commencement of Zechariah's ministry in 520 B.C., or thereabouts, had been years of sad judgments among God's people. The church had languished in captivity, her prophets were removed from her, Zion was broken down, the glory of her former days departed and the rebuilding of the temple was at a standstill. The Jews who had returned from exile were a discouraged remnant, ready in the face of so many obstacles and difficulties to give way to sloth, faint-heartedness and despair.

This situation gave occasion for the writing of the book of Zechariah—a book rich in encouragement and exhortation and full of magnificent prophecies relating to Christ and the preservation, enlargement and final glory of His Church. It is clearly a portion of Scripture peculiarly adapted to instruct and strengthen the the Church in every period of spiritual weakness and struggle. The understanding of its teaching will forbid despair even in the darkest hour. Surely there is no inspired book which we can less afford to neglect today!

Yet the truth is that this book, which Luther termed "the quintessence of the Prophets," is one of the least known in Scripture. When one considers the commentaries that have been written on Zechariah from Luther and Calvin down to the last century, it is an astonishing fact that not one such commentary appears to be in print in Britain at the present time. This, no doubt, partly explains our neglect of Zechariah, for without expository guidance into his language, imagery and symbolism, the average reader will often be at a loss to follow the meaning. It needs to be explained how the grove of myrtles (1 : 8) colourfully represents the state of the Jewish church at that time, why the horn (1 : 18) was thought of as a symbol of power, and the chariots (6 : 1) as a symbol of authority and judgment. Such symbolic language characterizes almost the whole book. Similarly Zechariah—accommodating his language to the understanding of his times—uses Jewish conceptions to express New Testament truths, e.g., the conversion of the Gentiles (8 : 20-23) is signified by the coming of the nations to Jerusalem, and the joy of the Church in her final perfection (14 : 16) is figuratively represented by the keeping of the feast of tabernacles.

After examining a variety of commentaries on Zechariah we came to the firm conclusion that for general purposes the work by a once prominent American divine, Thomas V. Moore (1818-1871), is the best, and fully worthy of C. H. Spurgeon's commendation as 'A capital book.' Moore, a graduate of Princeton Theological Seminary and a pupil of Dr. J. A. Alexander, was doctrinally and academically well equipped. He was moreover gifted with an

* This commentary, pp. 250, will be available Feb. 25th, 1958.
  price 9/-.

unusually vivid style and possessed the ability to present the truth in a spiritual and arresting manner.

Moore, following the natural divisions of the book of Zechariah, divides his exposition into various sections. At the head of each section there is a careful and illuminating analysis ; this is followed by a verse by verse exposition and the section ends with a series of ' Practical Inferences' drawn from the passage. This method is eminently successful in its clarity and conciseness. The reader is never left in doubt of his meaning, is never wearied by irrelevancies or disgressions, and is not presented with mere ' devotional thoughts ' instead of solid exposition. The ' Practical Inferences' contain, in brief sentences, a wealth of homiletical material and thus contribute to making the work ' most useful to ministers' (C. H. Spurgeon). Here is a brief selection of ' Practical Inferences ' :—

' What we have to do for God in life should be done quickly, for life is rapidly passing and to evil and good there come alike the swift shadows of the sunset.' (1 : 5).

' There hangs above each sinner a crushing weight, poised and ready to descend with overwhelming destruction.' (5 : 7).

' Christians should be happy. No people have a better right or better reason to rejoice.' (9 : 9).

' Prayer is the barometer of the Church. When the spirit of supplication is low, there is but little of the Spirit of God.' (14 : 10).

' However secure nations or men may think themselves in sin, their sin will be sure to find them out. Never has sin more proudly entrenched herself than in godless, but magnificent Tyre. Never has every element of earthly prosperity seemed more completely under control than in her case. And yet they were all swept like chaff before the whirlwind of the wrath of God, when the time for the fulfilment of His threatenings had come. Hence though nations seem long to flourish in their sin, let not the child of God be impatient. Let him remember that two hundred years passed away after the utterance of these threatenings against Tyre, and she seemed stronger than ever, and yet when the day of doom had dawned, the galleys that left on their stated voyages the peerless queen of the seas, when they returned found her but a bare and blackened rock, a lonely monument of the truth, that our God is a consuming fire.' (11 : 3-7).

' It is not only unwise, but it is wicked to be disheartened because of the external feebleness of the Church, compared with the work she has to do, and the enemies she has to encounter. God is her strength, her glory and her hope, and to despair of her is to deny God.' (4 : 10).

The first six chapters of Zechariah contain a series of eight visions given to the prophet. These visions, while having an immediate relevance to the Jews, announce 'great principles of divine procedure' equally applicable to the Church in every age. While explaining the symbolic picture Moore presents these principles in their clearest form. Short quotations from his exposition of the first and fifth visions will illustrate this :—

Ch. I, v. 8. 'Zechariah sees a grove of myrtles, a beautiful shrub, whose leaves exhale their richest odour only when bruised. This was a symbol of the theocracy, the Jewish Church. The Church is not a cedar, in its queenly pride, or an oak in its giant strength, but a lowly myrtle, humble, unpretending, and exhaling its sweetest graces when bruised by the weight of affliction. Such was the existing state of the theocracy, and hence the despondency of the people, who thought that so lowly a thing must be wholly overshadowed and destroyed by the proud and godless powers of the world.

' But in the midst of these myrtles he sees a man on a red horse, whom we afterwards discover to be the angel of Jehovah, that divine person whom we trace all along the history of the Old Testament. . . It is the second person of the mysterious Trinity, the great Head of the Church. The fact is thus symbolized that He is in the midst of the Church, unseen, and hence though seemingly so feeble, she has this inhabitant as her glory and defence. The celerity and strength of every agency connected with the Church, is set forth by the horses, the red colour of which signified the fervor of at once the zeal and the wrath of these agencies . . . The surrounding angels on horses set forth the fact that God has provided every species of agency for the supply and defence of His Church . . .

'The attendant angels are sent to spy out the conditions of the whole earth, and bring back the report (v. 11) that all nations were in peace and prosperity. But Judea was lying in desolation, Jerusalem in ruins, and the temple but partially rebuilt . . . It was time for God to work, and hence the divine angel begins (v. 12) to intercede for His people. Here, then, was an additional fact of great comfort. Not only does Christ dwell in the midst of His people, and watch over all that afflicts their condition, but He intercedes for them, and His intercession is never in vain . . . '

Ch. IV, v. 2. 'The golden candlestick represented the Theocracy, the Church of God, an image of great beauty, showing her mission to be a light-bearer in a dark world. The material, gold, indicated the purity, preciousness and indestructibleness of all that pertained to her. The seven lamps, and seven times seven tubes, indicated by the use of the number of perfection, the manifold modes by which grace was to be imparted. The olive trees represented the source of that grace, the Spirit of God . . . God has provided an unfailing source of strength for His people. Their supply comes not from a dead reservoir of oil, but a living olive tree, that is ever drawing from the rich earth.

' Here, then, were these lamps burning continually, lamps that man's hand did not make, and does not feed, and yet supplied from a source that is exhaustless, the living trees that stand beside the candlestick. Now, if the strength to do God's work comes from God, the weakness of man is no obstacle. Zerubbabel may have but few visible resources, but the work was one that after all was to be completed by God, and not by man . . .

There is not space to quote from Moore's masterly exposition of the great prophetical passages which are so prominent in Zechariah. The incarnation of Christ (2 : 10), His offices as a King and Priest (6 : 13), His character (9 : 9), His rejection, betrayal, and death, (11 : 8-14 ; 13 : 7), the calling of the Gentiles (8 : 22), the punishment of the Jews (11 : 14-17), the conflicts and final victory of the Church, these are all subjects gloriously foretold by the Holy Ghost. The closing chapters of Zechariah, containing references to events which are evidently not yet accomplished, are notoriously difficult. The principles of interpretation which Moore adopts in his cautious exposition ·of these profound portions of Scripture are most helpful and his conclusions provide much food for thought.

The study of this commentary will not only bring the teaching of Zechariah vividly to light, it will leave a profound impression of the wealth and riches contained in Scripture and cause the reader to go back to other old expositors whose works have been so long neglected.

THE WRITTEN MINISTRY OF A. W. PINK

Arthur Pink, who was a native of Nottingham (where he preached his first sermon about 1908) and who died in Stornoway, Scotland, on July 15, 1952, was in many respects an unusual man. He was unusual in what he did. After a widespread ministry, including pastorates in Australia and the U.S.A., he spent the last sixteen years of his life in seclusion devoting his powers exclusively to writing. In 1922 he originated a monthly magazine, " Studies in The Scriptures," and for thirty years he remained not only the Editor but practically the only contributor to its two dozen pages. The magazine (which terminated in December, 1953 when the late Mr. Pink's articles were exhausted) was concerned solely with the exposition of Scripture, and the manner in which its quality and variety were sustained by one man over such a period is unprecedented in this century at least. " Studies in The Scriptures " was unique. Mr. Pink was also unusual in his outlook. That is to say his view of the Scriptures, of doctrine, and of Christian practice, was not the view of the 20th century—nor even of many of his contemporary evangelicals. Few men have travelled so widely yet remained so uninfluenced by prevailing opinions and accepted customs. By independent study of the Word of God he arrived at the settled conclusion that much of modern Evangelism was defective at its very foundations and at a time when Puritan and Reformed books were being thrown out he recognised and advanced the majority of their principles with untiring zeal and ability. He was, in some ways, a Puritan born out of time. Had Mr. Pink lived in better days his reputation would probably have fared very differently, as it was his outlook did not make for popularity and he was thus comparatively little regarded. But events have justified his outlook. Two world wars were quite in accordance with his views of human depravity and the progressive decline of our nation was to him the inevitable consequence of the prevalence of a Gospel which is able neither to wound nor heal.

As an expositor of Scripture Mr. Pink was well equipped

He was familiar with the whole range of revelation and could thus divide the truth with due weight, emphasis, and proportion. His writings display no favourite doctrines or favourite passages. He is rarely side-tracked from the great themes of Scripture—grace, justification, sanctification, etc. One looks in vain for any quaint theories on prophecy and kindred subjects. The work of God The Father, and God The Holy Spirit receive their true emphasis as well as the work of The Son. The various graces that are displayed in the Christian life are not lop-sidedly portrayed ; humility and joy, godly-fear and assurance, these are all given their lawful place. He is equally devastating in dealing with errors ; he does not in his desire to escape Arminianism fall into Hyper-Calvinism. In his ability to distinguish a true conversion experience, to detect false peace, to administer the consolation or exhortation which a believer needs in his various conditions, Pink approaches the Puritans.

The importance of Pink's writings has lately been increasingly recognized in the United States—this has been principally due to the initiative and foresight of *The Bible Truth Depot*, Mifflinburg, who have done much to make his works available in the U.S. As well as printing several of his best books they have done a splendid work in reprinting in booklet or tract form many of Pink's best articles out of " *Studies in the Scriptures.*" By arrangement with our friends at *The Bible Truth Depot* we have now a good supply of these available for distribution in this country. Tracts of this sort have been almost totally unobtainable for a long time. It may well be that Pink's influence will soon become widely felt.

As a tract writer Pink, in our opinion, has not been equalled in this century. His style is direct, and arresting ; his spirit is searching and serious. He sees a truth plainly and expresses it clearly. Moreover he possessed in an eminent degree that quality essential to all good tract writers—the ability to seize on the particular needs of the time. In December, 1937, when the vast majority were absorbed in the contemporary events in Europe, he commenced an article in these words—" We are not going to waste the spiritual reader's time nor our space by a consideration of the latest doings of Hitler, Mussolini, and Co. . . . It is something far more solemn than anything occuring in the political realm that we are now going to write upon, namely, *the soul-deceiving character* of most of the ' Evangelism ' of this degenerate and apostate generation. . . ." The following quotation likewise displays his characteristic insight :

" It is true that there are not a few who are praying for a world-wide Revival, but it appears to the writer that it would be more timely, and more scriptural, for prayer to be made to the Lord of the harvest, that He would raise up labourers who would fearlessly and faithfully preach those truths which are calculated to bring about a revival."

The sale of these tracts and booklets by Mr. Pink is of an entirely non-profit making character and we would exhort all our readers to make every possible use of them. A form advertising the titles available, with prices, will be found with this issue except in the case of U.S. readers who should order supplies direct from *The Bible Truth Depot*, P.O. Box, 86, Mifflinburg, Penna., U.S.A.

"THE GODHOOD OF GOD"*

A. W. PINK.

Faith is that which gives God *His proper place*. And if we give God *His* proper place, we must take *our* proper place, and that is in the dust. And what is there that will bring the haughty, self-sufficient creature into the dust so quickly as a sight of the Godhood of God! Nothing is so humbling to the human heart as a true recognition of · the absolute sovereignty of God. The chief trouble is that so much that passes for faith today is really only maudlin sentimentality. The faith of Christendom in this twentieth century is mere credulity, and the "god" of many of our churches is not the Father of our Lord Jesus Christ, but a mere figment finite mind *can* understand, whose ways are pleasing to the *natural* man, a "god" who is altogether "such a one as" (Ps. 50: 21) those who profess to worship him, a "god" concerning whom there is little mystery. But how different the God which the Holy Scriptures reveal! Of *Him* it is said, His ways are *"past finding out"* (Rom. 11: 33). To particularize:

1. The "god" of the moderns is altogether lacking in *power*. The popular idea of today is that deity is filled with amiable intentions but that Satan is *preventing* the making good of them. It is not God's will, so we are told, that there should be any wars, for wars are something which men are unable to reconcile with *their* ideas of Divine mercy. Hence, the conclusion is, that all wars are of the Devil. Plagues and earthquakes, famines and tornadoes, are not sent from God, but are attributed solely to *natural* causes. To affirm that the Lord God sent the recent Influenza epidemic as a judgment scourge, would be to shock the sensibilities of the modern mind. All such things as this are a cause of *grief* to "god" for "he" desires nought but the happiness of everybody.

2. The "god" of the moderns is altogether lacking in *wisdom*. The popular belief is that God loves everybody, and that it is His will that every child of Adam should be saved. But if this be true, He is strangely lacking in wisdom, for He knows quite well that under existing conditions the majority will be lost . . .

3. The "god" of the moderns is lacking in *holiness*. That *crime* deserves punishment is still allowed in part, though more and more the belief is gaining ground that the criminal is really an object of pity rather than of censure, and that he stands in need of education and reformation rather than of punishment. But that SIN—sins of thought as well as deed, sins of the heart as well as the life, sins of omission as well as commission, the sinful root itself as well as the fruit—should be *hated* by God that His holy nature burns against it, is a concept that has gone almost entirely

* An extract from the booklet of the same title. Available price 6d. pp. 31.

out of fashion ; and that the sinner himself is *hated by God* is indignantly denied even among those who boast most loudly of their orthodoxy.

4. The " god " of the moderns is altogether lacking in a *sovereign prerogative*. Whatever *rights* the deity of present-day Christendom may be supposed to possess in theory, in fact they must be *subordinated* to the " rights " of the creature. It is denied, almost universally, that the rights of the Creator over His creatures is that of the Potter over the clay. When it is affirmed that God has the right to make one as a vessel unto honour, and another as a vessel unto dishonour, the cry of injustice is instantly raised. When it is affirmed that salvation is a *gift* and that this gift is bestowed on whom God pleases, it is said He is *partial* and unfair. If God has any gifts to impart, He must distribute them evenly, or else bestow them on those that *merit* them, whoever they may be. And thus God is allowed less freedom than I, who may disburse my charity as I best please, giving to one beggar a quarter, to another a dime, and to a third nothing at all if I think well.

How different is the God of the Bible from the " god " of the moderns! The God of Scripture is *all-mighty*. He is one who speaks and it is done, who commands and it stands fast. He is the One with whom " all things are possible " and " who worketh all things after the counsel of *His own will* " (Eph. 1: 11) . . .

The God of Scripture is *infinite in wisdom*. No secret can be hidden from Him, no problem can baffle Him, nothing is too hard for Him. God is *omniscient*—" Great is our Lord, and of great power: *His understanding is infinite* " (Ps. 147: 5). Therefore is it said, " There is no searching of His understanding " (Is. 40 28). Hence it is, that in a revelation from *Him* we expect to find truths which transcend the reach of the creature's mind, and therefore the presumptuous folly and wickedness of those who are but " dust and ashes " undertaking to pronounce the reasonableness or unreasonableness of doctrines which are *above* their reason!

The God of Scripture is infinite in *Holiness*. The " only true God " is He who hates sin with a perfect abhorrence, and whose nature eternally burns against it. He is the One who beheld the wickedness of the antediluvians and who opened the windows of Heaven and poured down the flood of His righteous indignation. He is the One who rained fire and brimstone upon Sodom and Gomorrah and utterly destroyed these cities of the plain. He is the One who sent the plagues upon Egypt, and destroyed her haughty monarch together with his hosts at the Red Sea. So holy is God and such is the antagonism of His nature against evil, that for one sin He banished our first parents from Eden ; for one sin He cursed the posterity of Ham ; for one sin He turned Lot's wife into a pillar of salt ; for one sin He sent out fire and devoured the sons of Aaron ; for one sin Moses died in the wilderness ; for one sin Achan and his family were all stoned to death ; for one sin the servant of Elisha was smitten with leprosy. Behold therefore, not only the goodness, but also " the *severity* of God " (Rom. 11: 22). And *this* is the God that every Christ-rejector has yet to meet in judgment!

The God of Scripture has a *will* that is *irresistible*. Man talks and boasts of *his* will, but *God* also has a will! Men had a will on the plains of Shinar and undertook to build a tower whose top would reach unto heaven ; but what came of it ? God had a will, too, and *their* willful effort came to naught. Pharaoh had a will when he hardened his heart and refused to allow Jehovah's people to go into the wilderness and there

331

worship Him, but what came of it ?   God had a will, too, and being Almighty *His* will was performed.   Balak had a will when he hired Balaam to come and curse the Hebrews ; but of what avail was it ?   The Canaanites had a will when they determined to prevent Israel occupying the promised land ; but how far did they succeed ?   Saul had a will when he hurled his javelin at David, but instead of slaying the Lord's anointed, it entered the wall instead . . .

Yes, my reader, and *you* had a will when you formed your plans without first seeking counsel of the Lord, and therefore did He *overthrow* them.   As well might a child seek to prevent the ocean from rolling, as for a creature to try and resist the outworking of the purpose of the Lord God—" O Lord God of our fathers, art not Thou God in heaven ? and rulest not Thou over all the kingdoms of the heathen ? and in Thine hand is there not power and might, so that none is able to withstand thee ? " (2 Chron. 20: 6).

The God of Scripture is *absolute Sovereign*.   Such is His own claim: " This is the purpose that is purposed upon the whole earth: and this is the hand that is stretched out upon all nations.   For the Lord of hosts hast purposed, *and who shall disannul it* ? and His hand is stretched out, and who shall turn it back ? " (Is. 14: 26, 27).   The Sovereignty of God is absolute and irresistible : " All the inhabitants of the earth are reputed as nothing: and He doeth according to His will in the army of heaven, and among the inhabitants of the earth: and *none* can stay His hand, or say unto Him, What doest Thou ? " (Dan. 4: 35).   The Sovereignty of God is true not only hypothetically, but in fact.   That is to say, God *exercise* His sovereignty, exercises it both in the natural realm and in the spiritual.   One is born black, another white.   One is born in wealth, another in poverty.   One is born with a healthy body, another sickly and crippled.   One is cut off in childhood, another lives to old age.   One is endowed with five talents, another with but one.   And in all these cases it is God the Creator who maketh one to differ from another, and " none can stay His hand."   So also is it in the spiritual realm.   One is born in a pious home and   is brought up in the fear and admonition of the Lord ; another is born of criminal parents and is reared in vice.   One is the object of many prayers, the other is not prayed for at all.   One hears the Gospel from early childhood, another never hears it.   One sits under a Scriptural ministry, another hears nothing but error and heresy.   Of those who *do* hear the Gospel, one has his heart " *opened* by the Lord " to receive the truth, while another is left to himself.   One is " ordained to eternal life " (Acts 13: 48), while another is " ordained " to condemnation (Jude 4).   To whom He will God shows mercy, and to whom he wills He " hardens " (Rom 9: 18).

A New Publication by The Sovereign Grace Book Club

The Five Points of Calvinism.   Articles by H. Bonar, J. Gill. J. Edwards, J. Calvin, A. Fuller.   Containing also *Let Patience Have Its Perfect Work*, by T. Goodwin.   (16/6).

Obtainable from the English branch of the Sovereign Grace Book Club, 1. Cliff House, Weston Lane, Southampton.   Cheques and postal orders payable to T. E. Watson.

Wickliffe Press, Wickliffe Avenue, 104 Hendon Lane, Finchley, N.3.

THE
BANNER of TRUTH

(11th Issue)

Subscription for six
issues, $1.25.

EDITOR:

IAIN MURRAY, B.A.
78B Chiltern, Street,
London, W. 1.

ASSISTANT EDITOR:
ERROLL HULSE.

*   *   *

"Thou hast shewed thy people hard things;
Thou hast made us to drink the wine of
astonishment.   Thou hast given a banner to
them that fear Thee, that it may be displayed
because of the truth."   Psalm 60 : 3-4.

*   *   *

CONTENTS

M

INFORMATION FOR READERS

This magazine is not a periodical, published at fixed intervals, but is designed rather as a booklet which can be of permanent usefulness and reference. The time of publication is therefore determined by the amount of edifying material which we have available for printing and not by our committal to any particular dates. We trust this will help to preserve the quality of the contents. Back numbers are available except issues 1 and 2. Subscribers to the magazine will, from time to time, be freely sent news of books published by The Banner of Truth Trust.

U.S. price for 6 issues $1.25 including postage.

A sample copy will gladly be sent to any of your friends whom you believe would be interested. All money received is put to the cause of spreading the truth. We gratefully acknowledge the assistance given to date in this respect by our subscribers.

JULY 1958

ADVICE ON READING

RICHARD BAXTER (1615-1691).

" **Make careful choice of the books which you read : let the holy scriptures ever have the pre-eminence, and, next to them, those solid, lively, heavenly treatises which best expound and apply the scriptures; and next, credible histories, especially of the Church . . . but take heed of false teachers who would corrupt your understandings.**"

1. As there is a more excellent appearance of the Spirit of God in the holy scripture, than in any other book whatever, so it has more power and fitness to convey the Spirit, and make us spiritual, by imprinting itself upon our hearts. As there is more of God in it, so it will acquaint us more with God, and bring us nearer Him, and make the reader more reverent, serious and divine. Let scripture be first and most in your hearts and hands and other books be used as subservient to it. The endeavours of the devil and papists to keep it from you, doth shew that it is most necessary and desirable to you.

2. The writings of divines are nothing else but a preaching of the gospel to the eye, as the voice preaches it to the ear. Vocal preaching has the pre-eminence in moving the affections, and being diversified according to the state of the congregation which attend it : this way the milk comes warmest from the breast. But books have the advantage in many other respects : you may read an able preacher when you have but a mean one to hear. Every *congregation* cannot hear the most judicious or powerful preachers : but every *single person* may *read* the books of the most powerful and judicious ; *preachers* may be silenced or banished, when *books* may be at hand : *books* may be kept at a smaller charge than preachers : we may choose books which treat of that very subject which we desire to hear of ; but we cannot choose what subject the preacher shall treat of. Books we may have at hand every day and hour ; when we can have sermons but seldom, and at set times. If sermons be forgotten, they are gone ; but a *book* we may read over and over, till we remember it : and if we forget it, may again peruse it at our pleasure, or at our leisure. So that good books are a very great mercy to the world : the Holy Ghost chose the way of writing, to preserve His doctrine and laws to the Church, as knowing how easy and sure a way it is of keeping it safe to all generations, in comparison of mere verbal traditions.

3. You have need of a judicious teacher at hand, to *direct* you what books to use or to refuse : for among good books there are some *very good* that are sound and lively ; and some are good, but mean, and weak, and somewhat dull ; and some are *very good* in part, but have mixtures of error, or else of incautious, injudicious expressions, fitter to puzzle than edify the weak.

FORERUNNERS OF THE ENGLISH REFORMATION

"Salvation considered as coming from man is the creating principle of all error and all abuse. The excess produced by this fundamental error led to the Reformation and the profession of a contrary principle achieved it. This feature must stand prominently out in an introduction to the History of the Reformation." Dr. Merle D'Aubigné.

An overall view of English church history reveals a natural division into a series of cycles. These cycles may be compared to a succession of advancing and receding tides. They begin with awakening, lead to spiritual progress and prosperity, then terminate in declension and apostasy. The length of these periods may vary greatly, but the general features remain the same.[1] The first such cycle began with the introduction of Christianity into Britain in the first century of our era and its powerful conquest over the satanic evils of Druidism. This cycle ended in the fifth century when the British church had become corrupted by Pelagianism and was fearfully judged by the invasions of the Saxons (A.D. 449). For the following one hundred and fifty years no visible church existed in England, till with the advent of the Celtic missionaries (notably Aidan who evangelised Northumberland A.D. 635-651) began a new period of spiritual prosperity. But again this was succeeded by doctrinal error and decay of piety. The church entered the long "Dark Ages", and was visited by such judgments as the invasions of the Danes and Vikings (A.D. 835 onwards) and the Norman Conquest (1066), which brought the English people for the first time under complete Papal domination.

In the fourteenth century a revival of the truth seemed a forlorn hope, but this, in fact, proved to be the period when God began to prepare the nation for the great Reformation which was to come two centuries later. A study of the leaders of this preparatory work will provide us with lessons well fitted to guide us today, and the way in which they faced a situation somewhat similar to our own should make their lives of peculiar interest to us.

The walled city of Oxford, surrounded by woods and lazy streams, perhaps possessing in the early fourteenth century some 1,500 students and boasting an academic pre-eminence second only to that of Paris, was the starting point of this revival. It was here in the early years of that century that a young student from Chichester, Thomas Bradwardine (c.1290—1349), was awakened to the truth of the Gospel. He narrates his experience in these words

---

[1] "Histories are but the advertisement, memorial and token of the work and judgment of God, of the way in which He upholds, governs, hinders, advances, punishes and rewards the world and specially men as each may deserve, be it evil or good."—*Martin Luther*.

—" I was at one time, while still a student of philosophy, a vain fool, far from the true knowledge of God, and held captive in opposing error. From time to time I heard theologians treating of the questions of grace and free will, and the party of Pelagius appeared to me to have the best of the argument. For I rarely heard anything said of grace in the lectures of the philosophers except in an ambiguous sense, but every day I heard them teach that we are the masters of our own free acts, and that it stands in our own power to do either good or evil. And when I heard now and then in church a passage read from the Apostle which exalted grace and humbled free will—such, e.g. as that word in Romans 9, " So then it is not in him that willeth, nor in him that runneth, but in God that sheweth mercy," and other like places— I had no liking for such teaching, for towards grace I was still unthankful. . . . But afterwards, and before I had become a student of theology, the truth before-mentioned struck upon me like a beam of grace . . . wherefore, also, I give thanks to Him who has freely given me this grace."

Henceforth the determining influence in Bradwardine's life was to make known to his fallen age the truth of the grace of God. He was the first to go further than seeking the reform of mere external abuses. He went to the root of the matter by tracing the decadence of the church to her Pelagian doctrine, her denial of man's total depravity and her ignorance of the sovereignty of God.

Bradwardine's abilities soon brought him into prominence. In 1325 we find him a proctor of the University, and his theological lectures at Merton College soon earned him the title of " The Profound Doctor ". These lectures, which were eagerly listened to and circulated through all Europe, were later expanded into a famous treatise—" *De Causa Dei Contra Pelagium* " (*Of The Cause of God Against Pelagius*). This was a book which the Puritans were to make use of in the seventeenth century Arminian controversy. A godly Archbishop of Canterbury, George Abbot, secured its publication in printed form in 1618 in a folio volume of nearly 1,000 pages.

A few quotations from this great work will illustrate its nature and spirit. "As in the times of old 450 prophets of Baal strove against a single prophet of God; so now, O Lord," he exclaimed, " the number of those who strive with Pelagius against thy free grace cannot be counted . . . the will of man (they say) should precede and thine follow ; theirs is the mistress and thine is the servant . . . alas, nearly the whole world is walking in error in the steps of Pelagius. Arise O Lord and judge thy cause." Bradwardine defines predestination as " God's eternal fore-ordination or predetermination of his will respecting what shall come to pass." God's will is not conditional, depending on man for its fulfilment, but it is "universally efficacious and invincible . . . it cannot be impeded, much less can it be defeated and made void by any means whatever." To drive this truth home, Bradwardine goes on—" If you allow (1) that God is able to do a thing, and (2) that he is willing to do a thing, then (3) I affirm that thing will not cannot, go unaccomplished. God does it now or will certainly do it at the destined season; otherwise he must either lose his power or change his mind." "If the will of God could be frustrated and vanquished, its defeat would arise from the created wills either of angels or of men, but could any created will whatever, whether angelic or human, counteract and baffle the will of God, the will of the creature must be superior in strength to the will of the Creator." From such solid reasonings as these Bradwardine concludes "Whatever things come to pass, they are brought to pass by the providence of God."

In 1338 Bradwardine was appointed a chaplain to King Edward III and the duties of that office called him from his lecture rooms at Oxford to accompany the King on his French campaigns. He was present at the famous victory of Crécy and the capture of Calais. Such was his moral influence upon the King and his troops, that many contemporaries attributed the English success to the holiness of their chaplain rather than to the valour of their army. Bradwardine's services to the King led to his appointment in 1348 to the Archbishopric of Canterbury; but this, unfortunately for the nation, was a position he was never to exercise, for returning to England on the 19th August, 1349, he fell a victim to the Black Death then raging and died at Lambeth on the 26th of the same month.

This deadly plague which suddenly swept perhaps a third or half of the English population into the grave, proving a terrible blow to the agriculture and economy of the nation, may have been the means of awakening another Oxford student to eternal realities. At any rate we learn from Wycliffe's later writings that it made an impression on his mind that could not be effaced. John Wycliffe (c.1324—1384) was at this time in his twenties, having come up to Oxford from his ancestral home near Richmond in the North Riding of Yorkshire to study for the priesthood. None of the traditional events of his early life, his date of birth, his first college at Oxford and his first written works, are free from uncertainty. It is likely he was influenced by the moral earnestness and theological erudition of Richard Fitzralph (The Chancellor of the University from 1333 to 1347); it is just possible he heard Bradwardine lecture and it is certain he was greatly helped by the latter's writings.

The first clear historical fact relating to Wycliffe's career is that in 1361 we find he had risen to the distinguished position of Master of Balliol College. Though he resigned this position after a brief tenure on being presented to the living of Fillingham, in Lincolnshire, it is nevertheless evident that he continued to spend much of his time teaching in Oxford up till the summer of 1381. Sometime between 1365 and 1372 we know he became a Doctor of Theology. About the same time he first became known as a public figure, not so much as a spiritual leader, but as a patriotic champion of England's secular rights against Papal encroachments. In the employment of the Crown he attended sessions of Parliament and, by denying the Pope's right to exercise authority in secular affairs, successfully advocated the rejection of Papal taxation. On behalf of the Government he treated with the Papal delegates at Bruges in 1374 and after his return was promoted by the King to the Rectory of Lutterworth. Wycliffe's insistence on a division between spiritual and secular offices aroused the wrath of the English prelates (men who were accustomed to holding wealthy political positions) but for the moment Wycliffe's Parliamentary friends shielded him from danger. The Papal bulls sent to condemn him in 1377 had no effect. The following year angry rivalry in the Vatican led to the election of two Popes and the resultant schism within the Papacy which lasted for half a century diverted the Vatican's attention from the English Reformer. Wycliffe was given three years respite and now with his eyes fully open to the real nature of the Papacy and the true needs of his times, he appeared as a spiritual Reformer. He denied transubstantiation, spoke of the Papacy as Anti-Christ, alleged that since the year 1000 all the doctors of the church had been in error, and threw himself into an attack on Pelagian theology. But his work was not merely negative; in a series of tracts and books he poured forth the substance of his former studies. He began the vitally important work of training students to itinerate and preach the Gospel,[1] and above all, he took the momentous step of shaking the dust of ages off the Latin Bible and translating it into English. These activities were the beginning of a great movement. Although Wycliffe was compelled to leave Oxford in 1381 and died at Lutterworth in 1384, it was not before he had raised a testimony to the truth that nothing could silence. " He filled all England and almost all Europe with his doctrine," wrote Bishop Newton. His followers, " the Lollards " (as they were called) were to stand fast through a hundred and fifty years of bitter persecution till the Reformed Church of England espoused the faith they had suffered to preserve.

It appears that the doctrine which inspired this fourteenth

---

[1] The aims of faithful ministers, Wycliffe taught, should be :—" firstly, that the law of God may be steadily known, taught, maintained and magnified; secondly, that great and open sin which reigneth in diverse states be destroyed and also the heresy and hypocrisy of Anti-Christ and of his followers; thirdly, that very peace and posterity and burning charity be increased in Christendom and particularly in the realm of England, for to bring men readily to the bliss of Heaven."

century awakening was chiefly the sovereignty of God and the belief in God's electing grace. Perhaps no other age in English church history has produced two such predestinarians as Bradwardine and Wycliffe. They were men who understood the truths which their age needed; they grasped the remedy which the errors of their times required and they were not afraid to apply it. " It was Wycliffe's conviction," writes Dr. Merle D'Aubigné, that " to believe in the power of man in the work of regeneration is the great heresy of Rome, and from that error has come the ruin of the church. Conversion proceeds from the grace of God alone, and the system which ascribes it partly to man and partly to God is worse than Pelagianism."[1] Professor Lechler in his summary of Wycliffe's theology refers to " one peculiar feature " which " runs like a scarlet thread through the whole system of Wycliffe's thinking—we mean the thought that the Church is nothing else than *the whole number of the elect*. It is to this thought," he continues, " that we have to direct our attention before every other, for this concerns the eternal ground of the Church while all other parts of the discussion relate to its temporal manifestation and life.

"According to Wycliffe, the eternal ground or basis of the church, lies in the *Divine election*. He always defines the Church to be the communion or the whole body of the elect. In other words, he places himself in deliberate opposition to the idea of the Church which prevailed in his time and expressly disapproves of those notions and forms of speech according to which men took the Church to mean the *visible* Catholic Church—the organised communion of the hierarchy. Wycliffe on the contrary seeks the Church's centre of gravity in the past eternity, in the invisible world above; for to him the Church is essentially Christ's body or Christ's bride, according to the well-known apostolic figures. A soul is incorporated with Christ, or betrothed to Christ, not by any act of man, not by any earthly means and visible signs, but by the decree of God according to His eternal election and foreordination. The Church, therefore, has in the visible world only its manifestation, its temporary pilgrimage; it has its home and its origin, as also its end, in the invisible world in eternity. Every individual devout Christian owes all that he possesses in his inner life to the regeneration which is the fruit of election. It is only by virtue of the gracious election of God that the individual belongs to the number of the saved . . . Wycliffe carries back conversion, salvation, and membership of the Church to the election of grace, i.e., to the eternal and free decree of God in Christ."[2]

One or two quotations from Wycliffe will illustrate his position. He refers to Holy Scripture as " The faultless, most true,

[1] *History of The Reformation of the Sixteenth Century,* vol. V p. 95, 1865, Collins edit.

[2] *Lechler's Life of Wycliffe*, pp. 315-316, R.T.S. edit. 1904.

most perfect and most Holy Law of God, which it is the duty of all men to learn to know, to defend, and to observe." Faith in Scripture is the gift of God, " Christian men receive their faith of God as His gracious gift; He giveth them the knowing and the understanding of truths . . . giving them grace to assent in their hearts to those truths. . . . The Holy Ghost teaches us the meaning of Scripture." This grace is not given to all; " There are two classes of men," he observes, " who stand over against each other, since the world's beginning to the world's end. The first class, that of the elect, begins with Adam, and descends through Abel and all the elect to the last saint who, before the final judgment, shall contend for the cause of God. The second class is the reprobate. . . ."

Wycliffe encountered the arguments always used against defenders of the truth. " It maketh dissension and enmity," said some. To this he replied that there is a kind of peace which the Author of the Gospel came not to establish, and that the only peace which may be innocently left unbroken, is that which is founded on right principles. "His views and rebukes were uncharitable," said others. If his reproofs were uncharitable, replied Wycliffe, then the life of Christ, of his Apostles, and of the prophets who preceded them, must set a dangerous example to the Church. "Almighty God," he observes, " who is full of charity, commandeth the prophet Isaiah, to cry and cease not, and to shew the people their great sins. . . ."

Wycliffe's life and work is one of the great turning points of Church history. When he died the Reformation had begun. Minds had been enlightened, souls converted, and preachers sent to the corners of the land. By " the seriousness of his language, the holiness of his life and the energy of his faith," he left an example that multitudes were to follow. " He must have been," says J. C. Ryle, " singularly filled with the Holy Ghost." In Bohemia his teaching resulted in a great revival, led by John Huss. Even on the Continent, therefore, the way to Reformation was in great measure prepared by his work. As a bold and fearless witness to the truth when it was least popular Wycliffe reminds us of an Old Testament prophet. As an exponent of the doctrines of grace he anticipated the Reformers. " Wycliffe," writes D'Aubigné, " is the greatest English Reformer. If Luther and Calvin are the fathers of the Reformation, Wycliffe is its grandfather."

* * *

" It is the property of a good Christian, and of true grace, to observe what work God is doing, and to help on that work: what God is doing in the world, and to help that on ; what God is doing upon his own heart, and to help that on. ' O Lord,' saith the soul, ' help me! ' ' I will help thee, I will put my shoulder unto thy work as thou art pleased to put thy hand to my duty."—*William Bridge* (1600-1670).

THE FREE OFFER OF THE GOSPEL

Viewed in the light of the Marrow controversy.

The use of the term " offer " in the presentation of the Gospel was introduced occasionally by the Reformers and taken up by the Puritans to describe the manner in which God holds out salvation to all hearers of the Gospel call. " God invites all indiscriminately by outward preaching," says Calvin, and in this invitation " is the grace of God offered to us " (Calvin's Tracts, vol. III, p. 253-4, C.T.S. edit.). " The mercy of God is offered equally to those who believe and to those who believe not " (The Eternal Predestination of God, p. 79, Cole's edit.). The Reformed Confessions all endorsed this position. The great international Synod of Dort (1618), consisting of delegates from all the Reformed Churches, affirmed : " It is the promise of the Gospel that whosoever believeth in Christ crucified should not perish, but have life everlasting : which promise, together with the injunction of repentance and faith, ought promiscuously, and without distinction, to be declared, and published to all men and people " (Ch. 2, art. 5). Likewise the Westminster Confession (1646) : " He freely offereth unto sinners life and salvation by Jesus Christ, requiring of them faith in him, that they may be saved " (Ch. 7, art. 3).

But it is perhaps true to say that, in Britain at any rate, it was not until the early eighteenth century that the lawfulness of this term "offer" was first fully discussed. This came about in Scotland through the famous " Marrow " controversy—a controversy in which, among other issues, the universal Gospel offer was called into question. The dispute was occasioned by the re-publication of a Puritan work, " The Marrow of Modern Divinity," in 1718. The book was condemned by the General Assembly of the Church of Scotland, and those who approved its teaching—" the Marrowmen " as they were nicknamed—were called upon to defend and elucidate the free offer of the Gospel. Three great preachers, Thomas Boston (1676-1732), Ebenezer Erskine (1680-1754) and Ralph Erskine (1685-1752) contributed most to this defence and left a permanent mark on Scottish evangelical preaching.

The question at issue was whether or not there is a universal call to all sinners to receive Christ with a promise (or offer) of mercy to all that do so. The opposers of the Marrow-men denied this universal call and offer, and maintained rather that only the conscious sinner, the convinced and the contrite, have a warrant to come to Christ. Christ is only to be held forth, they said, to prepared and penitent sinners; none are to be called to believe on the Saviour but those possessing these inward marks. Now the Marrow-men replied that such a restricted presentation of the Gospel was Scripturally defective and practically harmful. Defective in that it made the sinner's warrant to believe turn on his inward qualifications instead of solely on the divine command and promise. Harmful in that it leads to bondage. The hearer is directed to his own heart rather than to Christ and becomes involved in questionings whether he is so truly humbled for sin as to have access to the Saviour. The convicted, doubting soul, feeling nothing but his hardness and impenitency, may thus be led to regard any approach to Christ as presumption—for he believes he has not been called and that Christ has promised him no welcome.

It was against this background that the Marrow-men sought to defend a universal Gospel offer which all sinners *as such* have a warrant and obligation to believe. They taught that it was:

(1) *A Free Offer.* " Christ invites all without distinction, even the worst of sinners, to this spiritual feast: Isa. 55 : 1, ' Ho, every one that thirsteth ,. . .' ; Rev. 22 : 17, ' And whosoever will, let him take of the water of life freely.' These are gospel-invitations, clogged with no conditions, comprehending all who are willing to receive Christ, whatever their case is or has been " (*Boston's Works*, edited by McMillan, vol. X, p. 95, 1854 edit.). To the objection that Isa. 55 : 1 refers only to conscious sinners who are thirsting after Christ, Boston replies that the context shews that the thirsting ones invited are such as are spending money for that which is not bread and their labour for that which satisfieth not, they are not thirsting after Christ but after satisfaction in an empty creation—a thirst after happiness which is natural to all mankind. Similarly on the text " Come unto me, all ye that labour and are heavy laden " (Matt. 11 : 28), Boston says : " The words, labouring and heavy laden, do not restrict the invitation to such as are sensible of their sins, but they denote the restlessness of the sinful souls of men—their hearts being full of unsatisfied desires " (*Gospel Truth Accurately Stated And Illustrated* from the writings of the Marrow-men by John Brown of Whitburn, p. 289, 1831 edit.). He supports his statement with these reasons: (a) The words agree to all out of Christ and none have any right to restrict them. All who are out of Christ labour seeking their satisfaction in the creatures—"All things are full of labour . . ." Eccles. 1 : 8. They all carry a burden of sin and wrath. The word properly signifies a ship's lading, which, though insensible of it, may sink under the weight. (b) The words in other Scriptures are without controversy applied to the most insensible sinners, Isa. 55 : 2. "Ah, sinful nation, a people laden with iniquity ! " Were they sensible? far from it, for, " Israel doth not know, my people doth not consider " (Isa. 1 : 3-4). (c) All without exception that hear the Gospel are called to come to Christ, Rev. 3 : 20. And if any¬

one be not called, they have no warrant to come; and if so, unbelief is not their sin, as in the case of the heathen; which is absurd.[1]

(2) *A Particular Offer.* "The general call and offer of the Gospel reaches every individual person (who hears it), and God speaks to every sinner as particularly as though he named them by his name and surname. Remission of sins is preached to *you,* we beseech *you* to be reconciled, the promise is unto *you*; and for my part I do not know what sort of a Gospel men make, who do not admit this" (E. Erskine in *Gospel Truth,* p. 355)

(3) *A Real and Sincere Offer.* God is not offering something which He is unwilling to bestow. "God offers Christ cordially and affectionately in the gospel; his very heart goes out after sinners in the call and offer thereof. It is not possible to conceive anything more affectionate than the words in which he bespeaks sinners, Isa. 55 : 1-3; Ezek. 33 : 11; Hos. 11 : 8. God's whole heart and soul is in the offer and promise of the Gospel" (E. Erskine, *Gospel Truth,* p. 365).

"Many do not consider, nor believe that Christ is knocking at the door of their hearts for admission, and therefore they do not bestir themselves to receive him. But believe it, it is no fancy, but the most certain reality, and therefore I say to you and to each of you : 'To you is the word of this salvation sent' . . . Christ is willing to come into every heart.[2]   Why does he demand

---

[1] In thus stressing the freeness of the Gospel the Marrow-men were not ignoring the necessity of a preparatory work of conviction in the sinner, but they were denying that conviction provides the warrant to believe. "It is a truth till men be convinced of their sin, they will not prize the Saviour, but Jesus is offered to all without exception. In the preaching of the Gospel he is presented to the careless and impenitent, as much as to the most contrite and convinced. Indeed, if Christ were not offered to sinners *as such,* penitent persons would absolutely despair, for who is more hardened in their own reckoning than themselves ? " (*Gospel Truth,* p. 486).   They quoted with approval Samuel Rutherford's dictum—" reprobates have as fair a warrant to believe as the elect have." (*Boston's Works,* VII, p. 487).

[2] The sense in which Boston uses this expression is discussed on page 14. To show that Boston was not alone in believing such language to be in accord with the strictest orthodoxy we add the following striking quotation: "God does not here (Hosea 13: 14) simply promise salvation, but shews that he is indeed ready to save, but that the wickedness of the people was an impediment in the way. 'I will redeem them,' as far as this depends on me. What, then, does stand in the way ? Even the hardness of the people; for they would have preferred to perish a hundred times rather than to turn to the Lord . . . We may learn from this passage, that when men perish, God still continues like himself, and that neither his power, by which he is mighty to save the world, is extinguished, nor his purpose changed, so as not to be always ready to help; but that the obstinacy of men rejects the grace which has been provided, and which God willingly and bountifully offers."—*John Calvin* on *Hosea* (1559). Calvin Trans. Soc. Edit, pp. 476-7.

open doors, but because he is willing to enter ? Though the house be not worthy of his presence, though he has received many indignities from it and in it, yet he is willing to grace it with his royal presence. . . . See the glory of his willingness to save ! His whole word is full of demonstrations of this " (*Boston's Works,* III, pp. 102-106).

(4) *A Commanding Offer.* " Sinners must come in. ' Compel them to come in ' (Luke 14 : 23). Sirs, ye not only may come, but ye must come, even the worst of you. Ye are not only desired to come in, but ye must not abide without. Consider, ' This is his commandment, that ye believe ' (1 John 3 : 23). Ye are peremptorily commanded to come in. Therefore I charge you in his Name to come in, and not disobey his peremptory command. Those that were first bidden to this supper, they would not come, but they sent their excuses : but were their excuses sustained ? No ! God passes a peremptory sentence against them (Luke 14 : 24), ' None of those men which were bidden, shall taste of my supper.' We dare admit no excuses in this matter, bring them from whence ye will, whether from God's greatness, your own vileness, or the world's incumbrances. Whatever your case be, ye are commanded of God to come ; and his commands are not to be disputed, but obeyed . . . This is the duty God has commanded you : (John 6 : 29) ' This is *the* work of God, that ye believe on him whom he hath sent.' This is the great comprehensive duty : If ye do this, ye do all ; if ye do not this, ye do nothing. . . . ' He that believeth not shall be damned ' (Mark 16 : 16). (*Boston's Works* VI, pp. 288-9).

(5) *An Urgent and Solemn Offer.* " It is in this world only the call takes place (Matt. 28 : 18-19). As for those who are gone into the other world, the call can reach them no more; they are prisoners without hope . . . This Gospel is the Lord's farewell sermon to the world. It is God's last grace to the world (Heb. 1). No other dispensation of grace shall ever the world see more. Now, Sirs, the last ship for Immanuel's land is making ready to go; therefore now or never ! (Heb. 10 : 26-27). . . . The more frequent, and the more solemn offers that are made to sinners, the greater is their contempt which they pour upon the Son of God. And every sermon will add to their account; so that I doubt not but many of us, if they hold on as they are doing in slighting Christ and his ordinances, the day will come, in which they will wish from their hearts they had never lived where sermons were to be heard. And reflections on these will cut them to the heart for ever more ! Of all vengeance that which follows a despised Gospel is the most dreadful. ' But I say unto you, that it shall be more tolerable for the land of Sodom in the day of judgment than for thee.' . . .

O children of the house of hell, close with the offer of adoption into God's family ! I beseech you to accept it, nay, I charge

you to come out from among them this day, and enter into God's
family through Jesus Christ, under the pain of God's eternal
displeasure " (*Boston's Works* V, p. 358; II, p. 453; III, p.99;
I, p. 651).

Two main questions will probably occur to many after reading all these quotations.

*Firstly, Does this evangelism differ from Arminianism ? Is there
any real difference ?* We answer that it does differ and differ profoundly in these leading respects :

(a) Arminians deduce from the offers and invitations of the Gospel
that man has the ability to respond; for, they say, the sinner cannot be called upon to do what is out of the compass of his power.
The Marrow-men, in contrast, asserted the true distinction
between what a man *may* and *ought* to do, in point of warrant,
and what he *can* or *will* do. They affirmed God's right to call
and command, but also man's sinful inability to repent and believe.
None taught human depravity more clearly than Boston and the
Erskines.

(b) Consequently the Marrow-men held that only God's internal
regenerating work can make the external Gospel call efficacious.
This internal work is confined to the elect. " Many are called (by
an outward call), but few are chosen " (Matt. 22 : 14, cf. Acts
13 : 48). E. Erskine classes among " damnable and soul-ruining
errors " the Arminian opinion that sufficient grace is given to every
man that hears the Gospel to repent if he chooses (*Gospel Truth,*
p. 349).

(c) Arminians generally hold that the universal offer of salvation
includes a declaration that Christ made atonement for every man
and that God intends to save each one if men will let Him. The
Marrow-men did not teach this. They affirmed that while the
Gospel offer expresses God's revealed purpose to save all who
believe on His Son, it does not express God's unrevealed and
sovereign will as it relates to election and the extent of the atonement. Although God's secret will regulates all His dispensations
towards His creatures, it forms no part of the rule either of our
faith or of our duty. The unconverted are not called upon to believe
that they are elected or that Christ died for them in particular.

The Marrow-men denied universal redemption. According
to Boston Christ did not die " to render sin remissable in all
persons and them savable," rather He made " full satisfaction in
behalf of the elect " (*Works* VII, p. 241). " Let Arminians maintain at their peril their universal redemption," says Ralph Erskine,
" but we must maintain at our peril the universal offer " (*Gospel
Truth,* p. 385).

(d) Arminians hold that God loves all men equally and alike; the
Marrow-men affirmed that the universal expression of God's

benevolence and compassion contained in the Gospel offer was not the same as His electing love.

Secondly, If Christ's death was only for the elect, how can the non-elect be offered a pardon, when, as far they are concerned, no atonement has been made ? In reply to this difficulty, we can only say that we believe that, while Scriptures do teach the general invitations of the Gospel *and* the particular and special work of Christ, they do not choose to reveal clearly how both truths are consistent with each other. Nor is it necessary that they should do so, for our conduct is not to be governed by our understanding of all the grounds and reasons of God's procedure but by His commands.   A minister should preach a full, unfettered Gospel because God has commanded it to be preached to every creature. He has forbidden his ministers to exclude any man from the offer (Mark 16 : 15). " The sole ground or warrant for men's act, in offering pardon and salvation to their fellow-men, is the authority and command of God in His word. We have no other warrant than this; we need no other ; and we should seek or desire none; but on this ground alone should consider ourselves not only warranted, but bound, to proclaim to our fellow-men the good news of the kingdom, and to call upon them to come to Christ that they may be saved " (*W. Cunningham's Historical Theology,* vol. II, pp. 347-8).

But if we grant our inability to harmonize a limited atonement with unlimited offers of Gospel mercy that is no proof of any real *inconsistency* between the two. We are bound to believe that they are consistent with each other though we may not be able to perceive and develop this consistency. This is a point at which the scriptural believer recognizes that his faith is not a human system but that it contains depths and reasons fully known only to the mind of God. At the same time we can go as far as saying this : The Gospel offer contains nothing that is not absolutely truthful. All who comply with its directions shall certainly be saved. If some will not comply the cause lies in themselves. The decree of reprobation leaves men to do as they like and it is only their sin that hinders them from trusting in Christ.

Finally, we can observe that the sincerity of God's offer even to the non-elect is in accordance with the truth that God does *desire, delight* and *approve of* things which, for other reasons, He has not *determined* to carry into effect. This distinction can be illustrated from God's commandments. His commandments express what He desires should be done. When the Israelites disobeyed them He cries—" O that my people had hearkened unto me." " O that thou hadst hearkened to my commandments ! then had thy peace been as a river . . ." (Psa. 81 : 13; Isa. 48 : 18; Deut. 5 : 29). Unmistakably such verses express what was God's desire. Yet we must say that though their actions were, *in their own nature,* displeasing to God, He had nevertheless willed and permitted such conduct for wise and holy ends. Similarly with the Gospel offer. God desires that everyone should believe it; He has no pleasure in the death of the wicked (Ezek. 33 : 11) but delights in their conversion[1]—thus Christ yearned for the salvation of the people of Jerusalem (Matt. 23 : 37). Yet this desire, in the case of the non-elect, is for the fulfilment of something which in His inscrutable counsel and sovereign purpose He has not actually decreed to come to pass. This distinction between God's desire and His will, or, more correctly stated, between the will of God's benevolence and His decretive will, underlies the free offer of the Gospel.[2] His benevolence and compassion, expressed in the universal call to repentance, extend to every creature even to those whom He has not decreed to save. At this mysterious evidence of the unsearchable character of God's ways the humble believer stops and says with Calvin " we go no farther than the Lord leads us by his Word."

[1] " God delights in the conversion and eternal life of the sinner, as a thing pleasing in itself, and congruous with his infinitely compassionate nature, and therefore demands from man as a duty due from him to turn if he would live."—*Francis Turretin* (1623-1687), Professor of Theology at Geneva. Quoted in W. G. T. Shedd's Dogmatic Theology, vol. II, p. 483 (1889 edit.).

[2] This distinction may be a new one to many readers but it is far from novel. *Calvin*, in expounding 2 Pet. 3:9 (God is " not willing that any should perish "), distinguishes between God's wish or revealed will and His determinate (hidden) purpose in the following words: " But it may be asked, If God wishes none to perish, why is it that so many perish ? To this my answer is, that no mention is here made of the hidden purpose of God, according to which the reprobate are doomed to their own ruin, but only of his will as made known to us in the Gospel. For God there stretches out his hand without a difference to all, but lays hold only of those, to lead unto himself, whom he has chosen before the foundation of the world." *Commentaries on The Catholic Epistles*, p. 419.
A helpful exposition of the texts relating to the above distinction will be found in a recent booklet entitled *" The Free Offer of The Gospel"* by *Professors Murray* and *Stonehouse* of Westminster Theological Seminary; pp. 27, price 25 cents., obtainable from Lewis J. Grotenhuis, Belvidere Road, Phillipsburg, New Jersey, U.S.A.

APPENDIX

Quotations from The Puritans on The Free Offer of the Gospel.

" Will you have a proof of Christ's earnest suit to gain the hearts of sinners ? His whole life upon earth was a great proof of it ; His doctrine, so full of pathetical invitations, proves it ; the joy of His heart at the success of the gospel ; His tears and sorrows for the obstinacy of unbelievers ; His labours and travels to gather sinners to Him ; His admirable encouragements put into general invitations ; His dreadful threatenings to all that reject His motions ; His commissionating and qualifying, continuing and encouraging His ministers to carry on His suit in His name: all these things make up a full demonstration that Jesus Christ is an earnest suitor for union and communion with the souls of sinners."—*John Flavel* (1627-1691) *Works*, vol. IV, p. 120, 1820 edit.
" ' Behold I stand at the door and knock; if any man hear my voice, and open the door, I will come in to him . . . ' (Rev. 3: 20). This expression

extends the gracious offer of Christ, and brings in hope to every hearer . . . as if Christ should say, I will have this offer of my grace to go round to every particular person; if thou, or thou, or thou, the greatest, the vilest of sinners, will hear my voice, and open to me, I will come into their souls. And hereby all objections are obviated; as for example, 'I am the greatest of sinners,' saith one; 'I have been a self-cozening hypocrite,' saith another; 'I have resisted grace too long, and doubt the time of mercy is past,' saith a third. The ground of all these, and a thousand more objections, is taken away by the gracious extent of Christ's offer in the text: for who is he that can limit where Christ does not ? "—*Flavel*, vol. IV, p. 143.

[The above quotations are from Flavel's exposition of Rev. 3: 20— an exposition extending to 251 pages. We personally see no weight in the objection that this passage in Revelation is addressed to the church and not applicable to the unconverted—for the *visible* church contains believers and unbelievers, elect and non-elect. Flavel's use of this text is common amongst the orthodox Puritans, c.f. *David Clarkson's* treatise on Rev. 3: 20, entitled '*Christ's Gracious Invitation To Sinners*' (Works, vol. III, pp. 34-100), and *Obadiah Sedgwick's* '*The Riches Of Grace Displayed In The Offer And Tender Of Salvation To Poor Sinners.*' William Dyer, John Cotton and Increase Mather also wrote on this text. Ed.]

" Though the efficacy and benefit (of Christ's death) be intended to believers, yet God's offer of Christ, and the publication of the gospel, is general: Isa. 55: 1; Rev. 22: 17. No man can plead that God left him out . . . God hath expressed enough of His will to show man his duty, though not enough of His will to tell man His pleasure and secret intention . . . ' Secret things belong unto the Lord . . . ' (Deut. 29: 29). The proposal of Christ in the gospel, that is a revealed thing, and it belongeth to the creatures.

That God is serious and in good earnest in these offers, appeareth—
1. By His entreaties. He beseecheth you to take Him as well as offereth Him: Ezek. 33: 11, 'Turn ye, turn ye from your evil ways; for why will you die, O house of Israel ? ' 2 Cor. 5: 20, ' Now then we are ambassadors for Christ, as though God did beseech you by us.'
2. Because it suiteth more with His delight that you should take hold of these offers and not refuse them: Ezek. 33: 11, ' As I live, saith the Lord, I have no pleasure in the death of the wicked.' Merely as it is the destruction of the creature, so God doth not any way approve of it, though, as a just punishment, He delighteth in it. If you look to God's approbation your accepting grace more suiteth with it than your refusal.
3. Because He is angry that you do refuse: John 5: 40. He is grieved that men, through their own folly, neglect that which should do them good: Matt. 23 37, ' O Jerusalen, Jerusalem . . . how often would I have gathered thy children together, even as a hen gathereth her chickens under her wings, and ye would not ? ' He meant by His outward ministry, though not inward call. He was mighty solicitous and earnest in that. So though God use all the means with us, and give us all the light that possibly can be unto His will, excepting saving light, we turn unto our own way."— *Thomas Manton* (1620-1677) *Works*, vol. III, pp. 330-335.

" They who are judged at the last day " (for not receiving the Gospel) " will be speechless and have nothing to reply . . . Because *they despise an overture of a treaty about peace and reconciliation* between God and their souls. God who hath no need of them, nor their obedience or friendship, tenders them a treaty upon terms of peace. What greater condescension, love, or grace could be conceived or desired ? This is tendered in the gospel, 2 Cor. 5: 19. Now, what greater indignity can be offered unto Him than to reject His tenders ? Is not this plainly to tell

Him that they despise His love and scorn His offers of reconciliation ? . . .
It is life and salvation that He tenders, on whose neglect He complains
that men will not come unto Him that they might have life. Certainly there
can be no want of righteousness in the ruin of such persons."—*John Owen*
(1616-1683) on Heb. 3: 3, *Works* vol. XX, pp. 308-9, Goold's Edit.

" There is a twofold calling, one external only, consisting in the tender
and offer of grace, inviting of men to come in ; in which sense our Saviour
said, ' Many are called, but few are chosen.' The other internal and
efficacious also, when God with the outward offer changeth the heart,
making it to embrace Christ."—*Anthony Burgess* (1656), *Spiritual Refining*,
p. 582.

" Thou wilt confess one day, I might have had mercy. I was offered
Christ and grace. I felt Him knocking by His Spirit ; but I slighted Him,
grieved Him, and rejected Him, and now it is just with God to shut the
door of mercy against me."—*Obadiah Sedgwick* (1600-1658).

" Whatsoever be the Lord's secret decrees concerning the salvation of
some and condemnation of others ; yet the means of execution of those
decrees shall not be particularly revealed to the stumbling of any man,
but the offer of grace and declaration of God's goodness is so laid out in
common, that whosoever doth not embrace the same, is made inexcusable ;
for when God saith, ' O that my people had hearkened unto me ' (Psa.
81: 13), he that doth not answer the Lord, with, ' O that thou wouldest
frame this heart of mine to the obedience of faith,' hath nothing to say
if he be damned, for slighting of the offer so freely held forth unto him,
and pressed upon him."—*David Dickson* (1583-1662) *Commentary on the
Psalms*.

EXTRACT FROM A SERMON BY
R. M. McCHEYNE (1813-1843) ON PROV. 8 : 4

It is commonly thought that preaching the holy law is the most
awakening truth in the Bible ; and, indeed, I believe this is the most
ordinary means which God makes use of. And yet to me there is something far more awakening in the sight of a Divine Saviour offering Himself to every one of the human race. There is something that might pierce
the heart that is like a stone in that cry: ' Unto you, O men, I call ; and
my voice is to the sons of men.' (Prov. 8: 4) . . . Very often awakened
persons sit and listen to a lively description of Christ, of His work of
substitution in the stead of sinners ; but their question still is, ' Is Christ
a Saviour to me ? ' Now, to this question I answer, Christ is freely
offered to all the human race. ' Unto you, O men, I call . . . " There is
no subject more misunderstood by unconverted souls than the unconditional
freeness of Christ. So little idea have we naturally of free grace, that
we cannot believe that God can offer a Saviour to us, while we are in a
wicked, hell-deserving condition. Oh, it is sad to think how men argue
against their own happiness, and will not believe the very word of God!

' If I knew I were one of the elect, I would come ; but I fear I am
not.' To you I answer, Nobody ever came to Christ because they knew
themselves to be of the elect. It is quite true that God has of His mere
good pleasure elected some to everlasting life, but they never knew it till
they came to Christ. Christ nowhere invites the elect to come to Him.
The question for you is not, Am I one of the elect ? but, Am I of the
human race ?

' If I could repent and believe, then Christ would be free to me ; but
I cannot repent and believe.' To you I say, Are you not a man, before
you repent and believe ? then Christ is offered to you before you repent.

(*Continued on page* 21)

CAUSES OF APOSTASY FROM THE GOSPEL

John Owen 1616-1683.

[John Owen, one of the greatest of Puritan divines, was educated at Queen's College, Oxford, where he took his M.A. in 1635. While at College, his ambitions after political and ecclesiastical eminence were broken by his conversion, and in the year 1637, rather than conform to the unscriptural statutes of Archbishop Laud, he left the university and thus gave up, as far as he could see, at the age of 21, all hope of advancement. But after Laud's fall under the Long Parliament, Owen rose rapidly and after pastorates at Fordham and Coggeshall in Essex, he was made in 1651 Dean of Christ Church, Oxford. The following year he became Vice-Chancellor of the University. The Civil Wars had left the University bankrupt and in chaos. Owen reorganised it with conspicuous success, and, assisted by such Puritans as Thomas Goodwin, his preaching and teaching made a profound impression on many of the students. After the Restoration of Charles II in 1660, Owen led the Independents through the succeeding years of bitter persecution. He died in London in 1683 after a long and painful illness.

The following article is an extract from Owen's great work on Apostasy published in 1676. In it Owen examines the causes of the landslide from purity of doctrine, conduct and worship that took place after 1660. This book is one of the finest of Owen's works. Dr. Doddridge wrote— "Owen's style resembles St. Paul's. There is great zeal and much knowledge of human life discovered in all his works, especially in his book on Apostasy." Owen's complete works were last published in 1862 in twenty-four volumes. The Treatise on Apostasy extends to some two hundred and fifty-nine pages in Volume VII of this edition.]

Before taking up the main subject of his book Owen first demonstrates that there exists in persons and churches alike a universal proneness and readiness to relinquish and fall away from an orthodox profession of the Gospel. This inclination to turn aside from true doctrine he proves from the predictions of the apostles and from the experience of the Church in all ages : " No instance can be given of any Church or nation in the world, which ever received the profession of the Gospel, that did not sooner or later, either totally or in some considerable degrees, fall off from the doctrine which it reveals and the obedience which it requires." Even New Testament Churches, such as the Corinthian and Galatian, who from the ability, authority and infallibility of the apostles, had the most forcible reasons for constancy, often lapsed from their first profession. In the early centuries the Arian and Pelagian heresies provide " woeful evidence of the instability of professors," and again in our own times, says Owen, there is " sad evidence of the proneness of men to forego the truths of the Gospel after they have been instructed in them. . . . How great an inroad has been made on our first profession (whether for better or for worse the great day will discover), by that system of doctrines which from its author, and for distinctions sake, is called Arminianism ! As Pelagianism did gradually insinuate itself into the vital spirits of the body of the Church in those days, proving a poison unto it, so under its new varnish it will be received, until it diffuse itself into the veins and vitals of the present reformed Church. There is a demonstrative coincidence between the beginning of our visible apostasy from piety and the admission of these novel opinions, contrary to the faith of the first reformed Churches."

After laying down as a principle that " a defection from the truth of the Gospel once professed is a sin of the highest guilt, and that which will result in the most pernicious events," Owen proceeds to state seven general causes of apostasy : —

(1) *The enmity to spiritual things which is in man's mind by nature, abiding uncured under a profession of the Gospel, is the first spring of apostasy.*

" Men on various accounts may take upon themselves the profession of the truths of the Gospel whilst their natural enmity ("the carnal mind is enmity against God," Rom. 8 : 7) abides and predominates in their minds. Thus, upon the first preaching of the Gospel, many were convinced of its truth, and took upon them its profession, merely on account of the miracles that were wrought in its confirmation, whose hearts were not in the least reconciled unto the things contained in it (John 2 : 23; Acts 8 : 23). When our Saviour preached after his feeding five thousand with five barley loaves and two small fishes, the multitude being prepared in their minds by the miracle they saw, were so affected with his doctrine that they cried out, " Lord, evermore give us this bread," John 6 : 37; but upon his procedure to instruct them in heavenly mysteries, they put in exceptions to his doctrine, vv. 41, 52, 60, and immediately forsook both him and it, v. 66. And our Saviour assigns as the reason for their defection their unbelief, and adds that it was not given unto them of the Father to come unto him, vv. 64, 65, or the enmity of their carnal minds was yet unremoved."

Similarly in all ages, Owen argues, "many are prepossessed with notions of the truth of the Gospel in their education, by the outward means of instruction that have been applied unto them; but yet, notwithstanding this advantage, they may still abide under the power of this depravation of their minds." When exposed to errors such persons will therefore soon receive them, " because all error is some way suited unto the mind as thus depraved and there is somewhat in every error to recommend itself unto the vanity, or curiosity, or pride, or superstition of the carnal mind."

(2) *Spiritual darkness and ignorance, abiding in the minds of men under the profession of the truth, is a cause of apostasy.*

" Multitudes of those who profess the truth never had a view of its spiritual glory because of the darkness of their minds, and therefore have no experience of its power and efficacy, nor are their hearts and lives influenced and guided by it. When the doctrines of the Gospel are thus taken rationally into the unrenewed minds of men they have no stable grounds whereon to stand in the profession of the truth against temptation, opposition, or seduction. Mere notions of truth, or the knowledge of the doctrines of it, enabling us to talk of them or dispute for them, will preserve none from defection.

When men learn that they may know, and are satisfied with what they know, without an endeavour to find the life and power of what they know in their hearts, their assent to the truth will have no stability accompanying it. The immediate purpose (with respect unto us) of the whole revelation of the mind and will of God in the Scripture is, that it may put forth a *spiritual, practical power in our souls.* He who hath learned to be meek, humble, lowly, patient, self-denying, holy, zealous, peaceable, to purify his heart, and to be useful in his life, is indeed the person who is best acquainted with evangelical truth. That knowledge which does not present the things known, believed, and perceived, as *lovely, excellent,* and *desirable unto the will and affections,* is a " cloud without water," which every wind of temptation will scatter and blow away.

(3) *The innate pride and vanity of the minds of men is another means whereby they are inclined unto an apostasy from the profession of evangelical truth.*

The mind of man is naturally lifted up with high thoughts of itself. It exalts *imaginations* of its own, which it loves and dotes on. It makes *itself* the sole and *absolute judge* of what is divinely proposed unto it, whether it be true or false, to be received or rejected, without desire or expectation of any supernatural guidance or assistance. Wherefore, when men have taken on them the outward profession of the Gospel, they begin to find, upon inquiry, that the principles of its doctrines are unsuited to the natural pride of their minds. Hereon they give up themselves to the conduct and teaching of others, who have invented opinions more suited to the innate pride of their minds.

Hence it is that all those doctrines of the Gospel which are not absolutely reconcilable unto reason as corrupt and carnal, are by many so laden with contempt and scorn that it is sufficient to expose any man unto the contumelies of " ignorant, irrational, and foolish," who dares to avow them. Such are the doctrines of eternal predestination, of the total corruption of the nature of men as unto spiritual things by the fall, of the power and efficacy of the grace of God in the conversion of sinners. . . . Many can see no reason for the admittance of these things, and therefore (although they are fully declared in the Scriptures) they are so derided and exploded as that the very names of them are grown into contempt. But why all this scorn, all this severity ? Men may do well to consider, that not long since all the prelates of

England owned those doctrines as articles of faith which now they
so deride.

(4) *The work of Satan is to promote apostasy.* He was the
head of the first apostasy from God and ever since God hath been
pleased to make known the way of salvation by Jesus Christ his
two great designs and works in the world have been to keep men
off from receiving the Gospel, and to turn them aside who have
received it. His principal design in the world hath been, and
continueth yet to be, the corrupting of the minds of men about
the truth, and drawing them off from it, in part or in whole. So
the apostle intimates, " I fear, lest by any means, as the serpent
beguiled Eve through his subtilty, so your minds should be corrupted . . ." (2 Cor. 11 : 3).

(5) *Judicial blindness is connected with apostasy.* God does
not look on all these things as an *unconcerned spectator.* He tempts
none, but he rules all and overrules all events to his own glory. He
will not suffer men first to undervalue and then to reject and forsake the choicest of his mercies, such as his word and truth are,
without visiting them with some acts of his severity. Wherefore,
when men, from the corrupt principles mentioned, seduced by the
lusts of their own hearts, and entangled by the deceits of Satan,
do relinquish the truth, God, in his holy, righteous judgment, gives
them up unto *further delusions,* so that they shall complete their
apostasy, and grow obstinate therein unto their destruction. When
a people, a nation, or a church, have received the Gospel and the
profession thereof, not walking answerably thereunto, God may
forsake them, and *withdraw from them the means of their edification and preservation.* And this he does,—First, *By removing his
candlestick from among them.* This the Lord Jesus threatens his
back-sliding church withal, Rev. 2 : 5. God will deprive them of
the light and means of knowledge of the truth so that darkness
shall irresistibly increase upon them. Some of the instruments of
light, it may be, shall be taken away by death,* and some shall
lie under prejudices; the gifts of the Spirit shall be restrained or
withheld from others. Secondly, in this condition God " sends
them strong delusion," 2 Thess. 2 : 11, by *delivering them up to
the power of Satan and suffering false teachers to come among a
people* with such advantageous outward circumstances as shall
further their success. Lastly, God doth *judicially* smite persons with
blindness of mind and hardness of heart, that they shall not see,
nor perceive, nor understand. This effect of God's severity is
declared, Isa. 6 : 9, 10; and application is made of it unto the
Jews under the ministry of our Saviour himself, John 12 : 39-41,

*Not long after Owen wrote this in 1676, several of the leading Puritans
were removed by death: Manton and Greenhill in 1677, Thomas Goodwin
and Matthew Poole in 1679, Charnock and Brooks in 1680, T. Gouge in
1681, T. Case (the last of the Westminster divines) in 1682, and Owen himself in 1683.—Ed.

and that of the apostles, Acts 28 : 25-27, and is expounded, Rom. 9 : 7, 8. When things are come to this issue, then is the state of such apostates miserable and irrecoverable.

RECOVERY FROM APOSTASY.

What is the best way, means, or expedient, to be plied unto this end ? I say it is only the diligent ministerial dispensation of the word; the truth of the Gospel will be no otherwise preserved in a nation, church, or people, but by this means of God's appoint-ment. When God shall be pleased to give unto the people who are called by his name, in a more abundant manner, " pastors after his own heart, to feed them with knowledge and understanding;" when he shall revive and increase a holy, humble, zealous, self-denying, powerful ministry, by a more plentiful effusion of his Spirit from above; then, and not until then, may we hope to see the pristine glory and beauty of our religion restored unto its primitive state and condition. And if the preaching of the Gospel be the only sovereign, effectual means appointed by God for the change of men's natures and the reformation of their lives, *it is a vain expectation* that either of them will be wrought in such a way as to restore the glory of religion in the world, *unless provision be made for an able ministry to instruct the body of the people.* Here, then, must begin the cure of that lethargy in sin that the world is fallen into—namely, in the renovation of a powerful evangelical ministry.

McCheyne Extract.—(*Continued from page* 16.)

And, believer, Christ is not offered to you because you repent, but because you are a vile, lost sinner. ' Unto you, O men, I call . . .'

If Christ be freely offered to all men, then it is plain that all who live and die without accepting Christ shall meet with the doom of those who refuse the Son of God. Ah! it is a sad thing that the very truth, which is life to every believing soul, is death to all others . . . Oh, brethren, you are without excuse in the sight of God, if you go home unsaved this day! If you could die and say that Christ had never been offered to you, you would have an easier hell than you are likely to have! You must go away either rejoicing in or rejecting Christ this day ; either won, or more lost than ever. There is not one of you but will yet feel the guilt of this Sabbath day. This sermon will meet you yet. ' How shall we escape if we neglect so great salvation ? '—*Memoirs of McCheyne*, Moody Press edition, p. 196).

BAXTER'S GUIDE TO THE VALUE OF A BOOK—

While reading ask oneself :

1. Could I spend this time no better ?
2. Are there better books that would edify me more ?
3. Are the lovers of such a book as this the greatest lovers of the Book of God and of a holy life ?
4. Does this book increase my love to the Word of God, kill my sin, and prepare me for the life to come ?

REPRINTS OF TWO FAMOUS WORKS

Republished by *The Sovereign Grace Book Club,* 1124 Southeast First Street, Eastville 13, Indiana, U.S.A.

British Agent: Mr. T. E. Watson, 1 Cliff House, Weston Lane, Southampton.

Human Nature In Its Fourfold State by *Thomas Boston,* $4.95.

Thomas Boston was born at Duns, in Scotland, educated at Edinburgh University (1691-1694), and exercised his powerful and successful ministry at Simprin (1699-1707) and Ettrick (1707-1732). His life, characterised by habits of prayer, study and fasting, is recorded fully in his ' *Memoirs* ' which he wrote for his children ; in an introduction to the 1899 edition of this classic ministerial autobiography the Rev. G. H. Morrison wrote thus of Boston's ' Fourfold State ' :

" If ever a book was steeped in prayer, it was that ' Fourfold State.' From the Tuesday in January, 1712, when Boston first put pen to paper for its final draft, it was daily spread before a throne of grace, and found its place in every family fast. At times it looked as if the book would never see the light . . . and it was not till November, 1720, that Boston handled a bound copy of his work. Almost immediately it took hold. New editions were called for, and testimonies of its usefulness came pouring in. It was discussed in Edinburgh drawing-rooms. The shepherd read it on the hills. It made its way into the Highland crofts, where stained and tattered copies of the earlier editions may still be found. For more than a hundred years its influence upon the religious life of Scotland was incalculable. And to-day . . . there are great parts of Scotland in which one cannot move among the people, and catch the accent of their more serious talk, and listen to their prayers, without perceiving, howsoever dimly, that the influence of Boston's masterpiece is unexhausted yet. Nor need one wonder at the power of it. It is so orderly and clear, so rich in just and beautiful citation, so searching, and here and there so softening ; it is so strong in its appeals, so full, for all its doctrine, of warmth and human life; it is so couched in language of the homeliest and truest ring, rising at times into unquestionable eloquence, that the secret of its acceptance is not far to seek."

The book, as the title suggests, is divided into four main divisions. Man is considered in the state of innocence (prior to the Fall), the state of nature, the state of grace, and the eternal state. This is a work all can and should read. When John Brown of Haddington lay on his death-bed this was the book he exhorted his children to study. We hope it will again be widely read.

The Existence And Attributes Of God by *Stephen Charnock*, (1628-1680), pp. 802. $8.95.

"The existence of God is the foundation of all religion. Moses begins with the author of creation, before he treats of the promise of redemption. Paul preached God as a creator (Acts xvii. 24) before he preached Christ as mediator . . ." From such principles as these Charnock proceeds to an exposition of God's character and perfections which is unparalled in the English language. Conscious of the majesty and greatness of God as all the Puritans were, Charnock's work on this subject stands alone in its depth and intensity of light. The Puritans believed that low views of God were the ultimate cause of all errors and all sins and that the communication of a true knowledge of the Divine character is the supreme purpose of creation and redemption—it meets the sinner's greatest need and should be the foremost theme of the Gospel minister. Surely our times call for a recovery of this realization ; Charnock's message was never more needed.

The following quotations will give some idea of the character of this book :

"We are as far fallen from the holiness of God as the lowest point of the earth is from the highest point of the heavens . . . More distant we are from God by reason of sin than the vilest creature, the most deformed toad, is from the highest and most glorious angel."

"There is nothing under the heavens that the affections of human nature stand more point blank against, than against God . . . None seeks God as his rule, as his end, as his happiness ; man desires no communion with God ; he places his happiness in anything inferior to God ; he prefers everything before Him, glorifies everything above Him, judges God unfit to be conversed with and cares not whether He has a being in the world or not."

"The sovereignty of God as a lawgiver is most abhorred by man . . . As soon as ever it appeared in creation, the devils rebelled against it in heaven, and man would have banished it from the earth. This is the great quarrel between God and man, whether He or they shall be the sovereign ruler . . . The devil attempted to share God's sovereignty and tempted man to share it . . . Most of the errors of men may be resolved into a denial of God's sovereignty."

"Sin unlinks the dependence between God the sovereign and man the subject. Sin endeavours to subject God to the wills of men. God is deposed, and man enthroned ; God made a slave, and man a sovereign above Him."

"The devil directs his fiercest batteries against those doctrines in the Word, and those graces in the heart, which most exalt God and bring men to the lowest subjection to their Creator."

"Man is always gaining or losing something. The holiness, happiness and wisdom of saints is capable of increase and diminution . . . (but) if there were any change in God He would be sometimes what He was not, and He would cease to be what He was ; change implies defect, if God were changeable He were not infinite and almighty."

This large volume of Charnock will demand time, concentration and all the faculties—mind, will and heart—of the reader. It is pre-eminently a book for ministers and students. His style, unlike that of his colleague Thomas Watson, is not always the most readable ; his conceptions are profound and elevated and no half-hearted reader can expect to follow him. But to the serious reader this reprint will prove a lifelong treasure.

Other recent reprints of the Sovereign Grace Book Club are :

1. *The Returning Backslider.* A commentary on Hosea XIV by *Richard Sibbles ;* This same volume contains *God's Providence Unfolded In The Book of Esther* by *Alex. Carson.* $3.95.

2. *An Exposition of Galatians* by *John Brown, D.D.* $4.95.

" SERVANTS OF THE WORD."

Under the above title the six addresses given at the last Puritan Conference are now available in booklet form. Mimeographed, pp. 71, 2/6 or 3/- by post. The subjects dealt with at this year's Conference were: "The Puritans And The Lord's Day"; "The Savoy Conference, 1661 "; "Thomas Shepard's ' Parable Of The Ten Virgins ' "; " John Bunyan And His Experience "; " The Puritan Principle of Worship "; " Daily Life Among The Puritans." The Chairman of the Conference, Dr. Lloyd-Jones, in summing up said that there is no justification whatever for the difference that undoubtedly exists between Puritan daily life and that of Christians to-day. We desire to have the Christian life made easy, and to take it easily ; but only spurious Christianity comes easily ; true godliness demands self-discipline, self-examination and a serious single mindedness.

The next Puritan Conference, held annually at Westminster Chapel, London, S.W.1, is planned for Dec. 16th and 17th, 1958. We believe many of our readers will wish to obtain a copy of the above addresses from the *Rev. David Fountain, 275 Spring Road, Southampton.*

BANNER OF TRUTH PUBLICATIONS

❀

DOCTRINE

A Body of Divinity by Thomas Watson. pp. 226. $3.25. "One of the most precious of the peerless works of the Puritans." — C. H. Spurgeon.

The Doctrine of The Holy Spirit by George Smeaton. pp. 384. $4.50. ". . . provides in many ways the best practical teaching on this subject."— Dr. Martyn Lloyd-Jones.

SERMONS AND BIOGRAPHY

Princeton Sermons by Charles Hodge. pp. 400. $4.50. 249 Sermon outlines providing "an amount and quality of homiletical example and suggestion probably not surpassed in the same number of pages in the English language."—A. A. Hodge.

Select Works of Jonathan Edwards. Vol. I, pp. 180. $2.95. Contains a biography by Iain Murray, Edwards' account of the great 1735 revival at Northampton and three of his famous sermons.

Select Sermons of George Whitefield. pp. 128. $2.25. "Once let the evangelical ministry of England return to the ways of the 18th century and I firmly believe we should have as much success as before."—J. C. Ryle.

COMMENTARIES

Joel, by John Calvin. pp. 132. $2.25. An exposition of a most relevant book of Scripture by the foremost commentator of the 16th century.

Zechariah, by Thomas V. Moore. pp. 250. $3.25. "A capital book ; most useful to ministers."—C. H. Spurgeon.

Song of Solomon, by George Burrowes, pp. 456. $4.25. "I cannot speak too highly of this work . . . It has everything that should characterize a good commentary."—Dr. Martyn Lloyd-Jones.

Jonah, by Hugh Martin. pp. 386. $3.95. ". . . manifests the superb qualities which all of Martin's writings exemplify."—Prof. John Murray.

Jude, by Thomas Manton. pp. 378. $4.25. "If anyone wants to buy a good specimen of a Puritan divine, my advice unhesitatingly is, ' let him buy Manton.' "—J. C. Ryle.

(Available June 23rd, 1958).

❀

The Bible Depot, P.O. Box 86, Mifflingburg, Penna., U.S.A.

Wickliffe Press, Wickliffe Avenue, 104 Hendon Lane, Finchley, N.3.

THE
BANNER of TRUTH

(12th Issue)

Price 9d.

Subscription for six issues, 6/6.

EDITOR:

IAIN MURRAY, B.A.
78B CHILTERN, STREET,
LONDON, W. 1.

ASSISTANT EDITOR:
ERROLL HULSE.

＊　　＊　　＊

"Thou hast shewed thy people hard things; Thou hast made us to drink the wine of astonishment.　Thou hast given a banner to them that fear Thee, that it may be displayed because of the truth."　　Psalm 60 : 3-4.

＊　　＊　　＊

CONTENTS

361

INFORMATION FOR READERS

This magazine is not a periodical, published at fixed intervals, but is designed rather as a booklet which can be of permanent usefulness and reference. The time of publication is therefore determined by the amount of spreading the truth. We gratefully acknowledge the assistance given of edifying material which we have available for printing and not by our committal to any particular dates. We trust this will help to preserve the quality of the contents. Back numbers are available except issues 1 and 2. Subscribers to the magazine will, from time to time, be freely sent news of books published by The Banner of Truth Trust.

Subscription for 6 issues 6/6 including postage.

SEPTEMBER, 1958

BRITAIN'S SOLE PRESERVATIVE—
AN OUTPOURING OF THE SPIRIT

JOHN BROWN OF HADDINGTON.

Let our political managers project what schemes they will, for the reformation and salvation of our nation, they will but issue in vanity and vexation of spirit. The Lord hath rejected their confidences, and they shall not prosper in them. Nothing but a remarkable outpouring of the Spirit of God can prevent our superlative miseries, answerable to our heaven-daring national iniquities. As no civil socities have any existence in the future state, national sins must of necessity be punished with national judgments in this world, Jer. v. 9, 29 ; Hosea iv. 1-3 ; Isa. xxiv. 5, 6.

(1). The Jewish nation, to whose mercies and crimes those of Britain are peculiarly similar in different ages, were shut up to fearful judgments, for want of an effusion of the Holy Ghost. Not all the faithfulness of Moses, and their other governors, nor all the piety of Aaron and his sons, and of the faithful Levites in their church, nor all the laws which they received from God Himself, and the innumerable miracles which they saw and felt, could preserve that sensual generation, destitute of the Spirit, from tremendous ruin in the wilderness. Not all the fervent prayers and faithful sermons of Isaiah and his fellow-prophets, nor all the remarkable reformation carried on by pious King Hezekiah, could prevent the miserable calamities of the Jews in their time, as the Spirit was not poured out. Nay, not all the labours and miracles of Christ Himself, and of His apostles, and the pious lives and fervent prayers of many thousand Christian Jews, could, without the pouring of the Spirit on them, prevent the ruin of their nation in that period. Why, then, should we hope for deliverance by any other method ? Dare we pretend that we are dearer to God than His peculiar people, the seed of Abraham, His friend ?

(2). The sins of Britain at present are so great, many, universal, heaven-daring, heart-hardening, and conscience-stupefying, and, in every respect, so aggravated, that the nation can neither be duly convinced of them, nor the blood of Christ answerably applied for the remission of them, without a remarkable effusion of the Holy Ghost, John xvi. 7-14 ; Ezek. xxxvi, 25-29 ; Micah vii. 18, 19.

(3). The wicked manners of Britain have been so long continued, and are become so universal and fashionable, and are so much encouraged by such as should be reprovers and reformers, —and men's consciences thereby so much blinded, biased, or hardened, that there can be no national reformation of them, without a remarkable outpouring of the Spirit of God, Hosea iv. 1, 2, 6 ; Isa. i. 2-5 ; lix. 1-15 ; lvii. 17; Jer. v. 1-9.

(4). So many thousands of unsent, careless, indolent, unholy, and erroneous preachers in Britain, by their legal, Arminian, or blasphemous doctrine, and by their impious and unedifying example, lay a fearful bar in the way of all the ordinary work of the Holy Ghost, Hosea v. 1 ; Gal. iii. 2 ; Ezek. xiii. 22.

But, not withstanding all these things, an abundant effusion of the Holy Ghost would prevent our superlative ruin.

(a). It would excite and enable all the fearers of God, in the nation, to strive together in prayer for our preservation and proper relief, Zech. xii. 10 ; Isa. lxii. 1, 6, 7 ; Psalm cii. 17.

(b). In consequence of this, it would furnish our land with a proper number of well-qualified ministers, who, having received their mission from Christ, would clearly, faithfully, assiduously, and earnestly preach the gospel of His free grace, and by fervent prayer, holy example, and every other method, travail in birth to win souls to Him, Jer. iii. 15 ; Isa. lxii. 1, 6, 7 ; Psalm cxxxii. 9, 16 ; John xx. 21-23 ; Eph. v. 10, 13.

(c). It would furnish these faithful ministers with proper messages from God, suited to His own gracious purposes, and to the spiritual state of the hearers, and would enable them to deliver them in a lively, serious, and affecting manner, Ezek. iii. 3, 4, 10, 11, 17-21 ; xxxiii. 7-9 ; Mic. iii. 8 ; Acts xviii. 25, 28; Col. i. 28, 29; 1 Thess. i. 4, 5 ; 1 Cor. ii. 2-5, 13 ; iv. 2 ; 2 Cor. iv. 2 ; v. 11, 22; 2 Tim. iv. 2 ; Acts xx. 19-21, 26, 27.

(d). It would procure large and attentive audiences to hear these faithful ministers, Acts ii, xiii, xv. xix ; 1 Cor. xvi. 9 ; Acts xvi. 14; Isa. xlix. 1 ;lii. 15.

(e). It would, in carrying home the Word of God into men's consciences and hearts, convey to them the spiritual benefits of the new covenant,—conviction of sin, union to Christ, regeneration, justification, adoption, sanctification, and comfort, Luke v. 17; John vi. 63 ; Heb. iv. 12 ; 1 Thess. i. 5 ; ii. 13 ; Acts ii. 36-47.

(f). It would incline, direct, and enable those ministers and people to such an holy conversation towards God and men, as would adorn and enforce the preached gospel of Christ, and make others to consider and fall in love with it, 1 Thess. ii. 1-10; v. 12-25; Rom. i. 8 ; Acts ii. 41-47 ; iv. 13 ; Phil. ii. 1, 16; Matt. v. 16; Tit. ii. 9-14 ; iii. 8, 14 ; Psalm ci. 2-8.

(g). It would render all ranks, in their respective stations, active and skilful in spreading the knowledge of Christ and His truths, and in repressing the now fashionable abominations, Gen. xviii. 19 ; Josh. xxiv. 15; Deut. vi. 6, 7 ; Mal. iii. 16 ; Psalm ci ; 2 Chron. xvii. ; xix.; xxix. -xxxii. ; xxxiv.; xxxv. ; Song ii. 15; Tit. iii. 10, 11 ; Rev. ii. ; 1 Thess. v. 14; 2 Tim. iv. 2 ; 1 Tim v. 20.

(Continued on page 29).

REFLECTIONS ON REVIVALS

The ways of God in nature and in His Church bear some striking similarities. The life of nature is characterised by its seasons and changes—winter and spring, drought and rainfall. Just so is the life of the Church. Her spiritual life is not always at the same level; sometimes it is high and sometimes very low. Now when the Church moves out of a period of barrenness into a period of refreshing and new life that transition is generally described by the term revival. Strictly speaking the word means to *bring back to life* and thus refers to the re-awakening of Christians; but in popular use it has come to have a wider meaning and conveys the idea of a rapid and powerful work of the Holy Spirit resulting in multiplied conversions. In revivals that which the Spirit normally does in calling and convicting particular individuals is done simultaneously in many souls and what might ordinarily be the work of years is concentrated into perhaps a few weeks or months. Thus in a sense the day of Pentecost is repeated.

Revivals are a historical fact. The outpouring of the Spirit which established the Protestant Church four hundred years ago was the greatest revival since apostolic times. It was a revival at Cambridge towards the close of the sixteenth century, during the ministry of Perkins and others, that empowered the Puritan movement. It was a series of revivals between 1596 and 1638, under such men as Bruce, Welsh, Dickson and Livingstone, that preserved the Church of Scotland in her struggle with the forces arrayed against her. It was a revival—" one of the largest manifestations of the Spirit that almost since the days of the apostles hath been seen "—that mightily re-planted the Gospel in Northern Ireland in 1625. It was in the spirit of revival that the great New-England churches were born from 1630 onwards. And when the glorious seventeenth century had passed nothing could restore the situation until the Spirit was again poured out from on high. The work appeared in South Wales shortly after the conversion of Rowland and Harris in 1735; in 1739 it broke out in England under Whitefield and Wesley at London and Bristol; and in 1742 a remarkable revival occurred in Scotland at Cambuslang. This eighteenth century awakening spread far and wide (Yorkshire, Bedfordshire and Cornwall felt its power in an uncommon degree) and continued, with intervals, for a number of years. But by the close of the eighteenth century, and in the first half of the nineteenth, revivals appear to have been confined largely to North Wales (commencing at Bala in October, 1791) and to parts of Scotland (at Moulin, in 1798 and 1800; in Skye, in 1812 and 1814; in Lewis, in 1824 and 1835; at Kilsyth, Dundee and elsewhere in 1839-40). It was not until the memorable year 1859 that Northern Ireland, Wales and Scotland again witnessed revivals on a national scale. Nearly a century has passed since that time and we have not seen the like.

N

But we may yet live to see it, for revivals are God's means of preserving His Church and extending His kingdom when all other
means have proved hopeless.

SOME GENERAL CHARACTERISTICS OF REVIVALS

(1) *Rapidity and Suddenness.*   Revivals often commence
suddenly in a way which demonstrates that their origin is not of
man.   The Holy Spirit works in a mysterious and unexpected
manner not according to man's calculations : " The wind bloweth
where it listeth, and thou . . . canst not tell whence it cometh, and
whither it goeth." (Jn. iii. 8).   His operations may likewise be
glorious in their rapidity :

" In Scotland, the whole nation was converted by lump : and
within ten years after popery was discharged in Scotland; there
were not ten persons of quality to be found in it who did not profess
the true reformed religion, and so it was among the commons in
proportion.   Lo! here a nation born in one day . . . " (*Kirkton* on
the Scottish Reformation, quoted in *Lectures on the Revival of
Religion* by *Ministers of the Church of Scotland*, p. 9).

" This is certain, that it is a great and wonderful event, a
strange revolution, an unexpected, surprising overturning of things,
suddenly brought to pass . . .   Who that saw the state of things in
New England a few years ago, would have thought that in so short
a time there would be such a change ? " (*Edwards* on the 1740
Awakening in New England, *Works*, vol. I., p. 379, 1834 edit.).

" On Saturday, February 17th, 1739, Whitefield stood upon
a mount in a place called Rose Green, his first field pulpit, and
preached to about two hundred of these barbarous men (Kingswood
colliers) . . . his second audience at Kingswood consisted of two
thousand individuals; his third, from four to five, and they went
on increasing to ten, fourteen, and twenty thousand . . .   The first
evidence he observed, of having made any impression on his rude
auditors, was their deep silence ; the next, and still more convincing,
was his observation of the *white gutters* made by the tears which
fell plentifully down their cheeks black and unwashed from the
coal-pits . . .   In the middle of February, Kingswood was a wilderness, when the month of June arrived, it was already blossoming
like the rose."

(2) *Power.*   In times of revival the Spirit of God accompanies
preaching with a kind of irresistible force ; hearers feel themselves
in the immediate presence of God ; the Word of God becomes of
infinite importance to their minds ; simple truths concerning Christ,
the nearness of eternity and the awfulness of being in an unconverted state, have an over-powering influence ; and such cries are
heard as " O eternity, eternity !   O that I had no soul !   O that I
had never been born . . . "

There are innumerable illustrations of this fact. Let us be satisfied with one and hear something of what John Wesley saw at Everton, Bedfordshire, on Sunday, May 20th, 1759, when he went to hear the local minister, John Berridge. After speaking of the crowded church and a congregation made up of three times more men than women, Wesley writes :—

" The text was, ' Having a form of godliness, but denying the power thereof.' When the power of religion began to be spoken of, the presence of God really filled the place. And while poor sinners felt the sentence of death in their souls, what sounds of distress did I hear ! The greatest number of them who cried or fell, were men ; but some women and several children felt the power of the same Almighty Spirit, and seemed just sinking into hell . . . numbers wept without any noise ; others fell down as dead ; some sinking in silence ; some with extreme noise and violent agitation. I stood on a pew-seat as did a young man in the opposite pew, an able-bodied, fresh, healthy country man. But, in a moment, while he seemed to think of nothing less, down he dropped, with a violence inconceivable. The adjoining pews seemed shook with his fall . . . When he fell, B-ll and I felt our souls thrilled with a momentary dread, as when one man is killed by a cannon-ball, another often feels the wind of it . . . " (*Whole Works of John Berridge,* p. xxxv., 1864 edit.).

Such physical manifestations of power are *not* of the essence of revivals and indeed they can be produced by causes other than the Holy Spirit's activity, nevertheless it is a fact that such phenomena do frequently accompany genuine revivals. This should not surprise us, argues Jonathan Edwards, " Let us rationally consider what we profess to believe of the infinite greatness of divine wrath, divine glory, the divine infinite love and grace in Jesus Christ ; and then how reasonable it is to suppose, that if God a little withdraw the veil, to let light into the soul—and give a view of the great things of another world in their transcendent and infinite greatness—that human nature, which is as the grass, a shaking leaf, a weak withering flower, should totter under such a discovery ! Such a bubble is too weak to bear a weight so vast. Alas ! what is man that he should support himself under a view of the awful wrath or infinite glory and love of JEHOVAH ! . . . That external glory and majesty of Christ which Daniel saw, when ' there remained no strength in him ' (Dan. x. 6-8), and which the apostle John saw, when he fell at His feet as dead ; was but a shadow of that spiritual majesty of Christ which will be manifested in the souls of the saints in another world, and which is sometimes, in a degree, manifested to the soul in this world " (*Works,* vol. i., p. 368).

(3) *Multiplied Conversions.* " Thy people shall be willing in the day of thy power " is a text which has seen many glorious ful-

filments. Many ministers have experienced in revivals the meaning of the declaration of William Cooper, that he had, in the 1740 awakening at Boston, New England, more souls come to him in *one week* in deep concern, than in the whole *twenty-four years* of his preceding ministry. When John Wesley formed his first Methodist Society in London in July, 1740, it had 75 members; by 1741, 1,000; and by 1743 the London Society numbered 2,020. When William Grimshaw began his mighty ministry at Haworth in the wilds of Yorkshire in 1742 he had but 12 communicants. "How many have you now?" demanded the Archbishop of York not many years later. The reply was, "In the winter, from 300-400; and in the summer, near 1,200." In 1767 the Bala Association meeting of the Welsh Calvinistic Methodists was attended by some 200 persons; by 1814 it was attended by between 15,000-20,000! It is calculated that not less than a thousand people joined the churches of the Calvinistic Methodists in Montgomeryshire as a result of one sermon preached by Michael Roberts in 1819. Yet more remarkable is the fact that one sermon preached by John Elias at Pwllheli in 1832 was the means of ending a great spiritual darkness which had prevailed there for upwards of ten years and led to the addition of 2,500 persons to the church in Carnarvonshire in that year!

No doubt all these figures included some temporary professors, but be it remembered that, unlike our times, it was difficult two hundred years ago for any mere professor to get admission into the membership of an evangelical church. Professed converts were examined then by different standards than those of the present day. We believe such numbers as the above can be adequately explained only in the language of Scripture: "Come from the four winds, O breath, and breathe upon these slain, that they may live . . . and they lived, and stood up upon their feet, an exceeding great army" (Ezekiel xxxvii. 9-10).

SOME DANGERS WHICH MAY ACCOMPANY REVIVALS.

(1) *Unawareness of any danger is a foremost danger.* Because great blessings are present in times of revival it is possible to look upon revivals as almost ushering in a state of perfection—as a time when God does all and therefore all problems cease. This attitude, which Edwards refers to as "a grand error" (*Works*, vol. i., p. 398), displays a sad ignorance of church history and of human nature. Even the New Testament churches, born in the midst of the greatest revival and taught by infallible apostles, were liable to excesses, disorders and even errors. Several of the New Testament Epistles were occasioned by this very fact. "It may seem mysterious that God should permit a work of His own holy and blessed Spirit to be accompanied, marred, and perverted, by errors and abuses. But so it has been from the beginning" *Dr. Ashbel*

Green, of Princeton, in the excellent Appendix to *Sprague's Lectures on Revivals of Religion,* p. 489, 1833 edit.).

(2) *Attributing too little to the Holy Spirit is a danger.* By this we mean the failure of some to recognize in times of revival what is truly the Spirit's work and thus to withhold their support. This failure may be prompted (as perhaps it was in the attitude of the Secession Church to the Cambuslang revival of 1742) by an excessive pre-occupation with particular parts of Scriptural truth; or, more serious, it may be due to a plain disregard of the supernatural.

(3) *Attributing too much to the Holy Spirit is an equal danger.* This danger into which many have fallen, is displayed by the kind of person who says "Because such a thing was taught or done in a revival *therefore* it must be alright." In other words it is falsely assumed that because the Spirit is present He *must* be the author and endorser of all that takes place. The fact is that though revival in its origin is supremely a work of God, yet He still works through sinful and fallible men. Man is just as prone to error and excesses in revival as at any other times—perhaps more so, due to the inevitable excitement and to the special efforts of Satan to hinder the work.

(4) *Ignoring the possibility that even leaders of revivals may fall into errors is a serious danger.* Historical facts are perhaps the strongest argument here. There can be little doubt that in some ways the Moravians and their missionaries were leaders in the eighteenth century awakening. It was they who were instrumental in Wesley's conversion in 1738; it was their Society he first joined; it was the Moravians whom he then described as "a church whose conversation is in heaven." Yet in less than three years Wesley was to discover their three great errors, namely, he says, "universal salvation, antinomianism, and a kind of new, reformed quietism." It was these same Moravians who, in the words of Whitefield to Zinzendorf, "have been unhappily instrumental in misguiding many real, simple, honest-hearted Christians, and introducing a whole farrago of superstitions, not to say idolatrous fopperies, into the English nation."

The history of American revivals likewise bears eloquent testimony to the possibility of errors or excesses entering through revival leaders—Davenport in 1741, Marshall in the Kentucky awakening of 1800-1802, Finney in the "Western revivals" of 1825-1832, are memorable examples.[1]

---

[1] On these three men and the respective revivals in which they took part see the Appendix to *Sprague's Lectures,* pp. 387-392, 489-493; the Appendix to Andrew Bonar's 2nd edit. of *The Memoir of Dr. Nettleton;* and on Finney, *B. B. Warfield's Perfectionism,* vol. ii.

In defending the genuineness of the 1740 revival, even though it was mixed with some errors, Edwards gives some helpful reasons why God should sometimes thus permit His work to be marred. His explanation is two-fold :— (1) that the Church by learning the evil consequences of errors should in future be forewarned ; (2) that man might be humbled and God glorified.

" It would be such a revival of religion as never was," writes Edwards, " if among so many men, not guided by infallible inspiration, there had not been many notable errors in judgment . . .

" The errors and irregularities that attend this work may be accounted for, from the consideration of the infirmity and common corruption of mankind . . If God intends this great revival of religion to be the dawning of a happy state of His church on earth, it may be an instance of the divine wisdom . . .   For it is very likely to be of excellent benefit to His Church, in the continuance and progress of the work afterwards.   Their experience, in the first setting out, of the mischievous consequence of these errors may be a happy defence to them afterwards, for many generations, from these errors, which otherwise they might continually be exposed to . . .

" It is very analogous to the manner of God's dealing with His people, to permit a great deal of error, and suffer the infirmity of His people to appear . . . to teach them what they are, to humble them, and the more to secure to Himself the honour of such a glorious work." (*Works,* vol. i., pp. 397, 373, 374).

THE CASE OF JOHN WESLEY (1703-1791)

We have often been asked to comment on the place of this eighteenth century leader.   As we see it the following facts appear :

(1) Wesley by his untiring ministry of over fifty years did much good.   In the industry and devotedness of his personal life he was second to none.   " He has generally blown the gospel trumpet and rode twenty miles before most of the professors who despise his labours have left their downy pillows," wrote Fletcher in 1771.

(2) This good was done by the amount of truth which he taught, but with this was mixed the denial of election, of the imputed righteousness of Christ in justification, of the final perseverance of the saints, and the assertion of universal redemption,[2] of " free-will,"[3] and of the possibility and desirability of believers

---

[2] " Oh that there may be harmony, and very intimate union between us ! Yet, it cannot be, since you hold universal redemption." Whitefield to Wesley, Nov. 24th, 1740.

[3] "The Conference conceived that, by the merits of Christ, all men are cleared from the guilt of Adam's actual sin . . . that their souls receive a capacity of spiritual life, and an actual spark or seed thereof." Tyerman on the 1744 Methodist Conference. *Tyerman's Life and Times of John Wesley,* vol. i., p. 444.

receiving an instantaneous sanctification in this life--thus becoming "perfect" Christians.[4] Wesley had been brought up by parents who held the doctrine of election in abhorrence and the strange fact is that even after his conversion he never changed his views on this and other truths.

(3) Wesley's Arminian errors wrought considerable harm in his own day. They introduced a division into the evangelical witness of the nation which had been absent since the Reformation, divided the leaders of the awakening,[5] distracted their followers,[6] and produced disorder in his own Societies.[7] After his death his influence lived in Finney, in the leaders of the "Higher Life" holiness movement[8] and was partly responsible for the disastrous outlook which developed amongst evangelicals in the later nineteenth century respecting the doctrines of grace.

Wesley might have effected tenfold more good had he taught the whole counsel of God and he would certainly have been preserved from some of the consequences which followed his ministry.

CONCLUSION.

Doctrinal orthodoxy in itself will not necessarily lead to revival, but the presence or absence of orthodoxy will very much affect the character of a revival. It is false reasoning to argue that because God has sometimes blessed an imperfect ministration of His Word therefore soundness in the faith is of little importance. Where there is error or disorder harm will inevitably be done as well as good and the former may even exceed the latter . If rainfall becomes a thunder-storm the desolations may exceed the bene-

---

[4] A short time before his death Wesley wrote:—"I cannot but believe, that sanctification is commonly, if not always, an *instantaneous* work." (*Tyerman,* vol. i., pp. 402-3). "Is there, or is there not, any instantaneous sanctification between justification and death? I say, yes." (Ibid, vol. ii., pp. 596-7).

[5] The Reformation and Puritan leaders had been at one in these issues. Wesley's views made the separation between him and Whitefield (and most of the rest of the eighteenth century leaders) inevitable. It caused them "to build separate chapels, form separate societies, and pursue, to the end of life, separate lines of action . . . the gulf between Wesley and Whitefield was immense " (*Tyerman,* vol. i., p. 351).

[6] Doctrinal controversy amongst evangelicals hindered the awakening in England. In Wales, where there was no Arminianism, there was no distraction caused by this error.

[7] "The doctrine of entire sanctification, attainable in an instant, by the exercise of faith, was now (1761) troubling Methodism throughout the country" (*Tyerman* vol. ii., p. 416). On March 26th, 1763, William Romaine wrote to the Countess of Huntingdon:—"I pity Mr. John from my heart. His societies are in great confusion; and the point, which brought them into the wilderness of rant and madness, is still insisted on as much as ever. I fear the end of this delusion " (Ibid., vol. ii., p. 463).

[8] Cf. *B. B. Warfield's Perfectionism,* vol. ii., pp. 55 and 557, etc.

fits. It would not be hard historically to demonstrate that *the benefits, depth, and permanency of any revival are invariably in proportion to the degree of Scriptural purity held by its leaders and participants.* Dr. Archibald Alexander of Princeton spoke from experience when he said, " In a revival, it makes the greatest difference in the world, whether people have been carefully taught by catechising, and where they are ignorant of the truths of the Bible " (Appendix to *Sprague's Lectures,* p. 364).

But if revivals may have their dangers, let us finally remember the immense good which a revival can bring—multitudes saved, piety elevated in the church, atheism rebuked in the world and much more. Surely our land must soon see either revival or destruction! " Ah! my friends," says John Bonar, "we have not understood what it is for souls to perish : we have not understood what is the meaning of the souls of our children perishing—of the souls of our neighbours perishing—of unconverted men and women and children dying in their sins, else we could not cease to pray and labour, till the windows of heaven were opened, and the Lord ' rained righteousness on the people, and saving health on all our families '."

FLOWERS FROM A PURITAN'S GARDEN

This heading was the sub-title of a small book published by C. H. Spurgeon in 1883. The book consists of a collection of Thomas Manton's illustrations and similes, to which Spurgeon added some brief meditations. Spurgeon had long felt that there was an unusual value in Manton's illustrations, for he used them sparingly and when they were introduced it was not as ornaments but as a vivid means of making a truth clearly understood. In consequence Manton's illustrations are very natural and forcible. After many years' familiarity with the works of this great Puritan Spurgeon spoke thus in the preface to the above book :—

" I have come to know Manton so well that I could choose him out from among a thousand divines if he were again to put on his portly form, and display among modern men that countenance wherein was a ' great mixture of majesty and meekness.' His works occupy twenty-two volumes in the modern reprint : a mighty mountain of sound theology. They mostly consist of sermons ; but what sermons! They are not so sparkling as those of Henry Smith, nor so profound as those of Owen, nor so rhetorical as those of Howe, nor so pithy as those of Watson, nor so fascinating as those of Brooks ; and yet they are second to none of these. For solid, sensible instruction forcibly delivered they cannot be surpassed. Manton is not brilliant, but he is always clear ; he is not oratorical, but he is powerful ; he is not striking, but he is deep. There is not a poor discourse in the whole collection : he is evenly good, constantly excellent. Ministers who do not know Manton need not wonder if they are themselves unknown."

The following are a few of the " flowers " which Spurgeon gathered. It may be that the scent of them will induce some of our readers to purchase a whole garden—we mean *Manton's Commentary on the Epistle of Jude*! It would be a happy day if this writer's twenty-two volumes were again in print and all can help to that end by procuring this first volume of Manton's to be republished in Britain for over 70 years.

The doctrine, which the following quotations illustrate, will, in some cases, have to be arrived at by the reader's own meditation.

" The end of study is information, the end of meditation is practice, or a work upon the affections. Study is like a winter's sun, that shineth but warmeth not; but meditation is like blowing up the fire, where we do not mind the blaze but the heat."

" God seldom lighteth a candle, but he hath some lost coin to seek."

" There is a clock with which Providence keepeth time and pace, and God himself setteth it."

" A ministry that stayeth in the paint of words will beget but painted grace."

" Fruit that hath but little sun can never be ripe."

" Be watchful; the world is the devil's chess-board; you can hardly move backward or forward, but he is ready to attack you by some temptation."

" Laden boughs hang low. The nettle mounteth above its fellow weeds, but the violet lieth shrouded under its leaves, and is only found out by its own scent."

" Passionate outcries do only frighten easy and over-credulous souls, and that only for the present: proofs and arguments do a great deal more good. Snow that falleth soft soaketh deep. In the tempest Christ slept: when passion is up true zeal is usually asleep."

" Hard speeches have an evil influence in controversy, and do exasperate rather than convince. The dog that followeth the game with barking and bawling loseth the prey; and there is not a more likely way to undermine the truth than by an unseemly defence of it."

" When the sun is gone all the candles in the world cannot make it day."

" Sin is an ill guest, for it always sets its lodging on fire."

" To fix our confidence upon a dying world is folly. It is as if we were building our nests when the tree is being cut down, or decorating our cabin when the ship is likely to be dashed to pieces or already sinking."

" O ye ministers of the word, consider well that you are the first sheets from the King's press; others are printed after your copy. If the first sheet be well set, a thousand more are stamped with ease. See, then, that the power of religion prevail over your own hearts lest you not only lose your own souls, but cause the ruin of others."

"It is of advantage to others when we use vocal prayer, for it quickens them to the same exercise, as one bird setteth all the rest a chirping."

"The best of God's people have abhorred themselves. Like the spire of a steeple (the higher it rises towards heaven the smaller it becomes) we are least at the highest. David, a king, was yet like a weaned child."

"When men have much to say in a letter, and perceive that they have little paper left, they write closely."

" 'What if my master should come and find me idle?' said Calvin to his friends, who demanded of him why he wasted his body in such constant labours. Few are like-minded so as to put this question to their souls, 'Am I as I would wish to be should Christ come?' "

"We do not judge of men's complexions by the colour they have when they sit before the fire. We cannot judge of a man by a holy fit which he hath when he is under the influence of a sermon."

"Everything tendeth to the place of its original. Men love their native soil; things bred in the water delight in that element; inanimate things tend to their centre; a stone will fall to the ground though broken in pieces by the fall."

"God will open the sinner's eyes in the next world, not by a holy illumination, but by a forced conviction. 'Be sure your sin will find you out.' We forget it now, and think we shall never hear of it more; but God can make all occur to memory as fresh as if newly committed, and in an instant represent the story of an ill-spent life, and show us all the thoughts, words, and actions that ever we have been guilty of. The paper goeth white into the printing house; but within one instant it is marked within and without, and cometh forth stamped with words, and lines, and sentences, which were in no way legible there before, even so will it be with the soul when conscience is aroused at the last."

"The first appearances of error are many times modest. There is a chain of truths; the devil taketh out a link here and a link there, that all may fall to pieces."

"A wolf doth not worry a painted sheep, nor does the world annoy a mere professor. But when any are holy indeed, and of a strict innocency, they are hated, and contradicted, and spoken against."

"Sometimes God letteth his people alone till their latter days, and their season of fighting cometh not till they are ready to go out of the world, that they may die fighting and be crowned in the field. But first or last the cross cometh, and there is a time to exercise faith and patience before we inherit the promises."

OBSERVATIONS ON ERROR*

John Flavel (c. 1628-1691)

An error is any departure or deviation in our opinions or judgments from the perfect rule of the Divine law ; and to this, all men, by nature, are not only liable, but inclinable. Indeed men, by nature, can do nothing else but err; Psa.. lviii. 3, "*He goeth astray as soon as born*"; makes not one true step till renewed by grace, and many false ones after his renovation. The life of the holiest man is a book with many erratas; but the whole edition of a wicked man's life, is but one continued error; he that thinks he cannot err, manifestly errs in so thinking. The Pope's supposed and pretended infallibility hath made him the great deceiver of the world. A good man may err, but is willing to know his error, and will not obstinately maintain it, when he once plainly discerns it.

The word of God, which is our rule, must be the only test and touchstone to try and discover errors. It is not enough to convince a man of error, that his judgment differs from other men's ; you must bring it to the word, and try how it agrees or disagrees therewith ; else he that charges another with error, may be found in as great or greater an error himself. None are more disposed easily to receive, and tenaciously to defend errors, than those who are the heads or leaders of erroneous sects ; especially after they have fought in the defence of bad causes, and deeply engaged their reputation.

OBSERV. 1. There are divers sorts and kinds of knowledge. Some is *human* and some *divine ;* some *speculative,* and some *practical ;* some *ingrafted* as the notions of *morality,* and some *acquired* by painful search and study : but of all knowledge, there is none like that Divine and supernatural knowledge of saving truths revealed by Christ in the scriptures. Hence ariseth the different degrees both of the sinfulness and dangers of errors, those errors being always the worst, which are committed against the most important truths revealed in the gospel.

These truths lie enfolded either in the plain words, or in the evident and necessary consequences from the words of the Holy Scripture; scripture-consequences are of great use for the refutation of errors : it was by a scripture-consequence that Christ successfully proved the resurrection against the Sadducees, Matt. xxii. The Arians, and other heretics, rejected consequential proofs, and required the express words of Scripture only, hoping in that

---

*The following is an abridged extract from Flavel's great treatise " *A Blow At the Root; or The Causes and Cure of Mental Errors."* The complete work can be found in Flavel's Works, vol. III, pp. 419-492, 1820 edit. Flavel is one of the richest of the Puritan writers.

way to defend their errors against the arguments and assaults of the orthodox.

Some think that reason and natural light is abundantly sufficient for the direction of our lives. But certainly nothing is more necessary to us for that end than the written word ; for though the remains of natural light have their place and use in directing us about natural and earthly things, yet they are utterly insufficient to guide us in spiritual and heavenly things, 1 Cor. ii, 14. " The natural man receiveth not the things of the Spirit of God."

OBSERV. 2. *Error is binding upon the conscience as well as truth ; and altogether as much, and sometimes more influential upon the affections and passions than truth is.*

Error presents not itself to the soul in its own name and nature, but in the name and dress of truth, and under that notion it binds the conscience, and vigorously influences the passions and affections ; and then being more indulgent to lust than truth is, it is, for that, so much the more embraced and hugged by the deceived soul, Acts xxii. 4, 5. The heat that error puts the soul into differs from religious zeal, as a feverish doth from a natural heat; which is not indeed so benign and agreeable, but much more fervent and scorching. A mind under the power of error is restless and impatient to propagate its errors to others, and these heats prey upon, and eat up the vital spirits and powers of religion.

OBSERV. 3. *It is exceeding difficult to get out error, when once it is imbibed, and hath rooted itself by an open profession.*

Error, like some sorts of weeds, having once seeded in a field or garden, it is scarce possible to subdue and destroy them ; especially if they be hereditary errors or have grown up with us from our youth. It is a great advantage to truth or error to have an early and long possession of the mind. The Pharisees held many erroneous opinions about the law, as appears by their corruptive commentaries upon it, refuted by Christ, Matt. 5. But did He root them out of their heads and hearts thereby? No, no; they would sooner rid Him out of the world. The Sadducees held a most dangerous error about the resurrection ; Christ disputed with them to the admiration of others, and proved it clearly against them ; and yet we find the error remaining long after Christ's death, 2 Tim. ii, 18. The apostles themselves had their minds tinctured with the error that Christ should be outwardly great and magnificent in the world and raise His followers to great honours and preferments amongst men. Christ plainly told them it was their mistake and error ; " for the Son of man came not to be ministered unto, but to minister." Yet this did not rid their minds of the error ; it stuck fast in them, even till His ascension to heaven.

O how hard is it to clear the heart of a good man once leavened with error! and much more hard to separate it from a wicked man.

OBSERV. 4. *It deserves a remark, that men are not so circumspect and jealous of the corruption of their minds by errors, as they are of their bodies in times of plague ; or of their lives with respect to gross immoralities.*

Spiritual dangers affect us less than bodily ; and intellectual evils less than moral. Whether this be the effect of hypocrisy, the errors of the mind being more secret and invisible than those of the conversation, God only knows, man cannot positively determine.

Or whether it be the effect of ignorance, that men think there is less sin and danger in the one than in the other ; not considering that an apoplexy seizing the head, is every way as mortal as a sword piercing the body. The apostle, in 2 Peter ii, 1, calls them damnable heresies, or heresies of destruction. An error in the mind may be as damning and destructive to the soul as an error of immorality or profaneness in the life.

OBSERV. 5. *It is a great judgment of God to be given over to an erroneous mind.*

The understanding is the leading faculty, that guides, and the other powers and affections of the soul follow, as horses in a team follow the fore-horse. Now, how sad and dangerous a thing is this, for Satan to ride the fore-horse, and guide that which is to guide the life of man ? That is a dreadful, spiritual, judicial stroke of God which we read of, Rom. i, 26.

OBSERV. 6. *Error being conscious to itself of its own weakness, and the strong assaults that will be made upon it, evermore labours to defend and secure itself under the wings of reason and scripture.*

The great patrons of error do above all things labour to gain countenance to their errors from the written word. To this end they manifestly wrest and rack the scriptures to make them subservient to their opinions ; not impartially studying the scriptures first, and forming their notions and opinions according to them. But they bring their erroneous opinions to the scriptures, and then, with all imaginable art and sophistry, wire-draw and force the scriptures to countenance and legitimate their opinions.

OBSERV. 7. *God, in all ages, in His tender care for His churches and truths, hath still qualified and raised up His servants for the defence of His precious truths, against the errors and heresies that have successively assaulted them.*

When Arius,* that cunning and deadly enemy to the Deity of

*A man of subtle parts and blameless life, which made his heresy much the more spreading and taking.

Christ, struck at the very heart of our religion, faith, and comfort ;
the Lord had His well-furnished Athanasius in readiness to resist
and confound him.   And as He had his Athanasius to defend the
Deity of Christ, so He wanted not his Basil to defend the doctrine
of the Holy Spirit against Macedonius.

So when Pelagius was busily advancing *free-will*, into the throne
of *free-grace*, providence wanted not its mallet in learned and in-
genious Augustine, to break him and his idol to pieces.   And it
is highly remarkable (as the learned Dr. Hill observes), that
Augustine was born in Africa, the same day that Pelagius was
born in Britain.

When Gotteschalcus published his dangerous doctrine about
predestination, the Lord drew forth Hincmarus to detect and con-
fute that error, by evincing clearly, that God's predestination
forces no man to sin.

So, from the beginning and first rise of Popery, that centre and
sink of errors, we have a large catalogue of the learned and famous
witnesses, which, in all ages, has faithfully resisted and opposed
it ; and when, notwithstanding all, it had even over-run Europe
like a rapid torrent, or rather inundation of the ocean, and
Germany was brought to that pass, that if the Pope had but commanded it, they would have eaten grass or hay ; then did the
Lord bring forth invincible Luther, and with him a troop of
learned champions.   Since that time the cause of Popery has become desperate.

OBSERV. 8.   *There is a remarkable connection between errors,
one linking in and drawing another after it.*

Among erroneous sects there is always some central error, and
for the service of that one leading and darling error other lesser
errors are maintained.   Thus we see the whole troop of *indulgences,
bulls, masses, pilgrimages, purgatory,* with multitudes more, flow
from, and are pressed into the service of the Pope's supremacy
and infallibility ; so, in other sects, men are forced to entertain
many other errors, which, in themselves considered, they have no
great kindness for ; but they are necessitated to entertain them in
defence of that great, leading, darling opinion they first espoused.

Some cry up, and trumpet abroad the sovereign power of
free-will, even without the preventing grace of God, enabling men
to supernatural works, as if the *will* alone had escaped all damage
by the fall, and Adam had not sinned in that noble virgin-faculty.
To defend this idol they are forced to deny several other great and
weighty truths, such as particular, eternal election, the certainty
of the saints' perseverance, the necessity of preventing grace in

conversion : which errors are but the out-works raised in defence of that idol.

OBSERV. 9. *Nothing gives more countenance and increase to error than a weak or feeble defence of the truth against it.*

The strength of error lies much in the weakness of the advocates and defendants of truth. Every friend of truth is not fit to make a champion for it. Many love it, and pray for it, that cannot defend and dispute it. " *I can die for the truth* " (saith the martyr), " *but I cannot dispute for it.*" Zuinglius blamed Carolostadius for undertaking the controversy of that age, because (said he) *his shoulders were too weak for the burden*.

He is a rare and happy disputant, who can clear and carry every point of truth, of which he undertakes the defence. It were happy for the church, if the abilities and prudence of all her friends were commensurate and equal to their love and zeal. Every little sword, every weak or impertinent answer of a friend to truth, is quickly turned into a weapon to wound it the deeper.

OBSERV. 10. *Errors of judgment are not cured by compulsion and external force, but by rational conviction, and proper spiritual remedies.*

Who can force me to believe what I will not, or not to believe what I will ? The rational and gentle spirit of the gospel is the only proper and effectual method to cure the diseases of the mind.

OBSERV. 11. *Erroneous doctrines producing divisions and fierce contentions amongst Christians, prove a fatal stumbling-block to the world, fix their prejudices, and obstruct their conversion to Christ.*

Errors dissolve the lovely union of the saints, and thereby scare off the world from coming into the church. This is evidently implied in that prayer of Christ, John xvii. " That all his people might be one, that the world might believe that the Father had sent him." There is indeed no just cause for any to take offence at the Christian reformed religion, because so many errors and heresies spring up among the professors of it, and divide them into so many sects and parties ; for, in all this we find no more than what was predicted from the beginning, 1 Cor. xi. 18, 19. " I hear that there be divisions among you, and I partly believe it ; for there must be also heresies among you," etc. And again, Acts xx. 30, " Also of your own selves shall men arise, speaking perverse things, to draw away disciples after them."

These things destroy not the credibility of the Christian religion, but increase and confirm it, by evidencing to the world the truth and certainty of Christ's predictions (which were quite beyond all human foresight) that as soon as His doctrine should be propagated, and a church raised by it, errors and heresies should spring up among them, for the trial of their faith and constancy.

Nevertheless, this no way excuses the sinfulness of errors and divisions in the church. Christ's prediction neither infuses nor excuses the evil predicted by Him : for what He elsewhere speaks of scandals is as true in this case of errors ; " These things must come to pass, but woe be to that man by whom they come."

OBSERV. 12. *How specious and taking soever the pretences of error be, and how long soever they maintain themselves in esteem among men, they are sure to end in the loss and shame of their authors and abettors at last.*

Truth is a rock that the waves of error dash against, and evermore return in froth and foam : Yea, they foam out their own shame, saith the apostle, Jude 13. What Tacitus spake of crafty counsels I may as truly apply to crafty errors : " They are pleasant in their beginning, difficult in their management, and sad in their end and issue."

Suppose a man have union with Christ, yet his errors are but as so much hay, wood, straw, stubble, built (or rather endeavoured to be built) upon a foundation of gold ; this the fiery trial will burn up ; the author of them suffers loss ; and though he himself may be saved, yet it will be so as by fire, 1 Cor. iii, 12-15. The meaning is, he makes a narrow escape. Like a man who leaps out of a house on fire from a window or battlement and with great difficulty saves his life ; just so *errorists* shall be glad to quit their erroneous opinions which they have taken so much pains to build, and draw others into ; and then, O what a shame must it be for a good man to think how many days and nights have I worse than wasted to defend and propagate an error, which might have been employed in a closer study of Christ, and mine own heart! Keckerman relates a story of a vocal statue, which was thirty years a making by a cunning artist, which by the motion of its tongue with little wheels, wires, etc. could articulate the sound, and pronounce an entire sentence. This statue saluting Aquinas, surprised him, and at one stroke he utterly destroyed the curious machine, which exceedingly troubled the fond owner of it, and made him say with much concern, " Thou hast at one stroke destroyed the study and labour of thirty years."

Besides, what shame and trouble must it be to the zealous promoters of errors, not only to cast away so vainly and unprofitably their own time and strength, which is bad enough, but also to ensnare and allure the souls of others into the same, or worse mischief : for though God may save and recover you, those that have been misled by you may perish.

THE REFORMATION CONFLICT

Part I.

"It was doctrine in the apostolic ages which emptied the heathen temples, and shook Greece and Rome. It was doctrine which awoke Christendom from its slumbers at the time of the Reformation, and spoiled the Pope of one-third of his subjects . . . It is doctrine which gives power to every successful mission, whether at home or abroad. It is doctrine—doctrine, clear ringing doctrine—which, like the ram's horns at Jericho, casts down the opposition of the devil and sin." J. C. Ryle.

A short study of the historical events which led to the establishment of Protestantism in England is sufficient to reveal the momentous character of the conflict which it involved. The nation became divided between two masters, two ways, two systems of religion. Neither would accept the other nor could they both stand together.

It was doctrine which made the differences so immense and irreconcilable, and in particular the doctrines of God's grace and predestination versus the medieval dogmas of man's works and free-will. Here the division reached its clearest manifestation and it was here that the sharpest spiritual battles were to be fought. This is not surprising, for it was not so much the abuses of Romanism that concerned the Reformers as the Pelagian errors which led to those abuses. Luther saw the order aright when he wrote : " The devil begat darkness ; darkness begat ignorance ; ignorance begat error and his brethren ; error begat free-will and presumption ; free-will begat " . . . then follows priest, purgatory, pomp and pope, etc.[1] Justification it is true was the foremost question, but the Reformers knew well that justification could not be established as gratuitous unless seen in the light of God's gratuitous election and man's depravity and inability. These were the truths which shook Rome and made England a scene of glorious spiritual revival four hundred years ago.

One further consideration should perhaps precede the following narrative. The question of the source and origin of the English Reformation has sometimes received confused treatment. The fact is that the Reformation did not come from the clergy. They could not reform themselves. " The then existing episcopal power being at enmity with the Word of God, and the slave of its own abuses, was incapable of renovating the church. On the contrary, it exerted all its influence to prevent such a renovation."[2] Neither did it come from the crown. Henry VIII's divorce from Catherine of Aragon, with the resulting separation from the Papacy which took place between 1530-1534, gave Parliament the opportunity

---

[1] *Luther's Table Talk*, Bohn's Standard Library edition, p. 219.

[2] *D'Aubigné, Hist. of the Reformation in the 16th Cent.*, vol. V, p. 135.

to implement its desire to remove the grievances which the people
had long endured from the church.   But such an official, external
Reformation was a very different thing from a spiritual, living
movement.   Henry VIII and Parliament might separate the people
from Rome, but they could not unite them to Christ.   This proud
monarch, in fact, remained a slave to his passions, a docile disciple
of medieval scholasticism and a detester of a real Reformation.
In the transformation that took place in England in the sixteenth
century we must look at men only as secondary causes, the deliverance of the land came from a sovereign hand.   " The Reformation came from the Holy Scriptures, from God, from His mighty
grace and not from princes."   It was this spiritual movement
alone which could break the chains of time-worn prejudices which
had long held the nation in darkness.   The reappearance of Christian truth, the work of the Spirit of God in applying this truth
to men's souls, this was the cause of the English Reformation.

In May, 1521, the quiet of many an English village was broken
by the hammering of a proclamation to the door of the church;
this same proclamation was to be read on the doors of churches and
cathedrals all over the land.   It was a Papal bull published against
Martin Luther, enumerating in a series of articles the ' heresies '
of this German monk.   One of these articles charged him with
teaching that " Free-will, after sin, is a title and name only of a
thing ; and while man does that which lies in him, he sinneth
deadly."[3]   To this bull was added a command of Cardinal Wolsey,
the king's chief minister and the Papal Legate in England, ordering
the handing over of all copies of books or pamphlets by this
reformer.   The king wrote against Luther ; monks and bishops
preached against him ; but this did little more than increase the
excitement caused by his writings and actions.   Many a humble
Lollard believer doubtless rejoiced to find that God had raised a
preacher of those truths which he had long been taught to love.
In the two universities (recently refreshed by the new classical
learning brought by such men as Colet) students diligently compared
Luther's doctrines with the contents of the New Testament in

---

[3] *The Acts and Monuments of John Foxe,* vol. V, p. 666, Townsend's
edition.   Luther meant, as he elsewhere writes, that free-will, after Adam's
fall and the consequent depravity of the whole human race, is a mere
empty name without reality.   Man as a morally responsible being is still
free to do what he *likes,* but as a sinner he no longer *likes* to do what is
spiritually good; his will is thus in bondage to sin.   Luther, in his reply
to the Pope, said, " I hold, defend, and embrace with the full trust of my
spirit those articles in the said bull condemned ; and I affirm, that the
same ought to be holden by all faithful Christians, under the pain of
eternal malediction."   (Ibid. p.677).
    In his *Table Talk* (pp. 119-120) he asserts the necessity of the rejection
of free-will even more strongly ; " It is my absolute opinion," he says,
" that he who will maintain that man's free-will is able to do or work
anything in spiritual cases, be they never so small, denies Christ."

Greek, which Erasmus had published in 1516. About 1519 we find Erasmus writing to Luther that " there were many in England who highly approved his opinions." On March 8, 1521, we find Warham, Archbishop of Canterbury, complaining by letter to Wolsey, " I am informed that divers of that University (Oxford) be infested with the heresies of Luther . . . having among them a great number of books of the said perverse doctrine." In 1523 Bishop Fisher of Rochester wrote against Luther, especially endeavouring to defend ' free-will ' from Luther's attacks. That same year Tyndale—shortly to leave for the continent—was for the first time busily engaged in studying Luther's mighty tomes while staying at the home of Humphrey Monmouth, a London merchant. Meanwhile at both universities the reform movement was continuing to grow in strength and numbers. In 1524 at Cambridge, Latimer was converted, so was the eminent Dr. Barnes shortly afterwards, and George Stafford became the first to lecture openly out of the Scriptures, constantly urging on his hearers the study of Augustine.

It was probably in the early summer of 1526 that the first cargo of Tyndale's New Testaments was smuggled into London. Part of the responsibility for their distribution fell into the hands of Thomas Garret, a converted priest. Soon we find Garret in Oxford secretly circulating the New Testaments. Among other works which Garret counselled students to buy " as bokes very necessarie " was Luther's *De Servo Arbitrio*—" *The Bondage of the Will.*"[4]

This arrival of an English New Testament was the signal for an outbreak of persecution. Wolsey's agents were ordered to arrest Barnes at Cambridge and all others who were found with copies of the New Testament. At Oxford the leading evangelicals were cruelly imprisoned in an underground dungeon, until after six months four of them, overcome by fever and the severities of Popery, glorified God by their death. But Tyndale had done something which could not be withstood ; the Scriptures like a mighty river carrying the living waters of the Gospel had been let loose.

Before long, it is said, more than twenty editions of Tyndale's New Testament had been circulated all over the kingdom. Nothing could have alarmed the priests more. " Away with these new translations," they cried, " or else the religion of Jesus Christ

[4] See Foxe, vol V, Appendix no. XV. Erasmus' treatise against Luther, published on Sept. 1st, 1524, and entitled *Diatribe seu collatio de libero arbitrio* (*Discussion, or Collation, concerning Free-Will*) had called forth Luther's mighty reply in Dec. 1525; cf. the Introduction to the excellent new edition and translation of this work by J. I. Packer and O. R. Johnston, published by James Clarke & Co., 1957. " *The Bondage of the Will* "— which Luther regarded as his foremost book—was well known and used by the English Reformers ; we find, for instance, Grindal when Bishop of London referring to it with approval in a letter written in June 1562—cf. *Zürich Letters*, 2nd series, p. 73.

is threatened with ruin." Before, it had been comparatively easy to burn Lollards for having a few portions of the Scriptures handwritten in English (seven believers had been burnt for that crime at Coventry in April 1519), but now printed copies of Scripture were everywhere to be found—in parsonages and inns, cottages and convents. We cannot stop to trace the story of the persecutions of these years. "It is impossible," says Foxe, "to name all who were persecuted before the time of Queen Anne Boleyn (1533). As well try to count the grains of sand on the seashore!"

With the fall of Wolsey in 1529, following his failure to procure from Rome permission for the king's desired divorce, Henry's displeasure fell upon the Pope and the English clergy. The church was severed from Rome, and Papal authority was replaced by that of the king—to whom the clergy had to submit as "supreme governor . . . in all causes, as well ecclesiastical as temporal." In order to strengthen his position Henry attempted to conciliate the evangelical leaders who, he saw, were united with him at least in opposing Rome. Thus Latimer was court chaplain in 1530, and Henry's agents promised Tyndale and Frith a safe return to England. But Tyndale was not concerned about his personal welfare. "What matters it," he said, "if my exile finishes, so long as the Bible is banished." Such were also Frith's convictions. They were not concerned with Henry's church, and its prelates and hierarchy, but with a living Christianity. The king and the reformers could come to no understanding, and Henry, affronted by their boldness, determined to treat them in another manner.

Bilney, one of the leaders of the awakening at Cambridge, was burnt to death in 1531. So was Byfield the same year. The accusation against him was that he had brought a number of Tyndale's New Testaments from the continent. "With what intent," demanded Stokesley, Bishop of London, "did you bring into the country the errors of Luther?"—"To make the Gospel known," answered Byfield, "and to glorify God before the people." Tewkesbury, despite severe torture, maintained the same faith as his brethren and, with the words "Christ alone" on his lips, went to the stake on Dec. 20th, 1531. The persecution continued. Bainham was martyred in 1532 and Lambert condemned to death (though the sentence was not executed till 1538). Frith, who had returned to England that year to spread the Gospel, was arrested, and burnt in 1533. All the evidence goes to prove that these godly men were united in doctrine. Bilney was questioned on the church, whether it could err in the faith or not. Upon which he gave the answer adhered to by all the Reformers, that the true church, being the number of the predestinate, "can by no means err in faith: for it is the whole congregation of the elect; and so known only to God who knoweth who are His." Bilney was also questioned on matters relating to predestination. Clearly, as Toplady says, "he would never have been put to the test of such queries if he had not been considered as a known predestinarian."[5] Bainham, at his first trial before the Bishop of London, asserted that "all godliness is given of God by His abundant grace : the which no man of himself can keep, but it must be given him of God." Lambert when questioned on these same truths boldly replied, "Concerning free-will, I mean altogether as doth St. Augustine : that of ourselves we have no liberty nor ability to do the will of God ; but are shut up and sold under sin, as both Isaiah and Paul witness." Frith left his doctrine beyond question by writing *A Mirror to Know Thyself* during his last imprisonment. The following brief extract from this forceful treatise will be sufficient to show his position :

" The most glorious gifts concerning our souls, come from God, even of His mere mercy and favour, which He showeth us in Christ, and for Christ, as predestination, election, vocation, and justification : and albeit, M. More with his painted poetry and crafty conveyance, do cast a mist before your eyes, that you might wander out of the right way, endeavouring himself to instruct you, that God hath predestinated and chosen us before the beginning of the world, because He knew before that we should do good works, yet will I set you upon a candle, which shall shine so bright, and so clearly dispel his mist and vain poetry . . . This are we sure of, that whomsoever He chooseth, them He saveth of His mercy : and whom He repelleth, them of His secret and unsearchable judgment, He condemneth. But why He choseth the one and repelleth the other, inquire not (saith St. Augustine), if thou wilt not err. Insomuch that St. Paul could not attain to the knowledge thereof, but cried out : ' O the depth of the riches and wisdom of the knowledge of God ! how unsearchable are His judgments and how uncomprehensible are His ways ! ' "[6]

Bilney, Byfield, Bainham, Lambert and Frith, these were leaders of the first rank to fall in the English Reformation conflict, but the truth lived after them.

In 1533 Cranmer somewhat unwillingly found himself consecrated as Archbishop of Canterbury. Sincerely maintaining the unlawfulness of Henry's first marriage with his dead brother's wife, Cranmer had done more than anyone else to procure the King's divorce. His aversion to the Papacy was also known and thus

[5] *Historic Proof of the Doctrinal Calvinism of the Church of England,* in Toplady's works 1 vol. edition, p. 117. Of this work Bishop J. C. Ryle wrote, " The book remains to this hour unanswered, and that for the simplest of all reasons, that it is unanswerable. It prove irrefragably, whether men like it or not, that Calvinism is the doctrine of the Church of England, and that all her leading divines, until Laud's time, were Calvinists."

[6] *The Fathers of the English Church,* edited by the Rev. Hugh Richmond, vol. I, p. 368-370.

Henry deemed him the best man to be at the head of the Church of England. Cranmer (not yet fully in the light of evangelical truth) proceeded to attempt to reform the Church from within, a task in which he was supported by the new queen, Anne Boleyn, until her execution in 1536, and by Thomas Cromwell, Henry's leading minister until he also went to the scaffold in 1540. The Church was soon a house divided against itself. One party desired the reign of the Pope, the other the reign of the Scriptures ; the one was set on maintaining the dogmas of Romanism, while the other was determined to drive the Roman doctrines out of England. At first the leaders of the Roman party denied Henry's authority over the church, but, when this course brought More and Fisher to the scaffold in 1535, the rest led by Gardiner and the Duke of Norfolk submitted to the king's supremacy while remaining resolute in maintaining the old doctrines of Popery. Cranmer, for his part, submitted, believing that the crown was more likely than Convocation to promote the needed reform of the Church. "Convocation," as D'Aubigné says, "an old clerical body, in which were assembled the most resolute partisans of the abuses, superstitions, and doctrines of the Middle Ages, was the real stronghold of Rome in England."

How far apart the two parties were began to be illustrated when Convocation, called by Henry " to determine certain controversies which at this time be moved concerning the Christian religion," met at St. Paul's in June, 1536. The proceedings began with a sermon from Bishop Latimer in which he addressed the clergy in a fearless manner : " If ye will not die eternally, live not worldly. Come, go to ; leave the love of your profit : study for the glory and profit of Christ. Preach truly the Word of God. Love the light, walk in the light " . . . But these bold exhortations, made little impression. The clergy of the Lower House presented a ' Protestation ' to their lordships of the Upper House of Convocation, denouncing the ' errors ' of the evangelicals in a series of short articles. The prolocutor read the long list of articles charged on the evangelicals. " They affirm," he read aloud, " that no doctrine must be believed unless it be proved by Holy Scripture . . . that a man hath no free-will . . . that confession was invented by the priests " . . . The two parties in the church faced each other like opposing armies. Unfortunately we have no records of the debates which followed. " Oh, what tugging was here between these two opposite sides," writes Fuller ; at length 10 Articles were set forth, containing " a medley religion, to salve (if not the conscience) at least the credit of both sides."

The real issues at stake were not dealt with, but only postponed. Cranmer failed at this period to put new wine into old bottles, a true Reformed Church could not be formed until those bishops were removed who would not submit to Scripture as the sole rule.

Cranmer could not carry the clergy with him, hence the slowness of the Reform. "I have done more in four weeks," said Luther, "than these Englishmen in twelve years. If they continue reforming in that style, England will never be inside or out" (of the Papacy).

The year 1537 saw a great step forward. Cranmer obtained permission for the free circulation of Scripture, and copies of the Bible in English were ordered to be placed in every church. This distribution of Scripture was the decisive factor in the Reformation. " ' It was a wonderful thing to see,' says Strype. Whoever possessed the means bought the book and read it or had it read to him by others. Aged persons learnt their letters in order to study the Holy Scriptures of God. In many places there were meetings for reading ; poor people clubbed their savings together and purchased a Bible, and then in some remote corner of the church, they modestly formed a circle, and read the Holy Book between them . . . God Himself spoke under the arched roofs of those old chapels or time-worn cathedrals, where for generations nothing had been heard but masses and litanies. The people wished, instead of the noisy chants of the priests, to hear the voice of Jesus Christ, of Paul, and of John, of Peter and of James. The Christianity of the Apostles re-appeared in the Church."[7]

But Henry's permission to circulate Scripture was but to suit his own ends, to find justification for his separation from Rome. He vainly thought to maintain in his kingdom, side by side, two things in opposition to each other, the Roman doctrines, and the reading of the Bible. Dismayed at the widening divisions in religion among his subjects, Henry imposed the ' Six Articles ' in 1539. It was an attempt to enforce Popery. The evangelicals did not remain silent. Latimer protested, resigned his bishopric and was sent to the Tower. In Lent 1540 no small stir was caused in London by Dr. Barnes, Garret and Jerome, who preaching in turn at St. Paul's Cross, boldly declared the Reformed Faith. Bishop Gardiner lost no time in reporting them to the king, who commanded the three evangelists to read a public retraction at the Easter service the following Sunday. When the day was come, Barnes ascended the pulpit and read the official paper he had received. "Having thus discharged," says D'Aubigné, "his duty as a subject, he felt bound to discharge also that of a minister. He therefore preached powerfully the doctrine of salvation by grace, the very doctrine for which he was persecuted."[8] Garret and Jerome followed Barnes's example and all three were straightway confined to the Tower. They were martyred on July 30th in

[7] D'Aubigné, *The Reformation in Europe in the Time of Calvin*, vol. V, p. 268.

[8] *The Reformation in Europe in the Time of Calvin*, vol. VIII, p. 245

Smithfield. Others who continued to preach the truth were also arrested. "Among divers of the clergy of London taken up this year (1540), Richard Wisdom was one," writes Strype. "This man was a very painful setter forth of true religion . . . among charges laid against him were that he said 'that all traditions of men should be plucked up by the roots. That man hath no free will to do good.' "[9]

Yet still the truth could not be silenced in London. Foxe has given us an account of a powerful sermon preached the following year in the city, at St. Antholine's church, by Alexander Seton. "Paul says, of ourselves we can do nothing; I pray thee then where is thy will ? Art thou better than Paul, James, Peter, and all the apostles? Hast thou any more grace than they? Tell me now, if thy will be anything or nothing ? . . . Paul said he could do nothing. Scripture speaks of three things in a man ; the first is will, the other two are consent and deed. The first, that is will, God worketh without us, and beside us. The other two He worketh in us, and with us." And here he quoted St. Augustine, to prove that we can will nothing that is good. Moreover, he said, "Thou hast not one jot, no not one tittle, to do any good." Seton was tried and condemned, "the greatest matter laid against him," says Foxe, "was for preaching free justification by faith in Christ Jesu ; against false confidence in good works ; and against man's free-will."

These quotations do not exhaust the evidence that exists concerning the character of the teaching which prevailed amongst the early reformers. Prynne, for instance, tells us of men like Robert Legat and John Harrison who maintained in their writings " that free-will of her own strength can do nothing but sin," and this doctrine, says Prynne, they confirmed with their blood in the days of Henry VIII.[10] Thomas Hancock, who "in the latter time of King Henry, and the reign of King Edward, did much good in Wiltshire and Hantshire," was another who firmly held these truths."[11]

The dark years of persecution continued with little or no improvement till the death of Henry VII on January 28th, 1547. Weeping had been endured for a long night but a morning of joy was now to come.

(TO BE CONTINUED).

[9] Strype, *Memorials Ecclesiastical*, vol. I, p. 369.

[10] *William Prynne's Anti-Arminianism,* p. 79.

[11] Strype, *Memorials Ecclesiastical*, vol. II, p. 73.

THREE MORE REPRINTS

To be republished by the Banner of Truth Trust, Autumn, 1958.
Advance orders can now be received.

THE EPISTLE TO THE ROMANS

A Commentary by Robert Haldane (1764-1842). pp. 664. 15/-.

" It is with particular pleasure that I recommend this commentary on the Epistle to the Romans " writes Dr. Martyn Lloyd-Jones and in his foreword he gives us his reasons. Firstly, " the fact that I have derived such profit and pleasure from it myself." Secondly, while the commentaries of Charles Hodge and Haldane " both stand supreme on this mighty Epistle, there is greater warmth of spirit and more practical application in Haldane." Thirdly, the unusual value this commentary derives from the history behind it. This portion of Scripture more or less engaged Haldane's attention for nearly 30 years. He expounded it at Geneva in 1816 and as a result witnessed a widespread revival not only in Switzerland but also in France. In an age when the faith of old Geneva had been set aside and forgotten, nothing contributed more powerfully to a return to the spirit and doctrine of the Reformers than Haldane's exposition of Romans.

THE CHRISTIAN MINISTRY

With an inquiry into the causes of its inefficiency

By Charles Bridges. pp. 400. 13/6.

Why has the Church ceased to command the attention of the great majority of our nation?

Why does powerlessness characterise so much of the Christian witness of our times?

Why has much of the depth and unction of former days departed from us?

Though written over a hundred years ago Bridge's ' *Christian Ministry* ' goes to the heart of such questions, for the state of the Church will always be determined by the state of her ministers.

This work is divided into five parts—General view of the Christian Ministry; General causes of the want of success in the Christian Ministry; Causes of ministerial inefficiency connected with our personal character; The public work of the Christian Ministry; The pastoral work of the Christian Ministry. Within this compass there is a masterly treatment of such subjects as the minister's prayer life, his studies and reading, his sermons and preaching. The book is an outstanding ' Manual of ministerial responsibilities, privileges and encouragements.'

Biographical note :—

Educated at Queen's College, Cambridge, and ordained in 1817, Charles Bridges became one of the prominent Christian leaders of the last century. From 1823 to 1849 he was vicar of Old Newton, Suffolk, and later of Weymouth and Hinton Martell, in Dorset. As a preacher he was called upon for such important occasions as the Clerical Conference at Weston-super-Mare in 1858 (when he preached along with J. C. Ryle) and the consecration of the Bishop of Carlisle in York Minster in 1860. Renowned though he was in his own day for his pulpit ministry, his subsequent fame rests in the books which came from his pen—*An Exposition of Psalm CXIX* (1827), *Forty-eight Scriptural Studies* (5th ed. 1833). *Fifty-four Scriptural Studies* (1837), *Exposition of the Book of Proverbs* (1846), and a *Manual for the Young* (1849). His *Christian Ministry* went through nine editions within 20 years of its appearance in 1829 and has probably remained unequalled in its field. These works earned high commendation from many, including C. H. Spurgeon, who described all Bridge's writings as "very suggestive to ministers."

After his death a small selection of his correspondence was published in book form in 1870 and it reveals a man of deep Christian piety. "I never remember anyone" says the writer of the Foreword, "in whose presence it was more difficult to be irreligious, or even frivolous."

THE CONFESSION OF FAITH

A Handbook of Christian Doctrine by A. A. Hodge (1823-1886)
pp. 430.   13/6.

The Confession of Faith, drawn up at Westminster in 1646 by over a hundred leading Puritan divines, presents one of the finest concise statements of the Christian Faith. It is the purpose of the author in this book to analyse the chapters and sections of that Confession, to give proofs and illustrations of its teaching and to assist the learner and teacher by a series of questions appended to each chapter. The result is a fine handbook of Christian doctrine providing in simple language an exposition and explanation of all the leading doctrines of Scripture. Professor Patton of Princeton referred to this volume as "a very useful book, full of clear thinking and compact statements. It reveals Hodge's strong convictions, his power of analysis and his ability to make sharp and discriminating definitions."

A. A. Hodge, the eminent son and successor of Charles Hodge, was finely equipped for this work. After three years missionary work in India, and fourteen years as a pastor, he spent the remainder of his life teaching systematic theology in the theological seminaries at Allegheny (1864-1877) and Princeton (1877-1886). In this sphere he proved himself one of the greatest teachers that America has ever produced. Patton wrote of him, "His thought and learning were those of a genius and a saint, and he occupies a unique position among his peers. He held the Reformed theology as a sacred trust. He defended it with zeal, taught it with enthusiasm, and reflected it in his life."

Important Request to Readers

The Banner of Truth Trust would be glad to hear from a reader who could lend us any of the following books :

David Dickson's Commentary on the Psalms (the Scottish edition, i.e., nineteenth century edition).

Jonathan Edwards' Works (the Robert Carter, New York edition, 1881).

Albro's Life of Thomas Shepard (published in Boston, U.S.A., about 1870, in a series of volumes on the works of the New England Fathers. Does any reader possess the series?).

George Lawson's Commentary on Ruth and Esther (Rentoul's Philadelphia edition of about 1850).

The above editions are essential unless a better edition exists.

(Continued from page 2).

(h). By enabling multitudes to discern truth from error, and sin from duty, it would render unsound and indolent ministers despised and shunned as fearful plagues, and vile impious persons abhorred, and so ashamed to exert themselves in their wonted evil ways, Zech. xiii. 2-6; Psalm cvii, 42; 1 Sam. ii. 30.

(i). By means of these things, together with the fervent prayers of such as believed in Christ, many others would be daily added to the Lord, and to His Church, Isa. lxii. 1 ; 2 Thess. iii. 1; Isa. ii. 3-5 ; xlix. ; liv. ; lx. ; xliv. 3-5 ; Zech. viii. 20-23.

(j). In consequence of all this, the Lord would graciously defer, mitigate, or sanctify those fearful calamities which our nation in general, and each of us in particular, have richly deserved, Isa. xlviii. 9-11 ; vi. 13 ; Zeph. iii. 12; Dan. ix. 25 ; Zech. xiii. 9.

BANNER OF TRUTH PUBLICATIONS

●

DOCTRINE

A Body of Divinity by Thomas Watson. pp. 226. 8/-. "One of the most precious of the peerless works of the Puritans." — C. H. Spurgeon.

The Doctrine of The Holy Spirit by George Smeaton. pp. 384. 13/6. ". . . provides in many ways the best practical teaching on this subject."— Dr. Martyn Lloyd-Jones.

SERMONS AND BIOGRAPHY

Princeton Sermons by Charles Hodge. pp. 400. 13/6. 249 Sermon outlines providing " an amount and quality of homiletical example and suggestion probably not surpassed in the same number of pages in the English language."—A. A. Hodge.

Select Works of Jonathan Edwards. Vol. 1, pp. 180. 8/-. Contains a biography by Iain Murray, Edwards' account of the great 1735 revival at Northampton and three of his famous sermons.

Select Sermons of George Whitefield. pp. 128. 6/-. "Once let the evangelical ministry of England return to the ways of the 18th century and I firmly believe we should have as much success as before."—J. C. Ryle.

COMMENTARIES

Joel, by John Calvin. pp. 132. 6/-. An exposition of a most relevant book of Scripture by the foremost commentator of the 16th century.

Zechariah, by Thomas V. Moore. pp. 250. 9/-. "A capital book ; most useful to ministers."—C. H. Spurgeon.

Song of Solomon, by George Burrowes, pp. 456. 10/6. " I cannot speak too highly of this work . . . It has everything that should characterize a good commentary."—Dr. Martyn Lloyd-Jones.

Jonah, by Hugh Martin. pp. 386. 12/6. ". . . manifests the superb qualities which all of Martin's writings exemplify."—Prof. John Murray.

I Corinthians, by Charles Hodge. pp. 400. 11/-. ". . . shows Hodge's sure grasp as one of the very foremost theologians of the Word. Students of the Scriptures will find this volume a great asset."—W. J. Grier.

Jude, by Thomas Manton. pp. 378. 13/-. "If any one wants to buy a good specimen of a Puritan divine. my advice unhesitatingly is, ' let him buy Manton.' "—J. C. Ryle.

✱

78b Chiltern Street, London, W.1.

Wickliffe Press, Wickliffe Avenue, 104 Hendon Lane, Finchley, N.3.

THE
BANNER of TRUTH

(13th Issue)

Price 9d.

Subscription for six issues, 6/6.

EDITOR:

IAIN MURRAY, B.A.
78B CHILTERN STREET,
LONDON, W.1.

ASSISTANT EDITOR:
ERROLL HULSE.

*   *   *

" Thou hast shewed thy people hard things ;
Thou hast made us to drink the wine of
astonishment.   Thou hast given a banner to
them that fear Thee, that it may be displayed
because of the truth."   **Psalm 60 : 3-4.**

*   *   *

CONTENTS

BANNER OF TRUTH PUBLICATIONS
78b Chiltern Street, London, W.1.

The Confession of Faith by A. A. Hodge. pp. 430. 13/6. A commentary on the Puritans' greatest systematic statement of the Christian Faith —The Westminster Confession. A fine handbook providing in simple language an exposition and explanation of all the leading doctrines of Scripture.

The Christian Ministry, with an inquiry into the causes of its inefficiency, by Charles Bridges. pp. 400. 13/6. "Here must begin the cure of that lethargy in sin that the world is fallen into—namely, in the renovation of a powerful evangelical ministry."—John Owen. This was the book recommended by R. M. M'Cheyne "for keeping us in mind of our ministerial work."

A Body of Divinity by Thomas Watson. pp. 226. 8/-. "One of the most precious of the peerless works of the Puritans." — C. H. Spurgeon.

The Doctrine of The Holy Spirit by George Smeaton. pp. 384. 13/6. " . . . provides in many ways the best practical teaching on this subject."— Dr. Martyn Lloyd-Jones.

Princeton Sermons by Charles Hodge. pp. 400. 13/6. 249 Sermon outlines providing "an amount and quality of homiletical example and suggestion probably not surpassed in the same number of pages in the English language."—A. A. Hodge.

Select Works of Jonathan Edwards. Vol. I, pp. 180. 8/-. Contains a biography by Iain Murray, Edwards' account of the great 1735 revival at Northampton and three of his famous sermons.

Select Sermons of George Whitefield. pp. 128. 6/-. "Once let the evangelical ministry of England return to the ways of the 18th century and I firmly believe we should have as much success as before."—J. C. Ryle.

THE GENEVA SERIES OF COMMENTARIES

Romans, by Robert Haldane. pp. 660. 15/-. Great revivals of religion have generally been related to a rediscovery of this foremost New Testament Epistle. So it was in the sixteenth century and in the eighteenth. Haldane's exposition should be read by all who desire to see such a revival to-day.

Joel, by John Calvin. pp. 132. 6/-. An exposition of a most relevant book of Scripture by the foremost commentator of the 16th century.

Zechariah, by Thomas V. Moore. pp. 250. 9/-. "A capital book ; most useful to ministers."—C. H. Spurgeon.

Song of Solomon, by George Burrowes, pp. 456. 10/6. "I cannot speak too highly of this work . . . It has everything that should characterize a good commentary."—Dr. Martyn Lloyd-Jones.

Jonah, by Hugh Martin. pp. 386. 12/6. ". . . manifests the superb qualities which all of Martin's writings exemplify."—Prof. John Murray.

I Corinthians, by Charles Hodge. pp. 400. 11/-. ". . . shows Hodge's sure grasp as one of the very foremost theologians of the Word. Students of the Scriptures will find this volume a great asset."—W. J. Grier.

Jude, by Thomas Manton. pp. 378. 13/-. "If any one wants to buy a good specimen of a Puritan divine, my advice unhesitatingly is, ' let him buy Manton.' "—J. C. Ryle.

The Banner of Truth magazine is published at irregular intervals. Subscription for six issues, 6s. 6d., including postage.

NOVEMBER, 1958

THE REFORMATION CONFLICT
PART II

" Satan seeth now—blessed be God !—that some go about in deed and in truth, not trifling, but with the loss of all they are able to lose in this world, goods, lands, name, fame and life also—to set forth God's Word and His truth—and by God's grace shall do, and abide in the same unto the end : now therefore it is time for him to bestir I trow." Ridley to Bradford, April, 1555.

The accession of the young Prince Edward to the throne in 1547 brought with it the establishment of the Reformed Faith. Edward VI was England's Josiah, whom God gave at the appointed time; he was a king whose heart was tender and who trembled at the word and judgments of God. The Six Articles of 1539 were repealed; men like faithful Latimer were released from prison and many exiled ministers returned from abroad. Romanist bishops were deprived of their sees and their places were filled by advanced Reformers such as Coverdale, Ridley, Ponet and Scory. Several of the leading Continental Divines now came over to assist in the work of reform. The zealous John Knox was also in England by 1550. He declined the Bishopric of Rochester, but as a chaplain to the King he had leave to preach in all parts of the land, and this was a means of establishing many in the truth.

The doctrine of the Reformed Church of England was now laid down in the Homilies, in the Articles completed in 1552 and in the Catechism of 1553. What had been previously punished as heresy was now recognised as The Word of God. In the Articles we find free-will expressly denied, and predestination asserted as God's everlasting purpose " to deliver from curse and damnation those whom He hath chosen out of mankind . . . such as have so excellent a benefit of God given unto them be called, according to God's purpose, by His Spirit working in due season : they through grace obey the calling : they be justified freely . . ."[1] In the Catechism we read : " Immortality and blessed life God hath provided for His chosen, before the foundations of the world were laid." And again, " The Holy Ghost is called holy, not only for His own holiness, but because the elect of God are made holy by Him. The Church is the company of those who are called to eternal life by the Holy Ghost."[2]

[1]" The leaders of the English Reformation, from the time when the death of Henry VIII placed them firmly upon Protestant ground, profess the doctrine of absolute, as distinguished from conditional, predestination. . . . On this subject for a long period the Protestants generally were united in opinion." *Prof. G. P. Fisher of Yale, The Reformation,* p. 335. Conditional predestination means that God predestinated to salvation those whom He foresaw would believe or obey Him. The Reformers on the contrary held that such is man's hopeless state in sin and bondage that none can believe or obey unless they are first predestinated, and then regenerated by God.

[2]The 42 Articles drawn up at this time and the Catechism are to be found in *Liturgies of Edward VI,* published by *The Parker Society.*

Such was the unity now prevailing in the Reformed Church that some men—" sectaries," Strype calls them, " sheltering under the name of the Gospel "—who held the opinions of the Pelagians, found that in order to propagate their errors they had to gather congregations of their own. " These were the first that made separation from the Reformed Church of England," Strype records. The leaders of the Reformed Church regarded the propagation of free-will errors and unsoundness in the doctrine of predestination as a matter of such seriousness that " For the prevention of the spreading of these people, a commission was issued out in the month of January (1550) to one and thirty persons empowering them to correct and punish these men. Of which number was the Archbishop, and four other Bishops, and divers other Prostestants; and of the King's chaplains, Redman, Latimer, Coverdale . . . Dr. Parker."[3] As a result of this commission the teachers of the sectaries were summoned before an ecclesiastical court and examined in about 46 doctrinal articles. From this examination it appeared that the following beliefs and tenets prevailed among them—" That the doctrine of predestination was meeter for devils than for Christian men ; that children were not born in Original Sin; that there was no man so chosen, but that he might damn himself; neither any man so reprobate but that he might keep God's commandments and be saved; that St. Paul might have damned himself, if he listed; that learned men were the cause of great errors; that God's Predestination was not certain, but upon condition; that Adam was elected to be saved; and that all men being then in Adam's loins were predestinated to be saved; and that there were no Reprobates; that the preaching of predestination is a damnable thing . . ."[4]. Such was the desire for purity of doctrine amongst the evangelical Reformers that men who held such errors as these were reckoned totally unfit to instruct others.

In 1553 England's spiritual prosperity was suddenly reversed. On July 6th the young King died[5] and opened the way for

[3]See *Strype's Life of Parker*, vol. I, p. 54-55 (1821 edit.)

[4]*Strype, Eccles. Mem.* vol 2, p. 236-237.

[5]Edward VI died in the seventeenth year of his life, but he seems to have advanced more in godliness than many believers do in a lifetime. The following is the prayer which " he poured out to God a little before he breathed his last,"—" O Lord God, take me out of this most wretched and most troublous life, and receive me into the assembly of Thy elect; yet not what I will, but Thy will be done. Lord, I commend my spirit to Thee. O Thou, my Lord how happy and blessed would be my condition if I were with Thee! But for the sake of Thy elect preserve my life and restore me to my former health, that I may be able faithfully to serve Thee. Ah, my Lord, be kind and gracious to Thy people, and save the Kingdom of Thy inheritance! Ah, Lord God, preserve Thy elect people of England! Ah, my Lord God, defend this Thy realm and protect it from Popery, and maintain the true religion and pure worship of Thy name, that I and my people may be exalted to praise and celebrate Thy holy name. Amen." See *Philpot's Examinations and Writings, Parker Society*, p. 178.

Mary's ascension to the throne. Under this unfortunate, bigotted and bitter woman, brought up in the Church of Rome and surrounded by Popish counsellors, the land was once more plunged into darkness and Roman tyranny. This short reign, however, was to prove decisive in establishing Protestantism in England. To what extent the majority of the people had been affected by evangelical truth by 1553 is a questionable matter; but when the nation witnessed in the next few years nearly three hundred men and women adhere to the Reformed Faith at the cost of their lives, when it saw countless others suffer the loss of all possessions and exchange liberty for imprisonment or exile, then the spirit of the land was profoundly moved. When men saw England's noblest subjects going to the stake, when they saw the Reformed ministers sealing their preaching with their blood, when they saw common people persecuted not for crimes but for godliness, and when they saw the kind of spirit that animated the Roman Church and Mary and her Spanish husband, then it appeared more clearly than ever before that Romanism was a system displeasing to God and hateful to men, a religion which destroyed holiness, freedom and the truth. Many years were to pass before England began to forget the lessons she had learned under " Bloody " Mary.

It was clear to Mary and her counsellors in 1553 that the Roman doctrines of works, free-will, merit, etc., could not be restored without the suppression of the Reformed Faith. Not only were the leading evangelical bishops and clergy imprisoned and the doctrinal articles and catechism of the former reign abolished, but a series of various acts show that it was the Reformers' teaching on the doctrines of grace which the Romanists were determined to silence. An act, straightly charging persons with the penalty of heresy, was passed against the owning, possessing, reading, or selling of books by Luther, Calvin, Bucer, Martyr, Latimer, Cranmer, as well as several others—men who were all well known predestinarians.[6] An oath was enforced on all students residing at Cambridge that " You shall not keep, hold, maintain and defend any opinion erroneous, or error of Wycliffe, Huss, Luther . . . and that you shall namely and specially hold as the said Catholic Church holdeth in all these Articles, wherein lately hath been controversy, dissension, and error : as, concerning faith and works, grace and free-will . . ."[7] Yet not satisfied with this, such was the hatred of the Papists to the doctrine Bucer had taught in the University during the reign of Edward that his body was dug out of its grave and burned; then two Romanist doctors, Perne and Watson, endeavoured to blacken his memory by preaching against, and distorting the Reformers' doctrine of predestination.[8] " The truth

[6] See *Foxe*, vol. VII, p. 127.

[7] *Strype, Eccles. Mem*, vol. 3, p. 354-55.

[8] *Foxe*, VII, p. 280 and 284. " How perilous a doctrine is that which concerneth the fatal and absolute necessity of predestination," said Watson.

o

is," as Toplady says, " Queen Mary and her Spanish husband well
knew that ' Calvinism ' is the very life and soul of the Reformation;
and that Popery would never flourish till the Calvinistic doctrines
were eradicated."

The English Reformers, to a man, stood fast in maintaining
the truth. Some of the first martyrs had time while imprisoned in
London to draw up once more a confession of their doctrine.[9] This
confession included such statements as this—" Justification is by
faith only, which faith is not an opinion but a certain persuasion
wrought by the Holy Ghost in the mind and heart of a man ; where-
through, as the mind is illuminated, so the heart is suppled to
submit itself to the will of God . . . by this we disallow the Papistical
doctrine of free-will." To this document is annexed the names of
some of the most eminent Reformers, including John Rogers, who
went to his fiery grave in Smithfield on Feb. 4th, 1555—" as if he
was walking to his wedding "; and Robert Farrer, Bishop of St.
Davids, burnt in the market place at Carmarthen, March 30th,
1555, after telling the onlookers that " If ye see me once stir while
I am burning, then give no credit to the truth of the doctrine for
which I suffer." Another name attached to this confession is that
of John Philpot, Archdeacon of Winchester, who in his trial and
examination before five Popish bishops and other doctors of the
Roman Church, boldly affirmed his union with Calvin.[10] He, too,
died at Smithfield " thanking God that he was counted worthy to
suffer for His truth."

Again and again in the record of the death trials we find that
these same doctrines of predestination and free-will were involved.
Richard Woodman, who was burned in one fire with nine other
martyrs at Lewes in Sussex, answered his examiners in this manner
—" St. Paul saith, Romans 9; Ere ever the children were born, ere
ever they had done good or bad, that the purpose of God which

---

[9]*Toplady*,   p. 164, *and Strype, Eccles. Mem., Appendix of originals*,
p. 43.

[10]"Which of you all at this day," said Philpot, "is able to answer Calvin's
Institutions, who is minister of Geneva? . . . In that matter of predestination he is in none other opinion than all the doctors of the Church be,
agreeing to the Scriptures." See *Philpot's Examinations, Parker Society*,
p. 46, also p. 153, where Philpot says, " I allow the Church of Geneva, and
the doctrine of the same; for it is one, Catholic and apostolic, and doth
follow the doctrine that the apostles did preach; *and the doctrine taught
and preached in King Edward's days was also according to the same.*"
It is an incontestable fact that the English Reformers recognised their oneness in doctrine with Calvin and the Church at Geneva. In the reign of
Mary, Thomas Lever in exile on the Continent, wrote to Bradford imprisoned in London. After mentioning the towns he had visited he writes,
" I have had experience in all these places of sincere doctrine and godly
order and great learning, and specially of such virtuous learning, diligence
and charity in Bullinger at Zurich and in Calvin at Geneva, as doth much
advance God's glory, unto the edifying of Christ's Church, *with the same
religion, for the which ye be now in prison.*" *Strype, Eccles. Mem.,* vol. 3,
p. 241.

was by election might stand, not by reason of works, but by the grace of the caller, the elder shall serve the younger : Jacob have I loved but Esau have I hated." Upon which he was charged with denying free-will. Woodman then gave this plain reply, " If we have free-will, then our salvation cometh of our own selves : which is a great blasphemy against God and His Word." The Romanists being apparently vanquished in this debate, tried to recover their composure by saying that they did not seek to condemn him but to save his soul. Thereupon the prisoner ended his defence in this manner, " To save my soul? Nay, you cannot save my soul. My soul is saved already. I praise God therefore. There can no man save my soul, but Jesus Christ. And He it is that saved my soul before the foundation of the world was laid."[11] Another martyr, Richard Roth, when asked what he thought of his fellow-prisoner, gave this fearless answer, " I think him to be one of the· elect children of God."[12] Few gave a more glorious attestation to the Gospel than John Careless, who as a result of his sufferings died in prison. When at his trial he found himself questioned concerning predestination, he replied, " Let your scribe set his pen to the paper and you shall have it roundly, even as the truth is. I believe that Almighty God, our most dear loving Father, of His great and infinite goodness, did elect in Christ "—here he was interrupted, " Tush," cried his examiner, " What need all that long circumstance? Write, I believe God elected; and make no more ado." Careless, " No, not so, Mr. Doctor. It is a high mystery and ought reverently to be spoken of. And if my words may not be written as I do utter them, then I will not speak at all." His adversary gave way, and Careless went on to expound this hated truth."[13]

Richard Gibson, examined before the Bishop of London, was given a series of articles to profess or deny, his life depending upon his answers. One of these was, " A man hath by God's grace a free choice and will in his doings." Gibson denied it, and at length, wearied by his examiners, he declared he desired to hear no more of the Bishop's " babbling." He was burnt to death with two other brethren in Smithfield.[14] We find in the historical records repeated mention of the denial of free-will. Three persons were martyred at Beccles, in Suffolk, and among the articles for which they were condemned was this, " They affirmed no mortal man to have in himself free-will." We read of thirty-four people who were persecuted and expelled from the towns of Winston and Mendlesham in Suffolk, and among the reasons for this treatment there is the following, " They denied man's free-will, and held that the Pope's Church did err." Robert Glover, another martyr, testified that the

[11]*Toplady*, p. 187.
[12]*Toplady*, p. 177.
[13]See *Foxe*, vol. VIII, p. 168.
[14]*Strype, Eccles. Mem.*, vol. 3, p. 408-12.

elect can do nothing towards their salvation. They are, he says, "No bringers of any goodness to God, but altogether receivers. They chose not God first, but He chose them. They loved not God first, but He loved them first. Yea, He both loved and chose them when they were His enemies, full of sin and corruption."[15]

In 1556, after nearly all the leading Reformers who remained in England had suffered death, Strype records that Satan further attempted to weaken the cause of the Gospel by stirring up new sects and errors. "There were now," he records,[16] "abundance of sects and dangerous doctrines : whose maintainers shrouded themselves under the Professors of the Gospel. Some . . . denied the Godhead of the Holy Ghost, original sin, the doctrine of predestination and free election . . . Others held Free-will, Man's righteousness and justification by works, doctrines which the Protestants in the times of King Edward for the most part disowned . . . Therefore it was thought fit now by the orthodox to write and publish summary Confessions of their Faith, to leave behind them, when they were dead; wherein they should disclaim these doctrines, as well as all Popish doctrines whatsoever." Such a Confession was drawn up by John Clement, imprisoned in London, in which, says Strype, "the Protestants thought fit, notwithstanding the condemnation and burning of Cranmer, Ridley, Latimer, etc., for heretics, to own their doctrine as agreeable to the Word of God, and them as such as sealed the same with their blood. This Confession may be looked upon as an account of the belief of the professors in those days." This document drawn up by Clement on behalf of all the evangelicals was entitled "*A Confession and Protestation of the Christian Faith,*" and was dated April, 1556. (Clement died in prison shortly afterwards and was buried with John Careless in a dunghill.)

Towards the beginning, this confession exposes the manifold subtlety of Satan in corrupting the minds of men concerning the Gospel—"Some denying the doctrine of God's firm predestination and free election in Jesus Christ : which is the very certainty of our salvation. And as he (the devil) hath caused them to deny all these things, even so hath he made them to affirm many mad and foolish fantasies, which the Word of God doth utterly condemn : as free-will, man's righteousness . . . with divers such like; to the great dishonour of God, to the obscuring of His glory, the darkening of His truth, to the great defacing of Christ's death; yea, to the utter destruction of many a simple soul that cannot shift from these subtle sleights of Satan, except the Lord show His great mercy upon them. . . . I do undoubtedly believe in God the Holy Ghost, who is the Lord and giver of life, and the sanctifier of all God's elect . . . I do confess and believe that Adam, by his fall, lost, from himself and

[15]*Toplady,* p. 172-73.
[16]*Eccles. Mem.,* vol. 3, p. 363.

all his posterity, all the freedom, choice and power of man's will to do good : so that all the will and imaginations of man's heart is only to evil, and altogether subject to sin . . . Until the spirit of regeneration be given us of God, we can neither will, do, speak, nor think any good thing that is acceptable in His sight . . . As a man that is dead cannot rise up himself, or work anything towards his resurrection; or he that is not, work towards his creation; even so the natural man cannot work anything towards his regeneration.[17] This fine confession, which Strype gives in full, extends to many pages. It ends with the words, " Give the glory to God only, for He alone is worthy. Cleave fast unto Christ, and continue in His Word."

It is unnecessary to multiply similar instances of those who suffered for these truths. Toplady records them at length. My primary purpose is not to write history but to demonstrate the doctrine of the martyrs. The fact is that there is not a record of one martyr who did not hold these truths. The result of all the burnings in London, Strype tells us, was that those professing the Gospel increased considerably, or at least showed themselves more boldly towards the end of the reign. Men were exhorted to suffer for Reformed doctrine, even by their wives, Strype says, and " cared not for burning as a Popish judge confessed, ' You care not for burning; by God's blood (he swore) there must be some other means found for you.' " So greatly was the spirit of the people incensed against the persecutors that we find Bishop Bonner, for fear of the mob, resorting to burning martyrs in secret at night.[18] Such are the lengths to which man's enmity to the truth can go. On the death of Mary in 1558 the majority of the people were heartily ready for a Protestant ruler, and a Reformed Faith.

Four hundred years have passed since England witnessed these events. Time has dimmed men's memories and they act as if the happenings of those days have no bearing on the present. Such ignorance has cost us dear. The tide of popular opinion, which in 1558 was carrying the nation into a new era of spiritual and temporal prosperity, is now fast carrying us back to darkness and ruin. As Israel looked back to Egypt, so England looks back to Rome. The very Church which burned our martyrs, withheld the Bible from our people and trampled on our liberties is now favoured by thousands! Evangelicals are now a small minority— no longer are our spokesmen regarded as national heroes, no longer are our leaders men who command the attention of the throne, of Parliament and of the masses; no longer are our principles dear to the heart of many an Englishman. Like Samson we seem to be shorn of the strength we once possessed. Wherein lies the cause of such a change? Why has our influence gone? Has the truth lost

[17]*Strype, Eccles. Mem.*, vol. 3, p. 210-225. Another Confession drawn up by thirteen believers contains the same truths, see p. 228.
[18]*Strype, Eccles. Mem.*, vol 3, p. 461.

its power? The answer to all such questions is the same as it was in Daniel's day—" We have rebelled against Him; neither have we obeyed the voice of the Lord our God, to walk in His laws, which He set before us by His servants the prophets." Let us but return to God's Word, taking up again those doctrines wielded so mightily by our fathers, and we may yet live to inherit in our times the promise which they saw so gloriously fulfilled—" No weapon that is formed against thee shall prosper; and every tongue that shall rise against thee in judgment thou shalt condemn." (Isaiah 54, 17.)

PRECEPTS FOR MINISTERIAL STUDENTS

By C. H. Spurgeon.

1. Be sure you are called
2. Go in for a high ideal.
   Set before you something apostolic—Baxter, Bunyan, Whitefield. Have an ideal, and intend to reach it.
3. Make yourselves qualified for the best possible positions. To do this,you must continue to grow when you leave college.
4. Especially seek spiritual attainments.
   Be sure you are men of humility, prayer, faith, and of love for God and souls.
5. Overcome all mental and moral defects.
   Master your temper. Don't be sombre, don't be too light.
   Mental defects—Be careful of mental squints ; let the eyes of your mind look right on. Be logical, be accurate, be clear in your thinking as a crystal stream.
6. Study the most successful models.
   There is much in this. I made Whitefield my model years ago. Buy his sermons.
7. Try every method.
   With the people, with yourselves, hard study, days of prayer.
8. Be humbly willing to be corrected.
9. Be sure you feel what you preach, and preach what you feel.
   Get a red-hot heart, and preach to the heart.
10. Give sound matter, and plenty of it.
11. Put up with anything, even with cross-grained deacons and poverty.
12. Subject every desire in your soul to the one object of life ; be willing to forego high scholarship, or getting married, if these would hinder you in soul winning.
13. Seek grace to be always intense.
14. Ask Divine guidance about every little thing.
15. Be a pastor, be a saint, be an intercessor, be a martyr if necessary, and success surely awaits you.

THOMAS CHARLES OF BALA

"O! highly favoured country! I believe that you have more of the spirit and simplicity of the primitive Christians, among the rocks of Wales, than there is anywhere else at this day throughout the whole world."— Jones of Creaton to Thomas Charles, 1785.

No country entered more deeply into the benefits of the great eighteenth century awakening than did the principality of Wales, and perhaps nowhere else were the effects of that awakening so permanent and universal. The cause of this is not hard to find. Of all the blessings Wales enjoyed, the most conspicuous was the gift of a succession of powerful preachers and leaders. For over a hundred years following the conversion of Daniel Rowland and Howel Harris in 1735, the Welsh awakening was led by no common men. If anyone wishes to read of ministers who were hard students, early risers, fervent preachers, mighty in the Scriptures and in prayer, let them turn their attention to this period. In England the second generation of the Methodists were not of the same stature as their fathers. Whitefield had no successor. In Wales it was otherwise, as we shall see when we look at the life of one who belonged to the second generation of the Methodists.

Thomas Charles was born in South Wales on October 14th, 1755, and went to school at Llanddowror and Carmarthen. Though exercised with some convictions from his youth, it was not until 1773 that he was converted through hearing Daniel Rowland at Llangeitho. After this his heart being set on the Gospel, he seized the opportunity of a University education as a step to the ministry of the Established Church. From 1775 to 1778 we thus find him at Jesus College, Oxford. It was to this period of his life that he owed the mental preparation for his work, and it also brought him into contact with such English Evangelical leaders as John Newton and William Romaine.

Thomas Charles began his ministry in Wales in 1784. Nearly half a century had passed since Harris and Rowland had first

> ". . . hurled tremendous lightnings,
> Flaming with terrific sway,
> On the dark, benighted millions,
> Who in sin's foul regions lay."[1]

Harris's seraphic voice had now been silent in the grave for eleven years. Rowland was an old man whose labours were almost done. But by their preaching and the preaching of those who followed them, most of South Wales was enlightened with the Gospel and multitudes of converts were rejoicing in their Redeemer. In North Wales, however, the situation was far from bright. Some conversions had taken place there and a number had travelled south to

[1] Edward Morgan's translation of part of William Williams' Elegy on Harris.

hear the Gospel, but such was the violent hostility shown by the majority of the inhabitants that when Harris attempted to evangelise the North, he was on one occasion nearly killed and Rowland narrowly escaped being blown up by gunpowder. In North Wales not one minister of the Established Church favoured the Methodists, and such was the weakness of the Non-Conformists that in 1736 they possessed only six chapels in the whole area. It was to such an unpromising field of labour, to Bala a small town in the very heart of the North, that Thomas Charles was called to do his life work.

The unusual manner in which Charles was led to settle in the North deserves some explanation. On completing his course at Oxford he had found no openings in the anti-Methodist pulpits of the Established Church in his native land. Necessity, therefore, led him to accept the curacy of two churches in Somerset—the parishes of Shepton Beauchamp and Sparkford. But before going to his curacies in the autumn of 1778, Charles paid a holiday visit to a college friend in Bala; henceforth Bala was to claim an unrivalled place in his affections, for it was here he met the young and godly Sarah Jones. The story of their subsequent correspondence and courtship, of Charles' flying visits to Bala from Somerset and of Sarah's doubts and fears, is delightfully related in Volume I of D. E. Jenkins' standard *Life of Thomas Charles*. Charles' five years in Somerset were not easy ones. An unsympathetic vicar, ignorant parishioners, village hostilities and an insufficient salary, all helped him to learn with Luther that trials and temptations make a Gospel minister. The Lord had placed him in circumstances that would exercise the prayer and patience which were to be so indispensable in the future. His love to Sarah Jones was not the least of his trials, for the dependence of Sarah's parents on her abilities to run a general store made her presence in Bala a necessity. But, try as he would, no opening was given him to any Established Church in North Wales. At length he faced the choice of parting with the Church of England or with Sarah Jones. He chose the former, resigned his curacy in Somerset, and, casting himself upon providence for his future work, was married at Llanycil Church, Bala, on August 20th, 1783. Thus at the age of twenty-eight Charles settled in the heart of an area where Satan had long held sway.

He who came " to destroy the works of the Devil " now proved Himself to be mightily with His servant. For a time Charles exercised his ministry in Anglican churches around Bala, but the character of his preaching was too much for the clergy to bear and in March, 1784, he received his third and last dismissal. Now there was no course left but for him to turn to the Methodists, and his decision to do this marks not only a new era in his own life, but the beginning of a new era in the history of the Calvinistic Methodists in North Wales.

The awakening in Wales, as in England, had originated within the Established Church. But by this time the Welsh Methodists, while not assuming the title of a Church, were rapidly becoming a distinct body with their own itinerant preachers. It was to the ranks of these preachers that Charles joined himself in September, 1784, and after he had begun to preach far and wide throughout the North, he was quickly recognised, in the words of Rowland, as "a gift from the Lord to North Wales." We read of many being melted to tears by the power of his preaching; his knowledge and abilities gave a permanent lead to the Methodists in the North and the whole work received a new impetus. In April, 1785, Charles writes, "I am just this moment come home from three weeks' tour through Caernarvonshire and Anglesey. The fields here all over the country are white for the harvest. Fresh ground is daily gained. Whole neighbourhoods where the Word has been heretofore opposed call aloud for the Gospel. Thousands flock to hear and many in different parts of the country, we have good reason to believe, are effectually called."

Yet despite these promising prospects, immense difficulties had to be faced. The ignorant and godless state of the people was even worse than Charles had at first feared and the discovery of their condition, learnt from his early tours, distressed him beyond expression. Whenever he met a poor man or woman on the road he would stop his horse and earnestly enquire, "Can you read the Bible?" Only one in twenty could and very few possessed a copy. It became obvious to him that preaching alone could never remedy such a situation—"I find, through the ignorance of the Scriptures, that the terms which we very commonly use in preaching convey no idea to the bulk of our congregations."

The remedy which Charles was led to adopt was the institution of circulating schools. Originating in 1785 with one teacher, this project developed remarkably. In 1786 there were seven teachers; in 1789 fifteen schools, and in 1794 twenty schools. A school was only set up for six to nine months in any place, just sufficient time to teach young people to read the Scriptures, and then the schoolmaster moved elsewhere. In this way the schools exercised a far flung influence. This education, augmented in 1789 by the formation of Sunday Schools, was of an entirely spiritual character, and the scholars were all regarded primarily "as candidates for another world." Thomas Charles was one of the most successful leaders of children's work of all time, and if some of his methods of instruction were re-introduced today there is no reason why, given the blessing of God, we might not expect a similar success. The duty of memorising the Scriptures followed by public catechising was everywhere enforced. Acting on the principle that children are capable of far more than many imagine, Charles discovered that children of only five years old were capable of memorising many chapters of the Scriptures. Nor was such memorising mechanical. It was often accompanied and inspired by a deep love of the word of God.

A notorious English atheist, William Hone, was travelling in Wales about this time when he saw a girl at a cottage door reading the Bible. Going up to her he said, " Oh ! the Bible !" " Yes," answered the girl, " it is the Bible." " I suppose you are performing your task," commented William Hone. " Task ? What do you mean task ?" she asked. " I suppose your mother has set you so much to read," Hone replied. " Surely you would not otherwise read the Bible ? " " Not at all," was the answer, " I only wish I could read it all day long. It is my joy and delight, when my work is done, to get a few minutes to read this precious book."

This simple testimony was one of the principal factors in William Hone's conversion. Many adults were similarly affected by the speech of children; Edward Morgan gives one striking instance in the following narrative :—

" There was a certain town which seemed to grow worse and worse, increasing daily in all kinds of wickedness, though the Gospel had been regularly preached there for more than twenty years. The people, young as well as old, became more and more depraved. They ran into all manner of excesses, especially at the annual wakes. The most faithful and awful warnings were delivered from the pulpit, but with no effect. The state of things here was mentioned to Mr. Charles. Having considered the subject, he made up his mind to make an attempt to storm this stronghold of Satan in a way different from that of preaching. About two months before the wakes, he sent word to the teachers of their Sunday Schools, requesting them to get the children to search the Bible for texts which prohibit directly or indirectly such evil practices as dancing, drunkenness, fornication, etc., and to commit them to memory, saying that they might expect him there at the feast to catechise the children. The young people set to work, and there was a great deal of talk in the town and neighbourhood about the subject. When the time arrived, Mr. Charles went there, and most of the people of the place, led by curiosity perhaps in a great measure, went to hear what the children had to say on those subjects. The meeting began as usual with singing and prayer. Then Mr. Charles began to ask some questions on the points given them to learn. ' Is dancing, my dear children, a sin ? ' ' Yes,' said one emphatically, ' it was owing to dancing that the head of John the Baptist was cut off.' ' Is drunkenness set forth as bad and sinful in the Scripture ? ' ' Yes,' answered another, and repeated these words: ' Woe unto them that follow strong drink, that continue until night till the wine inflame them, and the harp and the viol, the tabret and the pipe are in their feasts; but they regard not the work of the Lord, neither consider the operations of his hands.' Isaiah 5: 11, 12. In this way he proceeded with them concerning the other sins and the answers were given with great propriety and seriousness. The people began to hold down their heads, and appeared to be much affected. Observing this, he addressed them in the kindest manner and exhorted them by all means to leave off their sinful practices, and to learn the word of God after the example of the children, and to try to seek superior pleasures and a better world. The effect was so great that all went home and the houses of revelling were completely forsaken."

It was not long before Bala became the headquarters of the Methodists in the North and Charles their acknowledged leader.[2] Indeed, he was shortly to become the most prominent minister in the land. Daniel Rowland died in 1790, and William Williams, Pantycelyn, Rowland's right-hand man and one of the last of the Methodist fathers, followed him the next year. Before his death, Williams, as if recognising Charles as his successor, sent him a dying exhortation—" Know, my dear brother, that now, as well as in the Apostles' time, errors are conceived and brought forth amongst many sects and denominations of people. But as Methodism has hitherto been kept clear from pernicious and destructive tares, I hope the Lord will preserve us to the end . . . Exhort the young preachers to study, next to the Scriptures, the doctrine of our old celebrated Reformers . . . They will see there the great truths of the Gospel and the deep things of God set forth in a most excellent and suitable manner . . . The larger and shorter Catechisms of the Assembly of Divines, with The Confession of Faith,[3] are deserving of the greatest respect and acceptance." A similar appeal was made to all the ministers of the Methodist connection by Williams in his Elegy on Daniel Rowland—

> " Take the place of Huss, and Jerome,
> Cranmer, Ridley, in the flame,
> Stand for Calvin and his doctrines,
> As did Daniel, in God's name;"[4]

Charles proved faithful to his trust, and in October, 1791, God honoured his ministry in an unforgettable manner. Returning to Bala from a visit to London he had found one hitherto vain young woman " in the greatest agony of soul-distress." Charles described what followed in the following narrative : " This case struck awe and terror into the minds of many; but still they were able to go on in their usual course, and no visible good effects appeared, till the first and second Sundays in October, which are weeks ever to be remembered by me. This glorious work began on a Sunday afternoon, in the Chapel, where I preached twice that day. I cannot say that there was anything particular in the ministry of that day, more than what I had often experienced among our dear people here. But, towards the close of the evening service, the Spirit of God seemed to work in a very powerful manner on the minds of

---

[2]The small town of Bala was well suited to this rôle. Its central situation and important manufactory of woollen goods made Bala's fairs and markets among the busiest in the North, and they were numerously attended from distant parts of the country. From two to five hundred pounds worth of woollen goods were sold every market day.

[3]This Confession—a fine handbook of Christian doctrine drawn up by the leading Puritans—with a commentary on it by A. A. Hodge, has now been republished by *The Banner of Truth Trust* at 13/6.

[4]This is D. E. Jenkins' rendering of the Welsh original: *Life of Thomas Charles*, vol. II, p. 72. It preserves the sense but not the beauty of the Welsh.

great numbers present, who never appeared before to seek the Lord's face; but now there was a general and a loud crying, 'What must I do to be saved,' and, 'God be merciful to me a sinner.' And about nine or ten o'clock at night there was nothing to be heard from one end of the town to the other, but the cries and groans of people in distress of soul. And the very same night a spirit of deep conviction and serious concern fell upon whole congregations in this neighbourhood when calling upon the name of the Lord."

In the three following years frequent awakenings and extraordinary outpourings of the Spirit occurred in several districts; indeed, for over forty years similar revivals continued to take place in North Wales. "I am persuaded," wrote Charles, "that unless we are favoured with frequent revivals, and a strong, powerful work of the Spirit of God, we shall in a great degree degenerate and have only a *name to live*': religion will soon lose its vigour; the ministry will hardly retain its lustre and glory; and iniquity will, of consequence, abound."

In the later years of Charles' ministry, while preachers such as John Elias were continuing to extend the victories of the Gospel, Charles' energies were directed more to consolidating the work. To this end he had two objects in view : firstly, the supply of Bibles to the Welsh people in their own language, and, secondly, the provision of literature to aid them in the study of those Bibles. Charles' struggle to make Welsh Bibles available for his people is a moving story. The details of how he first approached the S.P.C.K. in 1792 to print a new edition of the Welsh Bible, of how they reluctantly at length printed 10,000 in 1799—only to be immediately sold out —of how, despairing of this source of supply, Charles and some friends originated the great British and Foreign Bible Society, all these are matters which we cannot go into now. The first Welsh New Testament to be printed by the new Society was finished in 1806 and a contemporary paper reports its reception in these words :—" When the arrival of the cart was announced, which carried the first sacred load, the Welsh peasants went out in crowds to meet it, drew it into the town, and eagerly bore off every copy as rapidly as they could be dispersed. The young people were to be seen consuming the whole night in reading it. Labourers carried it with them to the fields that they might enjoy it during the intervals of their labour and lose no opportunity of becoming acquainted with its sacred truths." This intense love of the Scriptures was not to pass like morning dew. Five years later in 1811 we find Charles writing :—" The whole country is, in a manner, emerging from a state of great ignorance and ferocious barbarism to civilisation and piety ... Bibles without end are called for and read diligently, learned out by heart, and searched into with unwearied assiduity and care. Instead of vain amusements—dancing, card playing, interludes, quarrelling and barbarous and most cruel fighting, we have now prayer meetings. Our congregations are crowded and public catechising has become pleasant, familiar and profitable."

In the provision of literature to aid the study of Scripture, no Welsh pen was more usefully employed than that of Thomas Charles. In 1789 he published a Catechism which immediately earned him a widespread theological reputation; a second edition was called for in 1791. In 1799 he originated a quarterly magazine —*The Spiritual Treasury*. In 1803 he began his major work—a *Scriptural Dictionary*—and this was published some eight years later in four volumes.

" This dictionary," writes Edward Morgan, " is a magazine of useful, rich scriptural knowledge, and is of itself a valuable library. We hesitate not to say that next to the Bible, it is by far the best book in the Welsh language." Besides his own literary work Charles superintended the reprinting of old books such as the works of the Puritan, Walter Cradock; in 1803 he established a printing press in Bala itself and became largely responsible for the supervision and proof reading involved. In the next eleven years this press issued 55 editions of elementary school books, amounting in all to some 320,000 copies! Add to all this the part Charles played in seeking to improve the text of the Bible Society's Welsh Bible and the extent of his literary labours can well be realised.

Yet the whole time Charles continued to take the oversight of many churches and schools. To him fell the responsibility of presiding over the regular Association meetings of the preachers; his leadership was annually expected at the great Association meetings at Bala when thousands gathered to hear the Word preached; his wisdom drew up the form of ordination used when the first Calvinistic Methodist ordination service took place in 1811, and his enthusiasm enlisted Welsh support for the London Missionary Society and their missionaries in the South Seas. It is no wonder that these duties, interspersed with wearisome journeys and incessant preaching labours, told on his health. In crossing over Welsh mountains, in a freezing wind, in the winter of 1799, he sustained frostbite in the thumb of his left hand. Amputation followed and his life was endangered. In this connection the prayer of an old warmhearted Christian in the Bala prayer meeting was long remembered : " Fifteen years, Lord, wilt Thou not give him to us for fifteen years? For my brethren's sake this prayer is made, and for the sake of my neighbours, too." This prayer was remarkably answered for Charles lived till the autumn of 1814.

Many factors contributed to make the ministry of Thomas Charles so eminently useful and successful. He was endowed with fine natural abilities. Though not such a popular orator as Rowland or Harris he nevertheless possessed more mental and literary talents than either of these two leaders. He was the first Welsh Methodist —apart from Nathaniel Rowland—to enjoy a University education.

He was probably the only Welsh minister who was familiar with some of the great Continental Reformers such as Zanchius, Musculus, Vitringa, Witsius, Cocceius, Turretin and others. Among the Methodists of England and Wales there was no finer scholar and theologian than Thomas Charles of Bala. Moreover, on the practical level, by grasping and supplying the immediate needs of the people in the right way Charles displayed singular wisdom. Had it not been for the intellectual instruction given at this time to the people, the revivals would no doubt have tended to degenerate into mere emotionalism.

But far more important than these natural abilities were the fine spiritual qualities which characterised his life. He lived near to God, he cared nothing for a knowledge which did not lead to a closer fellowship with Christ, and he aimed at holiness in all things. The reader of his works will find how he constantly felt his dependence on the operations of the Holy Spirit—both in his studying and preaching : " When the Lord appears to our souls in divine truths, He teaches us more in one quarter of an hour than ten thousand years' study without His teaching. None can teach like Him." No one, Charles believed, dishonours Christ so much as a lukewarm professor : " In temptation, the Lord, Who is compassionate, pities us. In persecution, He suffers with those who are afflicted. In sudden and unexpected surprisals, He intercedes for His people. But in a cold, lifeless frame, He severely threatens : ' Because thou art lukewarm I will spue thee out of my mouth.' Words enough to make the best of us to tremble ! "

We have not space to assess the importance and influence of Thomas Charles except to add one word about his doctrinal position. From the start the Welsh awakening was a Calvinistic movement,[5] and it was in no small part due to Charles that it continued to bear that character. William Williams did not appeal in vain to Charles to preserve the doctrinal purity of the Welsh Methodists. Charles scarcely needed such an appeal for he had long felt the sweetness of the doctrines of grace. Back in his courting days we find him writing to his Sarah :— " I find it daily indispensably necessary to have a clear apprehension of the Eternity, unchangeableness, freeness and independency of God's love, to enable me to walk forward with any degree of confidence and comfort. God's love depends upon nothing out of Himself, but upon His own Sovereign will and pleasure *only*. Christ did not die for us to *cause*

[5]James Hutton, reporting something of the spiritual condition of Britain to Count Zinzendorf, in March, 1740, writes : " In Wales, some thousands are stirred up. They are an exceedingly simple and honest people, but they are taught the Calvinistic scheme."

" We are free in Wales from the hellish infection," wrote Harris to Cennick, in October, 1740, referring to Arminianism. Cf. *Tyerman's Life and Times of John Wesley*, vol. I, p. 299 and p. 321.

God to love, but God's love was the cause of Christ's propitiation."[6] Charles, like his Welsh contemporaries, saw no inconsistency between this faith and aggressive evangelism. Indeed, he writes, " Everything in the councils of heaven favours a *returning sinner*—election, particular redemption, vocation, justification, etc.—all, all are in his favour."[7]

In drawing up the questions to be put to those who were coming forward for ordination Charles saw to it that these truths were not passed over. Among the questions to be put to ordinands we find the following :—" What is your view of God's purpose and predestination? Of the fall and depravity of man? . . ." In his later years Charles regretted the signs of decline from the old orthodoxy. He writes thus to a young minister in 1813 :—" A salvation in covenant is but little known in these days, and therefore but little preached, but scouted and laughed at. Hence arise the prevailing notions about universal redemption, etc., etc., and a thousand other concomitant errors, which leave everything at random and in uncertainty. I hope the Lord will enable you and me more clearly to view a salvation in covenant—a covenant of peace which cannot be moved; and then we shall preach it warmly to others, and our success will be certain."[8]

In these days when the unsuccessful character of modern evangelism becomes increasingly apparent we should do well to look back to the life and message of Thomas Charles of Bala.

[6] *Jenkins' Life of T. Charles*, vol. I, p. 264.
[7] *Letters and Essays of T. Charles*, p. 388.
[8] Ibid, p. 392.

Bibliography:

By *Edward Morgan*—
  A Brief Memoir of the Life and Labours of Thomas Charles.
  Essays and Letters of Thomas Charles.

By *D. E. Jenkins*—
  The Life of Thomas Charles of Bala, 3 vols., 1,927 pages.

The earlier works by Morgan are the best introduction to Charles and give a fine idea of the man's spiritual stature. Jenkins' monumental volumes are more accurate and historical, essential to students of Charles but perhaps rather tedious in parts for the general reader.

In writing the above account I am also indebted to an MS. account of Thomas and Sarah Charles of Bala by S. M. Houghton, Esq., M.A., of Rhyl.

DEFECTIVE EVANGELISM*

J. C. RYLE (1816-1900).

"Which of you, intending to build a house, sitteth not down first and counteth the cost?"—Luke 14 : 28.

For want of "counting the cost," the hearers of powerful Evangelical preachers often come to miserable ends. They are stirred and excited into professing what they have not really experienced. They receive the Word with a "joy" so extravagant that it almost startles old Christians. They run for a time with such zeal and fervour that they seem likely to outstrip all others. They talk and work for spiritual objects with such enthusiasm that they make older believers feel ashamed. But when the novelty and freshness of their feelings is gone, a change comes over them. They prove to have been nothing more than stony-ground hearers. The description the great Master gives in the Parable of the Sower is exactly exemplified. "Temptation or persecution arises because of the Word, and they are offended." (Matt. xiii. 21). Little by little their zeal melts away, and their love becomes cold. By and by their seats are empty in the assembly of God's people, and they are heard of no more among Christians. And why? They had "never counted the cost."

For want of "counting the cost," hundreds of professed converts, under religious revivals, go back to the world after a time, and bring disgrace on religion. They begin with a sadly mistaken notion of what is true Christianity. They fancy it consists in nothing more than a so-called "coming to Christ," and having strong inward feelings of joy and peace. And so, when they find, after a time, that there is a cross to be carried, that our hearts are deceitful, and that there is a busy devil always near us, they cool down in disgust, and return to their old sins. And why? Because they had really never known what Bible Christianity is. They had never learned that we must "count the cost."

For true revivals of religion no one can be more deeply thankful than I am. Wherever they may take place, and by whatever agents they may be effected, I desire to bless God for them, with all my heart. "If Christ is preached," I rejoice, whoever may be the preacher. If souls are saved, I rejoice, by whatever section of the Church the word of life has been ministered.

* The following article is an extract from Ryle's volume on "*Holiness.*" This book may be obtained from the Banner of Truth offices, price 13/6, 14/8 by post. Ryle's remarks appear to have been prompted by the revival movement which began about 1873 and which was accompanied by a new emphasis in evangelism. For a fuller treatment of the same subject see the article by Dr. John Kennedy on "*Hyper-Evangelism*" in the 6th issue of *The Banner of Truth.*

But it is a melancholy fact that, in a world like this, you cannot have good without evil. I have no hesitation in saying, that one consequence of the revival movement has been the rise of a theological system which I feel obliged to call defective and mischievous in the extreme.

The leading feature of the theological system I refer to, is this : an extragagant and disproportionate magnifying of three points in religion—viz., instantaneous conversion—the invitation of unconverted sinners to come to Christ—and the possession of inward joy and peace as a test of conversion. I repeat that these three grand truths (for truths they are) are so incessantly and exclusively brought forward, in some quarters, that great harm is done.

Instantaneous conversion, no doubt, ought to be pressed on people. But surely they ought not to be led to suppose that there is no other conversion, and that unless they are suddenly and powerfully converted to God, they are not converted at all.

The duty of coming to Christ at once, " just as we are," should be pressed on all hearers. It is the very corner-stone of Gospel preaching. But surely men ought to be told to repent as well as to believe. They should be told why they are to come to Christ, and what they are to come for, and whence their need arises.

The nearness of peace and comfort in Christ should be proclaimed to men. But surely they should be taught that the possession of strong inward joys and high frames of mind is not essential to justification, and that there may be true faith and true peace without such very triumphant feelings. Joy alone is no certain evidence of grace.

The defects of the theological system I have in view appear to me to be these : (1) The work of the Holy Ghost in converting sinners is far too much narrowed and confined to one single way. Not all true converts are converted instantaneously, like Saul and the Philippian jailer. (2) Sinners are not sufficiently instructed about the holiness of God's law, the depth of their sinfulness, and the real guilt of sin. To be incessantly telling a sinner to " come to Christ " is of little use, unless you tell him why he needs to come, and show him fully his sins. (3) Faith is not properly explained. In some cases people are taught that mere feeling is faith. In others they are taught that if they believe that Christ died for sinners they have faith ! At this rate the very devils are believers ! (4) The possession of inward joy and assurance is made essential to believing. Yet assurance is certainly not of the essence of saving faith. There may be faith when there is no assurance. To insist on all believers at once " rejoicing," as soon as they believe, is most unsafe. Some, I am quite sure, will rejoice without believing, while others will believe who cannot at once rejoice. (5) Last, but not least, the sovereignty of God in saving sinners, and the absolute necessity of preventing grace, are far too much overlooked. Many talk as if conversions could be manufactured at man's pleasure, and as if there were no such texts as this, " It is not of him that willeth, nor of him that runneth, but of God that showeth mercy." (Rom. ix. 16).

The mischief done by the theological system I refer to is, I am persuaded, very great. On the one hand, many humble-minded Christians are totally discouraged and daunted. They fancy they have no grace because they cannot reach up to the high frames of feeling which are pressed on their attention. On the other side, many graceless people are deluded into thinking they are " converted," because under the pressure of animal excitement and temporary feelings they are led to profess themselves Christians. And all this time the thoughtless and ungodly look on with contempt, and find fresh reasons for neglecting religion altogether.

The antidotes to the state of things I deplore are plain and few. (1) Let "all the counsel of God be taught" in Scriptural proportion ; and let not two or three precious doctrines of the Gospel be allowed to overshadow all other truths. (2) Let repentance be taught fully as well as faith, and not thrust completely into the background. Our Lord Jesus Christ and St. Paul always taught both. (3) Let the variety of the Holy Ghost's works be honestly stated and admitted ; and while instantaneous conversion is pressed on men, let it not be taught as a necessity. (4) Let those who profess to have found immediate sensible peace be plainly warned to try themselves well, and to remember that feeling is not faith, and that " patient continuance in well-doing " is the great proof that faith is true. (John viii. 31). (5) Let the great duty of " counting the cost " be constantly urged on all who are disposed to make a religious profession, and let them be honestly and fairly told that there is warfare as well as peace, a cross as well as a crown, in Christ's service.

I am sure that unhealthy excitement is above all things to be dreaded in religion, because it often ends in fatal, soul-ruining reaction and utter deadness. And when multitudes are suddenly brought under the power of religious impressions, unhealthy excitement is almost sure to follow.

I have not much faith in the soundness of conversions when they are said to take place in masses and wholesale. It does not seem to me in harmony with God's general dealing in this dispensation. To my eyes it appears that God's ordinary plan is to call in individuals one by one. Therefore, when I hear of large numbers being suddenly converted all at one time, I hear of it with less hope than some. The healthiest and most enduring success in mission fields is certainly not where natives have come over to

Christianity in a mass. The most satisfactory and firmest work at home does not always appear to me to be the work done in revivals.

There are two passages of Scripture which I should like to have frequently and fully expounded in the present day by all who preach the Gospel, and especially by those who have anything to do with revivals. One passage is the parable of the sower. That parable is not recorded three times over without good reason and a deep meaning.—The other passage is our Lord's teaching about "counting the cost," and the words which He spoke to the "great multitudes" whom He saw following Him. It is very noteworthy that He did not on that occasion say anything to flatter these volunteers or encourage them to follow Him. No : He saw what their case needed. He told them to stand still and "count the cost." (Luke xiv. 25, etc.) I am not sure that some modern preachers would have adopted this course of treatment.

THE MARCH OF SALVATION

An allegory on " Things that Accompany Salvation."

By C. H. SPURGEON

Picture to yourselves the march of some ancient monarch through his territory. We read stories of Eastern potentates, in the olden time, that seem more like romance than reality ; when they marched with thousands of flying banners, and with all kinds of riches borne in their train. Now you are to take that as the basis of my figure, and suppose Salvation to be the sacred treasure which is being carried through the world, with guards before, and guards behind, to accompany it on its journey.

We will begin with *the advance-guard that has accompanied Salvation,* or rather *gone before it.* Then we will notice *those who accompany it by its side,* and conclude by noticing *the rear guard attending upon this Salvation of our God.*

First, then, IN THE MARCHES OF TROOPS AND ARMIES, THERE ARE SOME THAT ARE OUTRIDERS, AND GO FAR AHEAD OF THE OTHER TROOPS. So, in the march of Salvation, there is a certain body of great and mighty ' things that accompany Salvation,' which have far preceded it to clear the way. I will tell you the names of these stupendous Titans who have gone before. The first is *Election ;* the second is *Predestination;* and the third *Redemption;* and the *Covenant* is the captain of them all. Before Salvation came into the world, Election marched in the very forefront, and it had for its work the billeting of Salvation. Election went through the world, and marked the houses to which Salvation should come, and the hearts in which the treasure should be deposited. Election looked through all the race of man, from Adam down to the last, and it marked with sacred stamp those for whom Salvation was designed. ' He must needs go through Samaria,' said Election ; and Salvation must go there. Then came Predestination. Predestination did not merely mark the house, but it mapped the road in which Salvation should travel to that house ; Predestination ordained every step of the great army of Salvation; it ordained the time when the sinner should be brought to Christ, the manner how he should be saved, the means that should be employed ; and it marked the exact hour and moment when God the Spirit should quicken the dead in sin, and when peace and pardon should be spoken through the blood of Jesus. Predestination marked the way so completely, that Salvation doth never overstep the bounds, and it is never at loss for the road. In the everlasting decree of the Sovereign God, the footsteps of Mercy were every one of them ordained. As nothing in this world revolves by chance,—as even the foreknown station of a rush by the river is as fixed as the throne of a king,—it was not meet that Salvation should be left to chance ; and therefore God has mapped the place where it should pitch its tent, the number of its footsteps to that tent, and the time when it should arrive there. Then came Redemption. The way was rough ; and though Election had marked the house, and Predestination had mapped the road, the way was so impeded that Salvation could not travel it until it had been cleared. Forth came Redemption ; it had but one weapon, that weapon was the all-victorious cross of Christ. There stood the mountains of our sins ; Redemption smote them, and they split in halves, and left a valley for the Lord's redeemed to march through. There was the great gulf of God's offended wrath ; Redemption bridged it with the cross, and so left an everlasting pathway by which the armies of the Lord may pass over. Redemption has tunneled every mountain, it has dried up every sea, cut down every forest, levelled every high hill, and filled up all the valleys, so that the road of Salvation is now plain and simple. God can be just, and yet the Justifier of him that believeth in Jesus.

Now, this sacred advance-guard carried for their banner the Eternal Covenant. Election, Predestination, and Redemption,— the things that have gone before, beyond the sight, are all rallied to the battle by this standard,—the Covenant, the Everlasting Covenant, ordered in all things and sure. We know and believe that, before the morning star startled the shades of darkness, God had covenanted with his Son that he should die and pay a ransom price, and that, on God the Father's part, he would give to Jesus ' a number whom no man could number,' who should be purchased

by his blood, and through that blood should be most securely saved.
Now, when Election marches forward, it carries the Covenant.
These are chosen in the Covenant of grace. When Predestination
marcheth, and when it marketh out the way of Salvation, it proclaims the Covenant. 'He marked out the places of the people
according to the tribes of Israel.' And Redemption also, pointing
to the precious blood of Christ, claims Salvation for the blood-
bought ones, because the Covenant hath decreed it to be theirs . . .

And now comes SALVATION IN ALL ITS FULNESS. The 'things
that accompany Salvation' make a glorious march in the forefront
of it,—from Election down to these precious opening buds of virtue
in the sinner's heart. What a goodly army! Surely, the angels
do sometimes fly along in admiration, to see this bright array that
heralds Salvation to the heart. And now comes the precious casket
set with gems and jewels. It is of God-like workmanship ; no
hammer was ever lifted on it ; it was smitten out and fashioned upon
the anvil of Eternal Might, and cast in the mould of Everlasting
Wisdom ; but no human hand hath ever defiled it, and it is set with
jewels so unutterably precious, that if heaven and earth were sold
they could never buy another Salvation !

And who are those that are close around it ? There are three
sweet sisters that always have the custody of the treasure ; you know
them, their names are common in Scripture,—Faith, Hope, and
Love, the three divine sisters ; these have Salvation in their bowels,
and do carry it about with them in their loins. *Faith,* that layeth
hold on Christ, and trusteth all in him ; that ventureth everything
upon his blood and sacrifice, and hath no other trust. *Hope,* that
with beaming eye looks up to Jesus Christ in glory, and expects
him soon to come ; looks downward, and when she sees grim Death
in her way, expects that she shall pass through with victory. And
thou sweet *Love,* the brightest of the three ; she, whose words are
music, and whose eyes are stars ; Love also looks to Christ, and is
enamoured of him ; loves him in all his offices, adores his presence,
reverences his words ; and is prepared to bind her body to the stake,
and die for him who bound his body to the cross to die for her.
Sweet Love, God hath well chosen to commit to thee the custody of
the sacred work ! Faith, Hope, and Love,—say, sinner, hast thou
these three ? Dost thou believe that Jesus is the Son of God ? Dost
thou hope that through the efficacy of his merits thou shalt see thy
Maker's face with joy ? Dost thou love him ? Have you these three
graces ? If so, you have Salvation. Having that, you are rich to
all intents of bliss ; for God in the Covenant is yours. Cast your

eye forward ; remember, Election is yours, Predestination and Sovereign Decree are both yours. Remember, the terrors of the law are past ; the broken heart is healed ; the comforts of religion you have already received ; the spiritual graces are already in the bud ; you are an heir of immortality, and for you there is a glorious future. These are the ' things that accompany Salvation.'

Now you must have patience with me for just a few more minutes ; I MUST BRING UP THE REAR GUARD. It is impossible that, with such a vanguard, grace should be unattended from behind. Now see those that follow Salvation. As there were four bright cherubs that walked in front of it,—you remember still their names, —Humility, Repentance, Prayer, and a tender Conscience,—there are four that follow it, and march in solemn pomp into the sinner's heart. The first of these is Gratitude, always singing, ' Bless the Lord, O my soul : and all that is within me, bless his holy name.' And then Gratitude lays hold upon its son's hand ; the name of that son is Obedience. ' O my Master,' saith the heart, ' thou hast done so much for me ; I will obey thee.' In company with this fair grace is one called Consecration,—a pure, white spirit that hath no earthliness ; from its head to its foot it is all God's, and all gold. Linked to this bright one, is one called Knowledge, with a face serene and solemn . . . . .

Now, have you these four ? They are rather the successors of Salvation than the heralds of it. ' Oh, yes,' the believer can say, ' I trust I have Gratitude, Obedience, Consecration, and Know-ledge ! ' I will not weary you, but there are three shining ones that follow after these four, and I must not forget them, for they are the flower of them all. There is Zeal, with eyes of fire, and heart of flame, a tongue that burneth, a hand that never wearies, and limbs that never tire ; Zeal, that flies round the world with wings swifter than the lightning's flash, and finds even then her flight too tardy for her wish ; Zeal, ever ready to obey, resigning up herself for Christ, zealously affected always in a good thing. This Zeal always dwells near one that is called Communion. This, surely, is the goodliest of all the train ; an angel spiritualized, an angel puri-fied and made yet more angelic, is Communion. Communion calls in secret on its God ; its God in secret sees. It is conformed to the image of Jesus ; walks according to his footsteps, and lays its head perpetually on his bosom. And, as a necessary consequence, on the other side of Communion, which with one hand lays hold of Zeal, is Joy, joy in the Spirit ; Joy, that hath an eye more flashing than the world's merriment ever gave to mortal beauty, with light foot tripping over hills of sorrow, singing, in the roughest ways, of faith-fulness and love. Joy, like the nightingale, sings in the dark, and can praise God in the tempest, and shout his high praises in the storm. This is indeed a fitting cherub to be in the rear of Salvation.

I have almost done. Just in the rear is Perseverance, final, certain, and sure. Then there follows complete Sanctification, whereby the soul is purged from every sin, and made as white and pure as God himself. Now we have come to the very rear of the army ; but remember, as there is an advance guard so far ahead that we could not see them, so there is a rear guard so far behind that we cannot behold them yet. Let us just try to see them with the eye of faith . . . Hark, I hear the silver trumpet sound ; there is a glorious array behind ! A guard, far, far back, is coming, following the steps of the conquering heroes, that have already swept our sins away. Do you not see, in the fore part, there is one, whom men paint as a skeleton ? Look at him ; he is not the king of terrors. I know thee, Death, I know thee ; miserably men have belied thee. Thou art no spectre ; thine hand bears no dart ; thou art not gaunt and frightful. I know thee, thou bright cherub : thou hast not in thy hand a dart, but a golden key that unlocks the gates of Paradise. Thou art fair to look upon, thy wings are like the wings of doves, covered with silver, and like yellow gold. Behold this angel Death, and his successor Resurrection. I see three bright beings coming ; one is called Confidence, see it ! It looks at Death ; no fear is in its eye, no pallor on its brow. See, holy Confidence marches with steady steps ; the cold chill stream of Death doth not freeze its blood. See, behind it, its brother, Victory ; hear him, as he cries, ' O Death, where is thy sting ? O Grave, where is thy victory ? ' The last word, ' victory,' is drowned amidst *the shouts of angels.* These bring up the rear. Angels bear the spirits of the redeemed into the bosom of the Saviour,—

> " Far from a world of grief and sin,
> With God eternally shut in,
> They are for ever blest."

BUT WHEN ?

Reader, I dare say you mean one day to be a decidedly religious man. You hope one day to be a really serious Christian. But when is this to be ? I say again, When ?

Are you waiting till you are sick ? Surely you will not tell me that this is a convenient season. When your body is racked with pain, when your mind is distracted with all kinds of anxious thoughts, when calm reflection is almost impossible, is this a time for beginning the mighty work of acquaintance with God ? Do not talk so.

Are you waiting till you have leisure ? And when do you expect to have more time than you have now ? Every year you live seems shorter than the last : you find more to think of, or to do, and less power and opportunity to do it. And after all you know not whether you may live to see another year. Boast not yourself of tomorrow—*now is the time*!

Are you waiting till you are old ? Surely you have not considered what you say. You will serve Christ when your members are worn out and decayed, and your hands unfit to work ? You will go to Him when your mind is weak and your memory failing ? You will give up the world when you cannot keep it ? Is this your plan ? Beware, lest you insult God.

Are waiting till your heart is perfectly fit and ready ? That will never be. It will always be corrupt and sinful—a bubbling fountain, full of evil. You will never make it like a pure white sheet of paper and you can take to Jesus Christ, and say, " Here I am, Lord, ready to have Thy law written on my heart." Delay not, but begin as you are.

Oh, lingering reader, are not your excuses broken reeds ? Be honest ; confess the truth. You have no good reason for waiting.

Take the advice I give you. Resolve this day to wait no longer. Begin *at once to seek God*. *Repent of your sins*. Believe on Christ and be saved. " Behold *now is the accepted time ;* behold, *now* is the day of salvation." II Cor. 6 : 2.

J. C. RYLE.

Wickliffe Press, Wickliffe Avenue, 104 Hendon Lane, Finchley, N.3.

THE
BANNER of TRUTH

(14th Issue)

Price 9d.

Subscription for six
issues, 6/6 or $1.25

EDITOR:

IAIN MURRAY, B.A.
78B CHILTERN STREET,
LONDON, W.1.

ASSISTANT EDITOR:
ERROLL HULSE.

*   *   *

"Thou hast shewed thy people hard things;
Thou hast made us to drink the wine of
astonishment.   Thou hast given a banner to
them that fear Thee, that it may be displayed
because of the truth."   Psalm 60 : 3-4.

*   *   *

CONTENTS

421

PLEASE NOTE:—No further mail should be sent to 65a, Blenheim Terrace, N.W.8. The Editor's personal address is now 'Ayrsmoss,' 11 North Crescent, London, N.3.

ERRATA.—Page 7. Insert fig. [1] after Christ (line 8), and fig. [2] after Believers (line 11). The footnotes printed on page 8 should be transferred to this page.

Page 8. Footnote [1] and first half of footnote [2] on page 9 belong to this page.

Page 9. Before *Autobiography*, Vol. II, 225, insert fig. [1]. Transfer first footnote on page 10 to this page and alter its number to [2].

Page 10. Alter footnotes [2], [3], [4], to read [1], [2], [3]. Add to footnote [2] the page reference 327 after Vol. II. Insert as footnote to fig. [4], *An All-Round Ministry*, 304-306.

FEBRUARY, 1959

14th Issue

AN HANDFUL OF CORN

" There shall be an handful of corn in the earth upon the top of the mountains ; the fruit thereof shall shake like Lebanon : and they of the city shall flourish like grass of the earth." Psa. 72 : 16.

Having spoken of the permanence and universality of Christ's Kingdom, the psalmist here illustrates the way in which this Kingdom is going to reach such a vast extension. Though its beginnings be as small as a handful of corn sown in an unfavourable and exposed place—" the top of the mountains "—yet it will result in a harvest so great that when the breeze rustles through the rich ears of corn it will sound like the wind among the mighty cedars of Lebanon! And such will be the astonishing increase that " they of the city," i.e., the inhabitants of the spiritual Jerusalem who are the subjects of this Kingdom, shall be as plentiful as blades of grass! The principle here taught is that such is the *expanding power* of the Gospel, that no matter how small its beginnings, no matter how small is the remnant of believers who espouse its cause, no matter how unfavourable are the circumstances which attend its path, yet its fruit " shall shake like Lebanon."

God's people have often been as " an handful of corn upon the top of the mountains." It was so in the past and it is so to-day. But that should not discourage us. It was but an handful who turned the world upside down in the days of the Apostles (Acts 17 : 6), an handful evangelised Scotland and the north of England in the seventh century, an handful- spread the truth in the dark times of Wickliffe, an handful made this nation a Protestant land at the time of the Reformation. The men who have apprehended the principle contained in this verse have been those who " through faith subdued kingdoms, wrought righteousness, obtained promises . . . waxed valiant in fight, turned to flight the armies of the aliens." (Heb. 11 : 33-34). William Carey was such a man. He and his few colleagues from amongst the Calvinistic Baptists launched what was to be the beginnings of the great nineteenth century missionary movement on the sum of £13. 2s. 6d. ! " *Expect great things from God,*" was his watchword. Expectation of great things is still a Christian duty. God has pledged Himself to the growth and expansion of Christ's Kingdom—" Of the increase of his government and peace there shall be no end . . . the zeal of the Lord of hosts will perform this." (Isa. 8 : 7). An handful of corn can still result in a vast harvest. " We cannot even now tell whereto a humble effort to do good may grow," commented C. H. Spurgeon.

In our own field of labour—the circulation of Scriptural literature—we trust we have experienced something of the truth of this principle. Three and a half years have now passed since the first slender " Banner of Truth " was published in Oxford.

We had a list of a few friends who, we thought, might be interested and that was all.   In fact the magazine fell into the hands of a far wider circle than we had anticipated, and our little venture began to bear some fruit.   Then a year ago it became possible to commence publishing books and fourteen titles were made available during 1958.   We regarded the friends who subscribed to this magazine as the essential nucleus behind this expansion and we counted on your support and sympathy.   In response many of you have regarded yourselves as sharers in this work ; it is therefore our responsibility to inform you of something of the progress.   Twenty thousand books have now been sold.   The majority have been purchased in this country, but considerable quantities have gone to Australia, New Zealand, South Africa and America.   Supplies have also been sent to such places as India, Pakistan, Philippines, Japan, Formosa, Greece, Borneo, Denmark, France, Nigeria, Tanganyika, Rhodesia and Eritrea.   These books have sold in approximately equal quantities though the demand for one or two like Watson's " *Body of Divinity* " has been noticeable.   The *doctrinal* character of Watson's work makes this demand significant.   Among the purchasers the younger generation are conspicuous and large orders have been received from theological colleges.   For instance, one college in New Zealand ordered 64 copies of Smeaton on " The Holy Spirit."   These are facts which should encourage us all to greater effort.   The faith of our fathers has still the same expanding power !

The following notes will give a brief outline of our publishing programme for 1959.

The works which began to be republished last year will be continued, namely *Thomas Watson* on *The Ten Commandments* (8/- April) which continues his sermons on the Westminster Assembly's Shorter Catechism, and *Jonathan Edwards' Select Works,* Vol. II (10/6 June).   The latter volume will contain 10 of his sermons. *The Geneva Series of Commentaries,* will be increased by the addition of a new American commentary on *The Gospel of John* by *William Hendriksen** (21/- May), and by *Charles Hodge's* work on *II Corinthians** (10/- June).   Outside *The Geneva Series* we are republishing *Thomas Manton's* great commentary on *John XVII** (16/- July).   *The Christian in Complete Armour** by *William Gurnall* (15/- Abridged, March) will provide one of the finest works in practical divinity.   In the realm of doctrine the complete *Systematic Theology** of *Louis Berkhof* (25/- March) will be published for the first time in this country.   In some respects this will be the most important volume we have issued.   Later in the year, probably early autumn, we hope to republish *John Owen's* classic on the extent of the atonement, *The Death of Death.*   The

*Not for sale in the U.S.A.

remainder of the forthcoming books belong to somewhat different categories. *George Whitefield's Journals* (15/- August) will be the first autobiography we have reprinted. The subject of revivals will rightly receive considerable attention this year ; in that connection it is opportune that we should reprint *Sprague's* outstanding *Lectures on Revivals of Religion* (15/- April) and also some examples of true Calvinistic evangelism in a book entitled *Revival Year Sermons* (6/- March), being sermons preached by *C. H. Spurgeon* in 1859. Lastly a book designed to help the unconverted and to clarify central Gospel truths *The Way of Life* (7/6 May) by *Charles Hodge*. This is a book which can confidently be given to the unbeliever. All the above publication dates and possibly one or two prices are subject to alteration.

A great awakening and reformation is the need of our times. The fact that this is the true need is becoming widely recognised and dissatisfaction with modern thought is increasingly evident. It may be that the events of the present time will be regarded in future years as the first signs of the breaking dawn. "*Watchman, what of the night* ? The watchman said *The morning cometh* !"

BOOK REVIEWS

The books reviewed in these pages should be ordered from the Publishers concerned.

SYSTEMATIC THEOLOGY. By Louis Berkhof. Banner of Truth Trust. pp. 784. 25/-. Available March, 1959. *Not for sale in the U.S.A.*

Professor Louis Berkhof, late President-Emeritus of Calvin Seminary, Grand Rapids, served the cause of the Christian Church and of the Reformed Faith well. When he passed away suddenly on Saturday morning, May 19th, 1957, at the age of 83, it could be said of him that " after he had served his own generation by the will of God, he fell on sleep."

He was a man of many talents. He was particularly outstanding as a teacher and an author. After serving in two pastorates in the Christian Reformed Church, U.S.A., he began his long career as professor at Calvin Seminary in 1906. He had the priceless privilege of sitting as a post-graduate, for two years at the feet of the great men who then taught at Princeton Seminary. He gave 38 years of his life to Calvin Seminary. At first he occupied the chair of Old and New Testament—covering a wide field. Later he occupied the chair of Systematic Theology and it was here that he distinguished himself most. One who sat in his classes said : " His teaching was clear, concise, systematic. Having a systematic mind, he was by nature as well as training adapted for the chair of Systematic Theology . . . There was something massive about his intellectual equipment, as about his physique. Those who read his theological works know how much he could say, and say well, on a single page."

Berkhof stood in the great theological tradition from Calvin through Kuyper, Bavinck, the Hodges and Warfield. It is interesting to compare Charles Hodge and Louis Berkhof. Both made good use of their talents.

Continued on page 32.

A HUNDRED YEARS AGO

I.

C. H. Spurgeon and the 1859 revival.

"The old truth that Calvin preached, that Augustine preached, that Paul preached, is the truth that I must preach to-day, or else be false to my conscience and my God. I cannot shape the truth; I know of no such thing as paring off the rough edges of a doctrine. John Knox's gospel is my gospel. That which thundered through Scotland must thunder through England again."—C. H. Spurgeon.

The year 1859 contained little of a political nature to make it permanently memorable. The agony of the Crimean War and the shock of the Indian Mutiny were over. The American Civil War, with its repercussions on English trade, was yet to come. Across the Channel the conflict between France and Austria in the Italian peninsula was being fought without English interference. Victoria Regina passed the twenty-second year of her reign undisturbed, and in Westminster Lord Palmerston began his comparatively uneventful second ministry. But in the annals of the Christian Church this year stands out significantly as a veritable year of grace. Such a year Britain has not seen since, and its stirring episodes deserve lasting remembrance.

On a Tuesday evening, January 4th, 1859, twenty-four-year-old Charles Haddon Spurgeon addressed a vast gathering convened by the Young Men's Christian Association in the Exeter Hall. *"De Propaganda Fide"* was his subject, and it led him to plead the necessity of a revival: " We must confess that, just now, we have not the outpouring of the Holy Spirit that we could wish . . . Oh, if the Spirit of God should come upon those assembled to-night, and upon all the assemblies of the saints, what an effect would be produced! We seek not for extraordinary excitements, those spurious attendants of genuine revivals, but we do seek for the pouring out of the Spirit of God . . . The Spirit is blowing upon our churches now with His genial breath, but it is as a soft evening gale. Oh, that there would come a rushing mighty wind that should carry everything before it! This is the lack of the times, the great want of our country. May this come as a blessing from the Most High! " The desire was fulfilled. In the spring of 1859, kindled by the news of the revival which began in America in the winter of 1857-58, a widespread awakening began in Northern Ireland and in Wales. In the early summer it spread from Ulster to Scotland and by the end of the year Spurgeon could write, " The times of refreshing from the presence of the Lord have at last dawned upon our land."

Of all the preachers of that year of grace there was none more remarkably used than C. H. Spurgeon, and though London never became the centre of such revival scenes as were witnessed elsewhere, nevertheless there was no more influential voice in the whole land than that of the youthful pastor of New Park Street Chapel. Five years before, at the age of nineteen, he had left a small Baptist "cause" at Waterbeach, near Cambridge, to accept the pastorate of this London church.[1] It was a church that had fallen into serious decline. Not more than 200 people were meeting in a building designed for a congregation of 1,200. Within twelve months, however, the building was packed to capacity. By February, 1855, the enlargement of the old structure was an urgent necessity and the congregation therefore moved to Exeter Hall (capable of holding 2,500-3,000) till the alterations were completed in May. But the enlargement of New Park Street Chapel was utterly inadequate, for by 1855 the whole of London had become aware of the new preacher in their midst. "Since the days of Wesley and Whitefield," reported the newspapers, "so thorough a religious *furore* has never existed." In June, 1856, the congregation was forced to return to the Exeter Hall for its evening services and a fund was opened for a new building. In November a further move was necessary, and for three years the New Park Street church met in the Surrey Gardens Music Hall on Sunday mornings. On successive Sundays throughout this period Spurgeon's gospel filled this great building with between 5,000 and 9,000 people! At the same time Spurgeon was generally preaching about ten times every week. By 1859 he had preached in Scotland, Ireland and much of England. He turned down pressing invitations to go to America, but his sermons were read widely there and indeed in many parts of the world.

It was abundantly evident, therefore, that the power of the Holy Spirit was present in Spurgeon's ministry long before 1859. At the end of that revival year he wrote in the Preface of the fifth volume of *The New Park Street Pulpit*: "In the midst of these new displays of divine love, it is very pleasant to see the spots which have long been favoured retaining their wonted fruitfulness and rejoicing with joy unspeakable in progressing prosperity. Such is the case with the Church to which these sermons were addressed from the pulpit. Her bow abides in strength. . . . For six years the dew has never ceased to fall, and the rain has never been withheld." Yet, Spurgeon continues, "At this time the converts are more numerous than heretofore, and the zeal of the church groweth exceedingly." Undeniably, even in his ministry, it was a remarkable year.

Perhaps one or two events stand out. On March 1st he preached to an overflowing congregation at Whitefield's Tabernacle. On July 10th, following upon the death of a man by

[1] Spurgeon was born at Kelvedon, Essex, on the 19th June, 1834. His conversion took place in January, 1850. He first preached at New Park Street in December, 1853, and was offered the pastorate, which he accepted in April, 1854. With this congregation he remained till his death.

lightning on Clapham Common, Spurgeon preached in the open air to 10,000 people on " Be ye also ready." Two days later he preached to another open-air gathering at Rowland's Castle in a valley near Havant. Here the very hills took up the sound of his voice, and the breathless congregation could hear his moving exhortation coming back and echoing away in the distance— " Come, Come, Come, Come ! " The same month, on July 20th, Spurgeon preached in Wales for the first time, again in the open air, to a congregation of between 9,000-10,000. The inhabitants of Castleton, the village between Newport and Cardiff where this took place, had cause to remember the event till their dying day.

Such open air meetings in the country districts were a common feature of Spurgeon's ministry at this time. Even as late as October in 1859 we find him preaching in the open to a gathering of 4,000 at Carlton in Bedfordshire.

1859 was Spurgeon's last year in the Surrey Gardens Music Hall. For a certain time the owners had been deterred from open-ing the grounds and Hall on Sundays for entertainment by Spur-geon's intimation that the congregation would then cease to use the building. A valuable rent would thus be lost. But at length hoping to gain more by their entertainment programme they forced Spurgeon to act upon his word. In fact, after this the Music Hall " both morally and financially sank hopelessly," and was destroyed by fire in June, 1861. Many years later a hearer wrote the following impressions of those last services in the Music Hall : " I shall never forget the sermon on July 17th, 1859, ' The Story of God's Mighty Acts.' How he revelled in preaching that morning ! It was very hot, and he kept on wiping the perspiration from his forehead; but his discomfort did not affect his discourse, his words flowed on like a torrent of sacred eloquence. . . . I was present at the last service held in the Music Hall, on December 11th, 1859. It was very foggy, but the place was crowded, as much indeed as it could be. I had a front seat in the second gallery, and therefore enjoyed a splendid view of the people. Mr. Spurgeon preached an earnest sermon on declaring the whole counsel of God. There is always something sad about last things, and, as I came away, I felt that one of the happiest experiences of my youth belonged to the past. So also—in my opinion—passed away the most romantic stage even in Mr. Spurgeon's wonderful life."

Some of the memorable sermons which Spurgeon preached in the Surrey Music Hall during 1859 are shortly to be available again.[1] In them will be found the cause of the phenomenal success which attended his ministry. What was it that gathered and held a congregation of some 8,000 people? Was it advertisement, bright services, musical accompaniments, counselling rooms and follow up work? No; Spurgeon had none of these things !

[1] " *Revival Year Sermons*," 6/-, to be published by *The Banner of Truth Trust* in March, 1959.

The strength of Spurgeon's ministry lay in his theology. He rediscovered what the church had largely forgotten—the evangelistic power of so-called " Calvinistic " doctrine. In his speech on the laying of the foundation stone of his future Metropolitan Tabernacle, on August 15th, 1859, Spurgeon declared what was already generally known, " We believe in the five great points commonly known as Calvinistic. We look upon them as being five great lights which radiate from the cross of Christ." At the opening of the Tabernacle in 1861 addresses were given on these five points—Election, Human Depravity, Particular Redemption, Effectual Calling, The Final Perseverance of Believers. Far from being a hindrance to evangelism Spurgeon looked upon these truths as the driving force of a Gospel ministry. " Election I take it—and I am here speaking of the whole set of truths which group around this as their central sun—has not only a salting power, but exercises a flavouring and seasoning power over all our other doctrines. The purest evangelism springs from this truth. . . The doctrine which looks at first as though it would hush every exertion with indolence and make men sit down with listlessness and despair, is really the trump of God to awake the dead. Because it honours God, God will honour it."

Moreover, Spurgeon saw a vital connection between the proclamation of these truths and the outbreak of revivals. " In the history of the Church, with but few exceptions, you could not find a revival at all that was not produced by the orthodox faith. What was that great work which was done by Augustine, when the Church suddenly woke up from the pestiferous and deadly sleep into which Pelagian doctrine had cast it? What was the Reformation itself but the waking up of men's minds to those old truths? However far modern Lutherans may have ʰurned aside from their ancient doctrines—and I must confess so..ıe of them would not agree with what I now say—yet, at any rate, Luther and Calvin had no dispute about Predestination. Their views were identical, and Luther's " *Bondage Of The Will* " is as strong a book upon the free grace of God as Calvin himself could have written. Hear that great thunderer while he cries in that book, " Let the Christian reader know, then, that God foresees nothing in a contingent manner; but that He foresees, proposes, and acts, from His eternal and unchangeable will. This is the thunder stroke which breaks and overturns Free Will." Need I mention to you better names than Huss, Jerome of Prague, Farel, John Knox, Wickliffe, Wishart and Bradford? Need I do more than say that these held the same views, and that in their day anything like an Arminian revival was utterly unheard of and undreamed of.

And then, to come to more modern times, there is the great exception, that wondrous revival under Mr. Wesley, in which the Wesleyan Methodists had so large a share; but permit me to say

P

that the strength of the doctrine of Wesleyan Methodism lay in its Calvinism. The great body of the Methodists disclaimed Pelagianism, in whole and in part. They contended for man's entire depravity, the necessity for the direct agency of the Holy Spirit, and that the first step in the change proceeds not from the sinner, but from God. They denied at the time that they were Pelagians. Does not the Methodist hold, as firmly as ever we do, that man is saved by the operation of the Holy Ghost, and the Holy Ghost only? And are not many of Mr. Wesley's sermons full of that great truth, that the Holy Ghost is necessary to regeneration? Whatever mistakes he may have made, he continually preached the absolute necessity of the new birth by the Holy Ghost, and there are some other points of exceedingly close agreement; for instance, even that of human inability. It matters not how some may abuse us, when we say man could not of himself repent or believe; yet, the old Arminian standards said the same. True, they affirm that God has given grace to every man, but they do not dispute the fact that apart from that grace there was no ability in man to do that which was good in his own salvation. And then, let me say, if you turn to the continent of America, how gross the falsehood that Calvinistic doctrine is unfavourable to revivals. Look at that wondrous shaking under Jonathan Edwards, and others which we might quote. Or turn to Scotland—what shall we say of M'Cheyne? What shall we say of those renowned Calvinists Dr. Chalmers, Dr. Wardlaw, and before them Livingstone, Haldane, Erskine, and the like? What shall we say of the men of their school but that, while they held and preached unflinchingly the great truths which we would propound to-day, yet God owned their word, and multitudes were saved. And if it were not perhaps too much like boasting of one's own work under God, I might say, personally I have never found the preaching of these doctrines lull this Church to sleep, but ever while they have loved to maintain these truths, they have agonised for the souls of men, and the 1,600 or more whom I have myself baptized, upon profession of their faith, are living testimonals that these old truths in modern times have not lost their power to promote a revival of religion."[1]

In accounting for powerless preachers whose sermons affect no one Spurgeon said, "The reason is, I believe, they do not know what *the gospel* is; they are afraid of *real gospel Calvinism,* and theretore he Lord does not own them."[2] In speaking of the influence of these doctrines on his own church he wrote: "Among the many candidates for baptism and church membership who came torward every month there were great numbers of young people, and others of riper years . . . I was delighted to hear

[1] *The Life and Work of C. H. Spurgeon, by G. Holden Pike,* Vol. II, 315.

[2] *The New Park Street and Metropolitan Tabernacle Pulpit,* Vol. VII, 304-328.

them, one after another, not only express themselves clearly upon the great fundamental truth of justification by faith, but also give clear evidence that they were well instructed in the doctrines that cluster around the covenant of grace. I believe that one reason why our church has been, for these many years, so signally blessed of God is that the great majority of those who have been added to our ranks have been well established in the old-fashioned faith of the Puritans and the Covenanters, and therefore have not been turned aside or drawn away from us."[1] "Brethren," Spurgeon exhorted his fellow ministers, " in proportion as a ministry is truthful, other things being equal, God can bless it. Would you have the Holy Ghost set His seal to a lie? Would you have Him bless what He has not revealed, and confirm with signs following that which is not truth? I am more and more persuaded that, if we mean to have God with us, we must keep to the truth."[2]

Error concerning the above doctrines Spurgeon regarded as undermining the very Gospel itself. Arminianism—the error that Christ died for the salvation of all and that man must decide for Christ before God can convert him—he openly condemned: " What is the heresy of Rome, but the addition of something to the perfect merits of Jesus Christ, the bringing in of the works of the flesh, to assist in our justification? And what is the heresy of Arminianism but the addition of something to the work of the Redeemer ? . . . I have my own private opinion that there is no such thing as preaching Christ and Him crucified, unless we preach what nowadays is called Calvinism. It is a nickname to call it Calvinism; Calvinism is the gospel, and nothing else. I do not believe we can preach the gospel, if we do not preach just-fication by faith, without works; nor unless we preach the sovereignty of God in His dispensation of grace; nor unless we exalt the electing, unchangeable, eternal, immutable, conquering love of Jehovah; nor do I think we can preach the gospel unless we base it upon the special and particular redemption of His elect

---

[1] *The New Park Street and Metropolitan Tabernacle Pulpit,* Vol. VII, 302-303. The 1859 revival was itself an illustration of the connection between Calvinistic doctrine and revivals.

Andrew Bonar in his preface to the second edition of " *The Memoir of Dr. Nettleton* " (1783-1844), published in 1860, wrote: " Ireland, Wales and Scotland have been, during the past year, the theatre of the Spirit's mighty works, in a way not inferior to what was witnessed in the time of Nettleton. And let us not fail to note that the very same Calvinism which was wielded so effectually by Dr. Nettleton in his day, amid the scenes of revival wherein he was used as an instrument, has been used in our day, and in our land, by the Great Head of the Church. Who can say that Calvinistic doctrine has clogged the wheels of the chariot, when he casts his eye over the churches in Ireland, Wales and Scotland, where these have been the truths believed and proclaimed, while the Holy Spirit has come down in power and majesty ? "

[2] *C. H. Spurgeon's Autobiography,* Vol. II, 99,3. *Autobiography,* Vol. II, 225.

and chosen people which Christ wrought out upon the cross; nor can I comprehend a gospel which lets saints fall away after they are called. Such a gospel I abhor."[1]

About the year 1859 Spurgeon preached in Brighton. Not long after Brighton newspapers announced that he had given up his Calvinistic doctrines, whereupon Spurgeon sent the following lines to *The Brighton Examiner* : " The statement you have made with regard to my recantation of Calvinistic doctrine is a fabrication from beginning to end, and one which could only have been invented for malicious purposes. I am the same in doctrine as I have ever been, and I hope to remain faithful to the same grand truth until death."[2] After revising his early sermons for republication many years later Spurgeon wrote : " I was happy to find that I had no occasion to alter any of the doctrines which I preached in those early days of my ministry . . . as to the truths themselves, I stand just where I did when the Lord first revealed them to me."[3]

Spurgeon died in 1892. He lived long enough to see around him a terrible decline from sound doctrine. Towards the end he was regarded as " the last of the Puritans " and seemed to stand almost alone for the truth. " We feel," he declared, " that a hardening process is going on among the masses . . . Things are not now as in our early ministry . . . Why is this? Whence this distaste for the ordinary services of the sanctuary? I believe that the answer, in some measure, lies in a direction little suspected. There has been a growing pandering to sensationalism . . . I would condemn no one, but I confess that I feel deeply grieved at some of the inventions of modern mission work."[4]

In 1892 the tide of popular thought in the churches was very different from what it had been in 1859, and the theology of 1892 became, as Spurgeon prophesied, the theology of the first half of the twentieth century : " What is being done to-day will affect the next centuries . . . For my part, I am quite willing to be eaten of dogs for the next fifty years; but the more distant future shall vindicate me."[5] Now a hundred years have passed since the last great national revival. Surely the time has come for us to reconsider the fruits of the theological changes which have taken place since then. Have these changes really contributed to promoting more frequent revivals? to increasing the power of godliness? to convicting the world of sin? to filling churches with anxious hearers? Let us face the obvious fact—a great change has

---

[1] *An All-Round Ministry*, Addresses by C. H. Spurgeon, 350.

[2] *Autobiography*, Vol. I, 172.

[3] *The Life and Work of C. H. Spurgeon, by G. Holden Pike*, Vol. II,

[4] *Autobiography*, Vol. II, 158,

[5] *An All-Round Ministry*, 368.

taken place, is it for better or for worse ? Is the church empowered or impoverished by modern views of the gospel and of evangelism? If Spurgeon's was true Gospel preaching, then in how many places is the pure Gospel preached with power to-day? May the centenary of the 1859 revival cause many to consider such questions and to seek such an awakening as was witnessed throughout our land a hundred years ago !

The Universal Calls and Invitations of the Gospel Consistent with the Total Depravity of Man, and Particular Redemption

John Bonar*

" Unto you, O men, I call; and my voice is to the sons of man. O ye simple, understand wisdom; and ye fools, be ye of an understanding heart."
Proverbs 8 : 4, 6.

These are the words of Christ. They are the words of Christ to men in general—to all men—" to the sons of MAN." They are the words of Christ to all men—to every child of Adam, " To hear and to be of an understanding heart."

Now, we lay it down as part of Divine truth, that all men are by nature dead in sin, and utterly impotent to spiritual good ; and we lay it down as equally part of revealed truth, that Christ has a people—that he died for their redemption—and that their being brought out of their state of sin and misery into a state of salvation, is the direct fruit of his suffering in their room and stead.

If these things be so, if all men are dead in trespasses and sins, and yet all men are called—if Christ died for his people, to redeem *them* to God, yet salvation is offered to all—it follows necessarily that an obligation to spiritual duty is not inconsistent with total spiritual inability, and that a universal offer neither rests upon nor implies a universal atonement. Many think otherwise, and many who do not, are yet greatly perplexed by what such advance. On both of these points, therefore, we would now make a few observations, and having thus sought to clear the way to the full impression which the text should make, we would endeavour to do the thing which it expresses, and call all men everywhere now to repentance.

*John Bonar, the cousin of Andrew Bonar, was a prominent Scottish preacher of the last century. Ordained in 1826 he exercised a powerful ministry at Larbert and Robert Murray M'Cheyne became his assistant in 1835. Bonar died in 1863. The following sermon is taken from the Sept., 1844, issue of *The Free Church Pulpit*.

I. First, then, let us consider the call of the text to spiritual duty, as addressed to men—to all men—" to the sons of *man*."

Nothing more is required to vindicate this way of dealing with men, and to show that it is consistent with the highest wisdom, than that, as means, these calls should, in their own nature, be fitted to produce a right state of mind, and that they should be addressed to beings who, in their nature, ought to be moved by such calls. But many cannot be satisfied with this. In the pride of their heart they say, God could not call unless man could comply—nay, that it would be unjust in God to exhort, call, and urge, to what man had yet to get the help of God to do ; and, increasing in boldness as they advance in this course, they ask, whether it be not a mockery, unworthy of God, to call dead men to walk, and impotent to rise, and all to do what He knows no man can do without His special grace given to them ?

Now, if the inability of man was the inability of " natural brute beasts," as the apostle Peter speaks, and the call a call to the service of rational creatures—or if the inability was the inability of men, and the call a call to such to yield to God the service of angels or of archangels—or if the inability was the physical inability of a lame man to walk, and the call that he should rise and walk—though we would wish, even then, to speak with more reverence—there would be more weight in the vaunting words of these objections. But if the inability be the voluntary act of an intelligent being preferring the darkness to the light—if the inability be the inability of such a being to love his God, not with the love of an angel, but with all *his* heart, and all *his* soul, and all *his* strength—if the inability be that of a being who walks after the flesh, because he minds the things of the flesh, and not of the spirit —if the inability be that of a man who cannot find it in his heart to love and to serve the blessed God, and can find it in that very heart to give that love and service to the creature—then there is neither truth nor power in such statements, however vauntingly put forth as unanswerable.

And this *is* the real state of man. There is utter inability in him to spiritual duty, but it is just because sin is preferred. This inability is hopeless, but it is just because this is the governing power of the mind. There is utter helplessness in man, but this is just because this power will always prevail, if help does not come from God ; and there is in all this the deepest and darkest depravity, and that surely can never remove man from his obligation to serve God, or take away God's right to deal with man as a responsible being.

Such being the true nature of man's inability, it is evident that every hour of continuance in it is an hour of chosen rebellion, and, therefore, of deepest sin : and such being the true characteristics which every hour presents to God, there is no inconsistency in God demanding obedience, and no injustice in his punishing those who are not subject to his law, neither, indeed, can be ; and no mockery in his calling these men to turn from their sins.

That this is indeed the case will farther appear, if we consider the following plain truths, to which, as helping to a right judgment of the matter before us, we earnestly entreat your attention.

And, *first* of all, we would say, however startling it may appear at first sight, that *God can command what men are utterly unable to fulfil*—else, men must be able to keep the whole law of God in thought and word indeed, for God beyond all question does command this—else God could not command anything whatever which man could not perform—else God's right of sovereignty would be measured by man's willingness to comply with it, and God's moral government over the wicked would be at an end. *Secondly,* we would say, *God can blame and punish man for not doing what yet he* CANNOT *do*—else the more depraved man became, the less blameable he would become ; for, if total inability be a complete excuse, partial inability is a partial excuse ; and thus the more a man's heart is set in him to do evil, the less blameable he would become ; the more thoroughly hardened a man became, the less responsible he would be. *Thirdly,* we would say, *God can demand what man can do only by the aid of his Spirit*—else that which the Spirit of God works must be something which man, as the creature of God, is not bound to possess ; for if the Spirit only works in me, what is at that moment, and at every moment, my duty as a creature in such circumstances to be and to do—and the Spirit of God does this and nothing more—it must still be my duty to be in that state whether the help of the Spirit of God be sought or refused. In this case, as in every other case of a moral nature, my want is my wickedness—my weakness is my condemnation. *Fourthly,* we would say, *God cannot demand less of man—cannot demand other of man, than what his Spirit alone can work in the soul ;* for God cannot demand other than spiritual service—God is a spirit, and must be worshipped in spirit and in truth—God looketh on the heart, and any other service offered to him is a mockery—God is truth, and the Father seeketh such to worship him as worship him in spirit and in truth. And, *fifthly,* therefore, we would say, *God can and does demand of man, and cannot but demand of man—of sinful man—of man lost, undone, and dead—of man without strength, and utterly impotent—repentance and conversion ;* for, what is conversion, but just the right state of such a creature towards the blessed God ? What is the meaning of me not being able to convert myself, but just that I am so utterly depraved that I cannot love the ever blessed God, and do love the sin which he hates ; and what is this but darkest and deepest sin ? And what is repentance, but just that state which I cannot be without, for a moment, without in that moment involving myself in deeper rebellion, and contracting to my soul new guilt.

But still it may be said, if in *any way* man is so impotent and utterly unable, without special grace, to comply with the call of God, why should God use this way of dealing with him—why multiply, as the word of God does, calls, and exhortations, and warnings—why press him to turn and live—to make to himself a new heart—to repent and be converted ?   To this we answer generally, that such calls certainly do not imply an innate power of compliance, any more than the law being given implies an innate power of fulfilment—that the one and the other implies only that that state of mind to which these call men is the right state of mind which they should have towards God, and that this state of mind, therefore, God must claim, and claim every moment.   But, along with this, such calls and invitations serve the most important purposes, some of which we shall merely state.

1*st, They show us our duty and obligation—duty which lies on us at every moment—duty from which nothing can set us free.* This is the great design of all the calls of God to the sons of men. They set forth, not man's power, but God's claim—not what we are *able* to do, but what we *ought* to do—not our ability, but our duty.

2*nd, These calls of God show the connection betwixt the state to which we are called, and the enjoyment of the blessing promised.* There is a connection of co-existence, though not of cause and effect, and it is of vast importance to hold this constantly before us. As certainly as without Christ there is no salvation, so certainly without a personal union to Christ there shall be no salvation to us. As certainly as without shedding of blood there is no remission, so certainly without our washing in that blood shed, there will be no participation, and hence the gracious, and constant, and urgent call to " *take* " and live.

3*rd, These calls point out and hold before us what must be accomplished in us, if ever we be saved.* They shew us what we are perishing for lack of,—what, if it be never found in us, we shall never see life ; and what, if it is found in us, will certainly write us among the heirs of salvation.

4*th, These calls are all designed, intended, and most blessedly fitted, to shut us up to the faith now revealed—to the only way of life for fallen man.* In the gracious procedure of God, what is required as duty is promised as grace ; what He demands from us, He promises to work in us; and the demand is not to show us *our strength,* but to shut us up to *his promise.*

5*th, These calls and exhortations are intended to shew us what we ought to pray for.* Some have found out that *men* ought not *always* to pray. They have found out that, as we cannot pray without faith, so we should not pray till we know that we have faith ; and instead of being on their knees crying to God, have learned to argue on the uselessness and impossibility of unconverted men praying. We enter into no controversy, but we do know that one at least who was unconverted—who was in the gall of bitterness and in the bond of iniquity—was directed to pray, and that by infallible authority. " Pray God," said Peter to Simon, even when he perceived that he had neither part nor lot in the matter—" if peradventure the thought of thy heart be forgiven thee." Doubtless he that cometh unto God, must believe that he is—doubtless he that cometh acceptably, must come in the new and living way ; but, without fixing ought about precedence in things which, when they exist, brook neither the order nor the bounds which men would set, we would say that it is at once the duty and privilege of every soul to cry to God, and these calls, exhortations, and warnings teach them what they ought to pray for, and how they ought to ask it.

And finally, and above all, these pressing and urgent calls are designed by him who knoweth all that is in the heart of man, and how he clings to refuges of lies, to shut us out of all so-called neutral ground in spiritual things, and to shut us up to that in which all our safety lies, even the present and instant reception of Christ and conversion to God. The great delusion of men in general is, that they are doing something for their souls—that they are from time to time taking a step in advance, and that the path in which they are, will at length wind *its* way to salvation. The great anxiety of men is to get something to do, *in the mean time,* which may bear the look of religion, and yet let them alone to pursue their own course. It ministers to this delusion if you advise to read, as if, while reading, they might rest without an interest in Christ. Or if you advise to pray, as if, while praying, they may be satisfied without receiving. Or if you advise to seek, as if, while seeking, there was a degree of safety without finding. It meets this delusion, and there is no other way of meeting it, to leave no resting-place in all the accursed field of nature—to tell all men plainly that there are and can be no *mean times* with God—to say at once God requireth of us faith in Jesus Christ and repentance unto life, and thus to shut men up to that wherein safety can alone be found.

Yes ! what God requires—what he cannot but require, if compliance with his requirements is to include salvation, is conversion, saving faith, repentance unto life. Till this is done, nothing is done. Till Christ be received, death reigns. If you live on, separate from Christ, you but add sin to sin, and therefore treasure up wrath against the day of wrath. If you die in that state, you perish for ever, notwithstanding all your anxieties. If you pray and yet keep back your heart from God, you sin. If you worship, while yet you refuse to give yourself to the Lord, your very worship is mockery—all, all is sin and danger, and death, till you return to the Lord—till you yield yourself to him—till you repent and be converted. O most blessed day, when the sinner feels this—when at length he feels that out of Christ there is no resting-place for the sole of his foot, where for a moment he dares to rest—when he utterly despairs of salvation or hope from himself, and when utterly despairing of all other help, he casts himself into the " outstretched arms of Divine mercy," and, looking unto Jesus, says at length, " Save *Thou* me, and I shall be saved. Heal *Thou* me, and I shall be healed. Turn *Thou* me, and I shall be turned." That prayer shall enter into the ear of the hearer and answerer of prayer.*

II.   This brings me to speak, *secondly,* of the ground on which sinners are thus called and invited, and the warrant they have for instant compliance with that call.

Two things are evidently required, in order that these calls may be warrantably addressed to all, and all may have full warrant to comply with them.   1st, That there should be a Saviour provided —and 2nd, That that Saviour being provided, his salvation should be freely offered to us.   Christ is an all-sufficient Saviour—having all that sinners can need.   Christ as thus all sufficient is freely offered to all,—and this offer of Christ is conveyed to us, upon the testimony of God, and comes to each as " the word of salvation " sent to himself.

The call to come is thus itself the assurance of welcome.   As it would have been presumption to come without an invitation, so it is presumption to hestitate when that invitation is sent.   As it might have been a question whether we had been meant, if some only had been invited, so there is no room for hesitation, when the voice is to the " sons of man."   As it would have been a dark thing for us if none but those who had some previous good thing about them had been called, so it is most blessed for us that the call is

*As long as I am told that I must come to God, and that I can come. I am left to suppose that some good thing, or some power of good remains in me.   I arrogate to myself that which belongs to Jehovah.   The creature is exalted, and God is robbed of His glory.   If, on the other hand, I am told that I *cannot* come to God, but not also told that I *must* come. I am left to rest contented at a distance from God, I am not responsible for my rebellion, and God Jehovah is not my God.   But if we preach that sinners *cannot come,* and yet *must* come, then is the honour of God vindicated, and the sinner is shut up.   Man must be so shut up that he *must* come to Christ, and yet know that he *cannot.*   He must be told to come to Christ, or he will look to another, when there is no other to whom he may come.   He must be told that he cannot come, or he will look to himself.   This is the gospel vice, to shut up men to the faith.   Some grasp at one limb of the vice and some at the other, leaving the sinner open—but when a man is shut up that he must and he cannot, he is shut up to the faith—shut up *to* the faith, and then would he be shut up *in* the faith.   God is declared to be Jehovah, and the sinner is made willing to be saved *by Him,* in his own way, as sovereign in His grace.—*Professor Duncan's Speech in General Assembly of Free Church,* May 21st, 1844.

addressed by the authority of Him who calls to the lost, to the perishing, to the condemned, to sinners, even the chief ; and as surely as these words describe our true state and condition, so surely does the call of the gospel reach unto us, unto all of us.

This seems a most full and most blessed provision, meeting exactly the state of those who are utterly lost.   But many who would be wise above what is written are not satisfied with this. Those who think that universal commands imply universal power of our own to comply with these commands, think also that universal offers imply universal atonement as the ground of these offers.   Those who think that the call of God cannot be consistently addressed to men if they cannot themselves comply, think also that the salvation of Christ cannot be consistently offered to all unless the atonement was made alike for all—alike for those that perish and for those that shall be saved ; in a word, that as God's calling supposes ability in all, so God's offering supposes redemption wrought out for all.   Such men, feeling, however, that they cannot say this of redemption, viewed as actual deliverance from the punishment and power of sin, without being shut up to universal salvation, soon cut down the offer of the Gospel to the offer of pardon,—feeling that they cannot say of the righteousness of Christ, in its glorious fulness, of his active and passive obedience, what they say so boldly of his sufferings and death, they separate these, and cut down the ground of the Gospel offer to the death of Christ, —feeling that they cannot even say of this that it is universal in the way of a vicarious sacrifice and real satisfaction, they cut this down next, and say that the death of Christ does not secure any saving benefit to any, and is as much endured for the lost as for the saved, and, finally, feeling that any thing, whatever specific, might hamper them, they get quit of all by saying that the atonement is a great fact—a " general something "—equally done for all, but not securing saving blessings, or any blessings, to any : and as certainly, as fully, wrought out for Judas, who perished, as for Paul, who is saved.

Having thus, with impious hands, parted the seamless robe of Christ's righteousness, and separated what God hath joined, and then deprived even that which remained of any definite object, of any special design or saving power, to a troubled soul, it really does not matter much what they say of it, or what they do with it.   No ! What such a soul wants, is not a thing unconnected with salvation, but a thing bringing salvation.   What such a soul wants, is not a death only, but a life ; not an atoning sacrifice only, but a perfect righteousness ; not a sacrifice on earth only, but a prevailing inter-cession in heaven also ; not a crucified Christ only, but a risen, exalted, and reigning Christ also.   What such a soul wants is Christ as a Redeemer in all the fulness of his offices ; and what it wants to know is, whether *this Christ* is offered to it on the authority of

God. Now, we dare not say that Christ died for all in the same sense—we dare not pry into the secret book of God, and say that Christ's death was equally designed, in all that it did, for all—we dare not, with venturous hand, tear the robe of Christ's righteousness —we dare not separate betwixt his oblation and his intercession— we dare neither measure and mete what God hath left general, nor make universal what God hath made definite—we dare not say that Christ died as much for Judas and those who perish, as he did for Paul and those who in heaven are recording for ever his grace in loving them and giving himself for them—but we dare say that Christ is offered to all—freely, truly, fully, and, to all the ends of salvation, offered to all. We dare say that God is in Christ reconciling the world to himself, and not imputing to men their trespasses ; and, as ambassadors of Christ, yea, as if God did beseech men by us, as in Christ's stead we do beseech men to be reconciled to God. We dare say that, as there is nothing betwixt us and hell, absolutely nothing, but the mortal breath of this life, which may every moment be stopped, so there is nothing, absolutely nothing, betwixt us and Christ—that he standeth at the door and knocketh, and that, if any man will open, he will come in and dwell with him.

But here a proud objector will triumphantly say, and a trembling soul will sometimes also anxiously ask, How can you consistently offer what is not really designed to be given ? We answer 1st, that if the design of God actually to bestow what he offers, and to put every one to whom the offer comes into possession, *must* be *previously* known, there could be no probation and no moral government of God at all. We answer 2nd, that this is a difficulty that lies against every system, and against every system equally which admits and acknowledges the certain foreknowledge of God— indeed, against every system but the God-denying one of the fool, which says there is no God. We answer 3rd, that those who make this objection,have no advantage in point of a full, free, and direct offer of the salvation—even they cannot say that all receive salvation —even they cannot deny that God from all eternity knows who shall be saved—even they cannot say that God designs either the death of Christ or ought else to save those who from all eternity he knew would not be saved ; and even they, being as ignorant of God's foreknowledge as we are of God's decree, can as little as those whom they oppose assure *beforehand* as to what is the purpose of God. And we answer, lastly, that our views of the nature of the atonement, and the foreordination of God, does not in the least affect our free and full offer of the Gospel to all; because we do what God hath commanded us to do, knowing that he hath commanded, and that he will do as he hath said, and that whosoever believeth shall be saved.

But, still, an objector may say, *You* offer what is not there ;

there is nothing in your system except an offer ; there is nothing behind it ; there is no reality. But where is it, we ask, that there is nothing ? Is it in the original design and eternal purpose of God ? And is there more in the original design and eternal purpose of God in any system but that of universal salvation ? Or is it in the work of Christ that there is nothing ? There is glorious sufficiency in it. The atonement is complete ; nothing needs to be, nothing can be added to it. " His work is perfect "—the righteousness is perfect—the intercession is all-prevailing *to the very uttermost.* Or, finally, is it in the offer that there is nothing ? There is the most blessed certainty—the largest, the fullest extent in it—and what could there be more of in any offer ?

But, still, proud man, after all, returns, and asks, How can you sincerely offer what you say it may not be God's design actually to bestow ? And, growing more bold, he says, How can God offer that to all which is not meant for all ? This, instead of an offer of mercy, is but mocking and deceiving man. This is fearful language for man to use, but there is no foundation for it. No ! God neither mocks nor deceives any one. Where there is no confidence placed, there can be no deceit experienced. Wherever there is confidence placed, there the blessing is received. There is no deceit, and from this God shall stand for ever infinitely clear. No man, surely, would have God to fulfil his word of promise to those that do not believe it, and do not claim its fulfilment. And whosoever believes it, and claims the fulfilment, to him shall it be made fully and gloriously good, and good for ever.

Putting down, then, all such contendings against God, and escaping from the unwholesome atmosphere whence they spring, let us return to rejoice in the full warrant which every minister has to offer Christ to all—and the full warrant which each has to receive Christ for himself. Christ is set forth to us not only as a Priest, and not only as a Priest offering a sacrifice for sin, but as a Prophet, and a Priest, and a King ; and, as such, is made known to us to be received and rested on. The benefits of justification, adoption, and sanctification, are freely offered in him. This offer is to be made to " every creature under heaven," on the authority of God. They only who reject this offered grace perish in their sins ; they who believe it, and receive it, live and rejoice—joy in God, through Jesus Christ, by whom they have received the atonement.

Thus, without seeking to scan the unrevealed mysteries of the book of God's decrees—without defacing the works of Christ—without blotting out of the Word of God all that is said of God's sovereign grace and electing love—without destroying the object of faith, in order to make it acceptable to those who love not God —without reducing the blessed Word to a few portions of it, and

wishing to forget all the rest—without such things as these, there
is a full and blessed warrant to come to each sinner, wherever he is,
and say "unto you," the voice of Christ comes, "Turn and live."
"Look unto me and be ye saved." It is the command of God to
offer Christ,—"Go ye and preach to all nations." It is the command of God to receive him,—"This is the work of God that ye
should believe on him whom he hath sent." It is the invitation of
God to come to him ; and it is the promise of God, that whosoever
cometh shall in nowise be cast out. "The Spirit saith, come ;
and the Bride saith, come ; and whosoever will, let him come and
take of the water of life freely."

III. And now, therefore, we would fain do what thus we are
fully warranted to do—preach the gospel unto every creature.
"Unto you, O men, we would call ; and our voice is to the children
of man." Unto you is the word of this salvation sent, as surely,
as certainly, as directly, as if there was no other sinner in all this
world, or no other one to whom the voice of God had come. If
your name is not in the invitation of the gospel, neither is it in the
condemnation of the law. If your name is not in the call of God,
your nature is, and that is more certain than your name. As
certainly as you are lost— as certainly as you are condemned and
perishing—so certainly are you of those for whom as such, salvation
is provided, and to whom as such the invitation of God is sent.
Yes, Christ is God's gift to mankind sinners. The cross is God's
ordinance for the salvation of men, and Christ is dead for you to
come to—for you to live by. God calleth you by the ten thousand
expostulations and entreaties which he sends in his Word. Christ
calleth you by his sufferings— by his death—by his tears of compassion—and by his entreaties of grace. The Holy Spirit calleth
you by every one of those words of mercy and of warning, and by
every conviction and impression which they awaken in the heart.
Thy God hath found thee out, not with words of condemnation,
but with words of mercy. His words are all as fresh and full of
love as if first now, and first by you, they had been heard in human
language. With these words of gracious compassion doth he once
more overtake you—beseeching you to turn and live—assuring you
that in no wise you shall be cast out. O sons of men, his words
mean all that they say, and infinitely more than human words can
say ; they are drops of the compassion of God—who is a God of
truth, and with whom there is no variableness neither shadow of
turning. O how solemn then—how unspeakably solemn is the
situation of those to whom Christ's voice comes in the gracious calls
of his glorious gospel ! How solemn—how unspeakably solemn
our position this very day ! Here present this day to hear what
God the Lord will speak—called of God to lay hold of eternal life
—stripped of all vain excuses, and compelled to acknowledge that

God directly, personally, and earnestly beseeches us to be reconciled to him—eternal life in offer, Christ in offer, everlasting blessedness in offer, and every one either receiving or rejecting these offers. How dreadful is this place! The Lord is in this place and we have known it not. To the eye of man we seem but a congregation of men and women, of old and young, of richer and poorer, gathered together in the way to which men have become so accustomed—hastening to depart as if we had left but a common thing;—but God seeth not as man seeth. God sees here immortal souls—never-dying creatures—sunk in sin, and hanging on the sides of the pit ; —God reaches into the depth below and measures that awful word, " perish in their sins " ;—God sets forth Christ to be a propitiation through faith in his blood, and publishes anew the word, " Behold the Lamb of God who taketh away the sin of the world "—and God sees every soul in the act of receiving, or in the act of rejecting Christ :—God sees Christ either received, or Christ—*His* Christ —rejected in every seat, by every one! Yea, each one shall go out of these doors, either with the joy of Christ and his salvation received, or with the sin of Christ refused and rejected, cleaving to his soul. But, ah! what an infinite difference betwixt these two! What a difference now! What a difference at death! What a difference to all eternity! Refuse Christ, then, you may—many, many doubtless will—but know that God is infinitely clear of the blood of your soul. Refuse Christ you may, but know that his Word will cling to you; " I called but you refused ; I stretched out my hands, but ye would have none of my reproof." How often " I would, but ye would not." Refuse Christ you may, but be prepared to meet the deed—the deed of this hour—at the judgment-seat. What reason can there be for receiving him after, which is not equally powerful now ? What reason is there to think that you shall ever after be moved, if you can resist him now ? What cause have you to fear lest the Spirit who " taketh of the things of Christ and showeth them," being now resisted and quenched, will stop striving with you ? and what reason, therefore, to fear that the awful God-defying record of hardness and refusal *now* entered in the register above, will be the record read in " that day," and read as the just ground of your eternal and unchangeable doom ? Haste, then—escape,—grasp the hand of Christ yet out-stretched to save. Venture not to live another hour a rebel in the face of revealed mercy. And rest not until the voice of Christ to the sons of men be answered by you in the first breathings of the Spirit of adoption, " I will arise and return to my Father."—Amen.

THOMAS CRANMER (1489-1556) *

We have thus far seen the general agreement amongst the English Reformers on the relation between salvation and God's predestination. Man's works, they held, were not the cause of salvation, but faith, given by God according to His eternal purpose to the objects of His gracious choice. Though it would be a travesty of history to suppose that all the English Reformers saw and stated this with the same accuracy and fullness, nevertheless it was an underlying principle in the system of truth which they espoused. In the case of most of the sixteenth century leaders this fact scarcely needs demonstration, no one could mistake their views. But when we turn to one or two like Cranmer the evidence is perhaps not so apparent and as Cranmer, after all, was the most central figure in the English Reformation it is necessary that we should consider him in more detail. If his beliefs on this subject are in doubt our views on the doctrine which prevailed must be revised accordingly. There have been some who, recognizing Cranmer's importance, have sought to separate him from what they have regarded as the regrettable " Calvinism " of his contemporaries. It will be our concern in this chapter to question the justice of this separation and to see whether or not Cranmer was convinced on these points.

The life of Thomas Cranmer is hardly one that can be understood at first glance. In some respects he did differ from many of his contemporary Reformers. For one thing, he did not reach a position of influence so much by force of character as by having greatness thrust upon him. He went up to Cambridge about 1503, became a fellow of his College in 1510 or 1511 and until his fortieth year he had no prospects but those of an academic university life. All was suddenly changed by his unexpected encounter with Henry VIII in 1529. The Pope had refused to annul Henry's marriage with Catharine of Aragon, the king's wishes were thus thwarted and the question of his divorce had reached an impasse. Cranmer's suggestion of an appeal to the judgment of the Universities met with such royal favour, that he was called to leave his pupils and books at Cambridge, enter the king's service and shortly to become Archbishop of Canterbury and Primate of all England in 1533. It was a somewhat strange beginning.

Cranmer differed also from many others in the slowness with which he came to apprehend evangelical truth. His was no sudden crisis and spiritual experience, but a gradual development from one stage to another. At Cambridge, though he had begun to prize the Scriptures and to pray for the abolition of Papal supremacy in England, he took no part in the evangelical movement. After he

*Being the 4th of a series of articles on the English Reformers and the doctrines of grace. The series commenced in the 11th issue.

became Archbishop of Canterbury he had the painful task of watching evangelicals sentenced to the stake. Though he agreed with them in some things he differed in others and it was as late as 1546-1548 before he completely discarded the medieval notion of the corporal presence of Christ in the communion service. Cranmer was cautious, conservative and hesitant by nature and although this tendency was sometimes detrimental to him yet such was his sincerity and honesty that when finally persuaded of the rightness of a duty or principle he would always declare his mind.

Another factor which must influence our understanding of Cranmer was the unusual position in which he found himself. He did not have the unhampered liberty of action or speech in the degree possessed by the Continental Reformers. He was appointed to the office of primate of an unreformed national church by a despotic sovereign who intended to keep the control of ecclesiastical policy in his own hands. Cranmer had to work for reform within certain limits which were outside his control. A man of more light would doubtless have sometimes found the task unbearable, but the views of the English Puritans were not yet current and Cranmer never questioned the lawfulness of royal authority within the sphere of Christ's church.[1] The truth is that the connection between the crown and the Reformation in England was a great stumbling block to the cause of the Gospel and involved good men like Cranmer in many difficulties. Even the death of Henry VIII did not end these difficulties for the supremacy of all sovereigns over the national church was to remain a law of the land. Edward VI, being but ten years old on his accession, was too young to exercise the prerogative except through a regent. For two and a half years the regent, Lord Protector Somerset, was a true friend to Cranmer, but on the fall of Somerset in 1549, the regency of the unscrupulous Northumberland soon became an embarrassment to the Archbishop. Northumberland, like Jehu, assumed a zeal for Reform but at heart was out for nothing but his own ends. Throughout his career Cranmer was thus surrounded by political considerations which hindered the scope of his work. He could not act purely on principle, rather he had to weigh how far the government were prepared to go, how far the people were ripe for reform, etc. Retaining much of the medieval structure of the national church he felt called to preserve its unity and not to alienate the many who with patient instruction might join the Reformed cause. We must not forget that even in the reign of Edward VI the

[1] Those who like to praise Cranmer's moderation usually overlook the fact that in his interpretation of " the powers that be are ordained of God " (Rom. 13: 1) the Archbishop was very much of an extremist. His view of the Church's submission to the State was a serious error. A. F. Pollard in his *Thomas Cranmer and The English Reformation* says as much as can be said in Cranmer's defence, pp. 310-313 (1926 edition).

evangelicals were only a party within the national church and so they have remained, in varying degrees of strength, ever since.

Any estimation of Cranmer must bear all these factors in mind. He was called to a particularly difficult work. In judging how far he was successful in that work we shall be inevitably influenced by our own standpoint. If we admire the moderation and comprehensiveness of the Anglican system we may choose to think of Cranmer as " a greater man than any of his contemporaries." There can be no doubt that judged in terms of prudence and gentleness Cranmer excelled and these are virtues not to be despised. But if we regard the English Reformation as lacking in thoroughness and completeness our view of Cranmer's work will likewise be affected.[2] Even his warmest admirers must recognize the fact that he was a statesman as well as reformer and as such he was not prepared to act in advance of his times in the manner of a Luther or a Knox. He was also a scholar, one of the finest in Europe, and he was more at home in this rôle than in that of a systematic theologian. That even such a Christian leader as Thomas Cranmer possessed weaknesses serves to remind us that we are not to regard any man's views as the ultimate test of orthodoxy. To interpret Scripture in the light of traditional teaching is the very error which the Reformers denounced. Nevertheless it is not without importance for us to consider Cranmer's attitude to the doctrine of God's electing grace, nor without significance for us to see the unity of understanding which prevailed amongst English evangelicals in the great revival of four hundred years ago. The doctrine which bore such fruit is not something lightly to be forgotten. Let us then consider three lines of evidence which contribute to establishing Cranmer's position on these matters.

First, Cranmer's constant support of those who firmly believed and openly maintained the doctrine of absolute predestination demonstrates his willingness to advance this truth. Indeed, not only did the Archbishop support such men but, as we shall see, he deliberately appointed them to the most influential and powerful positions in the Church. In 1540 Dr. Lancelot Ridley, a man who

---

[2]Some of Cranmer's contemporaries regretted the failure to carry the purity of the Church's liturgy, government and order further during the reign of Edward VI than it actually went. Knox, for instance, strove for the cessation of kneeling at the Lord's Supper, and Hooper stood out boldly for the removal of the old episcopal vestments which he viewed as remnants of Popery. Hooper's stand involved him in controversy with Cranmer and Ridley of which J. C. Ryle wrote: " I believe that Hooper was much more far-sighted than his excellent fellow-labourers. He looked further ahead than they did, and saw the possibility of evils arising in the Church of England, of which they in their charity never dreamed . . . If Hooper's views had been allowed to prevail, one half of the Ritualistic controversy of our own day would never have existed at all." *Light from Old Times, pp. 86-87.*

"defended the cause of the Reformation with great energy," both by his zealous preaching and powerful writings (which were, we are told, "peculiarly obnoxious to the Popish party"), published a commentary on *Ephesians.* His Scriptural exposition of the opening chapter immediately classed him as a thoroughgoing expounder of the Reformed Faith. "Signs of God's predestination are these," he writes.[3] "First God of His goodness elects and chooses whom He will, only of His mere mercy and goodness, without all the deservings of man : whom He has elected He calls them for the most part by the preaching of the Gospel, and by the hearing of the Word of God, to faith in Christ Jesus : and through faith He justifies them, forgives sins, and makes them obedient to hear His Word with gladness . . . Of the contrary part, whosoever be not glad to hear the Word of God, but despise it, and care not to keep God's commandments but are all set to seek the pleasures and the glory of this world : whosoever is so affected, it is a token that they be not the children of salvation, but of perdition and eternal damnation : of these works that follow (the hearing of God's Word), we may have a conjecture, who be ordained of God to be saved, and who to be damned."

Continuing his exposition, on verse 4 of chapter 1, "according to the pleasure of His will," Ridley asserts, "no other cause is to be asked why God has elected and chosen us to be His children by adoption."

While Lancelot Ridley, for avowing such doctrines, was condemned by the Popish Bishop Bonner as a heretic, Archbishop Cranmer appointed him, in the following year, to the eminent office of being one of the six preachers in the cathedral church of Canterbury (1541). In this position Ridley continued to expound powerfully these same doctrines, as his later commentary on *Philippians* shows.[4] In this work he plainly declares that men have no ability to assent to the grace of God offered, God must first make their will, "ill of itself, to be good, conformable to His will." Another who preached and published these doctrines in writing during the reign of Henry VIII was Thomas Becon, for which boldness he was forced to flee from the country. Becon's books won renown, and in 1546 (when the Roman party was still predominant) we find them listed in a proclamation as prohibited books —along with books by others of the leading Reformers.[5] But Cranmer's estimation of Becon was such that when he returned to England in 1547, he was immediately made the Archbishop's private chaplain and also one of the six preachers at Canterbury.

[3]*The Fathers of the English Church,* vol. 2, p. 31, in which vol. is also contained a brief account of L. Ridley's life, p. 9.

[4]*The Fathers of the English Church,* vol. 2, p. 188-89.

[5]Foxe, vol. V., p. 567.

He, later in the reign, lectured in divinity at Oxford, " by the appointment, it may supposed, of Cranmer."[6]

" O where are the powers of free-will, if a man be without the Spirit of God? " writes Becon.[7] " Man has no power to seek for salvation, but rather continues still in his old wickedness, and seeks to be far from the face of God, coveting rather to be damned than he would once approach unto the sight of God ; sin has so slain his courage, Satan in him has so great dominion : yea, when he considers his wickedness, he is angry with God, hates God, and wishes that there were no God, that he might escape unpunished." How then can a man be saved in such a condition? Becon answers, " God alone is the author of our salvation, and He of His free mercy and abundant grace did choose us to be His heirs, before the foundations of the world were laid." Again, we find Becon writing that predestination is " the secret unchangeable appointment of God, before all beginnings, by His counsel and wisdom, to life everlasting concerning His elect and chosen people . . ."[8] This was the teaching of the men whom Cranmer appointed and it provides a pretty sure test of the Archbishop's doctrine.

In Edward's reign, such was Cranmer's determination to forward the Reformed Faith, that he brought over from Europe several of the leading Continental Reformers. Matthew Parker, later Archbishop of Canterbury himself, gives this account : " Archbishop Cranmer, that he might strengthen the evangelical doctrine in the Universities of Cambridge and Oxford, from which an infinite number of teachers go forth for the instruction of the whole kingdom, called into England the most celebrated divines from foreign nations, Peter Marytr Vermilius, a Florentine, and Martin Bucer, a German . . ."[9] These two men, as we shall see in a subsequent chapter, held and propagated the doctrines of grace in the clearest possible manner. As early as 1536 Bucer had dedicated his *Commentary on Romans* to Cranmer in which he

---

[6]See the Biographical notice of Becon, in *Becon's Early Writings, Parker Society*, p. x.-xi. An attempt to do justice to the importance of Becon's work was recently made in *D. S. Bailey's* book *Thomas Becon and The Reformation of the Church of England* (1952). Bailey writes : " he must be regarded as notable among the English Reformers for his work as a tract writer and propagandist. If the opposition which his writings provoked, and the ultimate success of the movement whose principles he so strenuously advocated, are any measure of the power of his pen, his contribution to the triumph of the Reformation in England, though intangible, can by no means be dismissed as negligible." p. 115.

[7]*Becon's Early Writings, Parker Society*, p. 72.

[8]Becon, *Prayers, Parker Society*, p. 616.

[9]I quote from Dr. Goode's *The Doctrine of the Church of England as to the Effects of Baptism in the case of Infants*, p. 65, (1849). William Goode was Dean of Ripon, and a forceful expounder of Evangelical truth in the last century. In this work he devotes over 100 pages to " the school of theology to which our Reformers and early divines belonged."

expounded these truths at length, so that Cranmer well knew the doctrine of the men whom he wanted in England. " Lay aside all delay, come to us as soon as possible. We will show that nothing can be more pleasant or acceptable to us than the presence of Bucer." So Cranmer wrote to Bucer on October 2nd, 1548.[10] After Bucer arrived in England in the April of the next year (following a second invitation from Cranmer), he was responsible as " the king's professor of divinity in Cambridge," for a leading part in forwarding the Reformation till his death in 1551. The same is true of Peter Martyr. Strype writes :[11] " As for the learned Italian, Peter Martyr, who is worthy to be mentioned with Melancthon and Calvin, there was not only an acquaintance between him and our archbishop, but a great and cordial intimacy and friendship : for of him he made particular use in the steps he took in our reformation. And, whensoever he might be spared from his public readings in Oxford, the archbishop used to send for him, to confer with him about the weightiest matters.[12] This Calvin took notice of, and signified to him by letter how much he rejoiced that he made use of the counsels of that excellent man." When Cranmer began to compile a Reformed Church law, the *Reformatio Legum Ecclesiasticarum* (a document containing important doctrinal statements), he chose Martyr to help him, and two others, Haddon and Rowland Taylor—who like Martyr held the doctrine of absolute predestination. Again on the accession of Mary, Cranmer, writing to the Queen, declared, " I, with the said Mr. Peter Martyr, and other four or five, which I shall chuse, will, by God's grace, take upon us to defend . . . all the doctrine and religion set out by our sovereign lord, King Edward VI, to be more pure and according to God's Word than any other that hath been used in England these thousand years."[13] So that it was to Martyr that Cranmer turned in a solemn crisis for aid in defending their common faith. Surely it is evident that the men who were most thoroughgoing in maintaining the Reformed Faith were the men whom Cranmer promoted and relied upon. Clearly these men propagated doctrine which Cranmer himself believed and desired to flourish.

Our second proof is more direct, and unanswerable. It comes

[10]*Cranmer's Remains and Letters, Parker Society*, p. 424.

[11]*Memorials of Archbishop Cranmer*, vol. 3, p. 318.

[12]There is no doubt that Peter Martyr had a supervisory influence over the formulation of the 42 Articles in 1552, which established the doctrinal position of the Church of England. *Dr. C. Schmidt* in his *Life and Selected Works of Peter Martyr*, says: " In the statement of faith of the English Church made by the Synod of London in the year 1552, the doctrines of Original Sin, Predestination and Justification were accepted in the way that Martyr, and with him all contemporary Protestant theologians in England had formulated them." Quoted by *Dr. G. P. Fisher, The Reformation*, p. 336.

[13]*Toplady*, p. 129.

from Cranmer's own pen. J. Hunt, by no means an exponent of
Reformed theology, writes in his *Religious Thought in England* :[14]
" It is a question that has been keenly discussed between Calvinists
and Arminians, which side could claim Cranmer, Ridley, Latimer,
and Hooper. If the question were to be determined by the general
tone and spirit of their writings, there can be no doubt that they
were Calvinists . . . As to Cranmer, if we take the notes on the
Great Bible to be his, which certainly we ought to do, the question
so far as he is concerned, is settled. He was a moderate Calvinist."

We have not been able to examine the notes to which Hunt
refers nor to verify if they are Cranmer's, but there is no uncertainty in the evidence for establishing Cranmer's views four years after
the publication of the Great Bible for we then find him writing
in the most decided manner.

The occasion was the publishing of *The King's Book* in 1543.
In 1537, following the compromising 10 Articles of the previous
year, a book had been drawn up by the Bishops and Cranmer
called the *Institution of a Christian Man*. It was a mixture containing both Reformed and Roman sentiments. A second edition,
somewhat altered to suit the Popish 6 Articles (1539) appeared in
1540. In this Cranmer had no hand. Then a third edition was
published in 1543 entitled *A Necessary Doctrine and Erudition for
any Christian Man*. " The same book," writes Strype of this third
edition, " was printed again, amended much both in sense and
language : yet not having any step in the progress of the Reformation, more than the former. Each edition expresses positively the
corporal presence in the sacrament : but in this is much added
about free-will, which it asserts, and good works."[15]   It seems
evident that the Popish Bishop Gardiner had the chief hand in
the alterations of this edition, though he flatteringly called it *The
King's Book*. Cranmer, dissatisfied with these alterations, made his
own private annotations in which his own doctrine is made plain
by his criticisms. I will give some examples. In the original
Institution of 1537, it was affirmed that God would never reject His
church or any member thereof ; to this the Popish party added in
the 1543 edition, " if fault be not in themselves." Cranmer rejects
this addition in these words, " This article[16] speaks only of the elect,
in whom finally no fault shall be, but they shall perpetually continue
and endure." Again, the *Institution* had asserted that all members
of the church who fell into sin would be restored by God, to which
was added in this third edition, " If wilfully and obstinately they
withstand not His calling." But Cranmer rejects this also in these
words, " the elect shall not wilfully and obstinately withstand God's

[14]Vol. I, p. 33.
[15]*The Fathers of the English Church*, vol. 3, p. 73.
[16]That is the article as it had originally stood in the 1537 *Institution*.
For these criticisms by Cranmer on *The King's Book*, see *Cranmer's Remains and Letters, Parker Society*, pp. 91-95.

calling." All members of the Catholic Church shall obtain remission
and forgiveness of sins, the 1537 *Institution* read; but the 1543
edition was altered to, all the members "following Christ's precepts,
and who when they fall repent shall obtain remission, etc." Cranmer's marginal criticism on this alteration is, "The elect, of whom
is here spoken, will follow Christ's precepts, and rise again when
they fall . . . Therefore in my judgment it were better to say thus :
The elect shall follow Christ's precepts, or when they fall, they shall
repent and rise again, and obtain remission, etc." In the article
on the work of the Spirit assuring us of God's favour, in *The King's
Book,* the need of our "applying our will to his motions" was
added to the original article of the 1537 edition. This Cranmer
rejects outright in these words, "Our faith and trust that we be
in God's favour and His own children hangs not of our own merits
and applying of our will to His motions."

One more quotation will suffice. Part of the 1537 *Institution*
reads as follows, the two words in brackets were added in *The
King's Book* :

"The penitent must conceive certain hope and faith that God
will forgive him his sins, and repute him justified, and of the
number of His elect children, not (only) for the worthiness of any
merit or work done by the penitent, but (chiefly) for the only merits
of the blood and passion of our Saviour Jesus Christ." Cranmer,
in his marginal annotations, sweeps aside the two additions, "Only,
Chiefly." "These two words may not be put in this place in any
wise : for they signify that our election and justification cometh
partly by our merits, though chiefly it cometh of the goodness of
God. But certain it is, that our election cometh only and wholly
of the benefit and grace of God . . . "

"I do not understand," writes Dean Goode, commenting on the
above, "how anyone can deny that these passages are decisive as to
Cranmer's views, and those taught by public authority in the *Institution,* on the following points, (1) that election is wholly and solely
of God's free and sovereign mercy, and that such as are elected
continue Christ's disciples to the end ; (2) that true Christian faith
is enjoyed by such only, and is indefectible . . . (3) that those who
ultimately perish never were members of the true Catholic
church."[17]

In his later writings Cranmer continued to express these same
truths. In 1551 he wrote, "I know this to be true, that Christ is
present with His holy church, which is His holy elected people, and
shall be with them to the world's end . . . neither Satan, hell, sin,
nor eternal death, shall prevail against them . . . But this holy
church is so unknown to the world, that no man can discern it, but
God alone." One final sentence from this godly man, "Our

[17]*The Doctrine of the Church of England as to the Effects of
Baptism . . .* p. 52.

Saviour Christ, according to the will of His eternal Father, when the time thereof was fully accomplished, taking our nature upon Him, came into the world, from the high throne of His Father, to give light to them that were in darkness and the shadow of death, and to preach, and give pardon and full remission of sins to all His elected."[18]

The third proof of Cranmer's doctrinal position lies in the public documents for which he was principally responsible in the reign of Edward VI. One of the most interesting of these documents was the Catechism, already briefly mentioned but deserving of more notice. This Catechism, generally ascribed to Bishop Ponet, was subscribed to by Cranmer and received royal sanction to be taught in all schools. It was designed, says Toplady, " as a larger display of those evangelical principles, which were virtually but more briefly contained in the articles. The reason is evident. The articles were intended for the clergy, who were supposed not to need so extended and minute a detail of doctrine. But the case was judged to be different with the laity . . . and therefore the Catechism was enjoined, as a kind of familiar and copious elucidation."

" The first, principal, and most proper cause of our justification and salvation," teaches this Catechism, " is the goodness and love of God, whereby He chose us for His, before He made the world. After that, God granted us to be called by the preaching of the Gospel of Jesus Christ, when the Spirit of the Lord is poured into us : by whose guiding and governance we be led to settle our trust in God . . . Whatever is in us, or may be done of us ; it altogether springeth out of this most pleasant rocke, from this most plentiful fountain, the goodness, love, choice and unchangeable purpose of God. He is the cause : the rest are the fruits and effects."[19] This was the kind of statement to which Cranmer set his hand. Clearly there is truth in Toplady's assertion that we must either believe Cranmer held the doctrine of absolute predestination " or charge the venerable archibshop with such extreme dissimulation and hypocrisy, as are utterly incompatible with common honesty."

The other public documents of Edward's reign speak with the same voice on these points The article on Predestination in the 42 Articles remained intact as the 17th of the 39 Articles. It is well known and easily accessible. I will therefore confine myself to a quotation from the lesser known *Reformatio Legum Ecclesiasticarum,* a work which received its last corrections from Cranmer's hand. After reproving those who use the doctrine to indulge in sin, the article goes on :—

[18]Quoted by *Toplady*, p. 129.
[19]*Liturgies of Edward VI, Parker Society.*

" But we, taught by the Holy Scripture, lay down this doctrine in this matter, that an earnest and correct contemplation of our predestination and election (respecting which it was appointed by the will of God before the foundations of the world were laid), that such an earnest and serious contemplation as we have mentioned of these things soothes the minds of pious men inspired with the Spirit of Christ, and beginning to experience a subjection of the flesh and members, and looking upwards to heavenly things with a certain most sweet and pleasant consolation ; since it confirms our faith of eternal salvation being about to come to us through Christ, lights up the most earnest flames of love towards God, wonderfully excites to thanksgiving, leads us as near as possible to good works, and draws us away as far as possible from sins ; since we are elected by God and appointed His sons ; which peculiar and excellent condition demands of us purity of morals and the highest perfection of virtue, and moreover lessens our arrogance, that we should not believe that the things which are freely given us by the gratuitous benevolence and infinite goodness of God are the produce of our own strength . . . "[20]

The three lines of evidence we have now examined all lead us to the same conclusion. However much Cranmer may have differed from some of his contemporaries in some respects there was no difference on these fundamental points. The faith for which Cranmer was burnt to death at Oxford on March 26th, 1555 (after two and a half years imprisonment) was the same faith for which Bradford had died at Smithfield, Hooper at Gloucester and Farrer at Carmarthen. The Word of God alone, the grace of God alone, the work of the Spirit alone—these great principles, sometimes known as "Calvinism," were the common possession of all the martyrs. This Gospel was their strength in life, their solace in death ; in vain did men strive to silence, imprison and burn it. Other gospels may appear to meet the needs of men while all is bright and times are prosperous, but let the times be desperate and the dark days of bloody tyrants recur, let fire and sword again encompass the church and then the truth of the testimony of the late Professor Froude of Oxford will again be realized :—

" *When all else has failed—when patriotism has covered its face and human courage has broken down — when intellect has yielded, when emotion and sentiment have become the handmaids of superstition . . . that form of belief called Calvinism has born ever an inflexible front to illusion and mendacity, and has preferred to be ground to powder like flint than to bend before violence, or melt under enervating temptation . . . Calvinism overthrew spiritual wickedness and purged England and Scotland, for a time at least, of lies and charlatanry.*"

[20]Quoted by Dr. Goode, p. 74.

BOOK REVIEWS—*Continued from page* 3.

Both had immense stores of knowledge, and were truly pious and thorough-ly devoted to God. Hodge wrote many books and numerous articles. Berkhof wrote 22 books, besides articles. The crowning fruit of Hodge's long career as a teacher was his three-volume *Systematic Theology*. Berkhof wrote his *magnum opus* at an earlier point in his long life, but he revised it and enlarged it a number of times. At first he preferred to call it *Reformed Dogmatics,* but later he termed it *Systematic Theology*.

There are points in which Berkhof excels Hodge, though the influence of the Princeton divine was undoubtedly more far-reaching. His work is, of course, more up-to-date. He deals with fresh challenges to the historic Christian faith which have arisen since Hodge's day. Not only so; he is also able to draw upon the fresh contributions made by men like Warfield and Vos, Kuyper and Bavinck. Moreover, his work is often more concise, compact and well-ordered. One virtue Berkhof shares with Calvin and Hodge—he gives us theology vibrant with life.

His last words in his last article for *De Wachter* were: " in the hour of death it is the forgiving grace of God which enables us to rest our heads in confidence, fills our hearts with the hope of eternal life, and causes us to look forward with holy joy to the eternal mansions which God has prepared for His own."

This is the finest one-volume *Systematic Theology* on the market. The Indices increase its usefulness to ministers and students. It is an indispensable tool to those who would possess the great treasure of divine truth which the Spirit has taught the church through the true theologians of the Word of God.   W. J. GRIER.

TEMPTATION AND SIN, by John Owen. Sovereign Grace Book Club, 1 Cliff House, Weston Lane, Southampton. pp. 322. 17/6.

It is one of the more hopeful signs of the times that the demand for Puritan books far exceeds the supply. The works of John Owen are much sought after and this reprint, containing his practical works on *Mortification of Sin in Believers, Temptation,* and *Indwelling Sin in Believers,* will do much to meet a great need. At no time are the Puritan writers more im-pressive than when dealing with the practical outworkings of their theology, and in this realm these three works are classics. Their re-publication is particulary opportune, coming as it does at a time when there are around us various theories about the method of sanctification and the nature of gospel holiness—theories which conflict not only with the Scripture but with each other and having as their only common factor the denial of the New Testament liberty given to Christians in matters of meat and drink.

The word ' mortification ' has become so commonly associated with the fastings and flagellations of monks and hermits that it has almost fallen out of use in evangelical circles. The mortification so earnestly pressed upon us in the first treatise, however, bears no relation to the Roman Catholic will-worship and neglecting of the body. Owen's idea of mortification is thoroughly evangelical. He shows that it is a work which can be performed only by those into whom God has instilled a principle of life. Because sin will remain in believers as long as they live, morti-fication is their constant duty. The author sees every uprising of sin as exceeding sinful ; ' Sin always aims at the utmost . . . Every unclean thought or glance would be adultery if it could ; every covetous desire would be oppression . . . it [sin] has no bounds but utter relinquishment of God and opposition to Him.'

The mortification of any one sin is shown to be successful only when sincerity and diligence are exercised in the opposition to all sin. Sin must be hated because it is sin, not merely because it wounds the conscience. Believers may keep their peace for a long time by ' applying grace and

mercy to an unmortified sin or one not sincerely endeavoured to be mortified.' Such a peace, however, is proved not to be the peace of God and
believers should not seek it. They should rather try to be affected by the
terrible guilt and danger of unmortified lust, to see its ability to harden
the conscience and to consider the awful nature of God's providential
dealings when He chastises His rebellious children. They should seek to
have the lust laid upon their conscences until they are filled with a longing
to be rid of it. It is only after this preparatory work that the author gives
directions to act faith on Christ as He is ' exalted and made a Prince and
a Saviour to give repentance unto Israel,' to consider the sufficiency and
fulness that is in Him. The use of such considerations to raise the expectations of His help will have the effect of engaging Him to our assistance
and of making the heart diligent in attending to all the means of grace
whereby life and vigour is imparted to the soul.

The second treatise is also a short one, based on the text ' Watch and
pray, that ye enter not into temptation.' Dr. Owen views entering into temptation as something different from ' the ordinary work of Satan and our
own lusts which will be sure to tempt us every day.' It is not merely to
fall as the result of temptation, for a man may enter into temptation and
not fall. To enter into temptation is to be entangled in it in such a way
as to know not how to get free. It occurs when Satan gets a particular
advantage over the soul and uses it to the full, or when ' lusts and corruptions meet with provoking objects and occasions, through the condition of
life that a man is in.'

It is against such an ' hour of temptation ' that the text exhorts us and
it is from this that a promise to be delivered is given on the condition of
watchfulness and prayer. There is no promise given in the Scriptures
to be delivered from being tempted at all. Promises are given, to be
kept while in temptation and to be delivered out of it. The promise with
which Dr. Owen is concerned in this work, however, is that given by
Christ to the Church at Philadelphia—' Because thou hast kept the word
of my patience, I also will keep thee from the hour of temptation ' (Rev.
3: 10). This being a greater promise than to be kept while in temptation,
the Christian is exhorted to the duty of watchfulness, the main part of
the treatise containing directions for the keeping of such a watch. A
chapter is devoted to the special circumstances when men usually ' enter into
temptation ' and another on keeping the heart. The author shows how
the natural temperament gives advantage to temptation, not only in those
who are of a hasty or morose disposition but in those who by nature are
gentle and easy to be entreated.

The treatise on Indwelling Sin is on a larger scale than the other two.
It was intended to stir up believers ' to watchfulness and diligence, to faith
and prayer, to call them to repentance, humility and abasement.' This
is a work which is thorough in its exposure of the plague of the heart and
will doubtless cause the reader much discomfort. ' It is to be feared,'
writes Owen, ' that very many have little knowledge of the main enemy
that they carry about with them in their bosoms.' It might be more profitable to read this treatise first, a true view of the character of indwelling
sin being required to show the urgency of the need of its mortification
and for watchfulness and prayer lest we enter into temptation.

This book has no entertainment value at all. The sole desire of its
author was to promote the godly life, and its directions are well fitted to
do that. It is a book for the serious and careful reader and for those who
at the time of reading are concerned not so much about their status
as about their condition.

CHARLES WALKER.

BANNER OF TRUTH PUBLICATIONS
78b Chiltern Street, London, W.1.

The Confession of Faith by A. A. Hodge. pp. 430. 13/6. A commentary on the Puritans' greatest systematic statement of the Christian Faith —The Westminster Confession. A fine handbook providing in simple language an exposition and explanation of all the leading doctrines of Scripture.

The Christian Ministry, with an inquiry into the causes of its inefficiency, by Charles Bridges. pp. 400. 13/6. "Here must begin the cure of that lethargy in sin that the world is fallen into—namely, in the renovation of a powerful evangelical ministry."—John Owen. This was the book recommended by R. M. M'Cheyne "for keeping us in mind of our ministerial work."

A Body of Divinity by Thomas Watson. pp. 226. 8/-. "One of the most precious of the peerless works of the Puritans." — C. H. Spurgeon.

The Doctrine of The Holy Spirit by George Smeaton. pp. 384. 13/6. ". . . provides in many ways the best practical teaching on this subject."— Dr. Martyn Lloyd-Jones.

Princeton Sermons by Charles Hodge. pp. 400. 13/6. 249 Sermon outlines providing "an amount and quality of homiletical example and suggestion probably not surpassed in the same number of pages in the English language."—A. A. Hodge.

Select Works of Jonathan Edwards. Vol. I, pp. 180. 8/-. Contains a biography by Iain Murray, Edwards' account of the great 1735 revival at Northampton and three of his famous sermons.

Select Sermons of George Whitefield. pp. 128. 6/-. "Once let the evan-

gelical ministry of England return to the ways of the 18th century and I firmly believe we should have as much success as before."—J. C. Ryle.

THE GENEVA SERIES OF COMMENTARIES

*Romans, by Robert Haldane. pp. 660. 15/-. Great revivals of religion have generally been related to a rediscovery of this foremost New Testament Epistle. So it was in the sixteenth century and in the eighteenth. Haldane's exposition should be read by all who desire to see such a revival to-day.

Joel, by John Calvin. pp. 132. 6/-. An exposition of a most relevant book of Scripture by the foremost commentator of the 16th century.

Zechariah, by Thomas V. Moore. pp. 250. 9/-. "A capital book; most useful to ministers."—C. H. Spurgeon.

Song of Solomon, by George Burrowes, pp. 456. 10/6. "I cannot speak too highly of this work . . . It has everything that should characterize a good commentary."—Dr. Martyn Lloyd-Jones.

Jonah, by Hugh Martin. pp. 386. 12/6. ". . . manifests the superb qualities which all of Martin's writings exemplify."—Prof. John Murray.

*I Corinthians, by Charles Hodge. pp. 400. 11/-. ". . . shows Hodge's sure grasp as one of the very foremost theologians of the Word. Students of the Scriptures will find this volume a great asset."—W. J. Grier.

*Jude, by Thomas Manton. pp. 378. 13/-. "If any one wants to buy a good specimen of a Puritan divine, my advice unhesitatingly is, ' let him buy Manton.' "—J. C. Ryle.

*Not for sale in the U.S.A.

The Banner of Truth magazine is published at irregular intervals.
Subscription for six issues, 6s. 6d., including postage.

Wickliffe Press, Wickliffe A· ·· ¼ Hendon Lane, Finchley, N.3.

456

THE
BANNER of TRUTH

(15th Issue)

Price 9d.

Subscription for six issues, 6/6 or $1.25

EDITOR:
IAIN MURRAY, B.A.
78B CHILTERN STREET,
LONDON, W.1.

ASSISTANT EDITOR:
ERROLL HULSE.

*　　*　　*

"Thou hast shewed thy people hard things; Thou hast made us to drink the wine of astonishment. Thou hast given a banner to them that fear Thee, that it may be displayed because of the truth."　　Psalm 60 : 3-4.

*　　*　　*

CONTENTS

APRIL, 1959
15th Issue

FAITH'S TRIUMPH

" Zebulun and Naphtali were a people that jeoparded their lives unto the death in the high places of the field." (Judges 5 : 18).

For twenty years Israel had groaned in bondage under the hand of Jabin, king of Canaan. His military hosts, led by Sisera and supported by 900 chariots of iron, held the land in complete subjection. The villages were depopulated, the highways deserted and there was " war in the gates " (Judges 5 : 6-8). No word came from the priests at Shiloh, no Joshua arose to smite the enemy, no arms were wielded by God's people—there was not " a shield or spear seen among forty thousand in Israel." Relief seemed hopeless. " God provides on purpose mighty adversaries for His Church, that their humiliation may be the greater, and that His glory may be the greater in their deliverance." (Joseph Hall).

The record of the deliverance is given in Judges, chapter 4. The ways of disobedience become too bitter to endure ; the people cry unto the Lord ; and a prophetess is raised up through whom the people learn judgment (4 : 5). Abuses are thus corrected and the Church reformed ; such is always the preparation for deliverance. Israel is now called to march with Deborah and Barak against Sisera—a remnant against a multitude, a band of footmen against a host of iron chariots. But the Canaanites were " men and not God ; and their horses flesh and not spirit " (Isa. 31 : 3). The enemy is confounded, the mighty Sisera flees and falls at length beneath the blow of a nail at the hand of a woman. A woman led Israel to fight and another woman thus completes the triumph. The Lord of hosts is never at loss for instruments. " He that had thought to have destroyed Israel with his many iron chariots, is himself destroyed with one iron nail. Thus do the weak things of the world confound the mighty." (Matthew Henry).

Yet this victory did not come without energy and action, and in the section of Deborah's Song, from which our verse above is taken, the manner in which the tribes of Israel supported, or failed to support, God's cause, is solemnly noted. Some are reproved and Meroz is cursed. There are times when inaction incurs a special guilt ; sloth is a sin which God hates. The commendation of Zebulun and Naphtali should teach us something about the character of true faith.

1. *Faith is an active grace.* They " jeoparded their lives unto the death." The degree and strength of our faith is sure to manifest itself by our works. That man who in the name of faith neglects the diligent use of lawful means needs to learn this lesson. Faith makes a man industrious ; faith takes the kingdom of heaven by force ; a faith which does not work is no faith at all. C. H.

Spurgeon tells us how he acted when first brought to love the Saviour's name: "I could scarcely content myself even for five minutes without trying to do something for Christ. If I walked along the street, I must have a few tracts with me; if I went into a railway carriage, I must drop a tract out of the window; if I had a moment's leisure, I must be upon my knees or at my Bible; if I were in company, I must turn the subject of conversation to Christ that I might serve my Master." Does this example of the energy of faith find some resemblance in us?

2. *Faith can act when times are worst.* No ordinary dangers faced Zebulun and Naphtali. Their case was desperate. Never in their history had Israel successfully faced chariots of iron, even the tribe of Judah when in her military prime had quailed before this fearful weapon. But, inexperienced in war though they were, and knowing nothing but defeat for twenty long years, Zebulun and Naphtali were still prepared to act though it cost them their lives. No matter how dark the skies may be, "faith," says an old Puritan, "is never non-plussed." "The profaneness of the times should not slacken but heighten our zeal. We should be holiest in evil times. In Noah's days when all flesh had corrupted itself, 'Noah was perfect in his generation and Noah walked with God' (Gen. 6:9). Athanasius stood up in the defence of the truth when the world was turned Arian. The more outrageous others are in sin the more courageous we should be for truth." (Thomas Watson).

Our problem is just the same as Israel's in the days of Sisera. God has again sold His people into the hands of adversaries. The judgment we have incurred is every bit as real and terrible as it was for the children of Israel under the hand of of Jabin. But if we find our punishment in this narrative, we also find our duty. God judges His people not to break them but to bend them to obedience and faith. Faith is the instrument of deliverance. Faith is the hand which takes hold of God's strength (Isa. 27:5). Faith acts not according to expediency but according to God's revealed will. Faith scorns self-pleasing and will jeopardize all to please God. Such faith, and in some degree it is the possession of every child of God, will never be disappointed. Let us take courage from the example of Zebulun and Naphtali. Like them we are but few, yet that should not dismay us because, as Matthew Henry says, "As long as any of God's Israel remain (and a remnant God will have in the worst times), there is hope, be it never so small a remnant, for God can make him that remaineth, though it should be but one single person, triumph over the most proud and potent."

A HUNDRED YEARS AGO

II.

THE DEATH OF JOHN ANGELL JAMES

The death of John Angell James on October 1st, 1859, stands out amongst the events which the centenary of that year serves to recall. For that event marked not merely the departure of a fore· most Evangelical Nonconformist Leader, whose influence had been vast and profound, but the passing of an era. In him was em-

bodied all that had been best in English Nonconformity and his preaching and writing had typified the finest characteristics of the first half of the 19th century. By 1859 Angell James had become the most notable surviving representative of an old school, and after his removal the leadership of Nonconformity fell into the hands of a new generation with a new outlook. The successor to James' pulpit was R. W. Dale (1829-1895). Like James he was to be a dominating influence amongst the leaders of his day, but it was a somewhat different kind of influence. Dale, while retaining broad Evangelical views, gave up belief in the verbal inspiration of the Scriptures, in the eternal punishment of the ungodly and " stood in the forefront of those who were throwing off the fetters of the old Calvinist Orthodoxy."[1] This change in thought which thus took place in the life of one church represented a revolution which was beginning all over the land. James' death was therefore more than the passing of a man. It was, in a sense, the end of an epoch. Henceforth there were to be convulsions and changes, new ideas and a new evangelicalism.

To those who think of 1859 only as a year of great revival these statements may come as a surprise. The truth, it would seem, is that while a spiritual movement, especially in Ireland, Wales and Scotland, swept many souls into the Kingdom of God, it was but of a temporary nature and not extensive nor profound enough to alter the direction in which the church and nation were drifting. The revival did not raise up young ministers and theologians by whom the church would overcome the inroads of error ; and this was a serious thing, for error was the greatest danger the church faced in 1859. That same year two books were published which

[1] *John W. Grant, Free Churchmanship in England,* 1870-1940, p. 69.

Q

revealed the intellectual forces which were about to deal devastating blows to the historic faith. One was scientific, Darwin's *Origin of Species;* the other philosophical, J. S. Mill's treatise on *Liberty.* The principle of evolution, development, progress, enunciated in the first book led to the implication that spiritual truth was not something which could be finally fixed and settled, but something subject to change, development and new discoveries. The second book called for emancipation from the bondage of old systems of thought and denounced the tame acceptance of traditions. That the church should have been, and was, imperilled by these new views is indicative of the low state of her strength. How·was it that such opinions were eventually allowed to prevail? How was it they were even taken up by so many ministers within the church herself ? There are things in the life of John Angell James which may help us to answer these questions.

Angell James was born at Blandford, Dorset, in 1785 and apprenticed to a linen draper at Poole at the age of 13. He was converted soon after and in 1802, through the assistance of Robert Haldane, entered the theological academy at Gosport. Here students were trained for the Congregational ministry and for the mission field and James received instruction for two and a half years. In the summer of 1804, while still a student, he preached to the Congregational Church at Carr's Lane, Birmingham, received a call to the vacant pastorate and began his life work at this church the following year. The congregation then numbered about 150 and were mostly elderly people. For the first seven years of his ministry James met with little success and much discouragement.[2] But a change was apparent by 1813, and from then on he rapidly came into nation-wide demand as a preacher. With a peculiar vehemence and earnestness he preached for the immediate conviction and conversion of his hearers and none was more honoured in the conversion of souls than the pastor of Carr's Lane. By 1859 his congregation numbered 1,800. After 1833 a breakdown in his health confined James' labours largely to the Birmingham area; this last phase of his life, which was also attended with family afflictions, was marked by increasing spirituality of mind and brought forth his two most valuable books, " *The Anxious Inquirer Directed* " (1834) and " *An Earnest Ministry The Want of the Times* " (1847). The first book had an immense circulation and influence. Upwards of half a million copies were sold before his death; and its usefulness can be judged by the fact that 27 persons gave hopeful evidence of conversion through the circulation of one copy in an American frontier town.

---

[2] This failure he attributed chiefly to his own lack of diligent study and of thorough preparation for the pulpit. Later in life he wrote, " I now deeply regret much misspent time, and greatly deplore that I did not, from the commencement of ministerial life, acquire the habit of early rising. Oh, what time I have slept away and for ever lost! "

The secret of the James' ministry was unconsciously revealed in the following words which he addressed to candidates for the ministry :—

" Preach Christ, my brethren, and for Christ's own sake. Exalt Christ, not yourselves. Exhibit Christ, in the divinity of his person, the efficacy of his atonement, the prevalence of his intercession, the fulnesss of his grace, the freeness of his invitations, the perfection of his example ; in all his mediatorial offices and Scripture characters ; and as the Alpha and Omega of your whole ministry. Christ has himself told you the secret of popularity and success where he said, ' And I, if I be lifted up, will draw all men unto me.' With this divine load-stone magnetize your sermons : here lies the attraction."

In the later years of his life James viewed with increasing dismay some of the tendencies of the times. " What think you of the state of our denomination ? " he wrote to a friend in 1840. " There seems to be , notwithstanding the great multiplication of our students, a great paucity of young ministers rising up of talent and power." In 1843 he writes : " It cannot be questioned that Popery and Puseyism are advancing in all parts of the world. Systems that we thought had grown old and effete, are renewing their youth ; controversies that we supposed had been settled, are reviving with all the fierceness of polemical war ; and elements of mischief which we imagined were extinct have burst into a flame." By 1851 matters are worse : " The state of religion in our country is low. I do not think I ever preached with less saving results since I was a minister ; and this is the case with most others. It is a general complaint. We have no diminution of Christian activity ; but individual piety is undevout and feeble . . . But there is a still more serious ground of apprehension in the minds of some of us, and that is for the orthodoxy of some of our young ministers. It is obvious to everyone that a spirit of scepticism is coming over our land from Germany and France, and all the great verities of religious truth are to be tried over again."[3]

None saw more clearly than James the need for a religious revival and great was his joy at the news of the awakening in America in 1857-58 and in Ireland in 1859. Writing a description of the latter event to a friend in the U.S.A., he says : " Presbyterianism in the sister Isle was a dull and torpid mass. Religious routine and heartless formality characterised the churches, because it characterised their pastors. Suddenly the Spirit has breathed upon the valley of dry bones, and the skeletons are being clothed with flesh and are standing up an army of living men." But his view of the situation in England was not bright, " There is very little stir in this country. People talk about revival, and that is all."

[3] These quotations and most of the material in this article are taken from the standard *Life and Letters of J. A. James,* edited by R. W. Dale, 1861.

This occasioned one of his last works, a pamphlet on "*What is the Spiritual State in our Churches?* It is significant that there was no demand for this pamphlet even though written by such a famous man. "By perhaps the generality of his brethren," writes his son, "he was thought too desponding. Time will show whether his views were groundless; but he did what he could to prevent his forebodings from coming to pass. He entertained them, however, to the last."

"*The State of the Churches,*" is an illuminating document. First James mentions what he considered the two excellencies of the church of 1859—her activity and her liberality. In these respects she outshone the church of 50 years before: "Those of us who were on the public stage at the commencement of 1809, and can remember what the aspect of things was then, can scarcely believe we are in the same church in the beginning of 1859, when we see night turned into day in our streets by gaslight, distance annihilated by railways, and intelligence conveyed by lightning . . . " He goes on to enumerate the development of Missionary work, Sunday schools, Tract Societies, etc. Then, turning to the other side of the picture, he deals at length with the things that caused his grief and alarm: earthly-mindedness, lack of self-denial, the low state of family religion, neglect of private reading of the Scripture, ignorance of doctrinal truth, lack of catechetical instruction, etc. From the many passages that could be selected from this section, the following will be sufficient to indicate how clearly James saw the signs of the times.

"I go on now to mention another of the faults of our churches in the present day, and that is an excessive regard to talent, genius, and eloquence in the ministry of the word. Ours is an age of man-worship, and idolatry of genius. The human intellect never made such advances as it has done in our times. The worship of talent, without vigilance, and a most sacred regard to the value and importance of truth, is likely, in this day, to injure our theology.

"Genius without virtue will only corrupt the world, and genius without truth will only corrupt the church. What a cry is there in our churches about talent! And I admit, that man being an intellectual being, must appreciate it . . . But what is to be guarded against is, exalting talent in religion, and especially in sermons, above truth, or to the neglect of truth . . .

"Let me ask, with what views are ministers often chosen to the pastorate, and heard in the pulpit? Nay, I may go a step further back, and ask, with what views are they trained by their teachers in the college? Is not talent enshrined in the schools of the prophets, as the object of idolatry; and does not modern training tend to cherish this feeling in the minds of our students? . . . When a pastor is to be chosen, how loud and how general the cry, 'We must have a man of talent.' The demand evinces a mental culture, that is itself a matter of congratulation; ay, but then there is another side of the question, and that is, a too great regard, in the spirit of the demand, for talent alone; it is the man of gifts rather than of graces, of parts rather than of eminent piety, sound orthodoxy, and earnest zeal, that is meant."[4]

Subsequent events soon proved the rightness of James' diagnosis. Thirty years later in the Down-grade Controversy, Spurgeon echoed the same sentiments only to find that they were even less popular than they had been in 1859. Whence came this great deterioration and decline? What were the factors which undermined the strength and influence which the Evangelicals had wielded in the first half of the 19th century? It has been customary to answer these questions purely in terms of the impact of science, philosophy and higher criticism. These were the foes, it is said, upon whom the blame must be laid. But such an explanation is far from adequate. These "foes" could never have done what they did apart from a *prior* failure within Evangelical ranks. When the day of battle came the trumpet gave an uncertain sound. The Evangelicals went out and found themselves smitten like Israel before the men of Ai (Josh. 7 : 4, 5). Having neglected the whole armour of God they found themselves no longer "able to withstand in the evil day." (Eph. 6 : 13).

There are two little-thought-of factors which contributed very largely to the above decline. The first Angell James recognised, but not, it seems to us, the second.

A New Emphasis in Theological Training.

Invariably it will be found that the prosperity of the church rises or falls according to the standard and kind of training she gives to her ministers. It was largely the training the Puritans received which made them so formidable in the 17th century. And when, after 1660, Nonconformists were shut out of the existing colleges and forbidden to establish new ones, their cause suffered heavily. At the beginning of the 19th century Nonconformist theological training had not recovered its 17th century efficiency, but it was recovering the right emphasis—men should be trained *to preach the Word*. Students were not allowed to forget that the object of their studies was to prepare them as preachers. "Know how to preach!" was the exhortation they received. "The chief design of your academical pursuits," wrote James to a student for the ministry, "is to prepare you more extensively to glorify God in the salvation of sinners. Let this thought be the constant inmate of your soul. Let it rise up with you in the morning and lie down with you at night   " After Springhill Congregational College was founded at Birmingham in 1838, James became its Chairman

---

[4] *The Works of John Angell James*, vol. ix, pp. 401-6. James' works were published in 12 vols. after his death.

ℚ*

and gave much of his attention to ministerial training. "It may be doubted," says one of his biographers, "if any one of his contemporaries had a more correct view of this paramount subject." But James' view—the view of the old school—was going out of fashion and the following anecdote will indicate the character of the new outlook. "At an anniversary meeting at Springhill College, Mr. James addressed the students on the subject of preaching. Dr. Gordon was also there, and made an effective speech, referring the students to the moral strength which Mr. James had attained, and quoting some Greek which Mr. James could not well understand—his mind was full of one idea, how young men were to become useful preachers—so he would have nothing of Dr. Gordon's encomiums or his Greek—he wanted to see the rising ministry aiming more at usefulness than high attainments in scholarship— though he did not undervalue learning. 'I want you,' said he, 'to be like Spurgeon, to preach as he preaches, in good plain Saxon style—and in his Evangelical strain, adapted to the wants and feelings of the common people.'" Unhappily the colleges all began to fall into the hands of men like Dr. Gordon!

Undoubtedly, one important cause in this change of emphasis and outlook was the affiliation of Nonconformist colleges with the University of London and the introduction of degree courses. James at first approved of this connection but he later came to see its dangers. This new system meant that theological students were subjected to a curriculum in which there was much that was quite irrelevant to the preaching of the Gospel; it gave a great impetus to the pursuit of learning, intellectual distinction, and academic prestige, but these were things which James viewed "as dust in the balance compared with sound theology, fervent piety, and preaching power." In an essay on "*Academic Reform*" with which he prefaced his book on James, Dr. John Campbell posed the question whether this adoption of London University degree courses was prejudicial to the interests of the colleges. He declared that it was. "That Denomination which shall make Preaching the *one great business* of its Academic Institutions will inevitably take the lead in the great work of evangelization, and ultimately triumph over every competitor. But if the really great want of the times is Preaching, ought it not then, for that reason, to be the great business of the colleges? Nothing within or without should be suffered for one moment to interfere with this." Then, after illustrating the kind of material which absorbed so much of the time of students taking degree courses, he asks, "What on earth have most of the foregoing subjects to do with the Preaching of the Gospel?" Such training sends forth "companies of tutors, rather than Evangelists and men 'eloquent and mighty in the Scriptures . . .'" The churches ask for *Preachers,* and they are offered B.A.'s, M.A.'s and L.L.B.'s! . . . I submit that the entire system is wrong.   The mind cannot without revulsion conceive of such a plan being laid down by the Lord Jesus Christ, or his Apostles, or even by the Fathers of the Reformation."

Not content with these general statements Campbell establishes his case with some striking figures.   In the twenty years previous to 1859 Springhill Theological College had 41 successes in the London University B.A. Examination.   But of these graduates only 7 were on the ministerial role in 1859!   Counting students who had taken other degrees and those who had taken none, only 34 Springhill men were exercising a ministry in Congregational churches in 1859!   On the other hand another college (Cotton End) where degrees were not taken, had 45 men in the ministry in 1859.   "The absence of Degrees at Cotton End has not impaired its efficiency as a Preaching School : Degrees have contributed nothing to the success of Springhill in raising up Pulpit Orators . . .   A Theological College might be the first in the land without a single graduate!"

It was not the need for learning which James questioned, but the necessity for that kind of learning which nurtures Gospel ministers.   The failure to pay heed to this was one great cause of the Evangelical decline in the last century.

A Diluted Theology.

John Newton, the Evangelical patriarch who died in 1807, was once in his latter years entertaining some friends to breakfast. " Pray, Mr. Newton," he was asked, " are you a Calvinist? " " Why sir," said Newton, " I am more of a Calvinist than anything else; but I use my Calvinism in my writings and my preaching as I use this sugar "—taking a lump, and putting it into his tea-cup and stirring it, he added, " I do not give it alone and whole ; but mixed, and diluted."[5]   There was value in the good man's comment but in the next 50 years the reliability of a " diluted " theology was put to the test.   In the first half of the 19th century, Evangelicals, apart from the Wesleyans, were almost all of a Calvinistic outlook. But, speaking generally, their Calvinism was of the same character as Newton's—not militant and clear cut, but moderate and quietly taken for granted.   The need for doctrinal precision and systematic theology was minimised and the emphasis in the best Evangelical circles was on experimental and practical preaching.   It was in the latter sphere that the great Nonconformist preachers of the first half of the century shone.   Angell James in this respect was typical of the others.   Theology was not his forte, in fact Dale even affirmed that " he could never give a thorough explanation of any point of doctrine."[6]   It is hard to fully accept the truth of Dale's statement, but at any rate it indicates where the weakness lay.

This weakness came out in James' attitude to the American revivalist C. G. Finney.   Finney's name was famous in alleged

[5] *The Autobiography of William Jay*, p. 272.
[6] *Life of R. W. Dale*, 2nd edit., p. 152.

revivals in the 1830's and it was Angell James who introduced his
' Lectures on Revivals' to this country with a recommendatory,
though somewhat cautious, preface. When a friend questioned the
wisdom of thus approving an Arminian author, James replied, " I
would so far agree with you as clearly to perceive a tendency in this
age to oscillate from the extreme of Antinomianism on one side of
the pendulum to Arminianism on the other . . . but I am still confident that, with all the palpable faults which attach to Finney's
books, they have done immense good in this country ; far more good
than they will ever do harm."[7]   So he wrote in 1840. But in 1843
we find him writing to a friend in America, " Our body has been
made a little anxious by the rising up in some quarters of a tendency to what is known I believe with you by the designation of
self-conversionism.   I think Finney's books have done a little harm
in this country, and I regret I ever gave a recommendation to his
lectures . . . The sentiment here that has given uneasiness is a virtual
denial of the Spirit's work in conversion . . .   I do not think it has
spread very widely here, but it is usually connected with revivalism,
which makes it seductive and mischievous."[8] Yet, in 1851, when
Finney was in England, James gave him the use of his pulpit!
" After all," he wrote to a friend, " there is so much deadness prevailing that one would welcome any instrumentality that is likely
to infuse a little more life . . . "[9] though he admitted, " I feel
considerable hesitation about encouraging his return to this country
for which a proposal is now being got up."   All this apparent
vacillation is partly to be explained by James' failure to apprehend
any serious danger in this direction.   " I believe," he said, " that
the system of Calvinism is not a mere vapour arising over the lake
of Geneva which a gust from Oberlin will dissipate."[10]   But it is
also to be explained by his moderate doctrinal position and diluted
Calvinism.   " I have long been of the opinion," he confessed in
1842, " that Calvinism, as it was put forth in the writings of the
divines of the 17th century needed to be accommodated more
closely to the mental economy and the Word of God."

This attitude, as history proves, was a downward path. Dale,
in his *History of English Congregationalism,* has some significant
comments on this theological trend among the early 19th century
Nonconformists. " The doctrines of Election, and a limited Atonement, were mentioned very occasionally, or dropped altogether.
They were not denied—they might be true—but . . . there was no
need to say anything about them.   Independents began to describe

---

[7] *Life and Letters of J. A. James,* p. 283.

[8] Ibid., p. 420.

[9] Ibid., p. 546.

[10] Ibid., p. 532.   Oberlin was the name of the American college where
Finney taught.   " So little importance did James attach to the minor
heresies of his day," says John Campbell, " that he rarely thought it worth
while to move either tongue or pen for their suppression."

themselves as 'Moderate Calvinists.'   They thought that while preserving the strong foundations of the Calvinistic theology and its method, they could modify some of the Calvinistic doctrines, which in their rigid form had become incredible to them.   But they were attempting an impossible task . . .   They had not learnt that theologians who begin with Calvin must end with Calvin.   'Moderate Calvinism' was Calvinism in decay.   The old Calvinistic phrases, the old Calvinistic definitions, were still on the lips of the Independents when George III died ; but in the spirit and tendency of their theology they were Calvinists no longer."[11]

The results of this doctrinal weakening, characteristic of so many 19th century English evangelicals, were devastating.   In the Church of England it removed the most effective barrier to the spread of Tractarianism[12] and in Nonconformity it prepared the way for Higher Criticism.   The collapse of Calvinism was not just the collapse of a time-worn system, it was nothing less than the collapse of all doctrinal Christianity.   When Dr. Peter du Moulin, a 17th century prebend of Canterbury, lay dying, he exclaimed, " Since Calvinism is cried down Christianity is in danger to be lost in the English nation."   Such words would have been equally true in the later 19th century.   " 19th century evangelicalism was not equal to the task of providing an alternate theology,"[13] a vacuum was left, and the doors were wide open for the advance of error.

If our commemoration of 1859 fails to remind us of these facts, if the centenary of the death of John Angell James passes unnoticed, we shall miss valuable instruction and overlook a key to the understanding of the present state of our churches and nation.

[11] pp. 587-8.
[12] The Romeward movement which began at Oxford about 1830, receiving its name from the 90 ' Tracts for the Times,' published by the leaders from 1833 to 1841.
[13] In fact the new evangelicals were not even conscious of the need of facing the difficulty they had created.   Dale wrote in 1877: " We have no theological system in the sense that Calvinism was the theological system of the Puritans . . . There are many among us who are satisfied with the variety and freedom of our present condition, and who have no desire that Congregationalism should be identified with any more uniform system of theological faith."   C.f. *Willis B. Glover, Evangelical Nonconformists and Higher Criticism in the 19th Century*, pp. 91-3.

. . . Some of you have never preached upon election since you were ordained.   The peculiarities of " the five points " are concealed.   These things, you say, are offensive.   And so, gentlemen, you would rather offend God than you would offend man . . .   But you say, " It will be dangerous."   What! God's truth dangerous?   I should not like to stand in your shoes when you have to face your Maker on the day of judgment after such an utterance as that.   If it be not God's truth, let it alone ; but if you believe the thing, out with it.   Keep back nothing; tell the whole gospel out.   Tell out man's responsibility : do not stutter at it.   Tell out divine sovereignty : do not refuse to talk of election ; use the word, even if they sneer . . .
C. H. SPURGEON, 1857.

MINISTERIAL TRAINING

A SKETCH OF THEOLOGICAL EDUCATION
in the 16th and 17th centuries.

"How shall they hear without a preacher? And how shall they preach except they be sent?" And how shall they be sent except they be trained? These are questions which bear an indissoluble connection to one another. If, in the appointment of God, the gospel cannot spread without preachers, so neither can preachers be sent without being trained. Even the apostles, who had an immediate call from the Lord Jesus Christ, were not sent till they were prepared, much less may we expect to find a departure from this procedure in anyone else. The training thus required is of a two-fold character. First, *intellectual*. The preacher is to teach, instruct, declare the whole counsel of God; he must therefore himself accurately know the Scriptures—in all their length and breadth. Secondly, *spiritual* or *devotional*. The heart must be prepared as well as the head; intellectual training alone will never make a true minister. Sound learning and godliness, education and sanctification, these are things which must go together. Biblical truth is revealed in order that it might be *believed, experienced* and *practised*.

Now before anyone can train in these two fields there are prior requirements necessary that God alone can give. There must be the possession of some natural abilities and powers of speech; there must also be a spiritual capacity, a love for the Saviour and such a hunger for the truth as will enable a man to undergo the discipline of study.[1] Given these pre-requisites, the purpose of training is to provide the stimulus necessary for their development and use, and, other things being equal, the character of that training will determine the student's usefulness in the ministry. Ever since the days when Paul taught for two years in the school of Tyrannus[2] the need for the consecutive and systematic instruction of students has been recognized, and it is true to say that the health of the church has aways been in proportion to the worth of the training received by her ministers.

It is this fact which gives such importance to the subject of theological colleges. We are not going to suggest for a moment

---

[1] "Two things are absolutely requisite to make a man a preacher, viz.,— (1.) *Special gifts,* such as perception of truth, simplicity, aptness to impart instruction, some degree of eloquence, and intense earnestness. (2.) *Special call*. Every man who is rightly in the ministry must have been moved thereto by the Holy Ghost. He must feel an irresistible desire to spend his whole life in his Master's cause."—C. H. Spurgeon.

[2] Acts 19: 9. Though Paul did not use the schoolroom exclusively for students there would doubtless be present a considerable number of them.

that a college training is indispensable to a minister, indeed there are times in the Church's history when a student is better off without college experience. When C. H. Spurgeon was called at the age of nineteen to what was soon to prove the most responsible charge in London, lest there should be any misunderstanding, he says, " I told the deacons that I was not a College man, and they said ' That is to us a special recommendation, for you would not have much savour or unction if you came from College.' " Such a reflection has often been unhappily true ! Nevertheless, it would be a great mistake to discredit the value of theological colleges because they have sometimes been perverted. Every man preparing for the ministry needs time, direction and spiritual knowledge ; a true theological college is designed to provide just these things. By burning midnight oil and by sheer determination some men have acquired individually all that they needed for a powerful ministry, but they are rare exceptions and would generally be the first to recommend to others the need of training under the eye of godly and zealous teachers. One of the greatest needs of our times is the need to recover a true conception of what a theological college should be and if there are no present day examples to guide us in this matter we can find ample sources of instruction when we turn back to the past.

It is no wonder the life of Europe was what it was in the early 16th century when we consider what kind of institutions controlled the training of men for the ministry. Until the time when Luther's lectures began to shake the classrooms at Wittenburg, the true purpose of theological training had been wholly buried out of sight. " In the universities," wrote William Tyndale, " they have ordained that no man shall look at the Scripture until he be noselled in heathen learning eight or nine years, and armed with false principles, with which he is clean shut out of the understanding of the Scripture . . . And then, when they be admitted to study divinity, because the Scripture is locked up with such false expositions, *and with false principles of natural philosophy,* that they cannot enter in, they go about the outside, and dispute all their lives about words and vain opinions, pertaining as much unto the healing of a man's heel as the health of his soul ! " Tyndale also complains of the complexity and uselessness of the multitude of text books to which students were subjected : " How is it possible that a huge mass of such books can train men up to live well, when the whole of one's life would not suffice to read them ? As if a doctor were to prescribe to a man labouring under a rapid disease, that he must read the works of *Iacobus a partibus* and all similar treatises, in order to discover in them how to restore his health, while in the meantime death will have carried him off, and there will be no possibility of helping any one at that rate . . . Let the great Rabbis study those huge volumes ; but, nevertheless, we must in the meantime provide for the ignorant multitude for whom also Christ died."

The Reformers were quick to realize that the church could never be reformed until steps were taken to alter the character of the existing colleges and, where necessary, to provide new ones. " It seemed a point of the first importance to reform those nurseries," comments the 16th century writer Melchior Adam, " that from them, as from a pure fountain, the streams of sound doctrine might water every corner of the nation." Cranmer thus brought over some of the best Continental divines to teach at Oxford and Cambridge, and Knox devoted much of his attention to the students at St. Andrew's. How different was the manner of instruction from the cold and dry lectures of medieval times ! James Melville, who as a student heard Knox at St. Andrew's in 1571, gives this description in his diary : " I heard him teache there the prophecies of Daniel, that summer and the wintar following. I had my pen and my little buike, and tuke away sic things as I could comprehend. In the opening up of his text, he was moderat the space of an half houre ; but when he entered to application, he made me so to thrill and tremble, that I could not hald a pen to wryt . . . er he haid done with his sermone, he was sa active and vigorous, that he was lyk to ding the pulpit in blads, and flie out of it."

Among the new colleges established in the sixteenth century none was more remarkable and influential than the Academy established at Geneva in 1559. This Academy, says Haüsser, " gave a new direction to Protestantism " and provided an example of thorough theological training that was to be widely followed. It was established in order to meet the incessant demands for preachers of the gospel that were sent to Calvin. In 1559 no less than 162 students were enrolled. Three out of every four of these came from France. In 1564 the number had risen to 300 and " the number increases daily," Beza wrote. Florimond of Raemond, a Catholic historian, relates the following explanation of how the students were drawn to Geneva : " One of the best people of Guyenne told me that one day when he was walking with some scholars, his companions, underneath the galery of the schools of Toulouse, the Holy Spirit descended upon them. He appeared neither as a dove nor as a tongue of fire. I do not know, said he, whether it was a white spirit or a black spirit. The fact is that five or six of the scholars, carried away by the same desire, packed their baggage and travelled day and night to Geneva."

There were no material comforts at Geneva to cause students to make such journeys. Even when the new buildings were completed in 1563 we read that " the students sat on long bare planks without backs, and used long bare planks in front of them as desks. There was no heating apparatus of any sort. There was no glass in the windows. Professors and students suffered a good deal from both draughts and from cold, but a slight alleviation of their misery was secured in November, 1564, when the Council ordered the gaping window spaces to be filled with oiled paper. A storm blew the paper to pieces, and after that, with some grumbles on the score of expense, the Council ordered the windows to be glazed."[3]

The curriculum was no less exacting. Work began at six in the morning in summer and seven in winter. The first hour was devoted to devotional exercises. Then on Monday, Tuesday, and Thursday lectures followed till 10 a.m., when a break for dinner was allowed. Every week-day afternoon there were lectures from one o'clock till five, with the exception of Saturdays when the students' only engagement was an afternoon meeting for theological discussion. Wednesday mornings were spent in public worship. Students were allowed to attend such classes as they pleased and some twenty-seven lectures were delivered each week. The spirit of the curriculum is embodied in the prayer with which Calvin began all his lectures, " May the Lord grant, that we may engage in contemplating the mysteries of His heavenly wisdom with really increasing devotion, to His glory and to our edification." No degrees were given.

That students should flock for instruction to a place so devoid of human attractions is indicative of the terrible earnestness which then existed in the hearts of many for the advancement of Christ's Kingdom. Conscious of the deadly struggle which was being fought out with error all over Europe, young men considered no hardship too great provided they might be instructed in the oracles of God and trained to carry the word of reconciliation to dying men. Geneva thus became the great missionary centre of the 16th century.

In England, after the accession of Elizabeth, the Puritans strove to conform the two Universities to the Genevan standard. Men like Sampson, Dean of Christchurch, Oxford, and Cartwright, Lady Margaret Professor of Divinity at Cambridge, exercised a wide influence on students before they were silenced for their failure to conform to Elizabeth's compromising ecclesiastical policy. To secure a college in which men might be prepared for the ministry according to Puritan views, Sir Walter Mildmay founded Emmanuel College, Cambridge, in 1584. On his next visit to the court he received the royal rebuke, " Sir Walter, I hear you have erected a Puritan foundation." " No, Madam," he replied, " far be it from me to countenance anything contrary to your established laws ; but I have set an acorn which, when it becomes an oak, God alone knows what will be the fruit thereof." None did more to

---

[3] *Hugh Y. Reyburn, John Calvin, His Life, Letters, and Work,* p. 284. I am indebted to Reyburn for other facts in this section.

EMMANUEL COLLEGE. c. 1688.

Apart from the Wren Chapel in the centre background this picture represents a view of the College as it was in Puritan times.

establish the Puritan movement than the men who came forth from this college; it became, as Spurgeon says, "the School of Saints, the nursing mother of gigantic evangelical divines."[4]

Laurence Chaderton, the first Master, jealously guarded the spiritual character of the college for 38 years and John Preston, his successor, faithfully preserved his trust till his death in 1628.[5] When James I sought to tempt Preston away from his post at Cambridge with the offer of a bishopric, he found his offer resolutely refused. What was a bishopric compared to training men for the ministry![6] The diligence of the Puritans at Cambridge during this period was a principal cause of the spiritual life which spread to all parts of England in the 17th century. Many of the best-known Puritan preachers were converted and trained at Cambridge — Richard Sibbes, John Cotton, John Preston, Thomas Goodwin and Thomas Shepard, are but a few of those who come into this class.

The average entrance age of students at Cambridge was sixteen. Rooms were generally shared between three or four. From the time of the early morning service at 5 a.m. religious and sober conduct was expected. Such pastimes as boating and swimming were unknown. The authorities frowned if students dressed in "silks and velvets, liker to courtiers than schollers." The curriculum was inspired to drill men into habits of mental discipline.[7] Edmund Calamy as a student used to spend 16 hours a day at his books! He later became one of the most popular preachers in London. William Gouge commenced at Cambridge his practice of studying 15 chapters of Scripture each day. Oliver Heywood tells us how he went up to Cambridge with the exhortation of his father ringing in his ears, "Often remember how short and precious your time is," and how he learned to prefer "Perkins, Bolton, Preston and Sibbes, far above Aristotle and Plato." After taking their degree students of Puritan views aspiring to the ministry would often seek residence in the house of some pious minister under whose experience and wisdom they would gain a maturity far be-

[4] The list of Puritans educated within the walls of Emmanuel is almost endless. During the Commonwealth Period no less than eleven heads of other Colleges came from Emmanuel!

[5] Chaderton, fearing lest an Arminian Master would be appointed by royal mandate when the office fell vacant through his approaching death, secretly resigned in favour of Preston in 1622. But strangely enough Chaderton lived till 1640 when he was about 94 years old!

[6] Such was Preston's eagerness to help students that Thomas Fuller referred to him as "the greatest pupil-monger in England." Emmanuel, at one point in this period, had 205 undergraduates. In 1622 there were 3050 students at Cambridge.

[7] "The great Puritanic authors must have been most industrious workers at the University, or they never would have become such pre-eminent masters in Israel. The conscientious student is the most likely man to become a successful preacher."—C. H. Spurgeon.

yond their years.   Many of the best Puritan ministers encouraged
this practice by taking in students.   How great a privilege was
thus enjoyed by men like John Angier who sat at the feet of the
Puritan Boanerges, John Rogers of Dedham!

In the 1630's Archbishop Laud did all in his power
to stamp out Puritan influence in the colleges at Oxford and
Cambridge.   Puritans were turned out of University posts
and not a few were forced to seek refuge in New England.
This persecution resulted in the furtherance of the Gospel.
Among the emigrants was John Harvard, a graduate of
Emmanuel College, and carrying with him to the New World the
imperishable memory of the value of his college days, he made
provision by his will in 1638 for the endowment of such a college
in New England.   Thus Harvard College was established at Newtown, Massachusetts.   The site was probably chosen in order that
the students might sit under the ministry of Thomas Shepard.
Shepard, another Emmanuel man, had been converted under Chaderton and Preston, and he was now in turn to become a spiritual
father to scores of others.   One Harvard student, referring to his
years under Shepard, declared, "Unless it had been four years
living in heaven, I know not how I could have more cause to bless
God with wonder than for those four years."   For many long years
Harvard was to remain the great training ground for ministers in
New England.   Without that acorn planted in Cambridge in 1584
how different the subsequent history of both England and America
would have been !   Under the shadow of that oak a generation of
men was raised up on both sides of the Atlantic, the like of which
has rarely been seen again.

After Laud's oppression and the Stuart tyranny had been
broken by the Civil Wars, one of the first concerns of the Commonwealth Government was to see that the best men were once more
placed in authority at the Universities.   To that end John Owen
was appointed Vice-Chancellor of Oxford University and men like
Thomas Goodwin were made heads of colleges.   The sun shines
brightest before setting and Oxford and Cambridge for ten or so
years before the restoration of Charles II in 1660 basked in the
brightest rays of the Sun of righteousness.   Philip Henry, who took
his B.A. at Oxford in 1650-51, "would often mention it with
thankfulness to God, what great helps and advantages he had then
in the University, not only for learning, but for religion and piety."
Matthew Henry, relating this account of his father's college days,
goes on to say how " serious godliness " was then esteemed and how
Owen and Goodwin would take it in turns to preach the University
sermon every Lord's Day afternoon.   A curious story survives of
an interview between Goodwin and a young student who was seeking admission to Magdalene College.   The story as given by
Addison in the 'Spectator' was intended to ridicule Goodwin, but,

shorn of its exaggeration, it serves to represent the kind of spirit which animated the President of Magdalene. The youth on going to the College for an interview " was received at the door by a servant who was one of that gloomy generation that were then in fashion. He conducted him with great silence and seriousness to a long gallery, which was darkened at noon-day, and had only a single candle burning in it . . . At length the Head of the College came out to him from an inner room, with half-a-dozen nightcaps upon his head, and religious horror in his countenance. The young man trembled ; but his fears increased when, instead of being asked what progress he had made in learning, he was examined how he abounded in grace. His Latin and Greek stood him in little stead ; he was to give an account only of the state of his soul, whether he was of the number of the elect, what was the occasion of his conversion . . . The whole examination was summed up with one short question, namely, Whether he was prepared for death ? "[8] To Addison such questions were amusingly ridiculous but to Goodwin nothing was of more serious importance. What value are mere literary attainments when the grace of God is absent? Happy would be the church be had she always such men preparing others for the ministry !

Students in Scotland were no less favoured in the provision they enjoyed for theological training in the later years of the 16th century and during the first sixty years of the 17th. The Scottish Reformers saw, perhaps more clearly than any, that there could be no powerful preaching unless there was a well taught ministry. When Knox died in 1572 his mantle rested on Andrew Melville. Melville, fresh from five years at the Academy in Geneva, returned to Scotland in 1574 and began his great work of bringing the Colleges at Glasgow and St. Andrews up to the level of the Continental schools. He gave a great impetus to establishing the right kind of theological training and his classes were the means of preparing such eminent preachers as Robert Bruce for the ministry. Edinburgh University was founded in 1583 and entrusted to the care of Robert Rollock. For twenty years Rollock laboured with abundant success, omitting " nothing which could impress the youthful mind with the knowledge and the fear of God." From his training came many of the best ministers of the day, including Robert Boyd of Trochrigg who became Principal of Glasgow University in 1614 and John Welsh whose apostolic preaching was attended by a great revival in Ayr. These were men mighty in the Scriptures and in prayer. Such was Welsh's love for secret prayer that he gave a third part of his time to it, and sometimes his wife would even discover him up in the night watches crying " Lord, wilt Thou not grant me Scotland ? "

In the twenty or so years preceding 1638, Scottish College

[8] *Works of Thomas Goodwin, Nichol's edition,* vol. II, p. xxxiii.

training languished under the high handed persecuting episcopal policy of James and Charles I. But in that year the Scottish nation could endure it no longer. The people rose in defence of their liberties and the General Assembly of the Church, once more taking control of the Universities, voted some of the best ministers in the land into positions of leadership at the Colleges. Consequently David Dickson, a man whose preaching had been widely used in revivals, was appointed in 1641 to spend the remaining 21 years of his life in professorial work at Glasgow and Edinburgh. And Samuel Rutherford was called from his harvest at "fair Anworth by the Solway" to become Principal of the New College, St. Andrews. Rutherford, say Wodrow, was "one of the most moving and affectionate preachers in his time, or perhaps in any age of the church." That men of such outstanding usefulness should thus be called to lecture students may seem strange to the modern mind. While souls were perishing was it right, it may be asked, that such evangelists should leave their pulpits for class-rooms ? But such a question only denotes the sad change that has taken place with regard to our views of the importance of theological training. The church knew better in the 17th century and had no cause to regret calling men like Rutherford from their parishes. Speaking of the of the latter's presence at St. Andrews, McWard wrote : " God did so signally second His servant's indefatigable pains both in teaching in the schools and preaching in the congregation, that it became forthwith a Lebanon out of which were taken cedars for building the house of the Lord through the whole land." What sweet days the church enjoyed when her evangelists were theological professors and her theological professors evangelists !

Rutherford is a fine example of the manner in which true learning and heavenly mindedness should go hand in hand. Folios and lectures did nothing to quench his zeal. An English merchant who visited St. Andrews, came away with the unforgettable impression of " a little fair man " who " showed me *the loveliness of Christ*." We know well from Rutherford's immortal letters the kind of exhortations his pupils would receive : " My Lord and Master is chief of ten thousand of thousands. None is comparable to Him, in heaven or in earth. Dear brethren, do all for *Him*. Pray *for Christ*. Preach *for Christ*. Do all *for Christ;* beware of menpleasing. The Chief Shepherd will shortly appear."

On the restoration of the miserable Charles II, his corrupt Scottish parliament quickly saw their need of silencing such teachers as Rutherford. He was ordered to Edinburgh on the charge of treason, but the summons, finding him on his death bed, received the memorable reply, " Tell them I have got a summons already before a superior Judge and judicatory, and I behove to answer my first summons, and ere your day come I will be where few kings and great folk come." On hearing the news, parliament put to the vote whether or not to let him die in the college. When it was carried to "put him out," valiant Lord Burleigh rose and declared, "Ye have voted that honest man out of the college, but ye cannot vote him out of heaven."

The year 1660 marked the end in Britain of a golden era in theological training. In that year the leaders of our nation repeated the sin of the Gadarenes—"They began to pray Him to depart out of their coasts" (Mark 5 : 17)—and Christ left them that our country might relearn by bitter experience what it was to be without theological colleges where faithful men might teach others also.

BOOK REVIEWS

SCOTTISH THEOLOGY In Relation To Church History Since The Reformation. Lectures by John Macleod. Free Church of Scotland's Publications Committee. Free Church Bookroom, The Mound, Edinburgh, I. pp. 331. 8/-.

Dr. John Macleod, the author of this book on "Scottish Theology," was himself an eminent Scottish theologian. He was inducted to the Chair of New Testament Exegesis in the Free Church College, Edinburgh, in 1906, at the age of 34. In 1913, however, he left the college to become pastor of a congregation in Inverness where he remained for seventeen years, becoming in 1927 Principal of the College at Edinburgh in addition to his pastoral work. In 1930 he was appointed Professor of Apologetics, Natural Science, Homiletics and Pastoral Theology, and remained in that position until ill health forced him to retire in 1942. He died in 1948.

Devoted as he was not only to the welfare of his own denomination but to that of Reformed Churches throughout the world, Dr. Macleod was one of those responsible for the setting up in 1937 of a special lectureship in the Free Church College which brought leading exponents of the Reformed Faith from other countries. He himself was held in great esteem and affection by theologians at home and abroad both for his vital godliness and for his deep understanding of and loyalty to the truth. Dr. Macleod had a particular interest in and affection for the Faculty of the Westminster Theological Seminary, Philadelphia and when they decided to celebrate the tenth anniversary of the foundation of the Seminary by inviting a distinguished theologian to give a series of lectures, the choice fell upon him. The subject was "Scottish Theologians in Relation to Church History since the Reformation." He delivered the lectures in 1939 and they were afterwards published, with some alterations, in this book.

The title may suggest that its appeal will be mainly to Scottish readers or to those with some acquaintance with Scottish Ecclesiastical History. This is far from being the case. The lectures were written with an American audience in mind and were enthusiastically received not only by the students but by the general Christian public. Their interest is more spiritual than national and they will be read with profit by all those whose delight it is to see the great spectacle of the Church of Christ standing on a rock and the gates of hell not prevailing against it.

The life of the Church in Scotland has been a life of constant warfare and in this it showed itself to be in true apostolic succession. The Church started with the blessing of being thoroughly reformed; and was truly Puritan in character and worship. It is not surprising then that Satan considered such a Church to be a foe worthy of considerable attention and that he launched upon her a series of powerful attacks. Peril and sword in the time of the Covenanters did nothing to separate her from the love of God.   Attacks upon her theology, however, were sometimes, and for a time, more successful and it is mainly about the faith of the reformers and their successors and the various deviations from that faith that this volume is concerned.   Although it is not a formal treatise on theology it deals with such subjects as the Inspiration and Authority of the Scriptures, the Covenant of Grace, the Atoning Work of Christ, the Work of the Holy Spirit, the method of evangelism, the free offer of the Gospel, Justification, Adoption and Sanctification.   When it is realised that this is not an exhaustive list of the subjects dealt with, some idea may be had of the scope of the book.   The various subjects arise naturally from the historical context.   Dr. Macleod had a penetrating insight into the real issue at stake in the succession of theological controversies that took place in Scotland over the centuries.   Such insight is shown in his dealing with the famous ' Marrow ' controversy.   The main question at issue was whether or not the gospel was to be offered to all, irrespective of spiritual condition, or whether it was to be restricted to the penitent.   Principal Macleod, of course, held firmly to a universal call to faith but shows the vulnerable side of the ' Marrow ' teaching with regard to the assurance which enters into faith.   The passage dealing with this is an excellent example of the tongue of the learned speaking a word in season to them that are weary.   The following quotation is particularly felicitous :

'. . . The full confidence to which the old Reformation doctrine of faith was meant to lead, though it is an eminently desirable attainment when it is in exercise, is by no means exclusively the faith that gives glory to the faithfulness of God.   Thus to insist upon it as the only shape that true faith takes is to mistake and give an inadequate or cramped view of the subject ; for the faith that is in grips with unbelief is faith as truly at work, though not so consciously triumphant in exercise as is the free and unshackled working of the faith that can boldly utter its challenge, ' O death, where is thy sting ? O grave, where is thy victory ? It creeps in under the covert of the worthy Name that it pleads and holds out against unbelieving fears.   So while it is wise and right to aim at and encourage the direct acting of faith as it lays hold of its object and says " Amen " to the word of promise, it is also wise and right to deal tenderly with the bruised reed and the smoking flax.   And such tender dealing calls for the recognition of faith, as faith, even when the beat of its heart is feeble and the believer himself is sorely tried with the whisperings of unbelief.   At the same time as tender consideration is called for the weakness of the weak they are not to be encouraged to rest satisfied with a meagre or poverty-stricken measure of attainment in the faith that glorifies the word and the heart of God.'

He had no sympathy with a latitudinarian attitude towards any doctrine but especially does he guard the doctrine of the Atonement which he looked upon as a transaction which definitely accomplishes the salvation of those on whose behalf it was made.   In the 19th Century there was a revival of the Amyraldian view of the Atonement.   The Amyraldians took up a position half way between Calvinism and Arminianism, holding as they do an Atonement which was universal in its extent and intention, although requiring the electing love of the Father and the effectual work of the Spirit for its application.   This deviation from the Reformed position may seem small but Principal Macleod regarded it as a most serious down-grade step and shows the practical result of it in the change in the method of presenting the Gospel message :

' It meant a new approach to the case of the anxious sinner when he was told that our Lord had died for him, and that he must right off receive this as the good news of salvation.   This method of approach to him hid from the enquirer that when it said that the Saviour had died for him it might prove that He had died either in vain, or with no intention to effect *his salvation. For the Universal Redemption which it taught was on its own showing a Redemption that did not secure life. In this respect the method of treating the anxious played with the use of deceitful terms, and did not compare well with the method that had been formerly in use. This older method told the sinner of a Saviour Who had died to save His chosen and called ones, and Who was now calling and inviting him to make proof of His saving power by taking Himself as the Lord his Righteousness, and so sheltering under the covert of His sacrifice and the shield of His intercession. The older Calvinism did not seek to assure the sinner that Christ had died his death until he had first, in the obedience of faith closed with Him as a Saviour in His office as Mediator. It could, as ' The Marrow' put it, tell him that Christ, Who died the Just for the unjust, was his for the taking, and that when he took this Christ as his own, he was in doing so guilty of no presumption. Methods that were borrowed from organised, almost mechanical, American Revivalism began to be so common in dealing with enquirers for salvation that they came to be looked upon as part and parcel of aggressive Gospel work. This hold in particular of such effort for the last sixty years and more since the great Evangelistic Campaign conducted in Scotland in 1873-74 by D. L. Moody and Ira D. Sankey.'*

Apart from dealing with theological questions, a good part of the book is devoted to pen-pictures of the evangelical leaders of each generation. The writer had his favourites and his paragraphs on James Durham, Thomas Halyburton and Hugh Martin particularly are calculated to arouse a further interest in these great men and their works. The first Senatus of the Free Church College and their immediate successors were high in his esteem, especially William Cunningham whom he calls a ' prince of divines and thinkers.'

This book is an admirable answer to the popular charges that theology is a purely academic subject and but distantly related to life and godliness, and that theological controversy is an evidence of a lack of the charity that suffereth long and is kind. Dr. Macleod shows that it is to the ' larger charity' of the second half of the 19th Century, when hospitality was extended to deviations from the Reformed Faith which would never have been tolerated in an earlier age, that we can trace the present state of the Church of Scotland, where the constitution ' leaves that Church with a Confession ' which no one of the ministry is bound to treat as his own creed.'

' Scottish Theology ' was the work of an unashamed enthusiast whose first devotion was to the Faith and his next to its most illustrious exponents. It is a most readable volume.

CHARLES WALKER.

THE WESTMINSTER CONFESSION OF FAITH. *Free Presbyterian Publications Committee,* 4 Millburn Road, Inverness, Scotland. pp. 436. 8/6.

It may be asked why a work already available should be reprinted ? The answer is that modern editions of the Westminster Confession have omitted the precious appendices which were formerly printed along with the Confession and the Catechisms. These appendices include such historic documents as *The Sum of Saving Knowledge,* generally attributed to David Dickson and James Durham and described by R. M. M'Cheyne as " the work which I think first of all wrought a saving change in me "; also *The Directory for Publick Worship* and *Directions for Family-Worship.* By thus reprinting in full the greatest volume that ever came from the pen of British divines the Free Presbyterian Publications Committee have done true service to the cause of Christ.

Lest any should regard the Confession as exclusively for Presbyterians we append the comments of C. H. Spurgeon: " Let wiseacres say what they will, there is more truth in that venerable Confession than could be found in ten thousand volumes of the school of affected culture and pretentious thoughtfulness. Want of knowing what the old theology is, is in most cases the reason for ridiculing it. Believing that the Puritanic school embodied more of gospel truth in it than any other since the days of the apostles, we continue in the same line of things ; and, by God's help, hope to have a share in that revival of Evangelical doctrine which is as sure to come as the Lord Himself."

EDITOR.

LECTURES ON REVIVALS OF RELIGION, by W. B. Sprague. Banner of Truth Trust, 78B Chiltern Street, London, W.1. pp. 472. 15/-.

This work was first published in 1832 by Dr. Sprague, who was a minister in the Presbyterian Church in the U.S.A. It was introduced to this country by two eminent ministers, one of whom was John Angell James, the great predecessor of Dr. R. W. Dale at Carr's Lane, Birmingham, and well-known author of " The Anxious Enquirer," a book greatly used in the conviction and conversion of sinners in the nineteenth century.

I am glad to commend such a book at the present time for the following reasons.

The first and most important reason is that I am profoundly convinced that the greatest need in the world to-day is revival in the Church of God. Yet alas! the whole idea of revival seems to have become strange to so many good Christian people. There are some who even seem to resent the very idea and actually speak and write against it. Such an attitude is due to both a serious misunderstanding of the scriptures, and a woeful ignorance of the history of the Church. Anything therefore that can instruct God's people in this matter is very welcome.

My second reason is that this particular book gives this instruction in an exceptionally fine manner. Dr. Sprague's own treatment of the subject is scriptural, theological, and balanced. Then to supplement that there is an Appendix of 20 letters by such great, saintly and scholarly men of God as Archibald Alexander, Samuel Miller, Ashbel Green and the seraphic Edward Payson dealing with their own experience in revivals. The result is a volume of outstanding merit and exceptional worth.

My third reason for commending it is that I do not know of any better preparation for the meetings that are to be held in 1959 in various places to recall the great Revival of 1857 - 1859, than the careful and prayerful study of this book.

An extract from the Foreword by DR. D. M. LLOYD-JONES.

ACKNOWLEDGEMENTS.

We wish to express our gratitude to *The Evangelical Library* for the photograph of J. A. James and to *Dr. Williams's Library* for the picture of Emmanuel College.

AN EXPOSITION OF EPHESIANS, Chapter 1 to 2: 10, by Thomas Goodwin. Sovereign Grace Book Club, 1 Cliff House, Weston Lane, Southampton. pp. 824. 27/6.

Dr. Goodwin was one of the pre-eminent teachers of the Puritan period and it was fitting that he should be chosen to expound the great Ephesian Epistle after his return from exile about 1640. Unknown circumstances led to an abrupt conclusion in the middle of the second chapter but his treatment of the first chapter—one of the most vital in the whole New Testament—is worthy of being numbered among the finest seventeenth century commentaries. This is not a popular work and we can hardly recommend it as an introduction to Puritan writings. Goodwin's thought is profound and his style is sometimes lacking in simplicity and directness. But the painstaking student will find this volume to be deeply rewarding and the riches of truth here displayed should stagger and absorb his mind long after he has turned from its pages.

The origin of this magazine was partly due to the inspiration gained from Goodwin on Ephesians and some readers will remember that our first issue contained an article extracted from this commentary.

This reprint contains Goodwin's unabridged exposition of the first chapter; the remainder is covered in a somewhat abridged form.

Some of Goodwin's characteristics are described in the following words by two of his friends in their Preface to the 1681 edition of his works:

"... Besides his eminent endowments, as to natural and acquired abilities, he had the happiness of an early and more than ordinary conversion, in which God favoured him with a marvellous light, especially in the mysteries of corrupt nature and of the Gospel ... And, indeed, that person is the best interpreter, who (besides other helps) hath a comment in his own heart; and he best interprets Paul's Epistles, who is himself the epistle of Christ written by the Spirit of God. He best understands Paul's Epistles, who hath Paul's sense, temptations, and experience ...

" He had a genius to dive into the bottom of points which he intended to treat of; to ' study them down,' as he used to express it, not contenting himself with superficial knowledge, without wading into the depths of things ...

" He had the happiness of high and intimate communion with God, being a man mighty with Him in prayer, to whom he had a frequent recourse in difficult points and cases; and such men wade further into the deep things of God who have such a leader ...

" He had a deep insight into the grace of God, and the covenant of grace; a darkness in which was anciently, and still is, the cause of great errors in the Church. He breaketh open the mines of the glorious grace of God, and the unsearchable riches of Christ; and the further you search into them the greater treasures you will find ...

" In the whole, he shews himself a ' man of God throughly furnished to every good work,' skilled in the whole compass of true divinity, speaking fully, clearly, and particularly to the points he undertakes to handle."

EDITOR.

REFORM !

Paul tells us that *the weapons of our warfare are not carnal, but mighty through God, to the pulling down of strongholds.* He probably had in his mind's eye the corvus, which the Romans employed in destroying fortifications, and certainly it aptly sets forth the work of Christians when attacking the citadels of error. We must sharply grapple the false doctrine, driving the sharp hook of truth between its joints; we must clearly understand the error, and study the Word of God, so as to be able to controvert it. The great corvus of Scripture is a mighty puller down. Then unitedly with earnest tug of prayer and faithful testimony, we must throw down piece by piece the mischievous system of falsehood, be it never so great or high. Stone by stone the wall comes down ; it is long and arduous work to destroy error ; many hands and hearts must unite, and then with perseverance all must labour and wait. Tracts, sermons, lectures, speeches, prayers, all must be ropes with which to drag the bulwarks down. God's blessing rests on the faithful endeavours of those who overturn the castles of error, and though their work may not speedily succeed, the great result is sure.

A Reformation is as much needed now as in Luther's day, and by God's grace we shall have it, if we trust in him and publish his truth. The cry is, " Overturn, overturn, overturn, till He shall come whose right it is." But, mark ye this, if the grace of God be once more restored to the Church in all its fulness, and the Spirit of God be poured out from on high, in all his sanctifying energy, there will come such a shaking as has never been seen in our days. We want such an one as Martin Luther to rise from his tomb. If Martin Luther were now to visit our so-called reformed churches, he would say with all his holy boldness " I was not half a reformer when I was alive before, now I will make a thorough work of it."

Reader, are you doing service in the Lord's war, which he is now waging ? You know the errors of Rome, are you doing anything to withstand them ? You see the Popery and iniquity of the National Establishment, are you in your measure exposing it ? Infidelity is still mighty, do you contend for God and for his Word ? Sin still reigns over millions, do you seek their salvation ? If not, why not ? Are you yourself on the Lord's side ? Oh may the grace of God lead you to trust in the great bloodshedding of Jesus, by which he has put away sin ; and then may his love constrain you to aid in dragging down the ramparts of evil.

C. H. SPURGEON.

THE WICKLIFFE PRESS

THE
BANNER of TRUTH

(16th Issue)

Price 9d.

Subscription for six
issues, 6/6 or $1.25

EDITOR :
IAIN MURRAY, B.A.
78B CHILTERN STREET,
LONDON, W.1.

ASSISTANT EDITOR :
ERROLL HULSE.

*　　*　　*

"Thou hast shewed thy people hard things ;
Thou hast made us to drink the wine of
astonishment. Thou hast given a banner to
them that fear Thee, that it may be displayed
because of the truth."　　**Psalm 60 : 3-4.**

*　　*　　*

CONTENTS

R

AUGUST, 1959
16th Issue

A HUNDRED YEARS AGO

III.

THE MINISTRY OF BROWNLOW NORTH

Towards the end of June a hundred years ago two men paced the deck of a vessel bound from Greenock in Scotland to Belfast. It was a fine summer evening and in the fading light the purple grandeur of the surrounding mountains and the dark water of the Clyde were an impressive sight. But the attention of the two passengers was doubtless absorbed with other things for this was to be no ordinary visit they were paying to Ulster. It is at the shorter of the two men we must look. He was a man of striking appearance, broad-shouldered, deep-chested, aristocratic in his bearing and dressed in the dark clothes of a country gentleman. Now in his fiftieth year, he was clearly a man of energy and strength and his serious countenance, square jaw and penetrating eye bore witness to his character.

How different Brownlow North was now to the youth who, thirty-one years before, had paid his first visit to Ireland! He was then a gay, careless, pleasure-seeker. Born in the London home of his grandfather, the Bishop of Winchester, in 1810; surrounded by aristocratic connections and church dignitaries; educated at Eton; destined, it seemed, to inherit the Earldom of Guildford; Brownlow North at that time had appeared to the worldly eye to lack nothing. That first visit to Ireland in 1828 should have sobered North for he there married a clergyman's daughter and before long faced the responsibilities of parenthood. About the same time his hopes of becoming the Earl of Guildford were dashed by the unexpected birth of an heir whose claims were superior to his own. But he had become too accustomed to reckless and extravagant living to make the changes which these altered circumstances necessitated in his expenditure, and soon, falling into debt, he left England with his family and sought relief at gaming-tables in France. He had found gambling a useful expedient before but now it failed him in the critical hour. In 1832 he was thus forced to send his family home, and volunteer for action in Don Pedro's Portuguese army. After many months in Portugal he returned to England at the end of 1833 and was forgiven. Yet though re-united to his family and henceforth avoiding debt his manner of life was unchanged. In the summer of 1835 he accompanied his brother-in-law to Scotland for the shooting season and so pleased was he with the social life and attractions of Aberdeen and the Scottish Highlands that he made that area his future home. It seemed he would live and die concerned about nothing but riding, shooting, billiards, dancing and such like. When godly souls on the Sabbath would be making their way to the house of God, Brownlow North would be seen departing for a day's fishing. But this career was arrested by a dinner-table rebuke he received from the saintly Duchess of Gordon in 1839. North became serious at last and going up to Oxford at the end of that year he applied himself with his customary energy and force of character to gaining an Arts Degree with a view to entering the Anglican ministry. But when almost on the eve of ordination and with the curacy of John Newton's old church at Olney already promised him, North's former excesses came to the notice of his Bishop. His fitness for the ministry was questioned and with typical candour North concurred to the Bishop's unfavourable decision. Thereafter he returned to Scotland and plunged back into his old life of pleasure and sin. Many have experienced temporary convictions and temporary reformation of character yet remained without the new birth. So it was with Brownlow North during his years at Oxford.

Not until he was forty-four did the great change come. One evening at the beginning of November, 1854, he was sitting playing cards as usual in the house he had rented for the shooting season on Dallas moors in Morayshire. Suddenly he was seized with a sensation of illness and an impression that he was about to die. " I said to my son, ' I am a dead man ; take me upstairs.' As soon as this was done I threw myself down on the bed. My first thought then was ; Now, what will my forty-four years of following the devices of my own heart profit me ? In a few minutes I shall be in hell, and what good will all these things do me, for which I have sold my soul ? " From that moment, though the illness soon passed, Brownlow North was a changed man. Sin, condemnation, and the world to come became intense realities to him and for seven months he remained in an agony of soul. His very physical frame was shaken and his countenance transformed. During this period he could read nothing but the Bible—even rising in the night to pore over its pages—and so absorbed was he in soul-distress that he knew nothing of all the newspaper reports of the battle of Inkermann and of the great Crimean campaigns. " It was in this prolonged period of anxiety of soul," says his biographer, K. Moody-Stuart, " that many of the truths which he afterwards preached with such amazing fervour and force were written by the Spirit of the living God upon the tablet of his heart, and burned into the very texture of his being. It was now that the thought of eternity was ever present to his distracted mind; now that he was taught that *God is* . . . It was now that he learned to hang for his life upon the naked word of God."

Immediately upon his awakening, North had laboured to undo the evil he had done. Family worship was set up, tracts were bought and carried wherever he went, his old companions were visited or written to and shown their peril. But not until a man has assurance of his own salvation is he prepared for extensive spiritual usefulness and that assurance he at last found in the third chapter of Romans. At Elgin, Morayshire, in the autumn of 1855 he began to make humble attempts at the salvation of the unconverted. At first it might just be a reading of Scripture and the peeling of an orange beside some bed-ridden pauper. Then in the sick-room he was led to exhort the dying and the careless; neighbours, on hearing of his presence, began to come in and listen, and in this unpremeditated manner Brownlow North soon found himself surrounded by perhaps sixty anxious souls crowded into a dwelling-house. One, listening to his burning words, declared she had listened to nothing like it since the ministry of " The Apostle of the North."[1] The news of North's conversion and new activities rapidly travelled far and wide. Worldlings were astounded and not a few Christians doubted the reality of such a change in such a person! But soon matters were to be put beyond a doubt.

Brownlow North's more public ministry commenced at the beginning of July, 1856, when he was invited to preach in Free Church of Scotland pulpits at Dallas and Forres. This quickly led to invitations from many churches in Morayshire and the adjoining counties. By the end of 1856 he had preached with great awakening power in many parts of the Highlands, including such centres as Fort William, Inverness and Aberdeen. In March, 1857, North came south to Edinburgh, and, declaring the truth in an agony of earnestness, roused the city in a manner that had not been known for several years. A newspaper reported : " As a spur to the regularly educated and regularly appointed ministers, and as a power-

---

[1] Dr. John Macdonald of Ferintosh, whose biography was written by Dr. John Kennedy of Dingwall.

ful living commentary on some of their most prevalent and fatal defects, Brownlow North seems destined to exercise a wide influence as a reformer. He has the good wishes of everyone who has heard him; and Edinburgh is flocking in thousands to his gatherings in the Tabernacle and elsewhere, to see the strange sight of a godless man of sport and fashion transformed into a fiery, weeping messenger of the Cross." Such was the commencement of North's ministry. "He was sent," says his biographer, "a preacher of the stamp of John the Baptist to awaken dormant souls, and break up the fallow ground, and by ploughing deep into men's consciences to prepare them for that flood of blessing which was to follow in the course of two or three years in the Revival of 1859-60."

The year 1859 was the most memorable in North's twenty years of ministry.

Such was the blessing now accompanying his labours that in the first two weeks of May "one hundred young men, besides many other persons, came to him, anxious about their souls." It was in the same month that he was, by the recommendation of such ministers as R. S. Candlish, George Smeaton, James Begg and John Bonar, recognized as an Evangelist by the Free Church of Scotland General Assembly. At that Assembly North was asked by the visiting moderator of the Irish Presbyterian Church to cross to Ireland and thus we found him bound for Belfast on that evening late in June, 1859. This visit was in a sense to be the special work of his life, for Ulster was in the throes of a great awakening and everywhere fields were ripe for the sickle which God had been preparing in the person of Brownlow North.

Four years earlier in 1855—the same year that North began to serve Christ—there had come to the parish of Connor, Co. Antrim, a new breath of faith and prayer. Nurtured by the faithful ministry of J. H. Moore, this developed and by 1858 a "calm, quiet, gradual work" of the Spirit was evident throughout the Connor district, "insomuch that when spring arrived it was believed that some hundreds had been savingly brought under its benign influence." This now proved to be the start of a work which was to spread rapidly all over Northern Ireland. That spread began openly to manifest itself on Monday, the 14th March, 1859, at Ahoghill, when, after an evening service "many fell down on their knees in the muddy streets and amid chilling rain, and poured forth earnest cries and prayers." Shortly after, revival broke out in the market town of Ballymena, three miles from Ahoghill, then at Broughshane, Coleraine, Portrush, Dundrod, Belfast and many other places. Often the outpouring of the Spirit was so sudden and so observable in the consequences that the very day on which it occurred was known. The characteristics of the revival were everywhere the same. "When the great outpouring came," says one eyewitness at Ballymena, "worldly men were silent with an indefinite fear, and Christians found themselves borne onward in the current, with scarce time for any feeling but the overpowering conviction that a great revival had come at last. Careless men were bowed in unaffected earnestness, and sobbed like children. Drunkards and boasting blasphemers were awed into solemnity and silence. Sabbath-school teachers and scholars became seekers of Christ together . . . " At Broughshane, "For about six weeks almost all agricultural operations, and indeed every kind of secular employment, were suspended, no man being able to think of or attend to anything but the interests of his soul. An overwhelming sense of awe and terror held in check the boldest sinners, while thousands who, till now, had lived as if eternity were a priestly fiction, seemed now for the first time to realise its truth and presence, and to feel as if the end of all things was at hand."

It was indeed providential that Brownlow North should have arrived in Ireland when these events were at their height. Knowing the depths of soul-distress himself, he knew how to counsel awakened sinners. His preceding labours in Scotland had given him close acquaintance with the Spirit's work, with the needs of young converts and with the danger of excesses that are liable to attend all spiritual movements. It is not surprising therefore that North now exercised a widespread influence on the course of the revival. During July and August we find him incessantly preaching throughout the length and breadth of Ulster. He was estimated to have addressed congregations of 4,000 to 5,000 in the market place at Londonderry, 7,000 at Portrush, 11,000 at Ballymena and 12,000 at Newtonlimavady! The Presbyterian minister of Portrush declared, "It were worth living ten thousand ages in obscurity and reproach to be permitted to creep forth at the expiration of that time, and engage in the glorious work of the last six months of 1859."

The above mentioned figures can be regarded only as approximate but lest they should seem quite incredible we need to remind ourselves of the insatiable thirst for the Word of God which a true revival brings. Infants memorize it, adults travel scores of miles to hear it, the labourer carries it with him in the fields, the factory worker has it beside him at the bench. That a thirst for a knowledge of God and Christ can exist so universally seems strange to us in our barren times, but it was so in Ulster a hundred years ago. Such was the spiritual hunger that the sale of " Scripture commentaries and such books as Watson's *Body of Divinity* " rose rapidly and we even read of a public house being turned into a book shop !

Professor William Gibson, the Moderator of the Irish Presbyterian Church during 1859, paid the following tribute to North's work. "Among those who visited us at this time none was more highly prized, either in Belfast or elsewhere, than Mr. Brownlow North. His striking spiritual history, his social status, and the wonderful success attending his labours, especially for the preceding two years in Scotland, all contributed to concentrate public attention on his evangelistic labours . . Having had frequent opportunities of hearing this eminent servant of Christ during his sojourn here, I can bear testimony to the wonderful power of his addresses. Thousands and thousands were gathered around him ; and whether under the canopy of heaven, or in the largest buildings that could be thrown open to receive him, he was ever ready to proclaim that truth which in his own case he had found inestimably precious."

Brownlow North continued his evangelistic labours right up to the week of his death in November, 1875. In December, 1859, he first preached in London and what was intended to be a brief stay lengthened into a period of five months of services. His preaching at the Exeter Hall, in theatres and at private ' Society ' meetings, was strikingly used to the conversion of many. Men like J. C. Ryle and C. H. Spurgeon were among the first to welcome him to the south. In 1860 North bought a house at Elgin and for many years it became his practice to itinerate for eight months of the year spending only the remainder at home. About 1865 he began to devote the majority of his time to England and in 1871 he changed his residence to London. As a preacher Brownlow North chiefly addressed himself to the unconverted. His natural earnestness was moulded into a spiritual force by his prayerfulness and reverence for the Scriptures. He commonly spent three hours every morning in reading the Bible and prayer. "The painful retrospect of a waste of valuable years " burdened him with a consciousness of the brevity of time and of what he might have been if he had followed Christ from his youth. This gave him an uncommon anxiety that others should not spend so much of their lives as he had done and thus, says K. Moody-Stuart, " he never lost an opportunity of speaking for Christ."

It remains for us to say something about the message which North preached. *The Being of God* was always the first truth that heralded his message. " In his hands the truth of God's existence became a tremendous and burning reality, borne upon the conviction and consciousness of his hearers with terrific force." North never took this truth for granted for he knew that, by nature, every man is " an unbeliever in the very existence of the God of the Bible." " I believe," he declared, " that Hebrews 11 : 6, is the *first verse* in the whole Bible that a man or woman requires to get into the heart. ' He that cometh to God must believe that *He is*.' Till you have got the substance of that verse into your hearts you are without saving religion in the sight of God." Next, *the immortality of the soul* was everywhere present in his preaching—" I can tell you to a minute how long your life is to be : it is to be as long as the life of God ! " He made the word " Everlasting " thunder in the consciences of his hearers. " I only remember," said one converted under his ministry, " that I felt that there was really a heaven and hell, and that Mr. North believed in both." The depravity of man, the peril of unbelief, the duty of instant acceptance of the salvation provided in the Gospel, these were truths he never wearied of repeating. Few excelled North in the manner in which he portrayed Christ freely offered to sinners and in the way he showed them their responsibility *then and there* to turn to God. There can never be aggressive evangelism where this note is missing from the message.

At the same time there were other sides to the Gospel North preached which distinguished him from men who, at first sight, might appear to be his successors. In his earnestness to invite sinners to Christ, North made no attempt to cover over those doctrinal truths least acceptable to human nature. He did not leave men with the impression that conversion lay within their own power, nor did he let them assume that Christ died to save all men universally. " Brownlow North did not preach universal redemption," says his biographer, " but regarded Christ as dying as the representative of His covenant people . . . His teaching was in all points most pronouncedly Calvinistic. Indeed, so much was this the case that it seems marvellous that it obtained such wide popularity . . . May it not be to this characteristic of his preaching that the stability of those converted under his labours is, under God, in great part to be attributed? "[2]

This aspect of his teaching came out clearly in his application of the Gospel to the unconverted. One hearer describes the close of one of his services in these words : " he entreated us all most earnestly to speak to Jesus there and then. He cried, ' Oh, speak to Him ! If you can say nothing else, tell Him that you hate Him, but speak to Him as you are.' I remember hiding my face in the pew, and saying that to Him, in deepest grief, and begging Him to change me."

The following striking incident gives us a similar insight into North's grasp of the truth : At the close of one of his services in Edinburgh, a young man asked to speak with him. Addressing Mr. North, he said, " I have heard your sermons, sir, and I have heard you preach often, now ; and I neither care for you nor your preach-

---

[2] Moody-Stuart further comments that while North derived his theology direct from his private study of the Holy Scriptures it was almost an exact photograph of what is known as the Theology of the Reformation.

ing, unless you can tell me why did God permit sin in the world ? "
" Then I'll tell you," the preacher at once replied ; " God permitted
sin, because He chose to do so." The man was taken aback by the
ready retort. " Because He chose it," North repeated, as the
objector stood speechless, and added, " If you continue to question
and cavil at God's dealings, I will tell you something more that God
will choose to do. He will some day choose to put you into hell.
It is vain, sir, for man to strive with his Maker : you cannot resist
Him ; and neither your opinion of His dealings, nor your blasphemous expression of them, will in the least lessen the pain of your
everlasting damnation, which will most certainly be your portion if
you go on in your present spirit. There were such questioners as
you in Paul's time, and what the Apostle said to them I say to you,
' Nay, but, O man, who art thou that repliest against God? ' " The
young man interrupted him, and asked, " Is there such a text, sir,
as that in the Bible ? "   " Yes, there is in the ninth chapter of
Romans ; and I recommend you to go home and read that chapter,
and after you have read it, and learned from His own word that
God claims for Himself the right to do whatever He chooses, and
does not permit the thing formed to say to Him that formed it, Why
hast Thou made me thus ?—to remember that, besides permitting
sin, there is another thing God has chosen to do—*God chose to send
Jesus.*"

A few days after this interview the young man returned. He had
gone home, read the ninth chapter of Romans, and, pleading for the
Holy Spirit to be his teacher, had learned the way of salvation by
grace. " I am happy, oh, so happy sir ; . . . the only reason why I
know I am forgiven is that, for Christ's sake, God chooses to pardon
me."

Having thus sketched a brief outline of the man who in Scotland, Ireland and England, was so greatly used in the awakening of
1859, it remains for us to comment on a question which the above
facts should naturally lead us to ask—How is it if Brownlow North
was such an outstanding figure in revival only a hundred years ago
that his name is practically unknown today? We suggest that the
principal answer to this question lies in the fact that North was one
of the last representatives of an old school ; when he died in 1875
it was just at a time when, through the powerful example of D. L.
Moody's campaigns (1873-74), a new style of evangelism was beginning to be popularized. The 1870's were a turning point in
Britain ; a new evangelical school was rising whose theology has
dominated evangelistic activity ever since. Once the " new evangelism " became the accepted norm it is not surprising that of the old
leaders all save John Wesley were soon forgotten. Moody eclipsed
North (just as Finney earlier in the century, in the United States,
had eclipsed Asahel Nettleton), but of these two men it was the one

we hear least about today who was the most Biblical and outstanding in his evangelism !

BIBLIOGRAPHY:

Brownlow North, Records and Recollections. By K. Moody-Stuart, 1878.
Brownlow North, His Life and Work. An abridgement of the above, 1904.
The Year of Grace, A History of The Ulster Revival of 1859. By William Gibson, 1860.

SMALL BOOKS BY BROWNLOW NORTH:

Ourselves, A picture sketched from the history of the Children of Israel. Third Edition, 1866.
" *Yes! or No!* " The substance of evangelistic addresses, 1867.
The Rich Man and Lazarus. A powerful exposition of Luke 16: 19-31.

The Banner of Truth Trust plan to reprint the last-named work before the end of 1959. We should be glad to borrow any books or tracts by North not mentioned above. Would readers kindly note this request.

Six Short Rules for Young Christians

I.   Never neglect daily private prayer; and when you pray, remember that God is present, and that He hears your prayers. (Heb. xi. 6).

II.   Never neglect daily private Bible-reading; and when you read, remember that God is speaking to you, and that you are to believe and act upon what He says. I believe all backsliding begins with the neglect of these two rules. (John v. 39).

III.   Never let a day pass without trying to do something for Jesus. every night reflect on what Jesus has done for you, and then ask yourself, What am I doing for Him? (Matt. v. 13-16).

IV.   If you are in doubt as to a thing being right or wrong, go to your room, and kneel down and ask God's blessing upon it. (Col. iii. 17). If you cannot do this, it is wrong. (Rom. xvi. 23).

V.   Never take your Christianity from Christians, or argue that because such and such people do so and so, that therefore you may. (2 Cor. x. 12). You are to ask yourself, How would Christ act in my place? and strive to follow Him. (John x. 27).

VI.   Never believe what you feel, if it contradicts God's Word. Ask yourself, Can what I feel be true, if God's Word is true? and if *both* cannot be true, believe God, and make your own heart the liar. (Rom. iii, 4; 1 John v, 10, 11).

BROWNLOW NORTH.

A CALL TO REFORMATION

J. G. VOS.[1]

Church reformation according to Scripture is a continuous process.

Ecclesia reformata reformanda est (" The church, having been reformed, is still to be reformed "). This follows from the fact that Scripture is an absolute and perfect standard, while the church at any point in its history on earth is still imperfect and involved in sin and error.

This process of reformation must be continuous until the end of the world. At no point may the church stop and say, " I have arrived. Thus far but no farther ! " Only in heaven can the church triumphant say that.

In this process of reformation there are certain historical stages and certain outstanding landmarks of progress achieved. For instance, the great historic creeds and confessions of the church are such landmarks of progress. The Westminster Confession of Faith, for example, marks true progress in the reformation of the church up to the time when that Confession was formulated.

Reformation Always Incomplete on Earth.

We may never regard this process as completed in our own day, or at any point in the earthly history of the church. We must always forget the things that are behind and press on to the things that are in the future; we must always strive to apprehend that for which we are apprehended of Christ Jesus. The church's doctrine, worship, government, discipline, missionary activities, educational institutions, publications, and practical life—all these are to be progressively reformed according to Scripture.

Reformation has always been a step-by-step process, and it must necessarily be such. Zealots would attempt to achieve everything at one fell swoop, but they only smash their head against a stone wall. God works by historical process—a gradual, continuous process— and we must conform to God's way of working.

Scriptural church reformation requires a searching self-criticism on the part of the church.

Not only is advance in study of the Scriptures required, beyond the landmarks of the past, but searching self-criticism on the part of the church is called for.

---

[1] Rev. J. G. Vos is Editor of *Blue Banner Faith and Life*, an American magazine bearing one of the most faithful testimonies to the truth in the world today. This article is reprinted from the *Blue Banner*, in slightly abridged form, by kind permission of Mr. Vos.

The church's subordinate standards must always be subjected to examination and re-examination in the light of Scripture. This is implied in our confession that only Scripture is infallible. If only Scripture is infallible, then everything else must be constantly tested and re-tested by Scripture.

Not only the church's official standards, but its life, its programmes, its activities, its institutions, its publications, must be subjected to a searching self-criticism on the basis of Scripture. These must always be tested and re-tested in the light of the Word of God. Such self-criticism on the part of the church is the corporate counterpart of the self-examination to which God in His Word calls every individual Christian.

Absolute Loyalty to Scripture Required.

Such self-criticism on the part of the church is difficult. It calls for effort, intelligence, learning, sacrifice, very great humility and self-denial, and absolute honesty. It requires loyalty to Scripture, a loyalty that is willing to go to any length in order to be true to the Word of God—a truly heroic and radical loyalty to Scripture.

Such self-criticism on the part of the church may be embarrassing and even painful. It may mean that the church, like Christian in Bunyan's *Pilgrim's Progress,* may find itself in By-path Meadow, and will have to retrace its steps humbly and painfully until it is back on the King's Highway again. Such self-criticism on the part of the church may be devastating to the special interests or projects of particular individuals or groups in the church. It may demonstrate that particular features of the church's standards, life or programme, are not fully in harmony with the Word of God, and should be re-considered and brought into harmony with that Word.

Past Reformation Attained by Self-Criticism.

For these and similar reasons self-criticism on the part of the church is often neglected, and even strongly opposed. Those who advocate it or seek to have it undertaken are likely to be represented as extremists, fanatics, enthusiasts, visionaries, troublemakers, and the like. Yet it is by such self-criticism that the reformations of the past have been achieved. Men like Luther, Calvin, Knox, Melville, Cameron and Renwick were concerned only about the judgment of God in His Word. They were not deterred by the adverse judgments and attitudes of men.

When the church has dared really to look at itself in the mirror of God's Word, in dead earnest, the church has been at its greatest, and has been influential in the world. It has gone forward with new life and vigour.

On the other hand, when the church has hesitated or refused to look at itself intently in the mirror of God's Word, it has been weak, stagnant, decadent, ineffective and uninfluential.

Constant denominational self-criticism on the basis of Scripture is a duty implied and recognized in our First Term of Communion. But is this really taken seriously? How much zeal, how much concern—I will even say, how much tolerance—is there for it today?

Shutting the Door Against Reformation.

There is a constant tendency in every church to regard the present state of affairs as normal and right. Thus what is in reality mere custom, comes to have virtually the force and influence of principle; while matters of principle come to be treated as if they were mere conventions or human customs, having only the authority of usage or popular approval. The sanction of present usage is regarded as sufficient to establish a matter as right, legitimate or even necessary. And conversely, the lack of present usage is regarded as sufficient to prove that a matter is wrong and improper.

This kind of stagnation, this attitude of regarding the status quo as normal, shuts the door against all true progress in church reformation. For the status quo is always sinful. It is always a falling short of the requirements of the Word of God. It is always something less than what God really requires of the church. Since the status quo is sinful, it may never be regarded with complacency, far less may it be regarded as the ideal for the church. It is a sin to absolutise the status quo.

The status quo always needs to be repented of. No matter how fine it may be, still it is sinful and needs to be repented of. To regard the status quo with complacency is one of the greatest sins of the church in our day—a sin which must grieve the Holy Spirit, and a sin which certainly prevents the church from making its true and proper progress in reformation according to Scripture. A church dominated by this idea cannot really move forward. It may indeed slide backward in defection and apostasy. At best it will only move in a fixed circle, always coming back to where it started from.

The Pattern of American Church History.

The churches of America, by and large, have moved in a fixed circle through their past history. We might also say, they have moved in a vicious circle. The pattern has been a slump followed by a revival followed by a slump, and so on. True progress is not made. The best that can be done, it seems, is to manage to get out of one pit after another. Nothing is more prevalent than this kind of stagnation in the church. Nothing is more difficult than to get any feature of the church's structure or activity really examined and reformed in the light of the Word of God.

True progress means building on the foundations laid in the past. But true progress does not mean being held in check by the dead hand of errors and imperfections of the past. There is only one legitimate check on true progress, and that is the check of Scripture itself. The true reformation of the church is a reformation on the basis of Scripture, it is a reformation within the bounds of Scripture, not a reformation beyond Scripture.

God Calls us to Reform the Church in our Day.

Are the church's official agencies, publications and institutions to reflect a cross-section of opinion as it actually exists in the church, like Mark Twain's "English as she is spoke"? Or are they to take their stand on the existing official standards of the church and maintain that line in confronting the public? Or are they to pioneer in denominational self-criticism on the basis of Scripture? Are they to blaze a new trail, going forward into new territory in the light of the Word?

These are difficult and serious questions. The tendency is to by-pass and ignore such questions as these. These questions are seldom faced. The tendency is rather to regard the status quo as normal. Or if not the present status quo, then at any rate the achievements of the past are regarded as normal. If we could just get back to the way things were in "the good old days" and maintain that standard, we are told, then everything would be fine.

But would it? Where have we been? This is 1959. How are we to be excused for having failed to advance beyond our forefathers in understanding the Scriptures? How can we say that the reformation of the church was completed in 1560, in 1638, or even in 1950? What have we been doing since then? Has our talent been buried in a napkin?

It is not difficult to admit that there are some evils in the church which need correction. But the tendency is to say that if we could just get back to the sound basis of a generation or two ago, everything would be just as it should be. What more could anyone ask? We could just hold that line for all time to come.

But that would not be doing our God-given duty. Our forefathers reformed the church in their time; God calls us to reform it in our time. We cannot rest on our laurels; we must strike out for ourselves, by faith, on the basis of the Word of God.

True Reformation seeks God's Honour and His Truth above all
other Considerations.

We live in a pragmatic age, an age impatient of truth, and
concerned mostly about practical results. It is an age impatient
of those who rate truth above results. Our age wants results and
is quite willing to believe that figs grow on thistles, if it thinks it
sees the figs.

Is the Time Opportune ?

I have heard, when someone sought to bring some feature of the
church under the critical judgment of Scripture, the objection that
the time was not opportune. "You may be right," the objector
would say, " but is this an opportune time to bring up such a matter? " Now, we should realise that truth is *always* timely, truth is
always in order, and that if we wait for an opportune time to bring
up truth that opportune time may never come. That more convenient season may never arrive. Always there will be some
reason that can be urged for not undertaking the reformation of
the church according to the Word of God.

God is the God of truth. He is light, and in Him is no darkness at all. Christ is King of the Kingdom of truth. To this end
was He born, that He might bear witness to the truth. He that is
of the truth heareth His voice.

Accepting the Status Quo is Sinful.

The too-ready willingness to accept the status quo as normal is
one of the great obstacles in the way of the real reformation and
progress of the church today. This attitude is sinful because it is
blind to the real sinfulness of the status quo. It fails to realise that
the status quo always needs to be repented of, always needs to be
forgiven by divine grace, and always needs to be reformed by the
church on earth. It fails to realise the truth of the statement of
Augustine that every lesser good involves an element of sin.

God's Holiness and Truth Require Continued Reformation.

At bottom, this complacent acceptance of the status quo as
normal proceeds from a wrong idea of God, an idea which fails to
reckon with His holiness and His purity ; and from a wrong idea of
Scripture, an idea which fails to realise the *absolute* character of
Scripture as the church's standard.

To place God's truth and honour first, above all other considerations whatsoever, requires great moral consecration. In this
matter it is true of the church as it is of the individual, that he that
loseth his life for Christ's sake shall find it.

THE LORD'S JEALOUSY AGAINST BACKSLIDERS CONSISTENT WITH HIS UNCHANGING LOVE [1]

GEORGE SMEATON (1814-1889)

" If his children forsake my law, and walk not in my judgments; if they break my statutes, and keep not my commandments, then will I visit their transgressions with the rod, and their iniquity with stripes. Nevertheless, my loving-kindness will I not utterly take from him."—Psalm lxxxix. 30, 31, 32, 33.

In the context, the Covenant between the Father and the Son is at large unfolded. The Eternal Son undertakes to come down to this world to put on our sin and our wrath, that God may love us as he loveth him. On this Mighty One our help is laid (v. 19), and when he comes, he is strengthened for the work given him to do. His Sonship is discovered when he cries, " Thou art my father;" and his every step in doing and in dying is taken in the room of all and every man whose person he sustained and for whom he acted as a surety; for they were given him by the Father. The believer, realizing this oneness with his Lord, says, I am Christ's righteousness, yea, as Christ, the well-beloved before the Father; and evermore he hears the Mediator saying, I am yonder sinner's guilt and sin, for I bore him on my person on the tree. It is then taken for granted (v. 30), that the seed of the Messiah shall go astray; but their sins, it is added, do not break the Covenant, which stands fast for ever more; for it was not made with us, but with the Son for us. For evermore the savour of Christ's sacrifice is as fresh as ever, and he ever cries, on behalf of all his own, Let them be brought back again white as ever—whiter than the snow. But we shall now, by God's help, analyse and open up the words as simply as we can. Notice,

I.

The seed of the Messiah stand in his relation to the Father, sons by Grace because he is the Son by Nature. *His children.* The full meaning, we take it, is, they are children in him; for the expressions *his children* and *his brethren* are interchangeably used—" He is not ashamed to call them *brethren,* saying, Behold I and the *children* which God hath given me." Heb. ii, 11-13. He raises all whom the Father hath given him as near himself as possible, to the rank of sons in the family of God, with a title to the heavenly glory. The foundation of our being children is, that Christ is God's only begot-

---

[1] Reprinted from *The Free Church Pulpit.*

ten Son in a sense peculiarly his own before the world was ; and we find the order of the Covenant, when he said—" I ascend unto my Father and your Father, and to my God and your God," not to *our* Father, for there is no such equality, but to my Father by nature, and yours by being found in me.   This relationship is Christ's of right, it is ours of grace through him—an undeserved boon ; and God becomes our Father only because he is the Father of one so near and dear to us.

Christ's Sonship is not a mere official Sonship, beginning when he took the flesh.   The relationship is from everlasting, founded in nature and not arbitrary ; and in like manner the love involved in it had no beginning, and can have no end.   The Son dwelt in the Father's bosom before the world was, dear to him as his own soul. Had the Sonship begun in time, as some men vainly speak, we could imbibe but little comfort ; for there might be constant fear, that what had a beginning might also have an end.   But when we see that the Sonship is founded in the very nature of the Godhead, and can no more change than God can change, a joy unspeakable is derived from the discovery.   And is not the thought an overwhelming one, that to us it should be given to stand within this bond between the Father and the Son—to be taken up, as far as may be, into this relationship, and remembered in inseparable connection with God's dear Son?

Do we look at the act of power put forth in calling us into the fellowship of his Son, Jesus Christ our Lord?   We are redeemed by power, as well as price, from being children of the evil one ; and if Jesus, by his cross, made Satan's title but an empty name, the question now is simply one of power—who is strongest ; and in the word of the gospel, Jesus goes throughout the world to claim his own, and by a mighty hand to dispossess the strong man armed of his lawful captive.

Do we look at the change in our relation to the Lord the Judge, in passing into the family of God?   When the Most High has seen the sinner consenting to be righteous in the Saviour's righteousness —to be saved in God's own way—sentence of acquittal is given forth by the holy Judge the very moment we believe on Jesus, and there is joy in heaven on account of it.   It is passed even now in the court of heaven, and the judgment-day will but proclaim it to all worlds, but not make it more perfect than it is now.   It is passed, moreover, in a man's own conscience, and then there is assurance, peace, and joy unspeakable, the glorious liberty of children in the family of God.

Do we look at the frame of soul with which the joint-heirs are imbued?   Though the Lord Jesus is in heaven till the times of the restitution of all things, yet is he ever with his children by his spiritual presence, till the end of the world. Their experience is not a mere dim resemblance of his own, but the very same in the measure in which they apprehend him. His peace is our peace— his joy is our joy, though he has an oil of gladness above his fellows —his spirit is ours, one spirit with him—his life is our life; we live, yet not we, he liveth in us—in a word, there is not one feeling or emotion that pervades the holy soul of the man Christ Jesus in the sanctuary on high, but vibrates in a greater or less degree through all the ranks of the redeemed, whether in the bliss above, or in their lowly dwelling place below—" I in them and thou in me."

Do we look at the love within which Messiah's seed are taken? They are more precious in God's sight than all the universe, and he loves them with a real father's love. It is not different love the Father bears to Christ's people from what he bears to him : " Thou hast loved them as thou hast loved me." (John xvii.. 23). Our capacity, indeed, is limited, but if we are Christ's we are loved with the very same love in kind, yea, taken within the bond of that very love that from eternal ages has knit the Father to his only Son. Lift up your heads ye drooping saints. The more you taste God's glory and desire him, will it not ravish your soul, that this God loves you, and has set the very love on you that he has set upon his Son?

Or do we look to the standard, the image after which God's children are to be conformed? They are to be conformed to that loveliest of holy scenes, the life, the character, the mind of Jesus— conformed to the image of God's dear Son. As they have borne the image of the earthy, they shall also bear the image of the heavenly; and at last they shall be like him, when they see him as he is. Yet a little while and the reviled sons of God shall shine brighter than the sun in a glory that will make kings and great men wonder.

II.

The Lord narrowly observes the new obedience of his children, and whether they will go astray. Allusion is made to that declension as proceeding step by step. When God says, " *If his children forsake my law*," he names the first step when they lose a relish for his presence and his holy will ; when he adds, " *and walk not in my judgments*," he names the next step when they walk no more with him, and lose the fear of God upon their hearts ; when he adds, " *if they break my statutes*," he shews that all comes to open high-handed sin at last, although the first step was but a loss of secret delight in God. Perhaps we may, with more advantage, advert here to the first commencement than to the open fruits of declension.

The sin that dwells in us comes on with noiseless step, disarming all suspicion, it may be under the guise of weariness, or suggesting delay in spiritual service, and it is little suspected, nay, spiritual slumber is accounted sweet.   Indwelling sin is of dreadful strength ; and if we cannot trace out all its windings and deceitfulness, if it is a friend within to every temptation from without, and wars in every power of the soul with the Most High, is not the most unwary soul most sure to fall?   Never did men occupy such an awakening position as the disciples in the garden.   The three were honoured out of all the sons of men to be with Christ in the crowning act of his obedience, when he formed his high and final act of choice to drink the cup which the Father gave him.   He had often been with them in Gethsemane's quiet retreat, as if he loved the scene of his future trial ; and now, when he was to gaze on the eternal hell not too great for one sin—when he was called to the highest act of his obedience, to choose, as man, whether he would be cast into the wrath of God as far as it could kindle on the Lord of glory—he wished to be refreshed by his disciples' fellowship and surely they will watch and keep him company.   Ah, no ! thrice that suffering one came back to get comfort in their fellowship, and his sweat was great drops of blood falling from his every pore upon the frozen ground, and they are fast asleep.   If it was his gentle complaint, " What, can ye not watch with me one hour? " O how many an occasion shall we trace as we look down from the heights of future glory, when we, too, enjoyed the same forbearance of Almighty love on our way to Zion.   We have begun this departure, if our thoughts turn not naturally and habitually unto God as the needle to the pole, or if less drawn by the cords of his constraining love than in other days.   We have entered on a path of declension, if, like the slumbering virgins, we have lost transforming views of the glory yet to be revealed in the presence of the Lord at his coming— if we press forward the less and not the more when accepted in the beloved.

O declining soul, you are not in *the same earnest effort*! The day was, when you ever saw some new perfecton in the Son of God, and sought some new occasion to commend him.   Where is the happiness you spake of?   You abuse the doctrine of conversion, if it is made a resting place for sloth, as if you might on that account be less in prayer, less in awe of God.   The almighty power of God on dead souls at first conversion—the very power by which the Saviour rose—must be as much as ever put forth on us from hour to hour ; and if God is waiting to carry on the work, are you unwilling to be the subjects of the same Almighty change?

You have ceased to seek *the same blessings,* although they are designed to be revealed from faith to faith till we are ever with the

Lord. When light from heaven first shone on you, you were eager to *win Christ himself;* now, though you feel your loneliness, you do not desire so much to apprehend him. O how different is it now! You once mourned over your thick darkness, and were not content with doctrines, without more glowing discoveries of heavenly things; but now you seek not *heavenly light* so much as you did then. As to *pardon,* again, through the imputed righteousness of God, the very highest attainment any child of God shall know on this side of Heaven, is to wash daily in the fountain, and yet hate sin as much as ever; but in your pride you will not daily be indebted to forgiving love, and in your unbelief you will not rely upon its freeness as you once did. Remember whence you are fallen. And if we speak of *strength for hourly duty,* the day was when you saw no reason why you should be weak when Christ is strong, or empty when it has pleased the Father that all fulness should dwell in him; but now, because God tries you whether you will labour for every blessing, and contend for it, you fall back discouraged.

Nor do you pursue the *same spiritual exercises.* As to private *prayer,* excuses multiply as years roll on. Every company and pursuit is not abandoned that unfits you for it, and the form is very irksome. If we ask how far you war with your *corruptions,* are you not weary of doing constant violence to your sinful nature, bolder now with little sins, less tender in your walk before the Holy One, and more careless in draining off corruptions daily, by slow degrees? And as to the measure in which you cherish *implanted graces,* time was when you strove to have them in the highest exercise, and were most of all afraid to have less of God and of his presence than on the day before. How different is it now!

You pillow your soul upon a time when your tears were turned into joy, your fears into peace, your sighs into songs of praise. You trust to past experience, to past recourse to Christ, and not upon himself as the refuge from the tempest now. What if you repose on a delusion, on an awakening which was but the savour of death unto death? It matters not what you once were, what are you now?

But notice here, again, that when the Lord so narrowly watches if we walk in *his law and judgments,* he means the law of liberty written on the heart, which neither can condemn nor justify a child of God. The children of God do not obey to be put among the children, for they are sons already, and they obey both in the rest above and here below with a love that casteth out the fear to which the law appeals. Obedience is Heaven begun, and the sons of God rejoice to see him take his honour, and call all worlds around him to esteem and love him, as most worthy. They are not under the law in whole or part, so far as it has sanctions, threats, or promises,

But let us bear in mind—for there may be ere long another Antin-
omian outbreak—that in the measure in which we win Christ, it will
be our meat to do the Father's will as it was his beforehand. Our
willingness to obey just shows how far we have tasted the sweetness
of the promises, how far we have apprehended Christ.

Let us bear in mind that every child of God is under high and
holy discipline, and that true grace is certain to be tried and sifted.
If Jesus learned obedience by the things he suffered, though he
were a Son, good cause there is that we too should be sifted. Remember that the Lord tried Israel for forty years, to prove what
was in their hearts; and if he cross our will, it is to try our faith
and patience—if heresy come in to deceive if it were possible the
very elect, it is to make manifest them that are approved. Let us
labour that, whether present or absent, we may be accepted of him,
and count it all joy to meet the trials which strengthen faith.

III.

God, jealous of his honour, cannot pass over the transgressions
of his children without chastisement. *Then will I visit their transgressions with the rod, and their iniquity with stripes.* This rod—
these stripes—may come in many a form, in personal affliction or
bereavement, in sorrow or reviling, in the buffettings of Satan or the
hiding of the Father's face. These visitations come not as the curse
of the law, for believers are not under the law, nor does their Father
disinherit them. God distinguishes between the persons of his children whom he loves and their faults which he punishes. "Thou
wast a God that forgavest them, though thou tookest vengeance
of their inventions." Ps. xcix. 8.

The afflictions which God sends to prove and try his people
come when they most ardently grow up into him, who is the head
in all things; but of these God speaks not here. The cross we are
to bear in following Jesus is felt most keenly when we are most alive
to God, for we must do violence at every point to the natural
aversion of our evil hearts, and to a world in open arms against our
God; but of that God speaks not here. The afflictions which he
speaks of here are punishments, and may be easily distinguished
from the other, because they come in seasons of departure from the
Lord. Upon these occasions, and even for sins of omission in which
we live more readily, the Lord allots, as his messages to Israel show,
a just recompense of reward. Have we to do with a God less
jealous now? If a holy God could not pass over one offence in
Moses, without making him bear the mark of his displeasure, we
have to do with one the same yesterday, to-day, and for ever; for
our God is a consuming fire. The Lord, who will not be mocked,
inflicts fit punishment for every declension, for all distrust of him.

Do ye make light of small departures from the Lord, because it is a day of grace? Do ye wink at decays of grace in yourselves, at sloth or unbelief or a defiled conscience, at lukewarmness in prayer or in holy love, as if God winked at them too? Ye shall suffer loss though ye may be saved so as by fire. Though God is at peace with us as Judge, his jealousy as the Holy One burneth with fire. It is told of a holy minister that he died imploring pardon, especially for his sins of omission. But more affecting than even the testimony of a dying hour, is the frown with which a God of love must visit them; and, if it be by spiritual judgments mainly that God now visits sin, the blighted religion in these souls of ours, the pointless sermons falling half-way to the heart, and the ease in Zion, may just prove that God is jealous. If any think that backsliding is a light matter because it is a day of grace, hold up the sin to the holy light of the Redeemer's countenance as he speaketh to the Seven Churches, and you will cry, who may abide the day of his coming? and who shall stand when he appeareth? for he is like a refiner's fire and like fuller's soap.

We have said that there is nothing properly penal in these frowning visitations of a Heavenly Father, for they have their source in his grace, and for their aim a return to himself. They are not from a Judge, but from a Father. The Lord has no pleasure in the sufferings of his children, but there is a glory in the connection between sin and punishment which never can be broken, and he will show that sin is an evil thing and bitter. When the warnings of Jesus in the garden could not keep the disciples awake, his rebuke was, Sleep on now and take your rest—he is at hand that doth betray me, implying, that the awakening providence of God would now compel their watchfulness. Alas! how many are never aroused till startled by tremendous judgments and alarming providences! God will deal in love with us if we can be drawn by the cords of love. But if kindness will not allure, the trials of a severer discipline will compel us to live near him, to cry unto the Lord in our distress.

Look at Israel, on entering the land of promise. Unmindful, after first success, of their work of vengeance on the doomed nations round them, they neither work *for* God nor *in* God; and when the angel tells them in Bochim, for their punishment, that they should not drive out those nations any more, such a day of weeping followed—such a day of repentance—as has seldom been in this dark world. But why did they not return to their first works? It seems that the courage once given them was not given again—the Lord was not with them in such measure any more. Is this a new thing in the earth? Ah! it is common to lose first love, but all do not regain their former place. Many are but blasted trees—melancholy monuments of what they were, or might have been. Some all zeal once are now lame in every effort, and what time is lost if ever they recover! Could I reach some young convert, ready to take a little slumber when the Sun of Righteousness has chased away the darkness of the night, as if the keen edge might be abated and all be well again, I would say, no quarter can be given in this warfare, till we see Jerusalem and the Lamb face to face. O, if any live as if they might safely be ever sinning and repenting, can you dread no danger?—is it only after a fall that ye will stand in awe, when our God is a consuming fire?

The Holy One can let alone men of the earth till the great day; but the Church, which is the only holy house in which he dwells— the renewed soul which is his temple—may not be left polluted. "You only have I known of all the families of the earth; therefore will I punish you for all your iniquities." Amos iii. 2. The jealousy of our God smokes on all sides of his chosen ones. What he can bear with for the present in the children of the wicked one, he cannot bear in those who are a people near him. Judgment begins at the house of God, on those who bear his image; for more heinous in God's account, and more ruinous to souls around them, is sin in God's people than in others.

By doubts and fears in a hesitating bosom, the Lord oft-times chastens his people, who once had joy unspeakable and full of glory. Satan is allowed to cast his fiery darts, and setting forth a long train of decays, with all their circumstances, takes occasion by some sickness greatly to terrify them, saying, What have such to do—the guiltiest among men to do—with life to come or with Jesus here. Their hands hang down—their songs in the night are silent. Is it not so with *many at this day,* as if wisdom's ways were not ways of pleasantness, and her paths the paths of peace? And in most cases —I say not in all—is it not because they have sinned away their light, and peace, and strength, and now they weep as they remember Zion. They would not keep awake when they might, and now they cannot imbibe the holy joy they fain would know again. They would not leave their spiritual sloth or worldliness when they might, and now they cannot let them go when they would. Who can stand before this holy Lord God? Oh! ye who live as if the Christ within were not to be the same holy image of the Father as the Christ without—who rather would be safe than holy—when put into the refiner's fire of James or of the Prophets, what but dross is left behind, after the wood, the hay, the stubble are burned up? Oh ye who think that free grace will cover another and another sin, instead of labouring to depart from all iniquity, call to mind with whom ye have to do; for the Lord is not mocked. Will ye provoke the Lord to jealousy? Ye who think it legal to take a single glance at your unweeded hearts—who will hear that Christ is *for* you, but who will not ruffle self-complacency by the thought that he is *in* you except ye be reprobates, ye cannot serve the Lord, said Joshua to such a people; "for he is an holy God—he is a jealous God—he will not forgive you your transgressions nor your sins." Lose not Israel-views of God—Old Testament views of God, for they are not to be forgotten, but carried with you when you think of God in Christ.

IV.

Our declensions do not utterly remove God's loving-kindness, because it is not founded on ourselves, but on another. It is striking to observe (v. 33), that the Lord changes the person, and when we expected to read, "*nevertheless my loving-kindness will I not utterly take from them*," he drops all mention of the sinner, and, reverting to the covenant, says, "*my loving-kindness will I not utterly take from him*."

The Father's love to the Son is the very foundation of the gospel. The Father cannot be an enemy to him who is his very heart. To shew that the Father cannot cease to love him, let us bear in mind that, when he came forth as Mediator, it was not a new affection that the Father bore to him, but the very same that had been borne to him before the world was. When he put off his glory and appeared eclipsed, self-emptied, humbled, the Father said of him, what had been upon his heart before time began, "This is my beloved Son, in whom I am well pleased." When he put on his people's sin, he met the anger of an offended Judge, not the enmity of an offended Father. Even when his God forsook him, as he hung surrounded with the terrific garment of our sin, and his human soul wanted all sensible comfort, he was the object, amid all his woe, on who Eternal love was resting. The great triumph of the cross is, that he who hung there was more pleasing in the Father's sight than even sin was hateful—*that the sin could be consumed, and yet the love remain entire.* Had this love not been as full as ever, as high as ever—had there been an interruption of it but a moment—our salvation had been hopeless. But while Christ took on him what was due to us, he did not lose, he could not lose, what was eternally his own : the light of everlasting love did not forsake, and could not forsake, the temple where it ever dwelt.

If, then, the Father's love was not abated when Jesus bore the garment of our guilt, and if a time shall never come when that love shall cool toward him or be withdrawn, never shall it cool toward his seed, who are taken within the bond of such a love. The love they enjoy is not different, but the same. At all times alike, and in all conditions alike—even in times of dreariest declension, God's love for ever rests on all who are joint-heirs with Christ, though at the time they do not feel it shed abroad upon them. Even then they are as much beloved as ever, and Jesus is to be heard saying, "Thou hast loved them as thou hast loved me."

These words, " My loving-kindness will I not utterly take from him," shew us, we believe, the *proper motive to be brought to bear on sad backsliders, and the Lord's way of restoring them.* While the mind of God is here revealed, it is not as if he kept the secret to himself ; he designs to give a spring of action unto us, to forestall undue despondency, lest the spirit fail before him.   If any presume on such words of tenderness—halt ! they are not spoken unto you, but to the downcast child of God, at a loss to know how God can love him with so little that is pure and lovely—ready to doubt how a worm, a rebel, an enemy, can be endeared to God.   When the declining soul is grieved with his own distempered heart, and his backslidings have reproved him, the Lord removes the cloudy day, by shewing that the only cause of the Divine favour is that, without a claim on our part, everlasting love rests on us because it rests upon the Son.   When sin is on the soul, we are prone to think that God is turned against us, and we dare not look again to his holy temple ; and to counteract this, God announces that he is unchanged—the very same he was at first.   God's voice at first was, This is my beloved Son, in whom I am so well pleased, that by him the guiltiest may come from wrath to grace—from sin to holiness—from death to life ;—in whom I am so well pleased, that in him all guilt is swallowed up, all wrath for ever hushed, and condemnation rolled away —all controversy between God and you forgiven and forgotten,—a heaven of light and glory is open over you, and the unveiled countenance of a friendly Father smiling on you with inexpressible complacency.   You then put on the Lord Jesus ; you become most dear in God's sight, as free from wrath as he is free, and partakers of a love which no creature can fathom.   What made you rest so sweetly under the refreshing beams of the Father's love so firmly anchor there, when nothing amiable in you drew forth the Divine complacency?   For his dear Son's sake alone, the sunshine of the Father's love first rested on your soul, and it is the same view of his unfathomable love in Christ that leads the downcast backslider to return.

The Eternal Father calls you, O backslider, to look up from the depths to him who giveth you his Son, and your warrant to embrace him now is not that ye received him formerly, but God's present gift, as if ye never heard that blessed name before.   Seek to be one with Jesus by receiving him afresh from day to day, if you would inherit God's love ; for it is by cleaving to God's dear Son anew, and not by leaning upon past experience, that ye find, to your soul's joy, no wrath upon his countenance, nor vengeance in his heart, but the very heavens and the skies raining down love.   The declining child of God is prone to think that God is turned against him as unworthy, and he is unworthy more than he ever dreamed of ; but in the holy of holies the merits of the Lamb are as fragrant as ever.

We are ever to realise that Christ puts in his righteousness to adjust the balance between God and us. The Father never removes his loving-kindness from him, and there is no propitiation necessary between the Lamb and us. O, if you think that your sins are higher than the grace of God, that you cannot again be rendered amiable even by God's dear Son, what is this but unmortified pride, because not beloved for what you are, or may have done? If a backslider refuse to lean his guilty soul on what he leaned at first, he will only pierce himself through with farther sorrow. However near we live to God, there is no other way of pleasing God, no other way of coming under the warm beams of the Father's love, than the plea from hour to hour to hour which is founded on his Son. And, after going backward, if you doubt whether the Father's smile again can settle on you—if you question whether God can again be pacified by what is laid up in Christ—you cast contempt as much upon the treasures of his grace, as if you hoped to be forgiven because your sins are small. Begin at the beginning, as if ye never knew the truth. Believe with all your heart that God has been more glorified by Christ than dishonoured by you—that the law is more magnified by the obedience of the greatest Being in the universe, than even violated by you; and look upon yourself as *in him* when he died, as *in him* when he rose, putting off our curse. Behold him, then, acquitted, and that you too were acquitted in him. Draw not your comfort or your confidence *from anything wrought in you* as a ground of faith, but look simply to God giving you his Son, and all the fulness of his Son, in the precious promises. Cast yourself on God's *self-moving grace without you,* and peace will fill your soul, *within.* Faith is the simplest act of leaning on the obedience of another—on Christ himself, our righteousness; it is the opposite of leaning upon aught within. Hear him saying to the Father, for you, " I have glorified thee on the earth." It is when ye thus look, expecting the Spirit to reveal the Son in you, to glorify the Lamb in your eyes, that you regain the joy you long for.

26

BOOK NOTICES

The catalogue enclosed with this issue contains latest information regarding Banner of Truth publications. Please circulate this catalogue, in designing it we attempted to go beyond mere advertising. Further free copies are available. All books listed are now available except *Edwards' Select Works*, vol. II, *John Owen's Death of Death* and *Whitefield's Journals* which are held up indefinitely by the present printing strike. Any readers overseas, including U.S.A., can obtain books direct from us at British prices unless otherwise stated.

The Way of Life, Charles Hodge, pp. 240, 7/6. Banner of Truth Trust.

We are particularly eager to commend this book to the attention of our readers. Some works are calculated to interest and assist only a certain group of readers, but in this case the appeal is universal and even if the contents can hardly be said to 'appeal' to the unconverted the book is nevertheless well designed to bring them to the truth. This is a book to clarify your own thoughts on the way of salvation and one which you can pass on to others.

The Gospel of John, William Hendriksen, pp. 775, 21/-. Banner of Truth Trust.

"It is good that this commentary on the Gospel according to St. John should now be made available in this country. For myself I have to say that it is the most satisfying commentary that I have ever read on this Gospel. Dr. Hendriksen is acknowledged and recognised as an outstanding New Testament scholar who is thoroughly up to date and fully aware of all modern movements of thought. He leaves nothing to be desired in that respect, but at the same time his outlook and teaching are thoroughly Reformed, Conservative and Evangelical.

There is an excellent Introduction, and a peculiarly interesting feature is the way in which he gives a synopsis of the argument of each section. At the same time there is a verse by verse commentary, and all bathed in the warm devotional spirit of a Pastor's heart.

Here is an invaluable aid for all

preachers, Sunday School workers and Bible Class leaders, and indeed for all who 'desire the sincere milk of the word that they may grow thereby.' "—Dr. Martyn Lloyd-Jones.

The Child's Story Bible, Catherine F. Vos, pp. 732, 25/-, Marshall, Morgan & Scott.

Some of us may well be suspicious of books which claim to present the Scriptures in story form. Such works have not infrequently presented error in a subtle and attractive manner and in any case what need is there to retell the Bible narratives in uninspired language ? The child's difficulty with Scripture, it may be said, is not one that can be met by a new version but only by the inward light of the Holy Spirit. We sympathize with such fears and approached this volume with caution. But it was not long before our feelings were radically revised ! So long as it is not used as a substitute for the Bible, here is a volume which provides an invaluable help to the mother who is labouring to bring up her children to love the Scriptures and the Saviour they reveal. There is nothing to which the child's awaking interest turns more naturally than stories ; this fact presents a golden opportunity to introduce Scriptural truth and if this opportunity is missed it is more than likely that the child will grow up to think of the Bible as a dull book which he could never understand.

Mrs. Vos' volume is really just a series of beautifully painted word pictures—covering events from Genesis to Revelation. She uses some imagination occasionally, as every re-teller

512

of Bible stories must do, but she does not confound fact and fiction by adding material which cannot be fairly surmized from the text. The aim is to seize the leading features of the Bible and convey them in story form. Mrs. Vos' selections and omissions are based on this principle and her choice is such as we would have expected from the wife of Geerhardus Vos, one of the greatest exegetes Princeton Theological Seminary ever possessed. (It will, incidentally, interest our readers to know that J. G. Vos is the son of these parents).

Some of these stories can be read to children of three years ; the book was particularly designed to be read by the seven to twelve age group, but it can be read with profit and enjoyment by Christians of any age.

The Volume is attractively produced with clear large print. The illustrations are bright but we deplore the two which supposedly represent the Lord Jesus Christ. These pictures did not form part of Mrs. Vos' original work and it is a pity they were ever introduced into this new edition. But these two pictures can easily be taken out and the value of the book will be all the greater. In a day when fine literature for children is very hard to find we prize this republication and commend it to all parents and Sunday School teachers.

Masters of The English Reformation, Marcus L. Loane, pp. 247, 12/6, The Church Book Room Press.

Those who have read other books by Canon Loane, such as his short biography of J. C. Ryle, will come to this book with keen expectations and they will not be disappointed. Here are finely written, moving, accounts of five foremost English martyrs—Bilney, Tyndale, Latimer, Ridley and Cranmer. Who can read of such men without being instructed and inspired ! The book contains plenty of solid historical information and is well documented, but it aims at interesting the average man and woman and in this respect it excels. It is high time we realised that *every* Christian should read church history. This is a book which makes a good starting point for the beginner and whets the appetite for more.

From our view point Canon Loane does not always do justice to the lack of thoroughness which characterized the English Reformation. He quotes R. W. Dixon's statement that Cranmer "preserved the continuity of the Church of England. He gave to the English Reformation largeness and capacity." Is not the case rather that Cranmer, with all his gentle Christian graces, had not the strength of doctrine or purpose of a Knox ? Expediency played too large a part in his policy. Cranmer, says the author, met the Roman party " so firmly from the Scriptures that in November, 1534, the Act was passed which laid it down that the King's Majesty ' justly and rightfully is and ought to be the Supreme Head of the Church of England.' " The impression is that such an Act had Scriptural authority. This is very misleading. The fact is that the government of the Reformed Church of England fell seriously short of the rule of Scripture, hence the necessity of the Puritan Movement.

However, the book professes to be biographical rather than doctrinal and as such it is worthy of a very wide circulation. We have read and reread it with much enjoyment. Although this book has been in print some years it is probably not so well-known as it ought to be and we are therefore calling attention to it again.

A Divine Cordial, Thomas Watson, pp. 94, 6/-, Sovereign Grace Book Club, British Agent : T. E. Watson, 1 Cliff House, Weston Lane, Southampton.

After a lapse of more than half a century there have appeared in less than eighteen months, reprints of three books by Thomas Watson. These are having a ready sale on both sides of the Atlantic. This is a heartening sign to all lovers of Puritan theology. It seems that Watson is forerunning his contemporaries in re-awakening interest in 17th century literature. To those who know the value of the writings of the one time pastor of St. Stephen, Walbrook, this renewed popularity is not surprising. For lively, pungent expositions of experimental religion Watson's works are likely to serve the Church till the end of time.

This present reprint was first published in 1663. It is a sweet exposition of Rom. 8 : 28. " All things work together for good, to them that love God . . ." and abounds in instruction and consolation. The tried, the afflicted, the lonely, the discouraged will all find this to be a true " *Divine Cordial.*" This is an ideal book to give to a sick friend. The print and lay-out of this work is particularly attractive, and it has been well edited for the publishers by T. E. Watson.

The Baptist Confession of Faith of 1689, pp. 54, soft covers, 1/6, from E. J. Harmer, 47 Albion Road, Tunbridge Wells, Kent.

The Philadelphia Confession of Faith, pp. 144, soft covers, 6/-, Sovereign Grace Book Club.

These two publications are in fact both reprints of the same Confession, the differing titles being due to the fact that in America the work assumed a different name. The Sovereign Grace Book Club edition contains some additional material—an appendix on believers baptism, The Philadelphia Baptist Catechism, and footnotes indicate the few divergencies in the Confession from the old Westminster and Savoy standards. The English reprint gives the 'proof texts' in footnote form whereas the American includes them in the text itself ; the former method aids readability.

Here then is the rock whence the Calvinistic Baptists were hewn ! We hope it will be well studied. Two

points occurred to us as perhaps particularly worthy of observation. The manner in which the Baptists of 1689 follow so much of the Westminster Confession (1646) reveals how close the 17th century Nonconformists were in their theology ! Closer than they have ever been since. When churches hold to free and sovereign grace there is a common unity which transcends differences in order and practice, but where grace is not central, as it is not today, we shall look in vain for unity among churches. Secondly, this old Confession shews us what Baptist theology was before smitten with Hyper-Calvinism in the 18th century. Nothing cut the nerve of aggressive evangelism more than the teaching that it is not every man's duty to accept the salvation freely proclaimed in the Gospel. It was only after Andrew Fuller (1754-1815) had gone back to the old truths of the 1689 Confession that the Baptist Missionary Society was formed in 1792 and Carey despatched to India. The subsequent departure of the great majority of Baptist churches into Arminianism was again a violation of the old Confession and we hope this reprint will serve to point many back to the truth as it is in Christ.

There is, however, one caution we would add. Though this Confession follows so much of the Westminster Confession, word for word, there are significant differences, notably the complete omission of the Westminster article on Reprobation in the section ' of God's Decree.' This omission reflects something of the theological weakening in progress within the churches at the time when this Confession was compiled.

A LASTING PEACE

R EADER, peace is a blessed thing. War is an immense evil. Peace ought to be prayed for night and day by all who love their country. But, after all, there is only one peace which is lasting, and that is *the peace with God which faith in Christ gives.*

There is no happiness compared with that which this peace affords. A calm sea after a storm, a blue sky after a black thunder cloud, health after sickness, light after darkness, rest after toil; all are beautiful and pleasant things. But none, none of them all can give more than a feeble idea of the comfort which those enjoy who believe in Christ, and have *peace with God.* It is peace which passeth all understanding.

It is the *want* of this very peace which makes many in the world unhappy. Hundreds have everything that is thought able to give pleasure and yet are never satisfied. Their hearts are always aching. There is a constant sense of emptiness within. And what is the secret of all this? They have no peace with God.

It is the *desire* of this very peace which makes many a heathen do much in his idolatrous religion. Thousands have been seen to mortify their bodies, and vex their own flesh, in the service of some wretched image which their own hands had made. And why? Because they hungered after peace with God.

It is the *possession* of this very peace on which the value of a man's religion depends. Without it there may be everything to please the eye, and gratify the ear—forms, ceremonies, services, and sacraments—and yet no good done to the soul. The grand question that should try all, is the state of a man's conscience. Is it at peace? *Has he peace with God?*

Reader, this is the very peace about which I address you this day. Have you got it? Do you feel it? Is it your own? Believe on the Lord Jesus Christ, and you shall have lasting peace. God says of the unsaved : " The way of peace they know not." Isa. 59 : 8, but of the Christian God says that " He will keep him in perfect peace, whose mind is stayed on Him because he trusteth in Him (God) " (Isa. 26 : 3).

J. C. RYLE.

THE WICKLIFFE PRESS